BTEC NATIONAL Business

Book 1

Roger Lewis

Peter Trevitt

Nelson Thornes
a Wolters Kluwer business

Published in 2007 by:
Nelson Thornes Ltd
Delta Place
27 Bath Road
CHELTENHAM
GL53 7TH
United Kingdom

07 08 09 10 11 / 10 9 8 7 6 5 4 3 2 1

A catalogue record for this book is available from the British Library

ISBN 978 0 7487 8126 3

Cover photographs by Rob Melnychuk/Getty Images and SUNNYphotography.com/Alamy
Page make-up by Pantek Arts Ltd, Maidstone, Kent
Printed and bound in Slovenia by Korotan

Contents

Core units

1

Exploring business activity   1

Types of business activity and ownership ■ How the type of business influences the setting of strategic aims and objectives ■ Functional activities and organisational structure ■ How external factors in the business environment impact on organisations

2

Investigating business resources   54

How human resources are managed ■ The purpose of managing physical and technological resources ■ How to access sources of finance ■ Interpreting financial statements

3

Introduction to marketing   99

The key concepts and principles of marketing and their application in the business environment ■ How and why marketing research is conducted by organisations ■ How marketing information is used by organisations ■ How marketing techniques are used to increase demand for products, goods and services

4

Effective people, communication and information   152

The importance of employing suitable people ■ How to communicate using appropriate methods ■ Different types of information and how it can be processed ■ Presenting information effectively

Specialist units

5

Introduction to accounting   196

The purpose of accounting and the categorisation of business income and expenditure ■ Preparing a cash flow forecast ■ Profit and loss accounts and balance sheets ■ Reviewing business performance using simple ratio analysis

9

Exploring creative product promotion   229

The constituents of the promotional mix ■ The role of promotion within the marketing mix ■ The role of advertising agencies and the media ■ Creating a simple promotional campaign

16

Human resource management   279

The factors involved in human resource planning in organisations ■ How organisations motivate employees ■ How to gain committed employee co-operation ■ The importance of managing employee performance at work

29

Introduction to the internet and e-business   331

How the internet has evolved ■ Using the internet and related technology for a range of business activities ■ The trends in the use of e-business ■ The key features of planning for the increased use of e-business at national, organisational and individual level

37

Starting a small business   372

Presenting the initial business idea ■ The skills and development needed to run the business successfully ■ The legal and financial aspects that will affect the start-up of the business ■ Producing an outline business start-up proposal

Introduction

Welcome to your new course, the BTEC National in Business. Starting a new course is exciting but can also be challenging. This book is designed to help you succeed.

The four core units (see below) give you an introduction to business activity, management of resources, marketing and communication. These are vital for the success of business organisations. The specialist units will prepare you both for work or further study in administration, marketing, human resources, accounting, ICT or the legal and management areas of business.

What must I do to pass?

There are 42 units available for BTEC National Business. The number of units you need to complete depends on which course you are studying.

Course	Units to be completed	Points needed to pass
BTEC National Award	6 (4 core + 2 specialist)	36
BTEC National Certificate	12 (4 core + 8 specialist)	72
BTEC National Diploma	18 (4 core + 14 specialist)	108

What grades are there?

Three unit grades are available. Always aim for a distinction.

Pass	Awarded for satisfactory achievement of all pass criteria	6 unit points
Merit	Awarded for satisfactory achievement of all pass and merit criteria	12 unit points
Distinction	Awarded for satisfactory achievement of all pass, merit and distinction criteria	18 unit points

How will this book help me pass the course?

Covering nine units of the new 2007 specification, this book has everything you need if you are studying for the BTEC National Award, Certificate or Diploma in Business. Simple to use and understand, it is designed to provide you with the knowledge and understanding you need to gain your qualification. We guide you step-by-step towards success, with case studies and activities to help you develop and demonstrate your understanding. Completing these will prepare you for the unit coursework assessments. We want you to get a distinction and have given hints on how to achieve this.

BTEC National Business Book 1 provides you with the following:

Core Units	Specialist Units
Unit 1 Exploring business activity	Unit 5 Introduction to accounting
Unit 2 Investigating business resources	Unit 9 Exploring creative product promotion
Unit 3 Introduction to marketing	Unit 16 Human resource management
Unit 4 Effective people, communication and information	Unit 29 Introduction to the internet and e-business
	Unit 30 Starting a small business

Is there anything else I need to do?

The secret of success

You will need to work hard and meet deadlines – you expect that. You will get good advice from your tutor as you go along, but here are a few brief pointers which will help you achieve your ambitions.

1 Be organised. Buy a set of files, at least one per unit, rewritable CDs and/or a USB memory stick. You will need a system for collecting, storing and retrieving your information.

2 Always back-up your files – don't learn the hard way. Never leave your printing until the last minute, the printer will either break down or run out of paper.

3 The business world is exciting and continually changing. Try to keep up to date, but remember that collecting information is not an end in itself, it is what you do with it that is important. Always quote the source and the date. Always support your opinions with evidence.

4 Your local high street is a living business, with everyday examples of everything you study in the classroom. Look and listen, this is business activity, management of resources, marketing and communication – the core units – at work.

5 Take advantage of all the support and advice that is available at your centre. Never be afraid to ask for help.

Whether you aim to progress into a career or into higher education, BTEC National will prove to be a valuable qualification. Believe in yourself and enjoy learning – Good Luck!

Features of this book

UNIT 1

Exploring Business Activity

This unit covers the following objectives:

- Types of business activity and ownership
- How the type of business influences the setting of strategic aims and objectives
- Functional activities and organisational structure
- How external factors in the business environment impact on organisations

This unit looks at what UK businesses do, who owns them, and the reasons why they exist; the various goals that UK businesses set themselves and how these differ between the public, private and voluntary sectors; how businesses organise their different activities so as to best achieve their targets; the factors from the outside world that affect business performance and how organisations respond to these.

Learning Objectives

At the beginning of each Unit there will be a bulleted list letting you know what material is going to be covered. They specifically relate to the learning objectives within the specification.

Grading Criteria

The table of Grading Criteria at the beginning of each unit identifies achievement levels of pass, merit and distinction, as stated in the specification.

To achieve a **pass**, you must be able to match each of the 'P' criteria in turn.

To achieve **merit** or **distinction**, you must increase the level of evidence that you use in your work, using the 'M' and 'D' columns as reference. For example, to achieve a distinction you must fulfil all the criteria in the pass, merit and distinction columns.

grading criteria	To achieve a **Pass** grade the evidence must show that the learner is able to:	To achieve a **Merit** grade the evidence must show that the learner is able to:	To achieve a **Distinction** grade the evidence must show that the learner is able to:
	P1 business organisations in terms of purpose, ownership, size and scale.	**M1** compare and contrast the ownership, aims and objectives of two selected businesses.	**D1** evaluate how the functional areas contribute to the aims and objectives of the two selected businesses.
	P2 describe the primary, secondary and tertiary classifications of business activities using local and national examples.	**M2** explain areas of growth or decline in the primary, secondary and tertiary classifications of business activities.	**D2** describe the purpose of setting aims and objectives for businesses.
	P3 describe the purpose of setting aims and objectives for businesses.	**M3** explain the interaction of functional areas and how they relate to each other in two selected businesses.	

case study 1.1 — Public to private: rail privatisation

In 1996 John Major's Conservative government controversially broke up and sold off British Rail which until then was owned by the state. The track and stations went to a new company Railtrack plc, whilst private operators such as Midland Mainline, Virgin and Connex ran the trains under contract.

activity

1. British Rail used to be state-owned. Why was this?
2. Which companies now operate the trains in your area?
3. Why did Railtrack plc find it difficult to maintain the railways effectively?
4. Write a brief argument either for or against selling off British Rail to private shareholders.

Public sector businesses are funded and run either by **central government** at Westminster or by **local government** at the town hall. Today the public sector tends to concentrate on services that are necessary or desirable, such as defence, law and order, education and health. In the past the state also took ownership of manufacturing industries such as ship-building, extractive industries such as coal mining, the railways and utilities such as electricity and gas. Local governments are responsible for essential services such as education, libraries and roads at a local level.

assignment focus

For this unit you will need to select two contrasting organisations to study; one should be a profit-seeking business and one a not-for-profit organisation.

Be careful to choose organisations that will provide sufficient detail to enable you to meet the grading criteria. If you already have a link with a business, perhaps as an employee, through work experience or through family or friends, then take advantage of this.

To achieve P1, for each business you have chosen:

- provide the business name and head office address
- describe the type of business, i.e. the products (goods/services) that it provides, the industrial sector to which it belongs, whether it is public, private, not-for-profit/ voluntary sector
- describe the business purpose, i.e. its aims, the customers it supplies (is it B2B or B2C?), how these are supplied and whether products are supplied at cost, below cost or at a profit. You could provide evidence of this by showing a summary of the final accounts (as in the Greenpeace and Tesco examples).

Go to the HSBC Group website (www.hsbc.com) to find out in which countries in the world it has offices.

On page 000 we look at how the construction company Alfred McAlpine has turned itself into a service business – a move from secondary to tertiary sector.

remember

Do not confuse local businesses with the local branches of national chains, e.g. the local Kwik Fit is part of a national organisation.

Case Studies

provide real life examples that relate to what is being discussed within the text. It provides an opportunity to demonstrate theory in practice.

An **Activity** that is linked to a Case Study helps you to apply your knowledge of the subject to real life situations.

Keywords

of specific importance are highlighted within the text and then defined in a glossary at the end of the book.

Assignment focus

is designed to help you achieve your grades through answering questions and undertaking research on the topics being covered.

Information bars

point you towards resources for further reading and research (e.g. websites).

Links

direct you to other parts of the book that relate to the subject currently being covered.

Remember boxes

contain helpful hints, tips or advice.

Acknowledgements

The authors and publishers would like to acknowledge the following people and organisations for permission to reproduce material:

Bob Rantaller and the Goldmajor Group; Department for Transport; EcoGen; Edexcel; Egg.com; EU Statistics UK; Fashion United; Friends of the Earth; Greenpeace; Investors in People; Leonard Cheshire; Marks & Spencer; Morrisons; Office for National Statistics; PepsiCo Tropicana; Pirate FM; Stagecoach; Tesco; Yahoo; Yorkshire Tourist Board.

Crown copyright material is reproduced with the permission of the Controller of HMSO and the Queen's Printer for Scotland. Licence number: C2006009492.

Photograph credits:

Digital Vision 2 (NT) p.274; Photodisc 54 (NT), p.274; Eric Vidal/Rex Features, p.328; Jim Forrest/Alamy, p.383; Paul Webb/Rex Features, p.383.

Every effort has been made to contact copyright holders and we apologise if any have been overlooked.

The authors would like to thank all those who have helped in this project, in particular the principals, colleagues and students at Southwark College and Bromley College, Lansana Keifala and Atsu Gbecki. Thanks also to Tunde Jegede for his time (and music) and to Stephanie Richards and Tracy Hall for their brilliant editing and proof reading skills.

We would also like to acknowledge the support and encouragement that we have received throughout from the team at Nelson Thornes and in particular from: Jess Ward, Vanessa Thompson and Nigel Harriss.

Finally, we wish to thank our families once again.

UNIT 1

Exploring business activity

This unit covers:

- Types of business activity and ownership
- How the type of business influences the setting of strategic aims and objectives
- Functional activities and organisational structure
- How external factors in the business environment impact on organisations

This unit looks at what UK businesses do, who owns them, and the reasons why they exist; the various goals that UK businesses set themselves and how these differ between the public, private and voluntary sectors; how businesses organise their different activities so as to best achieve their targets; the factors from the outside world that affect business performance and how organisations respond to these.

grading criteria

To achieve a **Pass** grade the evidence must show that the learner is able to:	To achieve a **Merit** grade the evidence must also show that the learner is able to:	To achieve a **Distinction** grade the evidence must also show that the learner is able to:
P1 describe the type of business, purpose and ownership of two contrasting organisations	**M1** explain the points of view from different stakeholders seeking to influence the strategic aims and objectives of two contrasting organisations	**D1** evaluate how external factors, over a specified future period, may impact on the business activities, strategy, internal structures, functional activities and stakeholders of a specified organisation
P2 describe the different stakeholders who influence the purpose of two contrasting organisations	**M2** compare the factors which influence the development of the internal structures and functional activities of two contrasting organisations	
P3 outline the rationale of the strategic aims and objectives of two contrasting organisations	**M3** analyse how external factors have impacted on the two contrasting organisations	
P4 describe the functional activities, and their interdependencies in two contrasting organisations		

grading criteria

To achieve a **Pass** grade the evidence must show that the learner is able to:	To achieve a **Merit** grade the evidence must also show that the learner is able to:	To achieve a **Distinction** grade the evidence must also show that the learner is able to:
P5 describe how three external factors are impacting upon the business activities of the selected organisations and their stakeholders		

Types of business activity and ownership

Types of business activity

We can categorise **businesses** according to:

■ **industrial sector** – the type of production carried out

■ geographical scale of their operations – whether they are **local**, **national**, **international** or **global**

■ form of ownership – whether they are in the **public**, **private** or **voluntary**/not-for-**profit** sectors.

The industrial sectors

Businesses are engaged in three distinct types of **production** with each type belonging to a different industrial sector.

■ Primary sector activities involve taking goods directly from nature. These 'extractive industries' include farming, fishing, forestry and mining.

■ Secondary sector activities comprise manufacturing and construction. These create semi-finished and finished products by using materials extracted by the primary sector or materials manufactured from these.

■ The tertiary sector consists of the service industries. These may produce either commercial services for businesses or direct services for the benefit of individuals and households.

Table 1.1 Business activities in the industrial sectors

Goods (the production industries)			Services	
Primary sector	**Secondary sector**		**Tertiary sector**	
Extractive industries: agriculture; forestry; fishing; mining; oil extraction; quarrying	*Manufacturing industries*: metals; chemicals; man-made fibres; engineering; food, drink and tobacco; textiles; footwear; clothing	*Construction industries*: building; civil engineering	*Commercial services*: wholesale and retail distribution; hotels and catering; transport; post and telecommunications; banking, insurance and finance; public administration	*Direct services*: education; health services; entertainment; police; veterinary services

Trends in the industrial sectors

Over recent decades, all industrialised countries have experienced growing employment in the tertiary sector whilst the number of employees in the primary and secondary sectors has fallen, as shown in Figure 1.1. In the UK, this trend is the result of:

■ the use of new technology in manufacturing

■ the decline of heavy industries such as ship-building, coal and steel – increasingly these goods are imported more cheaply from abroad

- the **outsourcing** of UK manufacturing to overseas producers often in China and the Far East where costs are lower
- a growing demand for services such as leisure and tourism paid for by an increase in our disposable income.

For example, the Eden Project in Cornwall, once a china clay quarry, is now a tourist attraction – a move from primary to tertiary sector.

Figure 1.1 Employment
in the industrial sectors,
1979–2004

Source: Office for National Statistics

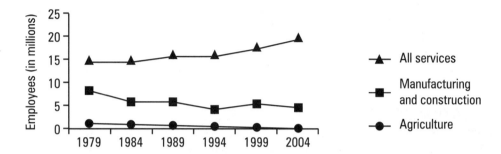

 Link

On page 42 we look at how the construction company Alfred McAlpine has turned itself into a service business – a move from secondary to tertiary sector.

Local, national, international and global business

The scale of business activity varies from local to worldwide.

- Local businesses serve the surrounding area and so tend to be relatively small. The independent corner shop is one example. *Yellow Pages* or *Thomson's Directory* will list others, such as plumbers, garages, hairdressers and restaurants.
- National businesses have sales outlets and distribution systems reaching across the country. National Express, as the name suggests, runs coaches nationwide.
- International businesses operate in more than one country. Arriva, for example, has expanded into a European operator. In addition to its UK operations, it also runs coach and rail services in the Netherlands, Scandinavia, Iberia and Italy.
- Global businesses operate in markets throughout the world. Household names such as Shell, Toyota, Avis, McDonald's and Levi Strauss are all global brands. Tesco, now with branches in Europe and Asia, is aiming for a global presence. HSBC calls itself 'the world's local bank'. What does this mean?

 remember

Do not confuse local businesses with the local branches of national chains, e.g. the local Kwik Fit is part of a national organisation.

i

Go to the HSBC Group website (www.hsbc.com) to find out in which countries in the world it has offices.

Gaining a wider market

Traditionally retailers have increased their scale of operations by setting up branches over a wider geographical area. Marks & Spencer, Tesco and Sainsbury all began as small local businesses and then expanded, first by establishing regional branches, then national and finally international branches.

Similarly manufacturers may gain access to new markets by setting up factories overseas. For example, the following now produce within the UK:

- Japanese car-makers Nissan near Sunderland and Toyota near Derby
- Daewoo electronics from Taiwan in Northern Ireland
- USA computer firms IBM and Compaq in Scotland
- Bosch electronics of Germany in Wales.

Buying into existing businesses through **mergers** or **take-overs** provides a more rapid means of expansion. Morrisons, for example, strengthened its position as a national grocery brand by buying Safeway, Wal-Mart of the USA gained access to the UK market when it bought into Asda and for a similar reason Banco Santander of Spain took over Abbey National.

'From bricks to clicks'
In recent years the growth of **e-commerce** (internet selling) has enabled some businesses to operate across international boundaries without the traditional need to have a physical presence in these countries. Amazon is one successful example of this trend.

On pages 30–33, we look further at business growth.

The public, private, voluntary/not-for-profit sectors

The UK has a **mixed economy** with some businesses operating in the public sector and controlled by the state and some in the private sector owned by individuals. Not-for-profit/voluntary businesses form a third sector seen as increasingly important to the regeneration of the country.

Table 1.2 The public, private, voluntary/not-for-profit sectors

Public sector	Private sector	Voluntary/not-for-profit
Businesses funded and run by the state provide public services. National government at Westminster ■ government departments, e.g. Home Office, DTI, Treasury ■ government agencies, e.g. Highways Agency ■ businesses such as BBC, Royal Mail. Local government at the town hall provides public services at a local level, e.g. roads, libraries, leisure centres.	Businesses owned by individuals and run for profit to reward the owner(s): ■ sole trader – one owner ■ partnership – 2–20 owners ■ private limited (Ltd) company – 2+ owners ■ public limited company (plc) – 2+ owners ■ franchises.	Run to provide a service to their members or to a group in society: ■ mutuals ■ charities ■ trusts ■ co-operatives ■ clubs and societies. May receive funding from government, the public or private businesses.

Public sector businesses are funded and run either by **central government** at Westminster or by **local government** at the town hall. Today the public sector tends to concentrate on services that are necessary or desirable, such as defence, law and order, education and health. In the past the state also took ownership of manufacturing industries such as ship-building, extractive industries such as coal mining, the railways and utilities such as electricity and gas. Local governments are responsible for essential services such as education, libraries and roads at a local level.

We will see that ideas about the extent to which the state should be involved in providing goods and services have changed over time.

Private sector businesses are owned by individuals, or groups of individuals. These are profit-making organisations whose owners (either sole traders, partners or company shareholders) risk their savings and other possessions in the hope of making personal gains.

Not-for-profit/voluntary organisations are becoming increasingly important and the government believes that they can play a central role in the future of the UK. They are run by private individuals but their ownership and aims are different from those of the profit-making private sector.

■ Not-for-profit organisations seek to provide a service for their members or for a group in society. They are not run for financial gain and any profit they achieve (usually called a surplus) is ploughed back to improve services in the future. Clubs, societies, unions, charitable trusts and workers' co-operatives are all examples. Well-known national examples of the not-for profit sector are the 'mutuals' including the building societies and some insurance providers.

■ The voluntary sector comprises those not-for-profit organisations relying to some extent on the work of volunteers who agree with their aims. Local voluntary organisations might be the tennis club or history society; national examples are RSPCA and RNIB, international examples include Amnesty International, Greenpeace and Oxfam. Often voluntary organisations perform a service that the public and private sectors do not perform adequately – perhaps because the state has insufficient funds, or perhaps because it is not a profitable activity and so is not attractive to the private sector.

Recent changes within the public, private and voluntary sectors

The three sectors of business ownership evolved to satisfy the wide range of needs within society. In a changing world the relationship between them has altered; some businesses have moved sector whilst businesses in different sectors have begun to work together in partnership.

Figure 1.2 Some recent changes in business ownership

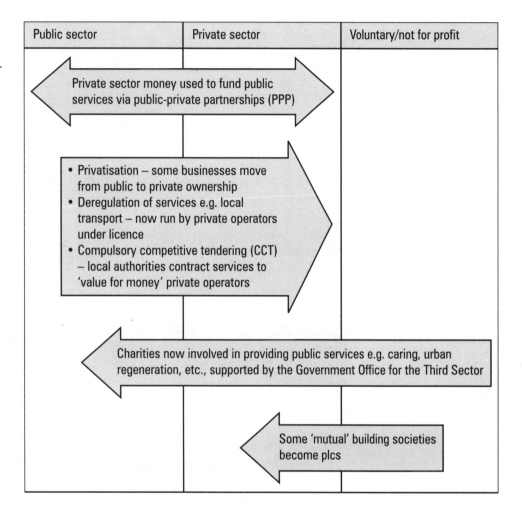

Public sector	Private sector	Voluntary/not for profit

Private sector money used to fund public services via public-private partnerships (PPP)

- Privatisation – some businesses move from public to private ownership
- Deregulation of services e.g. local transport – now run by private operators under licence
- Compulsory competitive tendering (CCT) – local authorities contract services to 'value for money' private operators

Charities now involved in providing public services e.g. caring, urban regeneration, etc., supported by the Government Office for the Third Sector

Some 'mutual' building societies become plcs

Public sector changes

The role of the public sector has been the subject of much debate over recent years.

In the past central government controlled businesses that they believed to be:

- necessary for the security of the nation – steel-making, coal-mining and ship-building, for example, should not be allowed to close
- essential services – transport and gas, electricity and water should be run for public benefit and not primarily for profit.

The National Health Service was provided free to all at the point of use. Organisations such as the BBC and Royal Mail provide public services – public service broadcasting, reliable mail delivery and access to government information and services.

More recently governments have become concerned about the cost to the taxpayer of supporting these services and sheltering them from competition. Today private sector business are encouraged to help fund these activities or, in some cases, to run them altogether. Recent trends have included:

- **privatisation** – since 1979 many central government-owned businesses such as BT, the water, electricity and gas companies, British Airways, BP and British Rail have been sold off. These now operate in the private sector as profit-making plcs. There is a view that these businesses run more efficiently if they are made to compete in the marketplace.
- **deregulation of public services** – restrictions have been removed to allow private businesses to run services that were previously operated by the state. Firms such as

Stagecoach and Arriva now run local bus services under contract. Under CCT (compulsory competitive tendering), local authorities engage the providers who give best value for money. This enables private contractors such as Cleanaway and Accord to provide local authority refuse collection

■ **public–private partnerships (PPPs)** – here private sector businesses help fund public projects such as London Underground, Crossrail, NHS hospitals and HM prisons. This is part of the Private Finance Initiative (PFI) designed to fund the New Labour government's public service reforms.

Figure 1.3 The deregulation of local transport provided an opportunity for Stagecoach to expand

case study 1.1   Public to private: rail privatisation

In 1996 John Major's Conservative government controversially broke up and sold off British Rail which until then was owned by the state. The track and stations went to a new company Railtrack plc, whilst private operators such as Midland Mainline, Virgin and Connex ran the trains under contract.

Railtrack charged the rail companies for its services and was also subsidised by the government. However, it was in a difficult position. On the one hand, as a plc, it had to make profits to reward its shareholders and to attract new investors; on the other hand, it needed to spend huge sums to provide a safe and efficient railway network.

When the Paddington rail crash in October 1999 led to the deaths of more than 30 passengers, Railtrack was accused of cutting back on safety standards in order to pay shareholders. In 2002 Tony Blair's New Labour government replaced Railtrack with Network Rail, a not-for-profit organisation.

activity

1   British Rail used to be state-owned. Why was this?

2   Which companies now operate the trains in your area?

3   Why did Railtrack plc find it difficult to maintain the railways effectively?

4   Write a brief argument either for or against selling off British Rail to private shareholders.

Voluntary sector changes

Building societies are 'mutual organisations' owned by their members – the savers and borrowers. They now operate in a similar way to banks but remain not-for profit organisations with all surpluses ploughed back to improve services in future.

Since the early 1990s, a number of building societies have converted into profit-making banks with plc status in order to raise more funds. The first to change was Abbey National, followed by others including Northern Rock, Woolwich and Halifax.

The Nationwide is the largest remaining building society. It claims that, since it does not have to pay a dividend to shareholders, it is able to provide a better deal for its customers in the form of higher savings rates and lower charges for loans and mortgages.

Check an independent personal finance website (e.g. www.moneyfacts.co.uk) or a weekend newspaper to find out the 'best buys' on savings and borrowing rates. How true is it that building societies provide some of the best offers?

As part of its deregulation programme, the government is encouraging the not-for-profit sector to run services for the national and local government. For example, in May 2006 the government created an Office for the Third Sector to support not-for-profit businesses founded for social purposes, referred to as 'social enterprise'. They believe that these organisations will be vital to the future of the UK.

Bulky Bob's is one success story. The business won a contract from Liverpool City Council to collect unwanted ('pre-loved') furniture in its fleet of purple vans. Forty per cent is sold to people on low incomes, as much as possible of the remainder is recycled. Everything that Bob collects would previously have been dumped in landfill sites. Under the agreement the council saves money, the environment and local people benefit. Bob's also gives work to the long-term unemployed and other excluded groups. By 2006 Bob's had 49 employees and a turnover of £809,000 a year.

The Minister Ed Milliband said, 'social enterprise is not an excuse for the government abandoning its responsibilities for funding public services.'

Business purposes

Why do businesses exist?

Businesses exist to provide the **goods** and **services** that people and other businesses need, want and are prepared to pay for. Walk along any high street and you will see signs of business activity – shops, buses, delivery vans, street cleaners and builders are all involved.

All businesses are engaged in production. They use inputs such as materials, labour and capital equipment (such as machinery) to produce outputs in the form of the **products** that customers demand. These products may be either goods or services.

Figure 1.4 Inputs and outputs in production

Inputs

Materials
Labour
Capital equipment

Outputs

Goods and services

Goods are tangible objects that we can see and touch.

- Consumer goods are produced for use by individuals and households. They include food, clothes and consumer durables (long-lasting goods) such as cars, refrigerators and DVD players.
- Industrial goods are produced for use by other businesses. These include raw materials, nuts and bolts, machinery, lorries and chemicals.

Services are activities that provide a benefit to individuals, to businesses or to both. Unlike goods, services are intangible.

■ Direct (or personal) services are provided for the benefit of individuals and households. They include the services of bank managers, doctors and entertainers.

■ Commercial services are provided for the benefit of businesses. These include transporting, warehousing, finance, business banking, insurance and telecommunications.

Figure 1.5 shows the commercial services that provide the **infrastructures** needed by businesses.

Figure 1.5 Infrastructures that support business

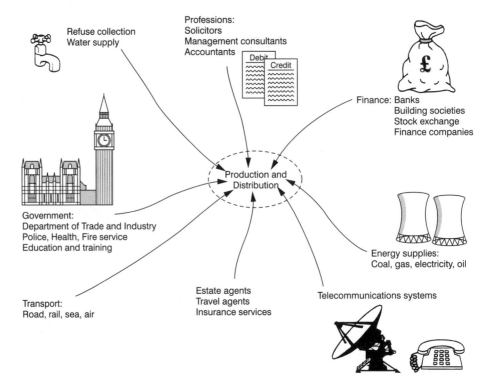

Businesses in all sectors exist to supply the goods and services that customers demand. Remember that this demand comes from individuals, households and communities, from other businesses and from central and local government via public spending. Demand becomes effective where customers are willing and able to buy.

Figure 1.6 Supply and demand

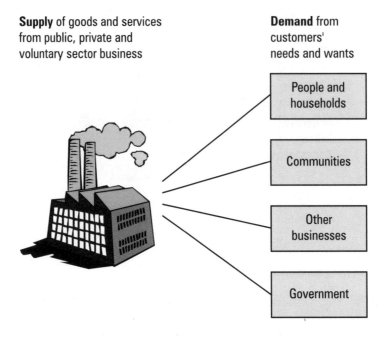

The way in which an organisation meets customer demand and the prices it charges for its products varies with:

■ the particular business activity and the nature and scale of its market

■ whether it is a public, private or not-for-profit business.

Supplying goods and services at profit, at cost and below cost

Private sector business

The main motivation for private sector businesses is to make profits for their owners, so that ultimately they must generate more money from selling their products than they spend on producing them.

Case study 1.2 shows how Tesco, the UK's most successful retailer, generates and uses its profits. Notice how the profits are used:

■ A percentage of profit is paid to the government's department of Revenue and Customs as corporation tax.

■ From the profits that remain, the directors will pay dividends to reward the company shareholders who own the business.

■ The remaining profit is retained and ploughed back into the business to fund future expansion.

> **remember**
>
> If you complete Unit 37, Starting a small business, you will need to identify a gap in the market for a product and plan to supply this profitably.

---

case study 1.2

Tesco plc: 'Every little helps'

In February 2006 Tesco announced record profits of over £2.2 billion. These were achieved not only through supplying customers with quality, variety and value in its core food business, but also through impressive growth in non-food items such as clothes and electrical goods, combined with expansion overseas. The company has also diversified into financial services, gas and electricity supplies, is an internet service provider (ISP) and an estate agent. The next plan is to challenge Marks & Spencer for leadership of the high street clothing market.

Tesco originally achieved success through fast turnover of stock at low prices – a small profit on a lot of items equals a lot of profit. Tesco's recent growth now means that it can now benefit from economies of scale by placing huge orders. This enables it to buy direct from producers (such as farmers) on very favourable terms. Tesco can then pass on these low prices to the customer.

Figure 1.7 Tesco plc – profit for 2006

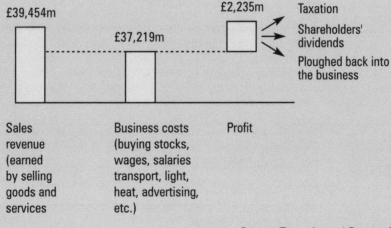

Sales revenue (earned by selling goods and services)

Business costs (buying stocks, wages, salaries transport, light, heat, advertising, etc.)

Profit

£39,454m

£37,219m

£2,235m

Taxation

Shareholders' dividends

Ploughed back into the business

Source: Tesco Annual Report, February 2006

---

activity

Log on to the Tesco website: www.tesco.com.

1 Look at the home page and make a list of the different types of operation in which Tesco is now involved.

activity
CONTINUED

2   In which countries does Tesco now have stores? What is its scale of business?

3   Click 'Investor relations' at the bottom of the home page to access the Corporate Affairs website. Clicking on 'Inside Tesco' brings up 'core purpose' and 'strategy' sections. What are Tesco's main aims?

Despite the need to make profits there may be occasions when a profit-seeking business is prepared to sell at, or even below cost. In March 2006, for example, 3 per cent of sales by the 'big four' supermarkets were below cost. There are a number of reasons why businesses may do this:

■   introductory offers – 'buy at this special low price for a limited period only'. This is a marketing tactic to encourage customers to try a new product in the hope that they will continue to buy when the price is later raised to a profitable level

■   in a price war or as a marketing ploy designed to steal customers from rivals. Ryanair's offers have included flights to Dublin for 1p and to Malaga for £2.98

■   as a 'loss leader', where one item is sold cheaply to attract customers who then buy further goods at full price, e.g. a supermarket may advertise below-cost turkeys at Christmas with this in mind

■   where there is no better alternative, e.g. late on a Saturday afternoon market traders may sell off fruit and vegetables below cost to cut their losses – the alternative is to throw them away

■   end-of-season sale items where the aim is to clear outdated, slow-selling stock and make way for new products

■   where the revenue is generated from sources other than the customer, e.g. newspapers or independent television companies subsidise their products from advertising revenue so that customers pay less than the cost of production

■   to enhance the service and thereby to boost corporate (or company) image, e.g. pharmaceutical companies may be persuaded to provide below-cost medication to developing countries, local shops may provide telephone top-up cards, stamps and electricity key-charging services for no, or minimal, profit

■   where contracts or the demands of regulators specify a given level of service, e.g. rail and bus operators may be required to run an off-peak service even though this part of the service is not profitable.

Large projects with high start-up costs may take time to build up a profitable customer base. BSkyB (now Sky), Eurodisney and Eurotunnel all took some years to achieve profitability. Any loss-making business is technically selling below cost. For example, the phenomenal growth of the Google search engine has made it one of the world's most visible brands. Tony Blair's reference to 'the Google generation' showed the extent to which it has become part of everyday language. In October 2006 it paid £885 million for the website Youtube. Yet Google does not charge us for searching the web – Youtube is also free.

assignment focus

1   How does Google make its money? How will it make money from Youtube?

2   In November 2006 First Direct bank announced that it would charge £10 for customers to use its current account. Most current accounts are free – why?

Public sector business

Public sector operations exist to provide necessary or desirable services to the community. They will need to generate sufficient funds to run these services but will not operate for financial gain. In general these services are provided to the user at less than cost. Successive governments decide which services should be provided by the state and each year raise the taxes needed to pay for these. The government uses a progressive taxation system (the 'Robin Hood' principle) to tax highest earners more in order to provide subsidised services for those in most need.

Central government spends around £8,000 a year for every man, woman and child in the UK.

Figure 1.8 Central government spending

Source: Budget 2007 Summary, HM Treasury

Where taxpayers' money is spent

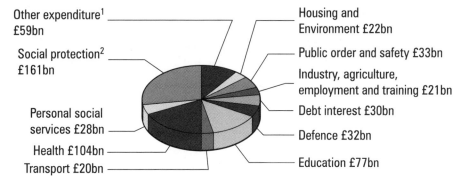

Other expenditure[1] £59bn

Social protection[2] £161bn

Personal social services £28bn

Health £104bn

Transport £20bn

Housing and Environment £22bn

Public order and safety £33bn

Industry, agriculture, employment and training £21bn

Debt interest £30bn

Defence £32bn

Education £77bn

Total managed expenditure – £587 billion

[1] Other expenditure includes spending on general public services; recreation, culture, media and sport, international co-operation and development; public service pensions; plus spending yet to be allocated and some accounting adjusments.
2 Social protection includes tax credit payments in excess of an individual's tax liability

Local authority library and education services, public transport for pensioners and the National Health Service provided by central government are all subsidised by public funds. Here users do not pay the full cost at the point of use; compare this situation with the fees paid by patients at private hospitals and by students at private schools.

'No such thing as a free lunch' – Milton Friedman
Governments are concerned to limit the cost of state services to taxpayers and to provide 'value for money spent'. Measures used in recent years include:

- privatisation and deregulation to enable private operators to take over some state services, (e.g. DHL on page 14), CCT to compel local authorities to contract out to efficient providers (e.g. Bulky Bob's on page 7)

- charges for services where possible, e.g. proposed charges for the ambulance service or asking students to pay their own university fees

- means testing in order to subsidise only the most needy

- closure of inefficient operations such as loss-making post offices (see pages 26 and 365)

- use of private funds for public services via public-private partnerships (PPPs).

Not-for-profit/voluntary sector business
Businesses in the voluntary sector raise money purely to pay the costs involved in carrying out their chosen activity. Oxfam, for example, funds humanitarian aid to developing countries in the form of food, clothing and education. On a local level, Mudchute City Farm in East London provides educational visits for inner city children. In meeting the demand from groups in the community, such organisations frequently provide a free service to the beneficiary.

The voluntary sector has a total income of over £15 billion, £4 billion of which comes from voluntary donations. The balance comes from corporate support (does the business you have chosen to study donate to charity?), state assets made available by the government's Office of the Third Sector and commercial operations, e.g. Oxfam runs shops and sells on eBay, the National Trust rents out properties, and local sports and community clubs operate bars and social clubs.

Many not-for profit businesses are viable commercial enterprises able to generate their own revenues by charging above cost. They differ from private sector organisations in that they plough back surpluses, as for example the building societies or, like the retail co-operative societies, return profits to their customers.

case study 1.3   Greenpeace

Table 1.3 shows how Greenpeace generates and spends its funds.

Table 1.3 Greenpeace's income and expenditure, 2003

Income	£000s	Expenditure	£000s
Subscriptions and donations	8,403	Expenditure expenses	4,458
Profit on merchandising, publishing and commercial events	152	Campaign information costs	688
		Cost of collecting subscriptions and donations	625
Raised by campaign groups	64	Cost of recruiting new supporters	1,035
Interest from investing surplus funds	19	Marketing costs	567
		Administration and management costs	405
		Surplus retained	860
Total income	**8,638**	**Total expenditure**	**8,638**

Source: Greenpeace Annual Review, 2003

activity

1 Why would a company form of organisation not be suitable for Greenpeace?

2 Give an example of a 'greener' method of production.

3 How do you think businesses themselves might benefit from using sustainable sources (and being seen to use these)?

4 Find examples of companies that adopt environmentally friendly policies. (They are usually proud of this and may use it in their promotional materials as well as in the annual report.)

In 2006 social enterprises in the UK generated £27bn in turnover. These are commercial operations but with a social mission. They aim to benefit the community whilst financing themselves from ethical commercial ventures. There is a mix here of provision below cost, at cost and above cost. For example:

■ Café Direct provides quality coffee to retailers whilst paying a fair price to growers. It is now the sixth largest coffee supplier in the UK.

■ Green Estate employs 42 people in Sheffield where it earns cash from regenerating run-down urban areas. It began with state funding but in 2006 generated £1.4 million from landscaping services and sales of recycled compost.

assignment focus

Consider using a not-for profit business for your unit assignment. The annual reports of national charities are freely available and details of activities and links appear on their websites.

Think about the following questions:

1 Should the government provide the services provided by charities such as the RNIB and RSPCA?

2 What do Amnesty International, Greenpeace and Oxfam do? Could private sector business provide these services adequately?

Supplying products in response to demand

Remember that customers include all of those who buy goods and services. They may be:

■ consumers – you and I, individuals and households wanting consumer goods and direct services for our own use

■ other businesses demanding industrial goods and commercial services to help them carry on production

■ central and local governments using taxpayers' money (public spending) to build roads and hospitals, equip the police, armed forces, and so on.

We can therefore identify:

■ **B2C** businesses selling to the consumer, the end-user. These are usually retailers such as Sainsbury's and NatWest, but could also be manufacturers or wholesalers selling direct

■ **B2B** businesses supplying industrial goods to other businesses, e.g. Rolls-Royce sells engines to aeroplane manufacturers, the London Brick Company supplies construction firms.

The supply chain for goods – supplying customer demand

A whole network of organisations and processes may be needed to supply a good to the end-user. Value will be added at each stage so that each business involved can sell the product on at a higher price.

Figure 1.9 A typical supply chain for a cereal

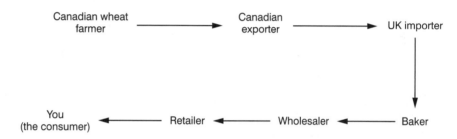

assignment focus

Procurers (buyers), producers, distributors, wholesalers, retailers and **e-tailers** (online retailers) all play vital roles within the supply chain. What are their functions? Which are B2B and which are B2C businesses?

Alternative supply chains for goods may be:

■ Manufacturer → Wholesaler → Consumer

Here the wholesaler also performs the retail function as, for example, when consumers buy from a carpet warehouse.

■ Manufacturer → Retailer → Consumer

Large retailers such as the major supermarkets buy direct from the manufacturers and growers and so perform their own wholesaling function. In the motor trade car manufacturers sell through franchised dealers.

■ Manufacturer → Consumer

At a local level, farmers markets allow growers to sell directly to the consumer. E-tailing (online retailing) enables direct selling by manufacturers such as Dell.

Missing out the specialist wholesaler and retailer should give a cost advantage that can be passed on to customers in the form of lower prices. This partly explains why online prices tend to be lower than those on the high street.

Notice that the supply chain ends with the consumer. Ultimately demand for B2B businesses is derived from consumer demand.

Supplying customers more efficiently

Efficiencies in the supply chain will improve business performance:

■ **Vertical integration** Here a business grows into other activities along the supply chain (as when a manufacturer such as Thorntons opens shops) to gain the value added at each stage for itself.

■ **JIT (just in time)** Stock is bought in just as it is needed. This avoids the costs of storage, wastage and tying up money in advance. Computer technology such as EPOS till systems (electronic point-of-sale) read bar code data, update stock records and automatically re-order supplies.

case study
1.4

The government as customer – will DHL deliver supply chain savings?

The NHS Purchasing and Supply Agency spends more than £4 billion a year on buying supplies for the National Health Service – everything from beds to bandages, medication to syringes, pacemakers to hip implants. These are delivered to hospitals by the 1,400 employees in the NHS Logistics Authority.

In July 2006 it was announced that US firm DHL/Novation will take over the responsibility for buying NHS supplies and is also likely to take over distribution. The company will be paid on the basis of the money it saves the NHS. Since DHL/Novation is large, it can save money by striking harder bargains with suppliers and the government hopes that these savings can then be used to provide more NHS services. By contracting out procurement (buying) and logistics (distribution), the NHS can also cut wages and pension costs.

Unison, the public sector trades union, is opposed to this 'further privatisation' and has threatened strike action. However, PM Tony Blair believes that the test of keeping the health service public is whether services are free to the user.

Smaller British healthcare suppliers are also worried that they may be forced into bankruptcy if prices are too low. These smaller companies are vital because they are the ones with new ideas and innovative treatments. They argue that since savings, not quality, is the target, jobs are at risk and patients may miss out on the latest care.

A government spokesperson said: 'We recognise the concerns of staff and are looking closely at the proposals before making a final decision.'

activity

1 Write a brief case for and against contracting DHL to work for the National Health Service.

2 Look at the McAlpine case study on page 42. Give examples of how the company supplies demand from central government.

3 Select two other areas of government spending apart from health. (Use the government spending figures on page 11.) For each area, name five items that the government will buy and identify five major suppliers.

4 Log onto the Rolls-Royce website and look at the Sourcerer site. This enables business customers to order Roll-Royce parts. What advantages do you think online buying provides for supplier and for customer?

Business owners

The legal structures of ownership to be found within the public, private and voluntary/not-for-profit sectors are illustrated in Table 1.2, on page 4.

Private sector businesses

Sole trader businesses are owned by one person who may keep all of the profits but has **unlimited liability** i.e. the owner is personally liable (or responsible) for all business debts.

Partnerships (sometimes called firms) are owned and run by between two and 20 partners who may share the profits. They are 'jointly and severally' liable for all business debts, i.e. each partner has unlimited liability (unless stated in the partnership agreement) and a decision made by one partner becomes the legal responsibility of all other partners.

Limited liability companies are owned by their shareholders and there is no legal limit to the number of shareholders a company may have. They differ from sole traders and partnerships in a number of ways:

■ A limited company exists in law and is separate from its owners. If you wished to take a sole trader or a partnership to court, you would be suing the owners of these businesses. In the case of a company, it is the company itself that is sued. It is, however, now possible to sue individual company directors where this is thought appropriate. An example is the (unsuccessful) case of 'corporate manslaughter' brought against the directors of the maintenance contractors Balfour Beatty following the Hatfield rail crash.

■ All limited companies must be registered with the Registrar of Companies at Companies House to whom financial information must be sent each year. This information is available for inspection by any member of the public.

■ Whereas sole traders and partners own and control their businesses, company shareholders elect a board of directors to run the company on their behalf. (In small companies, the shareholders may also be the directors.)

■ Unlike sole traders and partners, company shareholders are protected by limited liability. Should the business fail, their losses will be limited to the amount they have invested in the business; they cannot be called upon to forfeit their personal assets to repay business debts.

■ Those dealing with a company, therefore risk not being paid. For this reason a **private limited company** must display the word 'Limited' or 'Ltd' in its name, whilst a public limited company must display the letters 'plc'.

The differences between private and public limited companies are shown in Table 1.4.

Table 1.4 The differences between private and public limited companies

Private limited companies (Ltd)	Public limited companies (plc)
These may not offer their shares for sale to the general public and they therefore tend to be smaller than plcs. Examples include local and regional businesses, such as a garage, a farm, a builder, a coach company. Some companies start as private limited companies and become plcs when they need to raise further capital for expansion. This was the route taken by Manchester United in 1991. At the time of writing the new owner has enough shares to turn it back into a private company.	These may offer their shares to the general public, through the Stock Exchange – it is plc share prices that are displayed in the daily press. Plcs have the potential to raise huge amounts of capital and most of the larger companies have this form of ownership. They include household names such as Tesco, Marks & Spencer, ICI, the high street banks, as well as the privatised businesses such as British Airways and BT.

Franchises are sole traders, partnerships or companies that take on the brand and products of another business under licence. The franchiser (who owns the brand) uses this as a means of increasing its outlets and market, whilst the franchisee (who has permission to use the brand) gets a ready-made business with proven products, an established reputation and brand image. Examples of franchises include The Bodyshop, BSM (British School of Motoring), McDonald's and Domino's Pizza.

The public sector

The public sector is ultimately owned by the people of the UK and run for their benefit. Central government policy is decided by the elected government of the day. Once this policy passes into law it is put into effect by government departments and government agencies.

Central government departments are funded by Parliament and staffed by impartial civil servants. Departments include:

■ Treasury

■ Home Office

■ Foreign and Commonwealth Office

■ Defence

■ Trade and Industry (DTI)

- Health (DoH)
- International Development
- Transport
- Education and Skills (DfES)
- Work and Pensions (DWP)
- Culture, Media and Sport (DCMS)
- Social Exclusion
- Environment, Food and Rural Affairs (Defra)
- Communities and Local Government
- Constitutional Affairs
- Northern Ireland, Scotland and Wales.

Government agencies deliver the various government services for the UK government, Scottish Executive, Welsh Assembly or Northern Ireland Executive. A chief executive is responsible for day-to-day operations. Examples include the Highways Agency responsible for managing the road system and the Countryside Agency.

Local government policy is decided by elected councillors of the majority party. Local services are run from the town hall for the benefit of local people. For example, the major services listed by Islington Council in order of expenditure are: social services, environment and conservation, housing and leisure (including parks, leisure centres and libraries). Funding is from business rates, council tax and central government grants, with additional revenue raised via council rents, car parking charges and leisure centres.

To find information about the services provided by your local council and its spending, visit their website.

Voluntary/not-for-profit sector

These organisations are run on behalf of their members, their employees or the community. Paid employees or volunteers operate these on a not-for-profit basis with any surplus reinvested in the business.

The sector has a variety of forms of ownership:

- Mutual organisations such as building societies and insurance companies provide services for the benefit of their members, the savers, investors and policy holders. Profits (or surpluses) are reinvested – see page 12.

- Charitable trust status allows an organisation to escape tax liability so that more of their funds can be devoted to their chosen projects. For this reason many voluntary/not-for-profit organisations become registered charities. Trusts exist where appointed trustees hold and manage assets on behalf of a group of people. The National Trust, one of the UK's largest landowners, manages buildings and land for the benefit and enjoyment of the general public.

- Co-operatives operate in all sectors of the community, and they carry out a wide range of activities. They are owned by members who may be their employees or their consumers. Whilst some co-operatives have only two or three members, others have hundreds.

  - Retail co-operatives (the Co-op) for example are owned by their customers who receive a dividend each year based on their purchases. In 2006 they underwent a rebranding exercise to update their image.

  - Workers' co-operatives are owned and controlled by their employees who share responsibilities, decision-making and profits according to a set of internationally agreed principles. Worker co-operatives are growing in the UK with support from the Local Co-operative Development Agencies (CDA).

- Community Interest Companies (CICs) were introduced in 2005 as a means of business start-up for social enterprise businesses providing services to the community. There were 500 CICs registered by the end of 2006 and this is likely to grow.

- Social enterprises (such as Bob's, see page 7) are a growing sector with 55,000 businesses in 2006. These generate revenues from public services often under contract from local or central government

case study 1.5

The National Trust

The National Trust was formed in 1895 to protect coastline, countryside and buildings in England, Wales and Northern Ireland from uncontrolled development so that it is available for future generations to enjoy.

The property that the Trust owns is either donated, left as legacies or bought using the Trust's own funds.

The Trust is a charity and is completely independent of government funding, relying for income on membership fees, donations, legacies, and also upon revenue raised from commercial operations such as shops and holiday properties.

There are 3.4 million members and 43,000 volunteers. More than 12 million people paid for entry to properties in 2004, and 50 million visited the free open air properties.

In 2004 the Trust owned assets of £700 million consisting of: historic houses and gardens, industrial monuments, woods, beaches, farmland, moorland, islands, castles and nature reserves.

Source: The National Trust

activity

1   What is the advantage for the National Trust in being independent of government funding?

2   Give one major advantage for the Trust of having charitable status.

3   Why is a trust a suitable form of legal status for an organisation of this sort?

assignment focus

For this unit you will need to select two contrasting organisations to study; one should be a profit-seeking business and one a not-for-profit organisation.

Be careful to choose organisations that will provide sufficient detail to enable you to meet the grading criteria. If you already have a link with a business, perhaps as an employee, through work experience or through family or friends, then take advantage of this.

To achieve P1, for each business you have chosen:

■   provide the business name and head office address

■   describe the type of business, i.e. the products (goods/services) that it provides, the industrial sector to which it belongs, whether it is public, private, not-for-profit/ voluntary sector

■   describe the business purpose, i.e. its aims, the customers it supplies (is it B2B or B2C?), how these are supplied and whether products are supplied at cost, below cost or at a profit. You could provide evidence of this by showing a summary of the final accounts (as in the Greenpeace and Tesco examples).

Key stakeholders

Stakeholders are those people and communities who have an interest (or stake) in a particular business because they are affected by its activities. We can distinguish between:

■   internal stakeholders, those who work within the business, including: owners (sole traders, partners and those shareholders who participate in management), directors, managers and other employees

■   external stakeholders, including customers, suppliers, financial institutions, shareholders who invest but take no part in the running of the business, pressure groups, trades unions, employer associations, governments, commercial partners, local and national communities.

In practice, different stakeholder groups may have different, and sometimes conflicting, demands on a business.

Owners

Sole traders, partners or company shareholders own private sector businesses. These owners risk their own funds when they invest in a business and may be rewarded in a number of ways:

- income – sole traders and partners receive a share of profits in the form of drawings, whilst shareholders receive dividends

- capital growth – if the value of the business grows, the owners may be able to sell their stake in the business at a profit. A rising share price, for example, will benefit shareholders

- power and influence – shareholders can vote at the company AGM (annual general meeting) and influence policy decisions – environmental pressure groups buy energy company shares for this reason. A majority stakeholder can take over a company – this is how Wal-Mart gained control of Asda and how the Glazer family gained control of Manchester United.

Owners are a powerful stakeholder group and companies often state 'adding **shareholder value**' as one of their main objectives.

Employees

These work at various levels in the organisation. They include directors, managers and operatives.

Directors

Directors are employees whose job is to run the company on behalf of the shareholders. They set the **business objectives** and take strategic decisions about the 'direction' the business will take. In a small company, such as a family business, the shareholders may also be the directors, whilst in a large plc the shareholders will elect a board of directors to run the business.

If directors run a profitable business, they achieve a good salary, job satisfaction and prestige. There has been recent concern about 'fat cat' salaries paid to reward some company directors. (In July 2004 Sir Peter Davis left Sainsbury's with a £2.3 million performance bonus – the company reported its first-ever loss four months later.)

Managers

Managers are employees responsible for deciding on the tactics for achieving the organisation's objectives within a particular area, section or department. For example, a retailer such as Boots will appoint a branch manager to run each shop, while a college will appoint a manager to run the business studies and science departments.

Although managers have similar needs to other employees as mentioned below, they have more responsibility and are more highly paid.

Other employees

Operatives and clerical staff work under a manager or supervisor and are engaged either directly, or indirectly, in the production of the goods and services supplied by the business. They want secure jobs, good working conditions, satisfactory pay and pensions, good career prospects and a safe and healthy workplace.

The demands of employees will cost the business money and may put them into conflict with owners and their senior managers (the 'us and them' syndrome).

Customers

Customers buy the goods and services that a business produces and without them the business would not exist. Customers want a reliable supply of quality products at a reasonable price on suitable payment terms. In a competitive environment, businesses must be sure to keep their customers satisfied. Remember that customers may be consumers, other businesses or government departments.

Suppliers

Suppliers provide either stocks of goods or commercial services such as accounting, banking, electricity, water, security or maintenance. Those who supply on credit terms will want secure contracts with guaranteed and prompt payment. In 2005, the suppliers of MG Rover, knowing the company was in difficulties, refused to deliver parts unless cash was paid on delivery. The company ran out of components and ceased production.

Financial institutions

Banks and other financial institutions provide various forms of funding. They want the business to generate a profit so that any loans and overdrafts can be repaid and to gain a satisfactory return on these investments.

Pressure groups

These are concerned about specific issues ranging from the rights of motorists (the AA and RAC) to the abolition of foxhunting (League Against Cruel Sports). The TUC (Trades Union Congress) and CBI (Confederation of British Industry) act as pressure groups for employees and employers respectively, whilst charities such as Amnesty International (the plight of political prisoners) and Friends of the Earth (the environment) press their own concerns.

Local pressure groups may be set up to campaign on single issues such as opposition to a road development or a new superstore.

We look at the Highbury Community Association and Arsenal FC on page 21.

Trades unions

Trades unions are concerned about the pay and conditions of employment of their members, the employees in a particular industry or workplace. Most trades unions are affiliated to the TUC, a body representing the views of trades unions as a whole in the UK.

On page 14 we see how Unison represents NHS employees.

Employer associations

These represent the employers in a particular industry. They pass on information and set up agreements concerning matters of mutual interest such as rates of pay, conditions of work and procedures for resolving disputes. The Confederation of British Industry (CBI) represents the interests of employers at national level.

The CBI and TUC both act as pressure groups in working for their members' interests.

Commercial partners

Businesses frequently carry out their operations in partnership with other companies:

- Virgin's bank operates in partnership with Royal Bank of Scotland plc.
- Waitrose works with the delivery firm Ocado.
- In 2008 Liverpool will be the European Capital of Culture. The city is linking with public and private sectors organisations, such as: Hill Dickinson, United Utilities, Enterprise plc, Radiocity 96.7 and Northwest Regional Development Agency.

Central and local governments

Central and local governments have the power to block, promote and regulate business activity. They are concerned with the impact of business on the local and national economy, on people and on the environment.

- Local authorities can exercise control through local planning restrictions (Darlington Council rejected Tesco's plans) and the enforcement of public health and trades descriptions legislation. In turn they benefit from business rates.
- Central government receives revenue from businesses. HM Revenue & Customs taxes business profits and collects VAT, as well as PAYE (income tax) and NIC (National Insurance contributions) deducted from employees.

See pages 10–11.

Governments regulate employment, health and safety, consumer protection, competition and taxation. Business information, advice and grants are provided by the Department of Trade and Industry (DTI).

Local and national communities

Local residents and local businesses are concerned about the social costs and benefits of business activity. Costs include noise, light, atmospheric and water pollution, over-crowding and traffic congestion. Communities may benefit from better job prospects, regeneration of the locality and tourism.

Some issues affect people across the country particularly where there are social costs (costs borne by society as a whole rather than by the businesses that cause them). The growth of air traffic (one of the fastest growing sources of carbon emissions) is one such issue and social responsibility is a growing challenge for businesses:

■ Silverjet airline now charges a 'green levy' used to offset damage it causes to the environment.

■ In 2006 top band the Scissor Sisters took part in 'Global Cool' a carbon-neutral music event leading to the planting of 600 trees.

Links and interdependencies between stakeholders

Where stakeholder interests coincide they will work together. For example:

■ Employer associations support business owners, trades unions support employees.

■ The government's Department of Trade and Industry (DTI) will support:

  • business owners and managers by providing advice, information and financial help. The government wants successful businesses to boost national prosperity

  • employees via employment legislation

  • the consumer by promoting competition in the marketplace to keep down prices and drive up quality.

The Competition Commission investigation into the power of supermarkets (page 32) is an example.

The importance of stakeholders in influencing business activity

Some stakeholders are more influential than others. Workers in developing countries making clothes for fashionable brands can exert little power over their employers. Unionised workers such as those in the fire service, London Underground or Unison will have more power.

Pressure groups forced Shell to re-examine its corporate image when they publicised environmental abuses, whilst major shareholders have the power to remove company directors and influence strategic decisions.

The government is able to use the law to change behaviour by, for example, imposing environmental levies or health and safety regulations.

Conflicts between stakeholders

Different stakeholders have different, and often conflicting, needs. For example, traditionally businesses have suffered from an 'us and them' **culture** between employees supported by their trades unions on the one hand and top management representing shareholders on the other. Employee demands for better pay and conditions may conflict with the desire for higher profits so that industrial disputes, perhaps leading to strike action, may result. It is the task of the human resources function to resolve such problems.

One argument against privatisation of business (see page 6) was that it would create conflict between the needs of customers for effective, affordable services and the needs of shareholders to make profits. The take-over of Manchester United by the Glazer family in 2005 was supported by the shareholders who wanted to sell but opposed by fans who set up a pressure group to oppose the sale. Which stakeholder conflicts can you see in the DHL case study 1.4 on page 14?

case study 1.6

What a load of rubbish!

In August 2006 Arsenal FC closed their ground in Highbury, North London, and moved to their new ground half a mile away, built on the old Ashburton Grove refuse tip. The old ground with 38,000 seats was too small. The new 60,000-seater stadium will also generate revenue from its corporate, sports and gambling activities.

The development was only approved after lengthy discussions with a variety of stakeholders. It involved the relocation of 50 local businesses and the council waste recycling centre, the compulsory purchase and demolition of an industrial site and the construction of the new stadium together with 2,500 new homes (including 1,000 'affordable' dwellings.). Business and health facilities will be built in the surrounding area and overall 1,000 construction workers will be employed and 1,800 long-term jobs created.

By 2010 the existing ground will be converted into apartments and other amenities including a health centre and a public garden.

Figure 1.10 Stakeholder groups in Arsenal FC

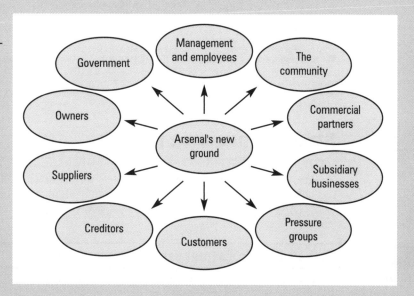

activity

1 a) Here are some stakeholders of Arsenal FC. Fit them under the correct headings on the diagram above:

   players, team manager, coaching staff, the Highbury Community Association, Robert McAlpine (the construction company), administrative staff, the fans, banks and other financial institutions, shareholders, local residents, local retailers, stadium and shirt sponsors Emirates, Newlon Housing Trust, Islington Council, the shirt manufacturers Nike, Sky, the department of Revenue & Customs, local shops

   b) Can you suggest others?

   c) Identify interdependencies and any possible conflicts between different stakeholder groups over the relocation of the club.

   d) Which stakeholder groups had conflicting interests? Briefly explain the different demands of these groups. Which stakeholder groups had power to influence the planning decision.

2 Re-read the Railtrack case study on page 6.

   Name other Railtrack stakeholders and explain why they had an interest in the business.

assignment focus

You may continue to study the two businesses that you used to complete P1 (on page 17) or choose two different contrasting organisations.

To achieve P2, you should identify and describe the various stakeholders of each business you have chosen.

To achieve M1, you must also explain the interest that each stakeholder group has in the business. Explain how each group tries to influence the way the business operates and the strategic aims and objectives that the business pursues. Give examples to illustrate this influence.

How the type of business influences the setting of strategic aims and objectives

Business **strategy** concerns the big decisions about where the business is going. Some organisations draw up a 'mission statement' as a summary of the standards, qualities and purpose of their business. Arriva's vision, for example, is 'to be recognised as the leading transport services organisation in Europe'.

We can distinguish between:

- strategic aims – broad statements of intent showing in general terms what the business wishes to achieve
- strategic objectives – more precise, quantified, plans of action which enable progress to be measured.

Strategic planning process

This process is carried out by businesses in all sectors.

In setting out the **strategic plan**, the directors will aim to move the business from where it is now to where it hopes to be at some specified future date. For example, your school or college will may have a five-year strategic plan covering aims for quality of teaching and learning, links with industry, etc.

Case study 1.9 looks (page 31) at Blacks five-point plan.

The strategic planning process has three main stages, as shown in Figure 1.11. Three levels of management will be involved in this process (Figure 1.12).

Figure 1.11 The strategic planning process

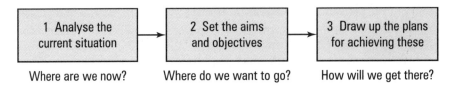

1 Analyse the current situation	2 Set the aims and objectives	3 Draw up the plans for achieving these
Where are we now?	Where do we want to go?	How will we get there?

For an explanation of PESTLE, see pages 43–51 and 132–133.

Stage 1: analyse the present situation

The directors assess the current position and performance of the organisation.

Quantitative analysis uses 'hard' measurable data to consider aspects of performance. This could measure volumes or quantities (eight new stores opened) or financial values (£100,000 profit). Such data may be further processed to provide valuable comparative information:

- over time, e.g. 10 per cent increase in profits since last year
- against competitors, e.g. **market share** is down 5 per cent
- against industry benchmarks, e.g. measures up to best practice.

Figure 1.12 Planning, level of management and monitoring

Planning	Level of management		Monitoring
Long-term corporate direction and mission Organisation-wide objectives, e.g. entering new markets, developing new products, buying new business, Corporate business plan	*Strategic* top-level managers/owner, long term, non-routine decisions involving risk	Strategic	**Benchmarking** against best practice, competitor analysis, changes in the external environment/ market place, PESTLE strategic assessment of customers surveys, continuous improvement
Financial budgets, personal targets on recruitment/ training, sales targets by region/product group, etc.	*Tactical* Middle management decisions at departmental or fuctional level	Tactical	Comparison of actual performance with plans, e.g. quality, wastage and customer satisfaction, sales targets, store or branch **appraisal**
Daily work allocation, staffing rota, breaks, work place health and safety, arranging cover for absent staff, stock display, etc.	*Operational* Day-to-day decision, usually routine with less risk	Operational	Staff punctuality and absenteeism, stock movement and replacement, staff behaviour, customer service, team/ individual appraisal

Ratio analysis pages 95–98 (also pages 220–227) and variance analysis (pages 79–80 and also page 199) are aspects of this.

Qualitative analysis judges business performance through 'soft' data based on attitudes, interests and opinions. It could measure satisfied customers, standards of service or staff morale. Where such data is captured via closed questions it may be quantified. For example when first direct, the online bank, claimed the best customer satisfaction among the retail banks it presented figures to support this. (Of course the validity depends upon the sample surveyed and the questions asked.)

Stage 2: set aims and objectives

Once it is clear where the business currently stands, aims and objectives will be set to move it forward.

The precise aims and objectives will depend upon the nature of the business activities, its ownership and scale. Profit, for example, will be a high priority for BA but irrelevant for Oxfam. Powerful stakeholder groups may also determine objectives. Many mission statements put 'adding shareholder value' as a priority (see Blacks pages 30–31). In a competitive market, the customers will have power, which is why first direct is concerned about customer satisfaction. For a rail company the government regulator can influence policy.

Cyert and March, in *A Behavioural Theory of the Firm*, also suggest that different management teams will have their own agendas, such as trying to gain the biggest salary or most power through 'empire-building' (building up their own sections).

Richard Cyert and James March (1992) *A Behavioural Theory of the Firm*, 2nd edition, Blackwell

We examine the strategic aims for public, private and voluntary sector organisations on pages 24–33.

Stage 3: planning strategies

Once the aims have been agreed, the organisation will need to create a plan – a series of objectives through which aims can become reality. These objectives become a working guide throughout the organisation. They should be quantified and ideally should be SMART:

- **S**pecific – they should clearly identify a product, activity, region, etc., e.g. 'We will increase sales of organic vegetables in the north-east'

- **M**easurable – it should be possible to determine when the objective has been met, e.g. 'We will increase sales of organic vegetables by 5 per cent'

- **A**chievable – the target must be one that employees can hit, i.e. it must be possible to increase sales by 5 per cent, otherwise employees are being set up to fail

- **R**ealistic – the target must not put unreasonable demands on employees or equipment. Sometimes the R stands for Relevant, meaning that the objective should be an appropriate one for the business to pursue and not a distraction

- **T**ime-related – the objective has a set time period or deadline, e.g. 'by the end of December'.

In drawing up the plan it is important to make sure that all activities are co-ordinated across the organisation. There must be:

- horizontal consistency – targets for each functional area should complement each other and not conflict, e.g. the production department must be able to satisfy sales targets

- vertical consistency – the SMART objectives for each functional area – finance (monthly cash **budgets**), sales (monthly turnover), human resources (recruiting and training staff), etc. – will need to be communicated (or cascaded) down from top level to supervisors so that all employees work towards them. Figure 1.13 shows the process.

Figure 1.13 Horizontal and vertical consistency

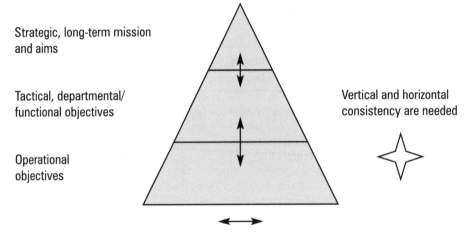

Strategic, long-term mission and aims

Tactical, departmental/ functional objectives

Operational objectives

Vertical and horizontal consistency are needed

Human Resources Marketing Production Administration Finance, etc. (Functions)
People Customers Processes/operations Financial (Perspectives)

> **remember**
> You will need to produce a financial plan if you study Unit 37, Starting a small business, as part of your course.

If all SMART targets are met, then the corporate objectives should be achieved.

Figure 1.14 illustrates how a one year financial plan will be drawn up to ensure horizontal co-ordination. The revenues and costs from the different departments must result in sufficient cash for the business to survive and sufficient profit to satisfy the shareholders.

Figure 1.14 The financial planning process

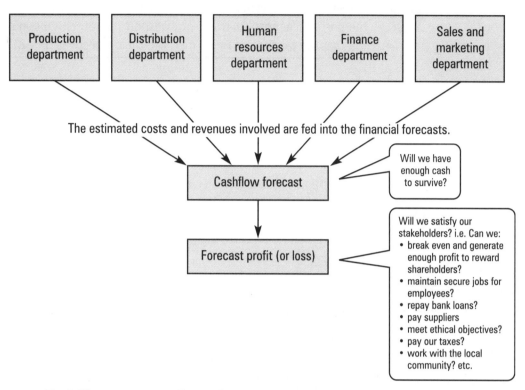

The directors set out the strategic objectives in the corporate plan

Managers of functional areas draw up tactics for achieving objectives.

| Production department | Distribution department | Human resources department | Finance department | Sales and marketing department |

The estimated costs and revenues involved are fed into the financial forecasts.

Cashflow forecast

Will we have enough cash to survive?

Forecast profit (or loss)

Will we satisfy our stakeholders? i.e. Can we:
- break even and generate enough profit to reward shareholders?
- maintain secure jobs for employees?
- repay bank loans?
- pay suppliers
- meet ethical objectives?
- pay our taxes?
- work with the local community? etc.

Public sector planning strategies

Service provision

The plans of public and voluntary sector organisations will be concerned with the effective provision of a quality service to the community. They are encouraged to operate efficiently to give the national or local tax payer value for money. This might mean:

■ taking opportunities to generate revenue – the police charge for security at sports and entertainment events, the library service rents out DVDs, local authorities charge for local car parking, schools hire out buildings

■ relocating to save money or create work. Many jobs in the north-east of England are now in the public sector.

Figure 1.15 English Heritage, which is responsible for Stonehenge, relocated from London to Swindon in June 2006 as a cost-cutting exercise

Quality assurance

Government departments and government agencies will set targets for the quality of state services. Published school league tables, inspector's reports and citizen's charters are ways of making public services accountable.

Privatised utilities, even though no longer state-owned, must still respond to government 'watchdogs' – regulators who review the services and prices charged for gas, water, electricity and rail services.

You can obtain citizens' charters for all local or national public services such as the post office, hospital trusts or transport operators. Obtain some and decide whether the targets are being met. Are their objectives SMART?

Service-level agreements

When private organisations (both profit-making and not-for-profit) win contracts to deliver public services, they agree to meet performance targets. In gaining the franchise to run South-West region trains in September 2006, Stagecoach agreed on the fares that it would charge and the level of service it would provide. The company must, for example, use profits from peak periods to subsidise loss-making off-peak services. This agreement protects the travelling public and Stagecoach will lose the contract if it does not deliver.

case study 1.7 — Two public concerns

The government is still responsible for the Royal Mail and the BBC. Nevertheless, both of these organisations are now competing with private sector providers.

Royal Mail

Royal Mail plc is wholly owned by the government. It consists of three separate businesses:

■ Royal Mail – the UK letter collection and delivery service deals with 84 million items each working day. In January 2006 the Royal Mail lost its 350-year monopoly when the UK's postal market became fully open to competition.

■ Parcelforce – the UK parcel delivery service. Parcelforce is now in competition with carriers such as DHL and White Arrow.

■ Post Office Limited – managing the nationwide network of 14,376 post offices and post office branches. At the time of writing there is a possibility that many unprofitable small post offices will close (many of the services are available online).

Revenue for the year ended 26 March 2006 was £9,056 billion, with £312 million profit before tax.

Source: Royal Mail Annual Report, 2006

Quality assurance

The three organisations publish citizens' charters. The postal regulator, Postcomm must approve all increases in the prices of stamps and the Consumer Council for Postal Services (usually called Postwatch), looks at consumers' concerns with the level of service.

BBC

The BBC is a public corporation. The content of programmes is independent of government but the trust is government approved. The Department of Culture Media and Sport (DCMS) sets the BBC's strategic aims which are:

■ sustaining citizenship and civil society

■ promoting education and learning

■ stimulating creativity and cultural excellence – including film

■ reflecting the UK's nations, regions and communities

■ bringing the world to the UK and the UK to the world

■ building Digital Britain.

▶

The trust will work with the heads of the various services to plan how these aims will be achieved.

Funding

No commercial advertising is allowed. An annual licence fee must be paid for each property with a TV set (not needed for a radio). Unlike terrestrial ITV, which is funded by advertising, the BBC is not free to the public.

The justification for the licence fee is similar to the justification for taxation. It enables the BBC to provide public service broadcasting that is of benefit to all sections of the community. Programme makers do not need to chase ratings to keep advertisers happy and this enables them to suit a variety of tastes.

Quality assurance

The BBC is regulated partly by Ofcom, the telecommunications regulator, and partly by its Trust.

Figure 1.16 The BBC's income and costs, 2005–6

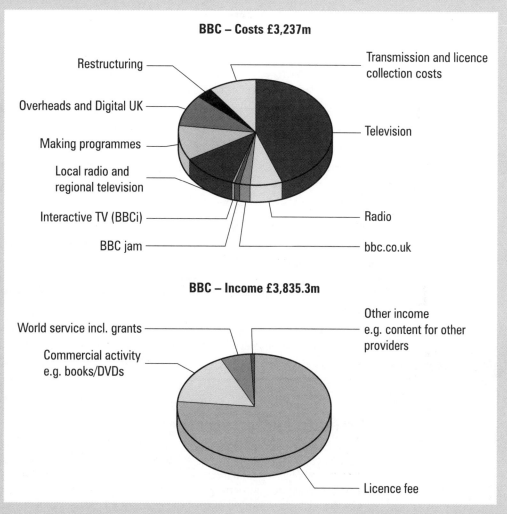

Source: www.wikipedia.org

activity

1 Look at the aims of the Post Office and the BBC. Why do you think they are in the public sector? Would their aims change if they were privatised?

2 Local post offices provide a public service. Should the government pay to keep them open even if they make a loss?

3 The level of the BBC licence fee is a matter of debate. What are the arguments for and against the fee, e.g. what is the alternative?

> *i*   The BBC website, www.bbc.co.uk, is an excellent resource for your BTEC course.

Strategic planning and the voluntary sector

Voluntary sector organisations generally exist to provide services that are not adequately provided by the public or private sectors. The Woodland Trust is an illustration.

case study
1.8

The Woodland Trust

Only 8 per cent of England is under woodland. The Woodland Trust's mission is to change that.

The trust aims to:

- buy and manage native woodland in the UK with the aim of conserving this and its wildlife for the benefit of people
- use volunteers to plant 12 million new trees between 2004 and 2009 – the 'Tree for All' campaign
- gain publicity and donations via the website (www.treeforall.org.uk) and via association with celebrities such as Clive Anderson, the Trust president
- make partnerships with industry to gain funding. Links include: Barclaycard, WH Smith National Grid, Transco and Ecover
- spread funding to benefit people around the country.

The Trust's woods are free for the public to visit and enjoy.

Source: Woodland Trust Annual Review, 2004

>   Go to the Woodland Trust website (www.woodland-trust.org.uk) and find their most recent annual review which can be viewed by following the link on the Publications page. Here you can find out what the Woodland Trust does with its funds.

activity   Why is the voluntary sector suitable for the Woodland Trust? (Think of the difficulties of operating in the private sector, or the reasons why the public sector might be unsuitable.)

Private sector strategies

Private sector businesses are found across the primary, secondary and tertiary sectors of the economy. Their owners (either sole traders, partners, or company shareholders) are primarily interested in gaining a financial reward from their investment in the business. The strategic plan will therefore concentrate on activities that will help to generate a profit, although this will frequently be balanced against the needs of other stakeholders.

Private sector strategic aims include the following.

Quality goods and services

Satisfying customer demand is the main purpose of business.

When we look at PESTLE analysis on pages 43–51 (also pages 132–133), we will see that markets change over time so that different products are demanded.

Profit maximisation

Traditionally it has been assumed that private sector businesses attempt to maximise their profits, i.e. to make the most profit possible by increasing sales revenue whilst minimising costs.

Businesses use a number of tactics for increasing sales revenue:

- providing products that people will buy in preference to competing products. This may involve branding to create identity and loyalty ('the real thing', 'the only flame-grilled burger'), innovation (new and more advanced products such as WAP mobile phones), affordable quality (John Lewis - 'never knowingly undersold') or lower prices. These attract extra revenue where demand is elastic (i.e. where the price reduction brings a significant increase in sales)

- gaining control of a market to reduce the number of competitors; this enables higher prices to be charged. Tactics may involve setting up 'barriers' that make it difficult for new firms to enter the market (perhaps by making exclusive agreements with suppliers who then cannot supply new businesses), buying up existing firms (e.g. in the grocery market Morrison has taken over Safeway, whilst Tesco is buying up local convenience stores) and putting firms out of business by taking their customers (local shops are hit when a new superstore locates nearby).

Costs can be minimised by:

- use of new technology to replace staff – the decline of employment in manufacturing over recent years is partly due to this

- introducing flexible working. This may take the form of part-time working, flexible hours, fixed-term contracts, home working or outsourcing. Where possible the idea is to convert staff wages into variable costs (costs directly proportional to production levels) rather than fixed costs related to time

- locating to economies where wage rates are low, e.g. India, China or Korea. Increasing globalisation makes this possible

- expanding the business in order to gain economies of scale – cost reductions that become available to large organisations, e.g. buying in bulk to gain lower unit costs (lower cost for each item)

- outsourcing – it may be cheaper to buy-in services run by specialist providers (e.g. cleaning, security, maintenance, delivery) rather than directly employing staff to run these in-house

- economy measures – achieved by monitoring costs and cutting back on unnecessary expenses ('belt tightening')

- delayering – flattening the organisational hierarchy by cutting out a layer of management. Middle managers are often the ones to go since their work may be carried out by computer technology or delegated (passed down) to staff lower in the organisation.

We look at organisational hierarchies on pages 35–36.

There are ethical dangers in seeking ever lower costs. In December 2006 it was reported that Bangladeshi workers were paid only 5p an hour to make goods sold by Tesco and Primark.

The importance of profit

The Tesco diagram on page 9 shows that businesses need profits in order to 'add shareholder value' – to reward their owners, reinvest in the business and attract future investment. However, there is evidence that in practice businesses aim for secure rather than maximum profits. Laura Tennison, CEO of JoJo Maman Bebe, is happy with a 6 per cent margin as opposed to the normal 12 per cent in the clothing industry. This allows her to build better relationships with suppliers by paying them fairly.

Sales growth

A business may attempt to increase sales in order to increase profits, to increase revenue or to gain a greater share of the market. The sales strategy will differ according to the market focus of the business.

A mass-market organisation will need to push sales volume and may use cost-cutting to tempt customers from rivals, or advertising to create awareness (in 2005 Magners did this with spectacular success).

A **niche market** business may focus on quality and be content with selling low volumes of high price goods. Aston Martin (currently owned by Ford) produces 450 cars a year.

Both high price and high volume can only be sustained by a monopoly (a business with little competition).

Break-even

Unless it is being subsidised (see Chelsea FC below), a business will ultimately need to cover its costs. The **break-even point** is reached when the sales revenue (or sales income) generated during a trading period exactly covers the costs so that there is neither a profit nor a loss. Sales beyond break-even will bring a profit, whereas failure to break even results in a loss.

The break-even forecast is a vital component in business planning and may help secure finance from investors.

 Link

We look at the break-even calculation in Unit 37, pages 76–77, 399 and 410.

Sky, EuroDisney and Eurotunnel all took some years to break even. They survived because they were able to raise sufficient funds either from share issues or by borrowing against their assets (the land, buildings and equipment they own).

Some loss-making businesses have rich benefactors to support them. In the 2004/5 season, Chelsea FC achieved a £140m loss, after investing heavily in highly paid players. The club survived because its owner, oil billionaire Roman Abramovitch, ensured the bills were paid.

---

assignment focus

1   How do you think the aims of Roman Abramovitch, owner of Chelsea FC, might compare with those of the major shareholders of Eurotunnel?

2   Why is it important for a small business to break even relatively quickly?

Survival

Whilst BT and BP think of profits in £billions, other businesses think only of surviving. ('Success would be still being in business next year,' – Barry Fry, Chairman of Peterborough United.) Most new businesses begin with survival as a main aim because two-thirds will fail within three years of start-up. Having cash to pay the bills is the key.

Ethical or social responsibility

Some private sector businesses combine social principle with profits – Body Shop, Innocent Drinks and JoJo Maman Bebe are examples. Many find that a responsible corporate image can help sales. Recently oil companies have rebranded as energy companies with Shell producing its 'Sustainability Report' and BP using 'Beyond Petroleum' as its **strapline**.

Notice that business aims will need to be modified over time to take account of changes in the external environment, in internal policies and in stakeholder demands.

---

case study 1.9

Black's Leisure Group plc – more than an outside chance

Black's is leader in the growing outdoor leisure market. Forecasts show continued growth of 5 per cent per year for the next five years.

In 2005 after reviewing their progress, the board strengthened their management team and set out their plan to take the company forward.

Their aims

Black's aims 'to create value for our customers, inspire them to enjoy the "great outdoors" and earn their lifetime loyalty, thereby generating attractive, sustainable shareholder returns.'

Their five point plan

■ Product development – a range of exclusive brands including Technicals for men, Freespirit for women and the ALS travel range

■ Format development – new Black's Out of Town stores – they give a sense of 'the great outdoors – indoors'; upgrade of Millets stores

■ Brand communication – new Millets advertising, truck advertising paid for by suppliers, new catalogues

■ Operational efficiency – improved recruitment, training and tills; control of store and distribution costs

■ New business development – two new e-commerce websites launched in 2006: www.blacks.co.uk and: www.millets.co.uk. A Freespirit website is proposed.

Monitoring and review

The 2006 annual report shows that the business is on course to achieve its objectives.

activity

1 Suggest examples of quantitative and qualitative analysis that Black's could use to assess their progress.

2 Identify strategic, tactical and operational aspects of the plan (the diagram on page 24 will help).

Growth

Businesses can grow internally or externally.

■ Internal or organic growth takes place when a business ploughs back (or reinvests) its profits. This is steady sustainable growth but may take many years.

■ External growth is achieved by either merging with, or taking over, other businesses. This provides a faster route to becoming a 'big business'.

Tactics for achieving growth may include:

■ **horizontal integration** – occurs when a business expands its present operations, as when Morrisons took over Safeway and when Lloyds and TSB merged into a single, larger bank. Such tactics provide increased market share and economies of scale

■ **lateral integration** – takes place when a business diversifies its product range to gain access to different markets. Philip Morris, owner of the Marlborough cigarette brand, has diversified into food products to counter the threat of legislation and compensation claims driven by anti-smoking pressure groups. Supermarkets have diversified from food into electrical goods, clothes, financial services, gas, electricity and even property

■ **vertical integration** – occurs when a business moves into other activities along the supply chain. A retailer may expand into wholesaling or manufacturing. The holiday company My Travel (formerly Airtours) operates all along the holiday supply chain by selling tickets to holiday-makers, operating ships and planes and running its own hotels.

How is growth measured?

Table 1.5 shows a number of ways in which growth at Tesco can be measured.

Table 1.5 Ways in which growth at Tesco can be measured

Year ended February	2002	2003	2004	2005	2006
Group sales, £m	25,401	28,280	33,557	37,070	43,137
Group operating profit, £m	1,322	1,492	1,778	2,064	2,280
Number of stores	979	2,291	2,318	2,334	2,672

Source: Tesco Five-year Summary

case study 1.10   Arriva

Arriva began as a motorcyle shop, moved into motor retailing and in 1980 bought the Grey-Green bus company. Like Stagecoach, Arriva benefited from the deregulation of local bus services. Today it is one of largest transport operators in Europe.

In 2003 Arriva stated that 'our business will grow through acquisition, better service delivery, innovation and marketing'. In other words, they will take over other businesses when this is appropriate and will also expand organically.

activity

1   What sort of integration occurs if:

   a) a bus company such as National Express takes over other bus companies?

   b) a bus company such as Stagecoach also runs rail operations?

   c) an airline such as easyJet has set up a call centre to sell its own tickets?

2   How exactly did deregulation benefit Arriva? (You may need to re-read pages 5–6.)

Level of profit

Investors expect businesses to increase profits from year to year. This can be difficult to achieve in a competitive environment. Tesco, however, has been highly successful in this respect; in 2005 they became the first UK company to make an annual profit of £2 billion.

Sales and market share

Figure1.19 shows that Tesco gained a larger share of the market than its rivals. In 2004, Tesco and Sainsbury's could have grown by buying their rival Safeway. However, the government's Competition Commission prevented this. The Commission will usually stop take-overs leading to a market share greater than 25 per cent if they feel that this will reduce competition and customer choice. What was the result of their 2006 investigation into UK supermarkets?

Figure 1.17 Tesco's market share

Source: TNS

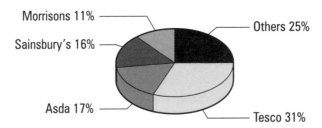

Morrisons 11%

Sainsbury's 16%

Others 25%

Asda 17%

Tesco 31%

Number of outlets

A retailer might wish to grow by opening more stores, both nationally and internationally. Similarly a manufacturer might open factories in other countries. This should also lead to a growth in market share. Domino's Pizza plc has announced, 'Quality growth is a vision ... our ambitious plans were realised with the opening of 50 new stores.'

Business value

The worth of a business can be measured in two ways:

■   by the bottom line on the balance sheet. This is the 'asset value' once debts have been paid. Asset value increases when a company ploughs back profits

■   by the total value of the company's shares on the stock market (Figure 1.18 shows Tesco's share price). This is called 'market capitalisation' and it will change as the share price rises and falls.

The prices of plc shares can be found in the media. **FTSE-100** (footsie) charts the rise and fall of the prices of the UK's 100 most valuable companies.

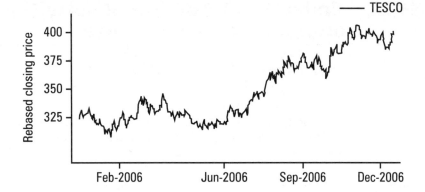

Figure 1.18 Tesco's share price, January to December 2006

If market capitalisation falls below asset value, the company is under-valued, the shares are cheap and the company might be ripe for a take-over. This is one reason why company directors are concerned about a falling share price.

Company directors aim to increase both asset value by reinvesting profits and the share price by all-round performance.

assignment focus

1   If one of your chosen businesses is a plc, plot its share price each week and look out for news items that may explain why its price rises and falls. Alternatively a website such as www.londonstockexchange.co.uk will provide a ready made chart for you.

2   Have the businesses that you have chosen to study grown? Take each of the measures of growth in turn and look at trends over the last two years. Some annual reports show a five-year trend.

3   Look for the FTSE-100 each day on the news or look it up in a newspaper or on the internet. What are the commentators saying about it?

Risks associated with growth

Overtrading
Expanding a business requires cash (more stock, equipment and staff). Expansion that is too rapid can leave a business with debts it cannot pay.

Diseconomies of scale
Sometimes a business grows too large to operate efficiently. Scale makes communication and decision-making more difficult. Where businesses have combined through merger or take-over, there may also be a lack of synergy, i.e. they may not fit well because of different cultures. Morrisons, for example, has experienced problems after taking over Safeway.

Solutions may include:

■   'down-size' by selling off some of the operations and concentrating on the core businesses, e.g. Boots reduced its services to refocus on healthcare

■   decentralise by setting up smaller divisions for different geographical areas or products

■   delayer by cutting out levels in the organisational hierarchy.

assignment focus

You may choose two of the business that you used to complete P1 and P2. Alternatively, you may choose two new businesses for this task.

To achieve P3 you should:

■   explain the terms 'strategic aims' and 'objectives'

■   identify the strategic aims and objectives of each of your chosen businesses. Provide the source of this information

■   give reasons that explain why each aim and objective is pursued by that particular business. (Remember that the form of ownership, other stakeholders, size, and industrial sector will be influential.)

Understand functional activities and organisational structure

Organisation structures

In order for a business to achieve its organisational aims and objectives, it will need to carry out a range of **functions**.

In a small business (perhaps a sole trader or partnership), the owner(s) will be directly involved in carrying out most or all of the organisational functions. A sole trader running a small corner shop, for example, is likely to undertake the tasks shown in Figure 1.19.

Figure 1.19 Functions of small businesses

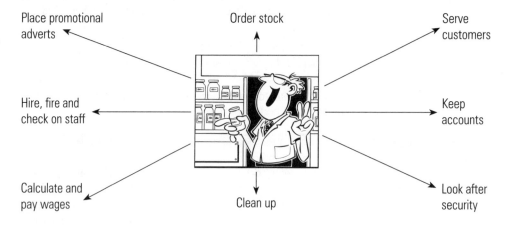

Place promotional adverts

Order stock

Serve customers

Hire, fire and check on staff

Keep accounts

Calculate and pay wages

Clean up

Look after security

Division of work into functional areas

In a larger business, division of labour becomes necessary and the work of the business is divided into separate functions, such as operations, finance, marketing, human resources and administration. Specialist staff are recruited to perform these different activities and separate departments, or functional areas, will be set up. The business will begin to take on a formal organisational structure.

The way in which different functions are organised is determined both by the size of the organisation and by the activities needed to achieve its goals.

On page 36 we look at the range of functions found across organisations and on page 38 at how these may work together to achieve organisational aims and objectives.

Purpose of an organisational structure

It now becomes necessary to identify how these employees will communicate. The purpose of the structure is to clearly identify the roles, levels of authority and lines of communication between employees, i.e. to show what the important functions are, who is in charge, who gives orders and who carries them out.

An organisational structure that is appropriate for one business will not suit another. For example, a manufacturer will need a production department whereas a retailer will not. Within a single business the structure will change over time in line with changing organisational needs.

An ideal structure is one that will help the staff to perform in the most effective way, whereas an unsuitable structure will hold them back.

The organisation chart

An organisation chart is a visual picture of the organisational structure. It shows the staff positions, their levels within an organisation and who they report to.

The horizontal lines show how the business of the organisation is allocated, for example, by functional area (VHF Radios, Figure 1.20), by geographical area (Arriva on page 41) or by specialism (McAlpine on page 42).

The vertical lines show the lines along which communication flows up and down the organisation.

Figure 1.20 The organisation chart of VHF Ltd, a manufacturer of radios

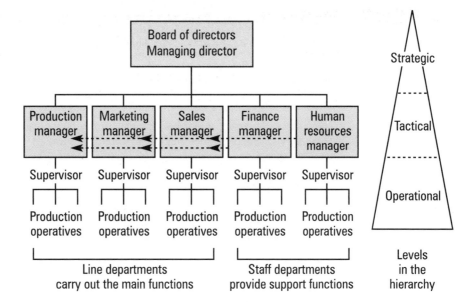

In VHF Ltd, five functional areas work together to achieve the business objectives.

- The 'line functions' of production, marketing and sales all help to achieve the main business objectives of making and selling radios.

- The staff functions support these main functions – the finance department ensures that there are sufficient funds, human resources makes sure that the business has the appropriate workforce.

Hierarchies and the line of command

Most organisational structures form a **hierarchy** (a structure with different levels of authority) similar to that shown in Figure 1.21.

Figure 1.21 Hierarchy and line of command

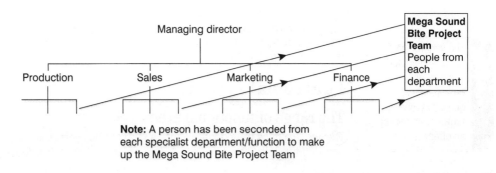

Note: A person has been seconded from each specialist department/function to make up the Mega Sound Bite Project Team

A chain of command (the scalar chain) runs from the top of the hierarchy down through each line department to the shop floor. Instructions flow from the top of the organisation downwards; employees at each level are managed by the line manager directly above them in their organisational function.

Figure 1.22 Tall organisational structure

Hierarchies may be tall, with many levels of responsibility, or flat, with few levels.

Tall hierarchies

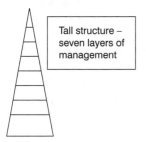

A tall organisation has many levels of management and supervision relative to the number of employees. Here there is a long chain of command from the top to the bottom of the organisation although, even in very large organisations, it is rare to find more than seven or eight levels of authority (Tesco has six). The presence of many managers/supervisors means that the **span of control** at each level is fairly narrow.

Tall structures tend to be formal and bureaucratic (necessary because of the generally large size) with many highly specialised functional areas.

Flat hierarchies

Flat organisations tend to be smaller and so less complex. The chain of command from top to bottom is short and this should simplify communication between employees at different levels.

Smaller organisations such as partnerships, co-operatives and some private limited companies have a flat structure whilst large organisations also increasingly seek to keep layers of management to a minimum (see Tesco on page 39).

In some cases, flattening an organisation may simply be a means of cost-cutting in disguise. Making an organisation 'leaner and fitter', 'slimming down' or 'right-sizing' are some of the euphemisms used.

Figure 1.23 Flat organisational structure

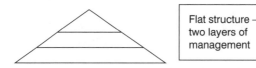

Flat structure – two layers of management

Span of control

The span of control is the number of employees over whom a manager or supervisor has authority.

Figure 1.24 Span of control

Manager

Subordinates

Wide   Narrow

Traditionally, the optimum span was considered to be between three and six people; thought to be the maximum someone could effectively manage. Narrow spans tend to create tall organisations, whereas wide spans are likely to be found in flat organisations.

When a large organisation delayers (flattens its structure by cutting out levels of middle management), the span of control for remaining managers will tend to widen giving them a greater workload. Some of these extra jobs are likely to be delegated – responsibility will be passed down to employees at lower levels.

Functional activities

The range of functional areas

The line functions to be found across a range of businesses include those listed in Table 1.6. The staff functions listed in Table 1.7 give support to the line departments.

> **remember**
> The various functional areas can only achieve organisational goals by working together as part of an effective system.

Table 1.6 Functional areas and activities

Functional area	Activity
R&D (Research and Development)	Research and development can involve: ■ invention – discovering new techniques and products. Both large and small businesses can come up with good ideas ■ innovation – ways of applying these ideas to make a product. This can be highly expensive and generally only very large organisations have R&D sections. The largest spenders are companies dealing in: pharmaceuticals, chemicals, transport and new technology. R&D is about developing new goods. Service providers tend to carry out product development (e.g. the Halifax developed Intelligent Finance, a new bank account) as part of the marketing process.
Link with other functions	R&D will work with design to achieve higher sales and market share through 'cutting edge' products. Ethical objectives may be achieved through environmentally-friendly products such as components that can be recycled.

Functional area	Activity
Design	Design translates the new idea from R&D into a product that can be marketed. It concentrates on appearance, safety, performance, cost and quality.
Link with other functions	Design will work with R&D as shown above.
Purchasing, sourcing or procurement	This section locates and buys in supplies of the right quality, in the right quantities, at the right time and at the right price.
Link with other functions	Goods must be purchased ready for production or for sale. These goods must then be delivered on time. Purchasing therefore links with production, or operations, and with distribution.
Production (or Operations)	In this context, production means manufacturing goods or assembling them from components in the factory or workshop. Notice that retailers selling own brand goods usually contract other manufacturers to make them to order. Tesco-branded mobile phones, for example, are produced by mmO2. Retailers and other service providers tend to carry out their core activity through an operations function (rather than a production function) since they do not actually manufacture.
	The production department of a manufacturer will produce goods to design specifications. It must purchase appropriate supplies and take delivery on time (often just-in-time). Production schedules are geared to satisfy marketing and sales targets – Dell, for example, manufactures computers to demand.
Link with other functions	The operations section of a service provider, such as a retailer, will similarly work with purchasing, distribution, marketing and sales to make supplies available to meet customer demand.
Marketing	Market research identifies customer needs and matches products with markets to achieve: higher sales and market share through clear targeting of the market, effective promotion and competitive pricing.
	Marketing activity is carried out through the 4 Ps to ensure: the right *product*, at the right *price*, in the right *place*. *Promotion* ensures that customers are informed about the product and are persuaded to buy it.
Link with other functions	Marketing should work with production, or operations, to ensure that goods sold can be produced on time and at the correct price.
Sales	The sales function involves taking and satisfying customer orders and dealing with customer accounts.
Link with other functions	Sales may be part of marketing or work closely alongside. As with marketing, sales must work closely with production (or operations) and with distribution if goods are delivered to customers.
Distribution (or Logistics)	The distribution function links the organisation with the supply chain by moving stocks of raw materials, components or finished goods into the business from suppliers. Where a business has it own warehouses, it will also move goods to factories or retail outlets within the business. Many organisations also distribute goods to customers after sale.
Link with other functions	The distribution section works closely with: ■ the production department of a manufacturer (the factory) where components are needed to meet schedules ■ the retail section of a chain of stores where the shop shelves need to be filled ■ the sales section might also need to arrange for delivery of goods to customers.
	Increasingly new technology and more responsive distribution systems allow businesses to save on storage costs by ordering goods for delivery just-in-time (JIT) for use.
	The importance of distribution can be seen when it goes wrong. In 2005, car production at MG-Rover finally stopped when the company ran out of components; suppliers had refused to leave stocks without payment. In 2004, Sainsbury's new £3bn logistics system was scrapped after it 'lost' large amounts of stock and shelves remained empty.
	Effective distribution, on the other hand, may improve customer satisfaction through efficient delivery times. The use of cleaner fuel, more effective journey planning and night-time journeys to avoid traffic congestion may help achieve environmental objectives.
	Frequently the distribution function is outsourced to specialist logistics firms.

Functional area	Activity
Customer service call centres	These provide the customer with the 24/7 support in the form of advice, information and action upon queries, complaints and sales transactions. To save costs the centres may be located at a distance from the business.
Link with other functions	Work closely with the marketing and sales functions in providing product information to customers and feeding back customer comments

Table 1.7 Staff functions and activities

Staff function	Activity
Human Resources (HR)	The HR function plans future staffing needs and helps maintain a suitable workforce for all sections within the organisation. HR will keep employee records, recruit and dismiss staff, comply with employment law, deal with health, safety and welfare, industrial relations, discipline and appeals, set up training and staff development and agree systems for monitoring and appraising employees.
Link with other functions	HR will help all functional areas across the organisation to get the right staff and improve their performance.
Finance	The finance function co-ordinates revenues and spending across all functional areas so that the business will have sufficient funds to survive and generate profits to reward its owners.
Link with other functions	Financial accountants record and report on the actual results of the business. They record the sales, borrowing and expenditure that take place across the various functional areas. They then draw up reports for the benefit of the shareholders. The yearly profit and loss account and balance sheet (which shows the value of the business) are required by law. Management accounting provides estimates for use by the various functional managers. This information allows managers to plan future action, make informed decisions and control business performance.
Administration	Administration includes the office function and may also be responsible for other areas, such as premises, security, catering and maintenance.
Link with other functions	This function involves setting up organised systems and routines so that the different areas within the business can operate smoothly. For example, the office in a college may distribute post, direct visitors, keep class registers and arrange for the maintenance of photocopiers.
MIS (Management Information Services)	This section gets appropriate and good quality (accurate and up-to-date) information to managers as and when they need it. The use of ICT enables them to collect and analyse data and produce detailed reports quickly. MIS will gather and process: ■ internal information about business resources, staff ■ performance, departmental targets, etc. ■ external information, e.g. industry benchmarks, competitor information, supplier prices, etc.
Link with other functions	This information will keep the various functional managers informed so as to take appropriate decisions in their day-to-day work. For example, MIS in a college will provide departmental heads with details such as class sizes, student attendance figures, success rates, the ethnic and gender mix of staff and students, the hours worked by lecturers, national benchmarks (standards to be achieved), and so on.
IT services	IT services provides technical support by installing, upgrading and maintaining the hardware and software in the business IT network. It may also provide support with design and maintenance of databases, websites and intranets.
Link with other functions	The section will give support across the organisation but may work particularly closely with MIS and administration.

Managing functions in small and micro businesses

In a sole trader or small partnership, the owners themselves might carry out many or most of the functions themselves, perhaps with the help of one or two employees. Small businesses that have developed an organisational structure will tend to combine a number of functions under one manager, e.g. sales, marketing and customer service are likely to be linked. Look at the structure in your college or school, for example.

Depending upon the business activity and size, it is also likely that specialist functions such as IT services will be outsourced, whilst a function such as R&D (research and development) may not be found at all. This can be expensive and tends to be carried out by larger organisations.

Relationships between functional activities

Interdependency of functional activities

When a gardener at NASA (North American Space Agency) was asked by a visiting president what his job was, he replied, 'Putting a man on the moon'. The point is that each employee should play their part in helping the organisation achieve its goals. It is a team effort with success achieved by the functional areas working together. How well they do this depends upon:

- the organisational structure and whether this promotes effective communication and workflow
- the style of management and their attitude towards employees – successful businesses listen to staff and make them aware of their contribution
- the culture of the organisation – the way in which the management and workforce do things.

Tables 1.6 and 1.7 indicate where functional areas are likely to be interdependent.

---

case study 1.11

It's a flat world

Tesco is now the world's third largest retailer (after Walmart of the USA and Carrefour of France). A number of factors have contributed to this.

Chief Executive Sir Terry Leahy believes that listening to customers, rewarding staff and encouraging staff loyalty and progression are important; a number of people who began at the bottom have worked up into top management.

However, he also emphasises that the organisational structure plays a vital part. Tesco is a flat organisation with only six layers between the trolley pushers and the chief executive. This means that directors are not remote figures and communication through the organisation becomes easier.

Tesco has decentralised control. Directors recognise that decisions about stores in Thailand are better taken by people on the spot. They know the problems, understand local conditions and so can act more quickly and effectively than head office in England.

Source: Sir Terry Leahy, from his speech to The Institute of Directors, April 2005

activity

1 Tesco sells FMCGs (fast moving consumer goods) and so has to keep the shelves continually stacked. Which functional areas work together in achieving this?

2 What services do you think Tesco human resources staff may provide for staff in the marketing department?

Flow of work

Getting a job done is likely to involve a number of functional areas and will need an efficient flow of information between them. For example, when a retailer sells by telephone or by mail order, five functional areas may work together in directly meeting customers' needs:

- Marketing arranges advertising. This may be done through newspapers or popular magazines. Catalogues may be sent through the post or distributed via agents. These must provide accurate product and pricing information and the company must be able to deliver.
- Sales takes orders. Orders taken by phone are keyed into the computer. Information about stock availability and advice about deliveries can be given immediately because the computer system is linked with the stock and storage sections.

- Delivery, distribution or logistics. Companies do not normally use their own transport, but instead use specialist external carriers, such as Royal Mail or White Arrow. This avoids the cost of maintaining vehicles and paying drivers. However, some companies use their own couriers to deliver goods. Goods can be returned or exchanged in the same way.

- Finance receives payment. There may be flexible methods of payment, ranging from cash on delivery to 50-weekly instalments. The credit controllers need to control their cash flow and monitor debt repayments very carefully.

- Storage and warehousing. It is important to minimise the costs of storage, to update stock records, and re-order goods as necessary. All information is immediately available to management as part of the management information system.

assignment focus

The objective is to get the right goods, (those which have been ordered), to the right customer at the right time. The process involves five functional areas and these must be co-ordinated.

1 Draw a diagram to illustrate the information flow between the parts of the system.

2 Where might things go wrong? Where might delays occur?

Outsourcing/contracting-out business functions

Rather than employing its own staff to fulfil each function, a business may decide that it is more effective or cheaper to outsource (buy-in) the service from an outside business. This is now common practice in a number of functional areas:

- Administration – Specialist firms may be contracted to run security, catering, cleaning, as well as the maintenance of equipment such as photocopiers or computers.

- Finance – Typically small businesses have engaged an accountant to produce their year-end accounts. Larger organisations may outsource their payroll to an external provider.

- IT – Frequently consultants may be brought in to help set up a new MIS system or design a business website. Nick Jenkins of Moonpig.com buys in IT services.

- Delivery – Using Royal Mail, DHL or White Arrow is a long-standing form of outsourcing. The delivery of Waitrose home deliveries by Ocado is a more recent example.

- Production – Increasingly the lower costs available from manufacturers in the Far East are attractive to UK producers. James Dyson ultimately stopped production of his 'bagless' vacuum cleaners in Malmesbury and outsourced to Malaysia. Cost was the reason he gave.

- Supply chain – Specialist firms are able to achieve more efficient sourcing of products. This is the reason the NHS sought to contract DHL to buy-in supplies for its hospitals (see page 14).

- Call centres have been a massive growth area in recent years. Location is unimportant if the service is right. Again it is the lower prices in countries such as India that have attracted UK firms (see Case study 1.12).

- Public sector services – The compulsory competitive tendering (CCT) system compels local authorities to give service contracts to external providers who give best value for money. Accord, for example, collects refuse for Islington Council. The Home Office has outsourced the running of some prison services to the security company, Group 4.

Outsourcing has a number of advantages. An organisation simply pays the agreed rate and the job is done. Human resources issues such as staff training, payroll, providing cover for sickness, recruitment of new staff and redundancy are the responsibility of the contractor.

There are disadvantages too – it has been reported that 1 in 10 employees in Scottish call centres work for organised criminal organisations.

See Case study 2.1, page 60, about call centres and the outsourcing of customer services.

Factors influencing the organisational structure

The ideal organisational structure will enable managers and employees to communicate effectively as they work towards meeting business objectives. However, what is right for one business will not be right for another. Business size, the external business environment and the objectives set out in the strategic plan will all influence the organisational structure.

Business size

The size of the business will influence the height of the hierarchy. We have seen that small businesses tend to have a flatter structure. Business size may also determine whether control is better centralised or decentralised.

- **Centralised control** In smaller businesses, sole traders and partners will provide or directly control most of the functions themselves. Small to medium companies, such as VHF Radios (page 35), will set up specialist functional areas, but the board of directors still retains central control over these. Centralised control allows speedy decision-making as fewer people are involved and less consultation is needed. This can be important when responding to changing business conditions.

- **Decentralised control** As organisations grow over different geographical areas or diversify into different products, it becomes difficult and inefficient to take every decision from the top. Large nationals and multinationals may be conveniently split into separate product or geographical divisions; the directors retain overall control, but responsibility for specific decisions is delegated to lower levels of management. For example, Arriva plc has created three geographical divisions (Figure 1.25).

Large global organisations such as ICI have introduced a still greater degree of decentralised control with a structure based upon product areas. These in turn are split into geographical operations. Figure 1.26 shows how ICI's Polyurethane division is structured. The division's managing director will still work within the guidelines set by the main ICI board, but is largely autonomous and is accountable for divisional costs and profits.

Figure 1.25 Arriva's decentralised control

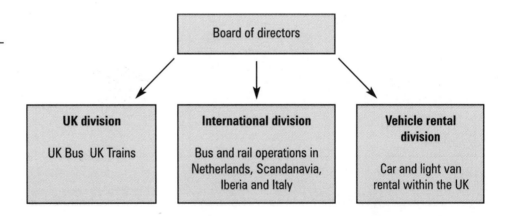

Figure 1.26 ICI's Polyurethane divisional structure

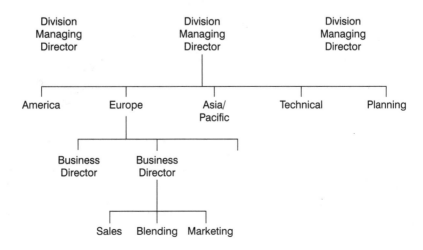

The business environment

Businesses will need to respond to the opportunities and threats from the changing external environment. New challenges may require a change in the organisational structure.

---

case study 1.12   **Alfred McAlpine plc**

McAlpine made its name as a construction company but since the millennium new business opportunities have been presented by:

- the growing trend for large organisations to outsource their business support services
- the New Labour government's Private Finance Initiative (PFI) designed to attract private funding and management for public sector projects (see page 6).

As a result, McAlpine is no longer just a construction firm: 'things have changed. This is now overwhelmingly a service business.' (McAlpine Business Review)

The senior management team (consisting of seven directors) has been reshaped to provide more effective leadership and control and the business has been restructured with a division for each area of activity (Figure 1.27)

Figure 1.27 Divisional structure of Alfred McAlpine plc

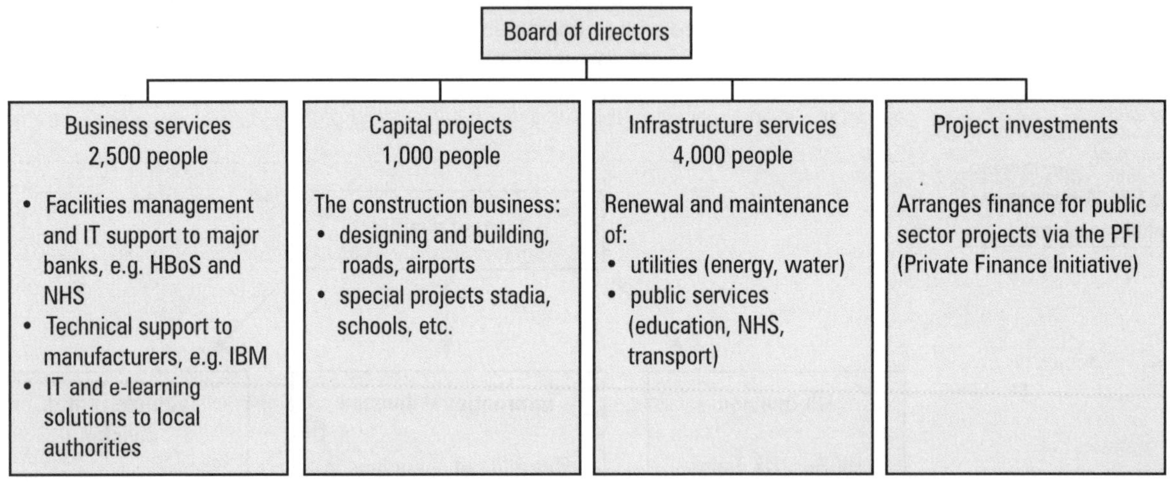

Board of directors			
Business services **2,500 people**	**Capital projects** **1,000 people**	**Infrastructure services** **4,000 people**	**Project investments**
• Facilities management and IT support to major banks, e.g. HBoS and NHS • Technical support to manufacturers, e.g. IBM • IT and e-learning solutions to local authorities	The construction business: • designing and building, roads, airports • special projects stadia, schools, etc.	Renewal and maintenance of: • utilities (energy, water) • public services (education, NHS, transport)	Arranges finance for public sector projects via the PFI (Private Finance Initiative)

activity

What sort of integration has McAlpine used in order to grow?

assignment focus

You may use two of the businesses that you used to complete P1, P2 and P3. Alternatively, you may choose two new businesses.

To achieve P4 for each business you have chosen:

- identify the different functional activities carried out and describe what is involved. An organisation chart will help
- describe ways in which they work together to meet the objectives of the organisation.

To achieve M2, explain why each business has developed its particular organisational structure. Compare the influences that determine the structure used by each business.

Strategic plans

The structure of the business must be capable of delivering the business aims. For example, if the aim is to grow into the European market, then it is logical to set up a European division (as Arriva did – page 41). Where there is to be a growth in sales, then a higher level of specialisation may be needed to deal with the extra work.

Alternatively a move to outsource some of the functions may simplify the structure.

How external factors in the business environment impact on organisations

The business environment is dynamic (continuously changing). Businesses can rarely control these changes but must nevertheless respond to any opportunities or threats that arise.

Influences on business from the external environment are sometimes called **PEST** factors because they can be found under the headings: **P**olitical, **E**conomic, **S**ocial and **T**echnological. Where **L**egal and **E**nvironmental factors are identified separately, we speak of **PESTLE** factors. This is how we approach external factors in this book.

Political factors

Political factors relate to the actions and views of the government at Westminster, local authorities, the government of the European Union (EU) in Brussels and governments of trading partners.

■ Financial policies might include raising the tax rate, providing grants to encourage regional development or subsidies to enable the rail industry to keep down prices. High taxation threatens business profits by removing spending power from consumers but may create demand through government spending on state services.

■ Environmental policies are now high on the political agenda.

 See Environmental factors on page 50.

■ Development and regeneration is encouraged and approved by government. Spending on new transport links, for example, can create demand for construction companies such as Balfour-Beatty or Hanson (see page 53).

■ Foreign affairs can involve making treaties abroad, providing foreign aid or declaring war. Some businesses might suffer through disruption to overseas trade links whilst others benefit from demand for defence products.

Party politics

The policies that governments announce in the Queen's speech each year may be business-friendly or unfriendly so that the result of a general election may be significant for a particular business.

Margaret Thatcher's deregulation and privatisation policies (see page 5) gave opportunities for business growth, while the restrictions placed on the development of out-of-town shopping malls under John Major's government hit the growth of large retailers such as Asda. New Labour's public private partnerships have enabled companies such as McAlpine to finance state projects including hospitals and schools, whilst public health initiatives have resulted in legislation to curb advertising by tobacco firms and fast food chains.

Remember that a threat to one business may be an opportunity to another. Whilst increased security at airports may deter people from flying, it also creates an opportunity for firms such as Ultra Electronics who manufacture surveillance equipment.

Economic factors

Economic factors relate to the wealth of the country and to our ability to buy goods and services. There is a link here with political factors since the government of the day will attempt to create a stable economic situation in which businesses can operate effectively.

Economic factors include the following.

The labour market, employment and unemployment

People in work have the money to buy goods and services. Conversely unemployment will reduce spending power.

Businesses demand suitably skilled workers and are influenced by the level of wages and the skills gap (the shortage of trained workers, such as plumbers, relative to demand). Immigration from the enlarged EU is helping to meet some of these needs.

Pay and personal wealth

The average UK salary was around £23,000 in 2007. As the level of disposable income (income available for spending) grows, so too does demand for consumer goods and services – this is good for business. However the pressure of increased spending may push up prices and create inflation.

You can search the Office of National Statistics website (www.statistics.gov.uk) for the up-to-date statistics on a wide range of subjects linked to your Business course, including employment figures, average earnings and inflation.

Interest rates and the cost of credit

Disposable income is not all about pay – it can be increased by borrowing. Retailers, manufacturers and the banks have all gained from the boost in demand created by cheap credit. However, the level of personal debt has become a major problem in the UK and the Citizens' Advice Bureau dealt with 1.4 million debt problems in 2005.

Inflation: public enemy number one!

Over recent years governments have made the control of inflation a priority. An inflation target – currently 2.4 per cent a year – is set and it is the job of the Bank of England to achieve this.

The Bank's Monetary Policies Committee (MPC) sits each month. If necessary it will put up interest rates to 'damp down' consumer demand – people will buy less as credit becomes more expensive and inflation should fall.

Alternatively, if inflation is low, the MPC may feel able to stimulate demand by reducing interest rates. The policy is effective because the high street and internet banks will respond to bank rate changes by putting their own rates up or down.

Whilst it is necessary to control inflation, high interest rates themselves can present a threat to businesses. They increase the cost of loan repayments, reduce demand from new customers and may reduce employment if staff are laid off. Added to this, customers may find it difficult to repay existing loans or mortgages so that banks may suffer from bad debts (debts that cannot be collected).

Not all of the MPC members will agree with a decision: The 'Hawks' wish to put up interest rates at the merest hint of inflation, whilst 'Doves' prefer to keep rates as low as possible.

Look up the Bank of England website at www.bankofengland.co.uk to see how inflation is changing and to keep up with MPC decisions.
What level is bank rate at present?
What is the present level of inflation?

assignment focus

1 In which ways are high interest rates a threat to your chosen businesses?
2 Work out the annual repayment on your businesses' loans (see the balance sheet) based on bank rate. (They will actually pay more.)

Changes in supply and demand

Consumers will buy goods and services if they have sufficient disposable income as well as confidence in the future.

Changing patterns of supply and demand can lead to fluctuations in activity known as the trade cycle.

■ Boom – Here customer demand is high, businesses take on staff as profits rise. If demand rises faster than industry can supply, then the economy 'overheats' and prices will rise. A high rate of inflation (rapidly rising prices) is undesirable because:

  ▪ it becomes difficult for businesses to plan

  ▪ the purchasing power of money is reduced, hitting people on fixed incomes

  ▪ UK products become uncompetitive abroad.

■ Slump – Rising prices will eventually cause demand to fall and staff to be laid off. The economy slows into recession and eventually into a slump where there is little demand.

Figure 1.28 Trends in economic growth

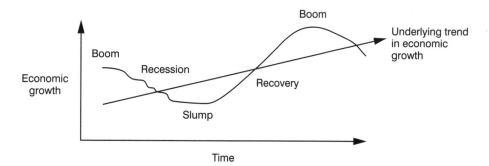

Competitive pressures at home and abroad

The business world is intensely competitive. Consumers have a range of choices and will constantly move their custom to get the best deals. The ability of customers to shop around and compare prices on the internet makes these choices possible, undermines customer loyalty and increases competition.

Globalisation of markets

The globalisation of markets provides opportunities for suppliers to compete. Cost can be reduced through outsourcing of manufacturing to the Far East and of call-centre services to India (see page 60). There is a threat to those businesses unable to adapt.

Continuous cost-cutting (the race to the bottom) introduces ethical issues since low cost may mean low pay and poor conditions for suppliers.

Energy prices

The dwindling supply of the world's resources of fossil fuels is struggling to keep up with demand. A rise in oil, gas and electricity prices – up 38 per cent in 2006 – is the result. This in turn threatens businesses via increased transport and production costs, whereas the oil companies and pipeline operators, such as Hunting, gain.

This situation provides an opportunity for the development of alternative fuels (perhaps organic fuel made from sugar cane or maize), electric cars or renewable sources of energy such as wind or wave power. Companies like Shell and BP (see page 51) are exploring these sources whilst continuing to search for new oil supplies.

Social factors

The way that we live – our attitudes, views, beliefs and lifestyles – influences our buying habits. For example: businesses may be affected by fashions, the crime rate, people's aspirations, the growth in the employment of women, the religious and ethnic mix of the population, standards of education, awareness of the environment and healthy eating (e.g. McDonald's now advertises 'free range egg' in its breakfast, Heinz has reduced fat, salt and sugar in its tinned soups).

The answer is blowing in the wind?

Following the Kyoto Protocol, the UK government introduced measures to reduce greenhouse gas emissions.

The Climate Change Levy (CCL) introduced in April 2001 is a tax added to business energy bills. The aim is to encourage organisations to reduce energy consumption and so cut down on carbon emissions. Exemptions exist for transport fuels, charities and organisations with a small energy requirement.

The EU emissions trading scheme (March 2003 until December 2006) gave businesses a carbon dioxide emissions quota. Those emitting less than their target could sell unused quotas to firms that had exceeded their targets. By 2005, 7 million tonnes of CO_2 had been saved.

Figure 1.29 Windpower is 'carbon-neutral'

Source: Rob Ayres, EcoGen

activity

1 Which stakeholders are likely to gain and lose from this measure?

2 In what ways is energy used by the businesses that you have chosen? Are they exempt from the Climate Change Levy? Have they published any policies indicating how their carbon footprint will be reduced?

Ageing population

A fall in family size allied to an increase in life expectancy means that the UK population is getting older. This is a problem for the pensions industry and a drain on the tax-payer. B&Q has employed older workers for some time and finds them effective and reliable. The government passed anti-age discrimination legislation in October 2006 to give employees the right to work beyond pension age.

You can find up-to-date figures on the age of the UK population on the Office of National Statistics website (www.statistics.gov.uk).

The colour of money

Businesses see a market opportunity in chasing the 'grey pound' spent by the increasing number of older people in the population. For example, Saga provides services such as holidays and car insurance exclusively for the over-50s, whilst 1960s model Twiggy has boosted clothing sales at Marks & Spencer. There is a growing demand for anti-ageing products ('make the earth move not your teeth!') and a high proportion of city bonuses are spent on plastic surgery.

case study
1.14

Pebble-dashing goes to the wall

Richard Duggleby of Yell, publisher of Yellow Pages, says that new headings reflect the services we demand in modern society whilst those removed are 'no longer relevant to the way we live today'. Rising incomes, new technologies and a multi-cultural society have driven the changes.

Table 1.8 Headings in *Yellow Pages*, 2006

New for 2006	What's been left out
Airport transfers	Bellfounders
Colonic Hydrotherapy	Briefcases
Satellite Navigation	Cherished Car Plates
Refrigerated Transport	Electric Shavers
Children's Entertainer	Fish Smokers
Coffee Shops	Football Pools
Oven Cleaning	Gamekeepers
Soundproofng	Lighthouses
Talent Agencies and Management	Meat Smokers
Wood Timber and Laminate Flooring	Pebble Dashing
Armenian Restaurants	Typewriter Ribbon Manufacturers
Polish Restaurants	Video Libraries

activity

1   Say which of the PESTLE factors are responsible for any five of the new entries or omissions.

2   Are the goods or services provided by your chosen business listed in *Yellow Pages*? Does your business have an entry?

Other colours used to identify market segments in society are:

- The green pound – spent by environmentally aware consumers. In 2005 the Co-op reported that UK spending on ethical products had risen to £29.3 billion.

- The pink pound – spent by gay consumers. With the law now recognising civil partnerships this has become an established segment

- The brown pound – spent by Asian and African-Caribbean consumers. In 2004 the disposable income of ethnic minorities was £32bn. Research shows that Asian consumers have a far higher percentage of subscription TV and personal computers than the UK average, whilst black women are the highest spenders on hair care products. O2 has sponsored Asian community festivals, offers cheap calls to India and Pakistan and Bollywood ringtones to try to win over this market.

assignment focus

1   Which market segments do your chosen businesses target?

2   Do they appeal to any of the colour-coded segments above? If so, identify the products concerned.

Culture and immigration

The enlargement of the EU has continued the trend for immigrants to seek a home and employment in the UK. The resulting mix of cultures provides opportunities for businesses to provide a wide variety of goods and services – the *Yellow Pages* listings on page 47 reflect these opportunities as does the 'brown pound'.

A new bank has been set up in Birmingham to cater for Britain's 1.8 million Muslims. This will operate in line with Islamic Sharia principles, will not invest in products deemed to be unethical and will operate without the use of interest. Rather than lending money, the bank will buy an item and then sell or lease it to the customer. Other branches will open in London and Leicester and telephone, internet and postal accounts will be available.

Hosting of major sporting and cultural events

Sporting world cups, European Championships and the Olympic Games can all provide significant business opportunities within host nations and beyond. The delay in completing London's new Wembley stadium has benefited Cardiff, with the city's Millennium Stadium hosting concerts, cup finals and football league play-off games.

Extensive media coverage spreads the benefits of international events beyond the host country. The German economy grew at its fastest rate for five years after it hosted the 2006 football World Cup. However, all of mainland Europe gained with £1.25 billion going into the UK economy from sales of related products (including 6,000 foam wigs sold by Sainsbury's).

London 2012 – a race against time?

The successful London bid to host the 2012 Olympic games promises carbon-neutral and environmentally sensitive growth to an area of east London that is currently an industrial wasteland.

Transforming the Stratford area by 2012 will add 10 per cent to the output of the UK construction industry, create 30,000 jobs, 100,000 new homes in the 'Thames Gateway' area and boost tourism for the country as a whole.

In addition to the Olympic village and new stadiums, there are three major transport projects:

- the high speed Channel Tunnel Rail Link (CTRL) to Europe for 2007
- extensions to the east London rail line
- Crossrail – a rail link from Heathrow airport in the west, through central London into Kent and Essex in the east.

The government hopes that retail opportunities and the prospect of rising land prices will encourage private businesses to invest in the schemes.

assignment focus

1   Can you think of any arguments against staging the Olympics in London?
2   Is either of your chosen businesses likely to benefit? If so in what way?

Celebrity culture

The use of famous faces in marketing campaigns (see page 231) is a well-tried tactic for selling goods and services. Clearly the images and personalities to which we respond will change with our attitudes and lifestyles. The concern over healthy eating, for example, has caused fashion house Prada to move away from 'stick thin' models.

The artist Andy Wharhol once observed that everyone wants their '15 minutes of fame' and increasingly successful businesses are being built upon the desire of ordinary people to achieve celebrity status. Youtube (show your own movie clips), *Big Brother*, *The X Factor* and quiz shows (get on TV) and radio phone-ins are all based upon getting the audience into the act.

Technological factors

When the Beatles sold a million records they were made of vinyl. Today's hits are increasingly likely to be digital. Technology constantly changes and business need to adapt in order to survive.

The internet has caused a revolution in how business is done. Businesses must keep up, but being ahead of the game does not always pay. A number of early internet companies (the dot coms) failed because dial-up connections were too slow and inconvenient for their services. Later entrants to the market have benefited from the development of high-speed broadband. Nick Jenkins of Moonpig.com (design your own cards) believes this factor is critical to his success.

Link | The internet is considered in detail in Unit 29.

Telephony developments

Mobile phones now routinely combine additional functions such as file transfer, whilst new technology is providing customers with ever more ways of getting online:

- Wireless application protocol (WAP) enables users of mobile phones and portable computers to receive e-mail and web-based information whilst on the move.
- 'Hot spots' are areas where wireless (not plugged in) applications, such as notebook computers can access the internet.
- Personal digital assistants (PDAs) are pocket-sized personal organisers, such as the Blackberry, which combine a calendar, diary and address book.

Technological advances also give rise to:

- new materials and processes used in manufacturing and construction – compare the view from a modern sports stadium with sitting behind a pillar at an old one
- new scientific developments such as the growing of GM crops or stem cell technology
- transport developments, e.g. in 2006 Ryanair became the first airline to announce that it was safe for passengers to use mobile phones on its flights
- communications advances – downloaded music is replacing CDs, DVDs have replaced videos. The internet has provided the opportunity for development of download sites such as iTunes and a major threat to record companies who find their products easily copied. A survey in December 2006 found that one in four people admitted to illegal downloads.

Legal factors

Legal factors relate to the law of the land and are therefore related to political decisions.

The effects of national and international law

A raft of UK and EU laws regulate businesses within the UK. Those involved in foreign trade are also bound by international law. Whilst the Institute of Directors (IOD) and the Confederation of British Industry (CBI) are concerned about the cost to industry of complying with legislation, other stakeholders clearly benefit.

- Employment law provides employees with rights and protects them from unfair treatment in the workplace.
- Health and safety law makes the workplace safer for employees, customers and other visitors.
- Environmental law is designed to protect our surroundings against harmful emissions and anti-social disposal of waste.
- Consumer protection law regulates the quality, quantity and safety of the goods and services that we buy.
- Taxation law sets out the requirements to draw up accurate accounts, pay income tax, corporation tax, National Insurance, VAT and customs duties.
- The Data Protection Act regulates the treatment of personal information held by businesses about individuals.
- Competition law promotes fair competition within markets. At the time of writing, BAA seems likely to be investigated for having a monopoly in the ownership of UK airports. It may be compelled to sell an airport to another business.
- Government 'watchdogs' regulate the privatised industries to protect customers against poor service and unreasonable price rises. For example Ofwat regulates the water industry and Ofcom regulates telecommunications.
- Local councils can decide on local building regulations, planning permission and the granting of licences. They can also enforce public health and environmental law.

In Unit 37 we look at specific laws that will affect a small business.

Environmental factors

Environmental factors may relate to energy needs, (e.g. in 2005 hurricane Katrina disrupted the US oil supplies and drove up world oil prices), pollution of the environment by industry and the need to recycle waste. Global warming can be seen as a threat or an opportunity; it depends on your point of view. What is your view?

The new awareness about the environment is opening opportunities for new and existing businesses:

- Ecover washing-up liquid
- B&Q's new range of solar panels and wind turbines
- Clearview Stoves – wood is the energy of the future
- farmers' markets for local produce – a niche, but growing, market based on the knowledge that the carbon footprint involved in transport is smaller for local goods.

In response to demands for zero waste, the Eden Project in Cornwall has developed a new biodegradable cricketing box made from hemp. At present this is being tested – it would be interesting to find out how.

As we stated earlier, environmental policies are now high on the political agenda. EU carbon trading schemes, for example, encourage manufacturers to reduce emissions of CO_2. Targets are set for local authorities to work towards zero waste so that less household refuse is dumped in landfill sites. These policies threaten businesses that cannot comply but provide an opportunity for those in the recycling industry.

Defra (the government department responsible for the environment) will plan to combat threats to the farming industry from infections such as foot and mouth disease and avian flu. The Environment Agency will attempt to monitor the effects of climate change upon the growing seasons and the coastline.

The impact of PESTLE factors

In setting out its business plan, an organisation will conduct PESTLE analysis to look at the external opportunities and threats that face it. We have seen that a particular factor may threaten one business but provide an opportunity for a rival.

The SWOT analysis for Eclipse Pottery on page 405 includes PESTLE factors under the headings of opportunities and threats.

New organisations

New organisations constantly spring up in response to PESTLE opportunities:

- Tyrrell's Potato Chips (thicker than crisps) aims to satisfy the lifestyle demand for quality products. Owner Will Chase believes that the products are price insensitive for two reasons:
  - for health reasons (a social factor) many people now eat crisps only as a treat. They are therefore prepared to pay a premium price for a quality product
  - growth in disposable income (an economic factor) also helps.
- Exclusively online businesses such as Trainline (rail information) or Moneyexpert (comparing financial services) could not exist without cheap PCs and the internet (technological factors).
- Steven Henderson's spur was environmental and economic. He set up his S-Plant company to convert waste cooking oil into bio-diesel after reading about global warming and rising fuel prices. The fuel is used in his father's tractors.

Winding up of existing organisations

Those organisations that cannot adapt will ultimately fail. Burger King blamed a disappointing 2006 in the UK on failing to respond to the desire for healthier food – something that McDonald's had done more successfully.

A number of high street retailers seem likely to struggle as e-commerce continues to grow in popularity. John Lewis has grown by setting up its own on-line operation. Similarly Virgin and HMV Music have developed music download sales.

The recent public interest in quality ethical brands has attracted the attention of larger established companies wanting to get in on the act. Take-overs by larger companies have included:

- Body Shop – now part of French cosmetics giant L'Oriel
- Toms of Maine (toothpaste) – now part of Colgate-Palmolive
- Rachel's Organic – taken over by Dean Foods of the USA
- Pret A Manger – one-third owned by McDonald's
- Green and Black's (chocolate) – sold to Cadbury-Schweppes
- Ben and Jerry's ice cream – owned by Unilever.

The new owners seek to enhance their corporate image by these acquisitions.

assignment focus

Which of the PESTLE factors have created the demand for these brands?

Revision of strategic plans

With the pressing need to combat global warming, the oil companies (criticised as being members of the 'carbon club') have drawn up revised strategic plans to take account of the need to develop renewable energy. Shell has produced its Sustainability Report, whilst BP talks of a time 'Beyond Petroleum'. Meanwhile both companies still actively search for new sources of fossil fuel.

case study 1.15 | **Emission impossible?**

The Shell Sustainability Report 2005 – Meeting the energy challenge states:

'We will:

- manage our GHG (greenhouse gas) emissions (target 5 per cent below 1990 levels by 2010)
- help customers reduce their emissions by providing more natural gas and advanced transport fuels
- invest in technology to capture CO_2 from fossil fuels
- work to build at least one large-scale business in alternative energy
- support policies that use markets to encourage GHG reductions.'

activity

1. Research Shell's environmental record in past years, e.g. in Nigeria. This shows why a change in corporate image was needed.
2. Shell is a powerful company. Why does it need to change in this way? Which PESTLE factors is it responding to?

Impact on stakeholders

The external factors have the potential to affect the various stakeholders in different ways. For example:

- Employees now find themselves protected by employment laws and with the right to take their employer to an industrial tribunal if a dispute cannot be resolved by other means.
- Customers have the right to question data held by organisations under the Data Protection Act and can expect better products and service as a result of consumer law. The increased competition introduced by the internet meanwhile provides greater choice at lower prices.

- Shareholders will benefit from global opportunities as James Dyson did from outsourcing vacuum cleaner production to Malaysia, whilst others (like Hanson below), will suffer if demand for their products fails.

- Employees will benefit when the economy is vibrant – in an extreme case 4,000 employees in the City of London received £1 million bonuses in December 2006. At the same time, workers making HP sauce in Aston, Birmingham, lost their jobs when the competition authorities allowed Heinz to buy the HP brand.

- The community may experience opportunities or threats. Advances in medical technology promise to cure a variety of ailments, whilst global warming has the potential to cause catastrophe – business and industry are responsible for two-thirds of the UK's carbon emissions.

Inconvenient for supermarkets

In real terms, food prices have declined since 2000. However, a number of stakeholders are concerned that supermarkets are too powerful. These include suppliers, small local retailers, communities and environmental pressure groups such as Friends of the Earth.

In May 2006 the government's Competition Commission (part of the Office of Fair Trading) decided to see whether supermarkets are operating in the public interest. The enquiry will take two years and will look at:

- how the 'big four', and especially Tesco, buy up small convenience stores to eliminate local competition. The number of local independent stores is declining rapidly

- the abuse of buying power to drive down suppliers' prices – low shop prices are achieved through low prices to suppliers

- the buying of large amounts of land to stop competitors opening stores

- selling items at below cost so that smaller businesses cannot compete.

Here the external influence is political and social. The government uses its influence to ensure that Tesco and the others are operating in the public interest.

Customers clearly like the supermarkets, so why are there dangers in them becoming too big? You can look on the internet to see the criticisms levelled at Walmart, the huge US retailer and part owner of Asda. You can also see why a number of towns have turned down planning applications from the big four.

assignment focus

If one of your chosen businesses is a supermarket or convenience store, research more about the Competition Commission enquiry.

Functional activity changes

Businesses may respond to changes in external factors by altering their functional activities. For example, firms may need to set up an e-commerce section, or a call centre function. Supermarkets have developed from exclusively self-service to include home delivery operations ('You shop we drop'). Demand has come with the change in working patterns and the growth in the number of working women (both social factors). The service has been made possible by the introduction of e-commerce (a technological factor).

case study 1.16

Hanson in the slow lane

Hanson is a multinational manufacturer of building materials; its aggregates section employs 3,700 staff in the UK.

The company blamed its lower profits in 2006 on the UK government's 'lack of action' on road building; 70 per cent of proposed new roads are still awaiting planning permission.

Other difficulties for Hanson have been an increase in pension costs and a £7.1 million loss on currency movements. The company also faces legal claims over the production of materials containing asbestos, although so far 70 per cent of these have been dismissed.

In response to slow demand for its products, the company aims to review its organisational structure and look at cost-cutting – this is likely to involve job losses.

activity

1 What are aggregates?
2 Identify the various PESTLE factors that have troubled Hanson. Under which heading does each belong?

assignment focus

Choose two of the business that you used earlier in the assignment.

To achieve P5 for each business you have chosen:

■ select three external factors that are having an impact upon these organisations
■ describe the effect both upon the organisations and upon their stakeholders.

To achieve M3, analyse how, in the past, various external factors have affected the two busnesses.

To achieve D1, you should select one of the organisations and evaluate how external factors may impact upon this business during the next five years. Mention how these are likely to affect: the activities of the business, its strategy, internal structures, functional activities and stakeholders.

UNIT 2

Investigating business resources

This unit covers:

- How human resources are managed
- The purpose of managing physical and technological resources
- How to access sources of finance
- Interpreting financial statements

Businesses need to be able to manage their resources if they are to be successful. This unit looks at the four main resources:

- human – it is essential to recruit and retain suitably qualified and experienced staff
- physical – especially maintenance, refurbishment and safety
- technological – legal requirements and protecting intellectual property
- financial – a business needs to manage its finances in order to control costs.

Finally, the unit considers how to interpret financial statements in order to determine the performance of a business.

grading criteria

To achieve a **Pass** grade the evidence must show that the learner is able to:	To achieve a **Merit** grade the evidence must also show that the learner is able to:	To achieve a **Distinction** grade the evidence must also show that the learner is able to:
P1 describe how human resources are managed in a selected organisation	**M1** assess how managing human, physical and technological resources can improve the performance of a selected organisation	**D1** evaluate how managing resources and controlling budgets can improve the performance of a business
P2 describe the main physical and technological resources that need to be considered in the running of a selected organisation	**M2** analyse the reasons why costs and budgets need to be controlled and explain in detail problems that can arise if they are left unmonitored	**D2** evaluate the adequacy of accounting ratios as a means of monitoring business health in a selected organisation using examples
P3 describe where sources of finance can be obtained for starting up a selected business	**M3** interpret the contents of a given profit and loss account and balance sheet and explain in detail how accounting ratios can be used to monitor the financial state of the given organisation	

	To achieve a **Pass** grade the evidence must show that the learner is able to:	To achieve a **Merit** grade the evidence must also show that the learner is able to:	To achieve a **Distinction** grade the evidence must also show that the learner is able to:
grading criteria	**P4** give the reasons why costs and budgets need to be controlled		
	P5 interpret the contents of a given profit and loss account and balance sheet		
	P6 illustrate the financial state of a given business by showing examples of accounting ratios		

How human resources are managed

Human resources

How does your teacher manage you? How does the head teacher or principal manage your teacher? We are all employees in one way or another, but are we good employees and how easy or difficult is it to manage us?

Staffing to meet changing business demands

In any organisation the first responsibility of anyone concerned with human resources is to make sure that there are sufficient qualified staff to enable it achieve its aims and objectives. Stand in any large store and you will hear announcements such as, 'Would X go to the checkout' or 'Y to section …'.

Here is one example with which you will be familiar. A store has busy periods during the day (lunchtime and early evening), on Thursday nights (late night shopping) and Friday and Saturday over the Christmas period. How could this be staffed so that staffing costs (wages) could be kept under control and customers are provided with a fast service? More staff would need to be employed when demand is high/busy (peak periods) and fewer staff during off-peak periods when demand is lower and the store is less busy.

The store could:

■ only employ full-time staff, but this could mean that there are too many staff during the less busy off-peak periods

■ employ a mixture of full-time, part-time and temporary staff. Fewer full-time staff would need to be employed, part-timers could be employed to cover the busy periods on Thursday, Friday and Saturday. (TK Max calls these 'associates' to show they are as much valued as full-time staff.) Short-term temporary contracts could be given to staff who only work over Christmas.

Staffing in most retail stores (where 20 per cent of staff are full-time and 80 per cent are part-time) and restaurants is organised this way. Charities such as Oxfam employ a large number of volunteer (unpaid) staff to work in their charity shops.

1   Do you have a part-time job? When are you employed? Why are you employed at these times?

2   What type of staffing arrangements does your organisation have? For example, are more people employed during busy periods? Are part-time staff employed at busy times?

For M1 and D1 you will have to assess whether the system works. For example, what are the consequences of over- or under-staffing for various stakeholders? How could the system be improved?

Co-ordination of team resources to meet targets

It is the responsibility of managers to make sure that the team has all the resources necessary to complete its tasks and meet its targets. In a retail store, this means providing customers with the products they need when they need them. Are the facilities satisfactory, e.g. clean, tidy, well laid out? Is the equipment well maintained and suitable, or does it break down? Is there sufficient stock available and in the right place? Have fast selling lines been restocked? Do shelves get tidied/recovered regularly, etc. Do the staff have sufficient knowledge of the products to answer customer queries? Are there sufficient well-trained staff to cope, or is there a staff shortage? Do staff look bored? Are they keen to help or do they ignore customers?

The resources need to be co-ordinated to make sure that tasks are completed. The manager will need to plan the staffing and allocate the work to the right people. What could happen if staff do not turn up, machines break down, equipment or stock is not available? These are all symptoms of an ineffective management. There should be a contingency (back up) plan if things go wrong.

A manager's people skills – leadership, communication and interpersonal – are often the key to motivating a team and developing a team spirit. People are an essential part of the marketing mix. Creating an effective team will help the organisation achieve its aims and objectives and improve performance.

Check this out the next time you visit your organisation. Are the shelves empty or well stocked and tidy? (Take care – these may be slow or poor selling lines which no one wants.) Do they have a range of goods, have particular sizes etc? Are there sufficient staff? Are they working or hiding? Ask a difficult question. Do they know the answer? What do your observations tell you about the quality of the management?

Monitoring of team performance

Research has shown that an effective team is likely to have these characteristics:

- focus on customer targets and goals
- relatively small with good leadership
- high level of help, support and trust amongst members
- ideas and experiences are shared
- all team members work to the same objectives
- work roles are clearly defined and everyone knows what they should do
- absenteeism and sickness rates are low
- morale and motivation are high, members enjoy working with one another
- team members seek agreement rather than argument
- open communication with a high level of participation in decision-making.

To achieve this level of effectiveness, the team leader and team members will need to be properly trained and developed, and there needs to be a clear system of **incentives** and reward for successful teams. There will need to be a balance between the achievement of any team tasks and the needs of the individual team members. Every aspect of the team needs to be monitored to ensure that it achieves optimum performance.

Table 2.1 Advantages and disadvantages of team working

Advantages	Disadvantages
Staff are able to share ideas/experience/ workload	Some employees do not like working in teams
Teams can achieve synergy, i.e. a team working together can achieve more than the same number of individuals working separately, or 1 + 1 = 3	Can take away individual initiative
	Decision-making can take longer as a consensus is needed
Help and support can be given to each member	Conflict can occur if the team members are incompatible
Enthusiasm, commitment and job satisfaction tend to rise	Weaker/stronger members can be frustrated
Tasks can be completed more quickly and effectively	Needs clear direction and targets
	May not be appropriate in some situations
	Team leaders need effective training

---

assignment focus

1 Does your organisation use teams to achieve tasks?

2 How are the teams structured?

3 How well do they perform?

4 If your organisation does not use teams, could it? Should it?

5 Do staff appear to work together, or help and support each other?

Monitoring is important because it is a way of comparing actual performance with any standards or targets which have been set, e.g. sales targets, stock control and customer service. Monitoring of staff time-keeping and absence is essential to meet targets and make improvements. Operational monitoring focuses on the individual. It will include checking and recording absenteeism, punctuality and time-keeping (arriving late and leaving early). Behaviour, attitude to work and customer service skills may be noted and could form part of a performance **appraisal**. Here the worker and line manager discuss past performance, including strengths and areas for improvement and agree the targets to be achieved before the next review. A successful appraisal can lead to a pay rise. At the tactical level, the emphasis is on team or departmental performance, e.g. Are deadlines kept, quality maintained and improved, targets achieved, budgets adhered to?

Do staff in your organisation appear to be monitored? New staff are monitored closely to ensure they are performing effectively.

Liaison with other departments

Good liaison – communication and contact between groups or departments – is essential for the smooth running of any organisation. You have probably heard people say, 'I blame the system' whenever anything goes wrong. Every organisation is a system or a set of inter-related or connected parts, managed to achieve a common purpose. The parts or sub-systems may be departments, functions, different teams or separate locations. Most problems occur at the boundary (or interface) between these, e.g. between production and personnel, between chilled and frozen food, between the buyer and the supplier, etc. It is important that managers liaise closely with their colleagues in other sections/departments to minimise conflicts and smooth out any problems. In retail clothing shops, the conflicts seem to be over the amount of display space and the number of staff allocated to each section. These could be solved by good liaison and communication to achieve good working relationships.

Good liaison/relationships with suppliers is also vital to ensure that shelves remain stocked or raw materials are delivered on time.

Establishment of professional culture

The culture of an organisation can be summarised by the sentence, 'It's the way we do things here.' Do your classes always start and finish on time? Do you always turn up on time? What happens if you don't? Do you care? Do the staff care?

The culture of an organisation is the set of customs, values, attitudes and behaviour adopted and shared by its members. It may be seen in the way management treat workers, how colleagues treat each other, how staff treat customers, workers' attitudes towards the product they sell or the service they provide, even the clothes people wear at work and the language they use. The culture sets the standards for the organisation; it gives support and provides guidance. Winning companies have a strong set of values which are reflected in everything they do. They strive for excellence and continuous improvement.

Does your organisation do this? Do you? Do staff in your organisation say, 'Sorry, I can't do that. It's more than my job's worth'?

See page 312 on organisational culture.

assignment focus

In your organisation:

1 Who makes all the key decisions? Are lower level staff involved in decision-making? What decisions can operatives make?

2 Does the organisation stress the rules and procedures? Or is it more flexible and informal?

3 Do staff work in teams?

4 Do staff feel valued, or is getting the job done more important?

5 Is there a staff uniform? Do all staff wear it, or just the operatives?

6 How do managers address staff, and vice versa? Are first names used? Is there a professional culture or is it too casual? Is there a formal or informal atmosphere?

7 Do managers and operatives share the same canteen with the same menu?

8 Do managers and operatives share the same rest room facilities?

9 Separation of professional and private activities. Are staff allowed to bring their friends to work, make private telephone calls, use the internet for private purposes or make private photocopies? Are mobile phones allowed at the workplace? This is a cause for concern in many workplaces where staff have been sacked for sending or receiving private e-mails or misusing the internet.

Provision of appropriate incentives

An incentive at work is anything which motivates or influences staff to increase production or sales. An effective system of managing incentives and rewards is often vital if the organisation wants to motivate its staff and improve performance.

Financial incentives

For most people, pay is a major reason for going to work. Pay certainly plays a part in motivation, but it is not always clear what part. Employees may have different priorities. It could be job satisfaction or the 'fun of working as part of a team with a cheeky grin' (source: www.virgin.co.uk).

Pay opens the door to many other things which may motivate, such as status and self-fulfilment. Payment is usually associated with motivation where it is linked with performance. An extreme case is piece-work where there is no basic pay and payment is entirely based on output. Home-workers in the fashion trade or casual agricultural workers, such as fruit-pickers, are often paid in this way. More usually, basic pay is supplemented by performance-related pay in the form of a bonus or commission for good results. Financial incentives to sell may motivate the employee but are not always good for the customer. Can you think why?

The traditional image of the car salesperson as a 'shark' came about in this way. Someone who is desperate to sell because they need the commission is unlikely to give the customer the best advice. Linking pay to performance may give employees an incentive to work more effectively. However, it may not be appropriate for all kinds of work. Profit-sharing schemes are another form of incentive. Some companies, e.g. John Lewis, try to encourage employees/partners by letting them share in the year's profits. In this way they can see a link between their work, the performance of the company and their pay.

Non-financial incentives

There is a growing trend for rewarding staff with non-financial incentives such as prizes for exceeding sales targets (popular in sports shops such as Footlocker), sales person of the month with a picture on the company intranet or magazine (Nationwide), etc.

How are staff paid in your organisation? Are there financial and/or non-financial incentives? Do they work?

Evidence seems to show that performance is improved by:

- profit-sharing schemes
- increasing staff participation (involving, consulting)
- good job design, i.e. creating jobs which people find interesting
- sharing gains/profits with staff.

Performance-related pay (PRP)

This is a method of linking an employee's pay to the work they perform or the output they achieve. Other performance indicators such as improvements in productivity or quality can also be used. PRP would normally be based on the achievement of targets set at an appraisal interview. Failing to meet targets would mean no PRP, i.e. no extra pay! It could therefore be a major incentive to improving performance, both for an individual and the organisation.

Does PRP work?

The evidence is that it can work in the appropriate situation. However, its effects are not always clear. It is not suitable for all jobs because it can be difficult to measure performance, especially in parts of the service sector. It can be divisive – why did they get it and not me? Many companies are unsure what the effect of PRP is in terms of motivation.

Opponents of the system have pointed out that an anagram for performance-related pay is 'mere end of year clap trap'. They claim that assessing overall performance and sharing the rewards motivates people more. What do you think?

 Link

For more about incentives, see Unit 16, page 298.

For more about incentives, see Unit 16, page 298.

assignment focus

1 Does your organisation use financial or non-financial incentives to motivate or reward staff? Should it?

2 Does your organisation use PRP? Should it?

Creativity and initiative

Do managers encourage their staff to be creative and act on their own initiative? To achieve this, staff need to be empowered, so that they are able to make their own decisions and accept responsibility. Employees need to be encouraged to think for themselves and to act accordingly. This requires:

- staff to be fully trained
- managers who are willing and able to delegate
- a culture where staff are fully valued and appreciated.

Some organisations are now promoting themselves with the strapline 'Our staff are fully trained to deal with all your questions. One phone call is all it takes', i.e. their staff are empowered to make their own decisions. Some teams, particularly in car production, can decide on membership and the allocation of work.

Empowerment has been seen as a way of enriching the job. It has also been seen as an excuse for dumping responsibility on employees at a lower level. Cashiers in clothes shops have responsibility for hangers and plastic bags. What do you think?

assignment focus

1 From your observations, are staff in your organisation empowered? Does it work?
2 Are staff encouraged to be creative and act on their own initiative?

Outsourcing versus in-house decisions

Rather than employing its own staff to provide each function, a business may decide that it is more effective or cheaper to outsource (or buy-in) a service from another business. Thus specialist firms may be contracted to run security, catering, cleaning, payroll, delivery services and the maintenance of equipment such as photocopiers or computers. Similarly, consultants may be brought in to help set up a new MIS system or design a business website.

Outsourcing has a number of advantages. An organisation simply pays the agreed rate and the job is done. Human resources issues such as staff training, payroll, providing cover for sickness, recruitment of new staff and redundancy are the responsibility of the contractor. However, not all outsourcing is successful. In 2000 Sainsbury set up an IT outsourcing deal with Accenture. This was scrapped in 2004 at a cost of £140m.

case study 2.1

Location is not important

Call centres (telephone services providing help and information to customers day and night) have grown dramatically since the late 1990s. Since location is not important, centres can be set up away from business to take advantage of lower costs. By 2003, businesses were making further cost reductions by outsourcing to low-cost providers abroad. India with its highly educated, English-speaking, low-wage workforce became especially popular.

Direct marketing companies also make use of cheap international calls to sell double glazing, loans and kitchens through sales staff in Bangalore and Mumbai.

The NatWest bank has tried to take advantage of these concerns by advertising 'No call centres outside the UK', whilst the GNER rail company announces that it is proud to have call-centres in Newcastle.

activity

Call centres are popular with the banking and insurance industries because costs of providing customer service are reduced.

1 What are the advantages and disadvantages for customers? (The alternative may be to go into a high street branch, write or telephone during business hours.)
2 Find out who carries out security, cleaning, canteen and maintenance services in your school or college. If these services are outsourced, why do you think this is?

Maintenance of operation

Adequate resources to meet tasks

Once aims and objectives have been decided and strategic and tactical plans have been drawn up, the organisation would need to make sure that all resources are available when they are needed in the short, medium and long term. Does your classroom have everything that is needed? Do you?

Goods out of stock, goods not delivered on time, waiting too long to get served, computer does not work, etc. – these are examples of where management has obviously failed to provide adequate resources. You will probably be able to think of many others. Have you complained or taken your custom elsewhere?

For its operations to run smoothly, every organisation will need to make sure that it has enough of the right resources in the right place at the right time. What resources are needed will depend entirely on the output of the organisation, e.g. a dry cleaners will need chemicals, plastic bags, hangers, etc. The resources are:

- staff – a very expensive and valuable resource. Should the staff be full-time, part-time or temporary?
- equipment, e.g. computers, fork lift trucks in a warehouse, delivery vehicles
- materials and goods for sale – good relationships need to be developed with suppliers
- working capital – sufficient cash to pay day-to-day expenses
- facilities – the buildings or premises.

For more about working capital, see page 82.

Two examples will help to show how these resources need to be co-ordinated:

Question: What do your local Thai restaurant or hairdresser both need to do to maintain an effective business and achieve their objectives?

Answer: Provide quality services and products, i.e. satisfy or exceed customer expectations with an excellent meal or a good cut.

They require:

- enough competent, trained staff, who are able and willing to give excellent customer service
- equipment and facilities, such as ovens, scissors, heating, lighting, seating, etc., which should be clean, hygienic and well-maintained, meeting or exceeding health and safety requirements
- sufficient supplies which should have been purchased in advance to meet demand, weekends are the busiest (planned)
- faultless administration, e.g. booking arrangements – 'Yes we are expecting you'
- sufficient working capital to pay day-to-day expenses.

Monitor, trouble-shoot, problem-solve

Managers cannot stand back once the plan has been constructed and the resources have been put in place. They must be actively involved in controlling, co-ordinating and directing operations. Although some managers are never seen on the 'shop floor', there are those who manage by walking around, taking a hands-on approach. When does walking around become interference? Which type of manager do you – as a customer – prefer?

Ideally managers should monitor/check/control all activities. They should be able to locate/identify problems and sort them out (trouble-shoot). If they cannot, there must be systems in place to check that everything is working. There should be someone available with the authority to handle problems or sort out complaints, i.e. make decisions. Does this sound like your restaurant or hairdresser?

assignment focus

1   On your last visit to the organisation you are investigating you discovered that goods you wanted were out of stock. Can you say why? What did you do about it?

2   Do managers in your organisation walk around? Are managers visible? Could you speak to one if you had a complaint? Would it be any good?

3   What would long queues in your organisation be a sign of?

Monitoring of performance and future planning
Are the aims and objectives being achieved? Are all the resources in place and working? Or perhaps there are breakdowns or shortages? Have these problems been dealt with?

There are three basic levels of management and decision-making in many organisations Figure 1.12 on page 23 is an example of possible planning and monitoring that may take place.

**assignment
focus**

How could you tell that your organisation was being run effectively? What criteria would you use?

The purpose of managing physical and technological resources

Physical resources

Buildings and facilities

remember

Keep thinking of the consequences if physical resources are badly managed and something goes wrong. Afternoon TV seems dominated by adverts for InjurylawyersRus.

Everywhere we look new buildings seem to be constructed. Perhaps your centre is having a new extension or a new open-plan computer suite. Physical resources are the buildings, equipment and facilities needed to provide goods and services. They include classrooms, car showrooms, offices, shops, railway and industrial premises and your selected business. The image and reputation of a business often depends on the quality of its premises. Badly maintained premises say, in effect, 'We are an unsuccessful business'. How often have you said, 'I don't like the look of that place' and taken your custom elsewhere? Customers demand high standards. It is the responsibility of management to provide them. In large organisations, a whole department headed by a specialist premises or facilities manager may be responsible.

Management at a retail store, for example, will want to create a relaxing atmosphere for their customers so careful thought will go into the layout and design. Fixtures and fittings such as shelves and rails will be used to display goods and reinforce the brand image. Window displays will be designed to show the products to best advantage and tempt customers inside. You should look at the management of the physical resources as an integral part of the overall management process designed to achieve corporate objectives.

Physical resources are an essential part of the **marketing mix** ingredients, Place and Physical evidence – see Unit 3, page 107.

**assignment
focus**

You need to describe the main physical resources involved in the running of your organisation.

1 Is the building clean, safe and healthy? i.e. Is the Health and Safety at Work Act (HASAWA) being obeyed?
2 Describe the premises.
   a) Are they old or modern, brick or concrete and glass, etc.?
   b) Where is it located? Include a map and/or photograph.

Materials and waste

Look at how goods are unloaded. Is there a queue of lorries when you arrive to shop at your local supermarket at 9.30 on Saturday morning? How are waste materials disposed of? Is there a green policy for recycling glass, plastic, cans, cardboard? In a hospital, how does it dispose of medical waste? How often do the cleaners change the water when cleaning a ward? How quickly is spillage cleaned up in a supermarket? How are toner cartridges disposed of? Reducing waste can provide substantial cost savings.

Plant and machinery

These are the physical tangible assets used by the business to carry out its activities, e.g. a kiln in a pottery or a fork lift truck in a warehouse. They can include lifts and escalators,

1   Does your organisation make and/or sell products?

2   What waste does it produce? E.g. packaging, chemicals, food past its sell-by date, etc. Is it bio-degradable (rot or break down over time) or will it remain forever in a landfill site?

3   How is waste disposed of? How much is recycled or reused?

For M1 and D1, you could look at how the system could be improved, food retailers claim huge savings just by ordering and rotating stock more effectively to meet sell-by dates.

ovens in the bakery section, dry cleaning equipment, heavy lifting equipment, etc. Who is responsible for repair, maintenance and cleaning? Is it done by internal staff or by a specialist outside company, i.e. is it outsourced? Is it properly guarded or protected? The type of equipment used will depend entirely on the activities of the business, e.g. computers and printers in an office, scissors and hairdryers in a hairdressers.

Check out the Health and Safety Executive website at www.hse.gov.uk to find the number of accidents caused by plant and machinery in your industry.

1   What plant, machinery or equipment is used in your organisation?

2   Do staff appear properly trained to use the equipment?

3   Does it break down? Is it safe?

For M1 and D1, you could look at how the use of plant and machinery could be improved. However if you say 'my organisation does not have any plant and machinery' then this will have little or no importance/relevance in improving the performance.

Equipment including ICT

Information communications technology (ICT) hardware and software has changed the way we all work, even three-year-olds play CBeebies games on a laptop. How many computers are there in your centre or at your workplace? Is the space too hot or is it air conditioned? Workspaces need to be specially designed or adapted for computer use. All electrical cables need to be safe. Specially trained staff need to be available (in large financial institutions this could be 24/7 all year around) to support, maintain and advise on these systems. Large supermarkets use the bar codes on products to check out the goods at the tills (these are linked to the head office and the suppliers and can provide an effective way of reordering and recording sales). Staff need to be properly trained to enable all stakeholders to benefit. 'Do you need help with packing?' Do you get eye contact with customers? Or checkout staff? Managers need to achieve a balance between the use of ICT and customer contact. Does your organisation succeed?

Planned maintenance and refurbishment

Does the building look cared for? Are the staff areas as well maintained as the public areas? Who is responsible? For example, do the local staff do minor repairs and maintenance? Does head office or an outside company do the major work? In a restaurant, are the outside of the windows clean? If not, what do you think the areas you cannot see are like?

Maintenance is carried out to make sure that:

■ the premises, plant and machinery comply with health and safety legislation

■ the premises are fit for the purpose they are intended

■ the image of the organisation is protected/improved

■ premises, plant and machinery do not deteriorate or break down.

Planned/preventative maintenance

Regular maintenance is carried out in advance to prevent any breakdown of the facilities resulting in loss of production or sales. It can either be done internally by the facilities or premises team, or it can be outsourced.

Reactive maintenance

Repairs are carried out or parts replaced when something breaks down. This approach can result in lost production and is often less cost-effective than a planned approach.

Refurbishment

Refurbishment may simply mean brightening up the premises to attract extra customers or a complete 'makeover'. It is often associated with a change of management or ownership. For example, the new management/owners of a restaurant may want a new image for the premises. This could involve new internal layouts and designs, redecoration, new fixtures, fittings, signage, etc.

---

assignment focus

1   How often is maintenance carried out in your organisation?

2   How long does it take before something is repaired?

3   Has it been refurbished? Does it look any different?

Health and safety

Emergency provisions are covered by health and safety legislation, e.g. clear fire exits, regular fire drills, clear instructions for emergency evacuation, regularly serviced fire extinguishers and emergency lighting.

---

assignment focus

Investigate the emergency provisions for your organisation.

1   How often are fire drills carried out?

2   Would part-time staff know what to do in an emergency?

3   Are fire exits clear? Are exit routes clearly marked?

Insurance

Insurance provides financial cover or protection against the risk of fire, theft, flood, etc. Every employer must have employers' liability insurance in case compensation has to be paid to an employee who is injured or contracts a disease as a result of their work. Public liability insurance is also recommended to cover against any claims made by non-employees, such as students, patients, customers, guests, etc., whilst they are on the premises.

A certificate of employers' liability insurance must be displayed at the premises. Where is it kept in your organisation? Where is all the student data stored at your centre, on the premises? Is a back-up copy kept off-site?

Security

Security is required to protect people, equipment, premises, stock, trade secrets and cash. Maintaining security is now a major concern for many organisations, with security guards a familiar sight in almost every high street. Entry and exit searches are commonplace. Many businesses search their staff.

---

assignment focus

For M1, consider how more effective management of the physical resources in your organisation would improve its performance (defined by its aims and objectives). Could you make any suggestions for improvement?

For D1, you need to evaluate how the management of physical resources fits in to the process of managing all resources, e.g. if the business is based at a person's home and they visit customers, are physical resources relevant?

Table 2.2 Security checklist

Features	Comments
CCTV	
Security guards: How many? How often do they patrol?	
Searches on entry/exit	
ID cards compulsory	
Metal grille or shutters, e.g. shop fronts	
Fire/burglar alarms	
Panic buttons next to the tills	
Specialist features, e.g. time locks for banks	
Double entry doors, e.g. in off licences	
Internal door entry locks	
Security tags on products	
Perimeter walls and fencing, patrols, dogs	

Technological resources

What is intellectual property?

The software you use, the music you listen to, this book you are reading or company names such as Virgin, Coca-Cola or McDonalds are all the **intellectual property** (IP) of the creators of the products.

The intellectual property owned by the organisation such as fashion designs, drawings, text, music and video are all part of its intangible assets. As with physical property, intellectual property has to be managed to protect the organisation from theft or illegal copying which could damage its sales and reputation.

'IP allows people to own their creativity and innovation in the same way that they can own physical property. The owner of IP can control and be rewarded for its use, and this encourages further innovation and creativity to the benefit of us all.' (source: www. intellectual-property.gov.uk)

What does it say around the edge of the music CD or DVD you play? If it says nothing, it is probably illegally recorded. What about the software you use – is it legal or illegal? Your centre will need a licence for each copy of Microsoft Word ©® it uses. There need to be as many licences as there are computers/site users.

Anything which is unique to an organisation, its products and services gives it a competitive advantage and needs to be protected.

There are four main types of IP:

■ registered designs

■ copyright

■ trade marks

■ patents.

Registered designs

Design refers to the appearance of the product – the lines, colours, contours, shape, feel or materials/ingredients of the product itself or its ornamentation. The design is part of the image, branding and marketing of the organisation. When a design is registered, it means that it is unique and no one else can use it. If they do, they could be liable to legal action and a claim for damages. A registered design is an important commercial asset which can be sold or licensed to another organisation. Ralph Lauren, Levi, Monsoon and H&M own unique designs.

Copyright ©

Owning a **copyright** gives the creators of literary and artistic material, music, films, sound recordings and broadcasts, including software and multimedia, CDs, DVDs and video the ability to control how the work is used, copied, performed, distributed online, broadcast, etc. The purpose of copyright is to give a monetary return (royalties) for the effort and cost of creation. Without such an incentive, people may be reluctant to develop new work.

For example, in the front of this book you will find 'Text © Roger Lewis and Roger Trevitt' and 'Original Illustrations © Nelson Thornes Ltd'.

The singer Cliff Richard whose earliest songs such as 'Living doll' and 'Summer holiday' were recorded in 1958 is trying to get copyright protection beyond the current 50 years. The song writer is already protected for 70 years. He says the royalties (money) he receives every time his records are played will stop in 2008 and this is part of his pension.

Counterfeit computer games and software, music, golf clubs and clothing, can badly damage the sales of the original creators of these products.

'The Swedish high-street fashion chain Hennes & Mauritz is suing British value retail chain Primark for plagiarising clothing patterns on dresses, shirts and babywear. Primark is being accused of copying H&M's dragon and flame pattern, a particular floral print, a Petrol Club branded badge design, a graffiti pattern and a target-style design. This court case marks a new phase for fashion legislation. Last year the courts were advised to use new European regulations that protect designers' rights and this is the first case of its kind.'

Source: www.fashionunited.co.uk, 10 March 2005

In March 2007, two of the authors of the book *The Holy Blood and Holy Grail* failed to prove a breach of copyright by Dan Brown, author of *The Da Vinci Code*. (He did not plagiarise.) They now have to pay legal costs of £3m.

---

assignment focus

Who is affected by these examples? What are the positive and negative effects?

Trade marks ™

A trade mark is any sign or symbol, which can be used to identify a brand, perhaps to differentiate it from its competitors or to create an image, e.g. Figure 2.1 shows the trade mark for our publishers Nelson Thornes.

A trade mark is used as a major marketing tool by the brand/trade mark owner to reinforce customer loyalty. Do you buy brand name trainers? The sign or symbol could be a name such as Nike; a logo, the Adidas three stripes; a slogan 'Just do it'.

The trade mark can also be the use of a colour. What is the colour of your organisation's name? Is it used consistently?

Music artistes, including Metallica and Eminem, have released albums early into stores when pirated material got onto free peer-to-peer services. (*Source*: Reuters Los Angeles/Yahoo News)

Have you illegally downloaded music? If everyone did this, how would artists get paid? Why should they bother to record?

In the UK, a trade mark can only be registered if it can be shown graphically, i.e. in words or pictures. Companies have had difficulty registering smells and sounds.

Figure 2.1 The trade mark of Nelson Thornes

Patents

A patent gives the sole right for a limited period (20 years) to the inventor or the inventor's employer to make, use or sell a specific invention. This must be a new product or process that can be made or used in any industry. The patent holder can stop other people from making, selling or using the product without permission. A patent gives the inventor an opportunity for making money which could repay any research and development costs. Because patents only give protection for a limited time, pharmaceutical companies in particular have to continually research and develop new products to ensure their long-term survival, which is why they fight so hard to protect them during their lifetime.

The Patent Office in London can grant a patent for exclusive rights in the UK only. The EU Patent Office is in Munich.

See www.patent.gov.uk.

---

case study 2.2 — The French connection

FCUK® products were protected by registered design. The brand created by Trevor Beattie in 1997 became very popular. However, by 2004 the novelty was fading – 'tired and tacky' was how the ad industry described it. A £3m campaign was launched to replace it using the new slogan 'Something beginning with F'.

Bach lacks bite
Disputes over patents, designs and copyrights are settled in court.

In October 2006 Matthew Fisher claimed that he had co-written the melody to the multi-million seller 'A whiter shade of pale' and should therefore receive a share of the royalties. The judge threw out the case.

In court both Gary Brooker, who holds the music copyright, and Matthew Fisher freely admitted that they had plagiarised the works of Bach. Unfortunately J.S. Bach died in 1750 and his music is not protected by copyright.

activity

1   Why was the FCUK brand so successful initially?
2   To whom did it appeal – which target market?
3   Such an image may not have been acceptable some years earlier. Which PESTLE factor has changed to allow its use?
4   Ringtones freely use fragments of popular classical music. How is this possible?

Legal protection

Copyright, Designs and Patents Act 1988

The Copyright, Designs and Patents Act 1988, protects the intellectual property of organisations and individuals. The main features of the Act are as follows.

- Exclusive rights for artistic, musical, dramatic (e.g. plays) and literary (books, song lyrics, computer programs) works last for 70 years after the death of the creator(s). But not the singer!
- Broadcast and recording rights last 50 years.
- Film rights last 70 years.

In 1992 the Copyright (Computer Programs) Regulations defined software as literary works so they were covered by the Act. For example, 'About Micosoft Word' on the Help menu states that any 'unauthorised reproduction or distribution of this program will be prosecuted to the maximum extent possible under the law.'

Computer Misuse Act 1990

This Act says that any unauthorised access of a computer is illegal. A person may be found guilty of breaking the Act if, for example, they use a user name or password without permission. If found guilty, the penalty may be a fine or imprisonment.

Registered Designs Regulations 2003
These regulations include new directives from the EU on the registration and protection of designs.

Trade Marks Act 1994
This Act sets out the details for registering trade marks and how they can be protected.

Patents Act 2004
This Act applies to 'all businesses which hold patents to protect their intellectual property' (www.dti.gov.uk). The changes will help with the way patents are enforced and how disputes with alleged illegal users (copiers, counterfeiters, etc.) can be resolved.

---

case study 2.3   **Polo case dismissed**

In July 2004, the Court of Appeal rejected a claim by Nestle to register a trademark showing the shape of the Polo Mint without the word 'Polo' or any indication of colour or size. Mars, a competitor, said the shape is 'devoid of distinctive character'. The judge said, 'This is an appeal with a hole in the middle. It is dismissed.'

Source: Martin Hickman, *Independent*, 27 July 2004

Figure 2.2 Do you recognise this?

activity

We eat 100 million Polos a year.

1   Why did Nestle want to register the shape?

2   Why did Mars object?

Technological resources have to be managed like any other resource. Organisations continually monitor the marketplace to make sure that no one is using their IP illegally and will take strong action against anyone who allegedly does so. Large organisations would have a legal department to carry out this function, e.g. pharmaceutical companies such as GSK fight to protect their patented drugs from being copied, the EU has stated that only ham made in Parma in Italy can be called Parma ham. Should all Cornish pasties be made in Cornwall? Ginsters use this as a major feature of their advertising.

For 20 years, the American brewing company Anheuser-Busch, the world's largest brewer, has been trying to stop the small Czech brewery, Budejovicky Budvar, based in Budweise from using the name 'Bud' to market its own beer, Budweiser. In 2003, the UK Court of Appeal ruled that both companies may use the Bud and Budweiser name. Both brewers have the right to use both the trade marks in the UK.

Source: Richard Adams, *Guardian*, 18 February 2003/www.american.edu

In 2007, Mel Gibson successfully prevented a beer called Braveheart from being sold.

assignment focus

What intellectual property resources does your organisation possess?

a) Does it have any trade marks – ™? Are there any names which are registered – ® – or work which is copyright – ©? Does it own any patents?

b) Can you include examples such as a photo of the name or logo in your assignment showing the symbols? Make sure you ask permission to use them otherwise you could be in breach of copyright, i.e. breaking the law.

For M2, check the web to see if your organisation is complaining or being complained about over its IP.

a) What is management doing about it?

b) Why is it important to manage and protect IP?

c) What could happen to a business if its products were copied by poor quality fakes?

For D1 you will need to look at how important the management of IP is in creating sales/profits/revenue (achieving its objectives) for your business.

How to access sources of finance

assignment focus

You need to describe where finance can be obtained for starting up a new business. You could use the business plan you produce for Unit 37.

The need for finance

Anyone starting up a business will need finance (money). They should consider four basic questions. The answers to these would determine the type and source of finance needed:

- What do they need the finance for? e.g. to obtain premises or buy stock.
- How much will they need?
- How long is the finance needed for?
- How much control and profit would they be willing to give up in return for extra investment capital?

What is the money for?

The need for start-up finance

Before it can begin to operate, a business will need start-up finance to buy essential items. A sole trader setting up a small corner shop for example will need premises, shop fittings, a till, possibly a small van and stock to sell. There will also need to be a float of cash for the till and some money in the bank to pay for day-to-day expenses.

The items that a business owns are called assets. They can be subdivided as follows:

- **Fixed assets** These are the 'tools' with which the business works. They are items that may cost a substantial amount but which last for some time, normally a few years at least – in our example the premises, delivery van, shop fittings and till. They are physical resources and will need to be properly managed and maintained; they are valuable assets. They are also an essential part of the Place and Physical Evidence elements of the marketing mix of the corner shop and contribute to its image and reputation.

- **Current assets** These are the items that will be used from day to day; their value will constantly change. In the example, stock, cash in hand (the till) and cash in bank are current assets. Having sufficient current assets helps with Processes and Physical Evidence in the marketing mix.

See pages 88 and 218 where assets are shown on the balance sheet.
See Unit 3, page 107 for the marketing mix.

How much money will a business need?

The need for finance is affected by a number of factors including the nature of the business and the proposed scale or size of the operations. A manufacturing concern, for example, may need expensive specialist machinery, while a business providing a service may only need a home office, a computer and a telephone.

How long is the finance needed for?

■ Long lasting fixed assets such as buildings and premises are best financed by long-term loans and commercial mortgages.

■ A shortage of working capital (e.g. the business does not have sufficient cash to pay its suppliers) would be best financed by bank overdraft or trade credit.

How much control is the owner willing to give up?

Finance may be available from **venture capitalists** or **business angels** (see below) but only if the owner is prepared to give up some control and a percentage of profits.

 See page 73 for a summary of sources of finance.

 Useful sources of information on business finance

■ Click on finance on the homepage of Yahoo where you will find comparisons of loan rates, credit cards, mortgages, insurance, etc.

■ Bank websites all have a section on finance for new businesses, perhaps you could share the task of searching through these with other members of your group.

■ The Business Link website, www.businesslink.gov.uk, is an excellent site on sources of finance for starting up a new business. (It also provides good advice for the business plan in Unit 37.)

Here are five questions from the interactive questionnaire on the Business Link website (Home > starting up > finding and managing the money > get the right finance for your business needs):

1   What do you need to finance? A new start up business?

2   Will any part of the finance be used to buy premises?

3   Are you prepared to give up part of your business to raise more finance? (This is one of the favourite questions on the BBC programme Dragon's Den: 'We will give you £100,000 in return for 60 per cent of your business.' How would you answer?)

4   Can you provide security for loans? Lenders will need some security for their money. They will want to know, 'will we get our money back?' Loans are frequently tied (secured) to business assets such as premises or equipment. If none are available, the personal assets of the trader, partners or directors will be used as security (e.g your home; What happens if you do not have any security? Then you must be prepared to give up part of your business. Try the quiz). Before granting a loan, a bank will usually wish to see whether the owners are also willing to risk a fair amount of their own money. If they are not, the bank will want to know why.

5   How much money do you need? To answer this question you need to have prepared a **cashflow** forecast and a budget.

 See page 207 for cashflow forecasts and budgets.

assignment focus

1   Answer the five questions above for your selected business.

2   Which sources of finance would you suggest?

www.bbc.co.uk/dragonsden contains tips on how to present your business idea and an online application if you want to be on the show, this reads like the assignment for Unit 37!

Internal sources

Owner's savings

Most small businesses begin with the owner investing their own savings. Even banks would be unprepared to lend to someone who is unwilling to risk some of their own money. If the owner does not have enough savings, they could:

- remortgage their home (take out another mortgage using their home as security)
- sell some personal possessions
- borrow from family and friends.

Using personal savings gives the owner 100 per cent control and 100 per cent of the profits. The downside is that, if the business fails, the owner could lose everything, both business and personal assets.

Capital from profits

Once a business is up and running, it will hope to make profits. These profits belong to the owners as a reward for their hard work and risk. For sole traders and partners, these profits may be their livelihood; in a company they are paid to shareholders.

When profits are put back into the business as opposed to being distributed to the owners, they are called ploughed back profits and are the single most important source of finance to business in general. The advantage is that it is permanent capital, does not need to be repaid and there is no interest charge for its use.

External sources

Overdraft

The bank may allow a business to overdraw – take out more than the business has in their current bank account. Beware, although some banks have a 'buffer zone' before charges are made, once this is exceeded charges can be very high – £30 per transaction, plus high interest is not unusual. It is worthwhile for any business to shop around and negotiate an overdraft limit. Many banks give free business banking for the first year. Overdrafts may allow the business to pay day-to-day expenses at times when the business does not have money available, but this can only be a temporary, short-term solution, e.g. to overcome a one or two month cashflow problem.

In 2007 banks were investigated for overcharging. What is the result of the investigation? Did you claim compensation?

Check the bank websites, e.g. Lloyds TSB, Barclays, HSBC, etc., for what they can offer to new businesses.

Business loan

A bank may advance/provide a business loan for periods of up to ten years (it will require security). This will allow the purchase of fixed assets – items which will provide increased benefits, e.g. sales – over a limited period of time. Loans have to be repaid with interest, whether or not the business is making a profit or indeed if the business is still trading. Generally businesses (and households) should keep their fixed outgoings as low as possible (do not get locked in to a contract with 2,000 free texts a month for only £60 if you only use 700).

Commercial mortgages

A business may buy premises using a mortgage from a bank. Typically a mortgage will have a repayment period of 25 years. A deposit is required and the business will have to demonstrate that it is capable of repaying the loan. The property acts as security – it will be repossessed and sold if repayments are not made.

<div class="sidebar">

remember

Inheritance is a favourite source of funds for student business plans. It is acceptable as start up finance, i.e. a relative has already died. It is not acceptable in month 3 and month 6 of a cashflow forecast, unless you have inside knowledge of when they are going to die!

remember

If the business fails, they could lose all their money.

</div>

Venture capital

Venture capitalists or venture capital trusts (VCTs) are willing to risk large sums of money, usually £2m plus, in businesses which they think will give them a high level of return/profit (a minimum of 25 per cent) over a fixed period of time. 3i –formerly Investors in Industry – provides finance for smaller businesses by buying their shares.

A business angel is a rich individual looking for an opportunity to invest smaller sums (a minimum of £10,000) in a small company by buying some of its shares. In return for the investment the angel will receive a percentage of the profits. The dragons in the *Dragon's Den* programme would be business angels. The disadvantages are that the owner may lose some control over the business and will have to share the profits. However, this is in return for increased initial investment.

Any outside/external investor would expect to see a rigorous well-researched business plan with a cashflow and profit and loss forecast. An existing business would also have to provide the profit and loss account which it sends to the Inland Revenue (tax office).

Hire purchase

Hire purchase (HP) allows a business to acquire an asset by putting down an initial deposit and paying the balance with interest over an agreed period of time. After the final payment, ownership of the asset passes to the business. Should the business fail to maintain the payments, the asset passes back to the finance company.

Leasing

With this arrangement, a business pays a rental to secure the use (often temporarily) of assets such as vehicles, mechanical diggers for building sites or computers. The business does not own the assets but has the benefit of using them without the expense of having to spend large amounts of money 'up front', i.e. on start up. This can help the initial cashflow and also means that the business is not left with an outdated asset soon after purchase. If a business is uncertain of its future, short-term leasing may be more attractive than outright purchase.

Mark McGuiness, a building contractor, says, 'We don't want to tie up our money in fixed assets we may only use occasionally, so we lease or hire them for the duration of a job.'

Factoring

This is becoming a popular way of turning debtors into cash. The factor, usually a bank, will immediately forward 80 per cent due on an invoice. When the debt finally becomes due, the factor will collect the whole amount and forward the remaining 20 per cent less a commission for the service. This means that a business can offer credit to its customers but it does not have to wait for payment.

Share issues

A company can issue shares as a way of raising finance. A shareholder (individual or institution) is the owner of shares and thus part owner of the company. They will have given money to the company in return for a share of the profits (dividend). Share capital which is recorded on the balance sheet does not have to be repaid. Only a company which is registered on the Stock Exchange as a public limited company (plc) can issue shares to the public to raise finance. Private limited companies can also issue shares but only on a very restricted basis, i.e. not to the general public. For example, four colleagues may each invest an equal amount of money into a business. Each would have 25 per cent of its shares and receive 25 per cent of the profits. Each would probably be a director. The main advantage of issuing shares is that it increases the capital initially available to the business without any loss of control to outside institutions

What is the most appropriate method of raising funds?

- Through normal trading, that is, through selling and ploughing back profits.
- By borrowing.
- By raising new capital.

Ploughing back profits

Remember that if a business is able to generate sufficient funds it will have no need to borrow or to raise new capital; because it will be able to withstand short-term fluctuations in its cashflow.

Where there are sufficient profits, capital can be built up by 'ploughing back' profits so that the business grows naturally (organically). This must be balanced against the need for drawings by sole traders or partners, or dividends by shareholders. If drawings or dividends are too large these may cause cashflow problems.

Borrowing

Where a business decides to borrow, then the length of the repayment period should be related to the life of the item being bought. If a business needs temporary working capital then short-term finance is appropriate (Table 2.3).

Table 2.3 Short-term sources of finance

Working capital needs include:	Appropriate methods of finance
Purchase of stock. overheads such as wages, rent, rates, light and heat, telephone, petrol, insurance, advertising, etc.	Trade creditors – used for obtaining stocks perhaps on 30-day credit. Bank overdraft to provide cash when it is needed. Technically an overdraft is repayable on demand. Factoring debts to gain some payment from debtors immediately from a factoring company.

From time to time a business will need to invest in fixed assets such as premises, equipment and vehicles. These represent a long-term investment and any funds raised to pay for them should also be long-term (Table 2.4).

Table 2.4 Long-term sources of finance

Fixed assets	Appropriate methods of finance
Land and buildings Vehicles Machinery Equipment Fixtures and fittings, etc.	Mortgage – long-term loans used for buying land and property Long or medium-term loans – used to buy fixed assets such as cars, equipment Leasing – an alternative to buying which means that large sums are not spent at once Hire purchase – buying over a period of time. The asset is owned only after the final payment. Again this spreads payments.

Table 2.5 New capital

Requirements	Way of raising new capital
To fund new projects or business expansion To buy fixed assets To provide permanent working capital where a business is continually short of funds.	A change of business ownership for example taking on partners, forming a company, or floating on the stock market Issuing new shares.

assignment focus

You need to describe the sources of finance which can be obtained to start up a specific business.

1 Collect leaflets and brochures from banks and other financial institutions.

2 Use appropriate financial/government websites to download financial information directly related to starting up your business (start up capital).

3 Compare the sources, e.g. interest rates and other charges, whether security is needed, length of the loan, etc. and write up your findings.

Interpreting financial statements

Link See page 38 for the main activities of a finance department.

Costs and budgets

Managing budgets

A budget is an agreed plan that serves as a target for a future period (e.g. daily, weekly or monthly). It may be set for sales, purchases, production, expenditure, etc. An organisation will create a budget so that it can control and monitor its operational activities. A budget will be based on past experience and forecasts of what is likely to happen.

There are:

■ quantitative budgets, which show estimated numbers of units, e.g. we may estimate sales of 5,000 DVDs or that 10,000 CDs need to be produced. Sales, materials, production and labour budgets are often quantitative in the first instance (see Table 2.6)

Table 2.6 A quantitative sales budget, volume of units

April units	May units	June units	July units	Aug units	Sept units
5,000	6,000	10,000	10,000	8,000	6,500

■ financial budgets, which show estimated costs and revenues and are expressed in pounds, e.g. we may estimate sales revenue of £500,000 a year (see Table 2.7).

Table 2.7 A financial budget based on the sales volumes in Table 2.6
Sales budget (revenue) here is the forecast revenue based on a sale price of £6 per unit, e.g. April units 5,000 × £6 = £30,000

April units	May units	June units	July units	Aug units	Sept units
£30,000	£36,000	£60,000	£60,000	£48,000	£39,000

Ultimately, all budgets are expressed in financial terms.

Budgeting is part of management accounting. There is no legal requirement to set a budget and the figures are drawn up by managers for internal use only. For this reason, budgeted information is likely to be sensitive. It is usually only available to those who need to know and you will find it difficult to obtain real-life examples for your studies. How might this affect your analysis?

Why is budgeting needed?

The budgeting process involves managers in drawing up detailed estimates for their areas and turning these into targets for the coming months. The aim is to make sure that the different sections of the business are working together, i.e. co-ordinated and controlled effectively to achieve the overall goals of the business. A large business such as Tesco will set store budgets from its head office at Cheshunt. Store managers may set budgets for each product line – fruit, fish, etc.

Planning, control and decision-making

The job of business managers involves carrying out the policies set by the directors. The managers are involved with planning, control and decision-making and the budget acts as a framework within which they can perform these functions:

Planning

The budget is part of business planning because it sets out clear objectives to be achieved in the coming period, e.g. sales to be achieved or costs not to be exceeded. Managers must use the resources within their section (staff, money, equipment, time, etc.) as effectively as possible so as to meet the targets that have been set.

Control

Managers will regularly monitor actual performance against the budget to see if the targets are being met. Any variances (differences) between the budget and actual performance will need to be investigated and explained. It may be that someone is not working hard enough, perhaps the targets are unrealistic or perhaps the forecasts are inaccurate. Whatever the reason, questions will need to be asked and suitable action will need to be taken.

Decision-making

Decisions are taken at the planning stage and during day-to-day operations. For example, the budget may only be agreed after a number of different possibilities have been considered. When a section is not meeting its targets, the manager will need to decide what to do about this. Perhaps costs will need to be reduced or managed to keep them within the budget, or income increased.

Cost centres and profit centres

Some business may be too large to be managed directly from the top, which is why businesses are organised into different departments each headed by a manager. The various sections or departments within an organisation may be made into cost centres or profit centres. This makes it possible to set targets for them and to monitor how well they are performing.

Costs managed to budget

A cost centre is a section within a business to which costs can be attributed. A college library, the maintenance section of an engineering works or the distribution section at a high street retailer might be cost centres. A manager will be responsible for seeing that the costs are kept within the allocated budget, i.e. that costs are managed to budget. Some managers may be given the responsibility of managing their own budgets; they are sometimes called 'budget holders'. Their permission is needed before money is spent in their department.

Classifying costs

Here is one way of classifying costs:

- Fixed costs; e.g. rent, business rates, heating, lighting, salaries of administration staff or telephone line rental, do not vary as the level of production sales changes. Fixed costs would be the same and would have to be paid whether or not the business is producing/selling zero units or 12,000. These costs are similar to the expenses in the profit and loss account.

- Variable costs do vary with the level of production/sales/output, e.g. raw materials, purchases of stock, wages of production workers (day workers in the building trades), printer paper and ink cartridges. These are similar to the 'cost of sales' in the profit and loss account.

Link See Greenco Ltd, Unit 37, page 399.

assignment focus

1   Which costs are fixed and variable in your home? Why do you need to control them?

2   Which costs may be fixed or variable in the organisation you are investigating?

Break-even charts

Link

See page 399 for information on break-even charts.

case study 2.4

Taking a break

The Students' Union want to run a day trip to the seaside. They need to know how many tickets they must sell to break-even. Research carried out by the students has provided four essential details:

■ sales price – each ticket for the trip will be priced at £15
■ fixed cost – the coach (including driver and fuel) will cost £300 for the day
■ variable cost – a meal will be included at a cost of £5 per student
■ capacity – the coach can take a maximum of 40 students.

The **break-even point** in units (in this case the number of tickets that must be sold) can be calculated by the formula:

$$\text{Break-even point (in units)} = \frac{\text{Fixed costs for the peirod}}{\text{Unit contribution (i.e. unit sales price – unit variable cost)}}$$

Therefore:

$$\text{Break-even point (in units)} = \frac{£300}{(£15 - £5)} = \frac{£300}{£10} = 30 \text{ units (or tickets)}$$

The break-even point can also be calculated as revenue required (£s):

BEP in units × unit sales price = Break-even point
30 tickets × £15   = £450

A break-even chart can be drawn to illustrate the relationship between costs and sales over different levels of output. There are two stages:

Stage 1: Set out the data in table format, as in Table 2.8. The shaded boxes show the four essential items of data. All else is calculated from these.

Table 2.8 The data for the break-even chart in table format

Estimates {	Maximum capacity 40 units	Fixed cost £300 for the day	Variable cost £5 per unit		Sales revenue £15 per unit		
	Output in units (tickets)	Fixed cost £	Variable cost £	Total cost (Fixed cost + variable cost) £	Sales revenue £	Profit/(loss) (Sales revenue – total cost) £	
	0	300	0	300	0	(300)	⎫
Results at different levels of output and sales	10	300	50	350	150	(200)	⎬ Loss
	20	300	100	400	300	(100)	⎭
	30	300	150	450	450	0	} Break-even
	40	300	200	500	600	100	} Profit

Notice that:

■ the output begins at zero units (the minimum customers possible) and ends at maximum capacity (40 is the most the coach can carry)

■ the units are shown in steps of 10 but any convenient interval (e.g. 5 or 20) could be used. Four or five rows of data is usually sufficient.

Reading the table:

■ If less than 30 students travel, there is a loss (calculate this for 29 tickets).

■ If 30 students travel, the trip will break even, i.e. Total cost = Sales revenue so that profit or loss = 0.

■ If more than 30 students travel, there is a profit (calculate the profit at 31 tickets).

Here the break-even point is shown exactly. However, often the final column may move from a loss at one level of output to a profit at the next. In this case, the break-even point is somewhere between these two points and the formula or chart can be used to find it exactly.

Stage 2: Plot a break-even chart using the data on the table, as in Figure 2.3.

Figure 2.3 Break-even chart

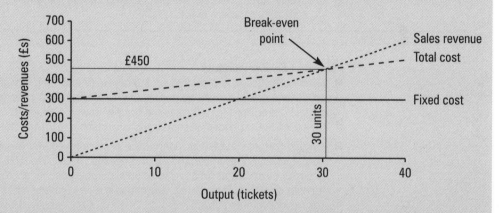

Notice that:

■ the x (horizontal) axis shows units of output (in this case the scale is from 0 to 40 units)

■ the y (or vertical) axis shows costs and revenues. The scale begins at £0 and must be sufficient to plot maximum sales or costs whichever is higher (in this case £600 sales)

■ lines are plotted for total cost and sales revenue. It is usual to also show fixed cost, although break-even can be shown without this. All lines are straight.

Reading the break-even chart:

The break-even point is located where the sales revenue and total cost lines cut (i.e. where sales revenue = total cost). Notice that the break-even point is shown:

■ on the x axis as 30 units (or tickets) need to be sold

■ on the y axis as £450 sales revenue to be generated.

The profit or loss is represented by the vertical distance between the sales revenue line and the total cost line. Attempt the readings at 10 units and 40 units and check these against the table.

activity

1   Use the figures in case study 2.4 to answer the following questions.

  a) What is the total cost at the break-even point?

  b) What is the total revenue at the break-even point?

  c) What will be the profit or loss if 20 tickets are sold?

  d) Would you expect there to be a profit or a loss at 25 units and at 35 units? Explain each one.

  e) Calculate the profit or loss at 25 units and at 35 units.

  f) Why does the chart extend only to 40 units (or 40 tickets)?

2   The £15 price of the day trip is too expensive for most students. However, the committee believe they can fill the coach if the ticket price is reduced to £12. A slightly smaller meal will be provided at a cost of £4 per person. The coach will still cost £300 and seat 40 people.

  a) Produce a table showing costs, revenues and profits at 0, 10, 20, 30, 40 units.

  b) Draw a break-even chart with a suitable title and labels.

  c) Calculate the break-even point by formula. Check this against the chart and table.

  d) Explain briefly whether the trip should go ahead, assuming that the aim is to break-even rather than to make a profit.

Fixed and flexible budgets

■ Fixed budgets stay the same even though there may be major changes in the level of production or sales. They do not identify or analyse fixed or variable costs. So with fixed budgets, predicted output/sales are compared with actual output/sales. This approach is only useful in situations where output/sales remain relatively stable.

■ Flexible budgets do take account of actual costs (fixed and variable) related to actual output/sales. For example, if costs rise because sales have increased, with a fixed budget this may be shown as an adverse or unfavourable cost variance. With a flexible budget it could be a favourable variance because it is recognised that to achieve increased sales may involve higher costs.

Income increased to budget

Profit centres are sections within a business which generate revenues as well as incurring costs. Here a manager will be responsible not only for controlling costs but also for seeing that sales targets are met. The canteen may be a profit centre if it charges for meals; the children's section in a department store or the local branch of a national company may be other examples. Income can be compared with the costs to see whether the centre is running at a profit or at a loss. If actual income is below the forecasted/budgeted target, then either income will need to be increased or costs reduced, e.g. unprofitable departments, courses, stores, etc. may be closed.

The benefits of budgeting

Budgeting brings a number of benefits to a business:

■ Managers understand their responsibilities. They have clear targets, know what their departments are trying to achieve and can then communicate this information to their staff.

■ The activities of the various sections are co-ordinated so that they all work together effectively. This means that managers work towards the objectives of their organisation. This avoids 'empire building' by managers working to their own agenda.

■ It enables the business to plan for the efficient use of resources (cash, stock and staff). Business performance can be monitored against the budget. This enables managers to identify problems in time and take corrective action quickly.

Monitoring budgets and variances

Once a budget is in operation, it will need to be regularly monitored to see if it is working. Managers will compare actual performance with the budget to see if there are any variations or variance, i.e. any difference between actual performance and the budget. If there are, then managers will want to know why

Variances may be:

■ favourable, where actual sales are higher than budget or actual costs lower than budget

■ adverse (or unfavourable), where actual sales are lower than budget or actual costs are higher than budget.

Table 2.9 Profit and loss account for MI5 Ltd (a major rival of KGB Ltd)

Sales	Budget £000	Actual £000	Variance	
Kitchens	100	110	10	Fav
Gardens	125	135	10	Fav
Bathrooms	250	270	20	Fav
Total sales	475	515	40	Fav
Costs				
Administration	250	240	(10)	Fav
Sales & distribution	70	75	5	Adv
Total costs	320	315	(5)	Fav
Profit = Total Sales − Total Costs	155	200	45	Fav

Notice in Table 2.9 that:

■ the variance = actual − budget. This means that higher actual figures give a positive variance and lower actual figures give a negative variance

■ for sales a positive variance is favourable (better sales than target) and a negative variance is adverse (lower sales than target)

■ for costs a positive variance is adverse (higher costs than target) and a negative variance is favourable (lower costs than target)

■ sometimes the current month may be adverse, but the year-to-date may be favourable and vice versa.

Managers will often set a limit within which variances are acceptable. After all budgets are based on estimates and it is unlikely that they will be achieved exactly. Perhaps a manager will only be concerned with variances of 10 per cent or more and regard any variance of less than this as insignificant.

Why do variances occur?

Variances can occur because of:

■ internal matters − the performance of individuals may be better or worse than expected. This may include ordering goods at the wrong price, wastage of materials, slow working. Alternatively there may be equipment faults. An adverse variance indicates a problem. Once the cause has been identified, then managers can take relevant action

■ changes outside of the organisation which alter the conditions of supply or demand (PESTLE factors) − perhaps materials or labour become scarce and their price rises, the market may change, the economic conditions may change. The business will respond to these as well as it can. In the meantime it may have to amend the budget to a more realistic level

■ incorrect budgets − perhaps the budgets are based upon inaccurate information. If this is the case, they will need to be revised and more realistic targets set. Managers may have been too optimistic or pessimistic with their original estimates.

For PESTLE factors, see Unit 1, page 43.

Table 2.10   Budgeted profit and loss account for Celtic Fringe (Hairdressers)

	December Budget	December Actual	Variance	Comments
Receipts				
Female	18,000	15,500		
Male	3,000	3,000		
Children	7,000	6,000		
Total Sales				
Costs				
Purchases	7,000	7,500		
Rent	1,100	1,100		
Wages	5,000	5,800		
Heating	600	950		
Lighting	450	630		
Total Costs				
Profit (Loss)				

1   Calculate total costs, total sales, profit (loss), all variances (favourable and adverse).

2   What problems could Celtic Fringe be facing? Why might these have occurred?

3   What remedies would you suggest? What effects could these have on the business?

4   What extra information would you find useful?

Cost control

Any company which tries to make a profit must be able to control its costs, i.e. keep its costs within the original limits of the planned budget. We are familiar with major projects such as the building of Wembley Stadium where costs exceeded the original budget by over £80m. In June 2007, the expected cost of holding the Olympics in London 2012 was £7bn over budget – the original bid was £2.4bn.

Managers must be responsible for keeping their spending within the original budgetary limits, otherwise projects may never get completed. (Are there unfinished home extensions near you because the budget ran out?)

When costs run out of control:

■ there could be a shortage of working capital, which could force the organisation into borrowing at a high level of interest

■ a higher than expected level of costs could force up prices and reduce competitiveness; this could reduce sales.

Too high a level of fixed and/or variable costs could reduce the net profit and gross profit and reduce the Rate of Return on Capital Employed (ROCE).

Link   For ROCE, see page 95.

Bidding to increase future resources

Any organisation aiming to expand will need extra financial resources. Internally, finance could be generated by more cost-effective sales, leading to higher profits which could be retained and ploughed back into the business. Externally, loans may be available through banks, whilst grants for specified purposes such as scientific development, off-shore energy and recreation could be obtained respectively via the EU, central government and local government.

case study 2.5 · Budgetary control: HM Prison Service

Objective

To plan, monitor, control, and adapt resources to meet agreed business objectives whilst remaining within notified limits.

Key risks

1   Inappropriate allocation of resources resulting in failure to meet objectives.

2   Poor decision-making as a result of inaccurate or inadequate information.

Exceeding any of these limits is considered by the Treasury and Parliament, to represent a serious failure of financial control.

Forecasts must be prepared monthly to highlight and anticipate variances from budgeted costs, to enable budgets to be fully used, and to provide an in-year control over the expected spend. Forecasts are the major way by which the Prison Service operates within the controls totals set by Treasury and Parliament.

In order to ensure that budgets are being used effectively in pursuance of the business plan, the Head of Finance must ensure that budget variances are monitored, reported to budget holders at all levels and corrective action agreed on a monthly basis.

Reports based on the current figures are prepared monthly at all levels of reporting. These reports must explain variances from budget and changes in forecast. If an overspend is being forecast the report should contain details of action being taken to reduce the overspend. If an underspend is being forecast the report should consider whether the underspend can be surrendered for reallocation to other units or whether additional outputs could be delivered within the unit to utilise the underspend.

Failure to forecast accurately can result in unnecessary action being taken to stop expenditure in other areas. Budget managers are expected to forecast any emerging underspends or pressures so that appropriate action (can be taken) to ensure that the Prison Service fully utilises the funds available to it.

Source: hmprisonservice.gov.uk: Guidance on Budgetary Control

activity

1   Explain the meaning of the terms 'overspend', 'underspend', 'surrendered for reallocation to other units', 'budget holder'.

2   Why are budget forecasts important? Why could forecasts go wrong?

3   What problems could occur with poor budgetary control?

4   Why would the Treasury and Parliament consider exceeding the limits a serious failure of financial control?

5   Why could controlling budgets effectively improve the performance of HM Prison Service?

The Business Link website, www.businesslink.gov.uk, gives details of grants available to young entrepreneurs (The Prince's Trust starting a business when you are young), to businesses in parts of the UK which are considered to be in need of extra assistance (assisted areas), and details of Town Improvement Grants available, e.g. for Bridgend and Porthcawl in South Wales.

Managers responsible for finance and development need to be continuously aware of these sources. Many businesses, including schools and colleges, employ people with specific responsibility for obtaining funding for capital projects through the EU.

Any bid for financial resources would need to be supported with a clear and logical budget, which shows evidence of robust cost and budgetary control. The funding institution would also want a cashflow forecast, profit and loss account figures and **balance sheets**, plus evidence that the organisation has appropriate reserves to cover emergencies or crises. If funding is given, the funding body would regularly monitor costs and budgets to ensure effective completion of any project.

Bidding for extra resources

Knowledge companies such as EKOT can provide information and write bids. This is what they offer:

Funding Obtaining funding for your organisation or project

- Identifying funding sources and opportunities
- Guidance on EU policy and procedures
- Obtaining information
- Developing partnerships for funding
- Bid writing and hitting the right buttons
- Practical hands-on bid support at all stages
- Bid training for managers

assignment focus

Go to www.princes-trust.org.uk. Download and complete the online enquiry form to present your case for extra resources. Prepare any documents you need to support your bid.

You could also use this activity for Unit 37.

Provision of appropriate liquidity/working capital

What is working capital?

How much money do you have in your pocket? Do you have enough for today's activities? What are your liquid assets?

Working capital represents the cash (or near cash) available to a business to finance its day-to-day activities. Without working capital, wages cannot be paid, suppliers' bills will not be settled, the mortgage will be in arrears and eventually the business may even have to close.

On the balance sheet working capital is shown as:

Working capital	=	Current assets	−	Current liabilities
Money available for day-to-day expenses		*Assets which can be quickly turned into cash*		*Those creditors who will need to be paid in the near future*

Current assets are also called 'liquid assets'. They are listed on the balance sheet with the least liquid (stock) first and the most liquid (cash) last.

The working capital cycle

The working capital cycle shows how cash circulates in a business as it trades. Current assets and current liabilities are central to trading activity, but other cash flows are also involved.

Ideally, trading activity will generate sufficient cash for all business needs through sales. However, the different demands on business cash and the uneven timing of receipts and payments may mean that cash from customers does not always flow in quickly enough. When there is a cash shortage, it will be necessary to raise extra funds by either borrowing, delaying payments or raising extra capital.

Why do working capital problems occur?

Some common reasons are:

- payment for purchases of stock are made ahead of sales, especially when sales are on credit
- the business needs to invest now for some future return, e.g. an investment in expensive fixed assets
- overhead payments coincide (all the bills come in together).

For example, it was announced in December 2006 that the Civil Service did not know how many people it employed and, because costs were so out of control, it had run up an overdraft of £250m

Managing working capital
It is important to draw up a cashflow forecast to identify possible problems and take appropriate action in advance.

See page 396 for how a cashflow forecast is constructed.

Appropriate action could include:

- reducing payments, e.g. by cutting/controlling costs, such as laying off staff, or finding cheaper suppliers and/or paying out lower dividends (costs managed to budget)
- delaying payments until cash is available by buying on credit, scheduling bills by paying in instalments, renting or leasing equipment to avoid up-front capital outlays
- increasing receipts through borrowing, raising more capital through shares or increasing sales revenue through product price changes (income increased to budget)
- collecting receipts more quickly by selling for cash rather than credit, implementing rigorous credit control policies, i.e. people pay bills on time. Do you?

Too much cash?
Although a business needs to have enough cash available to meet payments as they become due, having too much cash represents an inefficient use of funds – it is the equivalent of keeping your savings under the bed. Surplus cash should be put to use, either invested to earn interest, used to pay off loans and so reduce interest payments, or spent on assets which will add to the productivity of the business. Some companies buy back shares when they have the cash to do so.

Business management will need to balance the need for liquidity with the need to make the best use of resources.

Credit control
Slow payment by debtors can be a major problem, especially for small businesses with limited funds. They cannot easily withstand cashflow problems or afford to take legal action against defaulters. Many businesses would like to sell on a cash basis so as to guarantee immediate payment, but this may not be an option because customers may be unwilling or unable to place orders if credit is not available.

Provision of reserves to address emergencies
Using budgets enables decisions to be made in advance by identifying when problems are likely to occur, e.g. a cash shortage in the forecast cashflow. In this way, potential crises or emergencies can be avoided, e.g. cash reserves can be built up when the business is cash-rich or has a surplus of cash, such as during times when profits are built up. Local authorities do not allocate all of their funds at the beginning of the year but hold back some in reserve in case something unforeseen happens. Individuals do the same 'just in case, you never know when it might be needed'. Loans from banks may need to be agreed if cashflows or working capital appear to present a future problem.

The process of forecasting using past experience, analysis of current trends (such as the best-selling lines) and making assumptions about the competition is an essential skill required by managers.

> **remember**
>
> The working capital ratio and the acid test ratio (see pages 95 and 222) are both used in order to examine the liquidity of a business. Modern thinking suggests that the ratios should be as low as possible.

> **remember**
>
> Where credit is offered, it is vital to ensure effective credit control.

assignment focus

Look at the budgets on pages 79 and 80 and give reasons why budgets need to be controlled.

For M2, you need to explain in detail any problems that could arise if they are left uncontrolled.

Financial statements

The trading profit and loss account

To achieve P5, you need to interpret the contents of a **profit and loss account** and balance sheet.

This account shows the profits or losses made over the period of the account – usually one year – as a result of the business activities. It measures the financial performance as a result of its trading, e.g. for a retailer this would be the stock that it has bought and sold, for a manufacturer it would be the raw materials or parts it has purchased/used to make and sell its goods.

It shows the value of sales (turnover) made, the costs incurred in achieving those sales and any other business expenses for the period. The account is constructed from the account books of the business. Profits can be compared with the previous year or with competitors. The profit and loss account of limited companies must also show how much was paid in tax, how much was distributed to shareholders and how much was kept or retained in the business.

Profits or losses are calculated by comparing the value of sales with the cost of making these sales, so that:

$$\text{Profits or losses} = \text{Sales} - \text{Costs}$$

It establishes two key profit figures:

$$\text{Gross profit} = \text{Sales/Turnover} - \text{Cost of sales}$$

$$\text{Net profit} = \text{Gross profit} - \text{Expenses}$$

Explanation of the items in a profit and loss account

Table 2.11 A typical profit and loss account

	Profit and loss account for the year ending 31 July 2007	2007 £	2006 £
1	Sales or turnover; the money or revenue obtained from the sale or supply of the goods or service. There may be a note in the accounts showing, e.g. a breakdown of sales by area or brand which would enable managers to spot strengths and weaknesses in the pattern of sales. In 2006 Tesco sales were £43bn	140,000 3.7% increase	135,000
2	Cost of sales or cost of goods sold; these are the costs which can be directly attributed to the sales, they vary with the amount of sales. It is the cost of buying, acquiring, making or providing the goods which are sold. E.g. cost of stock, purchases, parts or raw materials, possibly the cost of hiring machinery, equipment or tools. This is how it is calculated (Opening stock + Purchases) – Closing stock = Cost of sales. This is how much a retailer would pay its suppliers. A 4.1% increase has produced a 3.7% increase in sales. Is this good or poor performance?	50,000 4.1% increase	48,000
3	Gross profit; Sales – Cost of Sales = Gross Profit. It is the money made from selling or making the product. E.g. if sales = £140,000 and the cost involved was £50, 000, then gross profit = £90,000. This is the profit before any business expenses are deducted. Items 1, 2 and 3 form the Trading Account which measures the trading performance. Less expenses or overheads; these are the indirect costs consumed or used up during the trading period. They are deducted from the gross profit. E.g. administration, distribution, wages, telephone, paper and cartridges, car and travel, etc. i.e., any cost involved in running the business. Salaries Heating and lighting Rent and rates Stationery and cartridges Administration	90,000 3.4% increase 70,000 7,000 15,000 4,000 3,000	87,000 40,000 6,000 14,000 3,800 3,000

▶

	Profit and loss account for the year ending 31 July 2007	2007 £	2006 £
4	**Total Expenses** = salaries + heating & lighting + rent & rates + stationary & cartridges + administration These can all be budgeted for. Actual performance can then be compared with the budget.	99,000 48% increase	66,800
5	**Net Profit** (Loss) = Gross Profit – Expenses Positive = Profit (Negative) = Loss Negative figures are usually shown in brackets. This business is making a net loss and would not be required to pay tax. In a company this figure would be called operating profit or profit before interest and tax (PBIT). Interest paid out on loans or received from investments Profit before taxation Taxation paid to the Inland Revenue Profit after taxation Dividends paid to shareholders, in return for their original investment Retained or undistributed profits, i.e. ploughed back profits. These are added to the reserves on the balance sheet under the profit and loss account	(9,000)	20,200

What does this account tell us?

1 *Turnover or sales* The value of the sales during the trading period. There has been a 3.7 per cent increase between 2006 and 2007. This could be due to a rise in the quantity sold or the price. What are the factors that could affect this figure? Externally these could be investigated using a PESTLE analysis. Internally, human, physical and financial resources need to be combined effectively to maximise sales.

2 *Cost of sales* The stock and other purchases made to achieve the sales have risen by 4.1 per cent. Managers need to be able to monitor and control costs effectively to improve gross profit, why have these variable costs risen e.g. has there been a rise in the cost of imported goods, perhaps there were problems with supply or a rise in wages.

3 *Gross profit* The business made a gross profit of £90,000 in the year ending 31 July 2007. It is unlikely that a business will make a gross loss. This would mean selling stock more cheaply than it was purchased. However it is quite possible, as this business demonstrates, for overhead costs to exceed gross profit, so the net profit figure will be negative, indicating a net loss. Rising gross profits show that the business is either in control of its costs and becoming more efficient or is able to raise prices and maintain sales. The higher the gross profit the better it is for the business.

4 *Expenses* This business has major problems with the very high salaries. The business spent an extra £30,000 on sales staff who appear to have achieved very little, are they worth it? Perhaps staff were hired because a new contract was expected. It is often more difficult to control overhead expenses than the direct cost of sales. Rent and rates for example are virtually fixed costs.

5 *Net profit* Due to the high level of salaries, the business made a net loss of £9,000 in 2007. It may be unable to repay any outstanding loans. No money would be paid to shareholders or ploughed back as retained profit. Costs need to cut. It is too late for control.

assignment focus

1   Fill in the missing numbers in the profit and loss account for Gross Stores a well known independent fish retailer in your area.

2   Explain the meaning of each item.

3   What are the main headline changes (the stories), e.g. in sales, gross and net profit etc. Write up these changes in a short article for your local newspaper. Include your own headline. Use no more than 50 words.

Table 2.12 Trading profit and loss account for Gross Stores (fish retailers), Year ending 31 July 2007

	2007 £	2006 £
Sales	180,000	135,000
Cost of sales		80,500
Gross profits	85,000	
Expenses		36,000
Net profits	47,000	

Purpose and use of the profit and loss account

The profit and loss account is used to measure trading performance and establish gross and net profit figures. Anyone who has an interest or concern in the business, i.e. any stakeholder, will want to see how the business performs financially.

- Managers would use the figures to carry out a financial SWOT analysis of the business, e.g. weak or strong trends in sales or costs which need to be controlled more effectively (salaries in the example above). They would need to identify why the costs directly associated with the sales have risen by 4.1 per cent and sales revenue has only grown by 3.7 per cent. Managers need financial information to be able to identify and solve problems, spot where problems are likely to occur, monitor and control costs.

For SWOT analysis, see page 131.

- Shareholders and the owners would be interested in gross and net profits, how much profit is paid out as dividends, how much profit is retained and how this is used.
- Investors would be interested in overall financial performance, whether it would be worthwhile buying its shares, how its performance compared with last year and how it compares with companies in the same sector. Investors would use the profit and loss account together with the balance sheet to work out financial ratios.

For ratios, see page 95 and Unit 5, page 220.

- Workers will want to know if there is a possibility of a pay rise or share of profits.
- The Inland Revenue uses the figures to calculate any tax that has to be paid.
- The bank would be concerned that the business could pay back any loans which were outstanding, or that the business was financially viable if it requested extra funds.
- Competitors would be interested in the financial performance of a rival, particularly the financial ratios such as gross or net profit margins.

remember

Budgets can be created for each item and compared with actual performance to detect any favourable or unfavourable variances on a regular weekly or monthly basis.

assignment focus

Tables 2.13 and 2.14 show the profit and loss account and balance sheet for Pizza DaActione plc for 2006 and 2007. Using these financial statements, prepare a brief written account of the financial health of the business (for P6 you will need to calculate financial ratios).

1   Describe and explain the purpose of each item.

2   Comment on the changes that have taken place, e.g. the 40 per cent rise in turnover/sales from £71,055,000 in 2006 to £99,562,000 in 2007.

3   Do you consider this business to be profitable? What evidence is there? Would you want a piece or indeed a slice of the action in this business? Why?

4   Obtain the most recent profit and loss account and balance sheet for the business you are investigating. Write a short report explaining the purpose of each item, the changes that have taken place, whether it is making a profit and whether it is viable – will it survive?

Table 2.13 Pizza DaActione plc: Group profit and loss account for the year ended 31 July 2007

	2007 £000	2006 £000
Turnover	99562	71055
Cost of sales	(70166)	(49454)
Gross profit	29396	21601
Distribution costs (2)	(2341)	(1789)
Administrative expenses	(4494)	(4404)
Operating profit	22561	15408
Disposals of fixed assets (3)	710	691
Profit on ordinary activities before interest	23271	16099
Net interest received/(paid)	(270)	55
Profit on ordinary activities before taxation	23001	16154
Taxation	(4965)	(3534)
Profit attributable to shareholders	18036	12620
Dividends	(2833)	(2214)
Retained profit	15206	10406
Earnings per share (4)	27.2p	20.1p
Dividends per share (5)	4.25p	3.35p

Table 2.14 Pizza DaActione plc: Group balance sheet as at 31 July 2007

	2007 £000	2006 £000
Fixed assets	65 429	42 739
Tangible assets	322	533
Investments	65 751	43 272
Current assets		
Stocks	4 086	3 362
Debtors	6 497	4 994
Cash at bank and in hand	5 382	6 812
	15 965	15 168
Creditors: amounts falling due within one year	(40 400)	(28 348)
Net current assets/(liabilities)	(24 435)	(13 180)
Total assets – current liabilities	41 316	30 092
Creditors: amounts due after more than one year	(3 454)	(582)
	37 862	29 510
Capital and reserves		
Called up share capital	6 919	6 783
Retained profit and other reserves (6)	30 943	22 727
Shareholders' funds	37 862	29 510

Notes to the accounts

1 Domino's and Pizza Hut are its main competitors.

2 Motorcycle riders, they get free training for their Compulsory Basic Training (CBT). This allows them to ride a learner legal moped.

3 Unprofitable outlets have been sold.

4 Earnings per share (EPS) shows the amount of profit earned by each share. Usually only a part is paid to shareholders the rest is ploughed back into the company as retained profit.

5 Dividends per share: the share of company profit paid on each share. Therefore a shareholder with 1,000 shares would get 1,000 × 4.25p = £42.50.

6 The reserves built up in the company, the figure comes from the profit and loss (PL) account

In Unit 37, you need to present information from a variety of sources. Financial statements can become much more meaningful when presented graphically. A breakdown of sales could be explained and presented using a pie chart, assets and liabilities could be shown and compared using bar charts.

www.advfn.com is an excellent site which helps you compare the assets and liabilities from a wide range of companies registered on the London Stock Exchange (LSE).

Go to the page which compares UK Food Retailers & Wholesalers Companies. Note that Sainsbury's has a much higher level of current assets (What could this say about stocks?), whilst Greggs has a higher level of cash. What other headlines can you see in the data? (NB LSE:TSCO is Tesco, LSE:SBRY is Sainsbury's, LSE:GRG is Greggs Bakery.)

The balance sheet

A balance sheet is a 'snapshot' of the financial state of health of a business on a specific date. This is indicated by the words in the heading 'Balance sheet of REAP Ltd as at 31 March'. It is a statement of the worth of a business, how much it owes and how much it owns. It shows whether the business can pay its debts, i.e. is it liquid/solvent (solvency/liquidity ratios). The balance sheet must balance because it shows what money the business has or has accumulated and how this has been used or invested. The information in the balance sheet comes from the account books or ledgers, which must also balance; if they do not, someone has made a mistake.

Figure 2.4 The balance sheet

Assets   Liabilities

The best way to analyse a balance sheet is to either examine the trends over a number of years or compare one company with another.

Elements of the balance sheet

There are three main parts to a balance sheet: assets, liabilities and capital.

Assets

Assets are resources owned by the business. They can be used to pay off a debt. On a balance sheet they can be classed as fixed or current.

- Fixed assets are those which bring long-term value to the business. They are owned by the business. There may be three types:

  - tangible assets, which include land and buildings such as shops, offices and factories, vehicles, office machinery, equipment, fixtures and fittings, etc. over time, these assets may appreciate (rise) in value, e.g. land and buildings, or depreciate (fall) in value, e.g. machinery. The balance sheet and profit and loss account will have to be adjusted to take account of these changing values.

  - intangible assets, which include intellectual property rights and goodwill, i.e. the value of the business image or reputation, represented in the brand name. It can often be difficult to put a monetary value £ on the intangible assets. How much is a brand name worth?

  - investments, e.g. shares held in other businesses.

Some companies, e.g. Tesco, use the term non-current assets instead of fixed assets in line with new EU regulations.

 For intellectual property, see page 65.

- Current assets consist of:

  - stock of materials or goods to be sold (the most difficult asset to turn into cash – it is the least liquid). As Tesco says, 'the value of goods held for retail sale in our depots and stores at the balance sheet date'. Too high a level of stock (or a rise) could mean that goods are not selling well and may have to be sold off cheaply. Stock also ties up cash and could create problems with the amount of working capital forcing the business into short-term borrowing at high interest rates

  - debtors (someone who owes the business money, e.g. customers) – a high level or a rise in debtors could mean that the business is having difficulties collecting its debts

  - cash in hand, cash in the bank and deposits – the most liquid asset. Too high a level could indicate that the business is not making its cash work hard enough to generate extra profits.

The value of current assets will change every day as stock is bought and sold and existing debtors pay. Current assets are the working capital of the business used for pay day-to-day expenses. It is the money used to pay immediate bills. How much money do you carry on you? Do you have sufficient liquid assets to pay your short-term debts, i.e. your current liabilities?

Liabilities

These are the debts owed by the business. On the balance sheet they are classified as:

- long-term liabilities – the 'amounts falling due after more than one year', e.g. long-term bank loans (perhaps 3–5 years) and mortgages (traditionally 25 years). Do you or your household have any long-term liabilities?

- **current liabilities** – the 'amounts falling due within one year', e.g.

  - creditors, usually suppliers who would normally expect to get paid within 30 days

  - overdrafts or short-term loans – overdrafts can be called in at any time, loans will have a deadline for repayment. These can be expensive – a good cashflow forecast and budget will help the business to identify any possible problems in advance

  - payments due including taxes (e.g. income tax and VAT) – there are penalties for late payment. Hopefully you will not have experienced this with late payment of an overdraft.

Capital and reserves

Theses are measured by:

$$\text{Total assets} - \text{Total liabilities} = \text{Capital and reserves}$$

It can include the called-up share capital, which is the amount of share capital received from the original issue of shares at the original price, plus any extra money received when the shares were issued (share premium account), any money from revaluing its fixed assets and money built up from the profit and loss account.

Shareholders' funds are the total of called-up share capital, retained profit and other reserves. This is the amount of money shareholders would get if the business ceased trading and closed down. It shows approximately how much the business is worth after any outstanding debts are paid. If you wanted to buy the company this is the lowest price it would accept! If you have a spare £40b, what about Tesco?

assignment focus

1 Table 2.15 shows figures extracted from the balance sheet for the Santos Hotel plc.

a) What form of finance do you think the Santos used to finance each of the following? (Give a different source in each case.)
- buying property
- buying stock from suppliers
- buying machinery
- providing day-to-day working capital

b) • What is the meaning of the term 'reserves'?
- What do you think these reserves might be used for?

c) Not all profits are retained in the business. Give two uses for profits not retained (both are mentioned on the balance sheet).

d) If the company were to be sold, how much money would be made available to the shareholders?

e) Imagine that the Santos wishes to gain the money owed by its debtors before payments is due. Which method of finance can it use?

f) Name one method of acquiring fixed assets which is not mentioned on the balance sheet

g) What source of funds available to Santos plc is not available to a sole trader or a partnership?

h) What are the main features of the accounts? How much is the business worth?

i) Calculate the current ratio and acid test ratio, comment on your results (see page 95).

2 Table 2.16 shows the balance sheet for Ohms Electric Shop, a small electrical store in your area which is resisting the spread of the big retailers such as Comet.

a) Fill in the missing numbers in the balance sheet.

b) Explain the meaning of each item.

c) What are the main headline changes (the stories), e.g. assets, liabilities capital and reserves, etc? Write up these changes in a short article for your local newspaper. Include your own headline. Write no more than 75 words. Use graphics where possible.

assignment
focus

Table 2.15 Balance sheet of the Santos Hotel plc

Sales	£000s	£000s
Fixed Assets		
Investment properties		4500
Tangible assets		76 291
Investments		80 791
		23 600
		104 391
Current assets		
Stocks	7013	
Debtors	11 007	
Cash in Hand	1450	
	19 470	
Less		
Creditors – amounts falling due within one year		
Loans and overdrafts	6591	
Creditors	13 312	
Dividends due	2003	
	21 906	
Working capital		(2436)
Total assets less current liabilities		101 955
Less		
Creditors – amounts falling due after more than one year		
Loans and debentures	4931	
Mortgages	11 315	
Other charges	486	
		16 732
Net Assets		85 223
Financed by:		
Issued Share Capital		2861
Reserves		82 362
Shareholders' Funds		85 223

Table 2.16 Balance sheet for Ohms Electric Shop

Sales	31 July 2007 £	31 July 2006 £
Fixed assets		
Shop premises	180,000	160,000
Fixtures and fittings	20,000	20,000
Vehicle		7,000
Total fixed assets	206,000	
Current assets		
Stock	4,000	6,000
Debtors	1,500	3,000
Cash in bank	5,000	5,500
Cash in hand	800	
Total current assets		16,000
Less current liabilities		
Creditors	7,000	4,000
Working capital = Current assets – Current liabilities		
Net assets = Fixed assets + working capital		
Financed by		
Capital		
Reserves	170,000	170,000

Purpose and use of balance sheets

In this section we will ask:

- Who are the users of financial information?
- What sort of information do they need?

The answer to the first question is that it is the stakeholders, the people who have an interest in the affairs of a business, who require financial information of one sort or another. Financial information is used both by those within the business, the internal stakeholders, and by those outside of the business, the external stakeholders.

Internal stakeholders

Internal users of information are those who run the business. They therefore include:

- directors
- managers
- other employees
- the owners, where they also run the business. For example, sole traders or partners will certainly run their own businesses. Similarly the shareholders in a small company may also be the directors.

In the case of larger companies, there is a clear distinction between the shareholders who own the company and the directors who run the company. In this case the shareholders are regarded as external stakeholders: they play no part in management, they are interested in the company purely as an investment and may not be particularly loyal if a better investment opportunity arises elsewhere.

---

assignment focus

1　If a business does not keep financial records, what sort of things do you think would go wrong from day to day? In the longer term?

2　Managers might ask, 'How much money is there in the business bank account?' Think of four other things they might need to know about business finances from day to day.

The purpose and use of balance sheets for internal stakeholders

Internal stakeholder groups need financial information in order to carry out their jobs effectively. A business will therefore keep those records which help its managers and directors to control the business, plan ahead and make informed decisions.

- *Directors* It is the job of the directors to set out corporate plans for the future of the company. They will also make strategic decisions about how these can best be achieved. Directors' decisions therefore concern the general direction of the business and include:
  - setting targets for profits
  - setting targets for expansion
  - aiming to increase market share
  - expanding the range of the company's products
  - recommending how much dividend the shareholders will be paid and how much profit will be 'ploughed back' into the business
  - deciding whether to issue more shares.

  None of these decisions can be taken unless the appropriate information is available. The directors will not usually be interested in the details of the day-to-day accounts. Rather they will need to see various reports and summaries extracted from the accounts. They will be interested in overall trends, e.g. how much profit is being made from year to year, the size of the wage bill, the sales totals at the various branches, the performance of the different departments, which products are selling and so on. They will monitor business progress by comparing performance figures from year to year, by comparing themselves with their competitors and by looking at averages for the industry.

  It is the directors' duty to manage the resources of the company in the best interests of the stakeholders. These duties are defined under two headings, which may lead to a conflict of interest.

- *Stewardship* This is the duty that directors have to the shareholders of the business. They have a responsibility to manage the shareholders' capital wisely and to ensure that they get an effective return on their money. Shareholders' interests are served by the company making high profits, paying out dividends and keeping the share price high. Many directors see this as their first priority, they are aware that they are elected by the shareholders and can lose their seats on the board if things do not go well.

- *General duty to stakeholders* The directors also have a responsibility to the other stakeholders, including the wider community. This is why the law insists that some financial information is made public. Rather than wanting high profits, the community may want more jobs, a better service, more investment, less pollution and a range of other things which may well reduce profits.

The directors of a company may set out their various aims in the company mission statement.

- *Managers* It is the job of the managers to carry out the policies set by the directors. Managers are concerned with planning, control and decision-making, often in a particular area of the business such as a department or a local branch. If the accounts are accurate, up to date and sufficiently detailed, then managers can extract the information they need. Regular management reports might include:

  - figures for each department

  - a breakdown of sales and costs

  - stock levels

  - the bank balance

  - amounts owed by debtors and when this is due

  - amounts owed to creditors and when this is to be paid

  - profit or losses for the month and for the year to date

  - comparisons between budgets (plans) and figures actually achieved.

- *Employees (other than managers)* Company employees will have access to the published company accounts which are made public at the end of each financial year. Employees of sole traders or partnerships have no such right to see their employer's accounts. At various times employees will be interested in:

  - profits – they may wish to know whether they are being rewarded in line with business progress, they may hold shares or there may be a profit-sharing scheme

  - predictions for future projects – this may help with questions about job security

  - how the business is spending its money.

External stakeholders

External users of information are those outside of the business who are affected in some way by the business and therefore have an interest (a stake) in its performance. External stakeholders include:

- shareholders who have put their money into the business purely as an investment

- potential investors who wish to know whether it would be wise to risk their money in the business

- creditors who are owed money by the business

- customers who buy the products of the business

- local and regional communities whose environment, health, house prices and services are affected by the business

- government departments, especially HM Revenue & Customs which regulates and taxes the business (formerly Inland Revenue and Customs & Excise).

The interests of external stakeholders are protected by laws which require businesses to disclose a certain amount of financial information available to them.

The purpose and use of balance sheets for external stakeholders

Each stakeholder group will have its own particular purpose and use for a balance sheet. At times the interests of one stakeholder group may well conflict with the interests of another group.

- *Future investors and lenders* Potential investors will wish to be sure that a business represents a sound investment. They will need to see summaries from the business' past financial records as a guide to past and possible future performance. For example:

- Investors considering purchasing new issues of plc shares will study the prospectus. This will show the details of the shares to be issued and the reason for raising new funds. It will also give information about the performance of the business in recent years as a guide.

- A bank or building society being approached for loan finance or a business angel or a venture capital trust (VCT) being invited to buy a stake in a company will need to see the profit and loss accounts and balance sheets – often for the previous four years. This will enable the investor to assess the financial strength of the business and to see how effectively it is being managed. An investor will also wish to assess the value of the business and determine which assets can be used as security for a loan (what the business can sell to raise money if a loan cannot be repaid in the normal way).

There may be a temptation for businesses requiring finance to 'dress up' the accounts to give a more optimistic picture. For this reason. prospective lenders and investors ask for the accounts as presented to the Inland Revenue, as these are unlikely to show artificially high profits. Why is this?

As well as reported results, investors may need to see management forecasts, such as the cashflow forecast and forecast profit and loss account. These are a vital part of any business plan as we see in Unit 37.

- *Creditors* A creditor is a person or an organisation to whom money is owed. The balance sheet identifies:

  - creditors to be paid within the year, also known as current liabilities. These may include suppliers of stock, the bank if we are overdrawn, tax due, and any bills outstanding

  - creditors to be paid after a year, also known as long-term liabilities. These may include term loans and mortgages.

  Creditors will be interested in the ability of a business to repay them. They may therefore look at the profit and loss account and ask 'Is the business profitable?' They may also look at the balance sheet – where two ratios are especially relevant:

  - the acid test ratio, which shows the ability of a business to raise money in the short term

  - the creditors payment ratio, which shows the average number of days the business takes to pay suppliers.

- *Government – HM Revenue & Customs (HMRC)* The government is a stakeholder in all businesses. It is interested in turnover (sales) and profits because these are the basis upon which tax (income tax and corporation tax), **VAT** (Value Added Tax) and **PAYE** (Pay As You Earn) are calculated. These departments are now all part of the HMRC – joined up taxation?

We look at ratios on pages 95 and 220.

What does the balance sheet measure?

The balance sheet measures:

- the wealth of the organisation, i.e. how much is it worth to the owners. The bottom line in the balance sheet shows how much it is worth if it were to be sold. It is measured by:

  Total assets – Total liabilities = Wealth of the organisation i.e. the shareholders funds

For Pizza DaActione plc, for example, this was £37,862,000 in 2007 compared to £29,510.000m in 2006, an increase of £8,352,000. Was Pizza DaActione an exception or did all Pizza companies experience a similar rise?

- how the assets have been paid for, funded or financed. We know the balance sheet measures fixed (non-current) and current assets, current and long-term liabilities and shows the capital and reserves which have been built up through profits. Assets are financed by the owners/shareholders capital (e.g. shares or equity) and borrowing. It is important that the amount of borrowing compared to raising finance through new share capital is closely monitored.

KeyNote or Mintel reports could be used to investigate trends in the home delivery/fast food sectors.
The KeyNote report *Fast Food and Home Delivery Outlets* has company profiles and a detailed analysis of market trends. Increasing use of the mobile phone for ordering is seen as a plus, whilst the ban on advertising junk food is a threat to future growth. Can you get a healthy pizza?

assignment focus

Obtain the balance sheets for two of your main competitors. How well have they done in the last year?

Always try to investigate the accounts of a business which you use as a customer. This will enable you to give a more personal view of its accounts based on your own experience. Look at the headline stories, e.g. 'Profits fall at XYZ'. If you have stopped going there, perhaps thousands of others have done the same. Why? D1 and D2 require you to evaluate a range of factors which could affect business performance or the financial health of an organisation.

Basic ratios

assignment focus

For P6, you need to illustrate the financial state of a given business by showing examples of accounting ratios. This means you should define and calculate solvency (liquidity) ratios, profitability ratios and efficiency ratios.

We show you how to calculate and interpret ratios in the specialist unit, Unit 5, Introduction to accounting, on page 220.

Table 2.17 Solvency ratios

Solvency (liquidity) ratios	2006	2007	Comments and interpretation
Current ratio $\dfrac{\text{Current assets}}{\text{Current liabilities}}$	2.1:1 £2.10p for every £1 of liabilities	2.4:1 £2.40p for every £1 of liabilities	This is worse. The business will have sufficient liquidity to pay its creditors, but why does it have high levels of stock, debtors or cash? Could stock be sold more quickly? Or cash used more effectively Tesco is about 0.6:1
Acid test ratio (liquidity ratio) $\dfrac{\text{(Current assets – stock)}}{\text{Current liabilities}}$	1.6:1 £1.60p of cash or near cash	1.5:1 £1.50p of cash or near cash to pay creditors	This is down, but may still be too high. Remember too high a ratio indicates an inefficient use of cash. The major supermarkets work at about 0.4:1

Table 2.18 Profitability and efficiency ratios

Profitability ratios	2006	2007	Comment
% ROCE $\dfrac{\text{Net profit x 100}}{\text{Capital employed}}$ How profit relates to the total funds invested in the business	11.4%	10.1%	There is a decrease here. The business is now a worse investment for its owners. However the return is just above the UK average for small businesses (10%).

Profitability ratios	2006	2007	Comment
Gross profit % $\dfrac{\text{Gross profit}}{\text{Sales}} \times 100$ The profit %, or margin related to sales, before expenses are taken away	50% This is 50p gross profit for every £1 of sales	45%	The gross profit % has been reduced perhaps by price cutting. As a result the business is more competitive so that sales may have risen. Any fall should be investigated. Supermarkets work at about 8%.
Net profit % $\dfrac{\text{Net profit}}{\text{Sales}} \times 100$ The profit on sales after all expenses have been deducted	4% This is 4p profit on every £1 of sales.	4.2%	Closely linked to the level of fixed and variable costs. Good cost control is essential to achieve a rise in the net profit %. What would happen to the % if sales rose but net profit remained the same. Supermarkets average 3.5–4%. 'Pile it high, sell it cheap' was the Tesco motto. Is Weatherspoons (public houses) trying the same approach?

Efficiency ratios			
Rate of stock turnover $\dfrac{\text{Cost of stock sold}}{\text{Stock}}$	$\dfrac{560}{40}$ 14 times	$\dfrac{836}{44}$ 19 times	The reduction in sales prices has resulted in an increase in the rate of turnover. The higher the figure the better, stock literally flies off the shelves. Sales are held to get rid of unwanted stock.
Debtor collection period $\dfrac{\text{Trade debtors}}{\text{Credit sales}} \times 365$ How quickly trade customers pay	30 days	35 days	On average customers are paying later. An increase shows that the situation is worsening. Credit control needs to be tighter and late payers must be chased. In supermarkets this averages about 8 days most customers pay immediately, i.e. a continuous cash flow = low liquidity ratios.
Creditor payment period (days) $\dfrac{\text{Trade creditors}}{\text{Credit purchases}} \times 365$ How quickly suppliers are paid	30 days	35 days	We are not paying our suppliers on time and the situation is worsening slightly. Supermarkets are very slow payers the industry average is about 90 days.

Table 2.19 Profit and loss account

Profit and loss account	2006 £000s	2007 £000s	Comment
Sales	1,120	1,500	An increase in sales of 34%
Gross profit	560	664	Gross profit up
Net profit	40	54	Net profit up

assignment focus

1   Use the financial statements for Pizza DaActione plc on page 87 to work out the solvency/liquidity ratios, and the profitability ratios.

2   You must use the formula and show your workings (how you arrived at your answer).

3   Give a brief description of your results.

For M3, you should interpret your results, e.g. have the ratios got better or worse? Why might this have happened?

Use the package of ratios to show how they can be used to monitor the financial state of the business. Be positive, stress the benefits.

Alternatively you can answer the same questions for the business you are investigating.

Limitations of ratio analysis

In interpreting ratios, we may need to look at a combination of factors – the present situation, the trend, the type of business, and so on. This can make ratio analysis complex.

Here are some possible limitations of using financial ratios to monitor the financial state or business health of an organisation:

■ Accountants may use different definitions for some ratios. For example there are a number of measures for capital employed, used in calculating ROCE. This can make it difficult to compare ratios between different businesses.

■ Changes in accounting policy, rather than performance, may explain some differences between years. For instance, the method of stock valuation will affect the level of profit.

■ Published accounts are summaries so it may be difficult, for example, to make exact comparisons between companies. It is important to use the notes to the accounts wherever possible, e.g. to find trade debtors (as opposed to general debtors) or credit sales (as opposed to total sales).

■ Changes in the economic environment, e.g. during periods of inflation when prices are rising, can make it difficult to put a realistic value on fixed assets such as premises and buildings. This can influence the ROCE. Changes in the ratios could be due to changes in prices and not actual performance.

■ Changes in competitive conditions, e.g. if the financial ratios for a business have improved but all its competitors have done much better, what can you conclude about its business health?

■ Not all the data needed to calculate ratios may be available so informed guesses may have to be made.

■ For stakeholders, financial ratios give a very limited view of the overall performance of the business. For example:

  • workers may consider a rise in gross/net profit, which has been achieved by keeping wages low, very poor performance

  • a local community which has suffered pollution, or had its local bus route or post office closed would not appreciate the headline 'Bus company profits rise'. Good financial ratios may appeal to shareholders, investors and banks but do they necessarily appeal to customers, workers and the local community? Perhaps the real acid test of measuring business health in an organisation would be to consider a range of indicators such as customer satisfaction surveys and environmental performance. How green is my business?

- There is no such thing as an ideal ratio and so analysis becomes a matter of judgement. Frequently it is the trend that is significant rather than the actual level of the ratio.
- Ratio analysis is usually only meaningful when performed as a comparison – either with other businesses in the same industry, with industrial averages or within one business over a period of time. Whenever possible comparisons should be based on like for like figures.
- Many small businesses never use accounting ratios, but instead try to maintain a positive cashflow.
- Financial ratios are most often used to monitor the performance of private and public limited companies. They are less useful for assessing the performance of charities or public sector organisations when profit is not a major objective.

If used with caution, accounting ratios can provide vital information about the financial strength of a business. However, remember that in any evaluation of business performance/ health, the analyst (you) will also need to look at information which is available in its annual reports, on the company and competitor websites, news websites and market surveys, such as KeyNote and Mintel.

As Disraeli might have said, 'There are lies, dammed lies and statistics (financial ratios).'

assignment focus

For M3, you should interpret the ratios you have calculated and say how they can be used to monitor the financial state of the organisation, e.g. by comparing one year with another or comparing your organisation with its main competitors.

For D2, you need to evaluate the adequacy (how good they are) of accounting ratios as a way of monitoring business health, e.g. is financial health the only criteria that should be used to comment on the overall business health?

Introduction to marketing

This unit covers:

- The key concepts and principles of marketing and their application in the business environment
- How and why marketing research is conducted by organisations
- How marketing information is used by organisations
- How marketing techniques are used to increase demand for products (goods and services)

Marketing is important in all industrial sectors and offers a wide variety of job opportunities. This unit introduces the basic principles of marketing and explores how organisations use marketing techniques in order to achieve their business objectives (covered in Unit 1). It looks at how marketing information is collected through marketing research, how it is analysed and used by organisations.

This unit has links with the specialist unit, Unit 9, Exploring creative product promotion.

grading criteria

To achieve a **Pass** grade the evidence must show that the learner is able to:	To achieve a **Merit** grade the evidence must also show that the learner is able to:	To achieve a **Distinction** grade the evidence must also show that the learner is able to:
P1 describe the key concepts and principles of marketing	**M1** compare the effectiveness of the concepts and principles applied to the marketing of products by the two chosen organisations	**D1** evaluate the concepts and principles applied to the marketing of products by a selected organisation and make recommendations for improvement
P2 describe how these key concepts and principles are applied to the marketing of products in two organisations	**M2** compare the analytical techniques used in supporting the marketing decisions of a selected business or product	**D2** evaluate the marketing techniques, research and analysis used by a selected organisation and make original recommendations for improvement
P3 describe how marketing research information is used by one of the organisations to understand the behaviour of customers, competitors and market environment	**M3** explain the marketing techniques used by a selected organisation and analyse why these techniques might have been chosen	

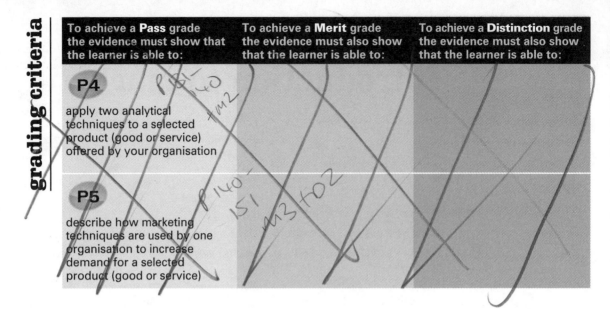

To achieve a **Pass** grade the evidence must show that the learner is able to:	To achieve a **Merit** grade the evidence must also show that the learner is able to:	To achieve a **Distinction** grade the evidence must also show that the learner is able to:
P4 apply two analytical techniques to a selected product (good or service) offered by your organisation		
P5 describe how marketing techniques are used by one organisation to increase demand for a selected product (good or service)		

The key concepts and principles of marketing and their application in the business environment

Principles of marketing

Marketing concept

From the cradle to the grave, everything from cots to coffins can be marketed. The marketing concept is a philosophy (way of thinking) in which the customer becomes the focus of attention for all the organisation's activities. The organisation is customer-orientated at all levels from the sales assistant to senior management. The concept involves creating and keeping customers by making sure that products and services match customers' existing and potential needs and wants whether online or offline.

The marketing of services is now as important as that for goods.

Marketing definitions

A dictionary definition of marketing is:

'the business of selling goods including advertising, packaging, etc.'

The 'etc.' is important because it is what marketing is about; the identification and satisfaction of customers' needs and wants. Advertising and packaging are only a small part of this process.

The Chartered Institute of Marketing (CIM) defines marketing as:

'the management process responsible for identifying, anticipating and satisfying customer requirements profitably'.

For Nestlé, this means finding out what consumers want and giving them a reason for buying a particular product.

This is done by a process called **branding**, which gives a product unique appeal, with a name, a pack design and a 'personality'. To survive and be successful every organisation, both profit and not-for-profit, must provide products and/or services that satisfy customer wants and needs, whether physical or emotional, such as supporting a charity.

Would a not-for-profit organisation agree with the CIM definition?

The marketing guru, Phillip Kotler, in his book, *Marketing Management*, emphasised the point that marketing must 'maximise the company's objectives', i.e. its main purpose is to help achieve the organisation's overall aims and objectives.

Two traditional views of marketing

- *The product approach* – when the business is exclusively concerned with manufacturing quality and efficiency, typified by the attitude, 'We don't need marketing, our product will sell itself'. Or 'we got so hung up on quality, we forgot about style'. This used to be the M&S approach which is now allegedly the UK's greenest retailer.

- *The technology approach* – these businesses are characterised by technological innovation. The Spectrum computer and the Sinclair C5 battery-powered car (now used as children's pedal cars at Camber Sands), were both invented by Sir Clive Sinclair. Now no one has heard of them. Although technically excellent, not enough attention was paid to marketing.

Customer focus

Today quality and technological innovation are still vital, but are combined with a marketing approach more focused on the consumer, e.g. meeting customer needs and building long-term relationships and loyalty. This is typified by Dyson products such as the bagless vacuum cleaner, Nokia mobile phones or perhaps the Sony PS3.

 Link

For loyalty, see page 148.

assignment focus

You need to describe the concept and principles of marketing, e.g. examine different definitions of marketing; are your organisations product, technology or customer-focused?

For your assignment it could be useful to choose organisations from different sectors, e.g. a retailer, manufacturer, charity.

The principles of marketing

For a business to be successful, its marketing should be based on these principles. It must:

- know its customers, who they are, what their needs and expectations are
- know and keep ahead of its competitors
- communicate effectively with its customers to develop the **brand** image
- be fully integrated with other functions such as finance, production and human resources and be part of the corporate business plan feeding through every level of the organisation
- be aware of legal, social and ethical constraints on its marketing activities
- plan and control all marketing activities so as to target the right message to the right consumer segment at the right time
- get the right products, to the right people, in the right place, at the right time, at the right price (when relevant)
- build in ways of tracking and evaluating the effectiveness of its activities and be prepared for continuous improvement.

Marketing activities

The selection of marketing activities carried out by an organisation will depend on its purpose and objectives, e.g. a charity such as Save the Children or Oxfam will relate its marketing to the cause it supports and concentrate its efforts on raising awareness or increasing charitable donations. Some charities use sport to raise money, e.g. the London Marathon and Great North Run. A manufacturer of machine tools for industry might target industrial buyers (i.e. B2B). A manufacturer can also market consumers (e.g. washing powders such as Persil; B2C) and retailers (B2B). A retail business would market to consumers (B2C).

Marketing activities are closely linked to creating an effective marketing mix which give it a competitive advantage over its rivals, by creating and keeping customers. Both profit and not-for-profit organisations now use the full range of marketing activities to achieve their corporate objectives.

 Link

The marketing mix is examined on page 107, and in Unit 9 on page 252.

Table 3.1 provides a possible list of marketing activities.

Table 3.1 Marketing activities

Type of organisation	Clothing retailer, selling physical goods	Charity, marketing an idea or cause	Manufacturer, marketing industrial goods to other businesses	Your centre
A selection of possible marketing activities	Marketing research, Advertising and promotion (B2C); choice of place: click, call in, call, catalogue. All aspects of the marketing mix	Marketing Research, Raising awareness; fund raising, public relations, cause-related marketing mix	Exhibitions, sponsorship, corporate communications (B2B), corporate hospitality at football and music events, etc.	

assignment focus

1   Make a copy of Table 3.1 and complete the column for your centre showing its marketing activities, e.g. open days, prospectus, etc.

2   What marketing activities are carried out by your two organisations?

For M1 and D1, you need to compare the effectiveness of these activities. Analyse whether they work and how could they be improved.

Marketing objectives

Marketing objectives are determined by the corporate top level or strategic goals of the organisation. For example, if the organisation intended to increase sales and had, after suitable market research, identified Poland as an appropriate place to start selling its products, then resources would need to be allocated to the marketing budget to achieve this. SMART objectives would need to reflect this goal, by identifying who are the potential customers (the majority still live in rural communities), their needs and wants, cultural differences, lifestyles, etc. SMART objectives could be created for individual stores or product categories.

SMART objectives are discussed in Unit 1, page 24.

Marketing objectives should be SMART and flow directly from the mission or vision of the organisation. Many, but not all, organisations draw up a mission statement as a summary of their long-term aims and objectives. It is a general statement of the standards, qualities and purpose of the business. Marketing objectives should relate directly to the mission. Here are two examples of mission statements. What marketing would be needed to achieve these?

Friends of the Earth

Friends of the Earth (FoE), the environmental charity and pressure group, has this mission:

'Friends of the Earth defends the environment and champions a healthy and just world'.

The charity promotes itself through advertising and direct mail shots and raises money through a gift catalogue, Christmas cards and sponsorship. Figure 3.1 is an example of an advert for FoE designed for your age group. Do you support environmental pressure groups?

Sainsbury's

Sainsbury's has this mission:

'To meet our customers' needs effectively by providing the best quality and choice to meet their everyday shopping needs and thereby provide shareholders with good, sustainable financial returns.'

Figure 3.1 Friends of the
Earth – raising awareness

"Gasping and panting, sweat
was dripping off my body..."

The mission needs to be implemented (acted on). Sainsbury's focus on three core areas: outstanding quality and choice, delivering great service and competitive costs. This approach requires SMART objectives. Here is a current example from Sainsbury:

- **S**pecific – the company should clearly identify a product, activity, region, etc., e.g. 'organic food, healthy eating and green living'
- **M**easurable – it should be possible to determine when the objective has been met 'we are looking for a 4–5 per cent footage growth, up from today's rate of 2 per cent' (this refers to the size and number of stores, it is the selling space, the Place in the 4 Ps)
- **A**chievable – the target must be one that the organisation can hit, otherwise it is setting itself up to fail. Find out in five years whether Sainsbury's achieved a 4–5 per cent growth in selling space.
- **R**ealistic – the target will not put unreasonable demands on the resources of the organisation, e.g. staff or finance. Sometimes the R stands for Relevant, meaning that the objective should be appropriate to current circumstances, Sainsbury's is currently no. 3 in the supermarket market share league table (after Tesco and Asda).
- **T**ime–constrained – the objective has a set time period or deadline. Sainsbury's has set a 'three to five year time frame' for opening new bigger stores, i.e. achieving growth in footage.

 Tesco opened 50 per cent of all new shopping space in 2006. Find out what the Competition Commission has said about Tesco in its 2007 report on supermarkets.

assignment focus

What are the mission statements for your organisations? Do they work? Are they true? What objectives do they have? Why do they need to be SMART?

Objectives must be precise and quantified to show the time span within which they are to be achieved. They should be attainable, realistic targets, which motivate the business and serve as the basis for its planning and decision-making. Every organisation will have its own marketing objectives which depend on its own needs and wants, and those of its existing and potential stakeholders:

- HSBC, for example, might wish to sell more financial products, such as mortgages. What marketing does it do? A 'green sale' – 'For every green sale product you buy, we'll donate to conservation projects around the world.'

- An organisation might want to increase market share (for example, by 4 per cent over the next 18 months). The market share is the proportion or percentage of the market served by a particular brand or business. Being 'no. 1' adds sales and status to a brand – the implication is it must be good. However, being 'no. 2' in the market can also be turned into a classic selling point, as the famous slogan 'We are Number Two. We try harder!' demonstrates. Pepsi and Evian are no. 2 in their categories.

- An organisation might want to maintain/improve product and business image. What image or mental picture do you have of politicians or used car salespeople ('remarketing'!)?

assignment focus

1   A company's image depends to some extent on the relationship between price and quality, e.g. premium, bargain, cowboy and economy. Can you name some retail outlets or products which come into each category? Which category do your products come in?

2   For M1 and D1, consider whether this image should or could be changed. Why?

Functions of marketing

The main functions of marketing are to:

- obtain and keep customers. This can be done, for example, by informing and persuading people to buy the product or, in the case of a charity, to contribute to the cause or by making people aware of the product through promotion

- help achieve the aims and objectives of the organisation, e.g. profit, sales or growth

- achieve a competitive advantage for the organisation by understanding the competitors and improving on their performance

- create a marketing plan which uses all elements of the marketing mix

- establish, maintain and develop the image and reputation of the organisation by using the marketing mix to create a brand.

Use of marketing principles

Every organisation will to a greater or lesser extent market its products. This marketing activity maybe online, offline or a combination of both, summed up in the 4Cs:

- Click for online activity
- Call for telephone operations
- Call in for face-to-face
- Catalogue.

Can you think of examples? Which method do you or your family use? Large retailers are now using all of these to market their products. Do organisations pay enough attention to each of these 4Cs? A phone call to a bank takes a minimum wait of 20 minutes with music you don't like, allegedly!

assignment focus

How do your organisations use marketing principles, e.g. what type of relationships are there (B2B, B2C, etc.)? What are the functions of marketing in your organisations? What are their objectives?

Table 3.2 Marketing principles for different organisations

Type of organisation	Marketing principles which may be used
Small business	Possibly operating in small markets, survival may determine the marketing strategy, defining and positioning the product are important as is identifying a target group. One person may be responsible for marketing
Voluntary organisation/charity	These are not-for-profit organisations with cause-related marketing. Objectives will be closely tied to funding/ donations. The charity market is competitive so image/ reputation is important
Government department/agency	The government provides services, benefits, allowances, etc. It is mainly concerned with promotion. Local government also tries to increase the take up of its services
Large manufacturing business	Could be marketing to other businesses (B2B) or consumers (B2C), e.g. double glazing. The product, its quality and price are important. 'People' are important in establishing relationships
Retail consumers	Any organisation which markets directly to retail consumers whether online or offline will use the full range of the 7Ps in order to distinguish itself from its competitors. It has to create a Unique Selling Point to attract and hold customer loyalty. It must be customer-focused. Brand image is important

Planning, control and evaluation processes

All marketing activities are a cost or expense for the organisation. They need to produce results. Expenditure has to be accounted for. SMART marketing objectives need to be implemented through a business and marketing plan. This will set out the targets to be achieved. The targets act as the guideline (or standards) against which performance will be measured. Evaluation methods need to be built in at the planning stage, e.g. current awareness of the product leads to a new advertising promotion campaign which creates new awareness levels. Careful control and monitoring will need to take place during the implementation stage.

See page 150 for a full explanation of this process.

Development of e-marketing

See page 144 for how e-marketing can be used to connect directly with individuals.

Today we are all familiar with promotional text messages on our mobiles and adverts on the computer. Virtually unknown 20 years ago, many public and private organisations now use e-marketing (electronic marketing via the telephone, mobile phone and/or computer) as a medium for their marketing activities. It is part of the wider activity e-business. It can include:

- all the traditional marketing activities, such as promotion, advertising, public relations, direct marketing and market research, plus newer types of marketing such customer relationship marketing (CRM). This concentrates on building a long-term relationship with the customer, using a customer database built up from loyalty cards such as the Tesco Clubcard, Nectar or the Boots Advantage Card.
- the full range of marketing relationships as shown in Figure 3.2.

See page 149 for more information on relationship marketing.

Figure 3.2 Marketing
relationships

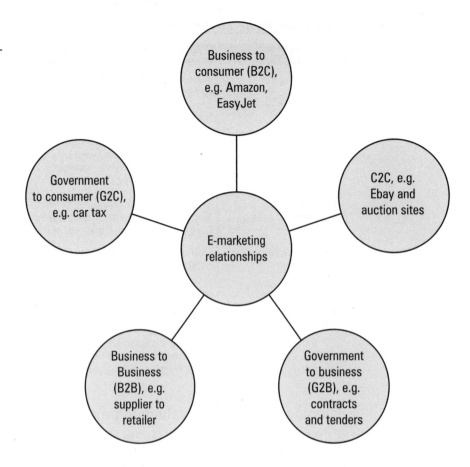

E-marketing is now an established part of the marketing mix. Many organisations are described as 'clicks and mortar', i.e. their products may be bought and sold through the computer (clicks) or at physical premises (the mortar). Manufacturers, retailers, charities, central government (through its anti-smoking and anti-drink and drive campaigns) and local authorities (e.g. promoting their recycling facilities) now all use e-marketing methods.

Figure 3.3 A government
anti-smoking campaign

Marketing mix

The marketing mix refers to the way in which the key parts of an organisation's marketing tools are combined (mixed) to achieve its objectives. Senior management will be responsible for marketing strategy; the marketing department will need to create the tactics (methods) to put the strategy into operation.

Figure 3.4 The marketing mix

The 4Ps

The traditional marketing mix of Price, Product, Promotion and Place – the 4Ps – was created to market goods. It has dominated marketing thinking for the last 45 years, yet is still only a guideline by which a business can create a strategy, The growth in the service sector and e-tailers (electronic retailers) such as Easyjet, who market through the internet direct to customers cutting out the intermediaries (such as wholesalers or retailers), have changed the way the marketing mix operates. See Table 3.3.

The 7Ps

Three extra Ps have been added to cater for this increase in the marketing of services, e.g. by opticians, hairdressers, banking and insurance, and the growth of online marketing.

- *People* Staff are the most important resource in an organisation. Well-motivated, efficient staff can give an organisation a competitive edge.
- *Processes* Consumers are increasingly concerned about how goods are produced and delivered.
- *Physical evidence* This refers to the premises, staff, quality of the website, etc., i.e. anything which affects the image of the organisation and how it is perceived.

This expanded marketing mix will need to be continuously assessed and adjusted for an effective and mutually profitable long-term relationship to be built up with customers.

Every business will mix the 7Ps differently depending on the:

- type of product, e.g. necessities tend to be marketed differently from luxuries or services
- nature and number of competitors, e.g. in highly competitive markets price may be a major factor
- marketing mix of competitors
- range of **market segments** – some businesses use a different marketing mix for each group of customers.

See Unit 9, pages 230–51 for more about the marketing mix.

Table 3.3 Activities and decisions involved in each part of the marketing mix

7 Ps	Marketing decisions and activities
Product (goods or services)	Developing new products, reviewing the existing product mix, adapting current products, packaging (design, colour) and green marketing, quality
Price	Short- and long-term pricing methods for existing and new products, discounts, high or low price policies, price versus quality
Place	Selection of outlets, methods of transport, online presence, location of premises
Promotion	Includes public relations, sponsorship, sales offers, advertising, branding, costs need to be weighed against expected benefits
People	Recruitment and selection, training and development, incentives, rewards and recognition, service with a smile!
Physical evidence	Layout and design of premises and website, are they user friendly and accessible, corporate communications (online/offline)
Processes	Links with the customer, converting prospects into customers with good customer care, before and after sales service, help and advice

case study 3.1 — Eclipse in Poland! Marketing in Europe

Eclipse Pottery (see page 404) is currently based in Cornwall. Since the expansion of the EU and the consequent arrival of many Polish people in the UK, Eclipse has decided to investigate whether it would be worthwhile opening an outlet in Krakov in Poland. The main tourist area is around the spectacular Market Square.

Eclipse has already carried out some preliminary secondary desk research into housewares (see below): 'low price is the main factor underlying purchases'. Polish people are described as 'practical buyers' for whom functionality is more important than fashion trends. High value tableware is usually bought as a present.

Eclipse has also discovered that Poles tend to celebrate their name day/saints day rather than birthdays. Currently, the top girls' name is Anna, the most popular boys' name is Piotr. Eclipse has decided to produce a small number of traditional-style plates, cups and saucers with the top 20 boys' and girls' names. It hopes to rent a stall in the *sukiennice* (Cloth Hall in the Market Square) alongside other souvenir traders selling amber jewellery, woodcraft, hand knitted woollens, etc. It will use a dragon to promote its products. Its first objective is to get its plates used during the *pierogi-*tasting festival held in August. (*Pierogi* are small pockets of pastry filled with cheeses, mushrooms, potatoes, etc.)

activity

1 What are the costs and benefits for Eclipse Pottery trying to open in Krakov?
2 Why might Eclipse need to change its marketing mix?
3 Does your organisation sell in Europe? Give examples of how this could affect its marketing mix.
4 Give examples of how culture might affect the marketing mix.

See www.euromonitor.com for housewares in Poland; www.epp.eurostat.ec for current economic data; and www.mintel.com for market research data. www.krakow.pl is an official site which lists business opportunities.

Website Audits

How do your organisations use their websites?

1 Print screen the home pages of your two organisations. What evidence is there that the key concepts and principles of marketing are being applied?

2 Compare the marketing mix of both organisations as reflected in their websites – their online presence. Does this relate to their offline presence?

3 Evaluate the sites using these criteria: user friendliness, accessibility, security, design and layout.

4 Who is their intended audience? Are the AIDA principles being applied?

5 Is there a privacy policy (legal constraint)? Why is it there?

6 Make recommendations for improvement.

Limitations and constraints on marketing

At one time, advertisers and promoters could make any claims they liked about their products. There were no constraints on what they could do. Some exaggerated claims were made, e.g. 7UP was originally sold as a hangover cure. The freedom did not last long. Can you think why?

Today there is a range of voluntary and legal (statutory) controls on marketing activities.

Legal constraints

There are many laws controlling marketing activity, e.g. so that it is not misleading, does not encourage harmful behaviour, does not cause offence and is not illegal by breaking the equal opportunities legislation. The overall purpose is to protect consumers and promote a socially responsible attitude towards society and its citizens.

Figure 3.5 Events such as the Leonard Cheshire VisABLE modelling competition helped to raise the profile of disabled people in mainstream society and to make it harder for companies to ignore disabled people in their advertising campaigns

Sale and Supply of Goods Act 1994

This Act amended both the Sale of Goods Act 1979 and the Supply of Goods and Services Act 1982. It applies to all goods including food, regardless of where they are bought, e.g. from shops, market stalls, door-to-door sales, home party sales, or catalogue mail order.

According to the Act, the seller must ensure that goods are:

■ *of satisfactory quality* This term has replaced 'merchantable quality' used in the previous Act. Satisfactory quality is defined as the standard that a reasonable person would regard as satisfactory, taking account of any description of the goods, the price if relevant and all other relevant circumstances. The quality of goods includes their state and condition plus fitness for purpose, appearance and finish, freedom from minor defects and safety and durability. Are you a reasonable person? What do you think is satisfactory?

- *reasonably fit for any particular purpose*, i.e. they must be able to do what the seller claims they can do, for example, an electric toaster should be able to toast four slices in one minute if this is how it was described.

The Act can be enforced as soon as a contract (written or verbal) has been made between the buyer and seller, i.e. when the buyer has made an offer and the seller has accepted. If the contract has been broken, buyers can either get their money back or have the goods replaced. They do not have to accept a credit note.

However, consumers are not entitled to anything if they did not see obvious faults at the time of purchase, or were told about faults but chose to ignore them, or ignored any advice which was given.

Trade Descriptions Act 1968

The Act applies to transactions between businesses and consumers (B2C) and between businesses (B2B). It makes it a criminal offence to:

- apply a false description to any goods. The description can be written or oral (curiously, second-hand car dealers have been prosecuted most often) and can apply to the quality, size and specification, ingredients or raw materials, features, date and place of manufacture
- apply misleading advertisements
- make misleading statements about the price
- apply a false description to facilities, services or accommodation.

People have a seven-day cooling off period in which to change their mind if they have been sold something in their own home.

Consumer Credit Act 1974

The purpose of this Act is to make sure that most businesses that offer goods or services on credit or lend money to consumers are licensed by the Office of Fair Trading.

Advertisements offering credit or hire facilities to consumers are controlled by the Consumer Credit (Advertisement) Regulations 2004. The aim of the regulations is to make sure that customers get a true picture of the nature and cost of credit terms being offered, e.g. the interest rates being charged. Companies offering loans only appear to advertise on daytime TV. Have you seen them? Have you been tempted to consolidate your debt?

Data Protection Act 1998

With the development of computer databases, a great deal of private information has been collected on individuals by organisations such as supermarkets, insurance companies and banks. The speed with which computers can search, sort and access data from great distances has meant that it is increasingly easy for this information to be passed on. It was recognised that there was a need to protect the rights of those individuals on whom data is held.

---

assignment focus

1   How is it possible for call centres to operate from countries such as India. How did the data get there?

2   How is it possible to get a text message which says, 'You have won £500, please contact this number to obtain your prize' but does not say it is a premium rate number at £10 per second and calls last 2 minutes?

There are eight data protection principles contained in the Data Protection Act 1998. They are all concerned with the processing of personal data. The Act only applies to data that can identify an individual, e.g. name, address, NI number, e-mail address, telephone number, etc. Personal data shall be:

- processed fairly and lawfully
- obtained for lawful and specified purposes
- adequate and relevant – not excessive (no unnecessary questions)
- accurate and kept up-to-date (inaccurate or incomplete data to be erased or put right)
- not kept longer than is necessary for the purpose for which it was collected
- processed so as to keep individual data private
- kept secure against any unauthorised use, accidental loss or damage
- kept within the European Economic Area (the EU plus Norway, Iceland and Liechtenstein) and not transferred outside unless similar protection exists.

The Act came into force in March 2000. Organisations have until 2007 to comply with all the provisions. Does your centre comply?

Identify and assess the impact of any possible legal constraints on the marketing activities of your business. Use the headings we have given here. Try searching for court cases with your company name. Many companies selling food have been sued for falsely labelling their products.

remember

You could avoid the issues covered in the DP Act if you do not collect personal data in any survey you carry out, i.e. if your respondents cannot be identified.

Voluntary constraints

Most promotion and advertising in the UK is covered by voluntary controls. It is self-regulated by the industry. Its key feature is to provide and maintain standards so that all advertising is legal, decent, truthful and honest.

The Advertising Standards Authority (ASA) is an independent voluntary body financed by the advertising industry to make sure that self-regulation works. It does not have statutory powers. It supervises all advertising, including that on radio and TV. Its role is to protect consumers' interests. It administers the British Code of Advertising Practice and the British Code of Sales Promotion Practice. Although the ASA tries to prevent the media from carrying objectionable advertisements, it does not enforce the law.

The ASA monitors advertisements on a daily basis and can investigate written complaints from the general public. If it is unable to stop offensive advertisements appearing, it can as a last resort refer the advertiser to the Director General of the Office of Fair Trading using the Control of Misleading Advertisements Regulations. Most advertisers stop running their advertisements before this stage is reached, e.g. the Authority took action over a TV commercial for Tango within days of acquiring its new powers to control TV advertising.

Although advertising is strictly controlled, the ASA still receives hundreds of complaints about false or misleading advertisements.

Phrases such as 'news flash' are not acceptable in TV adverts. If an advert is a 'take off' or parody of a real programme, then the actors from the programme cannot appear. Why do you think this is?

In the UK there are restrictions on political and religious TV advertising. Tobacco advertising is banned.

Since November 2004 the Advertising Standards Authority has been a one-stop-shop regulating all advertising. It has a very interesting website (www.asa.org.uk), which includes a complaint form.

Check the ASA website. Has there ever been a complaint made against your organisations? Why?

Pressure groups and consumerism

A pressure group is an organisation, or group of people, which attempts to influence important decisions. The group may be in favour or against a particular outcome. They range in size:

- from small, informal local groups set up for a specific purpose, e.g. 'Save our Police Station' is a familiar sight in many small towns where the number of supporters seems to be matched by the objectors
- to large national, even international, organisations, such as Friends of the Earth (FoE) or Greenpeace.

The Consumers' Association represents consumers' interests through its Which? magazines. The AA was initially formed to protect the interests of motorists, although the RAC now claims to be no. 1.

An important feature of the current marketing environment is the rise in consumerism. The term can either refer to the protection of consumers' interests and rights or describe the way consumers are becoming more sophisticated, more concerned with the total package of benefits they obtain when they purchase a product. Many people now identify with a brand, its image and values. It may define their lifestyle or personality, such as Nike trainers or a Rolex watch.

Environmental and social constraints

While marketing has specific social and ethical responsibilities, since the 1980s there has been growing concern for the environment. Some businesses may be too concerned with profit and are prepared to cut corners to achieve this.

Businesses can no longer afford to be anti-environment or anti-social. Indeed a positive approach can be used as a key selling point, as the Body Shop 'not tested on animals' policy has demonstrated.

case study 3.2 — M&S does good: competitors go green with envy?

In January 2007, M&S launched 'Plan A', a £200m 'eco-plan' which will have an impact on every part of the organisation.

'By 2012 M&S will:

- become carbon neutral
- send no waste to landfill
- extend sustainable sourcing
- set new standards in ethical trading
- help customers and employees live a healthier lifestyle.

M&S Chief Executive, Stuart Rose said:

"Every business and individual needs to do their bit to tackle the enormous challenges of climate change and waste. While M&S will continue to sell great quality, stylish and innovative products, our customers, employees and shareholders now expect us to take bold steps and do business differently and responsibly. We believe a responsible business can be a profitable business. We are calling this 'Plan A' because there is no 'plan B'."'

Source: M&S press release, 15 January 2007

activity

1   Why has M&S 'gone green'? What does it hope to achieve?
2   Do you care about global warming? Would you use M&S? How should your organisations respond?

You can find out more about M&S's Plan A by visiting the website, www.marksandspencer.com, and going to Media and then Press releases.

The demand for organic and Fair Trade products has risen because they appeal to people's conscience, e.g.

- Waitrose Foundation Avocados: 'The foundation helps the workers who grow our South African avocados and citrus fruits by raising money for health, education and social products.' (*Source*: Waitrose New)
- Café Direct is a Fair Trade product which guarantees a better deal for third world producers.
- Douwe Egberts Good Origin Coffee 'has an online tracking system which enables you to trace the beans back to the farm where they were produced and find out how the farmers, their families and the local environment are being supported.' (*Source*: Waitrose News)

The marketer needs to be aware of which stakeholders/pressure groups (the people and communities who have an interest in a business because they are affected by its activities) may be offended or pleased by a particular marketing activity.

1 Is there any evidence that your organisation has responded to stakeholders' views, e.g. by introducing new products or adapting existing ones?

2 You are an ambitious marketing executive in the marketing department of J4O2Shirts (J2O is a registered trade mark of Britvic plc). The company is about to launch its new 'Environmentally Friendly Natural Cotton Range'. You are fully aware that cotton production uses more pesticide and artificial fertiliser than almost any other crop and therefore has the potential for immense environmental damage. You also know that the hydrogen peroxide and caustic soda used in bleaching the cotton, if discharged into the river system, will kill fish. What are you going to do next?

Acceptable language

Whilst the language used in advertising has to be accessible to its audience, it also has to be legal, decent, truthful and honest. The Advertising Standards Authority (ASA) has the primary responsibility for ensuring that all advertising uses acceptable language, i.e. language which does not offend. Problems can occur when advertisements which are specifically created for one target group (known as the preferred readers) are seen by other groups (the negotiated readers) who interpret them in their own way and could take offence.

These are the rules on taste and decency published by the ASA:

'The advertising codes state that advertisements should contain nothing that is likely to cause serious or widespread offence.

The codes also require that special care is taken to avoid causing offence on the grounds of race, religion, sex, sexual orientation or disability.

When the ASA Council decides whether an ad complies with the codes, it will judge on the context, medium, audience, product and prevailing standards of decency.'

Source: www.asa.org.uk; Schools and Colleges Resources No. 2, Taste and Decency

This is how these rules are specifically applied to TV alcohol advertising:

- 'Advertisements must not suggest that alcohol can contribute to an individual's popularity or confidence, or that refusal is a sign of weakness. Nor may they suggest that alcohol can enhance personal qualities.

- Advertisements must not suggest that the success of a social occasion depends on the presence or consumption of alcohol.

- Advertisements must not link alcohol with daring, toughness, aggression or anti-social behaviour.'

Source: www.asa.org.uk; Advertising Guidance Note No. 6

1 Can you find examples of unacceptable language used in advertisements? Why do you consider it unacceptable?

2 Do you consider the rules on TV alcohol advertising to be about right, too harsh or too lenient? Give reasons.

3 Check the ASA website. Have there been complaints about your chosen organisation or industry? What about your competitors? This could indicate the degree of rivalry. (Check under adjudications – the ASA decision on each complaint.)

How and why marketing research is conducted by organisations

To achieve P3, you must describe how marketing research information is used by one of your organisations to understand the behaviour of its customers, competitors and market environment.

Marketing research

Most marketing decisions involve taking risks. Marketing research is the homework that needs to be done to understand and minimise the risks.

The Chartered Institute of Marketing (CIM) has defined marketing research as:

> 'the objective gathering, recording and analysing of all facts about problems relating to the transfer and sales of goods and services from producer to consumer or user'.

For example, this could mean obtaining data to identify customers' needs and wants; analysing competitors' strengths and weaknesses; or scanning the market environment for potential opportunities/threats. The information can then be used to reduce the risk when making marketing decisions. So the essential components are: gather the data, analyse it, make decisions.

Marketing research is concerned with the whole range of marketing activities; it includes all aspects of the 7 Ps which make up the marketing mix, consumer and competitor research, business/economic research and forecasts (PESTLE).

As a result of the Data Protection Act 1998, the Market Research Society has produced the following definition of classic survey (or market) research:

> 'the application of scientific research methods to obtain objective information on people's attitudes and behaviour based usually on representative samples of the relevant populations. The process guarantees the confidentiality of personal information in such a way that the data can only be used for research purposes'.

You may already have some knowledge of marketing research, e.g. being interviewed in the street or through omnibus surveys, where many companies contribute their own questions to a multi-part questionnaire (they always seem very long!) which then gets sent to your address. How do they know your home or e-mail address? Because you have told them, e.g. by having a loyalty card, signing a guarantee, signing a guest book, filling in an online questionnaire because you have won a prize, etc. (Source: www.marketresearch.org.uk)

Knowing, how, why, where, when and by whom any research was carried out is vital if we want to trust any of the results. For example, recent research by BP suggests climate change is a major opportunity, whilst research by Friends of the Earth suggests it is a major disaster. Any comments?

Qualitative and quantitative research

- Qualitative research is carried out to collect 'soft' information such as the attitudes, views, opinions and perceptions of people, e.g. why people buy or do not buy a product, what they think about the product, what are their views on the competitors. Generally, this information is collected using small samples so that people can be interviewed in depth. **Focus groups** are the most popular method for collecting qualitative data.

- Quantitative research is carried out to collect 'hard' factual numerical information, often using large samples to find out, for example, the number and type of people who use or might use a particular product. It answers the question of how many people buy the product. The characteristics of buyers are quantified numerically (their **demographics**, see page 142). Results could show the percentage or proportion of people in particular categories. Quantitative research is the most common method of presenting information to help with decision-making. For example, '62 per cent of customers said they preferred the 'own-label brand', '19 per cent of the resident population of Bromley is under 16' (www.statistics.gov.uk). Loyalty card databases contain a huge amount of quantitative data about our personal shopping habits.

Internal and external research

- Internal research is based on internal sources, i.e. those within the organisation (hard copy, electronic records and staff). It should always be the first line of enquiry for any market research investigation because it should be cheap, fast, convenient and exclusive to the company, i.e. information is secret and not available to competitors. Especially important will be the availability of 'back data' or time series data which can be used to analyse trends and make forecasts (primary data, which is usually a snapshot of the current situation does not have this advantage). Beware of 'information overload', where too many statistics with too much unnecessary detail may be collected. Only if internal sources are unsuitable should the business move to external sources.

■ External research investigates external sources, i.e. they do not belong to the organization, e.g. customers, news reports, trade journals, market analyses from companies such as KeyNote or Mintel, etc.

Primary research

When an organisation wants new, fresh and original data on a particular issue, it would have to carry out primary research. This is research carried out for the first time to collect first-hand or primary data from actual or possible users of a product (goods or services). Data could be collected in the street, at a workplace or online, i.e. 'in the field'. Primary research (or field research) is carried out for a specific purpose, will be original, up to date and belong to the organisation that paid for the research, i.e. confidential and not available to competitors.

Secondary research

Also known as desk research, secondary research is searching for data that already exists (secondary data), either published and available as hard copy/electronic sources outside the business or internally within the business. It has been collected by someone else for their own purpose. Secondary research investigates the sources of secondary data. It should be the starting point for all market research. However great care needs to be taken when using secondary sources and data. Always bear in mind that the data was not collected to answer your questions and this may have affected the data analysis and presentation. Computer searches are now the most popular method for collecting secondary data. Always remember secondary data is available to everyone including your competitors.

Primary and secondary research can be carried out both within (internal) and outside (external) an organisation. Here are some examples of data held by a small business. Can you give examples from your centre?

Table 3.4 Example of data held by a small business

	Internal	External
Primary data	Supplier and customer information e.g. response to special promotions, held on company database Historical back data on the 4Ps	Online questionnaire, both quantitative/qualitative data collected from website users Face-to-face and telephone interviews
Secondary data	Internal data is shared and is available on the company intranet Desk research on historical or back data, e.g. sales	KeyNote/Euromonitor/Mintel market research; specialist UK and EU online statistical data: epp. eurostat.ec

For more about primary and secondary research, see pages 117 and 123.

KeyNote and Mintel reports will show national and regional trends in buyer behaviour, with a quantitative section on consumer demographics (age, income, etc.).

Purpose and uses of marketing research

Every organisation will have its own reasons for carrying out primary and secondary marketing research, e.g. to reduce the risk of business failure, improve decision-making, forecast future trends in order to anticipate customer needs, define markets and identify buying habits, improve marketing planning. Essentially it is about collecting and analysing market data to create better products to satisfy customer needs.

Here are some examples of research that could be carried out. If you check out the websites of any marketing research company, you will find many more.

Try surfing under 'Marketing research companies', then go to Products or Research solutions.

- *Nature of the market*, e.g. the size of the market by volume or value, potential for future sales, analysis of trends, estimates and forecasts of market share, profiles of the market segment, e.g. the characteristics of the target population – lifestyle, interests, income, etc.

- *Product research* Organisations will want to find out if there is a gap in their product range, how this could be filled and whether there is a market for a new product. They may need to assess the impact of packaging and how well it stands out on supermarket shelves. They could compare their products with those of competitors to investigate buying habits, or investigate the best advertising media to use.

- *Competitor research*, e.g. who they are, whether they have similar products and what their prices are, how well they perform, how they will react to a new product/competitor, what their customers think, their strengths and weaknesses.

You can find out about competitors' products by using trade directories, telephone directories, web searches and personal observation.
See: www.marketresearch.org.uk; MrWeb.com is a good portal site for desk research.

- *Price research* This could include collecting data on competitor prices, assessing how customers view prices and whether a price change would be acceptable, e.g. what would be the maximum price consumers would be willing to pay, how to price a new product – very low (penetration) or very high (skimming).

- *Promotion research* This includes measuring the effectiveness of advertising before and after an advertising campaign, the impact of promotion on demand, using population data and targeting market segments to establish where to promote products, and looking at the effectiveness of aftersales service.

- *Place or distribution research* This includes the effectiveness of different outlets and channels of distribution, the suitability of new locations based on demographic and customer segment data, or the effectiveness of different supply arrangements.

- *Market environment* Market research reports produced by commercial companies such as KeyNote backed up with personal observation are good ways of obtaining information about the external environment. They often contain a SWOT and PESTLE analysis of the industry/sector.

- *Researching customers* To meet its customers' needs and therefore improve its chances of survival a business will need to know:
  - how many customers there are
  - how much they are willing to pay, including their buying habits and patterns of spending
  - what their needs, desires, expectations, likes and dislikes, attitudes and prejudices are
  - how it can best inform, persuade and convince customers to purchase the product
  - what motivates customers and what attracts them to particular brands; for example, it could be the quality, design, colour, safety, or guarantees given with the product.

Whatever decision is finally taken, the business must be certain that its decision is based on accurate and reliable marketing research.

Limitations of marketing research

- Marketing research can be very expensive, so it is important that the expected returns should justify the cost.

- It can be very time-consuming, although with the increasing use of electronic data collection this has become less important. Today an organisation will have to balance cost and time.

- When were the figures collected? What is the date of publication? Data, whether primary or secondary is always out of date, although, in relatively static markets this may not be a problem, where the marketplace is changing frequently (dynamic), e.g. mobile phones, marketing research needs to be continuous.

- Perfect knowledge is impossible to achieve, there is never enough information and it changes all the time.

- Have valid and reliable sources been used for any secondary research? (See page 120.) You should always try to use at least two unbiased sources.

- Is the sample representative and unbiased? Are there sufficient respondents/items? What is the level of accuracy?

- Has the research been professionally carried out using accepted codes of practice? Is the source politically neutral or biased?

- Has the data been obtained ethically? Have the relevant rules and procedures been followed to ensure data is secure? Has the data been collected, analysed and disposed of according to the Data Protection legislation?

- Which organisation collected the information? Is the source reliable and trustworthy? Anyone can publish almost anything on the internet. How do you know if it is true?

- Why is the data available? Who is the intended audience? What purpose did the collectors wish to achieve? For example, statistics about the safety of smoking prepared by a tobacco company, or statistics about the safety of mobile phones prepared by a mobile phone manufacturer are likely to be biased in their favour.

Primary research

Methods

The basic methods that can be used for collecting primary information are as follows.

Observation

Companies such as Marks & Spencer often observe customer behaviour when new products are introduced into their stores or the layout and position of products is changed. Mystery shoppers – people who are paid to be professional shoppers – are frequently used by a business to check out both the performance of its own staff and that of its competitors.

Questionnaires

A questionnaire is a list of structured questions which is distributed to a number of people either face-to-face as hard copy (printed) or electronic copy (online or computer assisted via e-mail or mobile), in order to collect demographic information such as age or income. They can be completed by the respondent (the person completing the questionnaire) or an interviewer can record the answers which the respondent gives.

Questions

- Closed questions have only two possible answers, e.g. yes or no; agree or disagree; true or false. They are good for providing quantitative information.

- Open questions do not have a predetermined answer. People are free to make their own comments. Although they are good for gathering qualitative information, they can be difficult to interpret.

Interviews

Interviews can be carried out:

- face-to-face, either individually or with groups
- by telephone/mobile
- online through interactive video focus groups.

Which interview to choose

A structured interview (the interviewer will ask a set number of prepared questions usually based on a questionnaire) with closed questions is quick and easy to carry out and is the easiest to analyse. However, the respondent cannot give extra information. The informal methods take time and are difficult to analyse because of the wide variation of replies possible with open questions. The best approach for a simple survey is a structured approach with both closed and open questions.

case study
3.3

Big Brother is Watching You plc: the Data Protection Act applied to marketing research

The Data Protection Act affects market research in three main ways:

- *transparency* – individuals must be clearly told why the data is being collected and how it will be used. This applies to all types of questionnaire and interview
- *consent* – individuals must agree to their data being collected (i.e. they must be able to refuse) and have the right to opt out of any later use of the data
- *security* – data must be kept secure at all times during the planning, collection, analysis and final disposal stages.

So how do we get compensated for giving away our most confidential secrets?

A loyalty card insider says:

'We know if you have just had a baby, if you are going on holiday and how much you drink. We can suggest new products and tempt you with extra points. We can move customers along the loyalty ladder until they get hooked into shopping frequently and buying every offer. We can put electronic chips in the store card so that the retailer knows when you are in store. We can, and some do, sew electronic tags into labels.'

The Tesco Clubcard started in 1995 is the electronic database that has helped Tesco to precisely understand its customers' needs and is a major reason for Tesco achieving its no. 1 position in retailing.

The Tesco Clubcard database is not just used by Tesco. It is also used by Coca-Cola, Nestle, Unilever, Pedigree (dog food), etc. to target, e.g. dog owners, and assess the response to promotional campaigns. 'It is now a big business in its own right' but 'personal details are never made public and the data is made anonymous before it is released to another company'. Do you care?

activity

1   Does your organisation have a loyalty card? Do you?

2   Who benefits the most, the customer or the organisation?

3   Would you tell your best friend how many calories you eat every week, what personal hygiene products you use or your romantic expectations? Every time you use a loyalty card, this private information is entered onto your database. Is it worth revealing everything about yourself to get double points?

4   Check out the Data Protection Act on page 110. Do you think the eight principles are being followed?

case study
3.4

Marie Claire grows up

The glossy monthly magazine *Marie Claire* was relaunched in October 2006. Focus groups had been used intensively to create the new look which 'delivered a clear understanding of today's 30-something, affluent woman and what she desires from a glossy magazine. The resulting new look is more grown-up, elegant and sophisticated, and focuses on *Marie Claire*'s core strengths: fashion, beauty, real life reportage, celebrity and trusted advice.'

activity

Why would *Marie Claire* choose focus groups and not structured interviews or closed questionnaires for its relaunch research?

Focus groups

A focus group is usually a group of five to ten people – supposedly ordinary or representative members of the public – brought together by a market research company in an informal environment to discuss different products, ways to increase public participation in local council decisions, etc. It is in effect a collective interview. The main purpose is to get a range of views about the 'product'. It is qualitative market research. Focus groups are increasingly used both face-to-face and online through chat rooms and blogs ('a personal online journal,' says the Economist.com).

 www.ipcadvertising.com gives a complete brand profile of all IPC magazines.

Table 3.5 The advantages and disadvantages of various methods of collecting primary data

Method	Advantages	Disadvantages
Observation Direct observation of a task or activity e.g. buying	Very accurate and can be easily controlled, e.g. accompanied shopping to find out what and how consumers buy	Very expensive and time-consuming
Face-to-face A personal interview between the respondent and interviewer	High response rate; flexible and easily controlled; extra questions can be asked; answers can be clarified; body language can be seen	Very expensive; needs trained interviewers; can take considerable time; can be biased unless people are carefully selected
Postal For a postal survey a clear questionnaire is needed	Costs can be controlled, people have time to respond, any area can be covered, people may be more truthful if the reply is anonymous, postcode research can be used	Very low response rate, i.e. number of replies, questions cannot be explained or answers verified
Telephone A structured set of questions is recommended (see CATI below).	Easy to carry out, fast and convenient, flexible, satisfactory response rate; people may be more willing to respond over the phone	Can be expensive, depends on time and distance; respondents have little time to answer; body language cannot be seen; can be biased
Internet marketing research Questionnaires downloaded or completed online or via e-mail	Can be used for qualitative/quantitative data gathering. Quick and easy to administer	Who is the respondent? Who is in the sample? Is it representative?
Focus groups Small group brought together for detailed discussion on a specific topic	Can be used for in-depth research with immediate reaction and feedback. Relatively cheap and easy to set up	May attract the same group of people who give answers they think the researcher wants. Is it objective?
Panels Do not meet together and there may be many hundreds of people involved. They use online forms with set questions.	Online can cover a wide geographical area and cover a variety of topics	Panel members need to be rotated to prevent set answers being given
Field trials and piloting Testing a product before going live	Can prevent costly mistakes later, relatively cheap and convenient, can test a range of features, immediate reaction	Results can be biased if the area is not chosen carefully

Choice of method

The choice of method will be determined by many factors:

- *Accessibility* How easy or difficult is it for the researcher to contact the respondents? Focus groups, for example, are often brought together by a market research company, such as Ipsos MORI, on the basis of e.g. people's age, type of job, where they live or lifestyle. The internet and e-mails are increasingly popular for both UK and overseas research. Students generally use convenience or judgement sampling.

For sampling methods, see page 121.

- *Fitness for purpose* Will the chosen method achieve the objectives which have been set for the research, i.e. is it fit for the purpose for which it is intended? The sample should be unbiased and representative of the population which is being investigated. It should be objective and reflect only the views of the respondents. Are there enough respondents to allow the researcher to make valid conclusions?

- *Validity* Does the research do what it is supposed to? Would a different group of people give different answers, possibly leading to a different conclusion? Would the same group give the same answers if you tried again? Research is valid if it measures what it is supposed to.

- *Cost* This depends on whether the organisation is carrying out the research itself or bringing in (outsourcing) an outside specialist. A typical budget would depend on the size of the sample, the expected response, the number of people involved, the timescale and deadline, degree of accuracy and reliability, whether local, national or international, where quantitative or qualitative (this usually costs more). Generally the more complex and difficult the research the more expensive it will be, particularly if trained interviewers are needed.

- *Time and reliability* Could the research be repeated by someone else? Would it give the same results? If it can be replicated, then the results are said to be reliable. With a dynamic business environment, primary research must be used immediately or else it becomes out of date. This is particularly true of online surveys where companies are offering turnaround times of 48 hours from submission of questions to presentation of results. Generally greater accuracy, reliability and shorter deadlines only come at a higher price. In practice it is a matter of balancing the cost and effort involved against the rate of response. Higher response rates are usually more expensive to obtain.

assignment focus

Which of the methods of primary research in Table 3.5 would be most suitable for collecting:

a) qualitative information

b) quantitative information

c) information about competitors

d) information about consumer likes/dislikes

e) information about users of the product living in Poland?

Types of sampling

A sample survey is a way of collecting primary information from a small part of the total number of individuals or items that could be investigated. The total is normally referred to as the population or universe. For example, for a local council it is every resident, in a hairdressers, it is every client.

The sample that is chosen should be representative, i.e. typical of the whole population. It is a cross-section. The purpose of sampling is to find out and make estimates about the population which are based on the results of the sample. Ideally a sample should be as large as possible and/or practicable, because a bigger sample will give more accurate results about the population.

The benefits of sampling a population compared to investigating every item (a census) are that the costs are lower, inputting and analysis of the data is quicker, and greater flexibility and control are possible.

A comparison of sampling methods is given in Table 3.6.

Table 3.6 Comparison of sampling methods

Sampling method	Advantages	Disadvantages
Random Every item has an equal chance of being chosen	Rigorous; known chance of selection allows further analysis to be carried out; unbiased selection method	Expensive and time-consuming if respondents are geographically spread out; a complete accurate/up-to-date sampling frame needed
Systematic The first item is selected at random. Subsequent items are then selected systematically	Random method; easy to administer in street interviews; does not need a detailed sampling frame	Call back is necessary when interviewing households, i.e. cannot substitute the home next door
Stratified The population is first divided into segments or groups, people are then chosen to represent the population	Sample should be more representative of the target population	Full details of the target population need to be known to create strata
Multi-stage sampling Carried out in stages, e.g. centres, courses, students	A complete sampling frame is not required; the last stages at each level can be sampled randomly	It must be possible to identify stages at each level
Cluster A cluster, e.g. a postcode, is chosen at random and every person is included in the sample	Samples clusters rather than individuals; little travel involved; whole cluster can be surveyed quickly	Needs a large number of small clusters
Quota People are deliberately selected because of their specific characteristics	Quick, cheap and easy, low travel costs, no call back necessary	Subjective; based on researchers' opinions; non-random so less rigorous
Convenience The researcher chooses the most convenient or accessible people to survey	Cheap and easy to carry out because the researcher does not have to search/travel for respondents; useful 'qualitative' snapshot	Results can be unreliable as the choice of respondents depends on the researcher. May be biased and unrepresentative
Judgement People are chosen who meet the needs of the survey	As Convenience	As Convenience

assignment focus

A retailer has carried out a survey of customers each Monday morning for the last three weeks. The results of the sample do not reflect the sales of the shop for the whole week. Can you suggest what is wrong with the sample, and how it could be improved?

Sample survey

Accuracy

Perfect accuracy is almost impossible to achieve with a sample survey. There are several possible reasons for this:

- The sample size is too small so there is not enough data to make conclusions about the population.
- Questions could have been badly worded or are difficult to understand.
- The sampling frame (the total database of people or items, i.e. the statistical population) is out of date or has other errors, e.g. in the Register of Electors (a list showing those people eligible to vote in elections) people may have moved.
- The sample may be unrepresentative of the population.

In order to make the sample survey as accurate as possible and so achieve its objectives it needs to be properly planned. Table 3.7 shows the stages involved in carrying out a survey.

Table 3.7 Stages in carrying out survey

Stage	
Identify the issues for investigation	This is the research topic, make it narrow and specific. When you evaluate your research, work through each stage
Define and set objectives	Make them SMART. Is there a target population? What is the research problem/issue? The objectives will determine the questions that need to be asked.
Identifying information needs	What secondary data is available? Is it reliable? What primary data is needed. Fix your deadlines.
Decide method of collection of data	Will a questionnaire be needed? If so, then pilot or test it before you begin. Remember to include an 'others' option. When you evaluate, do not be afraid to criticise your choice.
Decide on sample size and method	How many people? Be truthful and realistic. No one believes 100! Give your reasons for selecting or rejecting a method.
Analysis and evaluation of data	What analysis is needed to reach a conclusion, e.g. averages, range of data. Is the sample too small to make realistic assumptions? Was it biased? Is it valid and reliable?
Presentation of results	A simple questionnaire with four or five answers per question will give good opportunities for graphical presentation, e.g. charts, graphs, diagrams. Write the report so that each objective is covered.
Conclusions and recommendations	Based on the original problem/issue, research and analysis, what decisions have been made? What happens next?
Re-evaluate marketing activities based on the research	Would you carry out the research the same way again? Would you make the same decisions? Does the marketing mix need to be changed? Is it the same target market?

Sources of bias

Bias refers to any influence which makes the results obtained from the sample differ significantly from the actual or true results for the population. Bias can occur because:

- the list of items from which the sample is selected is inaccurate or incomplete, e.g. on the electoral register people may have moved elsewhere
- the sample is unrepresentative, or untypical, e.g. items could be selected because they are convenient or easy to reach, such as always asking your friends or family, or always going to the local shop, when you are asked to find people to answer a questionnaire.

assignment focus

Why might these sample surveys be biased?

a) A survey intended to show the volume of traffic in your local area which is carried out between 8 a.m. and 9 a.m.

b) A survey intended to show the age of all shoppers at WH Smith carried out between 10 a.m. and 11.30 a.m.

c) A survey on the use of local entertainment facilities carried out between 9 p.m. and midnight on Friday night

d) An online survey of views about downloading music conducted by a music download site

Electronic data collection

Using the internet

For the majority of companies the internet is now the main method of collecting quantitative data. A 'hybrid ' approach using e.g. telephone interviewing (qualitative) and the internet (quantitative) is becoming popular, as are blogs and online focus groups (chat based and video based).

Traditional face-to-face focus groups are still the most important method of qualitative data collection.

Source: Research Industry Trends Report; www.mrweb.com

Pop-up questionnaires are becoming a regular feature of many internet sites. Do you block them?

The advantages for companies distributing online questionnaires are lower costs (no interviewers or mailing are needed), higher speed and the ability to survey a larger number of more willing people (because people have visited a website freely). Any company with a website should be able to survey its customers online. The disadvantages may be that the company doesn't really know about the people replying and customers may well become irritated with seeing a questionnaire every time they visit. Questionnaires must be simple and capable of self-completion.

> **remember**
> - Always name your sources – include the publication or website, table or reference number and date. This will help you and the reader to check the data. Keep a record of all sources.
> - Always use the most up-to-date information.
> - The press releases section of websites, i.e. what the company has told the press, can be useful.
> - Try to use more than one source, so you can verify data. When you investigate companies, check the alternative websites. Companies only publish what they want the reader to see.

Computer-assisted telephone interviewing (CATI)

The telephone interviewer uses a computer and a computer-designed questionnaire. The respondents' answers are directly keyed in using a code. The computer is programmed to carry out the analysis of the data automatically, and results are available almost immediately.

Analysing data

Data has no meaning; it needs to be analysed or processed before it becomes information. This is data: 7, 15, 16, 23, 35, 43; knowing that it is next week's winning lottery numbers is information. Converting data into information is important because it provides the foundation for all subsequent marketing decisions, e.g. identifying market segments and targeting, PESTLE and SWOT analysis (including secondary research), product portfolio analysis, etc.

What is the average? What is the range of data (the difference between the highest and lowest figures)? What is likely to happen next year? These and other questions can now be answered using software programs such as Microsoft Access, which can handle large databases, or Microsoft Excel, which is a spreadsheet program capable of statistical analysis.

 The Market Research Society (MRS) has a useful introduction to market research with a dictionary/glossary of terms and guidelines governing research.

Secondary research

Importance

Provided the researcher is aware of its limitations, secondary research has considerable advantages, as Table 3.8 shows

Table 3.8 Advantages and disadvantages of secondary research

Advantages	Disadvantages
It can be a useful and effective substitute for expensive primary research	It may not be fully relevant to the new users needs
Because data already exists it can be relatively cheap to search	It may be biased and unrepresentative of a range of opinions, look at a variety of sources
It can provide historical time series data for trend analysis	Data may not be available for a particular topic or problem
It can show the overall national or regional situation, e.g. 'how people travel to work' in *Social Trends* can be compared to a simple class survey	It can be expensive to log on/register with specialist agencies for in-depth reports, e.g. KeyNote
It can be a good starting point for research	It could be out of date

Sources of data and information

Every business now has almost instant access to a vast amount of data. Much of the general information is free, although more specialised sources can be expensive, especially for private subscribers. Always remember that anything free on the internet is available to everyone, including your competitors. Internet data is secondary and can be provided by anyone. Always ask the questions shown on page 117.

News reports

These websites are a simple way of keeping up to date with current business news stories. It is now so easy to keep up to date that your tutor will expect you to have current information.

Sources of news reports:

■ TV news websites, e.g. www.bbc.co.uk, www.news.sky.com, www.itn.co.uk

■ Newspaper websites, e.g. www.independent.co.uk, www.telegraph.co.uk, www.economist.com, www.guardian.co.uk

■ The press release, news release or media section of any organisation website

■ Text alerts (mobile phone) and e-mail alerts

Trade journals

Specialist trade journals and magazines are published for virtually every industry and sector of business. These will help you achieve a better grade in your assignments. Many sectors such as hairdressing have specialist **trade associations** which can have very useful websites, e.g. www.habia.org.uk.

Trade journals:

■ www.theretailbulletin.com (the complete retail news resource!)

■ www.thegrocer.co.uk for up-to-date news and archive on the retail groceries sector

■ www.marketingweek.co.uk

Market analyses from specialist agencies

A major key to your success will be your ability to find information quickly. Your centre and local libraries will be your most important resource. It is essential that you get to know them as quickly as possible.

You will find the market reports published by KeyNote (www.keynote.co.uk), Mintel (www.mintel.co.uk), Euromonitor (www.euromonitor.com) excellent resources for achieving higher grades. Try also Verdict Research (retail trends) and Reuter's Datamonitor.

Hard copies are available in reference libraries, executive summaries or chapter headings are available online. Thomson Datastream (www.datastream.com) and Dunn & Bradstreet (www.dnb.co.uk) are online company search sites. You will get better access if your centre is registered.

Target Group Index (TGI)

Target Group Index (TGI) surveys use socio-economic groups to target people for marketing purposes. Although many characteristics can be used to classify people, such as education, age, sex, number of people in the household, or income, occupation is most frequently used to indicate which social class people belong to.

Online sources

There are sites which cover every aspect of the course.

■ Newspaper sites, e.g. *The Times*, enable you to access a complete range of business information on many topics.

■ A wide range of information is provided by both national and international institutions, for example, the EU. The Advertising Standards Association (ASA) is always interesting, e.g. in September 2006 it announced that it had banned adverts for WKD on the grounds that they could tempt young people into drinking. The ASA site is a very useful portal for a range of sites.

■ Both the Broadcasters' Audience Research Board TV figures by channel and the Radio Joint Audience Research Limited Radio audiences by station can be used for market **segmentation** and advertising research.

■ Company websites and annual reports may also provide useful data.

■ *The Times* – www.timesonline.co.uk
■ Eurostat (the statistics office of the EU) – cc.europa.eu/eurostat
■ Advertising Standards Association – www.asa.org.uk
■ Advertising Association – www.adassoc.org.uk
■ Broadcasters' Audience Research Board – www.BARB.co.uk
■ Radio Joint Audience Research Ltd – www.RAJAR.co.uk

assignment focus

A local company is carrying out media research for a new advertising campaign. Check out the audience figures for your local commercial radio stations.

remember

When searching try putting the word(s) 'definition' or 'case study' after your search entry.

Government statistics

The UK government produces a wealth of information which can be used in many units of the BTEC National course. It is secondary data based on primary research. It is a valid and reliable source which provides excellent information on:

■ customer analysis, e.g. number of potential customers, their characteristics and regional distribution

■ competitor analysis, e.g. a business could compare its own sales with those of the total market to find out its market share

■ market environment/PESTLE analysis, e.g. retail sales, employment, inflation, living standards. It is particularly good for regional data.

Government statistics:

■ On the Office for National Statistics (ONS) website, www.statistics.gov.uk, the 'Browse by theme' facility and 'Neighbourhood' statistics are very useful.

■ You will also find these central and local government sites useful:
  ▪ Department of Trade and Industry – www.dti.gov.uk
  ▪ Business Link – www.businesslink.gov.uk
  ▪ UK government – www.direct.gov.uk
  ▪ your local borough council – www.[name of borough].gov.uk
  ▪ Companies House – www.companies-house.gov.uk

■ Your local Chamber of Commerce may also be useful.

■ Hard copies of *Social Trends* (lifestyle issues, e.g. how we live, work and relax) and *Family Expenditure Survey* (how we spend our money), *Monthly Digest of Statistics*, *Annual Abstract of Statistics* (major economic trends), *Economic & Labour Market Review* (from Jan 2007), *Regional Trends* (compares economic activity in the UK regions) and *General Household Survey* are available in your local library; selected extracts are available online, e.g. from the ONS website.

■ KeyNote and Mintel reports provide similar information.

case study 3.5

Secondary research: stay at your desk!

Joseph and Oliver intend opening a new designer wear clothes shop in your local high street. They know that you are currently studying marketing and ask for your advice. Their questions are listed in the activity below.

They have asked you to write a short report based on the secondary research you carry out advising them on whether or not they should go ahead. They would appreciate some maps or charts.

activity

1 The questions:

   a) Who are their competitors?

   b) What are the current trends in clothing retailing?

   c) What is the age structure of the population?

   d) Who are likely to be their customers and will there be enough of them?

   e) What should they be aware of when using your data? What are your sources?

   f) Should they go ahead?

2 Now write your report.

assignment focus

1 With other members of your group, work together to create a database of websites that you have all used. Put in the exact address, which will allow you to connect directly with the site. Use a table similar to Table 3.9. You could add other columns such as the units where each website could be used. Include a 'star' system to rate their usefulness/ reliability.

Table 3.9 Database of websites used to gather information

Web address	Ease of use	Details of free information	Usefulness of information
www.statistics.gov.uk			

2 a) Give three advantages and three disadvantages of using secondary data.

   b) Why should a business look at secondary sources before starting primary research?

   c) Give three advantages of using primary research.

How marketing information is used by organisations

assignment focus

To achieve this outcome you need to complete two tasks:

■ For P3, you must describe how marketing research information is used by one of your organisations to understand the behaviour of customers, competitors and market environment. See pages 127–31.

■ For P4, you must apply two analytical techniques to a selected product in your organisation. Look at pages 131–40.

Using marketing research

Marketing information is used to inform decision-making and reduce risk. The more information an organisation has, the more likely it is that the decision will be successful. Marketing information aids decision-making; it does not make decisions, experience and good judgement are still essential.

Marketing research can be used by organisations to inform its decisions in six key areas:

- to achieve business objectives
- to understand customers' preferences
- to understand customers' lifestyles and aspirations
- to find out about competitors' activities
- to understand the market environment
- to find out about decision-making units (DMUs).

Business objectives

Here are two possible business objectives:

- *Open a new store* Because so much depends on the success of a new store, its location needs careful research before any decision is made. Initial secondary research into the population structure could be supported by competitor analysis and the relevant ACORN profile.
- *Target a specific group* Transport for London (TFL) engaged a market research consultancy, Dragon, to investigate potential segments which could be targeted/ encouraged to use public transport such as 'younger well off males' with a healthy lifestyle.

Customers' preferences

The chocolate bar, Yorkie, was developed after intensive research with customers. Bromley Council engaged Ipsos Mori to run focus groups to find out how local residents can become more involved in council affairs. Innocent Smoothies for Kids were developed after intensive primary research with consumers and their parents! All aspects of the 7Ps of the marketing mix should be determined by customers' preferences.

Lifestyles and aspirations

Knowledge about how customers' lifestyles and aspirations are changing will help the organisation develop new products, spot new market segments or target its advertising, e.g. Do you buy or read NME (New Musical Express)? Here are some facts about NME readers: they bought an average of 39 CD albums in the last year, 15 tracks downloaded in last month, 18 albums burned to computer/MP3 player.

Source: NME reader Profile; www.ipcadvertising.com

How could this information be used in the music industry?

assignment focus

Describe how marketing research is or could be used by your organisation to understand the behaviour of its consumers. You should include the lifestyle and aspiration classifications on pages 129–31.

Competitors' activities

The main reason for a business researching competitors' marketing is to develop and market its own brands more successfully. It will need to find out:

- who the competitors are by using trade directories, trade associations, website searches, local business telephone directories
- whether competitors have similar products and what their prices are
- how well they perform – most businesses check this by pretending to be customers or by observing their activities

- how they will react to a new competitor, e.g. will they cut prices or offer discounts. Following the launch of Yorkie by Rowntree Mackintosh (now Nestlé), Cadbury reacted by redesigning and relaunching their Cadbury's Dairy Milk range in a new chunky form

- how they produce, sell and distribute their products

- what their customers think, this can be done informally or by asking for references (take care, they will only say good things about the company)

- their strengths and weaknesses so that it can develop its own strategy and possibly use them as a benchmark.

The answers to these and other questions about competitors can help a new business to gain a foothold in its chosen market and keep an existing business ahead of the competition. The term 'competitive advantage' can be used to describe those factors which are unique to the organisation and give it an edge over its rivals. Any of the 7Ps can be used. Examples could be superior products or designs, exceptional service, 24-hour delivery, pioneering technology, etc. A business can achieve a competitive advantage by finding out precisely what their customers want and meeting their needs better than anyone else.

assignment focus

Describe how marketing research is or could be used by your organisation to understand the behaviour of its competitors, e.g. has it changed any of the 7Ps?

The market environment

Changes in the PESTLE environment are continuous. Being able to understand and predict these changes needs effective research to make the right decisions. Here are some examples of how selected food businesses have responded to changes in the environment for their products

- This is why Innocent Smoothies for Kids were created: 'We thought it was about time that kids got their own Smoothies, so we found some smart kids, asked them and their parents some questions. 100% fruit, no added sugar concentrates, preservatives and all that other junk' (*Source*: Innocent website). (See page 375.)

- The labelling on a packet of Walkers Crisps has been improved to give more nutritional information including guideline daily amounts (GDAs) of fat, salt, etc. for adults. In 2006 Walkers had to recall some packs because they may have included metal filings.

- Healthy eating is moving from the simple low calorie/low fat approach towards 'functional' foods with more specific health benefits, e.g. spreads and yoghurts that lower cholesterol, which is a major cause of heart disease. (*Source*: Mintel, *Healthy Eating*, August 2006).

- Polish food shops have opened, e.g. in Llanelli and Swansea to cater for the influx of Polish immigrants following the enlargement of the EU (*Source*: www.bbc.co.uk/ news/wales). A shop in Hither Green Lane in London specialises in English, African and Polish food.

assignment focus

Using appropriate market research reports, plus your own primary observations, describe the responses your organisation has made to changes in its environment, e.g. entering new markets, developing new products, changing its marketing mix.

Decision-making units (DMUs)

Who makes the decisions in your home: your parents, yourself, your partner, a brother or sister, or another family member? Does it depend on the type of decision, such as what breakfast cereal to buy, where to go on holiday, your clothes, a family car? Perhaps it depends on the product or who has the money? Is price a factor?

A decision-making unit (DMU) may be a formal or informal group. In an organisation, this could be the purchasing department, managers or owners. At home, a group of family members.

Within the group, people may take on different roles:

- *Influencers* either at home or in the organisation provide information, e.g. about alternative products or suppliers. They are aware of market conditions.

- *Users* are the people who will use the product, e.g. a new photo printer or photocopier, and may help the final decision by asking for particular features such as the ability to enlarge/reduce. They are interested in the product and may desire a particular make or model.

- *Deciders* make the decision, i.e. they authorise the purchase. It may be the managing director, it may be your parents, yourself or your children. These are the people who take action.

In an organisation there may be specialist buyers, but do they make the decision, particularly when senior managers have their own pet projects? To make a successful sales or marketing presentation, you must identify the key people. Keep your address book up to date, personnel move on.

Knowing which members of a group perform these roles is essential marketing information, both for B2B and B2C sales. It will determine how products are marketed and sold. Look at any promotional advertising. Who is it appealing to – the user, influencer or decider? Advertising for Disney World appears to be targeted at the users/influencers, i.e. children. In families, children can have a significant influence on decisions to purchase products such as take away meals, confectionary, toys and clothes. Pester power (children pester their parents) may be used by advertisers to generate extra sales.

If you have a part-time sales job, you will be familiar with the need to identify individuals in the family DMU to enable you to make a successful sale.

assignment focus

Analyse a recent promotional campaign run by your organisation by identifying the users, deciders and influencers.

Lifestyle and aspiration classifications

ACORN

ACORN stands for Alternative Classification of Residential Neighbourhoods. It is available through CACI Market Analysis Ltd. It classifies the UK population into five categories and 17 groups (see Table 3.10) and details 56 types. An entry would show demographics (housing, family type, education and work, ethnicity), financial background, personal interests, holidays, PC and internet usage (e.g. type 15 'Affluent Urban Professionals' use the internet twice as much as the UK average to book holidays online), media (low satellite TV usage but high readership of the *Financial Times*).

Table 3.10 The five ACORN categories

Category	% UK population	Group	% UK population
1 Wealthy achievers	26.6	A Wealthy executives B Affluent greys C Flourishing families	8.6 7.7 8.8
2 Urban prosperity	10.7	D Prosperous professionals E Educated urbanities F Aspiring singles	2.2 4.6 3.9
3 Comfortably off	26.6	G Starting out H Secure families I Settled suburbia J Prudent pensioners	2.5 15.5 6.1 2.6
4 Moderate means	14.5	K Asian communities L Post-industrial families M Blue-collar roots	1.6 4.8 8.0
5 Hard-pressed	22.4	N Stuggling families O Burdened families P High-rise hardship Q Inner city adversity U Unclassified	14.1 4.5 1.6 2.1

The classification was revised in 2006 to take account of social and economic changes over the last ten years (PESTLE), such as the population getting older and more educated, increased car ownership and commuting, more single parents, less unemployment.

A simple way to find out the lifestyle characteristics of your postcode area is to go to www.upmystreet.com. Put in your postcode and go to neighbourhood profiles.

Alternatively, if you want a full ACORN profile, where an entry would show demographics (age profile, socio-economic profile [level of education, type of employment], attitudes, housing, ownership of durables, leisure, food and drink), go to www.caci.co.uk. Registration is free, but you need to give details. (Get your centre to register.) The full ACORN brochure which lists all the types can be downloaded for free without registration.

Here is an example of the amount of detail you can find:

> 'ACORN Type 30: The striking thing about this ACORN Type's usage of packaged goods is the enormous amount of dog food purchased, more than double the average.'
>
> *Source*: www.caci.co.uk

How could a retailer use this information?

assignment focus

Log on to www.caci.co.uk and follow the onscreen instructions to find out how your post code is classified with ACORN (you need to register).

MOSAIC

The Mosaic system is similar to ACORN but is more detailed and uses more data. It can create a profile of a single postcode, i.e. approximately 15 households. It uses information such as census data, County Court judgements, credit ratings, etc. There are 12 main groups including stylish singles, mortgaged families, council flats. These are then further subdivided, e.g. low rise flats.

Cross Cultural Consumer Characterisation (4Cs)

Originally created by the Young & Rubicam agency (now owned by WPP) the Cross Cultural Consumer Characterisation, better known as the 4Cs, attempts to classify people from anywhere in the world into seven stereotypical groups or segments (Table 3.11). These groups are based on people's core motivational needs, such as survival, security or status, and is based on Abraham Maslow's hierarchy of needs.

For Maslow's hierarchy of needs, see page 295.

Table 3.11 The seven groups of the Cross Cultural Consumer Characterisation

Group	Core motivational needs
Explorer	Discovery
Aspirer	Status
Succeeder	Control
Reformer	Enlightenment
Mainstream	Security
Struggler	Escape
Resigned	Survival

The classification describes people's attitudes, motivation and possible purchases, including brands and own labels. For example, the majority of people are in the mainstream and tend to buy well-known family brands and special offers. Strugglers want to escape what they see as the tedium and boredom of everyday life. They tend to be major buyers of junk food.

The 4Cs website, www.4cs.yr.com, includes a very useful online questionnaire which you can complete to find out which category you are in.

---

assignment focus

1 Log on to the 4Cs website and complete the questionnaire. Compare your result with others in your class. Any comments?

2 How would this knowledge about you as a consumer help a business selling, e.g. sports clothing, mobile phones or music?

How these classifications are used to segment, target and position products

Marketers need postcode information to segment their market and target and position their products. Using the 4Cs, new innovative and expensive electronic goods are targeted at explorers and aspirers. Green products are aimed at reformers. Can you say why?

'Everyone' is no longer an acceptable answer to the question, 'Who are the customers?' Both ACORN and MOSAIC work using postcodes. Almost every business tries to get its customers postcodes by running competitions, creating loyalty and membership cards or giving free gifts (collect five tokens and send your name and address, etc.). This data can then be entered onto a database and form the basis for strategic marketing decisions.

Here is how the ACORN consumer profile can be used:

- increased understanding of customer behaviour and lifestyles
- better customer communication, with mail and advertising specifically targeted, particularly when combined with reader profiles (see pages 127 and 380)
- better knowledge of customer preferences in specific areas with better estimates of possible demand
- better knowledge of where new stores should be located and what products to sell.

Source: CACI

ACORN is used by banks, retailers (range of products), advertising agencies (to find the most effective media) and the public sector to identify the most deprived areas.

---

assignment focus

1 Describe how ACORN and the 4Cs could be used by your organisation to identify and understand the behaviour of its customers.

2 To complete P3, you need to bring together all the activities including your work from P2.

Analytical techniques

---

assignment focus

You must apply two analytical techniques to a selected product (good or service) offered by your organisation, e.g. you could carry out a SWOT analysis (page 131–2), a PESTLE analysis (page 132), a product life cycle analysis (page 135), etc.

For M2, you need to compare the analytical techniques used to support the marketing decisions for your selected business or product, e.g. extending the brand to prolong its life, introducing new products, reducing the product portfolio or diversifying. You could examine the advantages and disadvantages of each technique.

SWOT analysis

SWOT analysis is also known as situational analysis. SWOT stands for Strengths, Weaknesses, Opportunities and Threats. It is a technique used in business planning for comparing or matching an organisation's internal strengths and weaknesses with the opportunities and threats found in the external environment. This can help to identify both threats to survival and potential for growth.

Strengths and weaknesses are internal factors which a business can control:

■ A strength is a specific asset, skill or competence found within the organisation which would help it achieve its objectives. Factors critical for success include the product that will be sold, the financial, human and physical resources available to the business and the systems that exist for managing these. What does the business do best?

■ A weakness is a specific feature found within the organisation which could prevent it achieving its objectives. Perhaps the product is not able to compete because costs are too high, perhaps management is inexperienced or the business is unable to respond to change. Where could the business improve?

It must respond to external factors, opportunities and threats:

■ An opportunity is any specific feature in the organisation's external environment (PESTLE factors) that would help it to achieve its objectives. Are there any trends that could be exploited?

■ A threat is any specific feature in the organisation's external environment (PESTLE factors) which would prevent it from achieving its objectives. What could stop the organisation?

The SWOT analysis shown in Table 3.12 has been constructed following marketing research carried out for a local leisure centre, also see page 381.

Table 3.12 SWOT analysis for a leisure centre

Strengths	Weaknesses
Good opening hours – 6 a.m. until 10 p.m.	Will not take a cheque for less than £15
Good location close to college and shopping centre	Changing rooms can be dirty particularly after school groups
Full range of internal facilities	Pool can sometimes be too cold
Staff friendly, knowledgeable and helpful	Gym facilities get very crowded at peak times and can be poorly attended off peak
Wide range of classes for all ages swimming, aerobics, aqua aerobics, karate, dance, etc.	
Opportunities	**Threats**
	New Health and Safety legislation requires both male and female staff to be always on duty at the poolside
	A private sector leisure centre has applied for planning permission

Whenever possible each item should be weighted to show its relative importance. This can be done using a simple scale, e.g.

■ Strengths: 1 = least important to 5 = very important
■ Weaknesses: 1 = least significant to 5 = very significant.

assignment focus

1 Carry out a SWOT analysis for your organisation or product. Check KeyNote or Mintel first. To make the SWOT more effective, you should include the weighting shown above. How could your SWOT analysis be used?

2 Can you identify any opportunities for the leisure centre in Table 3.12?

PESTLE analysis

Opportunities and threats from the external environment can be classified under the headings political, economic, social, technological, legal, environmental, often referred to as PESTLE analysis.

 Link   Read Unit 1, pages 43–50 where PESTLE analysis is described in detail.

How can an organisation use a PESTLE analysis?

The PESTLE analyses in Table 3.13 are based on selected extracts from marketing research for the mobile phone sector and the healthy eating market.

Table 3.13 PESTLE analyses for the mobile phone sector and the healthy eating market

Factor	Healthy eating market	Mobile phones
Political	Government campaign against child obesity. UK ranked fourth worst in the world	Health concerns and protecting young children
Economic	Rising incomes and consumer expenditure. Market worth £5b	91.2% of the population has a mobile phone
Social	Healthy eating is a major lifestyle shift for particular socio-economic groups	New social lifestyles, texting and social arrangements 'on the hoof'. Is anything a surprise?
Technological	New methods of food technology have enabled manufacturers to create functional foods	Mobile phone technology at the cutting edge of innovation
Legal	The Food Standards Agency (FSA) has introduced new food labelling legislation	Ofcom, the telecommunications regulator, bringing in new legislation
Environmental	Concern over the excessive use of pesticides and high residues in foods	Environmental protests over the siting of phone masts. Are they dangerous?

Whenever possible each item should be weighted to show its relative importance either as a negative or unfavourable factor which could adversely affect the organisation or as a positive/favourable factor which could help. As with a SWOT analysis, this can be done using a simple scale, e.g.

- Favourable: 1 = least important to 5 = very important
- Unfavourable:1 = least significant to 5 = very significant.

assignment focus

1   Carry out a PESTLE analysis for your organisation or product. (Check KeyNote first.) Use a weighting system to show how important each factor is. How could it be used to help your organisation?

2   How could the PESTLE analyses in Table 3.13 be used?

Competitor and competitive

Competitors are rivals. Being competitive means wanting to win. Are you competitive? Knowing who the competitors are and how they will react, e.g. to a price change or a new promotion, and what are their strengths and weaknesses, will help an organisation to develop a strategy to gain a competitive advantage.

Michael Porter the pioneer of 'competitive strategy' suggested three areas in which a business can gain (and lose) competitive advantage. This may be through:

- *cost leadership* – reducing prices without reducing quality, e.g. by producing large volumes or becoming more efficient

- *differentiation* – creating a **unique selling point (USP)**, based on marketing research, so that a product is seen as distinct from its competitors. Tactics for differentiation include branding to give identity ('the futures bright'), quality ('lean burn engine'), customer service ('free 24 hour customer hotline'), economy ('we check our prices daily')

- *focus* – identifying a particular market segment or buyer group rather than attempting to compete in the market as a whole. A business is therefore able to reduce costs and maximise impact by targeting or focusing on a selected market, e.g. 18–30 holidays.

The power of consumers

Consumers have more power when there are many suppliers, i.e. they have more choice and can 'shop around'. What does the organisation have to do persuade them to stay loyal?

Competition or rivalry will be more intense when:

■ products are very similar, which is why every business tries to distinguish itself from its competitors by having a USP

■ customers have a large choice and can switch easily from one business to another. 'We always remember you have a choice' was once used by British Airways as its advertising slogan. In May 2007 BA set aside £350m for alleged price fixing

■ there are many competitors in a slow growing/saturated market. These businesses need to create a competitive advantage in order to survive.

---

assignment focus

How has your organisation attempted to achieve a competitive advantage?

Developments in the local, national and global marketplace

Walk along your local high street and everywhere you will see evidence of the changing marketing mix of almost every type of organisation. Traditional department stores are closing to be replaced by TK Max and Primark. Banks become pubs. New computer stores appear and disappear. Twenty-four-hour retailing is increasing. Groceries can be ordered online, e.g. at Tesco 'You shop, we drop' or Waitrose, Ocado (a top 10 internet cool brand, see page 147). Tesco also has a catalogue promoting its non-food range and is selling software.

Shopping habits and buyer behaviour are changing, e.g.

■ A once weekly shop has now become the norm for most families as the ownership of cars and freezers has spread and parking becomes more difficult and expensive in town centres.

■ New superstores and retail parks are built on the edge of towns, e.g. Tesco shoppers must have cars, and once the store has their details they can be targeted to buy Tesco car insurance.

■ Internet shopping and booking are increasing.

These and other factors are all forcing small shops to close. Is this a trend that should be welcomed? Do you support your local corner shop or post office?

---

assignment focus

Here is a good excuse for going shopping. You should monitor developments for your product in your local high street and online over a period of three months. Use a table like Table 3.14 to record your findings. Say why you think these developments are occurring. Are you pleased or disappointed?

Table 3.14 Monitoring development of a product

Elements of the marketing mix	Developments in the high street/local marketplace, with reasons
Place	
Product	
Price	
Promotion	
People	
Processes	
Physical evidence	

Analytical techniques

How to analyse local, national and international developments

Situation analysis is vital to the survival of any organisation operating in any marketplace. Every sector needs to be investigated separately. Knowing where to find good information on these developments and using it effectively is the key to marketing and business success. The first step in finding information about current developments in any industry or sector is to look at market research reports such as those published by KeyNote, Mintel or Euromonitor (useful for an international perspective).

See www.keynote.co.uk, www.mintel.com, www.euromonitor.com.

How these reports can be used

Here are four examples which show current developments, concerns or issues in the marketplace for their respective industries:

- *Bridalwear* (KeyNote) – growth of online bridal gowns, imports from China

- *Cosmetics and fragrances* (KeyNote) – animal testing, safety of ingredients, counterfeiting and blackmail. A Mintel Report headlined 'Copycat cosmetics cash in on premium brands' found that counterfeiting or parallel brands severely damaged the brand name and could damage the consumer. Edible cosmetics such as Jessica Simpson's Dessert range of 'lickable and kissable' shampoos and moisturisers are a reaction against synthetic beauty products. (Euromonitor).

- *Designer clothing* (Mintel) – changing consumer attitudes, e.g. they are becoming more choosy and fashion conscious; population is changing 'there are more over 55s acting 10 years younger' whilst 'kids are fashion aware younger', 'men are more likely to buy designer clothing' (see activity page 126)

- *Global brands* – Allegedly it is the ambition of every teenager worldwide to wear Levi jeans, eat at McDonalds and drink a Coca-Cola. The McDonalds restaurant in Pushkin Square in Moscow is its busiest in the world. These are global or worldwide brands. Are consumer tastes and preferences becoming the same?

assignment focus

You need to investigate local, national and international developments affecting the marketplace for your company/product. Carry out an initial investigation of the KeyNote, Mintel and Euromonitor websites. Follow this with a visit to your local reference library to check out the hard copies and also look at the relevant SWOT and PESTLE analysis. Carry out a similar search of the news websites.

The product lifecycle

The product lifecycle is a description of the life of a product, from its launch to its final withdrawal from the market. Using this analysis will help a business decide whether it is worth investing further in a product.

The product lifecycle model (Figure 3.6) shows how products may go through four possible stages during their life in the marketplace.

Figure 3.6 is a model; no scales are shown on the axes because both the time and the amount of sales will vary with different products in different markets. Fashion clothing, for example, may be launched in Paris or London in the spring, achieve maximum sales in the summer and be in decline by the end of summer sales. This is a three-month cycle. Chart music may be launched, peak and decline in three weeks (the music chart launched in 2007 which includes downloads has radically changed this).

Stage 1 – Introduction and launch

Introducing a new product into the market can be a very expensive process. During this stage, costs are likely to be very high and profits will tend to be low. In large businesses, new products may be supported by 'cash cows' elsewhere in the product portfolio (see the Boston matrix on page 137). This stage can be particularly difficult for a new business without an existing distribution network. Internet sales and direct selling have been particularly useful in enabling some businesses to overcome this entry barrier. Thorough marketing research

Figure 3.6 Product lifecycle

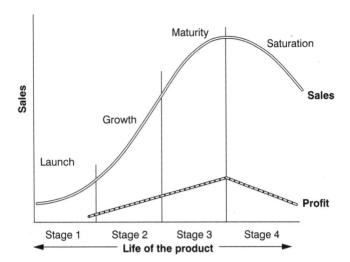

is needed before an organisation introduces a new product. Nokia has created its business strategy around the continuous introduction of new products.

Stage 2 – Growth and development
During this phase the product should be establishing itself in the market, sales and profits should be increasing and the initial investment should be paid for. If there is still little competition, profits could be at their highest.

Stage 3 – Maturity and competition
This stage is characterised by an increase in competition, which could lead to increased costs because of extra advertising and promotion. Sales of the product are still increasing but at an ever decreasing rate. Price cuts, special offers and discounts may be given in an attempt to stimulate sales. Some electronic companies only enter large mature markets where goods can be mass produced.

assignment focus

Is it worthwhile introducing a new product into a mature or saturated market, e.g. opening a restaurant in a high street where ten already exist?

Stage 4 – Saturation and decline
This stage is typified by declining sales and low profits. Even price cuts and advertising are not enough to tempt the consumer into purchasing. The business may attempt to relaunch the product in a different form (see the Marie Claire case study, page 118). Fragrances and aftershaves such as Charlie, Brut and Old Spice from the 1970s have made a revival according to research carried out by Superdrug.

To survive and grow, a business would want a **product mix**/portfolio with products at different stages of the product lifecycle, e.g. some reaching maturity with new products being launched. Does this apply to your organisation?

Assessment of the lifecycle approach
■ It is a record of past events. It cannot predict the future.

■ The stages shown here are only a general guide. Not every product will go through all the stages.

■ Some products may never get beyond the launch phase and fail immediately. For every successful product in the market, there are probably twice as many that have failed. Kit Kat, Liquorice Allsorts (100 years old), Bird's Custard (150 years old) and Lyle's Golden Syrup (considered Britain's oldest brand) are long-term survivors.

assignment focus

Draw a product lifecycle diagram for your organization. Identify at what stage some of its products are. Show these on the diagram.

Product portfolios

The product portfolio or product mix is the range of products sold or produced by a business. Car companies make sports and family cars, schools and colleges offer different courses. International companies such as Nestle or Proctor & Gamble have a wide product portfolio as a result of diversifying into a range of sectors. Although:

> 'there is an ongoing trend for manufacturers to slim down their brand portfolios to focus on a handful of megabrands rather than a wide range of individual products, e.g. Unilever's Dove campaign for Real Beauty.'

Source: euromonitor.com

Boston matrix

A useful technique for assessing the product portfolio/mix is the Boston matrix or Boston box (Figure 3.7), originally developed by the Boston Consulting Group, a leading firm of management consultants in the USA.

The horizontal (x axis) shows the market share compared to the largest competitor. The vertical (y axis) shows the growth in the market.

Figure 3.7 The Boston matrix

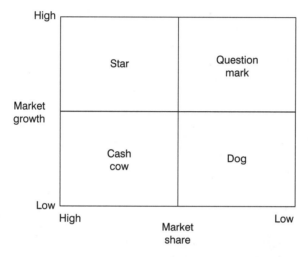

Stars

These are products with a high market share in a rapidly growing sector. Unless the product has achieved this position through heavy discounting it should be generating high profits. To remain a star in a competitive environment the product will continue to need heavy marketing expenditure.

Cash cows

Cash cows have a high market share in a slow growing, probably mature market. This should mean that the product has lower unit costs than its competitors. It should be generating a high level of profits which could be used to finance 'problem children/question marks'. Marketing expenditure would still be required to generate continued public awareness and repeat purchases.

Question mark or problem child

This product has a low market share in rapidly growing market. The organisation has to decide either to support it with heavy marketing, which could be difficult if it is not generating funds elsewhere, or withdraw the product from the market.

Dog

This product has a low market share in markets where there is little or no growth. A dog is probably reaching the end of its product lifecycle (the decline stage). Unless the market is expected to grow and the product can be rejuvenated or extended, there is little point in continuing to market and support the product. It should be dropped from the product portfolio.

*assignment
focus*

Put some of your organisation's products into a Boston matrix, explaining the reasons for your decisions.

Assessment of the Boston matrix

■ It can be difficult to define 'high' and 'low'. These can vary between industries, e.g. in markets where four or five large businesses dominate, e.g. UK supermarkets, 9 per cent may be considered a low market share, whereas in industries with a large number of competitors this would be considered very high.

■ The model assumes that an organisation is actively seeking either a bigger market share and/or rapid growth. What does the model say about businesses that want to stay small?

■ By focusing on market share and growth it ignores other factors which may be important, such as profit margins.

■ It can over-simplify the situation.

Here are some questions that can be answered using the Boston matrix model:

■ Do we have new products being developed to ensure the future growth of the business?

■ Do we have a balanced portfolio group of products?

■ How long is the present situation expected to continue? What information can we get from the lifecycle analysis?

*assignment
focus*

For M2, compare the analytical techniques used to support the marketing decisions for your business or product, e.g. what are the benefits and drawbacks of the techniques? Have products been introduced or withdrawn? Have any of the 7Ps been changed? why?

Diversification

Ansoff Matrix

H.S. Ansoff first described this in 1957 in the *Harvard Business Review*.

The horizontal axis shows existing and new products. The vertical axis shows new and existing markets. The matrix gives four possible strategies for increasing sales.

Figure 3.8 The Ansoff matrix

	Existing	Products	New
Existing Markets	**Penetration** Existing products in existing markets Low risk strategy	**Product expansion** New products in existing markets Medium risk strategy	
New	**Market expansion** Existing products in new markets Medium risk strategy	**Diversification** New products in new markets Highest risk strategy	

Link

See page 140 which looks at techniques used to increase demand for products.

Initially there are two key choices in the Ansoff matrix: to exploit the product or the market. To make a decision, a business would have to assess or screen the new markets and new products, then compare the potential benefits with those expected from continuing with existing markets and products.

Market-based strategies

■ *Penetration* This involves expanding market share in existing markets by using existing products. This can be done by:

- persuading current customers to buy more of the product; e.g. three for the price of two, an offer regularly adopted by Boots. These offers have the effect of improving the perceived value for money and frequently deter customers from switching to other brands

- converting non-users into customers, which could be achieved by extending and developing the image of the product, e.g. turkey is now sold as a year round meat, not just for a Christmas meal

- poaching customers from competitors; success will depend on their current loyalty to the competitor.

See the ladder of customer loyalty and the conversion model on page 148.

assignment focus

Boots increased its Christmas stock from 1,800 to 2,300 lines with an upmarket exclusive range including more gifts for men. 'We are the destination store for hurried Christmas shoppers,' said Boots.

Source: The Independent

Which Ansoff strategy is Boots following?

- *Market expansion* This involves using existing products to increase market share by moving into new markets. For example:

  - catering for different market segments, e.g. the J.D. Wetherspoon pub chain targets coffee drinkers in the morning. Woolworths has introduced a catalogue. Many stores have online shopping. BskyB is creating a database similar to Tesco to target the 14m homes that do not have Sky. Which Ansoff strategy is it taking?

  - entering new geographical markets, e.g. Tesco has entered Japan and Poland. IKEA and Body Shop have used franchises to increase sales.

Product-based strategies
- *Product expansion* This means either adapting the product so that it sells to more people in existing markets or introducing more products to existing customers. For example:

  - finding new uses for the product, e.g. turkey is now sold as mince, burgers, smoked and unsmoked in 'wafer thin' slices

  - changing pack sizes, e.g. one person Cuppa soups, mini-size cans of Pepsi and Coke which appeal especially to small children and are ideal for packed lunches

  - adapting existing products, such as introducing microwave varieties, e.g. micro chips in addition to oven chips

  - Tesco which made £1.1b profit in the first six months of 2006 has started selling computer software in its stores.

- *Diversification* New products for sale in new markets. This is the most expensive and risky strategy and requires intensive screening of both the ideas for new products and the opportunities in new markets. Many businesses find that the costs of development and entry are too high and prefer instead to diversify by acquiring the markets and products of another business, e.g. Morrisons take over of Safeway.

assignment focus

Use the Ansoff matrix to describe the marketing strategy for your product. What should happen next? Is your business following market- or product-based policies? Has it or should it diversify? Why?

Implications of social and technological change

How could organisations be affected? How could we as individuals and consumers be affected? How could society be affected by social and technological changes? The speed of technological change can be seen as a threat, global warming now dominates every headline with new weather records being set every year. If you are an optimist then you will see the biggest threats as the biggest opportunities, e.g. sales of solar panels, drought resistant plants and water butts for saving water. The world population is expected to double in your lifetime; currently over 50 per cent of the world population is living in poverty. What pressure will this place on our ability to provide the basic necessities of food, shelter and clothing? Predicting social and technological change is notoriously difficult. There will be winners, those who have made the right decisions – and losers.

Having already identified – in the PESTLE analysis – the social and technological changes taking place that affect the organisation and the sector in which it operates, the implications for marketing strategy and activities must now be considered.

Here are two trends which could influence marketing strategy.

■ *People are living longer* The proportion of older people in the population is increasing, not only in the UK but throughout Europe. SAGA is a company which specialises in providing services for the over-50s. What are the implications of this ageing population for marketing strategy? Most mainstream advertising and promotion seems to stop at the age of 35!

Look at the age distribution in your area on the Up My Street website.

■ *Health and lifestyle* Low salt, low sugar, high protein, healthy options, probiotics, the layered clothing look, new lifestyle magazines, health and fitness clubs, IPod mobile clubbing. Tastes and fashions are continually changing.

assignment focus

Identify the social and technological changes affecting your businesses. Give examples of how their marketing mix is responding to these changes. Could they do better?

How marketing techniques are used to increase demand for products (goods and services)

assignment focus

For P5, you must describe the marketing techniques used by your organisation to increase the demand for its products or services (pages 140–51). For M3, you must explain and analyse why these techniques have been used. For D2, you must suggest improvements, e.g. changing different aspects of the marketing mix.

Market segmentation and targeting

The majority of organisations try to increase demand for their products and services, whether they deal directly with consumers (B2C) or with other businesses (B2B). Charities attempt to increase donations or participation by volunteers. The government tries to increase the take up of its benefits; not everyone entitled to benefits actually claims. Manufacturers try to get retailers and wholesalers to stock more of their products.

Businesses which try to maximise profits will only attempt to increase demand if the expected revenue is greater than the cost of achieving it. Some businesses, however, are wary of increasing demand because of possible problems with supply or because they wish to stay small and exclusive

Importance

Businesses try to split whole markets into smaller units or segments so they can focus their marketing and other activities to target specific groups of people or other businesses. This should make it easier to achieve their business objectives. A market segment is a group of homogeneous or similar customers characterised, e.g. by age, income, geographical area (local, regional or national) and/or lifestyle. This may be demonstrated by the products people buy, their leisure activities, music or holidays.

The Co-op decision to invest £100m

Zoe Morgan is the first group-wide marketing director of the Co-op, 'We're seen as old-fashioned, low-profile, trusted but not professional enough.'

The Co-op is getting a £100m face lift, with new packaging, refurbished stores, new staff training, standardised fascias, unified shop fronts for the Co-op bank, supermarket and pharmacy chains, 'the only difference will be the colour'.

'This is a rebranding exercise, but the changes are not just cosmetic,' said Martin Beaumont, chief executive of the Co-op. 'We have a historic commitment to social causes, healthy eating, environmental care and other ideas that are back in fashion today'.

The famous Co-op 'divi' – an annual cash award to customers who sign-up for 'membership' (the loyalty scheme) will be extended to all Co-op products and services. This will bring the Co-op into line with its rivals.

Figure 3.9 Making an investment decision

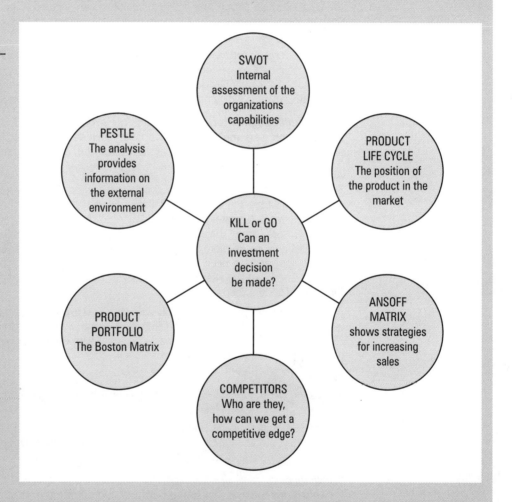

1 Evaluate the marketing techniques shown in Figure 3.9 and the research and analysis it may have used to arrive at a decision to spend £100m.

2 Carry out a similar investigation for your organisation, adding your own original recommendations for improvement.

Bases for segmentation

When creating a marketing strategy, it is important to target customer segments as closely as possible to match their needs. Very few companies have 'everybody' as their customers. Smaller businesses will usually try to find a niche (gap) in the market so that they can specialise in one or two segments in order to survive, e.g. West Country farm honey delivered direct to your home.

Segmentation, whether B2C or B2B, is important because it helps the business to create specific advertising and promotion, target direct mail shots, identify new marketing opportunities, customise the marketing mix and create a marketing strategy to match the needs of the segment.

Markets can be split into segments in many ways; the particular choice would depend on the type/size of company, the characteristics of the market and the type of product.

Here are some typical ways of segmenting a market in order to increase demand.

Geographic segmentation – where people live

With **geographic segmentation**, the market is split into homogeneous (similar) groups on the basis of where people live or where customers are located, e.g. countries, regions, urban or rural areas, postcodes (ACORN). An organisation can then target its marketing mix at a particular segment.

Proctor & Gamble, for example, produces and markets different flavours of Pringles in different countries to suit local tastes; salt and vinegar flavour allegedly does not appear in Belgium. Coca-Cola has deliberately pursued a policy of marketing the identical product worldwide, whereas Nokia has differentiated its mobile phones for different markets.

Demographic segmentation – who buys the product

Demographic segmentation uses variables such as age, gender, family type, income, size and type of household, occupation, ethnicity, religion, etc. to segment the market.

Age

This is particularly important. Many companies now produce and sell to specific age groups, e.g. children's toys and clothing manufacturers use gender and a 1–2 year age range such as 'suitable for 3–5-year-olds'. Older drivers get cheaper car insurance, students pay more! 'We only insure careful drivers,' says one company, which presumably means that other companies only insure more risky drivers with consequently higher rates! Any complaints? Many companies have been accused of deliberately targeting their promotion at young children. Check out the alternative websites for burgers, soft drinks, sweets, etc. Do you think they should be allowed to do this?

A Mintel report on pocket money says the UK's 7–10-year-olds get almost £417 million, while the 11–14-year-olds receive some £1.1 billion a year. 'Children are important consumers through their own purchases together with the pester power they exert over their parents,' says Jenny Catlin of Mintel.

Gender

Many products are gender-specific, such as health and beauty products or magazines. Can you think of other examples?

Some £30m is spent each year advertising female fragrances and £15m on male fragrances (Source: Keynote Cosmetics and Fragrances). A Mintel report 'Designerwear in the UK' shows that men are more likely to buy designer clothes than women.

Family type

Very often promotion is aimed at groups that represent the main stages in the family lifecycle. Here is an example of groupings from the Advertising Standards Association survey, 'The public's perception of advertising in today's society':

- teenagers 16, 17, 18 still at school
- singles aged 20–24
- parents with at least one child aged 5–14
- empty nesters aged 50–60 (children have left home!)
- the greys aged 65–75; with an ageing population 'grey' spending is highly significant.

A group particularly sought after are the 'DINKies' or 'dual income no kids'. Why do you think this is the case?

Psychographic and lifestyle segmentation

Lifestyle is our way of life as reflected in our activities, interests, habits, opinions and friends. We show it in what we wear, our mobile phone, the music we like. Our lifestyle affects our spending. The analysis works on the assumption that people in a particular segment will have similar attitudes, desires, expectations and buying habits. Marketing campaigns can then be created which specifically appeal to their motivations.

Some major market research companies have useful websites, e.g.

- AC Nielsen: www.acnielsen.co.uk
- Young & Rubicam: www.youngandrubicam.co.uk (good for their 4Cs)
- Taylor Nelson Sofres: www.tnsofres.com

Behavioural segmentation

This type of segmentation splits the market according to consumer behaviour, such as attitudes towards the product, buying habits, loyalty, usage and, most importantly, the benefits gained. This process examines the benefits that people hope to gain when they buy a product, e.g. do you buy toothpaste to clean your teeth or to give you 'fresh breath confidence'? (Colgate used this to create the advertising slogan 'The ring of confidence'.) What benefits do you expect from a product such as a mobile phone? Research shows fashion to be important. Does it matter to you?

Usage refers to the status of the user, e.g. first-time user, non-user, heavy user, occasional user, ex-user, etc. Identifying the category of user enables the business to create a marketing mix to target each segment. Essentially the objective is to convert non-users into users, and occasional users into regular users.

A particular group targeted by mortgage companies are first-time buyers. This group is trying to buy a home for the first time, i.e. they are trying to get on the housing ladder. They have particular financial needs and banks compete for their business by offering low initial rates of interest. They are important to the bank because on average over a 25-year mortgage people pay back three times as much as they originally borrow.

How can segmentation analysis be used?

Once the segments have been identified through research, an organisation will be able to:

- create a marketing mix for each group based on the research that it has done. Each of the 7Ps will be given a different emphasis. Promotion will play a bigger or smaller part in every marketing campaign
- analyse and profile customers, e.g. by age, income, consumer spending, financial status, etc., which can help with decisions about where to open new stores. WH Smith used this to identify new retail sites. Has it worked?
- develop sales and market potential forecasts
- stock those goods that potential customers have identified.

Conditions needed for successful segmentation

To work effectively, the target segment must be:

- *measurable* – it must be possible to measure the size of the segment using both the number of potential buyers and the amount they are willing to spend. This will enable the organisation to plan its provision
- *substantial* – the market segment must be large enough (by value or volume) to make targeting the market worthwhile. Ideally there should be prospects for growth
- *accessible* – e.g. there may be barriers to entering the market such as a lack of the necessary start-up finance; perhaps a high level of advertising is needed to change customer perceptions; entry may be controlled by law, e.g. mobile phone companies had to bid for a limited number of digital licences. The costs of entry must be less than the expected returns
- *unique* – each segment should have specific needs and characteristics, e.g. in one ACORN classification 75 per cent more people than average shop daily for their groceries yet they purchase fewer fresh foods than other groups. This uniqueness is important as it enables retailers to specially create a marketing mix directly targeted at that segment. Supermarkets would avoid this area because people do not buy in large quantities. However, corner shops do well.

case study 3.7   Music segmentation

Have you been to the music festivals at Reading or Glastonbury, or to the Proms? The music industry is an excellent example of how segmentation works in marketing, recording, performance, distribution, broadcasting, etc. The music industry is segmented in many ways: age, price, downloads, singles and albums market, genre, and so on. Genre can be further split up into blues, rock, classical, indy, rap, dance, etc. Dance can be divided further, e.g. house, garage and trance, and these can be subdivided further into 'niche' or smaller segment markets (see Table 3.15):

Table 3.15 Segmentation within the music market

House	Garage	Trance
Hard	UK	Please complete
Euphoric	2 Step	
Progressive	US	
Latino		

The top recording companies have separate labels, which concentrate on different genre.

activity

1   Why does the industry break down its market into smaller and smaller segments? What does it hope to achieve?

2   Which segment are you in? Would anyone know? Do you spend money on CDs and albums (see NME reader profile, page 127). Do you download? Could you segment the other music genre? Could you complete Table 3.16?

3   What type of segmentation does or could your organisation use? Give reasons.

---

i   Check out www.ttbblues.com and www.tundejegede.com

Design of the marketing mix to satisfy needs of the target group

Where do you buy your clothes? Perhaps M&S, Primark, Top Shop, Next, Gap, River Island, or none of these. Each outlet will specialise, i.e. target a particular group of customers, perhaps based on:

■ price – the average price tag at Primark is £4, or

■ age – M&S is perceived as aiming for an older age range, although it has made a major effort to appeal to a wider younger market.

Some products deliberately aim at creating an exclusive image with a corresponding marketing mix of high prices and a limited one-off range of fashions.

Greater individualisation afforded by e-business and e-marketing

E-business and e-marketing via the computer enable the seller to build up a comprehensive customer database for both consumers and businesses. This can be used to customise or personalise communication with individuals, which has always been the dream of every marketer. A customer database is a large store of information about each customer, sometimes called a data warehouse. It can be searched or mined for nuggets of personal information. Online communication, welcome pages and e-mails can then be personalised by name, recent purchase, past purchases, home address (nearest outlet) or people like you. This is one-to-one or personalised segmentation where every individual can be treated as a market segment.

case study

3.8

Posh and Specks Diner

The new restaurant recently opened in a local high street had beautiful laid out tables with silver cutlery; each place setting had three knives and forks, three glasses, etc. It did quite well in the late evenings but had very little trade for the rest of the day.

The problem was that the new owners did not appreciate that the restaurant market was segmented by time of day. Morning customers thought it looked too posh and expensive, lunch time customers wanted a quick snack without table service. Demand was much lower than expected. Their first objective was to increase demand.

The new owners decided to segment the market into three and target each group with a different marketing mix

- the morning and afternoon trade
- lunchtime trade
- evening trade.

activity

1   How would you change the marketing mix to target each market segment?
2   Do you think the conditions for successful segmentation have been met? See page 143.
3   What might be the results of this targeting?
4   What are the characteristics of target segments for your organisation?

case study

3.9

Woolworths Group plc: catalogue wars on the high street

In autumn 2006 following a £66m loss, Woolworths Group brought out a catalogue with over 6,000 items. This would rival Argos and Tesco, which had also brought out a catalogue. The group had identified a gap in the market for a children's toys to clothing range.

'Our Unique Selling point with the new catalogue will be that there are three ways to order for in-store free collection or home delivery,' said the chief executive.

activity

1   Check out the financial results for the Woolworths group for the last financial year. Has the new segmentation strategy worked?
2   Does, or should, your organisation have a catalogue? Who would it be intended for?

Database marketing can be a very efficient way of retaining customers and building a long-term relationship through customer retention management (CRM), which focuses on maintaining customer loyalty. It is equally effective in both B2C and B2B relationships.

See page 118.

How greater individualisation will work
It will:

- relate directly to individuals on a one-to-one basis. Organisations will profit from the total information held on customers through better efficiency and effectiveness
- monitor customers' buying habits

- improve customer service, e.g. by one-to-one target niche marketing – this involves knowing exactly what customers buy
- carry out customer profiling by age, postcode, etc.
- track customer preferences and buying patterns to improve customer and brand loyalty. The loyalty card now used by many consumers has enabled stores such as Tesco to build a database on 10 million people showing their shopping habits, frequency of purchase, use of special offers, price sensitivity (e.g. do people switch brands when the price goes up?), impact of adverts, own brand versus brand use, etc. BT knows your name and who your friends and family are, because you tell them!
- enable organisations to develop new products and services geared to the satisfaction of individual needs
- enable organisations to develop future marketing strategy by identifying trends.

Branding

Brand names are an essential part of the way a product is promoted and packaged. Every company will want the consumer to ask for its product by name. The purpose of branding is to differentiate products that are basically similar. It is an important feature of the non-price competition which exists in competitive markets. Each business is trying to establish its own name and reputation, e.g. companies making trainers such as Nike and Adidas concentrate entirely on using the brand name to sell the products. They will reinforce this by putting their names and logos on carrier bags, T-shirts and sweat shirts which the consumer then pays for. The major buyers of brand name fashion products are 16–25-year-olds. Which brand of trainers do you buy? What image do you have of the brand?

There are about 185,000 charities in England and Wales. The top 8 per cent get about 93 per cent of the income. Each of these needs a clear and distinctive brand and message.

From the manufacturers' and retailers' viewpoint, branding is important because it helps to create consumer loyalty and increase sales. If consumers can be persuaded to only buy, for example, High Track trainers, the company has effectively achieved a fully committed buyer and can use this to adjust its prices accordingly. What can you say generally about the price of branded and non-branded goods?

Branding importance in influencing buyer behaviour

Branding is used to give a product a specific identity or personality. It may consist of the name, logo, colours, pack design, slogan and music.

Branding helps to increase demand because

- it is an easy way of recognising or identifying products. Companies spend millions creating an image and reputation for their brand
- consumers tend to become attached and stay loyal to a brand. They are often reluctant to change
- people associate with the personality of the brand which is a reflection of the individual's lifestyle
- successful brands are known and trusted e.g. Persil. Cancer Research, the National Trust, Oxfam and the British Red Cross are considered the most valuable charity brands
- brands become the focus for advertising.

Brand building and positioning

There are six key elements to building a brand:

- *Name* This should be simple and easy to remember, e.g. Dell (computers), Sony (monitor), HP (printer). At the time of writing all three brands are in trouble. Dell had to recall four million laptops because the batteries exploded. Sony were delaying the launch of Play Station 3 (originally scheduled for March 2006) in Europe until March 2007. Ken Kutargi, Head of Sony's Global Computer Entertainment business, blamed the problems on mass producing the Blu-Ray disc drives (www.bbc.co.uk/news). How have Microsoft's Xbox 360 and the new Nintendo Wii console performed commercially? HP had problems in the boardroom after private detectives had been caught bugging the telephones of some of the directors.
- *Visual/graphic image* The logo and design should be simple and memorable, e.g. the Coca-Cola swirl, McDonalds golden arches, Adidas stripes.

- *Image and identity* These give the brand a personality. It should reflect the mission and vision of the organisation. What image do you have of your centre as a brand, does it deliver what it promises. The best way to create a long-term brand is to build a reputation based on quality and reliability. As Ronseal says, 'It does what it says on the tin' or 'You can trust Persil'.

- *Use the brand consistently* across all communication with stakeholders both online and offline.

- *Understand and gain the respect of the target consumers* by matching their needs as closely as possible.

- *Reinforce brand images*, e.g. mention the name as often as possible without it becoming irritating. Use a celebrity, but take care – not everyone will like them. Use well-known sounds, music or slogans/catchphrases, e.g. 'Hello Moto', sell the benefits – hair and beauty products seem to be highly scientific!

assignment focus

The brand can be the most important asset an organisation possesses.

1　What image do you have of Dell, Sony and HP?

2　Analyse (SWOT) your brand. What are its strengths? What does it say about the organisation? What are its qualities? Are the brand values clear? Do your friends and family feel the same about the brand as you do? Why are their differences?

'Cool brands'

Coolbrands are defined by brand consultancy Superbrands as:

> 'brands that have become extremely desirable among many style leaders and influencers. They have a magic about them signifying that users have an exceptional sense of taste and style.'

Source: www.thelondonpaper.com

The overall no. 1 was Aston Martin.

assignment focus

1　Which brands do you and others in your class consider cool? What qualities do these brands possess?

2　Are you investigating a cool brand?

Product positioning

The position of a product refers to a specific quality or characteristic of the product which is most often stressed in its advertising and is best known to the customer – its 'personality'. In other words, what immediately springs to the customer's mind when the product is mentioned. What image do you have of your brand?

Every business will attempt to achieve a unique position for itself, its products or its services, in the heart and mind of the consumer. It will do this by emphasising one or other of its main features – its unique selling point (USP).

As you read the following list of features, try to think of some product examples.

Some key features used to position a product:

- *Quality* – 'The best a man can get', Gillette sales of £267m in 2006

- *Who makes it* – 'We are the largest/smallest company so we try harder'

- *Price* – 'Never knowingly undersold', John Lewis

- *Physical characteristics* – biggest, smallest, sweetest Actimel is the no. 1 Pro Biotic

- *Who uses it* – e.g. a famous personality. What about Brad Pitt or Antonio Banderas for sunglasses?

- *Benefits from use* – 'cures headaches fast'

- *The location* – '1000 car parking spaces on the doorstep'

- *Value for money* – 'Fairy Liquid lasts up to 50% longer and lasts no time on shelves' (trade advertisement, *The Grocer*)
- *Image* – e.g. smart, attractive, friendly staff
- *Service* – 'The smiles are free' or 'We answer every call' available 24/7

Brand extension

This refers to methods that are used to extend or prolong the life of a product. Two techniques are particularly important. The first is repositioning which means changing the customers' view or image of the qualities and characteristics of the product. Here are some examples of repositioning:

- Lucozade – a sporty image and sweets
- Magners Cider – a premium drink with 538 per cent growth in sales in 2006 (*The Grocer*)
- Pot Noodle – the fuel of Britain (mined in Wales)
- Chocolate – organic and Fair Trade (Green & Blacks is no. 7 on the top 20 list of cool brands).

A classic technique for increasing demand is to extend the brand by introducing:

- new pack sizes and new flavours, e.g. Walkers Crisps now come in 14 flavours and three pack sizes: 34.5g 'single serve', 50g 'a big eat experience' and 175g 'for those sharing occasions'
- new ingredients and colours, e.g. new Fairy naturals with eucalyptus and anti-bacterial action. Is it still a washing-up liquid?
- other products with the same logo. How many products can you think of with the Nike logo on? Why does it do this?
- essentially the same product, which is differentiated (changed) to cater for different customer segments, e.g. shampoo for normal, dry, greasy or flyaway hair. The market is segmented by type of hair.

case study 3.10   Ralph Lauren

Ralph Lauren established the Polo brand in 1967 when he marketed wide extravagant ties. The original brand name became so successful that Polo, Ralph Lauren or RL can now be found not only on clothing (baby, boys and girls, men and women) but also on household items, gifts, perfumes and fragrances and sunglasses.

activity

1   Which branding strategy is Ralph Lauren following? Give reasons.
2   Which branding strategy or strategies are used in your organisation to increase the demand for its products or services?
3   Why are these strategies used? Could they be improved?

Branding and loyalty

The ladder of customer loyalty

Loyalty is important to every organisation from its customers, suppliers, providers of charity income, etc. It is the aim of every organisation to persuade people (consumers and businesses) to move up the loyalty ladder (Figure 3.10) and become permanent advocates, spreading the word about how good the business is.

Harley Davidson owners proclaim their loyalty to the brand by tattooing themselves with the logo. Do you demonstrate your loyalty to a brand? Do you wear anything with a logo on, i.e. are you an advocate?

The objective of every marketing activity must be to convert every prospect into an advocate. However, unless the organisation continues to build relationships with its customers, they could go elsewhere.

Figure 3.10 The loyalty ladder

Advocate
Totally loyal enthusiastic customers, also known as 'apostles'. They tell others how good the business is, i.e. word of mouth advertising, or show the brand name

Supporter
Enthusiastic but still passive

Client
The first-time buyer has been converted into a repeat customer, regularly purchases and is not drawn to your competitors

Customer
Prospects who become buyers. Businesses should make this process as easy as possible and encourage them to continue as customers – the process element of the 7Ps

Prospect
Also known as 'leads', these are people who have shown a positive interest in the business, but have not yet bought anything

Suspect
The business suspects this group might buy

The conversion model

This model looks at users and non-users of a brand. It examines consumer loyalty or how much people are committed to the brand, i.e. the likelihood of a repurchase by users or a first-time purchase by non-users.

Check out www.conversionmodel.com.

assignment focus

We are familiar with the concept of loyalty through the use of loyalty cards – stores try to keep customers returning by offering bonus points, vouchers, discounts, etc. Loyalty can be classified using degree of loyalty (0–100 per cent) or the likelihood of customers switching brands. Much advertising is designed to create brand loyalty, particularly when the product is cheap and competition is fierce.

1   How would you categorise yourself as a user of these products: Coca-Cola, Colgate toothpaste, Nokia mobile phones, Walker's crisps, your local leisure centre? Could you be tempted away from your favourite brand? What would it take?

3   Do you always buy the same brand or buy from the same shop?

4   Do you occasionally buy other brands?

5   Do you always switch brands, i.e. show little or no loyalty?

6   Would a loyalty card make you change your habits?

7   How loyal are you to the brands you are investigating?

Relationship marketing

Concept

The focus of marketing is changing. Traditionally the emphasis has been on short-term transactional marketing when just making the sale was considered success. There was little attempt at retaining customers or expecting repeat business. Customers were there to part with their money or 'open their wallets'. However, the costs of attracting new customers are 10 to 20 times higher, e.g. in publicity, special introductory offers, etc. than the cost of keeping or retaining customers. It makes good marketing and financial sense to build and manage relationships with customers with the goal 'once a customer always a customer'. The customer becomes the total focus of an organisations' mission and vision. Customer focus and customer orientation have become core values (see the Tesco website).

Relationship marketing differs from traditional marketing because it:

- emphasises the need to create long-term customer loyalty by retaining customers and so getting repeat business, rather than treating each sale as a one-off
- works on a longer time-scale, building and developing relationships with all of the organisation's stakeholders, including suppliers and the local community
- focuses on the customer rather than the product
- uses customer segments as opposed to market segments
- stresses service and quality performance ahead of product performance
- aims for long-term rather than short-term profits
- considers existing customers as important as attracting new customers. Nationwide uses this as a key feature in its advertising.

assignment focus

1 What evidence is there to suggest that your organisation practises relationship marketing?

2 Finance companies offer 0 per cent on balance transfers for three months. Mobile phone companies give 500 free texts to new customers. These offers are intended to tempt people away from their present supplier. Do you swap from one company to another to get the special offers?

Customer lifetime value (LTV)

LTV measures the value of customer loyalty. With the high costs of attracting new customers, there is every incentive for an organisation to keep its customers loyal and get them to spend more. Banks, for example, market heavily to attract new graduates. A LTV calculation shows why – stay with the bank for 40 years at £25,000 a year = £1m worth of business over your working life! Customers are now segmented by the value they give a business. For many businesses, 80 per cent of the profits come from 20 per cent of the customers. A family with two teenagers spends an average £150 per week in the supermarket. Are you average?

Planning, control and evaluation processes

When any marketing decision is made, e.g. launching a new product or entering a new market segment, it will need to be carefully and effectively planned and controlled.

The marketing planning process model can be split into a number of stages (Figure 3.11).

Figure 3.11 The planning, control and evaluation processes

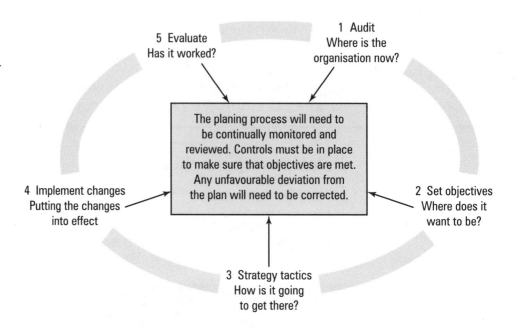

5 Evaluate
Has it worked?

1 Audit
Where is the organisation now?

The planing process will need to be continually monitored and reviewed. Controls must be in place to make sure that objectives are met. Any unfavourable deviation from the plan will need to be corrected.

4 Implement changes
Putting the changes into effect

2 Set objectives
Where does it want to be?

3 Strategy tactics
How is it going to get there?

Step 1: Audit

This is an analysis of the current position of the organization. It attempts to answer the question, where is the organisation now? What are its strengths and weaknesses? These will determine how it can take advantage of opportunities and avoid/minimise threats (SWOT). The marketing environment will need to be scanned and monitored (PESTLE analysis). This should be a continuous process as the external environment is always changing and cannot be controlled. Who are the customers? Are their needs being met? How effective is the marketing mix? What are the strengths and weaknesses of the competitors? Can the organisation achieve a competitive advantage? The purpose of the audit is to find out if there is a gap in the market and where improvements need to be made.

Step 2: Objectives

Objectives can be set for all levels in the organisation, e.g. corporate/strategic, (generally longer term and applicable across the whole organisation); tactical (where the focus would be on marketing).

For control and evaluation to be effective, these objectives need to be SMART. This will enable the organisation to compare, e.g. the performance/outcome of a decision such as trying to increase the demand for toothpaste in the 16–20 age group with the original quantified target. This process of monitoring and control will need to be continuous and corrective mechanisms need to be in place to make sure that objectives are being achieved.

For SMART, see Unit 1, page 24.

Step 3: Strategy and tactics

The strategy, or policy, follows from the audit, e.g. to enter new market segments, develop new products or reposition/relaunch existing products. Tactics are the methods and techniques that will be used to put the strategy into action. They set out how the objectives are going to be achieved, e.g. with a new marketing mix or rebranding exercise.

Step 4: Implement changes

This means putting the policies into action. Who will be responsible? What resources are needed? What are the timescales? Can it be done in-house or will it be outsourced? A full detailed plan is needed, perhaps based on a **Gantt chart** which shows the sequence of activities needed to complete the proposed change. Contingency arrangements need to be in place to cope with any unexpected events.

See Unit 9, page 277 for an example of a Gantt chart.

Step 5: Evaluate

Has the change worked? Did the change project achieve the objectives, e.g. have sales increased? Does the product have a new image? Are customers more loyal or are they switching to other brands?

assignment focus

1. You need to explain the marketing techniques which have been used by your organisation and analyse why these techniques might have been chosen, e.g. segmenting and targeting a specific group. How and why has it done this? Were the conditions for effective segmentation present?

2. How and why has it rebranded or positioned the product?

3. Has it used its website or database to create greater individualisation in its communications? Why?

4. Does it use the concept of relationship marketing? Should it? Why?

For D1 and D2, you have to make recommendations for improvements in the marketing of your products. What objectives do you have? How will you evaluate/measure your success?

Effective people, communication and information

This unit covers:

- The importance of employing suitable people
- How to communicate using appropriate methods
- Different types of information and how it can be processed
- Presenting information effectively

This unit gives you the opportunity to consider your own skills by looking at the qualities organisations look for in their employees: personal skills, communication skills and employability skills. It examines different types of information and how to communicate information effectively using appropriate methods.

The unit is linked to the specialist unit, Unit 16, Human resources management.

<table>
<tr>
<td>grading criteria</td>
<td>To achieve a Pass grade the evidence must show that the learner is able to:</td>
<td>To achieve a Merit grade the evidence must also show that the learner is able to:</td>
<td>To achieve a Distinction grade the evidence must also show that the learner is able to:</td>
</tr>
<tr>
<td></td>
<td>P1
describe the recruitment and retention process and documentation in a selected organisation</td>
<td>M1
analyse the employability, communication and personal skills required when applying for a specific job role</td>
<td>D1
evaluate the advantages to an organisation of employing suitable people to communicate information</td>
</tr>
<tr>
<td></td>
<td>P2
describe the main employability, personal and communication skills required when applying for a specific job role</td>
<td>M2
justify the reasons for using different methods for communicating business information</td>
<td>D1
assess the suitability of the three methods used for communicating and presenting information</td>
</tr>
<tr>
<td></td>
<td>P3
outline electronic and non electronic methods for communicating business information using examples for different types of audience</td>
<td>M3
demonstrate and justify the use of suitable presentation methods using information from three sources</td>
<td></td>
</tr>
<tr>
<td></td>
<td>P4
select information from three sources and manipulate it adhering to legislation for business purposes</td>
<td></td>
<td></td>
</tr>
<tr>
<td></td>
<td>P5
present the information from P4 using three different methods</td>
<td></td>
<td></td>
</tr>
</table>

The importance of employing suitable people

Human resources

People, or human resources (HR), are the most important resource in any organisation and, not surprisingly, there is a direct connection between the quality of the workforce and commercial success. To succeed, an organisation needs staff who are committed to meeting its aims and objectives, equipped to do so by adequate training and motivated by management to achieve their potential.

It is the job of human resources management to recruit, develop and retain quality staff. Within a small business, with perhaps one or two employees, responsibility for human resources will lie with the owner or with the partners. A small company may have one person whose job it is to look after issues relating to staff. Large organisations with many employees will have a whole section devoted to personnel.

Whatever the size or type of organisation, the aim is to make the most effective use of people. Toyota put it this way: 'The key to maximising quality and productivity lies in tapping the innate judgement and creativity of employees in the workplace.' All managers at all levels have the responsibility.

Recruitment and retention of staff

Recruitment

The first stage in the recruitment process is to identify the vacancy. New staff may be needed because:

- staff may have left the organisation because e.g. they have been dismissed, resigned or have been promoted
- the business is growing.

Once managers agree a vacancy exists and authorisation is given to fill it, then the job must be described and then advertised.

See Job description on pages 157 and 164.

Recruitment advertising

The organisation may already have the right people with the right skills to do the job, particularly if the training and development programme has been effective. In this case, it may appoint internally, which may of course leave a vacancy elsewhere in the business.

It is often necessary to make an external appointment and some organisations are compelled to advertise all posts externally. The process must be carefully planned to deliver the appropriate applicants. **Advertising**, together with the administrative costs of despatching application forms, checking returned forms, shortlisting and interviewing, can be time-consuming and expensive. This is why many organisations now recruit online. Most high street stores, for example, have online websites advertising for staff at all levels (from part-time sales staff to senior management), both locally and nationally.

- Look at www.virgin.com to see the qualities it wants in its staff.
- There are specific recruitment advertising websites, e.g. www.monster.co.uk.

Advertising in a range of media such as local and national newspapers, specialist magazines and online will help the organisation attract the right sort of people for the job by appealing to different market segments and simultaneously meeting their equal opportunities obligations. If it cannot recruit successfully, the whole process will have to be repeated, whilst the business carries on with a staff shortage.

Figure 4.1 shows an advert for administrative assistants for MI5. Applicants are advised to apply online, where there is a permanent online application form. Figure 4.2 shows the same advert on the internet. MI5 is responsible for protecting the UK against threats to national security.

Figure 4.1 Advertisement for administrative assistants at MI5

Source: News Shopper, Bromley edition

ADMINISTRATIVE ASSISTANTSSSSSHHH...

FROM £16,250 ACCORDING TO EXPERIENCE + BENEFITS, CENTRAL LONDON

Work at MI5, and you'll find everything you do at your desk will be crucial to the nation's security. From combating espionage to countering terrorist threats, we rely on information being in the right place at the right time. That means we depend on our dedicated team of Administrative Assistants to keep things well ordered and organised.

It's a varied role. Posted in one of our departments ranging from finance or records management to working as part of an investigation team, the tasks you'll carry out – filing, maintaining databases, drafting documents, organising meetings – might make you think this position's just like any other administrative role. In a way it is. The difference is that you'll be helping us to protect national security.

You'll need discretion. personal integrity, reliability, excellent organisational skills and be a flexible and co-operative team worker. You'll also need four GSCEs including English (Grade A-C) or equivalent, or relevant work experience of which you can give good examples.

To be eligible to apply, you must be a British citizen and one of your parents must be a British citizen or have substantial ties to the UK. Candidates must normally have been resident in the UK for at least 9 out of the last 10 years; this is particularly important if you were born outside the UK.

For national security reasons, you will need to be 18 years old, or above to apply. Your application may take around six months to process. You must limit those you tell about your application to your partner and/or immediate family.

Please visit www.mi5careers.gov.uk to apply. The reference number is A013.

Closing date for requesting application forms: 6 november 2006.

Closing date for returning application forms: 8 November 2006.

A matter of national security

www.mi5careers.gov.uk
The Security Service is committed to reflecting both equal opportunities and the society we protect.

assignment focus

1   Look at Figures 4.1 and 4.2. Which method do you think would be most successful in attracting suitable applicants?

2   Begin your research for P1 and P2 by looking for jobs which are suitable for you.

3   What employability, personal and communication skills are needed? What competencies would an applicant need to possess? Are there any special conditions which an applicant must fulfill?

Link

For employability skills, see page 159, for personal skills, see page 160 and for communication skills, see page 161.

Figure 4.2 The jobs page from www.MI5careers. gov.uk

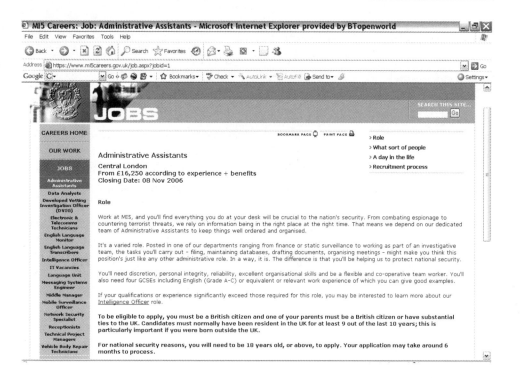

Staff retention

Some degree of labour movement into and out of an organisation is both useful and desirable because it brings in new staff with new ideas, skills and enthusiasm. On the other hand, too high a rate of movement can be expensive because of:

- recruitment, selection and training costs of new staff, e.g. it takes 18 months and costs £70,000 to train an engine driver

- efficiency costs caused by disruption – it may take some time before new staff can produce high quality work

- leaving costs – it may be necessary to make redundancy payments, pay notice periods or pay for holidays due.

The terms 'labour turnover' and 'staff turnover' are often used to describe the rate at which people leave an organisation and are replaced. They are calculated by comparing the number of people who leave with the average number of staff employed.

Suitably skilled staff

One major responsibility of HR is to make sure that there are always sufficient staff with the right skills to achieve the aims and objectives of the organisation, both in the short and long term. It will have to plan ahead and match its demand for labour with the available supply. This may involve employing a mix of full-time, part-time and temporary staff to meet its needs, e.g. extra part-time staff may be needed in a restaurant during the evenings and at weekends. Temporary staff may be employed in an office to cover annual leave. Retaining staff is important as new staff have to be trained.

Contracts of employment

There is a large body of law dealing with employment, e.g. equal opportunities legislation and minimum wage legislation. (What is the current minimum wage for under/over 18-year-olds?) Owners and managers must recruit legally, because breaking the law could result in severe penalties.

By law, an employee who works for eight hours or more a week must be given a **contract of employment** within two months of commencing employment (Trade Union Reform and Employment Rights Act 1993). This is drawn up by the employer and signed by the employee. It exists to give both parties a degree of protection, certainty and security and can be enforced by law.

case study 4.1 — Christmas staff

Additional staff are required during the run-up to Christmas to:

'provide advice and assistance to customers, shorten queues, open more tills, keep shelves and displays full, work in store stock rooms, and make sure that the stores are well maintained.'

Source: Game UK Sales Director

The recruitment agency Adecco estimated that it would cost retailers £150 million just to recruit temporary staff for the busy Christmas period. The Head of Adecco Retail said:

'Store and HR managers spend nearly 30 per cent of their time finding and managing suitable staff. The festive season is an increasingly strategic aspect of HR in the retail sector. The process can be one of a retailer's highest costs in terms of store management, time and resources.'

Source: www.theretailbulletin.co.uk

activity

1   How can suitable temporary or part time staff help an organisation achieve its objectives?
2   How can they be recruited?

All contracts must include the:

- name of the company and the employee
- job title
- date when employment began
- pay scale, hours of work, how payment will be made and at what intervals
- holiday entitlement
- terms relating to notification of sickness and sick pay, pension arrangements
- length of notice which an employee is entitled to receive and must give
- disciplinary rules, or where they may be found, appeals procedure and grievance procedure.

Other conditions which may be included are the need for medical examinations, working from different locations, the right to search employees, the need for confidentiality and the need to obey certain specific rules of the organisation. These could be set out in a separate staff handbook.

The above are called express terms, that is, they are openly agreed.

Personal or individual contracts

Many businesses have standard contracts setting out identical conditions and rates of pay for everyone in a particular job. However, personal contracts are sometimes offered to the senior managers of an organisation or people with specialist skills, e.g. you may have seen the term 'salary negotiable' in job advertisements.

Individual contracts are negotiated directly and privately with the individuals who are often asked not to reveal their salary to other staff. The key parts of a personal contract only apply to one employee.

They can include:

- a personal pay package
- personal bonus or commission rates
- special benefits such as improved car allowances and medical services.

Part-time workers may also be on limited personal contracts, but without the 'perks' or benefits offered to senior full-time staff.

Different types of employment contract are discussed in Unit 16, page 304.

The job description

Following an analysis of the job, a **job description** will be written which sets out: job title, grade (position on a pay scale), department, location, who the job holder is responsible to (manager's title), what the job holder is responsible for (e.g. staff, cash, equipment), job purpose and duties.

A person specification may be prepared which could include physical characteristics, qualifications, experience, aptitude and motivation. (Are you a self-starter, able to work on your own?)

assignment focus

Write a job description for a student on your course – you.

case study 4.2

'more reasons to work at Morrisons'

Figure 4.3 shows some extracts from the application for employment for Morrisons, the supermarket chain.

Figure 4.3 Extracts from an application for employment

1 Education

Dates (From/to)	Name and address of schools attended	Examinations taken (state level, dates and results)

2 Further education/qualifications

Dates (From/to)	Name and address of university, college, institution or employer	Examinations or courses taken, state dates and results

3 Positions of responsibility/other interests

Positions of responsibility (school, college or elsewhere)

Leisure interests

What, in particular appeals to you about working for Morrisons?

Which specific qualities do you possess that you believe make you a suitable candidate for a position at Morrisons?

Source: Morrisons

You are also required to:

- give your current or most recent employment details (work experience, etc. if a student)
- list your current responsibilities and reporting relationships
- give reasons for leaving/wishing to leave this employment.

In addition to the job details, there is also this question, 'If any time during the last five years is not fully accounted for in your employment record, please account for it here.'

activity

1   Make a copy of this form and complete all the sections.
2   Why do you think you are asked to account for any time you were not employed in the last five years?

assignment focus

1   You need to identify a particular job role in which you are interested.
2   You need to identify an organisation.
3   Write a covering letter for the application or check online.
4   Obtain the job description and fill in the application form for your chosen job. Complete the application form. With online application forms, you will need to keep scrolling to see what you have already written or download the form.

Identifying a job role

A useful place to start is the Connexions website: www.connexions-direct.com, which has a Jobs4U career database which explains the requirements for various 'job families', such as 'administration, business and office work', etc.

remember

Always make several copies of blank application forms before you begin to fill one in so you can practise before filling in the final version. When you are satisfied with a finished version, make a photocopy so you can refer to it at an interview.

Go to the Connexions website and find the Jobs4U database. Follow the link to 'marketing and advertising', which will give you this information:

'Most people in this sector are office based, but may have to travel, sometimes long distances, to visit clients and to attend exhibitions. This may mean working evenings and weekends at times and may involve staying away from home.

Having very good communication and presentation skills and creative ideas are important in this work. Candidates also need to be clear thinking, self-confident, flexible, with good negotiating and reporting skills.

Employers range from large companies and organisations to smaller businesses, advertising and public relations agencies dealing with different clients. Self-employment is usually possible. There are opportunities for part-time work.

Source: www.connexions-direct.com © Crown Copyright

Following another link to 'advertising media planner' will give you this information:

'An advertising media planner should:

- understand the role the media plays in advertising
- be good at teamwork
- have good communication skills
- be comfortable with numbers and statistics
- enjoy working with people
- have an interest in the media.'

Source: www.connexions-direct.com © Crown Copyright

Advertising media planners earn £15,000–£70,000.

Your centre or local Connexions will have various online questionnaires which will help you to identify a job role which interests you.

assignment focus

Explain the terms 'clear thinking', 'self-confident', 'flexible', 'good negotiating and reporting skills', 'good at teamwork', 'comfortable with numbers and statistics', in the bulleted list on page 158. Why do you think these skills are necessary?

Identifying an organisation

Do you want to work in the private sector, where making a profit is important, or perhaps a charity or the public sector? Would you prefer a large organisation where you might be 'a small fish in a big pond' or a small organisation, 'a big fish in a small pond'?

The graduates careers site, www.prospects.ac.uk, is helpful for P1 and in deciding on a university course!

Employability skills

Employability skills are general skills and abilities that can be transferred from one workplace to another. A good BTEC National qualification will help you get a job, go on to university or study for a professional qualification, e.g. in marketing or human resources (personnel). The range of units gives you the opportunity to find out which particular areas of business you would like to study further. Do you have a particular favourite? What qualifications are needed for the job you are investigating?

Experience of a similar role or similar industry

This would help new employees settle into a job more easily. They would make fewer mistakes and cause less wastage. They could quickly make a positive contribution to the achievement of an organisation's objectives.

Knowledge of products/services

This is vital in any customer-facing role. Many organisations use 'knowledgeable staff' as a key feature of their advertising and promotion. What would happen if staff were not able to give help or advice when asked?

The ability to meet personal and team/departmental targets

This requires good planning and organising skills, e.g. do you manage your time to achieve deadlines? Do you prioritise/organise tasks in order of their importance? Do you plan ahead? Can you do this as part of a team? Can you give examples of when you have used these skills?

Figure 4.4 Mock up of a job advert

We Want You

Do you have suitable qualifications; experience in similar role; knowledge of products/services; experience of specific industry?

Are you effective in meeting personal and team/departmental targets?

Do you have the ability to observe and raise professional standards of production/service delivery?

Ability to observe and raise professional standards

Many occupations and professional associations have codes of conduct which set out standards of professional behaviour, e.g. the Chartered Institute of Public Finance and Accountancy (CIPFA) code is based on five principles, namely integrity, objectivity, professional competence, confidentiality and professional behaviour. It applies to all CIPFA members.

For more information, visit www.cipfa.org.uk.

assignment focus

1 Explain the meaning of the five CIPFA principles. Why do you think such a code of conduct is needed?

2 What employability skills do you already possess or expect to possess by the end of your course? Do you have particular strengths or weaknesses? For M1, be prepared to give evidence of situations when you have used these skills.

3 How do your skills match the job role/job description you have chosen?

4 For D1, you need to evaluate how important it is for an organisation to recruit staff with good employability skills.

Personal skills

Patient

Patience is particularly important when dealing with difficult customers, complex tasks or routine tasks. It is closely linked with the ability to persevere – stick at a task until it is complete, without too much moaning or losing your temper.

Hardworking

This means performing the duties specified in the job description to the best of your ability. Employers appreciate staff who are hardworking, professional and take pride in their work.

Able to work as part of a team

Being able to work with colleagues, sharing ideas and workload to achieve team goals rather than personal goals, is now an essential skill. Team work is increasingly important in many workplaces where incentives/rewards are based on team rather than personal performance.

Interpersonal skills

This is our ability to relate to or work with other people. There will be many occasions, both during your education and at work when you will need good interpersonal skills to complete a difficult task. Active listening, positive communication and willing constructive participation are needed to get on well with people. When asked 'What is the most difficult part of your job', many managers say, 'Managing my staff'. However, they give the same answer to the question, 'What is the best part of your job?'

Co-operating with others

When liaising with managers and colleagues, always behave professionally and observe the formal boundaries. Being thought of as a good team player helps motivation and improves morale and is more likely to achieve your own objectives and those of the team.

Interviewing skills

Whether you are the interviewer or the interviewee, be fully prepared, listen, seek clarification when necessary and have a clear purpose. The content of an interview will depend on the context, e.g. recruitment, appraisal, promotion. The initial opening can be relaxed and inviting and simple open questions will achieve the best results. You may be interviewed as part of your evidence for M1.

For different types of questions, see Unit 3, page 117.

Negotiation

Negotiation is involved at all levels of the organisation, e.g. when trying to reach agreement over targets for sales and budgets. Team and one-to-one meetings are important because people can express opinions and reach an agreed conclusion. People are much more likely to work effectively if they are committed and feel they own the target achieved through good negotiation. Targets should always be SMART and where possible mutually acceptable. Do not be afraid to compromise.

Conflict

Some conflict can be constructive when it generates new ideas and clears the air. It can be destructive when it destroys relationships and breaks up a team. Learning how to resolve and manage conflict can be a powerful tool for handling difficult situations and bringing the best out of a team.

assignment focus

1   What personal skills do you already possess or expect to possess by the end of your course? Do you have particular strengths or weaknesses in your personal skills? For M1, be prepared to give evidence of situations when you have used these skills.

2   How do your skills match the job role/job description you have chosen?

3   For D1, you need to evaluate how important it is for an organisation to recruit staff with good personal skills.

Communication skills

Effective communication skills are the key to success in any occupation, both for the organisation (achieving objectives) and the employee (achieving personal ambitions).

Formal communication skills

Most business communication, whether written or verbal, is formal, i.e. it must follow certain rules or conventions. Formal written rules particularly apply to letters, e.g. the opening salutation, such as 'Dear Sir or Madam' and the closure 'Yours faithfully'. You would need to write formally when applying for a job.

Formal verbal skills are particularly important in meetings where there are specific rules about behaviour and the type of language used.

- In **formal communication**, it is important to use appropriate professional language.
- **Informal communication** skills are generally used between friends or colleagues.

Verbal skills

The way we use spoken words and phrases often determines whether or not communication is going to be successful, e.g. 'Thanks a lot' – is this a big thank you, or thanks for nothing, i.e. sarcastic? Do you talk too much or too little. Do you interrupt? Do you try to dominate a conversation? Do you take your turn? Do you use the same language with colleagues, managers, customers, friends and relatives?

Can you use formal and informal language, e.g. in meetings with colleagues or customers? Do you listen, contradict, agree, interrupt or take your turn? Do you take a positive constructive approach or are you negative and destructive? Do you change your use of language to meet the needs of your audience? Can you make/receive formal business telephone calls. Can people understand your messages on an answerphone? Can you deliver an effective presentation? Do you have any weaknesses which you need to improve?

Written communication skills

Can you spell? How good is your grammar and punctuation? Can you write formal reports and business letters? Can you write an effective conclusion or summary of your ideas?

Have you got a specific weakness, e.g. the use of 'their' (belonging to) and 'there' (place or position)? Mix these up on an application form or letter and you are very unlikely to get the job.

Listening skills

Are you a good listener? Knowing how to listen actively and respond constructively will be important to your success in the workplace. Employers want staff who can communicate with customers and clients by asking the right questions and listening to the replies.

Non-verbal communication skills

More commonly known as **body language**, **non-verbal communication** (NVC) refers to the way people communicate without the use of words. Good communicators know:

- how to use body language to project themselves
- how to interpret the NVC signals given out by others.

Here are some examples of body language: people deliberately shrug their shoulders, car drivers give V signs, football players often fake injury, some people twist their hair or fiddle with their ears.

Learning body language is the same as learning any language, it will enable you to understand and communicate much more easily with people.

Eye contact

Do you look at people directly? Do you look away when talking to your friends, work colleagues, teachers? How do these people look at you? There are many reasons why people do not look at each other, for example:

- they may be shy or insecure
- they may be telling lies, e.g. 'Sorry I'm late for work, but the bus broke down.'
- in some cultures it is considered rude to look directly at someone.

Body contact

Do you shake hands when you meet people? Do you greet people with a kiss on each cheek? Is your handshake wet and limp, which indicates a lack of interest in the meeting, or firm and positive? Do you touch people when you are talking? In Latin America this is considered a normal part of communication.

Facial expressiveness

When we smile, we use 15 facial muscles. The human face can change its expression more than any other creature's. We can show anger, pleasure, grief, happiness, sadness, disappointment, love or compassion. How do we use these expressions?

---

assignment focus

1 The group should divide into pairs. Person A, without using any words, should try to show these emotions – hatred, anger, fear, hope, love, joy, pleasure, disappointment. Person B must try and guess what emotion is being shown. Persons A and B should then swap roles.

2 Each pair should now try to agree on ten items they would take to an uninhabited desert island.

Head movements

Nodding the head usually indicates that a person agrees or says 'Yes'; shaking the head usually means 'No, I do not agree'. These movements do not mean the same in every country. Take great care in Bulgaria where these movements mean the opposite.

Gestures

These are movements of the head, hands or body which are made to express or emphasise an idea. For example, people:

- point their fingers when arguing
- shake their fists when annoyed
- shrug to say 'I don't know/care'.

Dress

The way people dress is an important signal about how they feel and behave. Their clothes are an extension of their personality. The confident person will wear bold and striking colours and patterns. The shy person will tend towards muted, neutral shades. By the same token, people judge us by how we are dressed. If you want to be taken seriously in business, you will wear a suit. Our appearance gives other people that important first impression. In business it is always best to dress the same way as other employees.

Posture

The way people stand or sit gives out different signals. For example, if someone sits forward in a chair, it generally means they are interested in the conversation. If they lean back and fiddle with their hands, this can be interpreted as 'I'm bored'.

Someone who stands up straight is assumed to be honest and positive, whereas a person who slouches and leans forward is thought to be the opposite. If a person stands close to you when talking, the impression is one of sincerity.

Social conventions

How people speak, behave or dress will differ between formal and informal situations. What are the social conventions at your centre, at work, in your home or when you visit elderly relatives?

Adapting communication techniques to audience requirements

Effective communication of information is always the responsibility of the sender who needs to choose the right words (whether the communication is written or verbal) and the best method of communication for the context/situation and content. They will also have to check whether the receiver has understood the communication and respond to any feedback.

See page 167 where we examine audience requirements.

Presentational skills

Presentational skills are very important at all levels in the organisation:

- strategically at board level, e.g. in meetings when making a case for extra resources, communicating with stakeholders or trying to get new business
- at the tactical level managers need to make speeches in front of an audience, their staff
- operationally, staff have to make presentations to customers, students have to make presentations to other students.

Besides positive body language, good personal and communication skills are needed to make an effective presentation. You will need to be confident and well prepared.

Ability to invite commitment to shared goals

Getting other people to agree to your suggestions or to operate effectively as part of a team requires persuasive language and the ability to motivate. Incentives or 'carrots' generally work better than penalties or 'sticks' – a little praise goes a long way. Do you have experience of managers, perhaps as part of a sports team or in a part-time job, who have the ability to inspire people into helping them achieve their goals?

assignment focus

You must produce a list of attributes (qualities or strengths) you already possess or expect to possess by the end of your course.

Complete a chart similar to Table 4.1. Break down each group of skills, e.g. under Communication skills: written, verbal, etc.

Table 4.1 My skills

	Specific skill	My evidence for this skill	Personal score, rate yourself on a scale of 1–5
Employability skills			
Personal skills			
Communication skills			

case study 4.3

Here today, gone tomorrow: Sample job description for a retail fashion buyer

Retail buyers purchase the merchandise that will be sold in their stores. The amount they buy depends on fashion, predicted sales and the available budget.

Choosing the right person will mean that the organisation may be 'able to maximise profits and provide a commercially viable range of merchandise at competitive prices'.

Over a year, here are some typical tasks:

- analysing fashion trends
- regularly reviewing performance indicators with sales
- managing plans for stock levels, reacting to change in demand and supply conditions
- meeting suppliers and negotiating terms of contract
- maintaining relationships with existing suppliers and sourcing new suppliers for future products
- liaising with other departments within the organisation to ensure projects are completed
- attending trade fairs, in the UK and abroad, to select and assemble a new collection of products
- participating in promotional activities
- writing reports and sales forecasts, and analysing sales figures
- liaising with shop personnel to ensure product/collection supply meets demand
- seeking merchandise feedback from customers
- training and mentoring junior staff.

In addition, buyers need to be excellent communicators, confident and have a flair for negotiation, influencing people and networking.

Pre-entry work experience will be advantageous. This could be a part-time retail job, an industrial placement or even work shadowing (observing an experienced member of staff).

activity

1 Obtain the application forms and job descriptions for your chosen posts. (You may need to download these from the organisation website.)

2 Use the job descriptions to draw up a list of requirements for the posts, e.g. what skills are needed, what abilities or competencies are needed.

---

remember

These are some useful 'power words' to use when applying for a job: arranged, completed, devised, identified, implemented, improved, managed, organised, performed, planned, prepared, produced, represented, researched.

Analysing the job description

Table 4.2 lists some examples of the skills that are needed to carry out the job successfully.

What does the job holder need to be able to do, i.e. what abilities or competencies do they need? In this example, they would need to have the ability to organise, make decisions, work to deadlines and meet targets, mix with a range of people (customers, suppliers), work as part of a team, lead, analyse trends and sales figures (numeracy). What are the current trends in female/male fashions? Could you predict what is likely to be in fashion six months from now?

What evidence would an applicant need to show that they possess the skills and competencies required for this job? It is not enough to say 'I have good interpersonal or team skills'. You need to give some practical examples of how you have used or demonstrated these skills, e.g. 'I worked as part of a sales team specially set up to promote a new range of fashion clothing'.

Table 4.2 Skills needed to carry out the job

Employability skills	Personal skills	Communication skills
Effectiveness in meeting targets, e.g. reviewing performance; managing plans, meeting project deadlines Knowledge of products, e.g. selecting and assembling new fashion collection	Co-operating with others, e.g. liaising with other departments and shop personnel Negotiating, e.g. terms of contracts, meeting suppliers Work as part of a team, e.g. participating in promotional activities	Writing reports; maintaining relationships; adapting communication techniques, e.g. to work abroad Presentational skills, e.g. to train junior staff

Getting the job – how to give a good interview

It is vital to prepare for an interview. Remember that you have got this far because of your original application. Now it is down to the impression that you make.

The object of the interview is to show your strengths. Points to consider are:

■ *Appearance* You need to reflect the image that the employer is seeking. (This is part of your ability to observe and raise professional standards of production/service delivery.)

■ *Manner* First impressions do count so, for example, wait to be asked to sit down. Speak clearly and look at the panel. Ask for clarification if you do not understand a question. Be polite but never be familiar. The panel will be friendly but it is a formal event.

■ *Achievements* These will already be on your letter, application form or CV. Be prepared to talk positively about these and to expand on what you have written. You should always keep a copy to re-read before the interview. Make your achievements relevant to the job in hand or a basis for future development.

■ *Personality* Your personality will come across, that is the point of an interview. It is natural to be nervous and some allowance will be made. Nevertheless the panel will expect you to be well prepared and to be able to answer reasonable questions courteously.

■ *Ambitions* You may be asked 'What do you hope to be doing a year from now?' Be ready for this; ambition shows drive and commitment.

■ *Value the job* Never admit that you just want to earn some money before you go off to Australia, or that you have applied for the job because there is nothing else about.

■ *Presence of mind* Often you will be asked to think on the spot about a particular job-related issue. A prospective teacher may be asked 'How would you reflect the school's equal opportunities policy in your lessons?' At this point it helps if you have read the documentation that the employer has sent you! The panel assumes that you are genuinely interested in the job and that you will be aware enough of issues to provide informed answers.

■ *The job offer* 'Are you a serious candidate for this job? If we were to offer you the post, would you accept?' You should be ready for this question, especially if you have made a number of other job applications.

Always prepare thoroughly. Find out all you can about the job and about the organisation. Look at business news websites. Be prepared for standard questions such as 'Why do you want to work for our organisation?' or 'Why do you want this job?' Take copies of your CV, covering letter and application form to the interview so you can refer to them if necessary.

assignment focus

1 For M1, practise interviewing (you have to prepare the questions) and being interviewed with a colleague. Perhaps this could be recorded; you can then work out how to eliminate any weaknesses and develop your strengths.

2 For D1, you need to evaluate the advantages to an organisation of employing suitable people to communicate information. You may find it easier to use the organisation to which you have applied. This will help put your ideas into a realistic setting. You could examine the various elements of the job role you have chosen and evaluate how important communication and information handling skills are in effectively fulfilling it. Look at your organisation's mission or objectives. How will employing the right staff help it achieve these?

How to communicate using appropriate methods

Communication is the bond that keeps us all together. It can be a source of intense pleasure or pain. In some situations, such as rock climbing, good clear, accurate communication can make the difference between life and death. A dictionary definition is: 'the imparting, giving or exchange of information, ideas or feelings; to succeed in giving information'. There must be at least two people and the process must be a success. If it is not, there is a failure, or breakdown, in communication.

Knowing how to communicate successfully with your tutor, manager, colleagues or friends will be the key to your success. Equally important is knowing when not to communicate.

Businesses need to communicate with a range of individuals and organisations, including their customers (e.g. through promotion), their suppliers, as well as their own employees. A properly structured corporate communication system requires clear and well-defined channels of communication to enable it to reach all stakeholders.

A simple model of communication

Figure 4.5 shows a simple model of the communication process, whatever medium is used. It will be particularly helpful for M2, M3 and D2. The simplest model of communication is one-to-one.

Figure 4.5 A simple model of communication

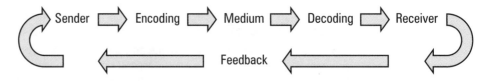

See page 238 on how the model can be applied to promotion.

At the end of this outcome, you will be able to fill in the boxes in Table 4.3 with the details for your presentation and other methods of communicating business information:

Table 4.3 Method of communication

Sender	Encoding	Medium	Decoding	Receiver
		e.g. verbal, non- verbal, written, non-written		
←	←	Feedback	←	←

Sender

This is the person(s) or organisation originating the message. The status and relationship between the sender and receiver will determine both the content of the message and the method and style of delivery. We are communicating with you through this sentence.

Encoding

This means putting your information into words, pictures, graphics, etc. so that the receiver will be able to understand your message. The sender will have an image of the receiver. It may be visual or just a mental picture (our image comes from teaching our own students face-to-face) and a purpose for the communication. Marketing research is used to get a better picture of the consumer as a receiver and to obtain feedback.

The process of encoding will depend on:

■ the complexity of the message
■ the purpose of the message, e.g. to convey financial information, report on progress, advertise, inform or create a corporate image
■ the relationship between the sender and receiver(s)
■ the chosen medium, e.g. face-to-face, text or e-mail, letter or telephone call, report, presentation.

Medium

The medium is the method used to send the message, e.g. verbal/written, formal/informal, electronic/non-electronic, etc.

Decoding

Decoding is the receiver's interpretation of the message. It depends on:

- the relationship between the sender and receiver, e.g. personal, B2B or B2C
- the type and nature of the message
- the style and tone of the language
- how well the message has been encoded.

Some messages can be recognised immediately, e.g. 'It's the real thing'; 'Have a break, have a ...'. (Answers: Coca-Cola; Kit Kat.)

Major advertising campaigns try to make a brand instantly recognisable by constantly repeating the same message. At work, getting a memo or e-mail addressed to Ms or Mr usually means trouble.

Receiver

The receiver is the person(s) or group intended to receive and understand the message. It may be your tutor, your class or your manager. With corporate communications, this could be any stakeholder. The number of receivers could range from one to millions. Should the message stay the same? Should the method of delivery change?

Feedback

Feedback is the response/reaction of the receiver to the message. Being willing and able to give feedback will greatly improve the quality of communication. Do you participate in class discussions? At gigs? Customer feedback is crucial to the success of an organisation. The real test is how much has been sold or how much given to a charity. Do you complain? People in the USA complain all the time? Do they get better service? Is quality of service linked to feedback? Is compliant an anagram for complaint?

Good communication always depends on the sender.

Audience requirements

The audience is the receiver or user of the communication, e.g. customers (B2C), staff or other businesses (B2B). It could be a group of new young trainees in a fast food restaurant, your group of students, customers who order on a website or members of a local sports club eager to hear last year's financial results. The sender/creator of the communication will need to understand their audience's needs or requirements to make the communication effective.

The choice of communication method would depend on the audience and their needs, the content and complexity of the message and the purpose of the communication.

Here are some factors which need to be considered when deciding on how to communicate whether using written/verbal, electronic/non-electronic, **multimedia** etc.

- *Age* For a younger audience, consider using cartoons, simple graphics, few words in a large font, colour. With an older audience, make it relevant. Think carefully about any music. Their tastes may not be the same as yours. Slow down the delivery.
- *Gender* Be aware of equal opportunities. Do not use stereotypes. Use a variety of images. Where necessary, use examples which appeal to both sexes. Look at magazines which are aimed specifically at women or men. What is the content? Who are the advertisers?
- *Ethnicity* Value cultural diversity. Cater specifically for different needs, e.g. are translation facilities needed? Do not use stereotypes. Use a variety of images. Find out about your audience in advance, e.g. in China the colour white is associated with death, whilst red represents pleasure, silence is often a mark of respect as is avoiding eye contact. 'Look at me when I'm talking to you'!
- *Special needs (presenter and/or audience)* Do materials need to be written in Braille or large print? Is an audio loop needed for people with hearing impairments? Is sign language required? With lip readers, make sure they can be seen and can see you. Check the lighting. Does the language need to be simple? Comic Sans is the recommended font for slow readers. Would charts and images be more effective than large blocks of text?
- *Readability and legibility* Is it interesting and able to be read? Is it clear enough to be read easily? Consider font style and size. Two slides can be better than one! Be aware that

not everyone has perfect vision. The bigger the font, the better. Use a simple font (Arial or Comic Sans). Where necessary keep the language simple. If you use a laptop, can everyone see it? Think about the lighting.

- *Attention span* How long can your audience concentrate? Do not change slides/OHTs too quickly – people need time to read. Watch the audience's body language. Check if they need more time, or is it OK to move on? Be aware constantly of audience reactions. Would you like to listen to yourself? Prepare thoroughly. Avoid long blocks of text.

- *Accessibility* The audience needs to identify with the communication, the words, graphics, charts, images, etc. It needs to be at the right level, too low and the audience will complain 'why are you talking down to me'. If the level is too high, the reaction is often 'I'm bored' because the audience cannot understand the content.

- *Interest* Getting your audience's attention and getting them interested is the key to any successful communication (look at AIDA on page 188). Whatever the method of communication – electronic or non-electronic – keep the audience interested by making the communication relevant to their own personal objectives as users of the communication.

- *Distraction avoidance* Make sure you get the main message across to your audience. Do not overload them with too much detail. Make sure there is nothing in the room that would cause distraction, e.g. mobile phones should be switched off. Make sure everything works before you start. Proofread everything that is to be printed.

- *Audience experienced/inexperienced* The experience of your audience will determine the content and knowledge level of a presentation. Although presenters are the experts because they have business/industry-related experience and knowledge and carried out the research, it is important to target the audience at the right level.

> **assignment focus**
>
> Who will be your audience? What are their needs? Begin creating your presentation. Give evidence to show how you have catered for their needs. (Hint: What are the advantages of your chosen methods? Why have you rejected others?)

Methods of written communication

Letter

Business letters are formal written communications with a letterhead, reference, date, sender address, receiver address, formal salutation such as 'Dear Madam' or 'Dear Sir', subject of the communication (e.g. you are overdrawn), the main body of the letter and a formal closing such as 'Yours faithfully', a signature and position.

Letters are personal, secure, confidential and provide a permanent record of events. They are user-friendly, relatively cheap and can be read many times at the reader's convenience (i.e. they are not screen-based).

Memorandum

Figure 4.6 is an example of a memorandum or memo.

Fax

Fax machines can either be 'stand alone' or combined with a printer, scanner and photocopier as an 'all in one' machine.

Despite the rise in e-mails, which are used mainly by personal customers, insurance, finance and construction still rely heavily on faxes for sending and receiving invoices, orders and contracts. 'With instant hard copy print outs, they are much simpler than e-mail and much more convenient when sending or receiving short documents,' said one loyal user. However, they can be less secure if they arrive at a machine which is unattended, so that anyone can see them.

> **remember**
>
> A report would be a useful way of presenting P2.

Report

Figure 4.7 is an example of a formal report.

Charts, diagrams, graphics and photographs could be added to a report to make it more meaningful for the audience.

Figure 4.6 A memorandum

Memorandum

To: You (student/job title or position/named person)
cc: (who will receive a copy)
From: Roger Lewis and Roger Trevitt (authors/job title or position)
Date: Today
Subject: Templates in Microsoft Word

There are templates or examples of styles of letters, faxes, memoranda and reports in Microsoft Word: click on File, New, General templates.

For examples of how to start a letter, click Insert, Autotext, Salutation. Closing shows possible endings, but note that this does not include the common closings used in UK businesses: Yours faithfully or Yours sincerely.

Keep paragraphs to the point. A memo is an internal form of communication, which in some organisations has been virtually replaced by internal e-mail.

Invoice

An invoice is a business document which shows a list of goods supplied and the cost of these to the consumer. It is one of a family of hard copy/electronic documents which are used in business to order, send/receive and pay for goods.

Invoices are used to record business activity and are an essential part of the communication paper trail used to keep track of orders and payments. Their details will later be added together to form the accounts of the business.

Flow charts

These show visually in words and shapes a sequence of activities that is needed to complete a task. Standard symbols are used, some of which are shown in Figure 4.8.

assignment focus

Construct a flow chart which shows how to make a cup of tea.

Publicity material

Publicity in all its forms is part of the marketing communication of an organisation. It can be either hard copy or screen-based. Effective publicity can inform customers of new products or future events or persuade them to switch brands.

When designing publicity material, it is useful to consider PASS, a mnemonic for remembering the four key elements that should be present in any publicity communication:

- **P**urpose
- **A**udience needs, e.g. Is this font too small? Is this better?
- **S**tructure, layout and design
- **S**tyle, e.g. formal, professional and businesslike, using graphics or images, use of language.

Electronic communication methods

Screen-based

Many organisations now use their intranet as the main means of communicating with staff, e.g. through notices, newsletters.

Figure 4.7 An example of a formal report

To: Kit Identi, Managing Director
From: K. Martins

Report on recruitment policy at Identikit plc

1.0 Terms of reference
This section should show the limits of the report and the precise areas which it should cover, for example:
Following the meeting held on 7 May these terms of reference were agreed:
1.1   To examine the present system of recruitment of senior managers
1.2   To suggest changes to the system.

2.0 Procedure
This section should show how the information was collected, for example:
2.1   *A survey was conducted of all job adverts which had been placed in the last two years, and who was* subsequently recruited.
2.2   A questionnaire was given to all senior managers, to find out their opinions on the present recruitment system. This had 20 open-ended questions which gave an opportunity for everyone to make a contribution.
2.3   The Personnel Manager and Deputy Manager were interviewed in depth, as a follow-up to the questionnaire.

3.0 Findings
This section should give the main findings of the report as a series of numbered headings, for example:
3.1   Survey of advertisements
Advertisements had only been placed in the two local evening newspapers, 'The Star' and 'The Echo'; these had produced only a small response.
  3.1.1 Advertisements 2000–2003
  Only 20% of these advertisements had produced a successful response.
  3.1.2 Advertisements 2004–2007
  These were more successful with a response rate of 40%. Most of these had come from the company website
3.2   Questionnaire results
All questionnaires were returned, fully completed. The general feeling was that in order to attract more candidates it was necessary to advertise more widely.
  3.2.1 National newspaper advertising
  All managers felt that it was necessary to advertise in the national press, particularly when there was a special feature on the clothing industry. There was no agreement on what newspapers should be used.
  3.2.2 Magazine advertising
  All managers suggested that the company should advertise in the trade magazine 'COVER UP', which is published every two weeks.
3.3   Interviews
The two interviews with the Personnel Managers confirmed the general findings.

4.0 Conclusions
This section should sum up the major findings of the report, for example:
Because originally vacancies had only been advertised locally, Identikit plc have only been able to attract a small number of applicants for any post. Most of the people who applied appeared to be well-intentioned but unsuitable. Website advertising had been more successful.

5.0 Recommendations
This section should contain the main and subsidiary recommendations which can be made as a result of the investigation that has been carried out, for example:
5.1   Identikit plc should advertise its senior management posts in national newspapers.
5.2   Identikit plc should advertise in the trade publication 'COVER UP'.
5.3   Identikit plc should set aside a budget to cover the increased cost this policy will incur.
5.4   Identikit plc must ensure that a standard format is used for all its advertisements.
5.5   Identikit plc should concentrate on recruitment through its website. It was noted that Sainsbury's now recruited entirely online and had cut its costs by £4m.

Figure 4.8 How to draw a flow chart

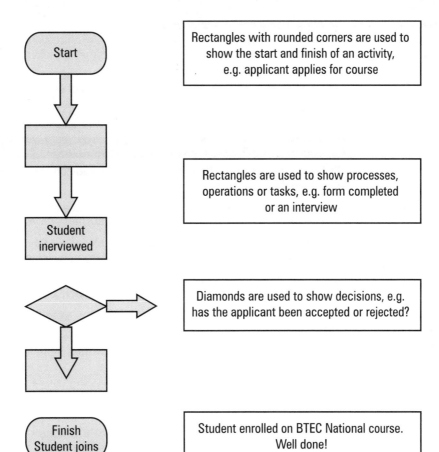

Start	Rectangles with rounded corners are used to show the start and finish of an activity, e.g. applicant applies for course
	Rectangles are used to show processes, operations or tasks, e.g. form completed or an interview
Student inerviewed	
	Diamonds are used to show decisions, e.g. has the applicant been accepted or rejected?
Finish Student joins	Student enrolled on BTEC National course. Well done!

Screen-based cash registers, tills and ticket machines are now a familiar sight almost everywhere. Tesco (or is it Tescopoly?) has introduced screen-based in-store promotional advertising. Screen-based financial trading is used across the world because of its speed and flexibility. Traders can communicate with clients continuously (Tokyo is 8 hours ahead of London, San Francisco is 8 hours behind us.)

This Barclays Capital website has an excellent series of demos which show how on-screen trading is done: www.barx.com.

E-mail

E-mail is the transfer of text, graphics, images, photographs and other information between computer users. They should be confidential. (In this respect e-mail is different from a bulletin board which is a general notice board.) Communication may be one-to-one, a person sending a private message to another person, or one-to-many, in which one person sends a message to many people connected to the network.

Two views on e-mail

- 'This is the best method of communication that has ever happened, I can contact all my staff immediately. One e-mail and all my stress has gone. I have told all my staff what they must do,' said Jill, a sender of e-mail.

- 'This is the worst method of communication that has ever happened,' said Alan, a receiver of e-mail. 'I have to look at my e-mail all the time – I am expected to reply – immediately. It is a continual source of stress.'

assignment focus

Supporters of e-commerce maintain that e-mail is much more secure than sending either written or telephone messages, both of which can be intercepted. Do you believe this? Do you buy or book online? Have your personal details ever been cloned/copied?

Strengths and weaknesses of using e-mail

A recent Microsoft survey found that 80 per cent of office workers now regard e-mail as essential. The three most popular uses of the internet are information gathering, education and e-mail.

Table 4.4 summarises the strengths and weaknesses of e-mail.

Table 4.4 Strengths and weaknesses of e-mail

Strengths	Weaknesses
The same message can be sent immediately to many people	Needs efficient filters to prevent junk e-mail
Fast and efficient and frees up time for other tasks	No face-to face or verbal contact with business colleagues, or friends
By using a laptop staff can keep in touch anywhere in the world	Messages tend to be written in e-mail jargon which can be misinterpreted
Complete files can be sent/downloaded with any message	Forces people to reply which can cause stress
There is a permanent record available on the hard disk	Unrestricted access can increase costs
	E-mail has the same legal liability as written material – beware!

Sixteen members of staff of the DVLA at Swansea were sacked for 'inappropriate use of e mails' (www.bbc.co.uk/Wales). Using e-mails or internet searches for personal reasons during organisation time is considered illegal.

In December 2006 an allegedly restricted e-mail – a Threshers off-licence voucher offering 40 per cent discount off all wines and champagne – ended up being e-mailed to over 2 million people. Threshers promised to honour all of them. How much was the free publicity and an instant database of 2 million people worth?

SMS (short message service)

In 2006, there were nearly 25 billion text messages sent in the UK. SMS is flexible and convenient, with all services – voice, messages, data, alerts – available through a wireless mobile. It is reliable, relatively cheap (depending on your provider and tariff) and selective – you know who is contacting you.

WWW (world wide web)

The web is now used for shopping, games, dating, entertainment, etc. We can buy, sell, find information and communicate. We all have a unique e-mail address, which is much shorter than our home address. It is used for business to business (B2B), business to consumer (B2C), government to business (G2B) and government to consumer (G2C) and customer to customer (C2C) communication. Yet whatever the relationship, the same principles of communication apply. There is a sender, who must be aware of the receiver/audience requirements. Being able to put these principles into practice so that the communication is readable, legible, accessible and meets the needs of the target group will ultimately determine its success or failure.

See e-business, page 105.

Methods of non-written communication

Organisations use different methods of non-written communication, depending on the nature of the business and who is the intended audience, e.g. staff, customers, suppliers, government agency, etc.

Telephone call

There are now 'more mobile phones in the UK than there are people', 'we spend 4 hours a day e-mailing, texting or phoning' (*Source*: literarytrust.org.uk). Mobile phones now appear to be used continuously for both business and pleasure. Are they safe? Are they a secure means of communication?

An effective business call will be well planned with a clear objective, e.g. to make a complaint or order a ticket. The style, tone and language should be geared to the needs of the listener/receiver.

The advantages of telephone calls are that they are easy and convenient almost everywhere, they can be made at any time and virtually any place, they give instant two-way communication, you cannot be seen, you do not need to be in the same place to conduct business. Do you always tell the truth when you ring to say, 'Sorry I cannot come in today, because … '?

The disadvantages are that you cannot be seen! Conversations can be overheard, they are not secure and there is no physical record (unless they are recorded 'for training purposes only'. Is this against the Data Protection Act?). They can be received at any time and virtually any place!

Video conferencing

This is a meeting between two or more people in two or more locations which takes place via a video link. People can see and speak to each other at the same time. These have become possible because of high speed **broadband** connections. The main benefits are the savings in time, travel costs and effort, People no longer need to be physically at a meeting to be able to participate.

On the downside, conference participants claim that it is difficult to pick up cues such as body language and asides, so discussion is often at a formal, exploratory level. There is also a time lag for the satellite bounce (watch any news presenter speaking to someone in the USA). Big deals are not usually closed in this way.

---

assignment focus

1 Construct a table like Table 4.5 which lists the different methods of written and non-written communication and also shows which method is suitable for different types of user.

Table 4.5 Methods of communication (1)

Method of:	Types of user
Written communication	
Non-written communication	

2 Construct a table showing the different methods of electronic/non-electronic communication and indicate which method is suitable for different types of user/receiver. For M2, analyse the advantages and disadvantages of each method of communication. Which do you use most often? Why?

What are the barriers to good communication?
Sender breakdowns

Communication can break down because the sender of the information has failed to convey the meaning and/or importance of the message.

The sender of the information could be at fault because:

■ the language could be too difficult or complex

■ there could be too much information ('information overload') so that the receiver misses the key points

■ the sender may be using threatening verbal or body language, e.g. shouting or being aggressive, so that the receiver does not listen

■ the sender could be 'talking down' to the receiver, so the latter is unwilling to listen.

Medium/method breakdowns

When the information is very detailed or complicated, then written communication is better than verbal messages, which can be misinterpreted. The general term for a method breakdown is 'noise', i.e. anything which disrupts communication between the sender and receiver, such as physical noise (e.g. a crackling telephone), small print, illegible writing, long words, jargon, etc.

Receiver breakdowns

The receivers of the information could be at fault because they:

- may deliberately choose to misinterpret the message because of their attitude, e.g. subordinates might not want to be bothered to wear safety helmets because the weather is hot

- do not listen because they do not want to hear the information, e.g. people do not like to hear bad news.

---

assignment focus

1   Say briefly which is the most suitable method of communication, giving your reasons, in each of the following situations:

   a) Explaining how a new machine operates (How would audience requirements affect this process?)

   b) Telling employees about the new sales targets (Would age, gender or ethnicity make a difference to the communication?)

   c) Giving the results of last week's record output

   d) Telling staff the names of the new people who have joined the organisation

   e) Keeping a permanent record of an interview

   f) Proposing a new method of working (Would staff experience make a difference to how this information was communicated?)

   g) Inviting people to the presentation you will be giving for M3

   h) A bank informing a customer that they are overdrawn (Does the audience/receiver make any difference?)

   i) A company informing customers of new products (Would the communication be the same information for each market segment?)

   j) Easyjet letting customers know of changes to flight schedules

   k) A company telling shareholders about its financial position in the last year

   Hint: Consider cost, speed, security, personal touch, whether formal or informal, user friendly, **accessibility**, permanent record, personal interaction, interaction between organisations, etc.

2   For M2, use the information on advantages and disadvantages of each method to suggest reasons why your chosen method is suitable for the types of user you have already selected. Add your reasons to the table you have constructed for the assignment focus on page 173.

Table 4.6 Methods of communication (2)

Method of	Types of user/receiver	Reasons for choice of method
Written communication		
Non-written communication		
Electronic communication		
Non-electronic communication		

Technologies

Information communication technology is moving so quickly that new software and hardware is being continually introduced.

Computers

Computers can be used to communicate in a variety of ways.

How many topics of communication are shown in Figure 4.9? How many would you use?

Figure 4.9 The Yahoo home page

Touch screens

Touch screens enable the users or receivers to obtain information directly from the screen without a mouse or keyboard. The screen will display a range of options, all the user does is activate one of these by touching the screen with their finger. They are particularly effective in high usage public situations, e.g. museums or a doctor's surgery where they provide a fast and secure information service. The user can interact immediately with on-screen instructions.

Digital broadcastlng

By 2012 all TV will be digital and you will require a set top box or aerial to receive it. 'Both sound and pictures are transmitted as computerised bits of information' www.(bbc.co.uk). Because the digital signal takes up much less space, more radio stations and TV channels will become available. These are likely to cater for smaller, precise market segments and attract specific audiences and advertisers.

DVD (digital versatile/video disc)

As the data is stored optically, DVDs store very large amounts of data as text, graphics, music, audio and multimedia. Many companies now include a corporate DVD as part of their job application pack. Bromley College has a student induction DVD. The Tour de France cycle race (which should start in London in 2007) used a DVD as part of its promotion campaign. Memory sticks are also performing the same function.

Mobile phones

There are now more mobile phones in the UK than there are people. They can transmit, receive and store data and voice messages, take photographs and send these to a computer. They can be used for text alerts for news, financial information, weather and traffic reports. Mobile phone technology is developing so quickly that, by the time you read this, it will already be out of date. There are as many tariffs as there are market segments. www.mirror.co.uk reported that OneCompare, the tariff comparison site, estimated that customers lost £1b a year by not switching, i.e. companies made £1b a year.

The internet and WAP (wireless application protocol)

WAP has now been largely overtaken by 3G services which allow mobile phone users to access the internet for news, business and financial information, etc. wherever they are. Who will benefit from this instant access to information?

 Link See pages 105 and 144 for more information on e-business.

Different types of information and how it can be processed

assignment focus

To achieve P4, you need to select information from three sources, e.g. company annual accounts or a government website and manipulate/process it, adhering to legislation for business purposes (i.e. it must be legal).

For P5, you will need to present the information from P4 using three different methods (see pages 185–91). These activities link with M3 and D2.

assignment focus

Describe the type of information you will be using and presenting.

Table 4.7 Types of information

Types of information	Characteristics
Verbal	
Written	
On-screen	
Multimedia	
Web-based? Numerical?	

Types of information

assignment focus

Describe the features of the three types of information you are using. If you are using internal/external, qualitative/quantitative or primary/secondary data, give your reasons, e.g. the strengths and weaknesses.

Table 4.8 Features of information

Feature of information	Description
Internal	Sales, Accounts, Marketing and HR records
External	
Primary	
Secondary	

Features of information

Current nature of information

Is it up-to-date, accurate, valid and reliable?

When information, ideas or opinions are in current use and generally accepted as valid, they are said to be common currency. A valid argument must be based on evidence. If you were making a presentation on the safety of mobile phones, your opinions should be based on evidence which is supported by more than one source, e.g. evidence which says they are safe and evidence which suggests they are unsafe, i.e. you should validate and cross-check your information.

How and why have you validated your information sources?

Life expectancy of information

In business, external and internal information, such as customer account details, is continually changing, i.e. it has a very short life span. Users and presenters of information must be completely up-to-date with current information to avoid making the wrong decisions. For example, you may have seen this on letters requesting payment, 'Please ignore this letter if you have paid within the last 24 hours.' Always check the publication date when using secondary data (both hard copy and electronic). Primary data is more is up-to-date, i.e. current.

Figure 4.10 A ten-point guide to protecting your identity online

> Operate on the internet in the same way as you do offline.
> Question why a website is asking for information.
> Never give online security details unless completely necessary.
> Look after your password.
> Never click on links in emails.
> Keep security software up-to-date.
> Remove spyware.
> Keep your internet connection secure using **encryption**.
> If it seems too good to be true, it probably is.

The full version of the Security Report: Online Identity Theft can be found at www.btplc.com.

Purpose of information

Table 4.9 The purpose of information

The organisation as a receiver of information	The organisation as a distributor of information
Updating knowledge	Communicating sales promotions
Informing future developments	Inviting support for their activities
Offering competitive insight	

The purpose of information is to meet the needs of the business and its stakeholders. It is a two-way process, with the organisation both a sender and receiver of information (see the model of communication on page 166).

A business has to know the needs of its customers, the activities of its competitors and its market before it can develop its business strategy. In order to gain an understanding of the market for a product or service it needs information.

An organisation requires information for many purposes, including the following.

To update knowledge

An organisation will need to update knowledge, e.g. about its customers through market research or the market in which it operates. Is there any new legislation, such as the **Disability Discrimination Act** or **Freedom of Information Act**? Are there new technologies or materials which could affect production? (Eastman Kodak has made 50,000 workers redundant because digital photography destroyed the market for traditional films.) Keeping up to date will enable the organisation to make comparisons with past events ('like for like' comparisons), e.g. are sales this week better or worse than this time last year. Keeping customers up to date about, e.g. account details or new products/services, is equally important.

To inform future developments

Information on future developments provides a foundation and guide for decision-making, e.g. on the appropriate volume of sales in targeted sections of the market. It can be used:

- to plan for the future – the more information a company possesses, the easier it is for it to achieve its objectives
- as a management tool to control budgets, e.g. comparing the difference between planned and actual promotional expenditure
- to make forecasts and estimates to inform future developments.

To offer competitive insight

The main reason for a business researching competitors is that it can develop and market its own brands more successfully. It will need to find out:

- who the competitors are by using trade directories, trade associations, website searches and local business telephone directories (secondary data). Do competitors have similar products and what are their prices?
- how well they perform – most businesses check this by pretending to be customers, by observing their activities or using professional mystery shoppers (primary data), e.g. Sainsbury's used this on its carrier bags: 'Our mystery shoppers regularly check the quality of our products and the service of our staff. Are you standing next to one?'
- what their customers think – this can be done informally or by asking for references (Take care – they will only say good things about the company.)
- how they will react to a new competitor, e.g. cut prices or offer discounts. When British Gas announced a 14 per cent increase, npower (which sponsors international test cricket matches) announced a price freeze and advertised with the slogan 'British Gas hit for six'. When it announced a further 22 per cent rise in 2006, how did your household react? A further 12 per cent is expected in 2007.
- their strengths and weaknesses so that it can develop its own strategy and possibly use them as a benchmark.

To communicate sales promotions

The best product in the world will not sell unless customers know it exists. For a sales promotion to be effective, it needs to raise **a**wareness, gain **i**nterest, arouse **d**esire and stimulate **a**ction (AIDA).

- See page 237 for an explanation of the AIDA concept.
- See page 238 for how the communication model is used in promotion.

To invite support for activities

Organisations trying to get funding from the EU or National Lottery; charities, such as the British Lung Foundation or ChildLine, inviting companies to sponsor or requesting volunteers and donations are inviting or asking for support for their activities. Any communication will need a competitive edge and the charity sector is very competitive. A charity will need information about the scale of the problems they are attempting to solve and knowledge of the funding sources. This is then used to communicate with stakeholders.

assignment focus

What is the purpose of the information you are gathering and presenting?

Information gathering

For information sources, see page 124.

Validation

The earth is round, although at one time the commonly held belief was that it was flat. Always validate (confirm) and corroborate any statements you make. The need to ensure that any data, however it was collected, analysed or presented, is valid and reliable means that rigorous quality control checks must be in place for every step of the process. For example, if you carried out the same survey again, would you get the same results? If not, can you rely on them as the basis for a commercial decision?

Always try to include more than one source. (Use the questions on page 117 to assess their reliability. This is source checking.) Double-check any calculations and proofread any text/ graphics. Be consistent, e.g. always use the same system to round numbers up or down.

Error management means learning from any mistakes you make, such as copying figures from one table to another incorrectly. Find out why you make mistakes and change your techniques.

Adherence to legislation

See Unit 2, pages 65–68 for more information on copyright and intellectual property.

Copyright

In your assignments, you will rely a great deal on source material. With new technology, it is very easy to download or scan information and merge this into your work. You must be aware of plagiarism (copying from other sources such as books, the web or indeed a friend) as this will adversely affect your grades. On the other hand, using a variety of sources effectively will enhance them. Either adapt material to your needs or, where you need to quote directly, use quotation marks and name the source.

Whether you use information from books, magazines, newspapers, or the web, you should always provide details of the sources you have used. Include the date of publication or the date the material was accessed from the web as a way of validating the material. The date is important because information on the site may change.

Always make sure that you are not breaking the law when you write or copy anything, for example who owns the copyright or the trademark? It is usually the author or creator of the work who has the exclusive right to use the material. Do you need permission to reproduce it? For example, when you search for images on the internet and find the image you want, it will have the phrase 'this image may be subject to copyright'.

Disability discrimination and equal opportunities legislation

Disability Discrimination Act 1995
This Act makes it illegal to discriminate against someone on the grounds of their disability. Under the Act, employers have an obligation to make 'reasonable adjustments' to working conditions or working arrangements which otherwise put disabled people at a 'substantial disadvantage'. For example, any presentation or sales promotion should be accessible to those who have a visual impairment.

Race Relations Act 1976 and Sex Discrimination Act 1975 and 1986
These Acts make it illegal to discriminate against someone on the grounds of race, sex or marital status. Discrimination occurs when people are excluded, i.e. assumptions are made, such as men are plumbers or women work in offices. Discrimination involves stereotyping according to race or sex. Take care when using images in a presentation.

Other legislation

Any presentation including all forms of advertising and promotion must be legal. Any individual has the right to complain if they feel they have been discriminated against. Advertisements have to be 'legal, decent, truthful and honest'.

Any text, image, graphics, photo, graph, chart, etc. which is used must obey the law. Use a variety of images in your presentation.

The Code of Advertising Practice (CAP) says:

> 'Marketing communications should contain nothing that is likely to cause serious or widespread offence. Particular care should be taken to avoid causing offence on the grounds of race, religion, sex, sexual orientation or disability. Compliance with the Code will be judged on the context, medium, audience, product and prevailing standards of decency.'

Source: www.asa.org.uk

Poster advertisements, which can be seen by everyone, usually get more complaints than when the same advertisement appears in a magazine.

The UK is a multi-cultural and multi-faith society. There are many religions and religious organisations that are very strongly supported and whose beliefs are very strongly held. It is therefore a very sensitive area of representation.

Have you needed to change your presentation to stay legal? Have you used quotes where material is copyright? Are your images legal?

Plagiarism and copying

When you use quotes, identify clearly where the quote begins and ends, and name your source.

Many examination boards and universities now require that work is submitted on disk. Software programmes are then used to see if anything has been copied. If copying is found the work is immediately failed.

Figure 4.11 shows the declaration you have to sign when you submit work to BTEC:

Figure 4.11 BTEC declaration

Source: Edexcel

Learner's Declaration

I certify that the work submitted for this Integrated Vocational Assignment is my own.

Signed: _____ Date: _____

Assessor's Declaration

I certify that the work submitted by the learner named above is original and has been completed independently.

Name of assessor: _____ Signed: _____ Date: _____

---

assignment focus

1. What legislation have you needed to follow when selecting and processing your information? For example, have you named your sources or copyright holder? Have you rejected particular images?

2. Has the data been processed legally? Does it obey equal opportunities legislation on sex, race, disability and age? Has it been deliberately manipulated to suit the needs of the presenter?

Processing methods

One key to your success is being able to process information effectively using the appropriate method. Sometimes it is important to use a computer; on other occasions it is sufficient, or even preferable, to work by hand. You will need to use computers during the course. Remember that information technology is one of the Key Skills. We do not attempt to teach you IT skills in this book, though many of the activities are designed to develop them.

The main applications you will use will be word processing, databases, spreadsheets, desktop publishing and PowerPoint. You may also use specialised packages, perhaps for accounting or design. There are many different products available, but in general they will work in much the same way and give equally good results. Whatever package you use, do save your work regularly and keep back-up copies (these words are written with feeling!). It may be that 'it wasn't my fault – the network crashed!', but if you have lost an afternoon's work that is no consolation. You have still lost it!

Copy and paste from source

You can copy and move graphics, text, images, etc. both within and between applications, to create the presentation which is most accessible and suitable for the audience. When copying from a website, you will probably need to use the text select tool to highlight the section you want to copy. Be aware when you paste back that the formats are likely to be different.

Manipulation and data handling

Many of the publications that you will be using to gather information, both hard copy and electronic, such as the KeyNote reports or www.statistics.gov.uk, contain many tables. To make these digestible (understandable) for your audience, you should summarise them or convert them into charts, i.e. manipulate them to suit your purpose.

Figure 4.12 shows a table of data from the Advertising Association's *Advertising Statistics Yearbook 2006*. The table shows the amount spent on advertising in millions of pounds per year (£m) between 1994 and 2005. We have used:

■ a line graph to show the trends in the data.

■ a bar chart to compare 2004 with 2005.

The data could be easily updated using the most recent figures.

Many different types of charts and graphs are available in standard spreadsheet packages or using the Insert Chart feature in Microsoft Word. You should try the press and hold feature to view a sample in advance. Most will not be suitable for your purposes. In your assignment (D2), say why you did not choose them.

Line graphs are good for showing trends. To create a line graph, highlight the data to be included, then Insert, Chart, Line, press and hold to see how it will look.

The horizontal bar chart in Figure 4.12 shows the advertising expenditure for 2004 and 2005. One year can be compared with the next.

Figure 4.12 Ways of manipulating information

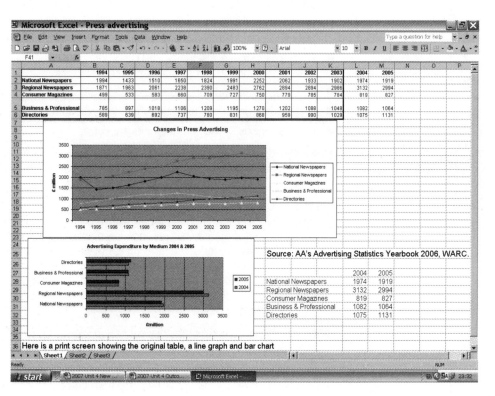

Do you prefer the line graph, or the bar chart, if so, why? Pie charts would not usually be used to show time-based data.

Enhancing information

The basic information for press advertising in Figure 4.12 can be enhanced by adding extra information, such as:

- *the average* You can find this in Microsoft Excel. Go to Insert, Function, Average, and highlight the national newspapers data with the cross cursor so the data is inside the dotted lines. B2:M2 should be showing in the number 1 box. The average is £1,877. This average is also called the mean or arithmetic mean

- *the range* This is the difference between the lowest and highest figures, or £916m. In this example, it is the difference in advertising expenditure on national newspapers between £1,336 (1994) and £2,252 (2000). It is particularly useful in showing the extremes of any data, e.g. knowing that the average daily sale of a shop is £1,500 is useful but also knowing that sales on Saturday are £4,700 and on Monday they are £300 will help the business plan its staffing (range £4,400)

- *the percentage change*, e.g. the percentage change in advertising expenditure in national newspapers between 2004 and 2005 is the difference between 1974 and 1919 (–55) divided by the original or base figure 1974 x 100 to create the percentage: –55 ÷ 1974 × 100 = –2.8%, i.e. the decrease between 2004 and 2005 was –2.8 per cent. These calculations can add greatly to the meaning and interpretation of data.

Try using different chart types (MS Word or Excel) with the data in Figure 4.12, e.g. Radar, Surface, Bubble, Cone, Cylinder, Pyramid, Doughnut, etc. Which are the most suitable/ unsuitable for presenting this information?

You will need to manipulate the charts to obtain the effects you want. The charts can be created in Microsoft Excel and copied across to your Word file.

Charts and diagrams: the rules

The purpose of graphics is to enhance or clarify text. Whether drawn manually or by computer, they should be clear, simple and useful.

- There must be a title.
- The source of the data must be given.
- The vertical (or y) axis should show the dependent variable, e.g. sales, costs or production levels.
- The horizontal (or x) axis will then show the independent variable, e.g. months, weeks, places.
- Keep scales simple. Use units of 10, 100 or 1,000 wherever possible. A computer will scale automatically, though you can alter this.
- Use a key to show different data.
- Use shading or colours to distinguish between different parts.
- Label each axis. Make sure the units are correct.

Line graphs
These are good for showing historical data and trends, but do not put more than five lines on the same graph as it becomes very difficult to distinguish them.

Pie charts
Pie charts are excellent for showing the relative proportions of data, i.e. for showing slices (segments) of the pie, but not for showing totals. They are good for a rough visual impression, but do not include figures unless these are specifically included. How does it work without colour? The chart can be manipulated to show real data and highlight a specific segment. They should not normally be used to show time series data, such as any figures with months, years, etc.

Bar charts
Bars can be vertical, horizontal, adjacent or separate. Individual totals can be shown.

Component or stacked bar chart
Totals can be directly compared, but parts can be more difficult to distinguish. With multiple bar charts, parts or segments can be compared but changes in the totals are more difficult to

distinguish. You should decide which feature is more important, changes in the components or the totals, then use the appropriate chart.

You should show evidence of how you have used mathematical/graphical processing methods in your presentation, e.g use print screen to show the spreadsheet. Give reasons for your choice.

case study 4.4

BTEC results

Read the information in Tables 4.10–4.12 about BTEC results.

Table 4.10 Results for BTEC Units 4 and 2

	Distinction	Merit	Pass	Fail
Unit 4	5	17	8	3
Unit 2	6	14	13	0

Table 4.11 BTEC results: summary of information

Type of information	Written, available as hard copy and on screen
Type of information	Written, available as hard copy and on screen
Features of information	Internal, primary, up to date, data will be kept on file by the centre and BTEC
Purpose of information	To inform all stakeholders of results
Information gathering	Internal, individual unit results
Adherence to legislation	All results are confidential and subject to the Data Protection Act. Results will be analysed for trends by age, disability, gender, ethnicity. Results only given to those with a 'right to know'

Table 4.12 Audience requirements for BTEC results

Audience	Audience requirements
Student	Individual results
Course team	Table showing individual/aggregate results
Senior management and governors	Presentation, aggregate results, table and charts
BTEC	Forms for all individual results
UCAS	Individual results
Employers	Individual results as part of a reference
Parents/guardians (if relevant, i.e. depends on student age)	Leaflet/newsletter, aggregate results, charts and individual highlights
Ofsted	Table, aggregate results, to compare with national benchmarks
Funding body	Table, aggregate results, to obtain funding
Local media	Press release aggregate results, charts and individual highlights

activity

1   Look at Figure 4.13 which shows six different charts representing the group results for Units 2 and 4 (Table 4.10).

a) Which chart shows the results for Unit 2 most effectively? Give your reasons?

b) Which chart shows the results for Units 2 and 4 most effectively? Give your reasons?

The charts were created using Microsoft Excel: highlight the data table, Insert, Chart, Chart types and Chart options.

Figure 4.13 Charts created from Table 4.10

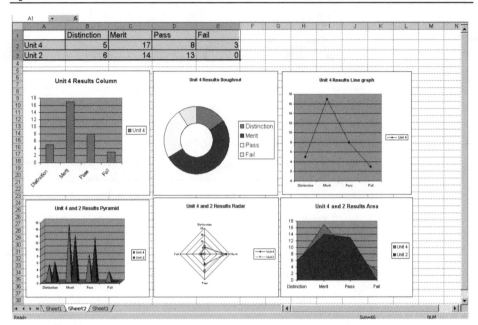

2   Table 4.13 shows results for Unit 1. Add these to Table 4.10 and produce suitable charts to show the full results.

Table 4.13 Results for BTEC Unit 1

Distinction	Merit	Pass	Fail
10	16	5	2

3   What are the key highlights of the results, e.g. 21 Distinctions? This information is required for a leaflet, press release and presentation.

case study
4.5

Local authority revenue and expenditure: Bromley

Look at this article from a local newspaper.

'Hey Small Spender!

The council provided services worth £573.3 million: Social Services £117.4m, Education £254.8m, Housing and Council Tax Benefit £89.7m. Other services came to £111.4m split into: Cultural, Environmental and Planning £57.1m, Housing £10.5m, Highways, Roads and Transport £19.2m, Central Services and Other £24.6m.

Its income came from: Non-Domestic Rates £99.4m, Council Tax £110.1m, Revenue Support Grant £99.3m, Grants £166.4m.'

Would anyone read this article, even though it contains vital information of direct concern to us?

Perhaps a table would be more effective? Look at Table 4.14.

Table 4.14 Bromley Council income and expenditure

Services provided £573.3m	Income received £573.3m
Social services £117.4m	Non-domestic rates £99.4m
Education £254.8m	Council Tax £110.1m
Housing and Council Tax benefit £89.7m	Revenue Support Grant £99.3m
'Other' services £111.4m	Grants £166.4m

Source: Based on figures from www.bromley.gov.uk

activity

In the Council Annual Report, the figures were presented as two pie charts. Draw the pie charts. Say which of the three methods you prefer and why.

assignment focus

1 Choose your three sources. Say why you have chosen them. (Hint: Use the headings: Types, Features, Purpose of information, Audience requirements.)

2 Select the information you need and process/manipulate it using statistical methods and charts. Name the legislation that you had to follow to stay legal. Give examples.

Presenting information effectively

assignment focus

For P5, you need to present the information from P4 using three different methods:

1 Who is going to be the audience – the users? What are their needs?

2 What is the purpose of the presentation? Do you have SMART objectives, e.g. to inform club members of the financial results for last year, to show the results of market research, to compare the cost of car insurance for new drivers?

3 For your three methods, you could produce:

■ a written report (including extracts from a spreadsheet, charts, graphics, images, etc.)

■ a leaflet

■ a web page.

4 Plan your presentation carefully. Define exactly what you want to achieve, e.g. do you want to inform or persuade your audience?

To achieve M3 you will need to make an oral presentation of the work you produce for P5.

For D2, you must also justify the method you have used for your particular audience. What are the advantages of your chosen method? What are the disadvantages of the methods you rejected? Why did you choose particular charts and images in preference to others? You could analyse the advantages and disadvantages of each method using the criteria covered in outcomes 2 and 3.

Presentation methods to meet the needs of the user

Who are the users of information? Who is the audience, e.g a specific market segment watching a TV programme or reading a magazine, perhaps colleagues/your group, managers at the workplace, customers instore/online or local newspaper readers? Any presentation/communication should be specifically created to meet the needs of the user.

We are exposed to business information all day, every day, including the junk mail we get through the post. Holiday brochures, leaflets from double glazing companies ('Just call us free now') and flyers all present business information. Presentation is about communication with stakeholders, either internal (your presentation) or external (B2B or B2C).

Remind yourself about the simple model of communication (page 166). Figure 4.14 below shows how it applies to presentations.

Figure 4.14 The model of communication applied to presentations

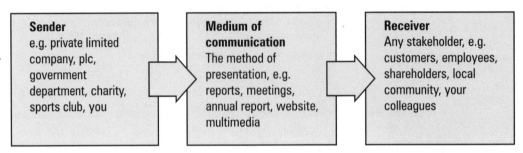

The decision always has to be which presentation method bests suits the needs of the audience and the complexity/purpose of the message. For example, communicating the importance of health and safety to a group of experienced workers requires a different approach to communicating the same information to a group of students! Would cartoons or simple, bold visual images be useful? If so, for which audience?

assignment focus

Which would you prefer? Give reasons.

Here are four ways of showing the results for Unit 4 BTEC National:

- a statement: 'Eight students achieved a Pass. Seventeen students got a Merit. Three failed. There were five Distinctions.'
- a simple table:

Table 4.15 Results for BTEC Units 4

	Distinction	Merit	Pass	Fail
Unit 4	5	17	8	3

- a vertical bar chart:

Figure 4.15 A vertical bar chart

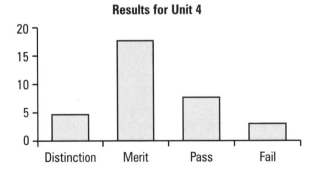

■ a pie chart:

Figure 4.16 A pie chart

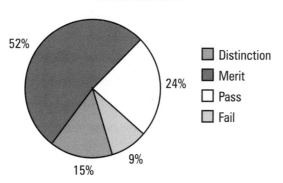

Results for Unit 4

52%

24%

9%

15%

■ Distinction
■ Merit
□ Pass
■ Fail

The charts were drawn using the Chart function in Microsoft Word. Highlight the data, then Insert, Picture, Chart, use Chart types and Chart options.

Documents

Traditionally printed documents have been the main means of communicating/presenting/recording business information. Internally, i.e. within an organisation, a written report may be used to present information to workers or managers. Externally, a company could report to its shareholders through its annual company report, which would normally be presented at an annual general meeting (AGM) of shareholders. You should look at an annual report such as EMI to find out how it is presented.

Document design

Documents (hard copy or electronic) can provide a permanent visual record of the activities of the organisation. Many documents such as student registers and those used for accounting purposes must be kept by law. Although they are a major means of communication and information, they can also be used to monitor and control activities and provide a check against possible mistakes.

Good clear documents are essential if a business is to succeed in achieving its objectives. Documents must be well designed and clearly laid out. They must be easy to read, user-friendly and, when necessary, available in several languages, large print or Braille.

Online forms are now a common feature of many company intranet (internal) and internet (external) sites. You probably have experience of job applications, UCAS, online banking and buying online. Have you found these experiences user-friendly?

The Financial Times provides annual reports at www.ft.ar.wilink.com.

See page 170 for an example of a report.

A good written report would have these features:

■ a front cover, with key details such as name of organisation (centre name), author name (you) and reference number (candidate number), title, company logo, the client, i.e. who the report has been prepared for (teacher), date. This may be the first contact that people have with the organisation. Do not put them off – impress them. Every report (assignment) should be presented with the same layout and it is worth spending time developing a style and format which represents the image you are trying to portray, e.g. a picture watermark may help. Once the right format has been found, use it all the time so that it becomes the house (your) style. This can be saved on the computer. What sort of image do you think is given by a poorly or badly presented front page?

■ a contents page, which lists the content with page numbers for each section (in an assignment this could be the outcomes). Number each page, put in a footer with perhaps a name and reference. The presentation (assignment) should be professional. This is how many businesses make their money

■ an introduction or summary page

■ an acknowledgements page, which includes the names of people who have given help, and written and internet sources.

Binding is important – the finished presentation has to make an impact. Remember the golden rule of communication is that the responsibility for delivering the message lies with the sender. The client/receiver cannot be held responsible for not understanding. First impressions count.

Leaflets, brochures and flyers

These are used extensively by organisations as part of their publicity and promotion. They can be used to persuade and/or inform.

The best way to design these is to use the **AIDA** approach:

■ **A**ttention – gain the audience's attention with a good headline: 'BTEC student becomes millionaire. Want to read more? Then see page 000. SAVE £££s.'

■ **I**nterest people in the product, topic or idea; use images, photographs, cartoons, etc.

■ **D**esire – arouse their desire with special offers, promotions, free gifts

■ **A**ction – invite questions, participation: 'call us or e-mail'.

---

case study 4.6 — Internet advertising

Internet advertising currently generates about £13bn a year (November 2006), and is forecast to reach £30bn by 2010. Companies would pay a company such as Google for every hit their website receives. This method of payment, however, is open to abuse, e.g. a competitor could continually hit the online advert creating large costs for the advertiser – many companies have gone bankrupt. In an attempt to stop this, (1) search engines will have to produce audited figures of genuine hits, (2) a payment by action method is to be introduced.

activity

How could this report affect internet advertisers and other internet stakeholders?

Leaflets can be produced on A5 or A4 paper, which may or may not be folded. Shading and colour work well but make sure the font and font colour can be seen – not everyone has your eyesight. Always check with a colleague before you print the final draft. It can be very expensive to put right any mistakes once you have gone to print – forget the contact details and no one will ever contact you! Always proofread; aim for zero mistakes in spelling, grammar and punctuation. Use the section on audience requirements on page 167 to ensure that your AIDA approach works.

---

assignment focus

Decide on your method of presentation. If you produce a leaflet, you will need a lot of computer time, so plan out your design by hand first.

For M2 and D2, give reasons for your choice of method, e.g. leaflets are simple and effective. They can include text (of various sizes) and images. Various colours can be used for the text and paper.

Use of style

The style of any presentation would depend on the:

■ objectives of the sender or presenter

■ needs and characteristics of the target audience

■ complexity of the content or message

■ method of communication, e.g. written or non-written.

The design of the style could include the font, text, colour, music, animation, video, images, graphics, tables, etc. Be consistent – an organisation would use the same basic style, its 'house style' across all its communication (e.g. leaflet, reports, web pages). Any variation would only be introduced to meet the needs of its particular audience.

Verbal/oral presentations

How to make an effective oral presentation
Before you start:

- decide on your objectives and make sure they are SMART so you can later evaluate the presentation. What are you trying to achieve?
- find out as much as you can about your audience, their characteristics and needs so they can be targeted precisely (this is the main purpose of marketing research).
- find out if there are any constraints, e.g. equipment or materials, cost, facilities, time/number of words.

1 Collect the information. Make sure it is accurate and up-to-date.

2 Obtain the evidence. You must be able to support any arguments you make.

3 Prepare all the materials you will need, e.g. notes, pictures, videos, specifically for the audience.

4 Try to think of what questions you might be asked. Then find the answers.

5 Try to think of where people could disagree with you. Then find the answers.

6 Make your presentation clear, interesting and simple. Would you like to listen to yourself?

7 Look at your audience and do not be afraid to smile. Use positive body language, stand up straight and do not slouch as it sends out a negative image.

8 Use visual aids such as an overhead projector (OHP) or multimedia computer linked to a projector and screen.

9 Always be positive.

10 Rehearse and practise your presentation several times.

11 Do not rush a slide show. People need time to look at it.

12 With a computer presentation, make sure you face the audience and position the computer carefully.

13 Use a large font on transparencies/slides, with few words.

14 Check that everything works before you begin. (Have the speakers been stolen?)

15 Dress specifically for the audience.

Try to avoid:

- over-running your time so you have to speed up
- forgetting any of your presentation materials on the day
- not checking that the disk you created at home works at your centre
- too much chatting and laughing with your friends
- drying up because you are nervous. Take a deep breath, smile and carry on. Remember everyone else will probably be nervous
- being too casual.

Role plays

Role playing is acting or playing different people in controlled, simulated situations in order to learn how to behave in real circumstances. Role plays are often used by the emergency services to test their ability to perform in a real emergency. Being a customer or sales assistant, or playing the interviewer and the interviewee are more familiar examples. Role plays allow the participant to give a practical demonstration of their personal skills. You will probably be interviewed as part of your evidence for M1.

Role plays help the 'actor' or trainee to develop skills which can be used in different situations, e.g. how to handle difficult customers or answer questions in an interview. The scenario (situation) used can range from very simple at the introductory level to highly complex as the trainee develops.

On-screen multimedia presentations

A multimedia presentation is a combination of at least two of the following: audio, text, graphics, images, video or animation. It should appeal to the emotions and add to the value of the message. The addition of sound will help people who have a sight impairment, but be aware that some people may have hearing impairments. Narrator converts words into speech – see Accessories, Accessibility, Narrator on the Start Up menu of your computer.

Audio

Sounds, music or speech can be added to a face-to-face or web presentation to enhance it. Keep the volume down – do not let it dominate. Make sure that sounds can be turned off, as not everyone may appreciate your choice of music, i.e. do not continuously loop the music. It is there to reinforce the images and promote the message. Most successful advertising is a blend of music, words and images. In Microsoft PowerPoint Help, search with Add Audio to see how you can add music or sound effects to a slide or animation presentation.

Sounds and music create an atmosphere. Think of the music and sounds in the films *Star Wars* or *Jaws*. What images do you have?

Video

Search Microsoft PowerPoint Help with Add Video to see how video/movies can be added to a presentation.

Since broadband has been introduced, with much faster download times, the facility to incorporate video into face-to-face and web presentations has greatly improved. However, when you create a website, check how long it takes before the video images appear. Most people switch off after about ten seconds! Images and video need a large amount of storage – copy to a CD or use a memory stick (always check that you have not left it in your computer). If you do not have a choice, split your files.

Whenever you make a presentation, whether professionally or as a student, check that the software used to create the presentation is compatible with the system for the presentation. What do you have at home? What is the presentation software, e.g. Windows 98/Windows XP/Apple for preparation, Windows for presentation?

Animation

Animation is the process of adding movement or effects to text, graphics or images. Animation can add character, interest, drama, etc. to make a presentation unique. A well-animated presentation is a very effective way of communicating a promotion message, delivering a business plan or showing the profit and loss account for the last year (animate so that each item is brought in separately and explained using Microsoft PowerPoint).

If you are using Microsoft PowerPoint, creating an attractive animated slide show is a relatively straightforward process.

remember

Check and check again that all the hard work you have put into creating your presentation is compatible with the software that will be used for making the presentation. Ask your tutor and the expert technicians.

Figure 4.17 Creating an animated slide show using PowerPoint

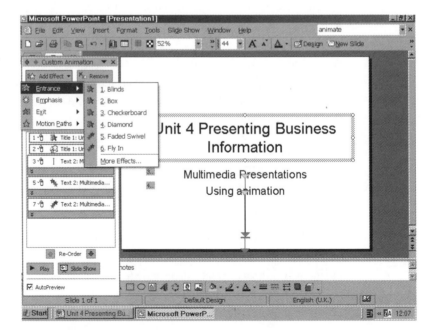

Use of images

Images can also be added from a scanner or camera, or direct from a mobile phone if you have the infra-red transfer facility. Which would you prefer: a lengthy description of how a hairstyle looks or a picture of the model?

Web-based presentations

Images on a website can sell products. However, before they can be used, they must be in the right format. JPEG (Joint Photographic Experts Group) and GIF (Graphics Interchange Format) are the most common. These are compressed files, which means they can be downloaded quite quickly and require less storage space. They are also available on most computers. JPEG is usually used for photographs. If images/video clips, e.g. those available on Yahoo, are copyright, either permission must be obtained before they can be used or the copyright owner must be thanked.

Hints on **web-based presentations**:

- Find out all you can about the possible users, e.g. Are they beginners? Or highly competent users? Young or old?
- Do not use too many different fonts.
- Use different font sizes to show the importance of the information being presented.
- Use bullet points rather than large blocks of text.
- Keep the background simple, so that it does not detract from the message. Red is considered a warm colour, whilst blue is said to be cold.
- Keep the colour scheme simple, both for the text and the background.
- Do not use too many colours and make sure the text is readable over the background. Yellow on white is very difficult to see!

These points also apply to slide presentations.

World Wide Web Consortium guidelines on accessibility

If you are unfamiliar with accessibility issues relating to web page design, remember that many users may be operating in contexts very different from your own. They may:

- not be able to see, hear, move, or may not be able to process some types of information easily, or at all
- have difficulty reading or comprehending text, not have or be able to use a keyboard or mouse, have a text-only screen, a small screen or a slow internet connection
- not speak or understand fluently the language in which the document is written
- be in a situation where their eyes, ears or hands are busy or interfered with (e.g. driving to work, working in a loud environment, etc.)
- have an early version of a browser, a different browser entirely, a voice browser, or a different operating system.

Source: W3C

assignment focus

As part of your evidence for P5, you should create a web page, this could include similar material to the report and/or leaflet.

Multilingual support

There are 23 official languages in the EU. There are only six at the United Nations (UN). Only meetings of EU leaders or ministers get full interpreter coverage, but the majority of documents are translated into all languages.

If you need to work alongside an interpreter, stop after every two or three sentences to allow for translation. Use subtitles and the translation facility on the computer if you are using a computer presentation.

If you are presenting to an audience which needs **multilingual support**, make the presentation visually interesting by using pictures, cartoons and objects with positive and constructive body language, e.g. smiling, hand gestures, etc. These will complement and reinforce the verbal delivery and help understanding. The text (words) should be kept simple and relevant. The context and examples should be geared to the age group.

Make sure that any interpreters or signers for people with hearing impairments are fully briefed. Documents may have to be translated.

'Croeso i Gymru' means 'Welcome to Wales' in the Welsh language. 'Witamy' is 'Welcome' in Polish. 'Konichiwa' is 'Hello' in Japanese. 'Ni hao' is 'Hello' in Chinese. World Hello Day is held in November. How many languages are spoken in your group? You could put the words for 'Hello' and 'Welcome' in as many languages as possible on a leaflet, web page or on a slide to begin your presentation.

case study 4.7 — Trends in advertising

Figure 4.18 is a graph showing the growth of internet advertising in £m. (This can be constructed using the relevant figures in Table 4.16 and Microsoft Word – highlight, insert, picture, chart – or Excel.)

Figure 4.18 The growth of internet advertising 1996–2005, £m

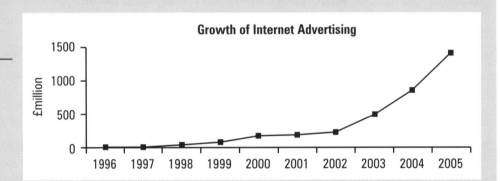

Table 4.16 Advertising media, by media sector, 1996–2005, £m

	1996	1997	1998	1999	2000	2001	2002	2003	2004	2005
National Newspapers	1510	1650	1824	1991	2252	2062	1930	1902	1974	1919
Regional Newspapers	2061	2238	2390	2483	2762	2834	2878	2962	3132	2994
Consumer Magazines	583	660	709	727	750	779	785	784	819	827
Business & Professional	1018	1106	1209	1195	1270	1202	1088	1048	1082	1064
Directories	692	737	780	831	868	959	990	1029	1075	1131
Press production costs	550	577	620	650	702	669	643	634	660	653
TOTAL PRESS	6413	6967	7531	7877	8604	8504	8314	8359	8742	8589
Television	3379	3704	4029	4321	4646	4147	4341	4378	4653	4820
Direct Mail	1404	1635	1666	1876	2049	2228	2378	2467	2469	2371
Outdoor & Transport	466	545	613	649	810	788	816	914	986	1043
Radio	344	393	460	516	593	541	547	584	606	579
Cinema	73	88	97	123	128	164	180	180	192	188
Internet	–	8	19	51	153	166	197	465	825	1366
Total	12080	13340	14415	15412	16984	16537	16772	17348	18472	18956

activity

1 Describe the main stories or trends in the data.
2 Calculate the percentage share of total advertising expenditure by each sector in 2005. Which is the highest?
3 What have been the main changes between 2004 and 2005?
4 Describe the growth in internet advertising.

Full details appear in *The Advertising Statistics* Yearbook 2006.

Output requirement

What does the final document or presentation need to include to achieve the desired effect? The answer depends on the needs of the audience, the simplicity or complexity of the message and the available budget. The first step is to have a clear idea of what needs to be said and the images/graphics that will be used to support the message. Several mock-ups could be created with different layouts.

Before you design your own presentation, collect leaflets, flyers, brochures, etc. Find the best ones to use as your benchmark (standard), then improve on them. Analyse why they are the best, e.g. is it the font style or size (typography), pictures (best [high resolution], normal or draft quality), graphics or paper quality? Do they use graphs, charts or tables to create a better image? How many colours are used? Colour can be expensive commercially. However, it can be an important factor in the perception of the presentation.

assignment focus

Using a separate file, experiment with the range of formatting features available in Microsoft Word. For example, look at:

■ Format, Background, Printed Watermark
■ File, Page Set Up, Landscape or Portrait.

The same approach can be applied to a slide presentation in PowerPoint. Keep editing. For most audiences, the fewer the words, the better. Be prepared for criticism and be willing to change. Between 50 and 70 words is the recommended maximum for a slide screen.

Combining information from a range of applications

Synthesising information

This means combining or bringing together all the information you have found to create a presentation which meets the audience's needs. Each element of the presentation, text, images, graphics, charts, etc., needs to be copied and pasted into one file, such as Microsoft Word, Frontpage or PowerPoint.

Once you have found the text/information you need, you will have to read through to select the main points. You can then produce a summary or edited version. Do not print the first article you find with the right title! Check the reliability of the source. If you are producing graphs or charts, check that you have entered the data correctly (your error management skills) before you proceed to the next steps. Make sure you use the correct chart for your needs and that it can be seen by the audience. Charts are an effective way of presenting financial information, as many people find large tables of figures difficult to understand. Using an average or percentage is also a useful method for summarising complex numerical tables.

You can now consider how the final version should look to achieve its purpose.

Include examples of how you have synthesised information, e.g. reducing a long article to a series of key bullet points or summarising changes in data by using averages.

If you are working with the Microsoft Office suite of applications, i.e. Word, Access, Excel, Powerpoint, Frontpage, you can copy and paste from one application to another. Excel is a spreadsheet program which is good for producing charts, graphs and diagrams. Word also has a limited chart function – click Insert, Picture, Chart. Once the relevant data has been input, the chart area, text and axes can be changed to suit your purposes. A variety of chart types can be produced, e.g. pie, horizontal and vertical bar. Click on the chart, click Chart on the toolbar to see the types that are available.

assignment focus

Have you demonstrated how you have used a range of applications and combined these effectively for the audience?

Specialist software

Pictures can be inserted from existing files, scanned in from a printer or directly from a digital camera. A software program, such as Adobe Photoshop, Photo Impression, Dell Image Expert, Microsoft Office Picture Manager or Paint, can be used to retouch, edit, add customised edges or frames, superimpose text on to pictures, eliminate 'red eye' effects, etc. Clip art can also be directly inserted.

assignment focus

To achieve M3, you must 'demonstrate and justify the use of suitable presentation methods using information from three sources'. You should prepare and deliver an oral presentation of the material you have produced for P3 and P4 to your assessor and your group.

Specialist hardware

Any office supplies outlet would have a wide range of materials and equipment for preparing an effective professional document-based presentation. Two pieces of equipment that a small business or home office would find useful are:

- a heat seal laminator for covering photographs, menus, certificates, handouts, maps, etc. with a plastic pouch or wallet. This process improves the appearance whilst also protecting the document. The finished product looks and feels more professional

- a comb binder, which is particularly good for binding documents with a large number of pages.

Overhead projector (OHP)
When you prepare an overhead transparency (OHT), check that the 'paper type' facility on the printer has been correctly set. If a photocopier is being used, check that:

- the transparency is photocopier-safe
- the correct photocopier tray is used.

Before you begin a presentation, switch on the OHP. Put the transparency on the glass stage of the OHP, check the image size and make sure it is in focus. You can do this by moving the mirror up or down. Make sure the glass is clean. Can everyone see? Do the blinds need to be closed? Should the lights be switched off? Always practise before any presentation and check that the equipment works. Be aware of health and safety issues, e.g. tape down any trailing leads.

During your presentation, look at your audience, not the screen. Look at the transparency on the OHP and use a pen or pencil pointed at the transparency to emphasise each point. Be aware that the whole of a transparency can be seen as soon as it is displayed. Use a piece of card to gradually reveal the points you want to make.

Remove each OHT when you finish. If there are long gaps, switch off the OHP. Keep the same sequence of OHTs in case someone wants to see one again. Put a sheet of paper between each transparency to avoid them sticking together.

What are the needs of your audience? Keep it simple. Do not put too much on each OHT. What do you need to do for people who are hearing and/or visually impaired? For people with dyslexia?

Computer projector

With this system, the computer is linked to a projector. Practise using the system before making any presentation. Become familiar with the controls, particularly the use of the wireless mouse and how to manually run the slides, as someone in the audience will always ask to see a particular one again. The key to success is practice and more practice and do not get flustered if something goes wrong.

Flip chart and display boards

Do you have good clear legible handwriting? Enough pens and paper? Flip charts can be prepared in advance or created during a presentation to summarise the discussion. Large display boards can be excellent as they allow any participants, guests, etc. to look at your materials in their own time at their own pace and, if you are available, ask any questions.

Interactive whiteboard

The interactive whiteboard is a large touch sensitive screen which allows the presenter – and the audience – to write and add their own contribution or comments to a visual presentation directly on the screen. This can be done using your finger or a special pen. It is linked through a projector to a computer. It can be used to access the full range of computer facilities including the internet. The final screen can be saved or printed.

remember

Murphy's Law says that if something can go wrong, it will. So be prepared. If you are using a laptop, check all leads and connections.

UNIT 5

Introduction to accounting

This unit covers:

- The purpose of accounting and the categorisation of business income and expenditure
- Preparing a cashflow forecast
- Profit and loss accounts and balance sheets
- Reviewing business performance using simple ratio analysis

Accounting is a vital part of any organisation. This unit will help you to understand and help to manage business finances. It looks at the importance of keeping accurate accounts, income and expenditure, how and why a cashflow forecast is prepared, how profit and loss accounts and balance sheets are prepared, and how to calculate financial ratios and use them to review business performance.

grading criteria	To achieve a **Pass** grade the evidence must show that the learner is able to:	To achieve a **Merit** grade the evidence must also show that the learner is able to:	To achieve a **Distinction** grade the evidence must also show that the learner is able to:
	P1 describe the purpose of accounting	**M1** analyse the cash flow problems a business might experience	**D1** recommend and justify action a business might take when experiencing cashflow problems
	P2 explain the difference between capital and revenue items of expenditure and income	**M2** analyse the performance of a business using suitable ratios	**D2** evaluate the financial performance and position of a business using ratio analysis
	P3 prepare a 6-month cash flow forecast to enable an organisation to manage its cash		
	P4 explain the component parts of a profit and loss account and balance sheet in a given organisation		
	P5 perform ratio analysis to measure the profitability, liquidity and efficiency of a given organisation		

The purpose of accounting and the categorisation of business income and expenditure

assignment focus

It may be useful to start with P2 (income and expenditure). P1 (the need to keep accounts) may become clearer when the range of business transactions is better understood.

Business record keeping involves:

■ book-keeping – keeping full and accurate financial records of day-to-day transactions

■ accounting – using the business books to produce reports on an organisation's financial performance for use by its managers and external stakeholders. These reports include the 'final accounts' consisting of the **trading account** and **profit and loss account** and **balance sheet**.

Link

On pages 214–15, we look at how the profit and loss account and balance sheet are prepared from accounting data.

On pages 220-27, we see how ratio analysis can be used to interpret and review business performance.

Financial versus management accounting

Financial accounting is the process of collecting financial data and using this to report on the historical (or past) performance of the business. This involves keeping accurate and detailed financial records and using these to draw up reports on business performance – Figure 5.1 illustrates this process. The final accounts, consisting of the trading, profit and loss account and balance sheet are the most important financial reports.

■ The information produced by the financial accounting process is needed by managers in order to run the business from day to day, telling them for example the bank balance, the amount owed by debtors and when this is due, the sales for the month, and so on. The final accounts show performance over the year and are also made available externally to: stakeholders who have a legal right to see them, e.g. the tax authorities and company shareholders

■ those who might use them to benefit the business – banks may need to see the final accounts over several years in order to consider loans or mortgages, a prospective buyer will need similar information.

Management accounting uses the business accounts to provide information purely for internal use by managers. This will help them draw up forecasts, set up plans and make decisions about the future. Such information is not normally available to those outside the business.

Management accounting is not subject to outside regulations. The information may, however, be shown to outside parties where managers believe that this will benefit the business. Cashflow forecasts, break-even and profit forecasts, for example, form part of the business plan shown to potential investors.

Which accounting records do businesses keep?

Precise accounting needs will vary with the type, size and ownership of the business. However, a typical business will keep the records shown in Figure 5.1.

The purpose of keeping business accounts

Businesses keep financial records in order to:

■ provide the information that managers need to run the business effectively

■ satisfy statutory (i.e. legal) requirements to report to external stakeholders on the financial position of the business. The legal requirements vary with the form of business organisation.

Figure 5.1 Business
record-keeping

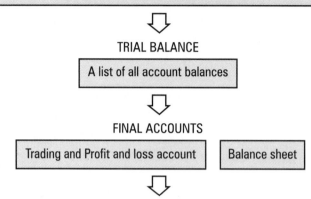

BOOKS OF ACCOUNT

creditor acounts (suppliers who are owed money)
debtor accounts (customers who owe money)
nominal accounts (income, expenditure, assets, liabilities, capital, drawings)
Cash book (money received and paid)

⇩

TRIAL BALANCE

A list of all account balances

⇩

FINAL ACCOUNTS

Trading and Profit and loss account   Balance sheet

⇩

INFORMATION TO STAKEHOLDERS (depending upon the legal form of business)

Internal use of accounting information by managers

The main financial aims of business management are to generate sufficient cash to enable the business to survive and to make sufficient profit to reward the owners.

The exact management requirements will vary with the type and size of the business. However, in general terms, the job of a manager is to exercise control over the business, plan for the future, measure performance and monitor progress. Correct decisions can only be taken where the appropriate information is available.

Planning

In drawing up plans, managers need to forecast what is likely to happen in different sets of circumstances. Such estimates are often based upon past experience and the business accounts can provide valuable details. For example, it is possible to see: the cost of electricity in a typical month, the cost of insuring the building for a year, the wage bill, and so on. This can be a starting point for setting up realistic budgets (or financial targets) for a coming period.

On page 207, we will look at how a cashflow forecast is prepared from estimated costs and revenues. This will form part of the business plan.

The final accounts (see pages 214–15) may play a vital part in securing finance for business plans. In addition to viewing financial forecasts, a bank may also wish to see the final accounts for the previous three or four years before granting a loan or mortgage. These will be the same accounts that were sent to HM Revenue & Customs and not 'dressed up' profit figures designed to impress the bank manager.

Monitoring and control

Once targets have been set, managers will monitor business performance to see how these are being met. For example, departmental heads may check sales, expenditure and profit against the agreed budgets on monthly basis. Any variances (differences between actual results and targets) will need to be investigated and any necessary action taken.

We also look at variance analysis in Unit 2 on page 79.

Managers work with information. The speed with which computerised accounting packages are able to process and report upon financial data increases the ability of managers to monitor and control the business. Case study 5.2 shows an example of credit control.

Measurement of financial performance

The final accounts measure financial performance over an accounting period. They consist of:

case study 5.1

KGB Ltd

Each month KGB Ltd monitors its profits against the budgets it has set. The results for month 4 are shown in Table 5.1.

Notice that:

■ Figures are shown for the current month and for the year to date

■ Variance = Actual results – Budget. A negative variance therefore results when the actual results are lower than budget.

■ Variances may be:

  ▪ favourable (FAV) where sales are higher than budget or costs are lower. Here the business is meeting or exceeding its targets

  ▪ adverse (ADV) where sales are lower than budget or costs are higher.

■ Managers will concentrate on adverse variances since these indicate that targets are being missed.

Table 5.1 KGB profit and loss, month 4

Sales	Current month				Year to date			
	Budget £000	Actual £000	Variance £000		Budget £000	Actual £000	Variance £000	
Kitchens	100	102	2	FAV	400	420	20	FAV
Gardens	125	130	5	FAV	500	538	38	FAV
Bathrooms	250	240	(10)	ADV	1000	962	(38)	ADV
Total sales	475	472	(3)	ADV	1900	1920	20	FAV
less **Costs**								
Administration	250	245	(5)	FAV	1000	975	(25)	FAV
Sales and distribution	70	74	4	ADV	300	315	15	ADV
Total costs	320	319	(1)	FAV	1300	1290	(10)	FAV
Profit/(loss)	155	153	(2)	ADV	600	630	30	FAV

activity

Write a brief memorandum to the finance director on these results.

a) Indicate which sections of the business are giving cause for concern.

b) Comment on the results for the month as a whole.

c) Comment on performance for the year so far.

■ the trading account, showing gross profit. This calculated is as: revenue from selling stock less the cost of buying this stock and putting it into a saleable condition.

■ the profit and loss account, showing net profit (or net loss). This is the final profit once business running costs (or overheads) have also been subtracted.

■ the balance sheet, showing the value or 'worth' of the business at a given point in time. This is calculated by the accounting equation:

  Assets – Liabilities = Capital

Assets are items of value owned by the business. Liabilities are amounts owed to those outside of the business, whilst capital represents the worth of the business to its owners – either partners, sole traders or company shareholders.

case study 5.2 — Solid Gold Pine

Lesley Jones, proprietor of Solid Gold Pine, keeps her business records on a computerised accounting package. One useful facility is the aged debtors schedule that allows her to control the amount she is owed by customers.

The latest report is shown in Table 5.2.

Table 5.2 Solid Gold Pine: account balances

A/C	Turnover	Credit Limit	Balance	Current	30 days	60 days	90 days	Older
Arfon & Griffiths	2300.00	1000.00	250.00	200.00	50.00	0.00	0.00	0.00
Colwyn & Co	3650.00	1000.00	550.00	0.00	0.00	500.00	50.00	0.00
Rock Relics Ltd	*5320.00	500.00	600.00	600.00	0.00	0.00	0.00	0.00
St Davids Crafts	4200.00	800.00	0.00	0.00	0.00	0.00	0.00	0.00
D Thomas	7500.00	1200.00	1000.00	150.00	750.00	100.00	0.00	0.00
Totals	22 970.00	4500.00	2400.00	950.00	800.00	600.00	50.00	0.00

activity

1 Who is Lesley's most valuable customer?

2 How much does St David's Crafts owe at the moment?

3 The credit limit indicates the maximum credit that a customer is allowed. Why has Rock Relics' account an asterisk (*) against it?

4 Lesley allows 30-day credit. Which customers should she contact urgently?

 Link

We cover final accounts on pages 214–15.

On pages 220–27, we will gain a more detailed assessment of business performance by using ratio analysis to interpret the final accounts.

Statutory (legal) reporting requirements – the use of accounts by external stakeholders

All businesses are required by law to draw up final accounts and to make these available to certain external stakeholders. The precise requirements vary depending upon the type of business organisation

All business must send a profit and loss account and balance sheet to HM Revenue & Customs at the end of the financial year so that tax can be calculated. Sole traders and partners will be charged income tax whilst companies will pay corporation tax.

Companies are also required by the Companies Acts (1985 and 1989) to:

■ keep accurate accounting records

■ draw up final accounts and present a summary to their shareholders at the annual general meeting (AGM)

■ send a summary of their profit and loss account and balance sheet to Companies House where they are made available for inspection by members of the public.

Larger companies must use external auditors – independent firms of chartered accountants – to ensure that their accounts provide 'a true and fair view' of business performance.

assignment focus

1   Select a UK-based plc to study for this assignment.

2   Obtain the latest annual report for your plc.

3   To achieve P1, produce a brief booklet aimed at trainees in the accounts section at your chosen business. The booklet is to be entitled 'The purpose of business accounting'. It should explain why your business keeps accounts, suggest the sort of information that will be recorded and the purposes for which this is used. Include both financial and management accounting uses.

Link   Reading Case study 5.4 on pages 205–06 will also help your understanding.

---

remember

The requirement placed upon companies to 'publish' their final accounts means that you will be able to obtain financial information about the company that you choose to investigate. (You are unlikely to find out similar details about a sole trader or a partnership, since these forms of organisation are entitled to keep their affairs confidential.)

■ Company accounts are available from company websites – usually in the shareholder or investor information sections. Print out only what you need.

■ Official printed copies are often more convenient and may be obtained via the company secretary – the website will provide the head office address.

■ WILink.com and the FT Financial Reports Service will post reports to your door. Both are free and efficient.

Categories of business income and expenditure

Each business works to a financial year: a 12-month period usually determined by the month in which the business began trading. For example, the financial year of Pizza Express is 1 July to 30 June, Tesco's year is 1 March to 28 February.

Remember that the final accounts that businesses must produce answer two fundamental questions (Figure 5.2).

In order to draw up these final accounts accurately we must understand the way in which business income and expenditure relates to the financial year in question and, in particular, the distinction between capital and revenue items.

Capital income

This is raised periodically when the business needs extra funds, perhaps for start-up or expansion. It provides long-term benefit to the business over a number of financial years and includes:

■ *capital invested by the owner(s)*, either sole traders, partners or company shareholders. Such funds are permanent in that they do not have to be repaid by a given date

■ *capital invested by business angels and other venture capitalists* such as 3is. These buy company shares but often with an agreement that the company will buy them back after a number of years

■ *loans* from relatives, directors, banks and other institutions usually repayable over a number of years

■ *mortgages* – loans raised to buy property repayable over periods up to 25 or 30 years.

Figure 5.2 Two fundamental questions which final accounts must answer

For business angels and venture capitalists, see Unit 2, page 72 and Unit 37, page 395.

Capital income appears on the balance sheet thus:

- Funds invested by owners are listed as capital.
- Mortgages and loans appear as long-term liabilities.

Revenue income

This is income generated by day-to-day trading and can be related to a specific financial year. It includes:

- *sales* – the value of goods and services sold to customers during business trading. The sales figure includes both cash and credit transactions made within the period – it is the legal date of the sale, rather than the date when money is received, that is important here
- *other items received* such as:
  - rent received – from subletting property
  - commission received for services provided
- *discounts received* – for prompt payment to suppliers.

Sales revenue appears on the trading account (see page 214). Other revenue items received appear on the profit and loss account (see page 214).

Capital expenditure

This is incurred when the business buys fixed assets. These will benefit the business over more than one financial year. Capital expenditure includes:

- tangible fixed assets purchased by the business. These are items we can touch, feel and see, such as land, buildings, office equipment, machinery, furniture, fixtures, fittings and motor vehicles. They will be of value to the business over a varying number of years – in the case of land perhaps for an indefinite period
- intangible assets which might include:
  - goodwill – the reputation, image and business contacts that make the business more valuable
  - patents and copyrights – intellectual property, i.e. distinctive ideas, products and designs owned by the business. They are protected by patent so that competitors may not copy them
  - trademarks – the business name and visual brand registered to protect it from unauthorised use by others. In 2006 the Coco Cola brand was valued at £35,327m according to *Business Week*

Figure 5.3 Tangible and intangible fixed assets

- long-term investments, such as investment in the shares of other companies, or in bonds where cash is deposited for a number of years to earn higher rates of interest.

Capital expenditure appears on the balance sheet as fixed assets (see page 215).

Figure 5.4 Business
expenditure

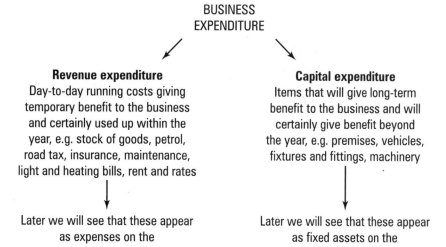

BUSINESS
EXPENDITURE

Revenue expenditure
Day-to-day running costs giving
temporary benefit to the business
and certainly used up within the
year, e.g. stock of goods, petrol,
road tax, insurance, maintenance,
light and heating bills, rent and rates

Later we will see that these appear
as expenses on the

trading and **profit and loss accounts**

Capital expenditure
Items that will give long-term
benefit to the business and will
certainly give benefit beyond
the year, e.g. premises, vehicles,
fixtures and fittings, machinery

Later we will see that these appear
as fixed assets on the

balance sheet

Revenue expenditure

This expenditure is incurred in running the business from day-to-day. Unlike capital expenditure, its value is wholly consumed (or used up) during the year in question. These are both the variable costs that change in line with production, and the fixed costs of running the different functional areas which tend to be unaffected by production levels. Examples of revenue expenditure include:

- the purchase of stocks, e.g. raw materials, components or semi-finished goods for manufacturing, supplies for use in construction, or finished goods for resale by a wholesaler or retailer
- premises costs (sometimes called establishment or estates costs), e.g. rent, rates, heating, lighting, insurance, maintenance and repairs
- administrative costs, e.g. telephone charges, postage costs, printing costs, staff wages, salaries, training and pensions
- selling and distribution costs, e.g. carriage (or transport) costs such as petrol or diesel, marketing costs such as expenditure on promotional campaigns, market research and sales staff
- finance costs, e.g. bank charges and the interest payments on loans, overdrafts and mortgages
- annual depreciation on fixed assets. Fixed assets cannot be charged as costs to the year of purchase because they are useful over a longer period – this is why they are capital items. However, they will not last forever. Depreciation (a fraction of their costs) is charged each year in an attempt to spread their cost over their useful life.

***assignment
focus***

The loss in value of a fixed asset is called depreciation. In 2004 Manchester United (then a plc) reported the following information.

Complete Table 5.3 by choosing from:

- years – 3 years, 7 years, no depreciation, 7 years, 75 years
- reason – wear and tear, age, obsolescence.

Table 5.3

Fixed asset	Estimated life (in years)	Reason for depreciation
Freehold land		
Buildings		
Computer equipment and software		
Plant and machinery		
Fixtures and fittings		

Purchase of stocks is a variable cost and appears in the trading account (see page 216), whereas costs associated with premises, administration, selling, distribution and finance tend to be fixed. These 'overheads' appear in the profit and loss account (see page 216).

The matching principle

When drawing up the profit and loss accounts accountants should include:

- revenue income generated in the period (regardless of when payment is received)
- revenue expense incurred in the period (again regardless of when payment is made).

Therefore all sales and costs for the period are included, whether they are on cash or credit terms.

Link   We will see later (page 219) that profit must not be confused with cash.

---

assignment focus

1. Identify each item as: capital income, capital expenditure, revenue income and revenue expenditure:

   a) buying a car, paying for petrol, servicing, annual insurance and road tax

   b) earning cash from sales of stock and receiving a bank loan

   c) renting an office, buying an office

   d) issuing new shares, receiving commission.

2. Monty buys Alf's window cleaning business for £750. It consists of: bicycle £150, ladder £75, buckets, etc. £25, list of customer names and addresses £500.

   a) Identify the tangible fixed assets and the intangible fixed asset of goodwill. Put a value on each.

   b) Are these capital or revenue expenses? Can you say why?

3. Turn to the balance sheet of JJ's Pies plc on page 218.

   a) Identify items of capital income and capital expenditure.

   b) Repeat this exercise for the plc that you have chosen to study.

Why is the capital versus revenue distinction important?

Table 5.4 summarises how income and expense items are classified.

If we confuse capital and revenue items then we do not give a 'true and fair view' of the business. Our accounts will be misleading because:

- profit is incorrect
- business value is incorrect.

Table 5.4 Classification of income and expense items

	Expense	Income	Final account
Revenue items relate to the year in question	revenue expense – on running costs whose value is consumed within the financial year	revenue income – sales etc. generated within the financial year	trading and profit and loss accounts – calculate profit for the period
Capital items relate to a longer period beyond the current year	capital expense – on fixed assets providing benefit beyond the financial year	capital income – either permanent capital from owner(s) or will be repaid over a number of years	balance sheet – calculates business value or 'worth'

case study 5.3 — Worldcom

In 2002 the US company Worldcom was found to have mislead its investors through inaccuracies in its accounts.

The case is complex, but essentially the company had treated some revenue expenses (overhead costs) as if they were capital items (fixed assets). The effect was to increase profits (because less costs were shown) and to show a higher business value (because more fixed assets were shown).

The company did this to hide its financial difficulties and reassure its investors. The US authorities took legal action against the company.

activity

1 If a major company such as Worldcom fails, which stakeholders may be affected and in what way?

2 Why does it matter if a business reports profits that are too high?

case study 5.4 — JD trading as Quicksands Sandwich Bar

When JD first set up as a sole trader business, she was interested in selling sandwiches, not in keeping accounts. It was hard work remembering to enter up her financial details regularly but she's glad she did. Here's what she records and why she does it:

Figure 5.5 Quicksands Sandwich Bar

■ 'I record everything – the savings I invested when I started, the mortgage I took out to buy the shop, the sales I make, the bills I pay for stock, insurance, rent, rates, light and heat, wages, etc., the cost of the furniture, chill cabinets and delivery van that I have bought ...'

■ 'My accountant needs these figures because every year I have to send details of my profits (my profit and loss account) and what I am worth (my balance sheet) to HM Revenue & Customs. If I don't do this, the HMRC will estimate my profits and I may pay far too much tax. Even now they may ask to see my records to make sure I am not cheating.'

■ 'I must charge VAT on my sales because I now exceed the annual sales threshold set in the chancellor's budget. I can claim back the VAT paid for supplies but any difference must be sent to the government. The VAT inspectors could enter and search my premises and take me to court if they suspected me of evading tax.'

■ 'When I decided to expand my business I asked the bank for a loan. They agreed because I could show them my accounts for the last three years (the same ones the tax people saw). They were reassured that I would be able to meet the loan repayments.'

■ 'The bank also looked at my expansion plans. I had used my accounts as a basis for these because I could see from them the costs and revenues likely to be involved.'

■ 'It's impossible to remember everything and I wouldn't be able to run the businesses without financial records.'

■ 'Profit is important – I need to sell my sandwiches for more than it costs me to make and sell them – that's how I earn a living. The accounts allow me to check how well I am performing so I can ask: are my sales up to target? are my costs rising? when must I pay my suppliers? have I got enough in the bank? etc.'

■ 'I need working capital, i.e. enough cash to pay the bills on time. To avoid problems, I draw up a forecast of my receipts and payments for the coming months. The business accounts provide information that helps me prepare this cash flow forecast.'

■ 'In future I may change to company status to raise more funds, although this would mean more regulation too. For example, I would need to comply with the Companies Acts and publish final accounts for the shareholders with a copy to Companies House.'

As JD says, 'If I did not keep accounts, Quicksands would sink.'

activity

1 List the items of capital expenditure and revenue expenditure that JD mentions. How do you distinguish between the two?

2 List the items of capital income and revenue income mentioned. Again say how you distinguish between these.

3 Why does JD keep accounts? Present your answer under two headings: Legal requirements and Management requirements.

4 How would the capital income of the business change if JD converted into a limited company?

5 What is the current annual sales turnover above which a business must register for VAT?

To achieve P2, you should explain the difference between capital and revenue items of expenditure and income. Do this as follows:

1   Turn to the annual report of your chosen plc. Locate the profit and loss account (probably called the Income Statement) and the balance sheet. If there is a choice, use the group (or consolidated) accounts.

2   Head your work: '[your company name] plc: capital and revenue'.

   a) Clearly explain the meaning of the terms: capital income, capital expenditure, revenue income, revenue expenditure.

   b) Illustrate each definition with examples from the plc final accounts.

   c) Briefly explain why it is important for an accountant to understand these terms.

Preparing a cashflow forecast

A business cannot survive without cash. Either it must generate enough cash through day-to-day trading, or it must be able raise funds from elsewhere. Another alternative is to reschedule payments, i.e. to arrange a delay until there is sufficient cash available.

The cashflow forecast

The cashflow forecast shows estimates of monthly receipts and payments over a forthcoming period – normally 6 or 12 months. This enables a business to estimate the cash available to it. This should mean that potential cash shortages are predicted well in advance so that action can be taken to prevent them occurring.

There are three sections to the cashflow forecast (see Table 5.6):

■   receipts – showing details of expected monthly cash in-flows

■   payments – showing details of expected monthly cash out-flows

■   a summary of the cash position comprising:

   •   net cashflow – total receipts minus total payments for the month

   •   opening bank balance – the funds in the bank at the start of each month. This is the previous month's closing balance. October shows zero because this is a new business

   •   closing bank balance – the funds in the bank at the end of each month. This 'bottom-line' is the most important figure.

Notice that the final two figures on the bottom line (September closing balance and Total closing balance) are equal. This shows that the arithmetic is accurate.

Reading a cashflow forecast

Warning signs might be:

■   a negative figure in the bottom line which indicates a cash shortage, usually shown in parentheses (brackets)

■   a reducing bottom line which may indicate that, although there are sufficient funds at present, problems may occur in future

■   a large and growing bottom line which shows a healthy cashflow. However, it may be inefficient to build up a large surplus of cash. It may be better transferred to a higher interest account, invested in new equipment, or used to pay off loans.

Greendale

Greendale is the trading name of Dale Green, a sole trader. His business will begin trading in October with a capital of £15,000 and a bank loan of £4,000 secured against his house.

The sales and purchases forecasts (Table 5.5) show that:

■ yearly sales should value £275,000. Customers will be allowed 30-day credit, hence payment will be received one month after sales are made

■ purchases of stock will cost £110,000 and suppliers insist on cash on delivery.

The business needs to buy equipment and furniture and fittings immediately and these capital expenses will be made in month one.

Dale has also estimated his monthly revenue expenses – the running costs. He has registered for VAT and estimated quarterly VAT payments. The bank has agreed an overdraft facility of £5,000.

Greendale's cashflow forecast (Table 5.6) shows all estimated monthly receipts and payments during the first year of trading.

Table 5.5 Greendale: Sales and purchases forecasts

Figures rounded to £	Oct	Nov	Dec	Jan	Feb	Mar	Apr	May	Jun	Jul	Aug	Sept	Total £
SALES	10,000	15,000	20,000	25,000	25,000	25,000	30,000	30,000	30,000	25,000	20,000	20,000	275,000
PURCHASES	4,000	6,000	8,000	10,000	10,000	10,000	12,000	12,000	12,000	10,000	8,000	8,000	110,000

Table 5.6 Greendale: Cashflow forecast for the period: October 20–8 to September 20–9

Figures rounded to £	Oct	Nov	Dec	Jan	Feb	Mar	Apr	May	Jun	Jul	Aug	Sep	Total	
RECEIPTS:														debtors
Sales (of stock)	0	10,000	15,000	20,000	25,000	25,000	25,000	30,000	30,000	30,000	25,000	20,000	255,000	20,000
Capital	15,000												15,000	
Loans, grants etc.	4,000												4,000	
Total Receipts (A)	19,000	10,000	15,000	20,000	25,000	25,000	25,000	30,000	30,000	30,000	25,000	25,000	274,000	
PAYMENTS:														creditors
Purchases (of stock)	4,000	6,000	8,000	10,000	10,000	10,000	12,000	12,000	12,000	10,000	8,000	8,000	110,000	0
Wages	1,000	1,500	2,000	2,500	2,500	2,500	3,000	3,000	3,000	2,500	2,000	2,000	27,500	
Salaries	6,000	6,000	6,000	6,000	6,000	6,000	6,000	6,000	6,000	6,000	6,000	6,000	72,000	
Rent/Rates	1,500	1,500	1,500	1,500	1,500	1,500	1,500	1,500	1,500	1,500	1,500	1,500	18,000	
Insurance	2,400												2,400	
Light/Heat			800			800			800			800	3,200	
General administration	1,000	100	100	100	100	100	100	100	100	100	100	100	2,100	
VAT			2,234			6,702			8,043			5,808	22,787	
Capital expenses	12,000												12,000	
Total Payments (B)	27,900	15,100	20,634	20,100	20,100	27,602	22,600	22,600	31,443	20,100	17,600	24,208	269,987	
Net Cashflow (A–B)	(8,900)	(5,100)	(5,634)	(100)	4,900	(2,602)	2,400	7,400	(1,443)	9,900	7,400	(4,208)	4,013	
add Opening Bank Balance	0	(8,900)	(14,000)	(19,634)	(19,734)	(14,834)	(17,436)	(15,036)	(7,636)	(9,079)	821	8,221	0	
Closing Bank Balance	(8,900)	(14,000)	(19,634)	(19,734)	(14,834)	(17,436)	(15,036)	(7,636)	(9,079)	821	8,221	4,013	4,013	

1 How much cash will flow into Greendale during March?

2 How much cash will flow out during June?

3 How much will be spent on salaries over the first year?

4 In which months will there be a cash shortage? (Hint: Check the bottom line of Greendale's cashflow forecast.)

5 In which month will this problem be at its worst?

6 The sales forecast estimates sales of £10,000 for October – so why does the cashflow forecast show October sales receipts as zero? (Hint: Re-read the case study details.)

7 There will be debtors of £20,000 (customers owing money) at the end of the year. Explain why.

Figure 5.6 Greendale's forecast bank balance

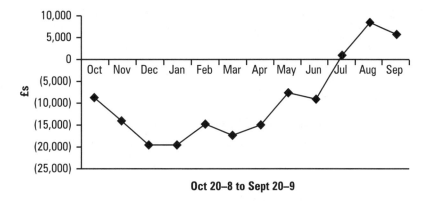

Oct 20–8 to Sept 20–9

What does Greendale's cashflow forecast tell us?

The forecast is produced on an electronic spreadsheet and charts have been linked to help illustrate the main trends.

The bottom line

Figure 5.6 shows that there will be a shortage of cash in each of the first nine months. Thereafter, from July onwards, there will be a cash surplus (if the business has managed to survive).

Over the year as a whole, receipts are expected to exceed payments, but money is not always there when it is needed.

Monthly net cashflow

Figure 5.7 shows that the Greendale's main difficulties can be traced to the first three months. March, June and September also have deficits. The main causes are:

- Credit is given to customers whilst suppliers are paid immediate cash. For example, in October there are no sales receipts yet £4,000 is paid to purchase stock.
- Sales have a seasonal peak period from April to June. The business starts up in October when sales are lower.
- The start-up costs, particularly the £12,000 capital expenses in October (for equipment, etc.), are a drain on cash in the early stages.
- Periodic payments such as VAT and light and heat cause shortages in certain months – in this case in March, June and September.

assignment focus

1 Why may a business such as Greendale offer credit to its customers?

2 New businesses often find it difficult to gain credit from their suppliers. Why do you think this is?

3 Greendale has registered for VAT. Look up the annual sales threshold above which a business must register.

4 Some businesses experience seasonal highs and lows in trade – Standard Fireworks makes 80 per cent of its sales in November yet must continue to pay overheads throughout the year. Can you think of other seasonal businesses?

Figure 5.7 Greendale's forecast monthly net cashflow

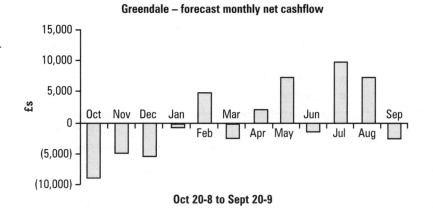

Greendale – forecast monthly net cashflow

Oct 20-8 to Sept 20-9

These problems are typical of a new business, and in reality Greendale's cash shortage will mean that someone will not get paid on time. The £5,000 overdraft limit is exceeded in each of the first nine months.

Depending upon who is affected this could mean: staff refusing to work, suppliers refusing to deliver stocks (as happened when MG-Rover failed in 2005), the electricity being cut off, and so on. Unless something is done the business will not survive.

Cashflow management

Ideally a business will generate sufficient cash from normal day-to-day sales. However, the different demands on business cash and the uneven timing of receipts and payments may mean that, as with Greendale, cash from customers does not always flow in quickly enough.

Cashflow problems

The major causes of **cashflow problems** across a range of business are shown in Figure 5.8.

Cashflow management is about controlling receipts and payments so that cash is available as and when it is needed. This involves using forecasts to identify problems ahead of time and then taking the appropriate action.

Figure 5.8 Cashflow problems

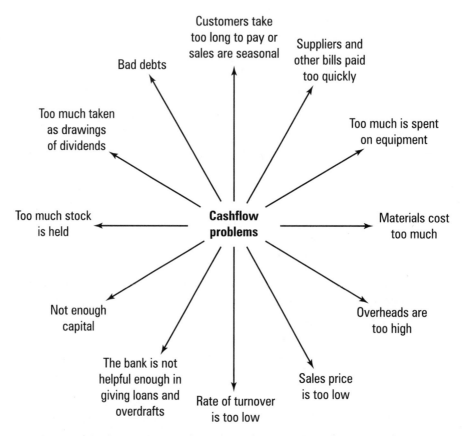

Solutions to cashflow problems

In general terms solutions to cashflow problems fall under four headings:

- *Reducing payments:*
  - cutting running costs – laying off staff, finding cheaper suppliers, using energy efficient vehicles, etc.
  - paying lower dividends to shareholders or lower drawings to sole traders and partners
- *Increasing receipts:*
  - increasing sales revenue by changes to price or by boosting sales volume.
  - raising more capital either from the owner(s) (sole trader, partners or shareholders), or from financial backers such as business angels or venture capital trusts
  - borrowing – loans to buy capital items, mortgages to buy property, overdrafts to meet short-term cash needs
  - grants are available for some start-up businesses

Figure 5.9

- *Delaying payments:*
    - negotiating credit with suppliers if possible
    - buying capital items (fixed assets) on credit to spread the payments
    - leasing rather than buying fixed assets
    - paying utility bills (gas, electricity) in instalments
- *Collecting receipts more quickly:*
    - selling for cash if possible, or on shorter credit periods.
    - giving discounts to encourage customers to pay promptly
    - good credit control to avoid late payment by customers and bad debts (non-payment)
    - factoring debts – the bank pays 80 per cent now, and the rest (less commission) when they collect the debt.

case study 5.6

Greendale – the solution?

There are a number of possible solutions to Greendale's cashflow problems. The finance director has set up the cashflow forecast on a spreadsheet to examine a number of 'what if?' scenarios. Immediately the alternative figures are entered into the spreadsheet the cashflow totals recalculate and the charts respond. Here are the conclusions:

- It is clear that either selling for cash or buying stocks on credit would immediately solve the problem. However neither is possible – customers demand credit and suppliers insist on a trial period before even considering credit facilities.

- The capital items may be bought on interest-free credit with 12 monthly payments of £1,000. This would help, but not completely solve, the problem.

- The VAT could be paid at the end of the year since Greendale is a small business. Again this would help, but not solve the problem.

- Figure 5.10 shows yearly expenses. There may be a way of reducing some of these:

Figure 5.10 Greendale's estimated payments, year 1

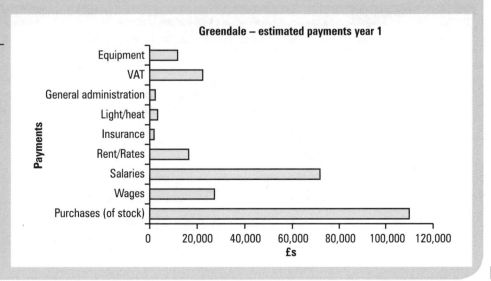

Ultimately the solution might be to bring in more finance to support the business until sales revenue increases sufficiently. Options are as follows.

- An injection of more capital would provide permanent funding suitable for both day-to-day working capital and for the purchase of capital items. If Dale has no more savings, he might take on partners or convert into a private limited company. In this case a business angel could be the solution (as it was for Innocent Drinks – see pages 375–76). However, bringing in new owners may mean loss of control; financial backers will usually wish to be involved in business decisions.

- The bank loan could be extended to help pay for the equipment – assuming further security is available. A loan would need to be repaid with interest over a number of years but would leave Dale in charge of the business. Loans are appropriate for capital expenses, but not for daily working capital needs.

- Extending the bank overdraft. This is an appropriate solution for a short-term problem such as this. Dale would incur a monthly interest charge and should not use this method for buying capital items. The rule when borrowing is that the length of the repayment period should be related to the life of the item being bought.

activity

1   Set up a cashflow model using an electronic spreadsheet. A template is provided on the Nelson Thornes website (www.nelsonthornes.com/btec). Set up charts such as those shown on pages 209–211. Save this model using a suitable name.

2   Enter the original figures for Greendale into your spreadsheet model and check that the totals correspond with those on page 208.

3   Now try 'what if?' scenarios to examine the solutions suggested in the case study above. Remember to start from the original figures in each case.

4   Suggest the most appropriate solution, giving reasons.

5   What are the main advantages of using an electronic spreadsheet for financial forecasting?

assignment focus

Valley Farms will supply local retailers with bags of organic produce. It will begin trading in July 20-8 with £25,000 of capital supplied by the owner Ms Verdi. She will employ two specialist managers each at a monthly salary of £2,000 and will draw the same pay for herself.

Market research shows the forecast sales volumes given in Table 5.7.

Table 5.7 Forecast sales volumes for Valley Farms

	Jul	Aug	Sep	Oct	Nov	Dec	Jan	Feb	Mar	Apr	May	Jun
Sales volume (units)	1,000	1,500	2,000	2,500	2,500	3,000	1,500	2,000	2,500	3,000	3,000	2,500

Supplies will be purchased from local producers at an average cost of £4.60 per unit, cash on delivery. The sale price will be £10 per unit and customers are likely to demand 30-day credit. The wages of sorters and packers will be paid at a piecework rate of £1.20 a unit.

Rent and rates will cost £1,200 per quarter with the first payment due in July; insurance for premises, contents and public liability will be available for an initial one-off premium of £3,000 to be paid at start-up.

Light and heat costs will be £1,100 a quarter with the first payment due in September. General administrative expenses are likely to be around £900 in July and £100 a month thereafter.

Various fixed assets will be needed including packing machines, a computer system, fixtures and fittings and a photocopier. These must be available immediately and are likely to cost £13,000.

1   To achieve P3, prepare a 12-month cash flow forecast for Valley Farms. Use an electronic spreadsheet model for this task.

2   To achieve M1, using the cashflow forecast, identify and analyse any cashflow problems that Valley Farms might experience.

3   To achieve D1, recommend ways in which Valley Farms might solve its cashflow problems giving reasons for your suggestions. A 'what if? scenario will illustrate how your recommendations will help.

4   Write an advice leaflet for use by the local Business Link. This should be called 'Cashflow' and should analyse the most usual causes of business cashflow problems and recommend with reasons the most appropriate solutions.

Profit and loss accounts and balance sheets

The final accounts

The final stage in the accounting process is to draw up the trading and profit and loss account and balance sheet for the benefit of both internal and external stakeholders.

■   The trading account shows the gross profit over a trading period.

■   The profit and loss account shows the net profit over a trading period.

■   The balance sheet shows the value (or 'worth') of the business at a point in time, in terms of assets, liabilities and capital.

As we have seen (page 200), the legal form of business organisation determines which external stakeholders have access to these reports each year. Managers needing to monitor weekly or monthly performance may wish to produce more regular reports.

Link

Figure 5.1 on page 198 illustrates the accounting process as a whole.

The trial balance

A trial balance sets out the figures from which the trading, profit and loss account and balance sheet are produced. It is drawn up by the book-keeper using the balances in the business accounts (see Table 5.6). It serves two purposes:

■   It checks the accuracy of the financial records. If the two columns (the debits and credits) do not balance, there is an error.

■   It provides a convenient list from which to compile the final accounts.

Table 5.8 How items are positioned on the trial balance

Debit balances	Credit balances	
Purchases of stock	Sales of stock	→ **Trading account** showing gross profit
Other running costs	Other receipts	→ **Profit and loss account** showing net profit
Assets owned by the business	Liabilities owed by the business	→ **Balance sheet** showing business value
Drawings or dividends taken out by the owners	Capital invested by the owners	

↑		↑
How the business used it funds	=	How the business generated its funds

As an example, we will look at Al Fresco, a sole trader, who has just completed his latest financial year. He has maintained accurate financial records and for convenience he lists his year-end figures in the form of a trial balance (Table 5.7).

Table 5.9 Trial balance of Al Fresco as at 31 December 200–

	Debit £	Credit £	Type of item	Final account
Sales		190,000	Trading income	
Sales returns	10,000			
Stock at 31 January 200–	19,500		Trading expense	Trading account
Purchases	120,000			
Purchase returns		12,000		
Discounts received		3,000	Additional income	
Discounts allowed	2,000		Overhead expresses	
Insurance	8,675			
Motor expenses	6,765			Profit and loss account
Salaries	17,500			
Light and heat	10,000			
General expenses	3,660			
Premises	150,000		Fixed assets	
Vehicles	4,800			
Debtors	18,000		Current assets	
Bank	5,700			
Creditors		9,000	Current liabilities	Balance sheet
VAT		3,000		
Mortgage		48,000	Long term liability	
Capital		140,000	Opening capital	
Drawings	28,400		Drawn by owner	
	405,000	405,000		

Explanatory notes (column heading spanning *Type of item* and *Final account*)

Additional information at 31 December 200–:
Closing stock £12,000   — adjustment — both trading account and balance sheet

Notice that each item on the trial balance appears once in the final accounts – going to either the trading account, the profit and loss account or the balance sheet.

The closing stock figure is an extra item needed to calculate accurate profits. It appears below the trial balance and comes from stock-taking (counting and valuing unsold stock) rather than from the business accounts. This appears twice – on both the trading account (Table 5.10) and on the balance sheet (Table 5.11).

Table 5.10 Trading and profit & loss account of Al Fresco for period ending 31 December 200–

The final accounts are drawn up in vertical format. Details appear in the left had column with totals to the right.

	£	£
Sales (less returns)		180,000
Opening stock	19,500	
Purchases (less returns)	108,000	
	127,500	
less Closing stock	12,000	
Cost of stock sold		115,500
Gross profit		64.500
Discounts received		3,000
		67,500
less Insurance	8,675	
Motor expenses	6,765	
Salaries	17,500	
Light & heat	10,000	
Discounts allowed	2,000	
General expenses	3,660	
Net profit		48,600
		18,900

The **trading account** – calculates **gross profit** on buying and selling stock

The **profit and loss account** – calculates **net profit (or loss)** after all other running costs

Table 5.11 Balance sheet of Al Fresco as at 31 December 200–

Balance sheet items appear in the order of permanence. The longest lasting (or most permanent) items are shown first.

	£	£
Fixed assets		
Premises		150,000
Vehicles		4,800
		154,800
Current assets		
Stock	12,000	
Debtors	18,000	
Bank	5,700	
	35,700	
less **Current liabilities**		
VAT	3,000	
Creditors	9,000	
	12,000	
Working capital		23,700
		178,500
less **Long-term liabilities**		
Mortgage		48,000
Net assets		130,500
As financed by:		
Capital (at start)		140,000
Net profit		18,900
		158,900
less Drawings		28,400
		130,500

net assets (assets less liabilities)

equals

capital (the value, or net worth, of the busines to the owner)

Notice that two figures, the closing stock and the net profit (or loss), are transferred to the balance sheet. These are shaded for convenience.

Profit and loss account

Profit is calculated on the trading and profit and loss accounts which follow one from the other. The heading 'for period ending ...' indicates the last day of the trading period over which these profits are calculated.

Profit is the result of revenue income less revenue expense.

The trading account

The trading account calculates the gross profit achieved from buying and selling stock. Gross profit is sales revenue less the cost of goods sold. In the example:

£180,000 – £115,500 = £64,500

Cost of goods sold equals opening stock (stock at start) plus purchases (stock bought in the period) less closing stock (unsold stock at the period end).

This account is used by traders such as wholesalers and retailers but is not relevant to service providers.

The profit and loss account

The profit and loss account calculates net profit over the trading period by subtracting business overhead expenses (the revenue expenses incurred over the period) from the gross profit. In the example:

£64,500 – £45,600 = £18,900

(Service providers not using a trading account would calculate net profit as sales less overheads.)

- Expenses not included in the profit and loss account are:
  drawings – personal expenses of the owner rather than business expenses
- capital expenses such as fixed assets.

A net loss

It is unlikely that a business will make a gross loss – this would mean selling stock at below cost price over a prolonged period. However, it is quite possible that overhead costs may exceed gross profit thus resulting in a net loss.

> **remember**
>
> Fixed assets are long-term items not consumed in the period. They remain of use for the future.

The balance sheet

The balance sheet includes capital income and capital expense. It shows the worth (or value) of the business at a given date by comparing the value of assets owned by the business with the value of liabilities owed to those outside the businesses. The heading 'as at ...' indicates that the balance sheet is a 'snapshot' of the business at a point in time.

- The top section shows: assets less liabilities equals net assets.
- The bottom section shows the owner's capital.

The balance sheet will balance, i.e. the two sections have the same total which represents the value of the business to the owner. In the example, this is £130,500.

Assets

Assets represent value owned by the business. They may be fixed or current.

For fixed assets, see page 202 and Unit 2, page 89.

Liabilities

Liabilities represent debts owed to external parties. They may be current or long-term.

For current and long-term liabilities, see Unit 2, page 90.

Working capital (or net current assets)

For working capital, see Unit 2, pages 82 and 83.

A shortage of working capital (a cashflow problem) may cause serious difficulties. In the example working capital is: £23,700, i.e. £35,700 – £12,000.

Capital

Capital is initially the value invested in the business by the owner(s). This will be increased each year when retained profits (profits not taken by the owner) are added. Any losses will be subtracted.

Sole traders and partners are entitled to take profits in the form of drawings (value in either cash or goods). Company shareholders are awarded a dividend by the directors.

In the example, the balance sheet shows capital at the start increased by profits and reduced by drawings. The closing capital figure – the bottom line – is the value of the business to the owner.

The published final accounts of limited companies

These are the accounts that you will be able to obtain because of the legal requirement for companies to publish their accounts. The format varies from that of the sole trader because of the difference in the form of ownership and in the needs of company stakeholders.

The example of JJ's Pies plc is provided with explanatory notes (Tables 5.12 and 5.13).

Table 5.12 Company final accounts: JJ's Pies plc: Group income statement

	2006 £000s	2005 £000s	Notes
TURNOVER	61,557	53,109	Sales of pies
Cost of sales	(34,101)	(28,054)	Cost of producing pies
GROSS PROFIT	27,456	25,055	
Distribution costs	(7,805)	(8,663)	Transport and storage
Administrative expenses	(13,785)	(11,888)	Running costs
GROUP OPERATING PROFIT	5,866	4,504	
Share of operating profit in joint venture	100	59	Profits from franchises
TOTAL OPERATING PROFIT	5,966	4,563	Profits from the pies
Profit on sale of fixed assets	775	–	Profit on selling some stores
PROFIT BEFORE INTEREST AND TAXATION	6,741	4,563	
Interest payable	(204)	(324)	Interest on loans
PROFIT BEFORE TAXATION	6,537	4,239	Net profit
Tax on profits	(1,958)	(1,404)	Corporation tax
PROFIT AFTER TAXATION	4,579	2,835	
Minority interests	(20)	–	Profits due to businesses holding shares in JJ's subsidiaries
PROFIT ATTRIBUTABLE TO SHAREHOLDERS	4,559	2,835	
	(1,757)	(1,018)	
Ordinary dividend			Share of profits paid to ordinary shareholders.
Retained profit	2,802	1,817	The remaining profit to be reinvested in the business. This becomes part of the reserves on the balance sheet.
Earnings per share	9.02p	5.60p	The profit that each share has earned over the year
Dividend per share	3.5p	2.0p	The amount of profit the directors propose to pay shareholders for each share they hold.

Table 5.13 JJ's Pies plc: Group balance sheet

	2006 £000s	2005 £000s	Notes
NON CURRENT ASSETS			*Fixed assets*
Intangible assets	1,430	2,386	*Goodwill and franchise fees*
Tangible assets	12,293	13,685	*Land/buildings, vehicles, equipment*
Investments in joint venture	339	307	*Share in Chez-Nous restaurants*
TOTAL FIXED ASSETS	14,062	16,378	
CURRENT ASSETS			
Stock	1,843	1,411	*Materials (ingredients)*
Debtors	12,233	10,702	*Owned by trade customers*
Cash at bank and in hand	3,721	3,885	
TOTAL CURRENT ASSETS	17,797	15,998	
CURRENT LIABILITIES	(13,380)	(12,919)	*Trade creditors (suppliers), tax and dividends due*
NET CURRENT ASSETS	4,417	3,079	*Working capital*
TOTAL ASSETS LESS CURRENT LIABILITIES	18,479	19,457	
NON CURRENT LIABILITIES	(7,749)	(7,756)	*Bank loans and mortgages*
NET ASSETS	10,730	11,701	*The value of the business*
CAPITAL AND RESERVES			
Called up share capital	2,660	2,546	*Funds raised by selling shares*
Share premium account	3,290	2,396	*Gains from selling shares at more than nominal value*
General reserve	3,000	2,500	
Profit & loss account	1,780	4,260	*Retained profits*
SHAREHOLDERS' FUNDS	10,730	11,701	*The value of the business*

Notice the change in terminology under EU accounting regulations:

- income statement = trading and profit and loss account
- non-current assets = fixed assets
- non-current liabilities = long-term liabilities.

assignment focus

1   What is happening to JJ's profits (before tax)?

2   Why is this happening (e.g. rising sales, lowering costs, both, etc.)?

3   How much was the company worth at the end of 2006? Has its value gone up or down?

4   Which other business does JJ's partially own?

5   JJ's balance sheet is presented in the order of permanence. Banks however, use the order of liquidity, that is with the most liquid assets first. Obtain the published balance sheet of a major bank to check this.

Cash versus profit

The purpose of cashflow forecasting is to measure the cash that we will have available at a given time. In doing this we take account of all cash inflows and outflows regardless of whether they are capital or revenue.

Profit on the other hand is about comparing the revenue income generated in a given trading period with the revenue expense incurred in making these sales. Here we include sales made in a period or expenses incurred regardless of whether they have been paid.

Case study 5.7 shows that cash and profit are quite different.

case study 5.7 — Park Stores

Park Stores will begin trading in July. Cashflow and profit forecasts have been prepared for the first six months.

Table 5.14 Park Stores: sales and purchases budgets

	Jul £	Aug £	Sept £	Oct £	Nov £	Dec £	Total £
Sales (on 30 day credit)	50,000	50,000	100,000	100,000	150,000	150,000	600,000
Purchases (paid cash on delivery)	35,000	35,000	70,000	70,000	85,000	65,000	360,000

Table 5.15 Park Stores: cashflow forecast

	Jul £	Aug £	Sept £	Oct £	Nov £	Dec £	Total £	Notes
RECEIPTS								Debtors
Sales	0	50,000	50,000	100,000	100,000	150,000	450,000	£15,000
New Capital	300,000						300,000	
Total Receipts (A)	300,000	50,000	50,000	100,000	100,000	150,000	750,000	
PAYMENTS								Creditors
Purchases	35,000	35,000	70,000	70,000	85,000	65,000	360,000	£0
Sales & distribution	10,000	10,000	10,000	10,000	10,000	10,000	60,000	
Administration	11,000	11,000	11,000	11,000	11,000	11,000	66,000	
Capital items (fixed assets)	280,000						280,000	
Total Payments (B)	336,000	56,000	91,000	91,000	106,000	86,000	766,000	
Net Cashflow (A–B) add	(36,000)	(6,000)	(41,000)	9,000	(6,000)	64,000	(16,000)	
Opening Bank Balance	0	(36,000)	(42,000)	(83,000)	(74,000)	(80,000)	0	
Closing Bank Balance	(36,000)	(42,000)	(83,000)	(74,000)	(80,000)	(16,000)	(16,000)	

Table 5.16 Park Stores: Forecast Trading and Profit and Loss Account for period ending 31 December 200–

	£	£
Sales		600,000
less Purchases		360,000
Gross profit		240,000
less		
Sales & distribution	60,000	
Administration	66,000	
		126,000
Net profit		114,000

Note: VAT has been omitted in this example.

Table 5.17 Park Stores: Forecast Balance Sheet as at 31 December 200–

	£	£	£
Fixed assets			280,000
Current assets			
Debtors		150,000	
Current Liabilities			
Creditors	0		
Bank O/D	16,000		
		16,000	
Working capital			134,000
			414,000
As financed by:			
Capital			300,000
add Net Profit			114,000
			414,000

1. Will there be sufficient cash in the first six months? Give details.
2. Does Park Stores expect a profit or a loss? Again give details.
3. Cash and profit are calculated differently. Which differences appear in the Park Stores case study?

To achieve P4, you need to explain the component parts of a profit and loss account and balance sheet in a given organisation.

Guy Roper has begun to draw up his final accounts, but is unable to complete them. He has asked for your help. Your tasks are to:

1. Complete the final accounts by providing the missing calculations and labels.
2. Write an accompanying explanation for Mr Roper of the purpose of the trading account, profit and loss account and balance sheet.
3. Include an explanation of each of the component parts within each final account.

Table 5.18 Trading and Profit & Loss Account of Guy Roper (Camping Supplies) for period ending 30 September 200-

		£	£
	Sales		
	opening Stock	38,500	
	Purchases	270,000	
		308,500	
less	closing Stock	20,000	
	?		
	Gross profit		
less	Insurance	4,250	
	Repairs	7,480	
	Postage and packing	4,750	
	Salaries & wages	150,050	
	Light & heat	2,540	
	Telephone	2,225	
	Finance charges	5,860	
	Advertising	6,790	
	Rates	8,750	
	General expenses	3,150	
	Net profit		

Table 5.19 Balance Sheet of Guy Roper (Camping Supplies) as at 30 September 200-

		£	£	£
	Fixed Assets			
	Land & buildings			250,000
	Equipment			17,500
	Fixtures & fittings			23,025
				290,525
	Current Assets			
	Stock		20,000	
	Debtors		35,320	
	Bank		10,750	
	Cash		1,110	
			67,180	
less	**Current Liabilities**			
	Creditors	26,000		
	Bank O/D	1,050		
			27,050	
	?			?
				330,655
less	**Long Term Liabilities**			
	Mortgage			82,000
				248,655
	As financed by:			
	Capital at start			230,000
	Net profit			?
				274,655
less	Drawings			26,000
				?

Reviewing business performance using simple ratio analysis

The final accounts show the absolute level of sales, costs, profits, assets, and so on. For example, the accounts of JJ's Pies tell us that profits and sales were greater in 2006 than in 2005. However, stakeholders may need more information in order to judge the financial strength and performance of a business. Managers, for example, may ask: How much profit do we make for each pound invested? How much profit do we get for each pound that we sell? Are we keeping our costs under control?' Such questions can be answered by using accounting ratios to show the relationship between business activities and results.

Ratios compared

Ratios are particularly useful as a basis for comparison. For example, the accounting ratios of a business may be compared with:

- previous results for the same business (notice that company accounts always provide the current and the previous year's figures)
- the performance of competitors
- the average for the industry
- targets set at the start of the year.

Types of accounting ratio

Ratios that can be used to measure business performance include:

- **profitability ratios**
- **liquidity (or solvency) ratios**
- **efficiency ratios.**

The use of the term 'ratio' is misleading because whilst some of the results are expressed as ratios, others are shown as percentages, days or rates of turnover. What they have in common is that they show the relationship between two or more figures normally taken from the final accounts of a business.

Profitability ratios

Gross profit % on sales (also called gross profit margin)

$$\text{Gross profit \%} = \frac{\text{Gross profit}}{\text{Sales revenue (or turnover)}} \times 100$$

Gross margin relates the buying and selling price of stock and so is used by manufacturers, wholesalers and retailers but not usually by service providers.

A gross margin of 20 per cent indicates that 20p gross profit is made on each £1 of sales. The ratio should be consistent from year to year and similar to industry averages.

Gross profit margin is altered by changes in selling prices, changes in the cost of purchasing stock or by a combination of the two. A business with a low gross profit margin will need a high rate of turnover to survive.

Net profit % (also known as net margin)

$$\text{Net profit \%} = \frac{\text{Net profit}}{\text{Sales (or turnover)}} \times 100$$

Net margin shows the relationship between net profit and sales. So, for example, a 5 per cent net margin shows that 5p net profit is made on each £1 of sales. This ratio can be used to monitor how overhead costs change over time. Net margin will normally change in line with gross margin; a greater rise than gross margin shows that overheads are being reduced, a smaller rise is a warning sign that overheads are increasing.

Again industry averages can be used as a guideline for target levels.

Net profit % is of interest to:

- managers who wish to see that profitability is in line with their targets
- customers and competition authorities who are concerned that companies are not abusing their power by making unreasonably high profits and that they are passing price cuts on to the consumer. In 1999 the Competition Commission launched an investigation into the profits made by UK supermarkets after comparing their profit margins with those in the US and France
- employees whose wages and salaries are a significant cost to a business. Employees may feel vulnerable if rising costs are driving margins down. Equally they may feel that they deserve better rewards if efficient working is keeping costs low
- shareholders who wish to see profitability as high as possible.

ROCE

ROCE (return on capital employed) is also known as the prime ratio.

$$\text{ROCE} = \frac{\text{Net profit}}{\text{Capital employed}} \times 100$$

For our purposes:

Capital employed = Closing capital (or net assets) + Long-term liabilities

ROCE should at least equal the interest that could be earned if the capital were to be invested safely elsewhere, e.g. the interest rate offered by a bank or building society or a similar business.

ROCE is of interest to:

- managers wishing to monitor performance
- shareholders/owners, who wish to see that their funds are being put to good use by the directors
- creditors, such as banks, who wish to see that the business can keep up interest and loan repayments.

Liquidity ratios

Liquidity ratios are sometimes called solvency ratios. Solvency refers to the ability of a business to pay its debts. A business is insolvent if the value of liabilities owed is greater than the value of assets owned. However, even a business with sizeable assets may still not be able to pay on time. For example, premises or equipment cannot be sold without damaging the business, and perhaps cash is tied up in stock.

Liquidity is the ability to turn assets into cash as and when creditors need paying, and it is crucial to survival.

The two liquidity ratios compare the current assets where money can be raised quickly with the current liabilities, those debts that need to be paid in the near future.

Turn to page 215 and remind yourself how working capital is calculated on a balance sheet.

Current ratio

This is also called the working capital ratio.

$$\text{Current ratio} = \frac{\text{Current assets}}{\text{Current liabilities}} \quad (\text{expressed as a ratio :1})$$

This ratio shows the value of current assets available to pay each £1 of current liabilities due. For example, a 2:1 ratio indicates that £2 of current assets are available to pay each £1 of current liabilities.

2:1 is sometimes said to be ideal but modern managers try to operate on as low a current ratio as possible. They argue that value tied up in stock, in debtors or resting in the bank is not actually 'working' at all.

Businesses able to generate cash sales from day to day (e.g. Tesco) can work successfully on a low ratio, but slow turnover businesses and those giving credit to customers usually need a higher ratio.

Acid test ratio

This is sometimes known as the quick ratio or liquid capital ratio.

$$\text{Acid test ratio} = \frac{(\text{Current assets} - \text{Stock})}{\text{Current liabilities}}$$

This ratio excludes stock because it may take time to sell and is therefore less liquid than the other current assets.

An acid test ratio of 1:1 (£1 of current assets excluding stock to £1 of current liabilities) is sometimes said to be ideal. However, again this depends upon the nature of the business.

Liquidity ratios will be of interest to:

- managers wishing to ensure that creditors can be paid whilst avoiding the inefficient use of business cash
- creditors interested in being paid on time
- auditors needing to certify that a company is a 'going concern'. When tunnelling problems delayed the opening of Eurotunnel, for instance, the auditors noted in the accounts that the business might find it difficult to survive.

Too much liquidity?

Although shortage of working capital can lead to cashflow problems, too high a ratio shows that managers are not making the most efficient use of the business resources (rather like keeping all of your savings under the mattress just in case). Surplus current assets tie up cash that may be better used elsewhere – perhaps in a high-interest investment, in new fixed assets to improve productivity or in buying back shares.

This is why businesses increasingly use JIT (just in time) delivery to keep down stock levels. This avoids the costs of storage and tying up money in stock-piling goods.

Efficiency ratios

Debtor collection period

$$\text{Debt collection period (in days)} = \frac{\text{Trade debtors}}{\text{Credit sales}} \times 365 \text{ (days)}$$

Where the accounting period is less than a year, the figure 365 will need to be adjusted, e.g. 182 days for six months.

The formula shows the average number of days that it takes to collect payment from customers. For example, if the collection period is 40 days, but the credit period is 30 days, then credit control needs to be improved.

Late payment by debtors is a major cause of cashflow problems, especially to small businesses. The debtor collection period is of interest to:

■ managers who need to control credit and ensure adequate cashflow

■ shareholders and potential investors who need to see that the business remains solvent

■ debtors (the customers)

■ creditors – they will not get paid if a business has cashflow problems because of poor credit control.

Debtor collection and creditor payment ratios

Sometimes precise figures may not be available for trade debtors and creditors (as opposed to total debtors and creditors) or for credit purchases and sales (as opposed to total purchases and sales). In this case, assumptions will have to be made, thus making the ratios less accurate.

Creditor payment period

$$\text{Creditor payment period (in days)} = \frac{\text{Trade debtors}}{\text{Credit purchases}} \times 365 \text{ (days)}$$

Again where the accounting period is less than a year, the figure 365 will need to be adjusted, e.g. 182 days for six months.

This formula shows the average number of days taken to pay creditors for supplies. If, for example, the payment period is 40 days when the credit period is 30 days, then efforts should be made to pay earlier, otherwise credit may be withdrawn or a valuable supplier lost.

The creditor payment period is of interest to:

■ managers who need to ensure adequate supplies

■ existing creditors who need to be paid

■ potential creditors who wish to see the business' payment record before allowing credit.

Rate of stock turnover (or rate of stock turn)

The rate of stock turnover shows the number of times that stock is sold (or turned over) during the trading period. Note that this should not be confused with 'turnover', which refers to the value of these sales.

$$\text{Rate of stock turnover} = \frac{\text{Cost of stock sold}}{\text{Stock}}$$

For our purposes, we will use the closing stock for this calculation. This figure is of interest to business managers – high turnover indicates efficiency.

There is often an inverse relationship between rate of turnover and profit margin.

remember Businesses try to hold as little stock as possible preferring to buy JIT (just-in-time) for the customer.

- A high turnover business, such as the grocery trade, will usually have low margins. Indeed retailers may intentionally cut margins to increase their turnover – the 'pile 'em high and sell 'em cheap' philosophy.

- A business with a low rate of turnover, such as a car showroom, requires high margins in order to survive.

Are the following high turnover/low margin or low turnover/high margin:

an antique shop, a computer retailer such as Dell, Argos, a manufacturer of specialised industrial plant for the car industry?

Ratio analysis: a worked example

Stanley Livingston is a sole trader. The final accounts for his first two years in business are shown in Tables 5.20 and 5.21.

Table 5.20 Trading and profit & loss account of Stanley Livingston for the periods ending 28 February 20–6 and 20–7

		28th February 20–6		28th February 20–7	
		£000s	£000s	£000s	£000s
	sales		1120		1500
	opening stock	0		40	
	purchases	600		840	
		600		880	
less	closing stock	40		44	
	cost of stock sold		560		836
			560		664
	Gross profit				
less	Overheads:				
	marketing	140		200	
	administration	200		210	
	establishment	120		150	
	finance	60		50	
			520		610
	Net profit		40		54

Table 5.21 Balance sheets of Stanley Livingston as at 28 february 20–6 and 20–7

		28th February 20–6		28th February 20–7	
		£000s	£000s	£000s	£000s
	Fixed assets				
	premises		300		300
	vehicles		100		100
	equipment		225		210
			625		610
	Current assets				
	stock	40		44	
	debtors	110		160	
	bank	15		10	
		165		214	
less	**Current liabilities**				
	creditors	70		100	
			95		114
			720		724
less	**Long-term liabilities**				
	mortgage		210		200
	Net assets		510		524
	As financed by:				
	capital (at start)		500		510
	net profit		40		54
			540		564
less	drawings		30		40
	Closing capital		510		524

Other information available:

- During his second year of trading, Stanley reduced his selling price in order to become more competitive.
- All sales and purchases are on 30-day credit.

Table 5.22 shows his profit and loss accounts. The ratio analyses are shown in Table 5.23 and 5.24.

Table 5.22 Profit and loss account for Stanley Livingston

Profit and loss account	200–6 £000s	200–7 £000s	Comment
Sales	1,120	1,500	an increase in sales of 34%
Gross profit	560	664	gross profit up 19%
Net profit	40	54	net profit up 35%

Table 5.23 Profitability and efficiency ratios for Stanley Livingston

Profitability ratios	200–6	200–7	Comment
% ROCE $\dfrac{\text{Net Profit}}{\text{capital employed}} \times 100$	$\dfrac{40}{720} \times 100$ 5.6%	$\dfrac{54}{724} \times 100$ 7.5%	There is an improvement here. The business is now a better investment for its owners. However the return is still below both the UK average for small busineees (10%)
Gross profit % $\dfrac{\text{gross profit}}{\text{sales}} \times 100$	$\dfrac{560}{1,120} \times 100$ 50%	$\dfrac{664}{1,500} \times 100$ 44.3%	The gross profit % has been reduced by price cutting. As a result the business is more competitive so that scales have risen and gross profit has increased. See also the comment on Rate of Stock Turnover (below)
Net profit % $\dfrac{\text{net profit}}{\text{sales}} \times 100$	$\dfrac{40}{1,120} \times 100$ 3.6%	$\dfrac{54}{1,500} \times 100$ 3.6%	The net profit % is unchanged despite a lower gross profit %. Overhead costs are therefore under control – see also the comment on the selling ratio. The profit and loss account showns that net profit has increased because of the higher gross profit
Efficiency ratios			
rate of stock turnover $\dfrac{\text{cost of stock sold}}{\text{stock}}$	$\dfrac{560}{40}$ 14 times	$\dfrac{836}{44}$ 19 times	The reduction in sales prices has resulted in an increase in the rate of turnover
debtor collection period $\dfrac{\text{trade debtors}}{\text{credit sales}} \times 365$	$\dfrac{110}{1,120} \times 365$ 35.8 days	$\dfrac{160}{1,500} \times 365$ 38.9 days	On average customers are paying late. An increase shows that the situation is worsening. Credit control needs to be tighter and late payers must be chased. The figure needs to be brought back to 30 days so as to avoid cashflow problems in the future
creditor payment period (days) $\dfrac{\text{trade creditors}}{\text{credit purchases}} \times 365$	$\dfrac{70}{600} \times 365$ 42.6 days	$\dfrac{100}{840} \times 365$ 43.5 days	We are not paying our suppliers on time and the situation is worsening slightly. The business should pay on time (there is money in the bank) so that suppliers do not withdraw credit facilities

Table 5.24 Solvency ratios for Stanley Livingston

Solvency (liquidity) ratios			
Current ratio current assets current liabilities	$\dfrac{165}{70}$ 2.4:1	$\dfrac{214}{100}$ 2.1:1	This is down to a more satisfactory level. The business will have sufficient liquidity to pay its creditors. The debtors figure is growing probably becase they are paying later. This needs to be watched (see debtor collection period).
Acid test ratio (liquidity ratio) $\dfrac{\text{(current assets – stock)}}{\text{current liabilities}}$	$\dfrac{(165{-}40)}{70}$ 1.8:1	1.7:1 $\dfrac{(214{-}44)}{100}$ 1.7:1	This is down, but may still be too high – there is £1.70 for every £1 due. Remember too high a ratio indicates an inefficient use of cash. The high debtors figure may be a problem

Calculating and interpreting ratios – some hints

There are three main stages when using financial ratios:

1   Extracting the figures from the annual reports or from the press – this can be more difficult for some company accounts where only summary details are given. It may be necessary to use the notes to the accounts in order to find the appropriate figures.

2   Calculating the ratios using the formulae – it is relatively straightforward to use the formulae once you have found the necessary figures. Always check your results to make sure that:

- they make sense, e.g. a gross or net profit ratio of more than 100 per cent is impossible

- there is an appropriate number of decimal places (one is usually sufficient)

- you indicate the units used, e.g. %, ratio :1, times, days.

3   Making comparisons and interpreting the results – this is the most demanding aspect as it requires not just doing but understanding. We suggest that you work in stages:

- First, state what has happened, i.e. has the ratio gone up or down significantly?

- State what this means to the business – for some ratios, e.g. ROCE, you will be able to say whether the situation is now improved or worsened.

- Suggest why the change may have happened, e.g. is a falling net margin to do with increasing overhead costs or with a falling gross margin?

- Suggest whether action is necessary and if so suggest what might be done, e.g. if net margin is falling perhaps overheads need to be controlled, if debt collection period is too high then there is a need for credit control, and so on.

Analysis of ratios

If used correctly, accounting ratios can provide vital information about the financial strength of a business. However remember that:

- there is no such thing as an ideal ratio and so analysis becomes a matter of judgement. Frequently it is the trend that is significant rather than the actual level of the ratio

- ratio analysis is usually only meaningful when performed as a comparison – either with other businesses in the same industry, with industrial averages or within one business over a period of time.

Ratio analysis is usually only meaningful when performed as a comparison, either with:

■ results from previous years (notice that annual reports provide the previous year's figures and sometimes a 5-year summary for comparison)

■ SMART targets set at the start of the year

■ other businesses in the same industry

■ industrial averages that act as a benchmark for good performance.

Limitations of ratio analysis

In interpreting ratios we may need to look at a combination of factors – the present situation, the trend, the type of business, and so on. This can make ratio analysis complex.

In using ratios, we must always be clear that differences in ratios are related with actual performance. There can be other reasons:

■ Accountants may use different definitions for some ratios, e.g. there are a number of measures for capital employed used in calculating ROCE.

■ Changes in accounting policy, rather than performance, may explain some differences between years, e.g. the method of stock valuation or depreciation will affect the level of profit.

■ Published accounts are summaries so, for example, it may be difficult to make exact comparisons between companies. It is important to use the notes to the accounts wherever possible to find trade debtors (as opposed to general debtors) or credit sales (as opposed to total sales).

assignment focus

B's Boutique operates as a sole trader. B's most recent final accounts and those of the previous year are shown in Tables 5.25 and 5.26.

Table 5.25 Profit and loss account account of B's Boutique for the year ending 31 December 20–6 and 20–7

		31st December 20–6		31st December 20–7	
		£000s	£000s	£000s	£000s
	sales		4,235		5,534
	opening Stock	250		315	
	purchases	1,335		2,225	
		1,585		2,540	
less	closing Stock	315		354	
	cost of Goods Sold		1,270		2,186
	GROSS PROFIT		2,965		3,348
	salaries	1,875		2,055	
	rent & Rates	175		187	
	leasing	105		118	
	interest	235		239	
	stationery	115		118	
	maintenance	97		97	
	general Expenses	45		54	
less	total Expenses		2,647		2,868
	NET PROFIT		318		480

▶

227

assignment
focus

Table 5.26 Balance sheets of B's Boutique as a 31 December 20–6 and 20–7

		31st December 20–6		31st December 20–7	
		£000s	£000s	£000s	£000s
	Fixed Assets				
	land & Premises		1,105		1,366
	fixtures & Fittings		115		258
	motor Vehicles		145		140
			1,365		1,764
	Current Assets				
	stock	315		354	
	debtors	400		675	
	bank/Cash	373		40	
		1,088		1,069	
less	**Current Liabilities**				
	creditors	225		325	
	Working Capital		863		744
			2,228		2,508
less	**Long-Term Liabilities**				
	loans		610		410
	net Assets		1,618		2,098
	As financed by:				
	Capital (at start)		1,300		1,618
	Net Profit		318		480
			1,618		2,098

Additional information:

■ All trading is carried out on 30-day credit.

■ The business operates in a highly competitive market and must price its goods accordingly.

1 To achieve P5, using the accounts of B's Boutique, calculate suitable ratios for profitability, liquidity and efficiency, for the two most recent years of 20-6 and 20-7.

   Display the results in table format to one decimal place. (You may find it convenient to use a spreadsheet for this task.)

2 To achieve M2, use the ratios for 20-6 and 20-7 to analyse the performance of the business.

3 To achieve D2, evaluate the financial performance of B's Boutique over the two years using all of the evidence available. Identify any problems and offer appropriate advice. Charts may help to illustrate your main points.

   Explain the usefulness and limitations of ratio analysis to the business.

   Prepare a presentation of your findings and be ready to present these to your group.

UNIT 9

Exploring creative product promotion

This unit covers:

- The constituents of the promotional mix
- The role of promotion within the marketing mix
- The role of advertising agencies and the media
- Creating a simple promotional campaign

You are already familiar with the promotional side of marketing as you are exposed to marketing communications every day, from a variety of different media. This unit introduces you to the different ways of promoting products and the sorts of decisions that need to be made about how to promote a product. You will have the opportunity to design your own promotional campaign.

This unit is linked to Unit 3, Introduction to marketing.

grading criteria	To achieve a **Pass** grade the evidence must show that the learner is able to:	To achieve a **Merit** grade the evidence must also show that the learner is able to:	To achieve a **Distinction** grade the evidence must also show that the learner is able to:
	P1 describe the promotional mix used by two selected organisations for a selected product/service	**M1** explain how the promotional aspect is integrated and used with the whole marketing mix of a selected organisation to achieve its business aims and objectives	**D1** evaluate and justify the use of an appropriate promotional mix with respect to business and marketing objectives for the selected organisation
	P2 describe the role of promotion within the marketing mix for a selected product/service	**M2** explain the relative merits of using professional agencies in ensuring the promotional success	
	P3 describe the role of advertising agencies and the media in the development of a successful promotional campaign	**M3** provide a rationale for a promotional campaign and make recommendations for improvement	
	P4 design a promotional campaign for a given product/ service to meet the needs of a given campaign/creative brief		

The constituents of the promotional mix

assignment focus

For P1, you need to describe the promotional mix used by two organisations for a selected product or service.

The promotional mix

Promotion refers to any marketing communication activities that are intended to inform, persuade or motivate, current and potential customers into buying or supporting a product or service. The customer can be another business (B2B – business to business, e.g. wholesaler, retailer) or a consumer (B2C – business to consumer).

Promotion is an essential part of the marketing activities of any for-profit or not-for-profit organisation. Charities, government departments, sole traders and plcs all carry out promotion to achieve their aims. It is one of the key elements of what is known as the marketing mix.

Link   We examine the role of promotion within the marketing mix on page 239.

The **promotional mix** is the combination of promotion methods used to communicate with target customers. The main methods of promotion are: **advertising** and **publicity**, **public relations**, sponsorships, sales promotion, personal selling, exhibitions, **direct marketing** and using the organisation's **corporate image**.

assignment focus

For D1 you will need to analyse how the different ingredients of the mix are combined to achieve the organisation's objectives. You are a target customer: how good are organisations at reaching/communicating with you? Which elements of the promotional mix most appeal to you?

Advertising and publicity

The Advertising Association defines advertising as:

> 'messages paid for by those who send them intended to inform or influence people who receive them'

Source: www.adassoc.org.uk

It is impersonal and the messages can apply to both goods, services and ideas or causes.

Advertising is any form of communication which is designed to inform and/or persuade businesses or consumers into taking action which meets the objectives of the sender. On any day we will be continuously exposed to advertising in all its forms, on the radio or TV, on the bus, on posters, through logos on clothing, bags and trainers, on the internet, your mobile phone, your junk mail and e-mails, newspapers, magazines, etc. The sender/advertiser could be a retailer, manufacturer, charity or government department (e.g. Department of Health 'Know your limits' anti-drink campaign).

remember
Remember AIDA (page 188) – the ultimate purpose of advertising is to get people to take action.

Advertising, in some form or other, has been in action for centuries. The red and white barber's pole is a reminder of the days when barbers doubled as dentists. Inn signs were important when customers could not read.

Advertising provides information to the buyer. It can be informative when it tells consumers about the product, what it does, how it works, what it costs and where it can be bought. It is persuasive when it is intended to tempt consumers to buy a particular product in preference to any other.

- To view TV and cinema adverts, find out the storyline and learn about the agency, go to www.visit4info.co.uk.
- *Marketing* is a very useful weekly magazine.

case study 9.1

Are these celebrities?

At the time of writing, Kate Moss (who was photographed allegedly taking illegal drugs in September 2005) and Shirley Bassey were advertising M&S, Ian Botham was advertising British Lamb and Weetabix, Wayne Rooney and Coleen were advertising George at Asda and Jamie Oliver was advertising Sainsbury's. Whatever happened to David Beckham who was on £18m a year with advertising and sponsorships?

activity

1   Why are personalities/celebrities used to promote products?

2   Why do organisations advertise?

3   Does your organisation use celebrities? Are they the right choice? Has the campaign attracted any bad publicity?

The main purposes of advertising are to:

■   increase demand, so that the business can sell more at any particular price

■   create or change the image, e.g. Kellogg's Cornflakes are in a package which conveys the image of a 'sunshine breakfast' (the 'look-alike' and 'me-too' own brand cornflakes are in an almost identical box). Adverts such as 'nothing is like' or 'the biggest small car in its class' are intended to hit a competitor's product

■   create brand loyalty so that customers will continue to buy the product in the long term

■   raise the profit/revenue by appealing to the emotions; e.g. charities are now advertising heavily

■   maintain and build the market share

■   increase awareness, gain attention, create an interest or desire for the product so that receivers of the message take action

■   change attitudes or the perception of the product.

Advertising is the main means by which a business can tell the public about the product and what it can do. The type of advertising medium that will be used depends on the content and purpose of the message and its target market.

Publicity is concerned with gaining public attention for goods/services. It is not necessarily paid for and may be unwanted and damaging to the reputation of the product/service. TV programmes such as Watchdog or Rogue Traders publicise bad companies.

assignment focus

1   Analyse the advertising being carried out as part of the promotional campaign mix you are investigating. What is the message? What media is being used? Who is it intended for? Has there been any good or bad publicity, either intentional or unintentional?

These tasks are helpful for P4:

2   What advertising do your competitors use, and can you say why?

3   What advertising do you intend to use as part of your promotional campaign? Why have you made this decision? What message will you be sending?

4   If you choose TV, what programmes? What times? Can you afford it?

5   If you go for magazines, which ones and how much space will you get for your money?

For M1, you should examine how the advertising is linked to other aspects of the promotional mix.

Public relations

Public relations is the process of communicating a specific message to an organisation's stakeholders. Its purpose is to achieve favourable publicity.

For stakeholders, see page 17.

Every organisation will have a file which contains a record of each time it has been mentioned in the media. The public relations (PR) department of an organisation (often included in the marketing department) has the responsibility for getting this publicity. Rock groups, politicians, personalities, presenters and plcs could all have people responsible for their PR. The purpose is to plan and control news to get good publicity and avoid bad publicity. Politicians use 'spin doctors' to turn or twist the adverse effects of a news story in their favour.

Public relations promotion involves:

- keeping the media informed of new products or changes to existing products
- providing press releases, stories, facts, lies, photos, secrets, etc., on behalf of the client to the media. These can result in excellent free publicity. However the sender has no real control over what the receiver will do with the information. Millions of press releases are issued each year; 95 per cent are ignored by the media
- lobbying – persuading journalists, TV presenters, etc. to write or mention the client, e.g. a travel article on Poland might say at the end, 'Our reporter, Holly Day, travelled to Poland courtesy of the Polish National Airline LOT', i.e. the trip was free in return for a free 'plug'
- companies sponsoring major sporting events. Corporate entertainment is an important feature of public relations. Potential clients could be invited to Wimbledon, the FA Cup Final or an England cricket test match. Could these invitations influence their decisions?
- community relations, e.g. the local theatre could give away free tickets to the current pantomime to the winner of the 'Name everyone in the theatre last night' competition! In 2006 Sacha Baron Cohen made the film *Borat* about a fictional Kazakh journalist. The President of Kazakhstan said. 'There is no such thing as bad publicity' and invited everyone to his country to see it for themselves
- organising a product launch or media event, the purpose of which is to achieve as much free publicity as possible, by inviting the press, TV, radio, the local MP, etc. Almost anything can be launched, e.g. a new album, the opening of a new crèche. Sustainable travel was the theme of the Green Canary Day media event organised by Canary Wharf and the Good Going Campaign.

Managing public relations

To be effective, PR must:

- be planned and controlled so that the right message gets across to the right people, i.e. those chosen or targeted by the organisation
- be ready to deal with any problems. Apologising and informing people why the train is late is good PR; doing nothing loses goodwill. What is your experience?
- have a specific message or objective which can preferably be measured, e.g. in column centimetres, or air time
- be developed over the long term to build up both the image and reputation of the organisation, its products, services and/or views and ideas.

assignment focus

What PR or publicity is currently in the news for your product organisation? Do an internet search of blogs and news sites to collect some examples.

Sponsorship

Manufacturers use sponsorship as a way of advertising themselves to the public. Sponsorship can mean giving financial support to an organisation, an event, an activity or a person.

McDonald's 'I'm lovin' it' (it's first global campaign) is already signed up to be one of the sponsors of the 2012 Olympic Games in London. (How will the ban on advertising high fat, sugar or salt products to under 16-year-olds affect this?) The International Olympic Committee (IOC) has already applied to register 2012 as a trade mark to prevent illegal use of the event and date. All advertising space within the London area will need to be secured for Olympic use for the duration of the games. Games-related words and images will only be allowed to be used by official advertisers. Ambush marketing where businesses pretend to be sponsors is strictly illegal. Banned words include gold, silver, bronze (is this a sun tan?), etc.

'Any unauthorised use of the Olympic Marks threatens London 2012's ability to establish a successful sponsorship programme and raise the funds necessary to host and stage the 2012 Games and to fund the Team GB.'

Source: www.london2012.org.uk

The owner of the Olympics Hair Salon in London said he would not change its name. If you intend opening a wedding planning business, do not use five rings as a symbol!

The main purposes/objectives of sponsorship are to:

■ raise customer awareness of the organisation and its products

■ raise the company profile and brand exposure

■ create, enhance or change an image, e.g. BUPA sponsor the Great North Run, charities use the event as a fundraiser

■ generate increased sales

■ widen the audience which sees the company's logo.

Companies now sponsor sports events, sports stars, plays, opera and pantomimes and TV programmes. Motorhead sponsor the North Hykeham under 10s football team! The 2007 London Marathon was sponsored by .... Can you remember the name? If you can't, who were the sponsors trying to attract?

A successful sponsorship can generate millions of pounds of extra sales. Local companies are increasingly prepared to sponsor local events.

Tobacco companies are no longer allowed to sponsor Formula 1 motor racing or advertise close to schools.

assignment focus

Who or what is sponsored by your organisation as part of its advertising/PR/publicity? Why? Or is your organisation sponsored?

Check out the corporate responsibility section of your organisation's website to answer the questions above.

Sales promotion

Sales promotion refers to the techniques and methods used by a business to sell its products to either consumers or other businesses. Its primary purpose is to get customers to take action and purchase a product.

The overall objectives of sales promotion are to:

■ encourage potential customers to buy the product

■ promote and/or maintain customer loyalty.

Business to business (B2B) trade promotion

The main purpose of trade promotions is to persuade businesses to stock and sell the product. There are several methods that can be used to achieve this:

■ *point-of-sale (POS)* displays set up near the till or check-out point. Retailers will be supplied with brochures, mock-ups of the product, leaflets and shop window displays which can be used to focus the customer's attention on a particular product. They appear to be very popular in chemists. Point-of-sale methods are extensively used, particularly in supermarkets, where evidence suggests that almost 30 per cent of purchases are the result of on-the-spot decisions. How often have you heard people say 'I only came in to buy three items and have ended up with a full trolley'? Tesco has decided to become a paperless shop. It is getting rid of all paper POS materials and replacing these with TV screens in the 'power aisles', where most people walk and make decisions

- *competitions* run by many suppliers especially for retailers as a loyalty incentive to get them to sell more of the product
- *discounts* offered to retailers when they buy in bulk or order in advance. They are particularly important when a business is trying to launch a new product. Wholesalers and retailers have to be persuaded to stock new and untried goods with uncertain profits.

On average, some 60 per cent of a sales promotion campaign budget for a consumer product, such as bottled mineral water, would be spent on point-of-sale and retail promotions.

Business to consumer (B2C) promotion

- *Vouchers and coupons* These can be a very efficient way of promoting sales as they cost the company very little. In 2005 Tropicana (juices) was offering '50p off your next purchase'. This promotion was run at the same time as a TV advertising campaign.
- *Samples and gifts* Sachets of just about everything are now stuck to magazines in order to tempt the consumer to buy the magazine and try the product. DVDs, CDs, floppy disks, seed trays and a bait box (this was attached to a fishing magazine) have all been available. Evidence suggests that any increase in sales due to the promotion is only temporary.
- *Discounts and competitions* These are also used to attract new purchasers or maintain the loyalty of existing customers.

Why do companies offer these inducements? Do you buy products because there is a gift attached? Crucially, do you stay loyal to your usual brand or do you switch if the competitor has a special promotion? All these offers are about keeping customers loyal.

See the loyalty ladder on page 148.

assignment focus

What sales promotion is being used by your organisations as part of their promotional campaigns?

Personal selling

In every civilisation wherever goods/services have been sold, the sales person has been central to the promotion mix. Today many students are part-time sales assistants. Do you or your friends feel valued as a key part of promotion?

Personal selling can take place face-to-face or over the telephone. Whether it's B2B or B2C, the process is the same. It is extremely important during the desire and action phases of the AIDA concept, e.g. when a purchase has to be made or a contract signed.

For AIDA, see page 237.

The benefits of personal selling come from the one-to-one communication. The message can be tailored to individual needs and feedback is immediate. Closing (making) the sale will require good communication skills with reassuring body language. Objections can be dealt with immediately and, once trust has been established between the buyer and seller, a long-term relationship can develop, both in B2B and B2C. But how much do effective sales staff cost to recruit, train and develop?

assignment focus

1   Describe the personal selling techniques used by your organisation?
2   The biggest assignment in the world ever? Can your group construct a giant family tree of the marketing mix, showing all the ingredients? It should end up covering a whole wall!

Exhibitions

Exhibitions are big business for many sectors of UK industry. They are particularly important for B2B trading where suppliers and buyers all come together to form a market at an exhibition centre such as the National Exhibition Centre (NEC) in Birmingham or Olympia in London.

There are many purposes of exhibitions, including to:

■ meet new customers

■ promote their image

■ launch new products

■ find out about existing and possible new customers and competitors

■ try out new ideas/products

■ build staff morale

■ network and develop contacts.

Being an exhibitor at a major trade exhibition can be used in promotional material. Being a winner at an exhibition is a selling point. Buyers get the opportunity to compare a range of products and meet the sales staff, although they often complain that they are too 'pushy' or over-aggressive. Both sellers and buyers agree that exhibitions are worthwhile, i.e. expenses are paid!

Are exhibitions value for money? Although exhibition costs can be expensive, the benefits, over the long term can be worthwhile particularly if the exhibitor can create a database of potential customers. This is best achieved by running a raffle or competition with name and address required. Local arts and crafts exhibitions are important for both sales and recognition.

According to its website, the National Exhibition Centre in Birmingham is the busiest exhibition centre in Europe, staging more than 180 exhibitions each year.

---

assignment focus

Is your organisation participating in any exhibitions as part of its promotion campaign?

■ Check out the exhibition websites, the NEC and Olympia websites.

■ The Audit Bureau of Circulations (ABC) has independent data on national and regional newspaper circulation and attendance at exhibitions. Checkout its website: www.abc.org.uk

---

Direct marketing

Direct marketing is any form of sales, supply or promotion made directly to the consumer. Included in direct marketing are direct mail, either off-screen or off-page mail order, tele-marketing, door-to-door distribution and direct reply advertising or selling. The internet is now a major focus of direct marketing.

There are two main advantages of direct marketing.

■ The market can be precisely targeted because the business contacts a known person directly.

■ Costs can be controlled and the business will know exactly what it costs to generate sales.

These are important points because most advertising campaigns tend to be hit and miss affairs, and the business does not usually know who has responded.

Direct mail

Used extensively by charities, financial services and book clubs, direct mail can be very precise. As computer databases become more efficient, individuals can be contacted directly with personalised mail. Much of the mail received is unsolicited 'junk mail', 'junk fax' or 'junk e-mail' (now known as spam), i.e. it is not asked for. The Data Protection Registrar is now getting an increasing number of complaints about some direct mail methods.

Databases are constructed on people who have, for example:

■ entered a TV, newspaper or radio competition and given a name, telephone number, e-mail address, etc.

■ joined a club or used a credit card in any shop. (Beware, store cards have very high interest rates and are being investigated.)

Almost all the transactions you make will be recorded somewhere – 'Smile, you are on camera'! There is one CCTV camera for every 14 people in the UK. Along with China and Russia, we are the most watched in the world.

Tele-marketing

Telephone marketing (tele-marketing) is increasing. It is cheap to set up, very persuasive on a one-to-one basis and the message can be varied.

Direct reply advertising

With this method, advertisements are placed in newspapers, on TV, fax machines, computers, mobile phones (check that you do not have to pay for receiving them), answer machines, etc. – 'You have been chosen ...!' Customers need to reply direct to the advertisement.

---

assignment focus

1   Give details of any direct marketing your organisation is doing in conjunction with its current promotional campaign.

For M1:

2   How can direct marketing help your organisation achieve its objectives?

3   How are the 4Ps of the marketing mix being used in this particular campaign?

Decisions about appropriate mix

In November 2006, *Marketing* carried the headline 'Nintendo in last-minute revamp of Wii launch ads'. Two weeks before the launch (intended for 8 December), Nintendo was allegedly 'unhappy with the original documentary style ads' and stepped in to reshoot them (stylistic changes) so that they would 'look more like ads' (*Source*: *Marketing*, 22 November 2006). The launch of all new games consoles has been very difficult. What criteria would be involved in such a decision?

Cost versus benefits

Whilst there will always be a budget for any promotional campaign – and the choice of promotional mix – it is better to judge the cost in terms of the expected benefits, such as increased awareness, market share or sales, rather than say, a particular medium is cheap or expensive. For example, although national newspapers may be 'expensive', if the expected return is greater than the cost, it is worth making the investment (spending the money). Does the promotion give value for money in cost per thousand?

See page 267.

Short term and long term

Since the mid-1990s, Cadbury has sponsored *Coronation Street*. It is rumoured that this sponsorship will stop due to changes in the Ofcom regulations and a shift in tastes towards premium chocolate. Who now sponsors *Coronation Street*? Is it still Cadbury or a major supermarket? Long-term brand building, awareness, recognition and loyalty are built on public relations and sponsorships. Advertising, sales promotions and personal selling are usually used to achieve short-term objectives.

Target market and exposure to media

Successful promotion means matching the target market to the media which they use. Market research is used to find out who are the customers, what are their demographics, their attitudes, interests and opinions (**AIO**).

For an explanation of demographics, see page 142, and for AIO, see page 256.

Newspapers, magazines, TV and radio produce reader and audience profiles. An effective promotional mix will communicate with the market using a range of media and promotional methods. The ban on advertising food and drink which are high in fat, sugar or salt to under 16-year-olds, introduced in 2007, will have a significant impact on the advertising revenue of music channels aimed specifically at this target segment.

Type of market

The promotional mix for business to business (B2B) would concentrate on building effective relations with the key decision-makers and influencers in the decision-making unit (DMU). Advertising in trade publications, exhibitions, sponsorships and corporate entertainment are particularly important. Trade promotion is important in the short run to persuade e.g. retailers to stock a product. Business to consumer (B2C) promotion would focus on those media used by the target customer.

For DMU, see page 128.

Changing conditions

Any organisation that promotes its products or services will need to be aware of its external market conditions. For example, should a charity be sponsored by a tobacco company? Or a company producing drinks high in sugar. Should a children's sports event be sponsored by a fast food restaurant? Would online advertising be more effective than traditional methods? The promotional mix needs to be continuously reviewed particularly when conditions are rapidly changing.

For external market conditions, see PESTLE, page 43.

Budget and timing

Every promotional campaign will operate with a strict budget. The size of the budget will determine what promotional methods and media can be used. Timing is equally important. TV and cinema adverts have long lead times and need to be booked well in advance; newspaper ads are more flexible and space can be booked at much shorter notice. Advertising agencies can be helpful in booking space and time slots across a range of media.

Communications model

We have dealt with this in detail in the section on communication in Unit 4, page 166.

Figure 9.1 looks at the communication model in relation to the choice of media that could be used by an organisation to convey its promotional message.

assignment focus

Produce a diagram similar to Figure 9.1 showing all the elements of communication for your two organisations.

Consumer response hierarchy

AIDA

AIDA is an acronym for **A**ttention, **I**nterest, **D**esire, **A**ction. It shows the reasons for using different methods of promotion for communicating with customers at different stages. It is similar to the loyalty ladder (page 148) because it shows how an organisation tries to convert non-users into loyal users:

Figure 9.1 The communication model applied to promotion and the choice of media

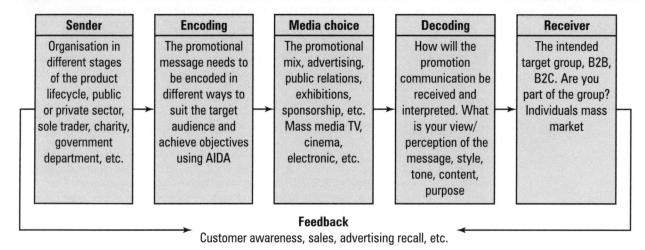

Sender	Encoding	Media choice	Decoding	Receiver
Organisation in different stages of the product lifecycle, public or private sector, sole trader, charity, government department, etc.	The promotional message needs to be encoded in different ways to suit the target audience and achieve objectives using AIDA	The promotional mix, advertising, public relations, exhibitions, sponsorship, etc. Mass media TV, cinema, electronic, etc.	How will the promotion communication be received and interpreted. What is your view/perception of the message, style, tone, content, purpose	The intended target group, B2B, B2C. Are you part of the group? Individuals mass market

Feedback
Customer awareness, sales, advertising recall, etc.

- **A**ttention/awareness – get the customer's attention through advertising. This is particularly true with new products at the launch phase of the product lifecycle (Figure 3.6). New cars, for example, are launched with a fanfare of publicity at international motor shows. Corporate/brand image can be important in gaining attention, e.g. dark chocolate Kit Kat 'piggy backed' the milk chocolate version. Simple posters in shop windows can be very effective for high street stores

- **I**nterest – gain their interest and commitment through public relations. Celebrities are frequently used to gain interest and public acceptance. Seeing your favourite personality using or endorsing a product may influence/convince people it is worth purchasing

- **D**esire – arouse their desire through special offers and sales promotions. These will need to be communicated through a range of media which directly appeal to the target audience. They may be connected with specific aspects of the marketing mix, e.g. the quality or price of the product

- **A**ction – get them to buy the product through effective personal selling techniques. There are three stages in the selling process:

  1 Opening the sale, e.g. use 'How can I help you?' rather than 'Can I help you?'

  2 Dealing with objections – anticipate what might go wrong and be prepared. A strong corporate brand image of e.g. quality or reliability can provide reassurance at this stage.

  3 Close the sale – remember nothing is sold until it is paid for.

Organisations with either a wide product portfolio or a range of target groups are likely to be using a variety of promotion methods

Figure 9.2

1   Is there any evidence that the promotional mix used by your two organisations uses the AIDA principles?

2   Do you go through the AIDA stages before you buy something, or do you buy on impulse?

The role of promotion within the marketing mix

Remind yourself about the 7Ps of the marketing mix in Unit 3, page 107.

Products and services

Product refers to the output of any business. This can either be tangible things, the physical goods, which you can touch, see or smell, such as a dishwasher or cod and chips, or the intangible services, such as the customer services that can be offered by the retailer. Different types of bank accounts or insurance policies are also called products.

Consumers buy particular products because they expect to get utility, i.e. satisfaction or benefits from using them. This satisfaction, the core benefit, must satisfy a need and can be obtained from any aspect of the product. For example, it could be the brand name of the dishwasher, the flavour or the 'packaging' of the cod and chips, the convenience of online banking, the security offered by insurance or the adrenaline rush from rock climbing. Whatever the reason or need, it is all part of the product – the ultimate retail therapy!

Industrial goods, whether machines, materials or equipment would be bought or hired by businesses for the same reason, i.e. they satisfy an industrial need.

Product range

The **product range** may also be called the product mix or product portfolio. The product range is the total number of product/service lines and items sold or produced by a business. The term 'width' is the number of product lines and 'depth' the number of items per product line, such as ten varieties of soup. A large supermarket, for example, could have thousands of lines, whereas a specialist supplier may have very few.

Most large companies, e.g. Nestle, will aim to have a range of products that cover as many market segments as possible. Car manufacturers make small, family cars, sports cars and 4x4s to cater for different lifestyles. Colleges and schools do this by offering a variety of courses that appeal to a wide range of people, although each course would be aimed at a specific target group. What do all your course members have in common?

In some cases, widening the product range will be achieved by the development of new products or by differentiating existing ones. Car companies, for example, make four- or five-door cars, with or without metallic paint, sporty wheel trim, automatic gearbox, sunroof, etc. – the so-called 'optional extras'. Special editions are sometimes made. Smarties, for example, are available in five standard packs – tubes, multipacks of three and five tubes (for supermarkets), cartons and mini-cartons. Each option requires a variation of the production process and will normally be offered at a different price. Promotion (communication) will need to be specifically created to cater for the needs of each target segment, e.g. the promotion of two-seater sports cars may be aimed at DINKies (dual income no kids).

1   What is the product range/mix of your organisation?

2   Which strategy has it followed?

3   Which product/service is being promoted?

New product development

Whenever there are changes in the marketplace, the business should respond. For example, as the location and age structure of the population change, this creates new opportunities for product development, so retirement homes are built to cater for the increase in the ageing population and new pension and life insurance schemes are introduced (no medical required and no salesperson will call).

People's preferences change, e.g. the growth in demand for organic products stems from a need for foods which are free from artificial pesticides and fertilisers and which promote careful consideration of the environment. Convenience foods are developed in response to changing lifestyles. Why is it that organic foods are still more expensive? Is it because retailers are exploiting this segment of customers who are willing to pay higher prices?

Telephone and internet banking have been introduced because people are 'cash rich and time poor'. Computer games and DVDs are also examples of products that have been created in response to changes in leisure habits. Or is it these technologies that are changing habits and lifestyles? At Dixons, the electrical retailer, sales of video recorders and 35 mm cameras have been discontinued due to a lack of demand and the rise in digital photography.

For an organisation to achieve its corporate and marketing objectives, it must increase or at least maintain its share of these changing markets. To be at the leading competitive edge of innovation, it will need to take risks by developing new products and improving existing ones. It will minimise the risks by carrying out thorough product and market trials before going ahead with a full launch. As a CEO of Unilever said:

> 'In the battle for competitive edge we define the need, create the brand and move it around the world at the marketing equivalent of the speed of light. Innovation is moving so fast that you need to be scouting ahead and creating markets.'

Instead of being consumer driven, i.e. responding to consumer needs, companies are now telling and showing customers what they need, e.g. Nokia.

How does a business develop new products?

A business will need to carry out market research to identify a gap in the market before it develops, launches and markets a new product. It will have to consider questions about promotion, price, place, packaging, people and processes (the marketing mix).

Evaluating and assessing new products: product and market trials

Once the business believes it has a sound idea it will need to carry out a product or market trial to find out if it is worth putting into production or developing further. It will need to look at:

- *quality and price* – quality may be associated with price, but words such as 'cowboy' (high price, poor quality) and 'bargain' (low price, good quality) suggest the relationship is not straightforward

- *quantity* – the potential size of the market and the volume of sales. This has to be large enough to justify the development costs, which in some cases can be considerable

- *timing* – this is often crucial to the overall success of a product launch, e.g. merchandise tie-ins with film or TV series (James Bond watch and car to coincide with the release of *Casino Royale*). The Microsoft Xbox360 and Nintendo Wii were released in autumn 2006. However, the Sony PS3 failed to launch in Europe until 2007, thus missing vital Christmas sales

- *position* – the new product's position within the existing product range (sometimes referred to as the product mix) and how it will be promoted.

The product trial

A product trial would usually use a prototype (initial version of a product/service) to find out if the product works, i.e. the prototype will be used to test consumer reaction. Several versions may initially be made and trialled on consumer panels. These panels should be representative of the intended market segment. The winner or highest-rated version will go forward for test marketing in a selected area. This was how Yorkie, originally called Rations, was developed.

Market trials

Before new products are introduced into the market, they are usually tried out on a very small number of people to find out what changes need to be made before any further money is spent on development. Many products get no further than this stage. A careful sample will need to be chosen. What appeals to one group may not appeal to another! The main purpose of a market trial is to identify and sort out potential problems, such as whether the quality is appropriate to the needs of the target audience or whether production/service costs could be reduced to give a realistic price.

A business could run a trial of, for example, new opening hours (we'll try it for a week first and then review it), a new service, proposed changes to an existing product, etc.

A field trial in a specific area could include a full press and TV campaign with promotional back-up, such as free samples. The data which a company obtains in this way will enable it to decide whether it is worthwhile to go for a total nation-wide launch. The test area should ideally be a small version of the target segment as a whole, i.e. with a similar range of ages, income, ethnic group, lifestyles, etc.

BT tests out promotions in any one of nine regional zones to find out how well they work:

> 'By careful monitoring of what happens we can make adjustments to the product, the make up of our target group, the message of our advertising or whatever, then comes national roll-out.'

Source: BT

Product failure

For every new product that succeeds in the market, there are probably 100 that fail, either because the market research was inadequate, or production faults occurred which could not have been foreseen.

Product features and variations

Unique selling points

A major objective of promotion in both the for-profit and not-for-profit sectors is to differentiate the product from the competition. Charities have to compete for donations and businesses have to compete for sales. Every organisation will attempt to achieve a unique position for itself, its products or its services, in the heart and mind of the consumer. It will do this by emphasising one or other of its main features – its unique selling points (USPs) or unique selling proposition to gain the consumers' attention and interest to achieve a sale. With an ever-increasing level of competition and more products competing for our attention, it is important to promote a product so that it stands out from its competitors. However, doing this can be expensive and an organisation will need to weigh the expected cost against the expected benefits.

Here are some key features or benefits which have been used as unique selling points. As you read the list, try to think of some product examples: quality, who makes it, price, product features, who uses it, benefits from use, location, value for money, image, service, brand name, logo, style and fashion, how long in business, services.

assignment focus

1 What USPs are being emphasised in the promotional campaigns you are investigating? How important are they in promoting/selling the product?

2 What USPs will feature in your promotional campaign?

What is the organisation selling?

The answer to this question – the USP – will determine the thrust and direction of its promotion. Look at these examples:

- Is Peugeot selling cars or adventure? 'Own one and you own the road, the Drive of Your Life'
- Are P&O Ferries selling the trip from Dover to Calais or a cruise?
- Does a sports club sell the sport or the social life?

The Nike campaign for trainers, under the slogan 'Just do it', is intended to keep Nike as a world leader in trainers, and people buying brand name trainers. But what is Nike selling – an image, a dream, 150 million pairs of trainers or a 10k run on a cold November evening? The Nike 10k attracted 30,000 runners, all of whom visited the website and bought the orange T-shirt. It also attracted protesters carrying placards stating, 'Say no to Nike sweat shops'. What does this mean?

What is your organisation selling? A fragrance or the Lynx effect!

1 What is your promotional campaign selling? Is it a product, experience, emotion, enjoyment or a promise of a better life? Take care, the Advertising Standards Authority has responsibility to make sure that adverts are legal, decent, truthful and honest. (Adverts for health clubs have often been criticised for failing to mention that people have to use more calories than they eat to reduce weight!)

2 What range of products does your business have?

3 Has your organisation brought out new products within the last year? Look at news or press releases on its website. How have these been promoted?

4 What is the key message of the campaign you are investigating?

Associated services and benefits

With increased competition and consumers becoming more sophisticated, even the idea of the product has changed. A new definition is:

Product = Core benefits + Tangibles/Intangibles + Augmented product
The key need e.g. colour, design, e.g. after sales
satisfied by the taste, brand name, service, well trained
the product, image, service etc. staff, credit
e.g. hunger, facilities, delivery
security

A promotion could emphasise particular features of the total product with each of its market segments in each of the media it uses. Can you identify the components of the total product you are investigating?

Product positioning

Product positioning refers to a specific quality or characteristic of the product which is most often stressed in its advertising and is best known to the customer – its 'personality'. In other words, what immediately springs to the customer's mind when the product is mentioned. Tropicana is '100% pure squeezed orange juice not from concentrate' (see Case study 9.4 on page 255).

1 How is the product positioned in the campaign you are investigating?

2 How much does the promotional campaign you are investigating stress or emphasise the product and the associated benefits in the marketing mix?

3 For D1, how is this helping to achieve the business aims and objectives?

Price

The price at which a business sells its products is an integral part of the marketing mix. Ask yourself the questions: How much would you expect to pay for a new microwave oven? Would you buy one for £40 or does this sound too cheap, i.e. it cannot be any good for that price? Do you associate price with quality? What about a £20 Easter egg for a member of your family? Does this seem expensive? What about a present for your best friend which costs £60 at Harrods in London and £20 in your local high street? Do you link the price with the place where it is bought, with quality or with value for money?

The seller of any product will have considered these and many other questions before deciding on the price at which to sell goods. £9.99 and £19.99 look and sound better than £10 or £20. (Actually they are only priced like this because it forces the shop assistants to open the till to give change.)

Pricing strategies

The pricing strategy that a business adopts will depend upon many factors. Below are some examples.

If the business is operating in a competitive market it could choose to keep its prices in line with its competitors, or try to undercut them. If the product is new and has only just been launched, a low introductory price could be chosen to tempt purchasers. Soft drinks are launched at 20p but within weeks are the same high price as other canned drinks. Marshall Cavendish, a publisher of weekly part-works, offers the first two weeks for the price of one, and a free binder!

If the business decides to maximise profits, this will have a different effect on price than if it decides to maximise its share of the market, i.e. the company's objectives are important.

Costs of production, both fixed and variable, can be significant, if the business chooses to adopt a cost-based pricing system. Look at the prices in your local sandwich bar – do they vary with the type of filling? Do you buy on price or the filling? Compare this with tins of paint in a local DIY store, where prices are the same whatever the colour.

In this section, we will look at pricing as one vital part of the company's marketing mix.

Pricing new products

When a business introduces a new product or relaunches an existing one, it has to make a decision about which price to choose.

Pile 'em high and sell 'em cheap

Here low price is the selling point. A small profit per item provides a worthwhile return where rate of turnover is high.

This is possible where supplies are inexpensive – perhaps through bulk buying. This may not be available to a small business with limited buying power, although, it may be used by a market trader buying and selling surplus or bankrupt stock. This is how Jack Cohen started Tesco.

Penetration pricing

With penetration pricing, prices are set very low to enable the company to gain a foothold in a very competitive market. Once this has been achieved, prices may be progressively or selectively raised. Gillette, for example, launched a new product with a cheap razor and expensive blades. Exporters have often used this method to gain a foothold in another market – low-priced Japanese motorcycles virtually destroyed the UK industry. In 2006, China was accused of dumping shoes into the EU at below cost. The EU put a tax on all their shoes. Are you paying more?

The method is most effective if demand is elastic, so that consumers are tempted away from their usual supplier. Many new products are initially offered at a 'special introductory offer price', particularly when there are many other suppliers of similar products.

Premium pricing (perceived value pricing)

This is putting a high price on a product to give the impression that it is high quality. Some products are in demand because they are expensive. This is used where the demand is inelastic. The Belgian lager Stella Artois is premium priced and advertises with the slogan 'Reassuringly expensive'. Are you reassured by high prices?

High prices are possible in niche markets. Small businesses selling limited quantities of speciality products (real ale, organic vegetables, hand-crafted pottery) may use this tactic. Check the price of organic vs non-organic vegetables.

Skimming pricing

With skimming pricing, prices are initially set very high to take advantage of some people's desire for a new product or design at any price. The term 'skim the cream' pricing is often used to describe this approach. Computer software packages, computer games, current chart music and DVDs are excellent examples of this type of pricing. The product may have a novelty or scarcity value, and the supplier may have little direct competition; perhaps because it is protected by a patent.

As with premium pricing, the high price may give extra appeal. Gradually the price will be reduced as competition appears. However, as consumers become more sophisticated, they will often delay purchasing until the price comes down. Would you buy the No. 1 chart hit six months later? Do you download?

The Competition Commission may intervene if it believes prices have been kept artificially high for too long, as happened with the makers of CDs.

Skimming is most effective if demand is inelastic, i.e. people want the product at any price. Marketers call these people 'early adopters' or 'must have' the newest mobile phone, the newest fashions in clothes or trainers. Do you consider yourself to be in this group?

Cost-plus pricing

Pricing methods which are based on the cost structure of the business are favoured by accountants because they are supposedly more accurate and reliable. The cost of production is used as a baseline figure and the price is then marked up by the required amount. For example, if a retailer buys a product for £35 and wants a return or profit of 20 per cent, it will add 20 per cent (the margin) to the buying price to get the selling price of £42. This is the 'added value' to the product.

If the business is trying to maximise its profits, it should use a form of cost-plus pricing. For this method to work successfully, all costs need to be accurately accounted for, particularly those associated with a change in the level of output. In many firms this is a very difficult process, which is why the simpler mark-up procedure is used. Cost-plus pricing tends to ignore the demand for the product and the competition.

Marginal cost pricing

Here prices may be varied to suit market conditions. For example, the last minute price of a package holiday may be lower than the advertised price – holding out for the original price may mean no sale at all. This is worthwhile as long as the marginal cost (the cost involved in making the sale as opposed to not making it) is covered.

Positioning pricing

With positioning pricing, prices are set which reflect the consumer's view of the product. For example, good champagne is supposed to be expensive. Therefore a cheap champagne will be associated with poor quality. If the business sets too low a price, consumers may not buy the product – it is all a matter of psychology! The lowest priced tender, for example, is often not accepted. Products are often repositioned at higher prices to change their image.

Demand-based pricing

Many businesses set their prices based on what they think the consumer is prepared to pay. There are many examples of where this technique is used – consultants vary their fees according to the client; market traders charge whatever they can get away with; jobbing gardeners look at the value of the property before deciding on a price; the local corner shop (which buys its supplies 'cash and carry') sets the highest price it can and if the goods do not sell it merely reduces the price. Travel companies and airlines such as BA work the same way – if unsold accommodation or seats exist, these are sold off cheaply, often on the internet where all pricing is dynamic, i.e. it changes with the level of demand and supply.

Competitive pricing

Competitive pricing is a situation where the business sets a price roughly in line with its competitors. Much will depend on the type of competition which exists for the product, particularly the number of sellers and the number of buyers. This process works reasonably well if the cost structures of the companies are roughly similar.

Most businesses are in competition and must be aware of the prices of competitors. The supermarkets 'check prices everyday', John Lewis is 'never knowing undersold' for in-store (not internet) sales.

Unless their product is highly distinctive many new businesses will begin by setting their prices at the levels charged by similar businesses. (How does the local hairdresser determine prices?)

Discount pricing

In many competitive markets, e.g. office machinery or office consumables, the published list or catalogue price is only the starting point for bargaining. Buyers and purchasing officers in most businesses should be able to obtain the goods for less than the advertised price, particularly if they intend dealing with the supplier in future.

Many firms can be forced into price cutting if they are short of cash or need to increase sales quickly.

Differential pricing

A business may sometimes charge different prices for the same product at different times, e.g. peak and off-peak telephone calls, rail travel and holidays. Prices in this case will be based on the **elasticity** of demand for the product.

A change in price could affect the sales/revenue for the product, consumers' perceptions on value, supplier and retailer margins, profit levels and cashflow forecasts, overhead costs and competitor prices. A business must always be prepared for a range of reactions when prices are changed, e.g. a competitor could follow a price change or ignore it.

assignment focus

1 What pricing strategy/strategies are being used by your organisation? Why?
2 How important is price in the marketing mix?

Place or distribution

The P for place is shorthand for the process of distribution – the way in which the seller gets the right goods and services to the customer, either consumers or other businesses, on time, first time, every time. To do this successfully, a business needs an effective logistics system to place the product at the point where it is required by the customer.

Distribution is a customer service that should satisfy the actual and perceived needs of the buyer. If it does not, the producer will soon go out of business.

Distribution channels

The **distribution channel** is the method by which goods and services reach the customer at locations where customers are able to buy them, e.g. at home or in shops. A whole network of organisations may be needed to supply a product to end users and other businesses. The more often a product changes hands, the more expensive it becomes because everyone in the chain needs to be paid, which is why buying online direct from the supplier is usually cheaper, e.g. Amazon.

> **remember**
>
> The channel of distribution can also be called the distribution channel, distribution chain or supply chain.

The chain of distribution may have four main elements (Figure 9.3): in all cases the producer and consumer are vital – someone must produce/supply the product and someone must demand it. Whether intermediaries are used depends upon the nature of the product, where it is made, and how it is to be made available to the consumer. Examples of different chains of distribution are given below.

Figure 9.3 The chain of distribution

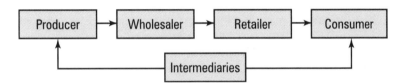

Producer → Intermediary → Consumer

In this chain, the intermediary can be a:

- *retailer*, e.g. clothing and footwear manufacturers who deal directly with large retailers; large supermarket chains, such as Tesco and Waitrose, buy direct from the farms and factories which produce and manufacture goods to their specifications

- *dealer* – car and motorcycle manufacturers, such as Ford, Honda and Suzuki, deliver directly to dealers for onward sale to consumers. Mobile phones are also sold through dealers. Whenever dealers are involved in distribution, there is always some concern over whether there is sufficient price competition. In the UK, the price of the original phone is subsidised by approximately £200; to compensate for this call charges are very high. Compare this with Norway, where the initial costs are much closer to the real price but call charges are very much lower

- *franchise* – this is a licence, given to a distributor or retailer, which gives the right to sell the products in a particular area. The franchisee (a retail outlet) will normally pay the franchiser a percentage of profits. Body Shop and McDonald's are well-known examples of companies that have grown quickly by granting franchises.

assignment focus

1 Does, or should, your business use the internet for distribution, selling or promotion? Is the current campaign on the internet or its website?
2 What distribution channels does it use? Give reasons.

Table 9.1 Advantages and disadvantages of short channels of distribution

Advantages	Disadvantages
Manufacturer is able to control and monitor the supply of the product. Dealers get financial help and support in return for an exclusive dealership, i.e. agreeing not to sell a competitive product. Manufacturer is able to respond quickly to changes in the conditions of demand.	Retailers can become very powerful and are able to negotiate very low prices. This has happened with many suppliers to UK retail chains. Lower prices, however, have not been passed on to consumers. The cost of distributing the product may rise (most lorries return empty from wholesaler. WalMart have been particularly successful in arranging suppliers close to wholesalers so that lorries can return full).

Producer → Wholesaler → Retailer → Consumer

When there is a large number of small retailers, the producer will usually deal with a wholesaler who buys in bulk, stores the products and sells them on to the retailer in smaller quantities. Because wholesalers buy large quantities direct from the manufacturer, they are able to negotiate much lower prices. They 'break bulk' and sell much smaller quantities to retailers who in turn sell individual packs to consumers. Wholesalers provide value by storing goods and making them available close to where they are needed by retailers.

A small grocer may go to the wholesaler, perhaps a 'cash and carry', to collect stock. This may be done fairly regularly to avoid the grocer having to devote space to storage.

The services provided by intermediaries are sometimes regarded as unnecessary. However, intermediaries can be essential in creating an effective demand. For example, if we have to travel to Canada for breakfast cereals, we may decide we do not want them after all.

Producer → Consumer

This is also known as direct sales or direct supply. Examples of **direct selling** would include the local baker; doctors; hairdressers and, increasingly, sales via the internet. IKEA is an example of a company which makes and sells its own products.

Table 9.2 Advantages and disadvantages of direct selling

Advantages	Disadvantages
Manufacturers can make bigger profits Manufacturer can be more responsive to consumers Consumers can buy from their own homes Manufacturers have total control over the product and its price	It is not profitable for low value items unless there are large sales Goods cannot be examined before being purchased Manufacturers will have to pay all the storage costs

The internet is now firmly part of the P for place in marketing and selling goods and services in the UK. Almost anything can be bought (and sold) online.

'You can buy anything on ebay, e.g. Loch Ness water or a human soul for £11.61.'

Source: *Evening Standard*

Nearly 10 million people, out of a total of 16 million home PC owners, regularly use the internet and 85 per cent of businesses. It is estimated that £40 billion of sales are now made via the e-commerce network worldwide every year, with European sales estimated at £10bn in 2006. Although sales to consumers are important, it is anticipated that its most valuable use in the future will be for business-to-business trade, e.g. finding suppliers.

Table 9.3 Advantages and disadvantages of using the internet

Advantages for the seller	Disadvantages for the seller
• Cuts out the intermediary wholesaler and retailer. • Can reach more people. • A large and powerful database can be built up which enables the service to be personalised, e.g. Amazon.com. the world's biggest Internet bookseller will suggest titles based on a customer's spending patterns. • Service is available 24 hours a day, 7 days a week without the need for staff. • Provides the opportunity for small/medium size businesses to trade internationally without having to relocate or set up complex distribution channels. • Small businesses with an effective net site can compete worldwide provided that price and delivery terms are customer focused. • It gives access to new markets.	• Pricing structures will need to be totally transparent across the world, there can be no price discrimination between countries. • Profit margins can be much lower than traditional distribution particularly when on-line costs are included. • High level of initial start up costs, particularly the advertising needed to attract people to the site, e.g. Amazon.com. uses radio, newspaper, magazines and other websites such as Virgin.net. • High initial technology costs but with the capacity for growth if the business expands. • Effective storage and distribution systems are needed.
Advantages for the buyer	**Disadvantages for the buyer**
• Wide range of choice which can be accessed from home or work. • The Internet is probably a classic example of a free market, pricing is dynamic and depends on supply and demand. It should always be possible to bargain for a lower price. • Can be accessed at any time to suit the user, e.g. airline tickets can be purchased 24 hours a day without the aggravation of phoning during office hours. • Many people do not want to spend their free time walking around shops to find a product. Cars can be bought and delivered to your door all through a PC, with a 40 per cent price saving. • Almost anything can be bought including a proposed site auctioning human eggs. The site is described as 'unethical and distasteful' (Evening Standard). • Provides a vast store of accessible information.	• Difficulty keeping credit card details secure (although no worse than phone systems), encryption or scrambling the data will help. A site which is secure should have an address beginning https//, a dialogue box appearing saying the site is secure and a padlock icon comes up. • Very few sites show the small fonts! • What happens if goods are faulty? Need to be changed? Is there a guarantee? Warranty? Does the customer have to pay for returning goods? • May be necessary to follow up a transaction with several phone calls if, for example, goods are not delivered on time. • What after-sales services exist when goods are purchased in another country? • What Data Protection legislation exists, e.g. in the USA personal details are much more freely available than in the UK.

Channel selection

The supplier will have to decide whether to provide the goods directly to the customer, or use an intermediary such as a wholesaler or retailer. Which decision is made will depend on the answers to these questions.

■ Who are the customers? For example, industrial users and large retailers would normally be supplied through short channels, while small retailers and consumers may require an intermediary.

■ What are their needs? For example, if the product requires complex, frequent servicing then a short channel may be preferred. Long channels would work for simple products. Consumers and businesses wanting convenience and 24/7 access would need online facilities.

■ Where are they situated and what outlets are available? For example, when customers are clustered together, retailers are possible. Online direct selling can be used for national and/or international distribution.

■ What are the characteristics of the product? For example, services must be supplied directly to the consumer – there cannot be an intermediary. Do goods have to be delivered immediately or can they be stored? Products with a short 'shelf life' need short channels, whereas durable goods can be stored with a wholesaler, enabling the manufacturer to cut storage costs.

Table 9.4 Comparison of costs and benefits associated with each decision

Direct to customer	Using an intermediary
• Gives the producer total control. • Provides immediate customer service. • Can be very expensive if the producer has to run its own fleet of transport. • Can be expensive if there are many customers with small orders, widely spread. • Producer can give the image it wants. • Gives good customer feedback and response. • All stock is readily available, but costly to store. • Centralised storage can be inefficient particularly with bulky or heavy products. • Will need to provide a range of customer services.	• Can be very expensive. • Provides storage facilities. • Able to provide small quantities. • May not give the image required by the manufacturer. • Can be important in large areas with few customers. • More difficult to control. • May only carry a few popular lines. • Intermediary or decentralised distribution is needed for high-weight, low-price goods. • Retailers can provide services such as free delivery and installation.

Many businesses now operate more than one channel of distribution in order to reach different segments of the market. For example, Next sells through its high street shops and via its catalogue; Dell computers are sold 'off the page' through the press and magazines, through telephone sales, via the internet and through a small business sales team.

assignment focus

1   Why do businesses use more than one distribution channel?
2   Which channels are used by the business you are studying?

Service distribution

The main differences between the distribution of goods and services are that:

■ services can only be provided direct to the customer, e.g. a dentist cannot work through an intermediary; a friend cannot go to the gym to train for you!

■ services are intangible, which means so they cannot be stored and have to be provided on demand. If you want the total experience of the Reading Festival, you have to go yourself.

Service industries, therefore, have to be able to spread the demand for their services. They do this by changing their marketing mix, e.g.

■ *Price* Peak and off-peak pricing is a key feature of many service industries, e.g. holidays are priced according to the season, rail travel and telephone call charges vary with the time of day. The purpose of these policies is to spread the demand.

■ *Product* Administration systems have been devised which help to spread the loadings, e.g. holidays, and dentists have to be booked in advance and staff are specially trained to give advice and help.

■ *Place* Services have to be provided where the customers are situated, e.g. hairdressers, dentists and plumbers can be found in any reasonably populated area. The provision of services is decentralised and therefore expensive.

■ *Promotion* Special promotions advertise the benefits of using off-peak facilities, e.g. no queues and no waiting at the restaurant (between 6 p.m. and 7 p.m.).

Many new businesses have been forced to seek alternative methods of distributing products where large firms have already tied up the existing market outlets. This can be a very expensive process, but also very rewarding as Haagen Dazs ice cream demonstrates. When Haagen Dazs could not distribute through traditional grocers (Walls had the rights to the freezers), it targeted off-licences!

Role of intermediaries (push and pull)

Push strategies involve the manufacturer persuading (pushing) wholesalers and retailers to stock their goods. When manufacturers directly target their intended consumers, they are trying to get them to demand their goods so that goods are pulled through wholesalers and retailers. An effective internet site often sees goods pulled directly off the suppliers shelves into the online shopping basket.

Packaging and product presentation

These are key elements in the process of creating a brand image. BP has 'green' garages and forecourt shops and prominently displays a yellow daffodil in its promotional literature. What does petrol smell like? Think of Toblerone and Smarties – these have all the qualities of good packaging. Packaging is an essential tool for distinguishing one brand from another.

The packaging, including shape, design, brand name, etc., are all part of the intellectual property of the business and can be a very valuable asset. See Unit 2, page 65.

The key features of packaging are as follows:

- *Colour* What colour is the Kit Kat pack? The colour associated with Cadbury's is purple, and with BP green. Some colours are said to be warm, while others such as blue are seen as cold or refreshing, e.g. toothpaste or chewing gum. Do you associate colours with emotions or feelings? The colour of the pack reinforces the image.

- *Shape and design* The shape should be instantly recognisable and enable the product to be differentiated from the competition, e.g. Terry's Chocolate Orange, Ferrari.

- *Distinctiveness or brand visibility* The graphics, logo, font style and size should all combine to give shelf 'stand out'. Look at the confectionery section in a newsagents. Which products stand out? Which do you buy? The Coca-Cola bottle is unique, distinctive and immediately recognisable worldwide. How does the pack reinforce the brand image? Do you shop in particular stores because you like being seen with their brand name on the packaging and carrier bags?

- *Size* Is the pack too small or too large? Can you get the spoon into the bottom of the coffee jar? Ergonomics is the study of how people and products/machines relate to each other. Do you sometimes feel that a product has been designed for someone else? Is it functional, convenient and easy to open?

- *Functionality and protection from damage* during every stage of the distribution process from the manufacturer/supplier to the wholesaler and retailer. During storage and transit, goods may experience a wide range of conditions, e.g. in temperature and humidity. Do you check every egg in the box? Do you find 'wrapped five times for perfect freshness' excessive? There needs to be a balance between what is environmentally friendly and what is necessary to protect the product. Can the product be handled and stored effectively?

- *Communication* Is it persuasive with clear text and visuals? Does it provide information? Do customers want to buy it? Does it include any necessary legal requirements, e.g. 'Smoking kills', the warnings on medicines, such as 'Keep out of reach of children'? Is there nutritional information? Does it provide instructions on how the product should be used? Is there information overload? Is it cluttered? Can you see it?

- *Message* What message does the packaging convey? Does the personality of the product show? Is the USP clearly stated, e.g. does the package and labelling convey a sense of luxury? Does it do 'exactly what it says on the tin'?

- *Integration with other elements of the marketing mix*, packaging and the way the product is presented are vital ingredients in any promotional campaign. (Tropicana, see page 255, changed its packaging to attract new users.) Cosmetics companies spend millions on the promotion, packaging and design. 'Our packaging can be seen everyday. It is continuous promotion, one long advert. At Christmas time when most fragrances are purchased, we go to great lengths to provide a gift wrapping service as part of the added value we offer. Our packaging must be extra special to match the image we are trying to create,' said a cosmetics industry spokesperson.

assignment focus

1   What are the packaging characteristics of your product?

2   Some products have excessive packaging. Does yours? Is it environmentally friendly?

3   How important is packaging in the marketing mix for your product?

4   For M1 and D1, how does it help your organisation achieve its aims and objectives?

case study 9.2

Responsible marketing

■ In an attempt to reduce binge drinking, the brewers Scottish and Newcastle (Kronenbourg, Fosters, Carlsberg) announced that it will state the number of units of alcohol in its products, urging drinkers 3 to 4 units a day for men 2 to 3 for women.

■ Coors (Grolsch, Carling) will also have responsibility **straplines**. Tobacco companies already have them: 'Smoking kills'.

■ Coke and Pepsi intend to label their soft drinks with nutritional information such as the amount of calories, fat and carbohydrate.

■ McDonald's, 'but not as you know it'!, conscious of accusations of allegedly contributing to obesity, sent mail drops to 17 million homes explaining its new healthier image. Did you get one?

■ Adverts for junk foods which contribute to obesity have been banned on TV before 9 p.m. Producers of children's TV programmes stated that the loss of advertising revenue meant that children's TV would be dramatically reduced!

activity

1   Why do you think that companies need to demonstrate a more responsible approach in their marketing to consumers?

2   How responsible is your organisation?

People

Staff are the most important resource in an organisation. Well motivated efficient staff can give an organisation a competitive edge. Creating a relationship with customers to 'earn their lifetime loyalty' (Tesco Strategic Vision) means delivering an effective service before, during and after the sale. With the present emphasis on customer focus and customer orientation, Tesco, being customer-centric, needs its staff to be well trained in customer service skills to deliver a consistently high quality service.

Consistency of image

For an organisation to provide a consistent high quality image, there must be systems to deliver features and benefits that enable a product or service to meet and satisfy customer requirements. It is the customer who defines quality. It is the customer perception of quality that drives sales and ultimately profits. The elements of service quality known as SERVQUAL include reliability, consistency, customer care, willingness and knowledge of staff, premises and facilities.

Quality and gap analysis

Gap analysis looks at the gap between, e.g.:

■ the service that you thought you would get and what was received

■ what the customer expected and what managers thought they wanted

■ the service promised and the service received.

Your expectations could depend, e.g. on what your friends have said, your past experience, your needs and the organisation's advertising. Have you sometimes expected a great meal or night out and felt let down by the service you got? Did you complain?

---

assignment focus

1 Have you experienced gaps in service quality? Do customers of your organisation find gaps? Can you explain why?

2 How important are the people to the success of your organisation? Are staff knowledgeable and helpful? Do they smile or look bored? How do they help your organisation achieve its aims and objectives? (M1, D1)

3 How important are people in the marketing mix for your product?

Processes

Consumers are increasingly concerned about how goods are produced and delivered. Are cosmetics tested on animals? Is your teak garden furniture from renewable sources? B&Q the DIY chain has made this a major feature of its marketing. How are complaints handled? is the process transparent and accessible?

Since January 2005 the EU has required companies in the food supply chain to keep a record of whom they buy their supplies from and whom they sell to.

Creating and maintaining a positive image

How easy or difficult is the buying process – before, during and after the sale – in your organisation? Are there queues at the check out? Are there sufficient staff? Are there different ordering/payment systems? Is the online experience user-friendly? Have you used the system? Does it work satisfactorily?

Achieving a positive image needs effective management and administrative control systems. For example, Primark and TK Max continually evaluate the 'shopping experience' to make the shopping process as enjoyable as possible. Display, layout and changing room facilities are regularly reviewed and monitored. The stores are regularly recovered (tidied up) and stock re-arranged by size, etc.

---

assignment focus

1 Identify the processes in your organisation which contribute to customer satisfaction.

2 How important are these processes to the success of your organisation? How do these processes help your organisation achieve its aims and objectives? (M1, D1)

3 How important are processes in the marketing mix for your product?

Physical evidence

This refers to the quality of the premises, website, advertising and promotion, etc., i.e. anything which affects the image of the organisation and how it is perceived. It is particularly important in the service sector; the outside of a restaurant needs to look inviting and clean if prospects are to become customers. Customer references are a useful way of providing evidence of satisfactory performance. (Restaurants display press and website reviews, when these are favourable!)

Promotional objectives

Business aims translated into marketing and promotional objectives

We know that an organisation could have a variety of corporate-wide aims, such as growth (getting new customers or persuading existing customers to buy more), maximising profit, providing a better service or an increase in market share (increase sales, launch new products). These would normally be set out in a corporate plan. Each aim requires a particular promotional message and a specific promotional strategy which would be implemented through individual functions or departments.

case study 9.3   Marketing 7Ps

Here is how the 7Ps have been combined to create the marketing mix for a well known high street bank and a local hairdresser.

Table 9.5 The marketing mix for a high street bank and a hairdressers

	High street bank	**Hairdressers**
Price	Interest rates vary between accounts depending on amount, level of risk and access required	Prices based on styles Experience expertise of stylist Peak and off-peak pricing Location and reputation
Promotion	Incentives to new borrowers and savers Advertising and sponsorship	Price discounts Senior citizen and concessions
Product	Savings and loans Overdrafts Insurance and mortgages Cheque accounts	Styles, cut, shampoo, highlighting, extensions, etc. Hair and beauty products
Place	Online and telephone banking, local branch	Head-to-head! Physical premises only
People	Well trained Corporate clothing (staff uniform)	Well presented competent and friendly staff who know their customers
Physical	Quality of premises Distinctive communications	Good location Clean and hygienic
Processes	Customer experience Online Telephone – long queues Face-to-face – long queues	Friendly greeting Good telephone booking system Customers well treated

activity

1   Construct a similar table showing the marketing mix for your products/organisations.
2   What is the role of promotion for the bank and the local hairdresser.

Figure 9.4 shows how a business plan can be turned into a promotional plan.

Figure 9.4 From business plan to promotional plan

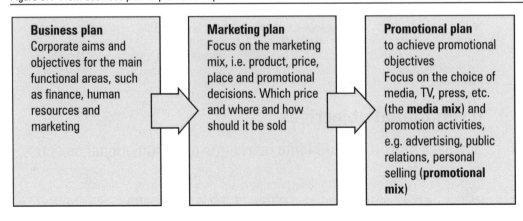

Business plan
Corporate aims and objectives for the main functional areas, such as finance, human resources and marketing

Marketing plan
Focus on the marketing mix, i.e. product, price, place and promotional decisions. Which price and where and how should it be sold

Promotional plan
to achieve promotional objectives
Focus on the choice of media, TV, press, etc. (the **media mix**) and promotion activities, e.g. advertising, public relations, personal selling (**promotional mix**)

See page 230 for further information on the promotional mix.

Figure 9.5 is an example from Unilever of how a corporate aim, e.g. 'to improve growth in all product categories' becomes a promotional objective, e.g. 'to achieve an overall increase in market share of 2 per cent for Dove'.

Figure 9.5 From corporate aim to promotional objective

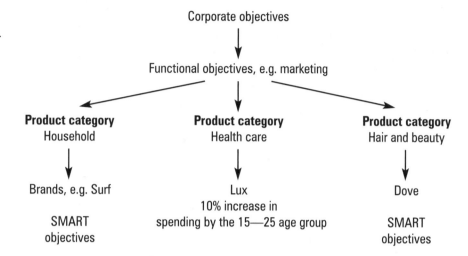

The corporate objectives will be turned into a strategy with objectives for each level (product category and brands) in the organisation. Action plans will be created showing how each objective could be achieved. The objectives should be SMART and vertically and horizontally consistent, i.e. integrated throughout the organisation with everyone working to the same goals. This should minimise internal conflict. Promotion and the other elements of the marketing mix will be used to achieve objectives.

An organisation cannot hope to achieve all its objectives at once. It needs to focus its promotional activities on its highest priority. Launching a new product or opening a new shop are immediate short-term aims needing short-term promotional activities. Building up awareness or changing attitudes are long-term objectives needing a long-term financial and promotional commitment.

AIDA sums up the main promotional objectives – see page 238.

Raising awareness of the product/service

The most wonderful product in the world will not sell if people do not know it exists. Since earliest times, the main purpose of promotional activity has been to make the market aware of the product, e.g. where it can be bought and what is the price. This provision of information is still a main function of local newspaper and radio advertising.

With new products or when products are being introduced into new markets, the first objective of any marketing launch campaign is to make potential buyers/users aware of the product or service. With existing products, it may be necessary to remind customers of the benefits of the product. For example, Tropicana Pure Premium juice (page 255) changed the packaging to bring in new users and remind lapsed users of the benefits of the brand.

See www.dynamic.logic.com/eyeblaster for an online case study of Florida orange juice.

All advertising media whether offline, such as TV, radio, newspapers, outdoor poster advertisers and cinema, or online, such as internet banner ads and pop-ups, claim to be able to raise awareness of the product/service if they are used as the communication medium.

'Smoking kills' and 'Don't drink and drive' are examples of public service promotion and illustrate the point that any organisation can promote its purpose and message. These are designed to raise awareness of the dangers of smoking and drinking. The action required is to stop.

Look again at Figure 3.1 on page 103. This Friends of the Earth advert is a good example of an advertisement designed to raise awareness of a current issue and was designed to be used on beer mats. It is aimed at a specific target audience, using images and text created to gain attention.

---

assignment focus

How is your organisation attempting to raise awareness through its current promotional campaign? Is it working?

Creating a distinctive market presence

In a highly competitive marketplace, it is very important that for-profit and not-for-profit organisations differentiate or distinguish their products/message from those of their competitors. The product has to be distinctive. It has to stand out from the crowd saying, 'Choose me!' Friends of the Earth, Comet and BhS are all trying to create a unique position for themselves. How do they do this? The brand name, message, logo and packaging can all be used to make a product stand out from its competitors. Advertising can be used to create an image, perhaps of quality, value or excellent service. The overall objective is to achieve customer loyalty. However, the image has to live up to the reality.

Many organisations operate in a very competitive environment. Why should the consumer choose one in preference to another? Do you make a decision on quality, brand name, price or another criterion such as a distinctive market presence? Andrex toilet rolls are advertised by a cute little puppy which has its own website: www.andrexpuppy.co.uk. Churchill Insurance (owned by the Royal Bank of Scotland), based in Bromley, uses a nodding dog. Which company advertises using a red phone?

---

assignment focus

1   What techniques is your organisation using to make its product/service achieve a distinctive market presence?

2   Promotion plays a major part in forming the image of a product which helps create a distinctive market presence. Where do you buy your clothes? Or music? Woolworths is one of the biggest sellers of music in the UK. Do you go there? How much does promotion influence what you or other family members buy? How important is it in the marketing mix?

Increasing market share

Market share is the proportion of the total market held by a business or product, e.g. Tesco's UK market share is 30.3 per cent. For an organisation whose primary goal is making profits, promotion would tend to emphasise those features which create and build sales. The purpose is to achieve a sustainable increase in market share so that the organisation can sell more without having to cut prices.

Many promotional campaigns are designed to keep customers loyal by reassuring and reminding them of the product, but also offering an incentive, e.g. 'Buy X and get 200 extra points at Boots'. The key purpose is to move the customer up the loyalty ladder from occasional user to being totally committed – 'Buy it again and get another 300 points' – to the point where the customer would not shop anywhere else (from being interested to taking action). Loyalty cards such as the Boots Advantage card, Tesco Clubcard and the use of the Nectar card by Sainsbury's are all intended to create loyal customers.

 Link   See page 148 for more information on the loyalty ladder.

The ability of an organisation to increase its market share depends on its own marketing mix, the activities of competitors and whether the market as a whole is growing. In stagnant markets, where sales have reached saturation, e.g. with fast food burger chains such as McDonald's and Burger King, one of the few ways to grow is to poach customers from the competition. Unless this can be maintained, any increase can only be temporary. The key to success is to make sure that new customers become permanent by creating a relationship with them. This process is called relationship marketing. The promotional campaign for Walkers crisps fronted by Gary Lineker has doubled sales in the last ten years.

Want to find out more? Check out www.walkers.corpex.com.

For relationship marketing, see Unit 3, page 149.

Promotional activities need to be planned and implemented to reinforce the mission, aims and objectives of the organisation.

These sites are very useful:
- TNS Superpanel reference library – www.tnsinfo.com
- www.theretailbulletin.co.uk

---

assignment focus

1 Does your organisation have increasing market share as an objective?
2 How does it try to achieve this?
3 Find out its market share by using KeyNote reports.

---

case study 9.4   **Tropicana**

'PepsiCo's success is the result of superior products, high standards of performance, distinctive competitive strategies and the high integrity of our people.'

'Our mission is to be the world's premier consumer products company focused on convenient foods and beverages. We seek to produce healthy financial rewards to investors as we provide opportunities for growth and enrichment to our employees, our business partners and the communities in which we operate. And in everything we do, we strive for honesty, fairness and integrity.'

Source: PepsiCo website

Figure 9.6 PepsiCo's advertising for Tropicana

Source: PepsiCo

The 2005 promotional campaign

B2C promotion

In 2005, there was a £4.5m TV campaign, press advertising, sampling, door drops, 8 million targeted direct mail shots, a 50p-off voucher and a competition with 31 BA Club Europe weekend breaks for two, one for each day in August (pity BA at Heathrow were on strike for three days!). For a chance to win, consumers had to register online to become a member of the Tropicana Breakfast Club. The competition was heavily promoted on radio, online and through *The Sunday Times*, with direct mail and sponsorship of the Simon Bates Breakfast Show on Classic FM. Tropicana spent approximately £15m promoting its products in 2005.

B2B support and advice

The company-recommended planogram (layout or graphical display of products) of Tropicana for instant consumption sales is, 'It should be located next to the sandwiches and other soft drinks to capture high value impulse purchases.' While the recommended planogram for take-home sales is, 'It should be next to milk in the dairy deck to capitalise on high footfall areas of the store and attract purchasers.'

Retailers were advised through the trade website press releases to stock up on 1-litre and 1.75-litre take-home cartons and the single serve instant consumption bottles.

What was the purpose of the campaign?

PepsiCo Trade Marketing Manager, Nicky Seal said that the campaign:

> 'will be highly engaging and appealing to loyal Tropicana drinkers. Supported by a huge media campaign it will also drive brand awareness, reinforce Tropicana's pure premium and number one positioning and ensure Tropicana is top of mind with consumers. We felt it was the right time to give the brand new packaging with a more modern refreshing look which will attract new buyers to the brand.'

activity

1   Why was a wide range of media selected?

2   What is the promotional mix? Why was a range of promotion methods chosen?

3   What was each part of the campaign designed to achieve? What are the objectives of the promotion?

4   Why was so much emphasis put on B2B communication?

5   Describe the marketing mix.

6   What is the role of promotion in this campaign?

7   Answer these questions for your own product.

Look at the marketing press, e.g. *Campaign*, *Marketing*. www.visit4info has all the adverts.

Targeting relevant audience

Promotional campaigns need to be directed at specific audiences. The publishers of this book, Nelson Thornes, target the Head of Business Studies in schools and colleges with their resources for Vocational Business Studies, as Figure 9.7 shows. This is a B2B promotion. Why haven't they targeted you as a consumer (B2C)? Can you identify the sweets?

Whilst some organisations focus exclusively on one target audience/market segment, others will differentiate their audiences and produce different campaigns for each group.

See page 140 on segmentation.

Attitudes, interests and opinions

Do you watch a particular TV channel or listen to a particular radio station? Perhaps you have a favourite magazine? Other people with similar likes or dislikes will also be watching or listening. Do your friends have similar attitudes to you? All of you are a market segment or target audience defined by a range of characteristics, i.e. your attitudes, interests and opinions (AIO):

- your attitudes (sometimes activities) could cover your views about sports, shopping, clubbing, gigs, holidays, etc.
- your interests could include food, music, friends, etc.
- your opinions could include those about education, your future, particular products, etc.

Figure 9.7 Nelson Thornes:
The B2B promotion

The AIO inventory is a technique which uses a set of statements to find out about people's attitudes towards a product, their interests and opinions, e.g.

■ I think my BTEC course will get me a better job.

■ I would only go on a beach holiday.

■ I would only buy brand names.

Answers would then be rated on a five-point scale like the one in Table 9.6.

Table 9.6 A five-point scale

Strongly agree	Agree	Don't know	Disagree	Strongly disagree

The information is used to build up a picture of a typical customer and segment the market. Promotion can then be targeted to appeal directly to a specific group.

Many campaigns have been aimed at changing attitudes or perceptions about a product. This is an image 'makeover' and can be very difficult to achieve.

1   What AIO is your campaign is aiming at: saving money? a beautiful home? value for money? a sense of adventure?

2   Does it appeal to you? Give your reasons.

Business to business (B2B) promotion

The objective of B2B promotion is either to persuade wholesalers/retailers to stock their products, i.e. it is push promotion or sell direct to customers. Any goods would normally be offered with a trade discount or incentive (see page 233 for trade promotion). An interesting example of pull promotion is Intel which sells its computer chips to other businesses, but advertises heavily to the public with the intention of getting us to demand that the computers we buy have 'Intel inside', i.e. Intel chips are pulled through the distribution system.

Here is an example of a B2B promotion: 'We use 22 million cans a day, 2,000 are filled every minute' (*Source*: *Marketing*, 22 November 2006).

For further information, go to www.canmakers.co.uk. and www.dba.org.uk.

assignment focus

1   What are the promotional objectives behind this B2B advert for cans?
2   Is it an example of push or pull promotion? Give your reasons.

Segmentation

Link   See page 140 for further information on segmentation.

A particular group targeted by mortgage companies are first-time buyers. This group is trying to buy a home for the first time, i.e. they are trying to get on the housing ladder. They have particular financial needs and banks compete for their business by offering either low initial rates of interest or '5 times your income'". They are important to the bank because on average over a 25-year mortgage people pay back three times as much as they originally borrow. Nationwide were advertising that all mortgage borrowers would get the same rates, but now differentiate between existing and new borrowers 'our competitors didn't follow us'.

assignment focus

1   Describe the marketing mix for your chosen product.
2   Describe the role of promotion within the marketing mix for your selected product or service. Use Table 9.7 to help you decide the importance of each of the factors.

Table 9.7 The importance of the 7ps in the marketing mix

	Low	Medium	High	Your reasons
Product				
Price				
Place				
Promotion				
Packaging				
People				
Processes				
Physical Evidence				

The role of advertising agencies and the media

Roles of advertising agencies

International advertising agencies such as J. Walter Thompson (Kit Kat and Nik Naks) or McCann-Erickson (Coca-Cola, Walls Sausages, Mastercard, but lost Bacardi) tend to work on mass market national/international brands.

To find out more about these agencies, go to:
■ J Walter Thompson – www.jwt.com or www.jwt.co.uk
■ McCann-Erickson – www.mccann.com or www.mccann.co.uk

An **advertising agency** is a specialist marketing business which will plan, create and carry out an advertising campaign on behalf of its client. The client which may be a private or public sector organisation, charity or political party will generally pay an agency a percentage of the total amount spent.

A full-service agency (one-stop shop) would handle each stage of a whole campaign including:

■ creative development, e.g. creating TV adverts – the agency would work closely with the client to find out their marketing needs and expectations (the creative brief is vital at this stage). Beware – an advertisement can be very creative and win awards for artistic quality, but if it does not sell the product it is a commercial failure – 'Great ad but what was it selling?'

■ analysing and buying media space and time – the agency will identify client needs and match these to the types of media, e.g. press, TV or outdoor advertising. It will then buy the space in the press or the time slots on the TV. An agency should have the knowledge, experience and expertise to identify the best media mix for the product

See page 261 for more information on types of media.

■ evaluating effectiveness – this stage must be carried out both before and after any campaign. Measures of effectiveness such as the number of people aware of the brand must be built in at the planning stage. An agency should have the capability to provide this research.

Agencies may specialise, for example, in media buying (booking space in newspapers/ magazines or time on TV or radio in advance of the launch of a new product). Industrial agencies work exclusively with manufacturers and suppliers of industrial goods, such as the mechanical diggers seen on building sites, and market these to companies such as Brandon Hire.

Small à la carte, or boutique, agencies may consist of two or three people who specialise in a particular sector or niche market, e.g. jewellery. Local agencies with local knowledge would be most effective for a small business with a local campaign.

Table 9.8 shows the major roles of a full service, or one-stop, advertising agency.

Table 9.8 Typical roles of advertising agencies

Production and traffic	Creative	Account planning	Media buying	Media planning
Make sure the work is completed on time to the required standard and all legal requirements are met, e.g. adverts must be 'legal, decent, truthful and honest' (www.asa.org)	Copywriters and art directors. Responsible for creating, writing and designing the ads, e.g. slogans, text, radio and TV scripts, voiceovers Adding pictures and graphics	Responsible for analysing any market research Identifying target segment/ audience Testing and evaluating the effectiveness of the advertising	Buy time on TV and radio Buy and schedule space in newspapers and magazines Bulk buying media space and time means cheaper rates	Make decisions about which media to use based on the client's campaign objectives and the media habits of the target audience, e.g. would radio or local press be more effective?

Graphic design and typography

The creative department is responsible for designing and creating the advertisement by taking the client's initial briefing about the product, adding its own ideas and turning them into reality. It will write the words (the copy), design and select the typography (plan and choose the size and type of font which best suits the product) and prepare the advert for printing. (Go to Format in Word to see a range of fonts.) Today these processes are often done using computer software, which can create any graphics and edit any photographs that are needed and design the most effective layout to convey the message. For a TV or cinema commercial, it would create a storyboard which literally sets out the story or sequence of images that would be used in the advertisement.

remember

Be aware of copyright in the use of fonts.

■ For information on copyright, see Unit 2, page 66.
■ For more about storyboards, see page 276.

A **copywriter** would write any words or lyrics used in jingles, e.g. 'Washing machines live longer with Calgon'.

There are usually four elements in the design of a print advertisement which together are intended to gain attention and interest, arouse desire and promote action (AIDA, see page 237):

■ the headline, which should be dramatic, eye-catching and memorable

■ the image, photo, illustration or graphics, which must reinforce the headline and copy and be appropriate to the needs of the audience

■ the copy (words), which are written to inform and/or persuade. These should complement the headline and image and could include a discount offer to arouse desire

■ the organisation details or signature, which would include the logo, addresses, telephone number, name, etc. The customer must be able to make contact to buy! The process must be easy as possible or the potential customer could go elsewhere.

See Unit 4, page 158, for a job description of an advertising media planner.

Production

Today this is almost fully computerised with copy and graphics sent via e-mail to an agency, where the finished product is scanned and set up digitally. The finished copy will be printed from a digital master copy.

Cost options

There are two major cost considerations:

■ Production costs include the number of colours (full colour is more expensive), technician and studio time for production and editing, celebrity endorsements, etc. Generally print adverts are cheaper to produce.

■ Media buying costs are determined by size of the advert, position, circulation, number of viewers or listeners, time of day (programme), number of time slots or newspaper insertions, etc. Rate cards are produced by the media to show how much an advertisement will cost according to size and position.

Additionally, the agency will need to be paid. Smaller agencies would normally be paid a fee for each project. Large agencies may be paid a commission by the media they use.

In-house vs outsourcing

One major decision will be whether the advertisement is produced in-house or prepared by an agency. In-house means the advertising is prepared internally. If the work is carried out by an outside/external company, it is outsourced.

Table 9.9 The advantages and disadvantages of in-house and outsourcing

For and against in-house	For and against outsourcing
• Know your own needs but can be subjective • Only internal resources available • More control • Could be less expensive up front • Experts only available in larger organisations • Less knowledge of specialist media and costs • Could work directly through the local newspaper/radio to create adverts	• More objective with wider experience • Access to wide range of skills • Close co-operation needed between client and agency account manager • More expensive, but the results could be worth it. Any decision should be based on value for money, i.e. effectiveness balanced against cost • Wide knowledge and experience of the marketplace • Can produce the whole campaign

Why use an agency?

Agencies should be able to provide staff with an expert knowledge of the ever-increasing complexity of the media. They are able to provide all the functions/research necessary to see an advertising campaign through from initial research to the scheduling and buying of media space. Specialist creative staff can create all types of advertisement. Because of their size, they are able to negotiate better rates with the media. An agency should have the knowledge, experience and expertise to identify the best media mix. On the other hand, there may be some loss of control and the process can be expensive.

How to choose an advertising agency

- Do you like their current campaigns?
- Do they have a portfolio of work?
- Are there references/testimonials?
- Who are the clients?
- Will they have time for you?
- Do they have the knowledge you need?
- What is the price and what are you paying for?
- Is the agency too big?
- Do you like them?

Advertising agencies advertise themselves in the trade press. How effective do you think they are? Check the trade press, Yellow Pages, etc.

---

assignment focus

1   What media are available locally? Investigate what free and paid-for newspapers/magazines (for discerning households like yours) are distributed. Find out the advertising rates.

2   What are the local commercial radio stations? Who listens to them? Is this your target market? How much does advertising cost? Do they provide help in preparing the advertisement? Check their websites.

3   How much would it cost to advertise on:

   a) a local bus?
   b) at the local cinema?
   c) in your centre prospectus?
   d) in your local church magazine? Good for wedding services and tuition!

4   Check out the services provided by your local advertising agencies. Find their websites using www.yell.com or the hard copy, Yellow Pages. What role would they play in the development of a successful promotional campaign?

Types of media

The media mix

Whether companies advertise locally, regionally, nationally or internationally will depend upon the available budget and the market, i.e. which segments are being targeted. Generally only those products with mass market appeal, distribution and demand would be worth advertising on a large scale. The majority of businesses (90 per cent) employ less than 20 people, so for these advertising is likely to be highly selective. However, remember that any website marketing has international potential.

The advertising medium is the means by which information is communicated to the public. The mass media are the means of communication which reach large numbers of people: TV, newspapers, radio and magazines and the internet are the primary mass media. The choice of medium will depend upon the product and the marketing objectives.

- *Local* – local paid-for and free newspapers, display and classified advertising, local radio, leaflet distribution, newspaper insertions or Royal Mail delivery, newsagents windows (good for services), local magazines and directories, buses and taxis, outdoor posters, shop window displays and signage, sandwich boards on the pavement (good for cafes), cinema, libraries, leisure centres (good for fitness clubs but check first, they might be competitors), church magazines (a target audience)

- *Regional* – regional terrestrial TV stations, commercial radio stations, regional editions of national newspapers, regional newspapers, e.g. Yorkshire Post, outdoor posters

See www.regionaladvertising.co.uk and www.itvregions.com.

- *National* – national TV and radio stations, newspapers and magazines, poster campaigns, web advertising, cinema
- *International* – satellite TV companies such as Sky can provide pure target audiences through their specialist channels. Newspapers such as *The Economist* and specialist magazines, e.g. *Access International* (a B2B heavy machinery magazine), have an international circulation. Internet and website promotions.

Television advertising

This is expensive but can be targeted at regions or specific groups according to education, age or lifestyle. Viewing panels are used to find out the nature of the audience for any particular programme and time slot. A points rating system is used to price the TV advert. Considerable information is available, e.g. people who use olive oil also drink wine, read, like holidays abroad, own a car, use mayonnaise and, would you believe, watch *Sex and the City*! So if you watch it, you are likely to see adverts for these products. Specific programmes are used to advertise specific products. However, do you switch channels when the adverts are on? The Broadcasters' Audience Research Board (BARB) has introduced a new electronic system for measuring audience appreciation of TV programmes, rather than just producing numbers of people watching. The social groups C1 and C2 watch most television.

Terrestrial vs satellite TV

There are five terrestrial TV stations but only three of these are commercial, i.e. rely on advertising revenue: ITV1, Channel 4 and Channel 5. There are now hundreds of satellite or digital stations some of which are 'free to air'.

The BARB publishes weekly and monthly summary figures of audiences for all major TV channels. Table 9.10 gives the figures for the week ending 12 February 2006. Some satellite channels have fewer than 5,000 viewers. These viewers would be total enthusiasts of e.g diving in the Gilli Islands; Dream Divers would advertise because it knows it has a pure audience for divers.

See Reach on page 266.

Table 9.10 BARB viewing figures for week ending 27 May 2007

Channel	Average Daily Reach		Weekly Reach		Average Weekly Viewing	Share
	000s	%	000s	%	Hrs: Mins per person	%
ALL/ANY TV	41,172	73.2	52,778	93.9	24:10	100.0
BBC1 (incl. Brkfast News)	28,067	49.9	47,098	83.8	5:16	21.8
BBC2	15,530	27.6	36,224	64.4	2:02	8.4
TOTAL BBC1/BBC2	31,215	55.5	48,546	86.4	7:18	30.2
ITV (incl. GMTV)	23,060	41.0	44,386	79.0	4:44	19.6
CHANNEL 4/S4C	16,552	29.4	39,333	70.0	2:09	8.9
five	9,541	17.0	27,904	49.6	1:17	5.3
TOTAL/ANY COMM. TERR. TV	30,658	54.5	49,178	87.5	8:10	33.8
Other viewing	25,086	44.6	39,373	70.0	8:42	36.0

Source: www.barb.co.uk

Want to find out more? Go to www.barb.co.uk.

Adam Stanhope, who started Rapture, the channel geared to 16-year-olds, says:

> 'Teenagers are the most valuable demographic group in the country, targeting is important, agencies don't buy airtime from small channels to get wider reach, they buy from them to get really pure audiences.' (*Source*: The Times)

What do you think is advertised during programmes about extreme sports, clubbing and computer games?

Newspaper advertising

There are national, daily and Sunday newspapers, provincial daily and evening newspapers and local weekly newspapers. Although local newspaper advertising is relatively cheap, nationals can be expensive because of the high circulation.

Newspapers can be used to target specific groups of people. *Sun* readers are in the C1 and C2 category, while the A and B groups read *The Times*. It can be very effective locally.

The cost of advertising in newspapers depends mainly on the size of the readership (circulation), the size of the advertisement, the number of insertions (the number of times an advert appears) and the page position.

Posters

Posters are generally used to display very direct messages, e.g. 'Vote for me!' Campaigns can be planned locally, regionally or nationally. They are frequently used to back up a TV campaign. Poster sizes vary from 2 to 50 square metres; the largest size gives a very large message! Nestle use posters extensively for advertising Polo, Yorkie, Kit Kat and Aero.

Outdoor advertising

Bus stops, taxis, street furniture, telephone/internet booths, wherever there is a space, there will be an advertisement. Sports events are increasingly popular – advertising space is already being sold for the 2012 Olympics in London. What does this say about the power of advertising?

- Check out the publication Media Week which carries details of 'roadside activity' classified by national/London posters and national/London buses.
- Look at maiden.co.uk, the largest outdoor advertising provider and www.oaa. org.uk for presentations on outdoor advertising.

Cinemas

Unless you arrive late, you cannot escape cinema advertising for Bacardi, Martini, jeans and the local Indian restaurant, which never looks like the one you use! (A parody of this has been used by McDonald's in its advertising.) Cinema adverts require long lead times. Do you still have a local cinema or a multiplex in your nearest large town?

Radio

Audiences, or market segments, can be targeted locally or nationally. As with TV, specific programmes and stations attract different types of people. In London, for example, Capital Gold plays 1960s and 1970s music, while Capital Radio plays contemporary music – each appeals to a different market. As with TV, advertising costs depend on the time of day and the size of the audience. Commercial radio reaches 75 per cent of all 15–24-year-olds. What station do you listen to? What would you advertise?

Table 4.16 shows that radio advertising has grown rapidly since 1996. The reason for this growth has been the blue chip (well-known) companies such as Kingfisher who have advertised Woolworths and B&Q. Dixons says:

> 'Growth has been driven by our High Street retailer Link which sells our mobile communications range. Link's younger target customers match the profile of many radio station listeners. Radio allows you to target a narrow lifestyle rather than a demographic group.'

It is flexible and personal as most people listen to the radio on their own. Many radio stations will help advertisers plan and develop their campaign without the need to go through an agency.

Table 4.16 on page 192 shows how advertising expenditure has changed over the last ten years.

Specialist media

There are approximately 7,000 magazines which appeal to quite specific market segments: sports, leisure interests, nails, catering and those planning a wedding (there are five *Bride* magazines for different ethnic groups), etc. Nike and Adidas, for example, advertise regularly in sports magazines. Clubs, churches and nurseries have newsletters all of which carry advertising. These specific local publications enable advertisers to target specific local target market segments. Trade publications (those intended for businesses) attract specific B2B advertisers plus recruitment adverts e.g. *The Grocer*.

Criteria for media selection

An advertising agency would research the most effective media for advertising a product including the cost, reach, coverage, etc.

Here are some criteria that could be used to enable an organisation to make its own decision.

Costs versus expected coverage

The decision about which media to use is based on the cost of the advertising and the expected response. For a small local business, a *Thompson Local/Yellow Pages* telephone entry plus a local newspaper advert could be sufficient. (A standard black on yellow whole page advert for London South East with a circulation of 253,000 cost £4,927 for the September 2006 edition.) A local car body repair business such as Heswell Bodyshop finds 'word of mouth' more than sufficient. 'We don't advertise,' said Matt the owner. What does this say about the role of promotion in the marketing mix?

Generally large businesses selling mass market products, such as washing powder, would use national mass media such as TV. The same advert may even be used worldwide, e.g. Coca-Cola. Small, local or niche market organisations would use local or specialist media.

Beware of using words such as 'expensive' or 'cheap' when describing the cost of advertising. They should be used in the context of the objectives of the campaign and the results achieved. (See the Tropicana case study page 255 and the YTB on page 270.) Measuring the success or failure of a particular medium can be very difficult. Many organisations ask their customers 'Where did you hear/find out about us?' Direct marketing companies often include a code number in their advertisements on TV or the press, to help them find out this information. Advertising recall surveys are often used to test consumer awareness of the product before and after an advertising campaign.

Effectiveness of selected communication channels

For any campaign, an organisation will have to decide which is the best medium to use to get its message across to its audience.

Promotional objectives

To achieve its promotional objectives, an organisation must have the right message, in the right medium, at the right time, for the right audience. Each medium has its own special characteristics, e.g. print adverts can be cut out and referred to again, internet adverts can be viewed and printed, radio and TV can be dramatic but can you remember the information? For example, the *Yellow Pages* for Bromley and Bexley has a 12-page Wedding Guide with sections on arriving in style, capture the day on film, dressing for the big day, a wedding planner checklist and helpful information on flowers, the reception, etc. An internet search produced images, video, photographs, music, helicopter rides (Matt and Helen), a country house with Thomas and Sarah, etc. Which promotional mix will achieve the promotional objectives requires careful analysis of the available media. Which is most likely to get the buyer to make a purchase or take action? Which would you prefer to search?

The Newspaper Marketing Agency (NMA) suggests that there are six roles for newspaper advertising:

Table 9.11 Advantages and disadvantages of types of media

Medium	Advantages	Disadvantages
Newspapers/ magazines	Good reach and frequency, can be targeted, daily, weekly, locally, by age, lifestyle, etc. complex messages can be delivered	Adverts have to compete, some magazines have to be booked a long time in advance. Newspapers are quickly thrown away
Cinema	Good for younger age groups, captive audience, can be localised	Expensive to produce Expensive for national coverage
TV	Can target nationally, regionally and by programme, mass market with high reach and frequency	Expensive to produce Expensive for national coverage
Radio	Good for local promotions, good reach and frequency, personal and intimate, relatively low cost per 1,000 listeners	Unless distinctive, may be part of the background, difficult to achieve national coverage
Outdoor	Good for geographical segmentation, good reach and frequency, wide range of opportunities (posters, buses, etc.), can be very large	Difficult to segment by age/ lifestyle, can only be used for simple messages, great for graffiti!
Direct mail	Can be targeted and personalised, costs are relatively low. Quick to produce and distribute. Results are easily measured with coded response	Most thrown away as junk mail
Internet	24-hour world wide reach and availability, can be revisited, immediate with short lead times on own website, may be personalised through database information to develop a long-term customer relationship	Pop ups may be blocked, expensive to achieve a high listing with search engines, initial development costs can be high

- call to action – getting the consumer to do (or not do) something, usually short term but can be long term
- depth of information – providing new and additional information about a brand, or to show new sides to the brand
- brand values – bringing the consumer closer to the brand through associations with which they identify
- (re)appraisal – creating a stir and forcing appraisal or reappraisal of a brand by presenting it in a surprising or shocking way
- extension – reminding consumers about a brand by repeating or developing established messages seen in other media
- public agenda – raising the profile of an issue/cause by provoking reaction and thought and by creating 'talkability'.

Source: www.fipp.com

Target audience

This is the segment that the advertiser wants to reach. It could be potential new customers (the primary market) or existing customers whose profile is already known through market research (the secondary market). Every media should have details of its readership or audience, e.g. for Virgin Radio 57 per cent of listeners are male, 53.1 per cent are in the ABC1 social group (source: RAJAR/Virgin Radio).

The key to success lies in matching the message to the audience size and type. Size may be measured by the number of readers/listeners or viewers, whilst type refers to specific segments, e.g. consumers may be segmented by age, income, lifestyle, etc. Businesses may be segmented by turnover, type of retail outlet, etc.

- For outdoor advertising, go to www.oaa.org.uk.
- For magazine audiences, go to the Periodical Publishers website at www.ppa.co.uk.
- Radio and TV stations have downloadable media packs which show the audiences.
- The Business Link website (www.businesslink.gov.uk) has an interactive questionnaire to help businesses select the right media.
- For newspapers, go to www.regionaladvertising.co.uk.

Focus of appeal

This can work on many levels, e.g. charities appeal to our emotions – 'Give just £2 a month and you could help'. Others work by appealing to our sense of adventure (cars), our need to be loved or part of a group (buying brand names for example – What would your friends think if you bought unbranded trainers?). Which of these images appeals to you – blue skies and warm beaches, babies and an attractive home, good food and drink, sport or perhaps an appeal to your conscience such as the advertisement for Friends of the Earth on page 103? The most successful adverts have a clear promotional message, with short, simple sentences, are believable and non-humorous. Most local radio adverts concentrate on where the product can be bought. However, adverts can appeal on many levels. Children enjoy humorous adverts with cartoons and animals.

Timing (minutes)

This is critical to the success of any campaign, as frequently media time and space have to be booked months in advance. Both time of day ('Looking for a loan' advertisements always seem to be in the afternoon, whilst 'Looking for a date' commercials are on late at night!) and day of the week are important, e.g. weekend colour supplements seem to be filled with health, beauty and fashion. Holidays are advertised in January.

Media buying and scheduling are essential functions in advertising agencies, particularly as TV advertising becomes fragmented with more and more commercial channels and correspondingly smaller but purer audiences. Cross-scheduling, where the media to be used in a campaign is timed simultaneously, is important when trying to communicate an effective message and gain an advantage over competitors.

Being able to book time or space may be a critical factor in determining the choice of media for a campaign. TV and cinema advertisements have a long lead time (the time between the booking and when the advert appears) compared to local media which is more flexible.

remember

You have a very short lead time (minutes) to plan your campaign for P4.

Circulation and readership figures

The *Sun* has a current estimated circulation of 3,298,000, with primarily a C1 and C2 readership. TV and radio measure the number of viewers and listeners.

C1 and C2 are social grades determined by the occupation of the head of the household. C1 is supervisory or clerical and junior managerial, administrative or professional. C2 is skilled manual workers.

Link

See the RAJAR extract on page 273 and BARB on page 262.

The figures are used to calculate:

- reach, coverage or penetration – usually taken as the percentage of the target group who are reached or exposed to the advert at least once during a particular campaign
- frequency – the number of times the target group have been reached.

- Look at the Channel 4 website: www.in4mer.com/advertising: 50 'spots' in the Midlands with 16 per cent of the UK population cost £60,000.
- www.capitalradiogroup.com has information such as the fact that Red Dragon FM reaches 318,000 adults each week which is 35 per cent of the population of the area. It has a 54 per cent reach of main shoppers with kids.

Cost per thousand

Cost per thousand (CPM, where M is the roman numeral for 1,000) is a method for comparing the cost of advertising across a range of media with different viewing/listening or readership data.

These formulae show how it can be done.

Press advertising

$$\text{Cost per thousand} = \frac{\text{Cost of full page advert}}{\text{Circulation}} \times 1,000$$

For example:

$$\text{Local paper} = \frac{\pounds1,800}{150,000} \times 1,000 = \pounds12$$

$$\textit{The Economist} = \frac{\pounds80,000}{1,000,000} \times 1,000 = \pounds80$$

TV or radio advertising

$$\text{Cost per thousand} = \frac{\text{Cost of advertisement}}{\text{Number of viewers/listeners}} \times 1,000$$

Perhaps additional information, such as the number of the audience in the target market, whether or not the audience actually look at advertisements and the reputation of the media would be useful. Most media have detailed figures of their audience. Local/regional press closely followed by *Yellow Pages* are the main choice of people looking for local services.

---

assignment focus

1 How have you selected and used the media you have chosen?

2 What criteria have you used?

3 How do you think your choice will contribute to the success of your campaign?

4 Calculate the cost per thousand.

You will need to decide on a media mix and promotion mix for your campaign in the next section.

Role of the internet

Internet advertising

In 1997, £8m was spent on internet advertising. In 2004, the figure was £653m. What is it now? This is the fastest growth of any sector and the trend is expected to continue. Existing websites can be used to advertise new products and special promotions. Banners and pop-ups can be good for increasing awareness. Do you block them?

The major difficulty for a small company is attracting new visitors to the website. Even being listed in the top 50 of a web search can be very expensive. How far do you scroll down?

Good web advertising has the potential to reach 30 million people in the UK alone, with the advert available 24 hours a day. Almost all major organisations have a website and the internet is in constant use for online searching and increasingly, purchasing. Companies such as Amazon and easyJet do all their business online. For others, selling over the internet adds another dimension to the P for place in the marketing mix. Thompson Holidays (owned by TUI, a German travel and transport business) advertise 'Click, Call, Come in, Switch on to Sky Digital'.

Disintermediation

Traditionally goods have been distributed from the manufacturer/producer to the consumer through intermediaries or 'middlemen' such as wholesalers, retailers, agents or dealers. The internet enables the supplier of goods/services to deal directly with consumers, the 'middleman' is no longer needed. This process is called disintermediation.

assignment focus   Who are the winners and losers resulting from disintermediation? (Consider the consumer, supplier, wholesaler, retailer.)

Direct marketing

This allows businesses to sell directly to consumers online, regardless of where the supplier or consumer is located. A Latvian website sells beer, wine and spirits direct to UK consumers without the necessity of paying UK taxes. A search for 'buying wine' in Yahoo produced 17.300,000 websites in 22 seconds. How much would it cost to get a website in the Top 10/100/1000? How far do you scroll down when searching?

The final step is one-to-one communication. Research suggests that people respond favourably to personalised communications which directly address their needs, e.g. home pages that welcome you by name and remind you of your last purchase. The individual has become the ultimate target segment, but does this make it more or less difficult to market products? Does there need to be a marketing mix specially for you? Any comments?

Link   See pages 105 and 144 for more information.

case study 9.5   Advertising on Yahoo

Under the heading 'Advertise with us' in the south-west corner of the Yahoo home page, there is a very useful section which covers internet advertising, including advertising online, planning a campaign, ad specifications, audience profiles and you as a member of the i-generation! According to Yahoo research their users are:

'Digitally Driven'

They embrace the fluid lifestyle that this technology enables them to enjoy.

Homogenous

The identity of the i-generation tends to be defined by collective interests and lifestyles, whether fashion or football, music or sexuality.

Self-Absorbed

For this generation, self-expression through creativity in personal life is high on their list of priorities.

Time-Pressured

Time remains the ultimate luxury for the i-generation. They lead extremely busy lives, making the internet a vital tool in managing their time more efficiently and effectively.

Brandist

The i-generation are brand experts and use those brands to define their identity. They have a sophisticated radar when evaluating brands, preferring understated stylishness to flashy or showy alternatives.

Social Sparks

"Social Sparks" are the instigators and opinion formers – a sub-set within the i-generation – and a key target for advertisers.'

Source: Yahoo

activity

1   Go to 'Advertise with us' on the Yahoo website. Are you one of the i-generation?

2   Use the information on the site to explain the benefits of disintermediation, direct marketing and one to one communication with internet advertising.

Creating a simple promotional campaign

assignment focus

You will need to design your own promotional campaign for your product/service. This should meet the needs of (be based on) your campaign/creative brief.

It could be a smaller business or a local campaign, e.g. a local cafe with an Italian theme, a new branch of a chain of health and fitness clubs, a new high street wedding service (with website).

Think carefully about every aspect of your campaign. You will need to justify it for M3.

Campaign brief

A campaign brief is a document that sets out the strategic requirements for the planning and management of a marketing campaign. It is a summary of the detailed research that will have gone into its production. It sets out three essential positions:

- Where are we now?
- Where do we want to be?
- How are we going to get there?

An excellent structure for a campaign is provided by the SOSTT + 4m approach, developed by P.R. Smith in the book, *Marketing Communications: An Integrated Approach*.

SOSTT + 4m

Table 9.12 SOSTT + 4m

S	Situation	Where is the organisation/brand now? What are the trends? Are there any past experiences? Who are the customers? Are there any significant PESTLE influences? etc.
O	Objectives	Where do we want to get to? These could be split into marketing objectives, e.g. increase market share, and communication objectives, e.g. influencing perception and attitudes towards the product.
S	Strategy	How does the organisation/brand get there?
T	Tactics	The details of the strategy, e.g. selection of media.
T	Targets	Audience, segments, i.e. who they are, where they are, etc.
M	Men (and women)	Who does what, e.g. in case study 9.6 some work will be done in-house by the Yorkshire Tourist Board (YTB) and some by the successful agency.
M	Money	The budget/financial resources – is it enough? How will it be spent? How much is there?
M	Minutes	What is the time-scale? When are the deadlines? A Gantt chart could help.
M	Measurement	How are the results going to be measured/monitored/evaluated? What lessons can be learned? What improvements could be made?

The following case study shows how this approach has been interpreted in practice. Every brief will be different depending on the type of organisation, campaign objectives, whether it is a product or service, size of the budget, etc. Even the layout may be different. However, in all cases, the purpose is the same – to plan and implement a successful campaign and give a framework for the creative brief.

case study 9.6

Yorkshire Tourist Board PR agency brief

Here is an example of a public relations (PR) campaign brief created by the Yorkshire Tourist Board (YTB) as part of the 'Make Yorkshire yours' marketing campaign:

1 Position statement (situation)

The marketing campaign began in January 2005. It was scheduled to run for 18 months with a budget of £2.8m. YTB want 'an innovative and engaging PR campaign to maximise coverage of the key communication messages'.

2 Communications objectives

Some of the aims of the campaign are to:

■ showcase the cream of Yorkshire tourism

■ boost awareness and understanding of Yorkshire's unique qualities. Visitors are invited to 'Make Yorkshire yours'

■ encourage people to find out more at the website and make more bookings online at www.makeyorkshireyours.com

■ encourage visits to the region

■ increase awareness of the region's outdoor pursuits and heritage.

3 Target audience

The priority is developing new audiences and reinforcing positive key messages to current visitors.

■ Primary market – couples aged 45+ years, both 'traditionals' and 'discoverers' (for a more detailed breakdown such as 'affluent older families in urban areas', look at ACORN on page 129)

■ Secondary market – couples aged 25–44.

4 Marketing campaign activity

This will include TV, press and magazine advertising, direct mail, online marketing through e-newsletters and advertising (an accommodation booking service will be available on the website) and public relations.

5 Key messages

'Make Yorkshire yours'. These promote Yorkshire as refreshingly modern, friendly, warm, great heritage, with something for everyone, plus log on to the website.

6 Agency activity

This sets out the time-scales (M for minutes). Both written communications, such as press releases and features in appropriate newspapers/magazines, and creative ideas, such as stunts and promotions are required.

7 Monitoring and evaluation

This will be done by measuring the amount and effectiveness of the press and event coverage using an Audit of Customer Expectations (ACE), i.e. what customers expect and what they experience.

Source: Yorkshire Tourist Board and www.makeyorkshireyours.com

activity

1 Identify the SOSTT + 4m in the case study.

2 Create a campaign brief using the SOSTT + 4m approach for your chosen business.

3 For M3, you must provide a rationale for your promotional campaign. Give your reasons for choosing particular objectives, your target audience and marketing activities. Say why you rejected alternatives. Why do you think it will work?

4 For M3, make recommendations for improving your promotional campaign.

Creative brief and selection of content

This is a brief document, no more than two written pages, which sets out simply what the promotion should do and how the target audience should respond.

Table 9.13 is an example for a fictional business called Eclipse, a craft pottery based in Cornwall. The time-scale for their promotional campaign is two months with a budget of £10,500. We will use the example of Eclipse throughout the rest of this unit.

Table 9.13 Eclipse creative brief

What are the aims of the campaign?	Create and measure awareness of the Eclipse brand. Gain exposure through the media (radio and newspapers). Maximise use of the budget.
What are the objectives?	Achieve a turnover of £36,000 in the first six months. Ten stockists under contract.
How will the marketing mix be used?	The total Eclipse package consists of price discounts to the trade and online purchasers. Promotions: ongoing press and radio. Place: web, retail outlets and direct from the pottery. Product: quality Cornish image.
Who is the target audience?	A chain of vegetarian restaurants. Local craft and gift shops. The Cornish community demographics 20–30, lifestyle ABC1. Visitors to the pottery.
What is the key message in the advertising? (the content)	Looks good, feels good, hand-made quality in Cornwall, original designs, adds style to your table 'Put your Cornish food on a hand-crafted Cornish plate', 'Relive your Cornish holiday'. Inform of stockist details, website and pottery address, plus logo.
Why should the audience believe us?	Local business with local knowledge. Using local products. Supporting local community.
What do we want the audience response to be?	Raised awareness, enquiries and sales through the web/outlets/pottery. A positive image of the products.
What tone and style should be used?	Gentle graphics, expressing quality and style With a daring edge that sets us apart
What is the budget?	Pre-launch/launch £10,500 over two months
Are there any constraints?	Larger budget, longer time period, need to generate revenue quickly, availability of guests, need to launch by Spring. Need to include all details and instructions for washing.
What communication mix should be used?	Advertising, public relations (launch party), direct mail shots to the potential trade customers, website loyalty features, sponsorship of local tourist events, e.g. pottery demonstrations linked to the local vineyard.
What media mix should be used?	E.g. newspapers, local radio, leaflets and flyers, website

assignment focus

Write a creative brief for your chosen business.

Campaign tactics

Reach the target group

The target group specified in Eclipse's brief has four segments:

- a chain of vegetarian restaurants
- local craft and gift shops
- the Cornish community demographics: 20–30, lifestyle ABC 1
- visitors to the pottery.

Eclipse now needs to work out how best to reach each of these target groups.

Who is your target group/audience/segment? Give your reasons.

Selection of appropriate media

This is the way the target segments are going to be given the message. The right choice of media is critical for the success of any campaign and even more so when the M for money (the budget) and the M for minutes (time-scale/deadlines) are very tight.

Eclipse has used these criteria to make its decision:

- which media has the type and size of audience that it needs
- cost of time – national, even regional, TV commercials are too expensive as are Lifestyle TV and the home shopping channel. Radio, despite being non-visual can create mental images and a one-to-one intimacy with the product. Advertisements are cheaper and very cost effective with good reach. At the time of writing, Carphone Warehouse and Budweiser were the most easily recalled radio adverts. Which radio/TV advert can you think of now? (Look in the weekly marketing press to find out what other people recall.)

See cost per thousand, page 267.

- cost of space – the price of advertisements in newspapers and magazines depends on the size of the advert and the circulation (size of the audience). The cost of making a TV or cinema advertisement can be very high
- ability to deliver the message
- potential return and value for money.

See page 140 for more information on segments.

The media mix is the range of media used to convey the advertising message. A typical large advertising campaign budget for a nationally distributed brand could be split between posters (5 per cent), radio (15 per cent), cinema (10 per cent), newspaper and magazines (20 per cent), TV (50 per cent). As a small local business, Eclipse will spend its budget on leaflets, trade promotion, local radio, local newspapers and a launch party (for public relations and possible networking). The decision would depend on the cost/size of the budget, the promotion message, target audience and potential return/value for money.

Leaflets

Leaflets, flyers and handouts are cheap and cheerful. They can be delivered by hand, by Royal Mail or distributed as newspaper or magazine inserts. Printing and distribution costs need to be checked. You will find *Yellow Pages* (www.yell.com) and the *Thompson Local* telephone directory will list suppliers. Eclipse will put flyers in local libraries and distribute them by hand outside the pottery and the craft shops. To make the flyer worth keeping, there will be a list of useful telephone numbers, such as tourist venues, registered cab companies, etc.

You could create promotional materials for your campaign, e.g. leaflets, flyers, newspaper advert, price list brochure with photographs of your product/service, business card, point-of-sale materials, multimedia, etc. The radio could want a creative brief. Be consistent: keep your font, logo and typography the same, and use it on all your materials.

Trade promotion

Eclipse has decided to spend part of its budget visiting possible retail stockists (B2B). This is called trade promotion. It is central to their policy of placing the product in craft and gift shops, but will mean giving substantial discounts on a 'sale or return' basis to persuade them to stock the tableware. The sales target could be achieved, but what might happen to revenue projections? Perhaps a mini trial launch in a few selected outlets could be tried to establish possible trading patterns before going live with a full launch. Point-of-sale (POS) promotion will consist of a large cut-out lion to raise awareness and attract attention. Interest will be aroused by a prominent product display and action will be driven by a 'Special introductory offer' on the Total Eclipse (AIDA).

Local radio

Eclipse hope to use part of their budget on a local radio advertising campaign.

case study *9.7*

Local radio: Pirate FM 102

Figure 9.8 The Pirate FM logo

Table 9.14 shows the radio listening figures from RAJAR (Radio Joint Audience Research Limited) which show Pirate having a healthy share of the radio audience in the local area. (note the west of Cornwall has a much bigger share). This would justify Eclipse's expenditure. Pirate advertising costs about £2.00 per 1,000 listeners.

Table 9.14 Pirate FM's listening figures

	Survey period	Adult 15+ 00s	Weekly Reach		Average hours		Total hours	Share of listening
			000s	%	Head	Listener		
Pirate FM Total	Y	608	185	30	3.7	12.3	2,272	15.3
Pirate FM 102 East	H	328	83	25	3.1	12.3	1,014	12.5
Pirate FM 102 West	Y	280	106	38	4.6	12.3	1,295	19.8

Eclipse are hoping to get publicity from inviting the breakfast show team to the high-profile launch party. Here are some of the services that can be provided for potential advertisers on the Pirate FM station. Eclipse are particularly interested in the section on 'Promotions and events':

Airtime campaigns:

■ A campaign of commercials individually produced to advertise your products and services
■ Short-, mid- or long-term, based on your objectives
■ Use for awareness or 'call to action'

Sponsorship and promotional opportunities:

■ Link your core advertising message or market positioning statement to a high profile
■ Pirate FM information sequence or programming feature
■ Use for short-term, high-impact advertising or for long-term name awareness

Promotions and events:

■ Pirate FM can help to bring your event alive with presenter appearances or promotional crew
■ Heighten the profile of, and gain maximum exposure for, your event

Source: www.piratefm102.co.uk

activity

1 Do you think that Eclipse should advertise on Pirate FM? Give reasons for your answer.
2 Should your choice of business use radio advertising?
3 Which station would you choose?
4 When would you advertise?
5 How many slots would you buy?

Give reasons for your answers.

Local newspapers

The website www.dailynewspaper.co.uk showed four local newspapers in Cornwall. Eclipse chose the *West Briton*, which is the highest selling weekly newspaper in Britain. It has a circulation of nearly 53,000 with 2.3 readers per copy and has the reader profile that Eclipse is after. Advertising costs vary with the size of the advert, number of insertions (weeks), position in the newspaper and whether it is mono or coloured.

The launch party

This will be held at the pottery. There will be a demonstration by the owners Della and Wayne, a display of the Eclipse range, opportunities to buy the products and an opportunity for guests to 'throw your own pot'. The guest list would include Pirate FM, local councillors, restaurant and shop owners, representatives from the local tourist board and Business Link office, plus other media. The key message (selection of content) will be demonstrating the product benefits of quality hand-made pottery with unique designs and high performance – dishwasher and microwave safe – a total sensory experience, to achieve word-of-mouth advertising (viral marketing). The invitations would need to be written into the activities in the Gantt chart. Eclipse would need an accurate estimate of guests to cater effectively. The number of guests would be strictly limited by the budget. However, any expenditure is a business expense and can be set against profits.

Suitable promotional materials and images

Eclipse will be using two images chosen for their dramatic impact and effect (Figures 9.9 and 9.10). They have high visibility and good 'stand out' from competitors. The images are immediately recognisable and with the logo will give Eclipse a strong brand identity.

Figure 9.9

Figure 9.10

Eclipse did not use a formal focus group because of budget constraints (see below). Instead these two images were chosen by family and friends (was this a good idea?) from an initial set of 12. The group was set up by Eclipse to:

- look at the images
- discuss the product and look at samples
- discuss suggestions for promotion.

The promotional message will be that Eclipse is quality tableware, hand-made in Cornwall. It looks good and feels good, with original designs it adds style to your table – 'Put your Cornish food on a hand-crafted Cornish plate', 'Relive your Cornish holiday'. It will also include stockist details, website and the pottery address.

The message could also emphasise the unique selling points of a product, e.g. Tropicana, '100% pure squeezed orange juice not from concentrate', 'HP invent' or reliability, safety and performance which feature in car advertisements. There is a proverb 'a good wine needs no bush', which means a good product doesn't need advertising. Do you agree?

Text and script

This needs to be written to complement the images – 'one picture is worth a thousand words'. Each medium (e.g. TV, press and magazine, direct mail, public relations) will require a different approach. Each audience will need a different focus. However, the approach should be integrated and complementary, with each medium supporting the other. Here are some issues that need to be considered.

- What are the objectives? What is the purpose? Remember AIDA.
- Is it informative, persuasive, or a combination of both?
- Gear the language to the needs of the audience. (Look at adverts in local newspapers/ specialist magazines such as *The Caterer* and the range of *Bride* magazines for different ethnic groups.) Remember KISS – keep it short and simple. Use paragraphs and a good headline. For many people, the promotion may be the first contact they have with the product. It has to gain immediate attention, interest and excitement. We all see hundreds of adverts/leaflets/flyers, etc. every day. They are competing for our money. Using colour with style and pace will help to create impact and visibility, but be aware of the special needs of the audience. Try to cater for all the senses, e.g. fresh bread baked at the supermarket, leather smells pumped into the air conditioning in the car showroom!
- Is it legal, decent, truthful and honest? (See the Advertising Standards Authority: www.asa.org.uk.)
- Sell the benefits and unique selling points (USP) rather than a specification (unless it is a technical product).
- Include the logo, strapline (e.g. 'Ginsters Cornish THRoUGH and THRoUGH'), contact telephone, e-mail, web address, etc. Make sure these details are accurate and available at the stated times. Word-of-mouth works both ways – 'I rang this number and it didn't exist.' If a business gets these details wrong, any promotional expenditure is worthless.
- Is it a trade or consumer promotion? Different styles, tone and language will need to be used with each audience.
- Find out how the competition/opposition promote themselves, e.g. who or what can be benchmarked as best practice in the craft pottery business? Perhaps a trade magazine such as *Ceramic Review* would help. (Is there a specialist magazine for your product? Check online.)

Stages of production

Once a brief has been created and the target segment(s) identified, promotional materials can be developed which are appropriate to the needs of the audience and the selected media.

Use of storyboards

This is a sequence of cartoons or sketches which can be used to produce an advertisement, presentation or animation. A well planned detailed storyboard can save both time and money at later stages of the production process when studio time, for example, can be very expensive. The earlier in the creative process problems can be spotted, the better.

Figure 9.11 A storyboard

Mock-up

This can either be a model, e.g. of a car or building, or a layout of printed materials. Leaflets, brochures, price and product lists, flyers, etc. can all be created as mock-ups to see if the design concepts, such as the position of the words and images, work. When attached to an A3 sheet they make an effective display.

Mock-ups and storyboards would be shown to the client or perhaps to a focus group for approval or further improvements before the final proof.

Final proof

The final version which is created must be accurate. Any text must be proof-read for spelling and grammar, accuracy and legality (e.g. copyright legislation). Any multimedia presentation should be checked for style and pace (make sure that the specific needs of the target audience are met). Use a checklist to make sure that each point in the brief has been covered.

Commercial agencies have to pitch (make a persuasive presentation) for a contract. For the Yorkshire Tourist Board contract, a brief presentation was needed to outline how communications objectives would be met and what tactics would be used. Creative proposals, targeting strategy, costing and time-scales were also required. Only three weeks was given to prepare the presentation.

Evaluating campaigns

---

assignment focus

To achieve D1, you will need to evaluate and justify a promotional mix with respect to the business and marketing objectives of your chosen organisation.

1 What are the components of the promotional mix?

2 What criteria will you use to evaluate the promotional mix?

3 How do these relate to the business and marketing objectives of your organisation?

4 What are the strengths and weaknesses of the mix including its use of the marketing mix?

5 Give your suggestions on how the promotion mix could be improved or changed to achieve their aims and objectives.

Much depends on what the promotional campaign was trying to achieve, e.g. increasing awareness, improving the image, changing perception or attitude towards the product, increase membership of a club, increase donations to a charity, number of hits on a website, etc.

Here are the aims of the Eclipse campaign:

■ create and measure awareness of the Eclipse brand

■ gain exposure through the media (radio and newspapers)

■ maximise use of the budget

■ achieve a turnover of £36,000 in the first six months with ten stockists under contract.

 Look at the Advertising Standards Authority website, www.asa.org.uk, under the adjudications section for examples of complaints made against advertisers. (High impact but are they legal, decent, truthful and honest?)

The evaluation of advertising is usually done using these criteria:

- Does it stand out against the background, e.g. on the printed page, in a commercial break, on a web page? i.e. what is its impact?
- Does the meaning and message come across to the target audience? Have you ever thought, 'Great advert but what was it advertising?'?
- Brand perception with existing brands or businesses – Have the customers' views changed, e.g. from a 'greasy spoon' lunchtime cafe to Italian theme?
- Has the advertisement aroused interest, created desire or led to action?
- Has the advertisement led to increased sales, profits, charitable donations, etc?

To measure any change, the evaluation of advertising needs to take place before and after the campaign. Recall is a method used to test effectiveness. In spontaneous recall, consumers are asked to name any advert which they have seen or heard in the last few days. With prompted recall, they are asked whether they have seen or heard a particular advert, in this case Eclipse.

Developing a promotion plan

The Gantt chart

The Gantt chart (Table 9.15) can be used to:

- identify and plan each activity
- monitor each activity, e.g. Were individual deadlines met?
- compare what was planned with the actual outcome/evaluation
- identify specific media (name of the newspaper) with specific costings.

Newspapers, e.g. the *Westmorlond Gazette*, specify that advertisements should be delivered as PDF files.

You can adapt Table 9.15 for your assignment.

Table 9.15 A Gantt chart for a promotion campaign

Step	Activities in weeks	1	2	3	4	5	6	7	8	9	10	11	12
1	Research and identify target group, see brief												D
2	Create the message to drive awareness, interest, desire and action AIDA												E
3	Select the media mix, e.g. local newspapers and radio depending on target group usage												A
4	Fix the timing and frequency for media exposure												D
5	Fix the budget												L
6	Select the promotion mix. Create promotion materials leaflets, with images and text												I
7	Organise trade promotion												N
8	Organise launch party												E
9	Work on radio advert with Pirate FM												
10	Organise newspaper advert												
11	Evaluation build in SMART targets to the initial brief												

Fix the timing and frequency

For an organisation with a large budget, these details would be arranged by an agency to maximise the impact of the campaign with the target audience segment. A small business would need to plan the schedule direct with the advertising media. The launch of a new product or a re-launch should be treated as a project, with full planning and implementation, using a Gantt chart or **critical path analysis** to make sure deadlines are met, e.g. it is essential to have the product/service available and fully operational (in stock or in the shops) before the advertising begins.

Link See page 404 for the Eclipse business plan.

Fix the budget

Although in the Eclipse example the budget has already been determined, in practice setting a promotional budget can be very difficult. Here are some methods which may help.

- Benchmark your competitors and spend the same.
- Spend whatever can be afforded – useful in small organisations with limited budgets.
- Spend what is needed to achieve objectives. How do you know?
- Spend a percentage of sales.

This sequence of activities is set for a 12-week period. Be aware of the timings for your campaign and the cost, e.g. a page in the *Sun* begins at £40,000.

The order of the activities can easily be changed. What matters is that the timings are accurate, particularly for critical activities, e.g. promotional materials must be produced before they can be distributed, launch party fully organised, etc.

Here is your invitation to the Eclipse launch party!

Figure 9.12

Eclipse

Welcomes you
To our Launch Lunch Party

Cornish clotted cream
Home-made honey and jam
Locally made scones
Cornish pasties

All eaten off **Eclipse** *original tableware*

Wines supplied by
Camel Valley Vineyards

With beers supplied by
Skinners Cornish Ales

Enjoy Your Total Eclipse Experience

Human resource management

This unit covers:

- The factors involved in human resources planning in organisations
- How organisations motivate employees
- How to gain committed employee co-operation
- The importance of managing employee performance at work

Employees are an organisation's most valuable resource because of the skills, knowledge and experience they bring to the job. Increasingly they need to be flexible and willing to learn new skills. Effective human resource management means getting the best out of employees to ensure the organisation meets its aims and objectives. This unit explains how human resource managers achieve this.

grading criteria

To achieve a **Pass** grade the evidence must show that the learner is able to:	To achieve a **Merit** grade the evidence must also show that the learner is able to:	To achieve a **Distinction** grade the evidence must also show that the learner is able to:
P1 describe the internal and external factors to be considered when planning the HR requirements of an organisation	**M1** explain why human resources planning is important to an organisation	**D1** Suggest, with justifications, ways of improving motivation in an organisational setting
P2 describe how the employee skills required in an organisation are identified	**M2** compare the use of motivation theories in an organisation	**D2** assess the importance of measuring and managing employee performance at work
P3 outline how an organisation's motivational practices and reward systems are informed by theories of motivation	**M3** explain how the results from measuring and managing performance inform employee development	
P4 describe how organisations obtain the co-operation of employees through the contract of employment and employee involvement techniques		

The factors involved in human resource planning in organisations

'Human resource planning is about the acquisition, utilisation, improvement and retention of an organisation's human resources [i.e. its staff, its people].'

Source: Edexcel

Changes are constantly taking place in the market for goods and services, e.g. 3g phones, Ipods, organic foods. In the workplace there are new materials and new technologies, e.g. key-operated tills have been replaced by point of sale scanners. (Do you trust these? They never seem to record special offers!) These internal changes affect the ability of the organisation to produce its goods and services. Businesses must respond to these new circumstances and manage their workforce effectively to achieve their aims and objectives.

Figure 16.1 Supply side and demand side changes

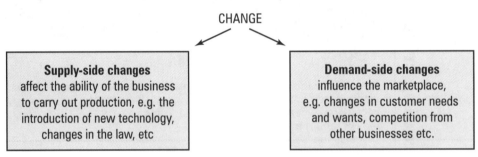

CHANGE

Supply-side changes affect the ability of the business to carry out production, e.g. the introduction of new technology, changes in the law, etc

Demand-side changes influence the marketplace, e.g. changes in customer needs and wants, competition from other businesses etc.

What growth is required?

What workforce is needed for this?

What is our present workforce?

Who will leave?

Who do we need to recruit?

What part can be played by flexible working, part-time working, new technology and staff training?

Businesses need to plan carefully for a change and to ensure that they have the right employees for their future needs. The HR plan is informed by information gained from both inside and outside of the business

HR plans are driven by the needs of the strategic plan of the business (how the organisation sees itself developing) for the period in question – the planning horizon.

Planners start from estimates of the future demand for the firm's products. Using this information, they will estimate the number of staff required to meet this and the skills these staff will need. The plan will then set out how these staff will be employed, what their conditions of service and pay will be, how they will be trained, motivated and monitored to ensure adequate performance. The plan must take account of both internal and external considerations.

When the train companies Arriva and First Great Western under-estimated demand, they were unable to provide enough drivers or trains. Over-estimating could result in too many staff.

Figure 16.2 The planning horizon

Figure 16.3 The stages in human resource planning

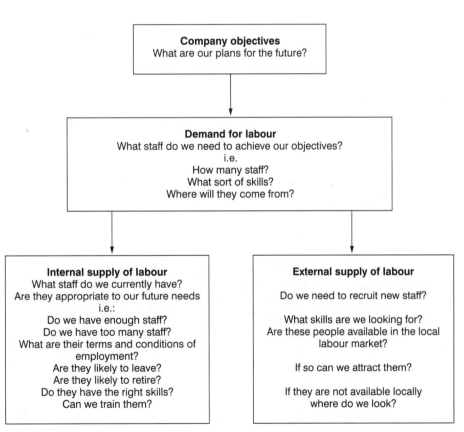

Internal planning factors
Organisational needs

Demand for products and services

Whatever the length of the planning horizon, e.g. six months (perhaps for seasonal demand), one, three or five years, an organisation will need to make estimates of the future demand for its products or services. Is it expected to rise or fall? By how much? Could it cope with a small change through using existing staff or through 'natural wastage', i.e. people leaving or retiring?

To estimate future demand, it will need to be aware of industry trends. Here are two examples taken from KeyNote Reports which provide excellent forecasts on trends:

- 'sales growth in fast food outlets is expected to decrease because of concerns over healthy eating' (Fast Food and Home Delivery Outlets)

- 'the branded coffee (e.g. Starbucks, Costa) and sandwich shop (e.g. Subway, Benjys) sectors are expected to grow between 7–11.8 per cent up to 2009' (Coffee and Sandwich Shops).

How would this information help an organisation with its human resource (HR) planning? Fast food outlets could reduce part-time hours. Coffee and sandwich shops could cope with the increase in demand, e.g. by giving existing part-time staff more hours or recruiting extra staff.

KeyNote reports can be found at www.KeyNote.co.uk.

New products, services and markets
The Ansoff matrix is used to help the organisation with its marketing decisions.

The Ansoff matrix is explained on page 138.

However, any marketing decision will have knock-on effects to other functions in the organisation. It could affect finance, production or, in this case, human resources – staffing.

Whenever a new product/service is introduced or the organisation enters a new market, it will need to ask, do we currently have the right staff? Do we need to train people? Do we need to recruit people e.g. with language expertise? In Wales there is a shortage of people with bilingual skills in Welsh and English. Retailers wishing to take advantage of the opportunities offered by e-commerce and internet selling will need suitable staff.

---

assignment focus

Just Desserts, which currently produces a range of organic yoghurts, intends diversifying by buying a chain of garden centres. It believes there are major business opportunities in global warming and climate change. Its business plan for the new venture (called Just Desserts), which will specialise in tropical and dry gardens, already has a financial, operational and marketing section.

1   What internal factors need to be considered when planning the HR requirements of the operation? Think about senior and middle management and operatives (workers).

2   What internal factors does your organisation need to consider?

Technological change
Where new technology is available, it may be possible to increase output without a proportionate increase in staff, e.g. in agriculture and car manufacturing. Automated production lines where machines/robots have replaced people are now commonplace. The majority of our bread, biscuits and cakes are now made entirely by machines. 'Hand decorated' or 'hand finished' is now a major marketing feature of some chocolate cakes. New technology/automation, whether considered from an internal or external point of view, can affect both the number of people employed and the skills that people will need.

An organisation will need to assess the HR implications on recruitment and training of introducing new technology. Not all employees welcome technology and could be resistant to change. A skills audit (page 291) could be a useful way of identifying individuals suitable for training.

Figure 16.4 New technology
has changed the way
businesses work

Staff training

Existing staff may be retrained as an alternative to employing new suitably skilled staff.
Training may enable staff to be re-deployed in other areas of the business. It may also be
used as a way of retaining and motivating the workforce.

Location of production

You may know of local examples of factories closing in your area, as production is moved
– usually overseas – because manufacturing costs are lower. Government offices are moved
out of London, because facilities costs are lower. Workers may have to be made redundant
as work is no longer available, or perhaps they can be redeployed (offered work in the new
location). The final decision on location may be based on whether there are sufficient suitably
qualified staff available, labour costs and the level of government incentives.

Many managers work a couple of days a week from home. Some get home early and then
check e-mails from a home PC. Others might spend the first couple of hours checking
messages and writing reports before travelling into work after the rush hour. Some employees
work full-time from home.

Teleworking is one way in which the location of production is changing as a result of new
technology, new services and increasing costs. These factors are increasingly important in
HR planning. Teleworking saves on expensive office costs. One desk is sufficient for several
workers since they are not all in the office at the same time. The practice of sharing desks is
called 'hot desking'.

Figure 16.5

Teleworking is likely to be popular because:

- people with young children are able to continue working
- many managers find it difficult to write reports or do work that requires concentration in the typical office
- disabled people with mobility problems will find advantages, as will old people and those who for various reasons are at a disadvantage in a face to face situation.

Employers can see advantages:

- BT sees 'teleworking' as a cheaper alternative than keeping open lots of small offices; office rent and running costs are dearer than PCs
- The evidence is that people work harder and longer if they work from home.

There may be a gain for society:

- It may reduce congestion on the roads as people work from home.
- Employment may be provided in remote areas.
- People may have the time to get involved with schools and other local activities instead of spending hours each day stuck in the traffic.

case study 16.1 — Teleworking

- BT has encouraged around 12,000 of its staff to work from home. Under its Options 2000 scheme, BT provides training and management support for all volunteers who work from home for a couple of days each week and meet a range of clients and colleagues in different locations on the other days. The Communication Workers Union is in favour and has ensured that BT will provide technical back-up and compensation for electricity, heating and other costs. The union has also pressed for guarantees on set working hours.

  BT systems engineer, Phil Howson, works for BT from his home in the fishing village of Mevagissey in Cornwall, almost 300 miles from head office. 'I could just as well do this job from France. It really doesn't matter where I am.' He works from his house via telephone, e-mail and BT's own intranet. Phil moved from London seven years ago. 'It seemed the right thing to do for all the family.' Since cutting office costs was a high priority for BT, the company was enthusiastic about the arrangement.

- IBM France found that its sales force was able to spend 45 per cent more time with its customers when they became a 'remote' workforce linked to the office by telecommunications networks. In turn this meant that less office space and facilities such as staff canteens were needed.

- The Telework and Telecottage Association is trying to persuade companies running call centres to employ workers from home. This could provide work for those in isolated communities, people with disabilities or those with caring responsibilities.

activity

1 Describe the factors involved in HR planning in the examples in the case study.
2 Find out if employees at your organisation work from home. Could they? Should they? Are there any other flexible working arrangements?

Succession and promotion of staff

Succession refers to the process of developing staff for promotion when their time comes. This fits with the image of a stable organisation where changes come steadily. In recent years organisations have needed to react to the 'challenge' of rapid change by breaking with traditional ways. They have:

- downsized – made staff redundant in an attempt to become more efficient and cost effective

- delayered – removed some levels of authority, especially in middle management so that organisations have become flatter. This has been helped by the introduction of information technology – the banks have reduced staff in this way

- filled some top posts by the process of 'head hunting'. Essentially this means stealing a star performer from another organisation by making them a better offer. There are employment consultants who specialise in this.

Although it has become common to recruit experienced people from outside the organisation, there are advantages to promoting from within:

- Employees are encouraged to remain loyal if they can see that they have career prospects if they stay.

- It ensures continuity of style – existing employees are aware of the 'culture' of the organisation.

Workforce profiles

A workforce profile is a description and analysis of the current staff. Relevant questions would include: What skills do staff have and how well are they performing? What age are they? How many are about to retire? What is the rate of staff turnover, i.e. how often and why do staff leave? Is there a balance of staff in terms of age, gender, ethnic background and disability? Is there a balance of full-time, part-time, temporary and casual staff?

Answers to these questions will help to identify training needs, problems in motivation and skills shortages and any need for new staff or less staff.

case study 16.2 — HR planning in Cornwall

Look at these four extracts from the Cornwall County Council workforce profile.

A

Figure 16.6 Employee age profile by gender

Source: www.cornwall.gov.uk, 2006

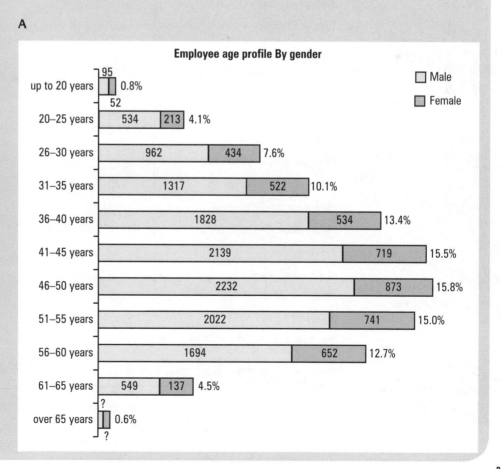

Employee age profile By gender

Age	Male	Female	%
up to 20 years	95		0.8%
20–25 years	52 / 534	213	4.1%
26–30 years	962	434	7.6%
31–35 years	1317	522	10.1%
36–40 years	1828	534	13.4%
41–45 years	2139	719	15.5%
46–50 years	2232	873	15.8%
51–55 years	2022	741	15.0%
56–60 years	1694	652	12.7%
61–65 years	549	137	4.5%
over 65 years	?	?	0.6%

Male ☐   Female ■

B

Table 16.1 Employees by Contract Type

	Permanent (Fixed Hours)	Permanent (Variable Hours)	Temporary (Fixed Hours)	Temporary (Variable Hours)	Fixed Term (Fixed Hours)	Fixed Term (Variable Hours)	Casual Hours	Totals
Totals	13216	3234	1105	324	532	1	1742	20154

Source: www.cornwall.gov.uk, 2006

C

Figure 16.7 Full-time/part-time employees

Source: www.cornwall.gov.uk, 2006

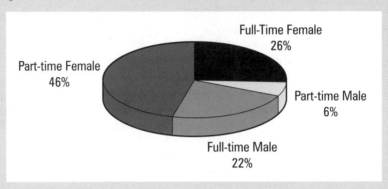

Full-Time Female 26%

Part-time Female 46%

Part-time Male 6%

Full-time Male 22%

D

Table 16.2 Reasons for Leaving, 1 April 2005 to 31 March 2006

Reason for Leaving	Number
Resigned – Leaving employer	1339
End of Contract	227
Resigned – Taking new post	219
Retirement – Normal	152
Retirement – Ill Health	49
Redundancy – Voluntary	28
Resigned – Maternity	17
Dismissal – Conduct	11
Dismissal – Ill Health	23
Retirement – Efficiency	6
Redundancy – Compulsory	14
Death	24
Dismissal – Performance	5
Other	157
Total	**2271**

Source: www.cornwall.gov.uk, 2006

activity

1 Describe the main features of each extract.

2 How many people left the council during the year? What are the implications for short-term recruitment planning?

3 Using extract A, describe what HR planning Cornwall has to do in the next 10 years.

External planning considerations

All organisations are affected by external (PESTLE) factors which are largely outside of their control. These factors will influence demand for the organisation's products and therefore its demand for labour. They will also affect its ability to retain existing staff and its ability to recruit suitable new staff.

For a full explanation of PESTLE, see Unit 1, page 43.

Supply of labour

Where is the labour going to come from?

If the human resources plan shows that labour will need to be recruited from outside of the organisation, then accurate labour market information, such as employment/unemployment trends, pay rates and the availability of skilled workers will be needed. If particular skills are in short supply relative to demand, then its price, i.e. wages, will be high. It might take time to train suitable staff. This is why Wayne Rooney cost Manchester United £27 million in August 2004.

Recruitment will move outwards: 'you begin locally, if you cannot find the person you want, you cast the net wider.' In a typical large superstore, 80 per cent of staff would be part-time, 20 per cent full-time. Most part-time staff would be recruited locally and given training within the business. Middle and senior managers could come from internal promotion within the company or be tempted away from competitors by an attractive pay and benefits package.

International

Top level senior executives are recruited worldwide.

The EU with its policy of free movement of labour, i.e. its citizens have the theoretical right to work in any country, has been a useful source of labour (it now has 25 member states). It is estimated that nearly 500,000 Polish people have moved to the UK since Poland joined the EU, which has helped the UK economy to continue growing.

The UK health and education services for example have recruited doctors, nurses, dentists and teachers from overseas. Premiership football clubs routinely recruit players and managers from around the globe. International recruitment is not a new phenomenon, even in the 1950s London Transport advertised in the Caribbean for bus and underground staff. Australia currently wants hairdressers and is advertising in the UK.

Industry trends will give an indication of future demand for the product and therefore of the derived demand for labour.

Labour market data for your local area can be found in the Economic and Labour Market Review (ELMR). (This is a merger between the Labour Market Review and Economic Trends.) Find it at www.statistics.gov.uk.

National, regional and local labour supply

Internet recruitment allows organisations to advertise any post anywhere in the world.

The majority of people who are recruited to work in an organisation will live locally. An organisation will need to know if an area has enough suitably qualified people available to meet its needs.

Check out the travel to work statistics at www.statistics.gov.uk.

<div class="sidebar">

remember

An HR plan could include recruitment, training and development, motivation and reward systems, performance measurement, redeployment (workers are offered new positions, tasks or places to work) and coping with redundancy.

</div>

Figure 16.8 A simple hierarchy of a typical large tall business

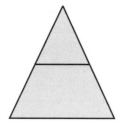

Top level senior management, because of the relatively few jobs at this level, people are willing to move home to further their careers. Posts are likely to be permanent, full time.

At the operative level, many jobs will be part time, even temporary or casual, most people will live and be recruited locally. Unskilled and semi-skiled jobs are filled with local people.

> **Full-time equivalents (FTE)**
> Assume one full-time person works 40 hours per week (hpw). There are ten part-time staff each with 4 hpw to cover peak periods when demand is high. These ten people are equivalent to one full-time member of staff.
> Beware newspaper headlines which shout, 'New store creates 100 new jobs'. Think FTEs, then the headline becomes 'New store creates 10 new jobs'. The alternative headline could be 'Three shops close, 12 full-time jobs lost'. Is the neighbourhood better or worse off?

Long-term and short-term trends

An organisation will need to investigate both long- and short-term employment trends before making a final decision.

Use www.statistics.gov.uk to investigate trends in employment/unemployment, vacancies, and occupations for your area. How might these affect an organisation's decision to expand or open a new business?

Labour costs

In order to attract employees, an employer must provide pay and conditions to match those in comparable jobs elsewhere. If an organisation considers its labour costs are too high in its present location; it might relocate production to lower cost areas and this might be overseas. In March 2007, Burberry – the iconic UK clothing manufacturer with a Royal Warrant (By Appointment to the Queen and the Prince of Wales) – closed its factory in South Wales and shifted production, possibly to China. A high profile campaign led by famous celebrities objected to the proposed closure.

In disadvantaged areas, e.g. where there is high unemployment, the government may provide help and support to attract new businesses.

Link   See pages 155 and 303 on employment contracts.

Government policy

The government runs several schemes to help businesses locate in particular areas.

■ There are nine Regional Development Agencies operated by the Department of Trade and Industry (DTI). Part of their purpose is to:

- promote employment
- enhance development and application of a skills action plan to ensure that skills training matches the needs of the labour market.

Manchester, Newcastle, York, Bristol, Nottingham and Birmingham are currently being promoted as Science Cities by the RDAs. They will receive funding over the next six years to further the development of their science activities.

■ Assisted areas are disadvantaged areas where extra selective finance is available which helps fund new investment projects that lead to long-term improvements in productivity, skills and employment. The map showing the proposed new assisted areas in the UK for 2007–2013 is available at the DTI website.

These schemes could be a deciding factor when an organisation is planning its human resources. Particularly as there may be financial help with premises, facilities and reduced taxation.

Visit the DTI website: www.dti.gov.uk.

assignment focus   Find out if your area is eligible for special help by searching your local borough/council website. How could this help an organisation with its external human resource planning?

Labour market competition

Organisations not only compete for a share of the market, they also compete for labour. Where there are shortages of specific skills, the competition for staff can be keen. Businesses enter the 'milk round' each year when they hold recruitment events to attract the best new graduates. Shell's image suffered following ecological damage to its oilfields in Nigeria, which directly affected its ability to attract staff. It adopted a new 'green' agenda in order to put this right.

Attracting the right staff will mean providing an attractive wage/salary plus benefits package, e.g. company pension scheme, car, regular bonuses, etc. People who have skills which are in high demand will get paid more.

Where there is a high level of local unemployment, it may be easier to recruit staff.

Changing nature of work

Consumers now expect services to be available 24/7, 365, e.g. call centres and superstores. Providing this level of service means that organisations need flexible and adaptable HR policies and workers who are willing and able to work with these new flexible working patterns.

An organisation will need a balance of staff to meet its needs: permanent full-time and part-time staff, temporary staff, casual staff and outside contractors.

> 'The rules on employing, permanent, temporary or casual staff are substantially the same.'
>
> *Source*: www.smallbusiness.co.uk

Permanent staff

Permanent workers can be full-time or part-time. Permanent staff have an open ended contract, i.e. there is no end date. Compare this with fixed-term contracts which will have an end date, e.g. a date when a project is complete. People on permanent contracts are the core workers needed by the organisation to carry out its activities. Most managers are permanent.

Temporary staff

Employers will normally hire temporary staff from an employment agency. They are used to cover short-term skill gaps, peaks in demand or staff absence. They are usually paid by the agency and have the right to a safe and healthy working environment and to be treated fairly under equal opportunities legislation.

Casual staff

Casual staff are often employed on an 'as and when required' basis, e.g. catering staff at a large banquet or dinner.

Flexible working practices

To meet the human resource needs of modern-day organisations, a number of different working practices have become common. Look at extracts B and C for Cornwall County Council (page 286) which show these. Here are some examples of flexible working practices which employers now use to achieve their objectives

- Job sharing is common in administration work. Here two workers share a single full-time post each working for part of the week. Employees may be able to vary days to suit individual needs whilst employers gain from a reduction in obligations and cost by employing part-time staff.

- Shift work is used when organisations provide a continuous service. Traditional examples include the public services (police, fire service, hospitals and public transport) and manufacturers and their suppliers. As organisations compete for customers, the emphasis on customer service has brought shift work to areas in the service sector. It is now common for large retailers to open long hours – sometimes 24 hours a day. Call centres (large warehouses full of telephone receptionists) enable us to phone for details of our bank accounts, insurance policies or travel details at any hour of the day or night. Can you think of other examples?

- Flexible working hours (flexi-time) enables employees, within limits, to vary the time that they start and finish work, as long as they work the total hours agreed each week or month. Employees can vary their working day to suit personal arrangements and to avoid the rush hour. The employer gains from staff satisfaction and motivation. It is also possible for staff delayed in travelling to make up work at the end of the day.

Link

On pages 155 and 303 we discuss the different types of contract of employment.

On pages 155 and 303 we discuss the different types of contract of employment.

assignment focus

Describe the external issues that affect human resource planning in your chosen business, e.g. does it have job vacancies? At what level? Does it have competitors? What does it do to attract staff? Does it recruit locally, nationally, internationally? How has technology affected its HR planning?

Search www.government-skills.gov.uk.

Employee skills

People as organisational resources

People, labour, or human resources, are an essential input necessary for a business to carry on production:

Some businesses may be run entirely by the owner or owners. However, most businesses need to recruit a workforce. Remember that employees operate at all levels within an organisation: as directors, managers, supervisors and operatives. Some will expect promotion and all will have and use different skills.

There should be correlation between the quality of the workforce and the productivity of the business:

> '... great people are the heart of our business.'
>
> *Source*: Domino's Pizza

> 'The key to maximising quality and productivity lies in tapping the innate judgement and creativity of employees in the workplace.'
>
> *Source*: Toyota Motor Corporation

Originally businesses used the personnel department to look after the welfare of staff. The change to 'human resources' came in the 1980s as businesses began to recognise that recruitment, training and motivation policies could make a real difference to business performance.

The job of human resources managers is to create and maintain a workforce that will enable the business to achieve its strategic goals.

Skill sets

This can refer to the skills possessed by an individual or by a team/organisation. The skill set needed by an individual may depend on the job and their position in the organisation. Operatives on the shop floor would require different skills from an administrative assistant. Finance and marketing managers have different skills. The skills required for jobs can be found in job descriptions and person specifications.

- Job-specific skills are those which are required to do particular jobs. They tend to be narrow and non transferable, e.g. you may learn how a particular business completes its invoices and files them. Another business may do this differently and if you changed jobs you would need training in the new system.

- Generic skills are those which once learnt may be applied in many different situations, they are transferable. The key skills of numeracy, communication and IT are transferable; when you learn these you are learning a technique. You can use these skills in any job. Are they part of your course? What skills do you need as a BTEC National student?

Transferable skills are needed because the changing nature of work means that people can no longer expect a job for life. Today's workers must be prepared for 'lifelong learning' and to adapt to new work situations. As a consequence, key skills that can be applied to any job are vital for your success and that of the business.

Look at Unit 4, page 164 for an example of the skill set required for a retail fashion buyer.

Jobs are sometimes described as skilled (formal qualifications or experience is required), semi-skilled or unskilled (no training is needed).

Skills audit

There are three steps involved in a skills audit:

1 What skills profile will be needed by the organisation to achieve its future aims and objectives? This is the most difficult part. It requires considerable research, e.g. PESTLE analysis, industry trends, etc.

2 What skills profile does the organisation currently have? – the audit

3 Is there a gap?

The skills gap is the difference between the skills required by industry and the skills available in the workforce. Where there is a shortage (a gap), a business will have to compete with other employers, train their own staff, look abroad or even relocate the business.

At a national level, the government sets up training schemes and gives incentives to maths and science teachers in an attempt to 'close the gap'.

Skill acquisition

If a skills gap is identified, the organisation can either prepare a training programme for its existing staff to acquire the necessary skills; or plan its recruitment to attract suitable external staff. You may have see notices saying, 'Closed 9–10 a.m. for staff training'.

For example, according to www.jobcymru.com, employers in Wales predict these skills will be needed in 3 years time: IT, managerial, organising own learning and development, Welsh language, leadership (based on the Future Wales survey). Currently they say their employees need a high level of skill in understanding customer needs, communication, ability to follow instructions, showing initiative, team working and flexibility. Do you have this skill set? Are they job specific or generic?

assignment focus

Collect three job advertisements from a local newspaper.

1 Study the job advertisements. Compare the difference in the skills needed. Which are low-skill and which are high-skill?

2 In which job is the range of skills required the greatest?

3 Explain which of the jobs would be the most difficult to fill.

4 What skills do you consider your organisation will need in one, three or five years time?

Impact of technology

Technology has helped reduce production costs whilst improving quality. The 'Friday car' was a product of manufacturing before automation was introduced. Manual workers become tired at the end of the week so the car made on a Friday afternoon was likely to be made with less care. Computers and robots do not need days off. Depending on the organisation, technology could create more jobs or fewer jobs and require more skilled staff to operate and maintain machines.

New technology is increasingly used in service industries. Examples include the introduction of automated telephone answering (press 1 for customer service, type in your PIN number ...), call centres (24-hour telephone advice lines) and online retailing, such as internet insurance, banking and travel services. Technology changes job requirements and staff need new skills, which can only be acquired through effective training. A good skills audit will enable an organisation such as Virgin Media to identify the human resource issues involved in providing 'digital TV, broadband, phone and mobile – all from one company'.

case study 16.3

Call centre – smooth operators wanted

Call centres were one of the fastest growing forms of employment in the 1990s. They consist of rooms full of telephone operators who provide a 24-hour link between businesses and their customers. It does not matter where these centres are located and this can give cost advantages. The new trend is to move them to low-wage economies such as India.

Alternatively – to lose a customer, please press …

This was the experience of a customer phoning a mobile phone company:

First a long promotion, then four options to select from.
The customer chose: 'If you are a pay-monthly contract customer and you would like to speak with a friendly upgrade adviser …
This led to: 'To enable us to give you information on our latest phones and tariffs, please state your name, your phone number …
and so on …

A problem with replacing people for automated enquiry services is that computers, whilst great at routine jobs, are hopeless at variety – the options they give us may not fit what we want. People, on the other hand, are flexible.

So why do companies use these IVR (interactive voice response) systems? The answer is cost – machines reduce staff. When you do speak to an employee, the machine checks their performance. It records the time operators take to respond, call duration and numbers of calls answered a day. The point is that labour is an on-going expense that is subject to moods, illness, tiredness, lateness and absenteeism. Technology is an initial expense but can work '24/7' and should ultimately bring savings

However, there is evidence that IVR also creates costs, and not only the cost of the contract. 'Non-completers' – people who get bored and put the phone down – represent lost sales.

activity

'IVR is the most hated management invention of modern times … employing a machine to answer telephone inquiries is a false economy,' said Simon Caulkin, writing in the Management section of *The Observer*, 29 August 2004.

What do you think are the human resource issues involved? Write as a customer and from the business point of view.

assignment focus

You will need to select a business for investigation. Ideally choose a business that you are familiar with. Perhaps either you, a friend or a family member works there. It will need to be large enough to enable you to meet the requirements of the unit.

1   Describe the skill profile of the staff employed in the business. Here you should include:

- examples of the specialist skills required within each of the main functional areas
- examples of low-skill work required within the organisation
- a summary of the general skills required at different levels in the hierarchy by directors, managers, supervisors, operatives.

The person specifications in job advertisements may provide one source of evidence,

2   Is this a high-skill or low-skill organisation?

3   Explain the internal and external factors involved in HR planning in your organisation.

Why human resource planning is important to an organisation

Government departments, local authorities, schools and colleges, construction and engineering businesses, etc. all need human resource plans to:

- estimate future staffing needs; e.g. what level and type of skills (job specific and generic) and how many staff will be needed

- help organise training and development of staff; this would be based on the gap between present skill levels; as shown by a skills audit, and estimated need

- plan for future developments in technology. Government departments are all predicting that their workforce will need e.g. e-business, e-government, and e-law skills to cope with the impact of technological change. HR planners will have to decide whether current staff can be trained or new staff will need to be recruited

- set objectives and targets for recruitment which can then be monitored and controlled to achieve corporate goals

- support and complement other parts of the corporate business plan, such as production or marketing

- avoid vacancies which could lose business to competitors, prevent the business from growing, reduce service quality and efficiency, put increased pressure on staff (Future Skills Wales)

- help the organisation achieve its corporate aims and objectives

- help to achieve customer satisfaction by having the right people

- cope with fluctuations in demand.

case study 16.4 — Design, creativity, inventiveness

One of the major concerns of today is the need for energy efficiency and sustainability. 'In the building industry, this is the key driver of our people planning.

The major constraint in our business is the acquisition of good people. We need people who can engage with the customer to find out what they really want. It is the customer who defines where we will be in three or five years time. Our people must be able to find building solutions which our customers can understand. We talk to our customers, to find out what skills we will need. We pick customers who are the best in the world. We pick people who are the best in the world, who buy in to what we believe, who naturally want to do stuff. So step 1 Do the right thing, step 2 Do it right. Our people are the key to our success.'

Source: Interview with a leading expert in sustainable building

activity

1 Do you believe that the customer should be the key factor involved in human resource – people planning? Explain your reasons.

2 Why is HR planning so important to this organisation? Is it important in your organisation explain? Why?

How organisations motivate employees

As you read this, ask yourself the question, 'Why am I doing this?' Is it because:

- you have to?

- you enjoy it?

- you think it might eventually be useful?

Figure 16.9

Motivation is the force that makes us behave in a particular way. In a business setting, motivation is about ensuring that employees put in the effort required to achieve the objectives set for them.

The extent to which the HR section will need to pay attention to motivation varies with the situation. Sir Clive Woodward, coach of the England rugby world cup winners said his players needed no motivation from him. Similarly firms may advertise for 'self-starters' – people who will drive themselves forward. Where work is more mundane, employers may need to understand how changes to the job, the culture of the organisation or the reward system may encourage employees to improve their performance.

Managers might be looking for better quality products, more efficient production ('more toothpaste out of the tube'), less absenteeism, lower staff turnover, etc.

Motivation theory

Over the years a number of management theories have been put forward in an attempt to explain the nature of employee motivation and suggest ways in which it may be improved.

Frederick Taylor's principles of scientific management

Taylor was an American engineer who studied production methods in the steel industry. He concluded that workers' main motivation was pay and that they needed close supervision.

He believed that complex jobs would be most efficiently performed if broken down into separate operations where little could go wrong. The whole job could then be completed in a series of stages by employees working together in a production line.

Taylor saw a number of benefits:

■ Each task would be so simple that it would require little training.

■ Since workers required little skill, they could be easily replaced if necessary.

■ If jobs are standardised, output could be easily measured, predicted and controlled.

However, by nature, production-line jobs tend to be low-skilled and repetitive and people do not always perform at their best in these situations. Disadvantages may be:

■ low motivation as a result of low job satisfaction – much of the job is outside of the workers' control, e.g. the speed of the production line may be set from outside

■ monotony resulting from stress and boredom may lead to errors, accidents or even employees putting a 'spanner in the works' to stop production

■ a breakdown in co-operation between workers and managers as an 'us and them' attitude grows up.

What sort of jobs do you think could and could not be successfully organised as Taylor suggested?

Taylor's theories led to the development of work-study analysis and work **appraisal** (he annoyed his wife by constantly timing her jobs in the kitchen).

Elton Mayo

In the 1920s Mayo conducted a series of experiments at the Hawthorn works of the American Electric Company in Chicago. He was investigating why, despite improved facilities and benefits, there was much dissatisfaction and poor productivity.

Mayo was surprised to find that as he made work conditions worse, workers actually produced more. He concluded that the employees were responding to the attention given to them, rather than to the physical working conditions. (His researchers were young men and the workers mostly women.) An increase in output by workers who perceive that they are being studied is now called the 'Hawthorne Effect'.

Mayo's studies suggest that:

■ people tend to respond positively when they are given recognition by management, sent on courses, etc. (will any course do?)

■ it is important to communicate with employees, and to at least discuss changes to the workplace. Consulting employees over important decisions, asking for suggestions and generally allowing them to influence matters is shown to motivate. Examples include employee representation on the board or through works councils – groups of worker representatives who meet with employers to discuss work-related issues

■ group cohesion, feeling part of a team, is important. Quality circles are an American idea, taken up by the Japanese before becoming popular in the UK and the USA once again. They provide a situation in which groups of employees can discuss work-related problems and suggest solutions.

Abraham Maslow's hierarchy of needs

Maslow first developed his 'Theory of Human Motivation' in 1943. Although not originally designed with the work situation in mind, the theory has since been used in an attempt to understand how employees can be motivated.

Maslow believed that motivation comes from a desire to satisfy a hierarchy of human needs (see Figure 6.10). We must first of all satisfy our basic needs for survival such as food and shelter. Thereafter we become interested in higher level needs such as job satisfaction and self-fulfilment.

People in developing countries, for example, will work hard for low wages because there is little alternative. Global companies have taken advantage of this to have their products manufactured in Korea, China and Malaysia. Conversely those with job security and on a reasonable salary may be motivated more by status or self-fulfilment – 'there is no more money but I will be running my own department'. Of course more money can often be the means of achieving self-fulfilment.

In practice, Maslow accepted that a variety of needs will exist at the same time, but suggested that once lower needs are satisfied then higher needs become the strongest motivators.

Figure 6.10 Maslow's hierarchy of needs

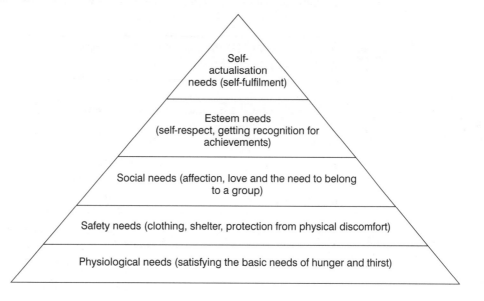

assignment focus

Try to use Maslow's theory to explain the following:

a) Immigrants from the enlarged EU come to the UK to perform agricultural work that residents will not do.

b) There has been a trend for some employees to 'downshift' – to move from high paying City jobs to less stressful work with less money out of town.

c) A footballer moves to a lower league club and takes a salary cut to get regular first team football.

d) Shell pays its employees well, yet in the 1990s its environmental reputation put off top graduates.

e) Steve Jobs of Apple is hugely wealthy yet he keeps working. Why doesn't he sit on the beach?

Frederick Herzberg's two factor theory

Frederick Herzberg's two factor theory, produced in the 1950s, concerns job design and satisfaction. From numerous interviews with accountants and engineers he concluded that two sets of factors are important in motivation (Table 16.3).

Table 16.3 Herzberg's two factor theory

Hygiene factors	Motivators
Reasonable pay Satisfactory conditions of work Benefits packages such as sick pay, pensions schemes, etc.	Responsibility Challenge Self-improvement
Without these, people are dissatisfied, but they alone do not lead to job satisfaction or provide motivation.	These provide job satisfaction and motivate people.

Hertzberg's theories suggest the following strategies will motivate:

■ *Job enrichment* Including motivators in the job, perhaps by giving employees more responsibility and involving them in decisions – so-called 'empowerment'. However, job enrichment should not be seen as a cheap way of increasing productivity – 'those who want their jobs enriched will expect to be rewarded with more than job satisfaction' (Charles Handy, *Understanding Organisations*).

■ *Job enlargement* Broadening the job by putting together a number of similar functions. The idea is to cut down on repetition by including a variety of activities.

■ *Job rotation* Employees swap jobs at regular intervals (a change is as good as a rest). This provides some variety and is made possible where the tasks are simple to perform. Ford do this with production-line workers.

Charles Handy (1993) *Understanding Organisations*, Penguin/Oxford University Press

assignment focus

1 How could Hertzberg's theories be used to improve the motivation of: a word-processing operator and a telephone receptionist?

2 Some features of the 'package' offered to new employees are listed below. Which of these are hygiene factors and which are motivators?

• Pay: a generous salary, overtime for unsocial hours, a commission or bonus to reward extra effort (performance-related pay)

• Conditions: reasonable working hours, flexibility such as opportunities for teleworking (from home), job sharing, flexi-time (varying start and finish times to suit)

• Maternity/paternity leave over and above the legal minimum

- Training opportunities: this will develop the employee and provide opportunities for promotion. A business with an approved staff development programme may qualify for the **Investors in People** (IIP) award

- Career opportunities: The firm offers a career structure allowing genuine progression routes to higher levels

- Fringe benefits or perks may include: a company car, sports facilities, a corporate box at high-profile sports events, private health insurance, generous company pension and staff discounts.

Douglas McGregor's Theory X and Y

In his book, *The Human Side of Enterprise*, McGregor put forward two extreme views about the way in which organisations manage their employees. He called these Theory X and Theory Y (Table 16.4).

Table 16.4 McGregor's Theory X and Theory Y

Theory X organisations	Theory Y organisations
Hold a traditional view. They believe that their workers are selfish, will not accept responsibility, are essentially lazy and work only because they have to. They have no loyalty to the organisation and need to be strictly supervised. They are motivated only by pay or by threats.	Have a positive view. They believe that their workers respond to encouragement and, given the right situation, will accept responsibility, can be genuinely creative, will accept change and can be motivated by work that is interesting. These workers will care about their organisation if it values their efforts.

McGregor believed that features from both styles had their place, although Theory Y seems likely to foster better industrial relations.

Douglas McGregor (2005) *The Human Side of Enterprise*, McGraw Hill Professional

assignment focus

1   Do the theories of Taylor, Mayo and Hertzberg incline towards Theory X or Theory Y?
2   Which view does the Japanisation of industry (page 298) represent?

David C McClelland – motivational needs theory

David McClelland's book *Human Motivation* (1988) identified three types of motivational need:

- *n-ach (need for achievement)* 'Achievement motivated' people respond to realistic but challenging goals, and seek advancement in their job. They need feedback on their progress, and want sense of achievement. According to McClelland, n-ach people get things done and are the most responsive to Herzberg's 'motivators'.

- *n-pow (need for power and authority)* These people wish to influence events and be seen to make an impact. They want to get their own way and have others acknowledge their position. Personal status is important to them.

- *n-affil (need for affiliation)* These people want to belong and are motivated by interaction with other people. They need to be liked and work best as part of a team.

McClelland's types are found to varying degrees in all managers and workers and the individual mix determines how a manager motivates, or how a worker becomes motivated. Do you fit any of these categories?

David McClelland (1998) *Human Motivation*, Cambridge University Press

Victor Vroom – Expectancy Theory

Vroom's Expectancy Theory, developed in the 1960s, suggests that two factors are important in motivation and both must be present (Table 16.5). For example, a sports car may be the reward for breaking the sales record, but the sales force will not be motivated to work harder unless they think that they have a reasonable chance of winning it. This may even be divisive. Team rewards may be better because everyone shares in success.

Table 16.5 Vroom's Expectancy Theory

Factors	In order to motivate:
Valence – the strength of desire	the employee must want what is on offer
Expectancy – the person's estimation of how likely they are to achieve this desire	they must also believe that they will succeed in getting this.

case study 16.5 — Motivation in the workplace

- Everybody at Thorntons – not just the Master Chocolatier and his team – is encouraged to come up with new product concepts. The pursuit of inspiring special foods is part of the fun of working at Thorntons.

  (*Source*: Thorntons plc Annual Report and Accounts)

- At the Toyota car factory at Burnaston near Derby and the Nissan motor plant near Sunderland, employees work in teams to manage their own work and to find ways to improve their procedures, (a process called *kaizen*). They each work to master every job at their worksite so that every member is multi-skilled and so can help or fill in for any other member of the team. The belief is that these extra demands are stimulating rather than stressful.

  (*Source*: *The Toyota Production System*, Toyota Motor Corporation)

activity

Read the examples in the case study of motivation in the workplace. Explain which theories are being used in each case.

Motivation – overview

Motivation may be provided by either:

- changing the working environment, including the job itself and the culture of the organisation. This will enable us to satisfy our internal 'needs'
- offering incentives which encourage and reward performance – these may be financial or non-financial.

Table 16.6 Providing motivation

Changing the working environment	Offering incentives
• participation (involving and consulting staff) • good job design • open-plan offices where all employees are on an equal footing without having to 'knock on the door' • delayering – organisations are becoming flatter so that there is now less of a gap between the bottom and the top of the organisation (although this may also be a way of cutting costs) • empowerment – employees are encouraged to take responsibility • staff training and development – to build confidence and open up career prospects	Financial, e.g. • profit sharing schemes • performance-related pay (PRP) including commission and bonus payments • employee shareholding • pensions schemes Non-financial, e.g. • parental leave • career breaks • flexible working

Reward systems
Financial rewards

Pay

People will certainly need reasonable pay and legislation exists to ensure minimum wages and to promote equal pay for equal work. At the time of writing, the average UK salary is around £23,000 a year.

Pay is a hygiene factor rather than a motivator. In 2004 Development Dimensions International surveyed 1,000 staff from large UK companies. Pay was given as the fifth most important reason for taking or leaving a job. More important than pay were:

- better promotion chances (43 per cent)
- more challenging work (28 per cent)
- a more exciting place to work (23 per cent)
- more varied work (21 per cent).

(People could choose more than one option.)

There are many other examples of people putting money down the list of priorities, e.g. big lottery winners who do not give up their jobs, or who return to work, others who use their winnings to set up in business or those who do a job that is more satisfying.

People will often work happily without pay; voluntary organisations and **mentoring** schemes depend upon this.

case study 16.6 — Because I'm worth it!

Disputes over pay are often about the 'pay differential' (they had a 5 per cent rise and we only had 2 per cent) rather than the actual amount. This is really about status rather than money.

In 2006, England footballer Ashley Cole fell out with his employers Arsenal FC because they would not pay him £50,000 a week. His salary at the time was £45,000 a week, less than some at the club but 100 times more than the average UK worker.

Cole said in his autobiography that the club did not value him. Nick-named 'Cashley' by the supporters, he now plays for Chelsea.

activity

1 Collect a number of job advertisements and compare the salaries offered for different types of work and different levels of skill, responsibility and experience. Notice that for some the salary will be negotiable. What will this depend upon?

2 Which career would you like to pursue? What qualifications will you need and what rates of pay can you expect? Is pay a factor for you? What else is?

Performance-related pay (PRP)

This involves measuring an employee's output and linking their pay to this. Variants of PRP include:

- piece-work payment based entirely upon output – no work, no pay, e.g. home-workers in the fashion business (often known as the rag trade) paid by the garment and fruit-pickers paid by the basket

- bonus or commission payments added to basic pay as a reward for meeting or exceeding targets. Performance payments to City bankers have proved controversial in recent years. Each December huge bonuses are paid to top performers. In 2006 over £21bn was shared out. Around 4,000 employees received over £1m each, with some pay-outs much higher. This is spent on property, cars, antiques, art, top of the range watches, designer clothes and vintage champagne.

Figure 16.11 'I wonder if they do extra large pockets?'

Firms argue that they must pay top money to get top people, although many appear to be rewarded for failure. Elmar Toime left the Post Office with £775,000 after the group missed all 15 of its service targets.

The Texan Marjorie Scardino is the best paid woman earning over £900,000 p.a.

PRP was traditionally used for production workers and sales teams whose performance is easily measured. Recent attempts to apply PRP to public service workers in the health service, local government, the police and education have been controversial. A major problem is that performance in these services can be difficult to measure. The pay incentive may also encourage behaviour that is not intended, and may be unethical.

case study 16.7 — Performance related pay

■ The financial services industry was forced to pay large sums in compensation to home-buyers who were mis-sold endowment mortgages in the 1980s and 1990s (these carry risk as they depend upon the performance of company shares on the stock market). Such mortgages were unsuitable for many clients, but were sold because they earned the best commission for the sales force.

■ A points system has been introduced in an attempt to measure police performance in North Wales. Officers get ten points for issuing a fine, ten points for an arrest, 20 points for a vehicle seizure. They lose five points for giving faulty intelligence.

activity

What problems might arise from rewarding the police for arrests, teachers for exam passes or hospitals for the number of operations performed?

Pension schemes

Occupational pension schemes (schemes offered by employers) can be a strong incentive for staff to join an organisation and remain loyal. However, things are changing. Whilst bosses of large companies may get huge amounts, pensions for employees in general will become less generous.

For some years UK employers have been worried about rising pension costs. The main problem is that people are living longer and so will be drawing their pensions for many more years than was originally predicted. 'Final salary' schemes – where the employee's pension is based on their salary at retirement – are the most generous. Firms are responding to the difficulties by closing these down: in 1995–2000, 650 such schemes were closed by employers, in 2001–2005 the figure had risen to 990.

In future people will have to save more for their retirement and work until they are older. The government has taken steps to raise the state pension age for women to 65.

Firms with a good pensions offer are likely to have loyal employees.

To find out how life expectancy is changing, go to www.statistics.gov.uk.

Profit-sharing

A minority of organisations share part of their profits with their employees as an annual bonus.

John Lewis, for example, operates 27 department stores, 180 Waitrose supermarkets and an online business, www.JohnLewis.com. The business is essentially a workers' co-operative, being jointly owned by its 63,000 permanent staff who are partners in the business. The mission set out by the founder is to 'run the business for the happiness of its members'. Each year between 8–20 per cent of profits are shared with the employees in direct proportion to their wages. The actual amount is decided by the partnership board after looking at the company's performance and the need for investment and development. 2006 was a record year, seeming to show that looking after staff can also mean looking after business. Workers are loyal to the business with staff turnover around 20 per cent a year compared to 40 per cent at rival retailers. This means that customer services levels are high.

Motivation at John Lewis is down to a number of factors:

- Staff are paid at market rates, but the profit-sharing scheme means that they are better rewarded than other shop workers. The scheme can add 25 per cent to their salary.

- Staff are listened to and are given a way of communicating their ideas to the board of directors.

- Staff have access to subsidised sports, social clubs and holiday homes.

Experts say that it is difficult to measure whether profit-sharing alone motivates staff since it is usually practised by companies with a general culture of employee involvement. It may be that motivation comes from other elements such as quality circles, workers councils, consultation programmes or from some combination of these.

Employee share options

Arun Sarin, chief executive of Vodafone, says that each time he meets with staff he is having a shareholders' meeting. Vodafone is one of a growing number of organisations that encourage their employees to invest in their company's shares. A price reduction is often offered as an incentive with the condition that the shares must be held for a specified length of time before they can be cashed in.

The winners

- In 2007, the 22,000 members of Marks & Spencer's Sharesave scheme gained a bonus of £56 million after rising profits had driven the company share price from 282p to 734p over three years. Twelve thousand employees received between £1,000 and £45,000 each. Chief executive, Stuart Rose, said, 'We're delighted that so many of our people have benefited – their faith in M&S has been rewarded.'

- In 2006, 60,000 HBOS staff were handed £67m in free shares, worth 5 per cent of annual salary. This was to reward workers for a 4 per cent rise in profits made from high street banking.

- In May 2006, Tesco gave £78m of free shares to 180,000 eligible staff. The shares are kept in a trust for five years, after which they will be sold free of tax. Chief executive, Sir Terry Leahy, said, 'Giving our people the chance to be shareholders is our way of saying thank you and ensuring they share in the success of the business.'

The losers

In a similar scheme at the electronics firm Marconi, many employees lost their savings when the share price crashed.

Mortgage subsidies

Financial organisations are often able to offer their employees low interest rates on loans and mortgages. This can be a valuable perk in a time of rapidly rising property prices. Over 25 years mortgage repayments are likely to be double the amount originally borrowed.

To find out the interest charged on a typical mortgage at present, go to either the website of a bank or an independent site, such as www.moneyfacts.co.uk. What are monthly repayments likely to be if £100,000 is borrowed?

Relocation fees

Organisations relocating to other areas will wish to take their key staff with them. Where this involves moving home, the considerable cost and disruption can be reduced by the payment of relocation fees. Included in this may be the physical cost of moving furniture, accommodation costs until housing can be found and survey fees and mortgage arrangement fees if a property is to be bought.

Company vehicles

A vehicle is the second most expensive purchase people will make. (What is the first?).

Sometimes a car is necessary for the job to enable a sales representative to travel to customers or a manager to get to different branches, for example. Alternatively a car may be a 'perk' of the job – a non-monetary benefit that has considerable value to the employee. This was once a means of paying value to an employee whilst avoiding the tax liability. However, the Chancellor has closed this 'loophole' in the law.

Loan advances

Staff needing to travel to work via rail may need to buy season tickets costing hundreds of pounds. Organisations, particularly in the public services, may be prepared to advance interest-free loans to enable staff to do this.

Staff discounts

Retailers will usually provide staff discounts which in total may represent a considerable saving over a period of time.

Non financial rewards

Child care

Increasingly, parents are choosing to work and employers are recognising that provision needs to be made. This can include crèche provision for children of pre-school age or play schemes for school holidays. Extended parental leave may be offered.

School fees

In order to attract highly skilled, and therefore highly paid, staff, the employment package may include help with private tuition fees.

Corporate clothes

Where uniforms are to be worn, these will normally be provided by the employer, although it may be the employees responsibility to launder them.

Flexible working

The traditional 9–5 day does not always meet the needs of modern organisations and a number of different working patterns have become common. A number of these also appeal to employees particularly those with caring responsibilities, including job sharing, shift work, flexi-time, part-time work and teleworking.

■ For job-sharing, shift work and flexible working hours, see page 289.
■ Teleworking is discussed on page 284.

Leave

Hours worked by UK employees are amongst the longest in Europe so a job offering generous leave can be attractive. There may be stipulations as to when this can be taken, however. Teachers, for example, cannot go away in term time, staff in seasonal businesses will similarly be restricted to 'slower' times of the year.

Healthcare

Long waiting lists for NHS treatment may make private medical treatment a valuable extra. Organisations may be able to strike favourable deals for their staff with private healthcare providers such as HSA or BUPA. One system is for the employer to pay the premiums on top of the normal salary and then deduct a payment to the medical firm.

Extended parental leave

Under the Employment Act 2002, parents of young and disabled children will be helped to stay at work. Support will be provided in the form of finance for working mothers, paternity leave for fathers and flexible working arrangements to help balance work and caring responsibilities. Employees who provide arrangements beyond the legal minimum are likely to gain the loyalty of their staff.

Career breaks

Employees may wish to take a break but with the view of returning to their job. Employers value effective staff and are now more likely to look favourably upon this. The reasons might include bringing up small children, volunteering work possibly abroad, study, alternative work or a secondment to another organisation. For example, a teacher might join a research or training initiative run by the Department for Education and Skills, and rejoin their school or college when this is completed. The skills gained may well improve work performance and motivation in future.

Salary sacrifice schemes

Employees may be prepared to negotiate a reduction in salary for extra leave.

Cafeteria incentive schemes

Here employees are offered a variety of benefits and encouraged to select from these.

Chapter Eight the web-design business put it this way:

> 'Always looking for new ways to incentivise and retain staff, Chapter Eight have today introduced a brand new employee benefits scheme.
> Our new 'cafeteria' scheme allows employees to mix and match a huge range of benefits to gain maximum benefit from our contribution to their development.
>
> In addition, the scheme also includes a payroll giving scheme administered by the Charities Trust.'

---

assignment focus

You will need to select an organisation for study. The choice is important as you must be able to gain access to the necessary information. You might choose to study the school or college that you attend, a work experience placement, an organisation where you are a customer or one where a member of your family is employed. You will need to contact the human resources department for information.

To gain P3, you should identify ways in which the organisation attempts to motivate its employees. Mention both motivational practices and reward systems. Recruitment advertisements may be one source of information. Explain which motivational theory is being used in each case.

To gain M2, you will need to make a comparison between the use of the various motivational theories in a workplace. For example, the employer may rely more heavily on one theory than upon another because of the nature of the work or the culture of the organisation, and you will need to explain this.

To gain D1, you should suggest ways in which the organisation might improve employee motivation.

How to gain committed employee co-operation

Contracts of employment

 Link

Contracts of employment are described in detail in Unit 4, page 155.

The workplace revolution – flexibility

It is becoming accepted that employers will need to develop flexibility in the workplace if they are to adapt and survive in the modern world. In recent years employers have found it necessary to makes changes to the terms and conditions under which employees work. This has meant a new workplace culture including:

- changes to contracts
- new methods of working.

Some employees welcome these changes but many feel threatened by job insecurity resulting from continual changes in the nature of work, the introduction of information technology and short-term contracts.

Employee and employer rights

Contracts of employment include express terms (see Unit 4, page 156) and implied terms. Implied terms are not set out in writing and not spoken of but are assumed to hold. For example, the employee has a duty of fidelity (trustworthiness) to the employer, and is expected to exercise due care. The employee in turn will expect to be supported if in a managerial role and will not be expected to do anything unlawful as part of the job.

Responsibilities of employees

The employee must:

- personally do the job and not ask someone else to substitute for them
- be honest and loyal
- obey all lawful instructions
- always behave correctly, following health and safety rules
- be careful and efficient in carrying out work
- be accountable for the employer's money, i.e. they must not cheat or steal from the organisation.

Responsibilities of employers

The employer must:

- refund expenses incurred in doing the job
- pay the agreed rate
- provide a safe and healthy workplace.

However the employer is not bound to provide:

- work
- education and training, except for health and safety and where it was originally agreed
- a reference.

Types of employment contract

Just as methods of working have changed, so too have the terms and conditions under which people are employed. People may be employed either full-time or part-time under a number of contractual arrangements.

Permanent contracts

Most organisations will have core employees engaged on permanent contracts, these may be full-time, fractional or part-time. The idea of a 'job for life' has become somewhat outdated since the 1980s, as businesses and their employees need to adapt to new technology and respond to increasing competition. Nevertheless permanent contracts remain the norm.

Fractional contracts

Pay and conditions of service are expressed as a fraction of those received by a comparable full-time employee. So, for example, in a 0.5 contract the part-timer works exactly half the number of hours of a full-timer and receives half of all entitlements such as holidays.

Source: National Association of Teachers in Further and Higher Education (NATFHE)

---

assignment focus

Look at the job adverts in the press and note the terms offered by prospective employers. What type of contract – permanent, full-time, temporary, etc – appears most frequently. Why?

The main change in recent years has been the rapid growth in part-time working. Many of the increasing number of women joining the labour force work part-time. They want flexibility and find that part-time work suits their needs. The government-sponsored Labour Force Survey has confirmed that most people who take part-time work do so out of choice and not because they cannot get full-time work.

Short-term (or fixed term) contracts

These may also be either full-time or part-time. Labour is one of the major costs of an organisation. When labour is plentiful, the short-term contract enables firms to meet present staffing needs without making a long-term commitment. As contracts expire, staff can be 'shed' if necessary, without the cost of redundancy. When there is a shortage of labour, this policy will be less successful.

Some posts are advertised as 'for one year initially', this may be a way of appointing someone for a trial period with a view to making the post permanent if all goes well.

Whilst short-term contracts suit some employees, for many, temporary contracts can lead to insecurity.

Temporary staff contracts

Sometimes staff are required for short periods of time either to replace employees who are absent or to help out in busy periods. Often temporary staff are employed by specialist agencies. Jobs covered in this way may include supply teaching, secretarial work, clerical work, nursing, and so on. Can you think of others? Often these staff are qualified professionals who may be looking for permanent posts or are simply looking to supplement their income.

Casual labour contracts

This is also a temporary arrangement but the term tends to be applied to manual or unskilled work. Staff may be hired and fired according to demand. Examples include seasonal work in agriculture, in the leisure industries (such as bar and hotel work) and some construction work. The work is usually hourly paid, although sometimes it is based on piecework – fruit pickers for instance are paid by the kilo.

---

case study 16.8 | **Working for Alliance & Leicester**

Sandra Hitching, director of human resources at Kelly Recruitment Services believes that, 'There is much more emphasis and awareness of the working mother. Many companies now provide part-time, flexi-time and home-working which enables mothers – and fathers – to have more balanced lives.'

A case in point is Lynne Turner, a qualified accountant who at 32 is senior finance manager of the Alliance & Leicester Building Society. She is the only woman in senior management working part-time – three days a week.

Julian Woodfall, human resources manager at the Alliance & Leicester says, 'Good people are hard to get, so we took the decision to ensure that part-time employees are not any worse off.'

For the past five years the society has provided the same pension scheme and pro-rata holiday entitlement for full-time and part-time employees. Banks such as NatWest allow mothers to work only in term time.

European legislation now gives part-time workers the same compensation and dismissal rights as full-time employees.

---

activity

1 Does this case study provide evidence that organisations can obtain the co-operation of employees through the contract of employment?
2 What rights and responsibilities do employers and employees have with a contract of employment?

Despite the existence of employment law and attempts at consultation and employee involvement, industrial disputes do occur. There needs to be a system in place for resolving these. There will be:

- **disciplinary procedures** – to take action against employees
- **grievance procedures** – where employees have a complaint against the employer
- appeals procedures – where each side may appeal against a judgement.

Disciplinary procedures

Disciplinary action may result from:

- failure to obey work rules – particularly serious if it leads to dangerous work practices
- breaking a contract of employment – constant lateness for instance
- unsatisfactory work performance after reasonable warnings.

Disciplinary action may result in:

- suspension – where a serious offence is alleged, it may be unwise for the employee to stay at work both from the organisation's point of view and the employee's (soldiers, police officers, teachers and surgeons are sometimes suspended, often on full pay, while allegations are investigated)
- warnings both oral and written
- dismissal. Which could be seen as fair or unfair.

There should be an agreed procedure which is fair, accessible, easy to understand, transparent and available to everyone. (Why is this important?)

Figure 16.12 shows a possible disciplinary procedure

Figure 16.12 A possible disciplinary procedure

An oral warning

↓

A formal warning if no improvement

↓

A final warning if no improvement

↓

Dismissal is a last resort

The employee may seek representation (perhaps from a trade union) during the course of disciplinary action.

Figure 16.13 Procedure when an employee is seen to be incapable of performing the job satisfactorily

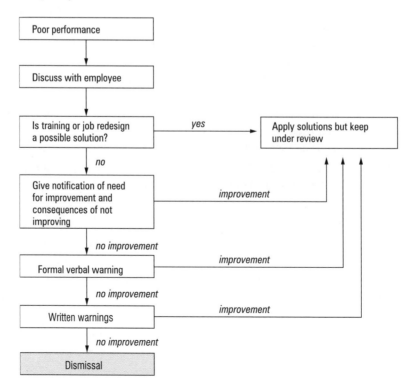

1   Obtain the disciplinary and grievance procedures for your organisation, either from your employer or for staff and students at your school or college. Does it follow the outline given here? Is anything missing or has anything been added?

2   Why are clear disciplinary and grievance procedures important for employees and employers?

Fair dismissal

An employee who is fairly dismissed has no grounds for complaint. Fair dismissal may be for any of the following reasons:

■   lack of qualifications – where an essential qualification is claimed but is not actually held, e.g. a driver needs a driving licence

■   lack of capacity to do the job – where performance remains poor and appropriate warnings and help has been given

■   conduct – such as continued absence or lateness without reason, fighting, stealing or unsafe behaviour

■   where continued employment would break the law, e.g. where a driver loses his/her licence

■   redundancy – if there is insufficient work or a job ceases to exist perhaps because of poor trade or a reorganisation then an employee may be made redundant.

Other substantial reasons include personality clashes which inhibit the working of the business, e.g. football managers may have their contracts terminated for this reason. Depending upon the circumstances compensation may be paid.

Summary dismissal, that is, immediate dismissal with no notice period, may be applied for stealing, fighting or dangerous work practices.

Unfair dismissal

This is where dismissal is against the law. The Employment Protection (Consolidation) Act 1978 states the conditions in which it is unfair to dismiss an employee:

■   where an employee of more than one year's standing becomes pregnant and is not taken on again after the baby is born

■   where a 'spent' conviction is the reason for dismissal. There is a period laid down after which criminal convictions are no longer relevant to a job application. For some jobs, certain convictions are never spent, e.g. fraud for an accountant, child molesting for the caring professions

■   where a worker is dismissed because of sex or race

■   where the employer does not follow the agreed procedures, e.g. an employee must be taken through the agreed disciplinary procedure.

From 1 October 2006, the Age Discrimination regulations made it unlawful to discriminate against employees because of their age. ACAS Chairperson, Rita Donaghy, said:

'It's easy to forget that age discrimination can affect all employees, from the youngest to the oldest. Rightly, there has been a lot of publicity about older workers – but we shouldn't forget that the new legislation will require employers to change their behaviour towards the younger generation as well. It is equally unacceptable to describe someone as being "wet behind the ears" as it is to call them "over the hill".'

Source: ACAS press release, 29 September 2006

Appeals within the organisation

Where an employee feels that they are being unfairly disciplined (victimised perhaps) then they may appeal using the organisation's appeals procedure.

Appeals outside the organisation

Legal disputes between employers and employees are dealt with by the Advisory, Conciliatory and Arbitration Service (ACAS) in the first instance. They will examine the evidence and try to assist both parties in reaching a settlement. Further appeals may be made to the court of appeal, the House of Lords or the European Court of Justice.

Grievance procedures

A grievance may be caused by:

- changes in the conditions and terms of employment
- health and safety problems
- bullying or harassment
- changes in working practices or working conditions
- lack of equal opportunities.

This is the procedure recommended by ACAS:

1   The employee informs the employer of their grievance in writing.

2   The employer invites the employee to a meeting to discuss the grievance where the right to be accompanied will apply. The employer notifies the employee in writing of the decision and notifies of the right to appeal.

3   The employee informs the employer if they wish to appeal. The employer must invite the employee to a meeting and following the meeting inform the employee of the final decision. (employees must take all reasonable steps to attend meetings).

Source: www.acas.org.uk

Union membership

A trade union is defined in law as:

'an organisation … whose principal purposes include the recognition of relations between workers and employers or between workers and employers' associations.'

Many of the rights that employees currently enjoy have been won as a result of trade union pressure over the years. Trade unions aim to represent the interests of their members through:

- negotiating with employers to improve pay and conditions through 'collective bargaining' – such agreements may determine the rates of pay nationally
- representing their members' interests in disputes with the employer, perhaps by giving advice and legal support
- providing education and training
- acting as a pressure group on government to gain legislation which will benefit their members.

With certain exceptions, an employee cannot be sacked for belonging to, or for failing to belong to, a trade union.

The attitudes of employers to trade unions varies, some are hostile, some welcome them as a positive influence. Do you belong to a students' union?

Codes of behaviour

You may be familiar with codes of behaviour. Most schools and colleges now have rules and regulations which govern student behaviour.

As we saw on page 160, many professions also have codes of conduct or practice which set out how their members should behave when carrying out their job. For example, the Market Research Code of Practice is a set of rules or guidelines created to regulate the industry. It sets standards and acts as a framework for all research activities. It sets out professional responsibilities, how researchers should behave and act. It is designed to make sure that research is carried out legally and ethically

Employee involvement techniques

Although reward systems can be an important way of motivating employees. good working conditions, communication and employee involvement in decision-making can be equally effective in helping the organisation achieve its aims and objectives. The amount of involvement depends on the size and structure of the organisation, management style and culture, and the issues to be discussed.

Search www.acas.org.uk with the keyword 'consultation'.

Membership of work groups

Look at Theory X and Theory Y on page 297. Which workers are more likely to participate in work groups?

Employee representatives on the board
Some organisations allow employees to attend board meetings as a method of consultation and involvement. For example, schools and colleges may have a staff member on the board of governors (does yours?). The John Lewis Partnership allows its staff to elect half of the board.

Staff associations
These are groups of employees formed to discuss staff welfare with management. They may discuss recreational facilities, canteens, etc., but rarely have the power to negotiate wages or conditions of employment.

Works councils
These are also known as Joint Consultative Committees (JCC). Under EU law, UK multinational firms operating in Europe need to set up works councils for their employees in EU states. This applies to all companies with over 1,000 employees and over 150 employees in at least two EU countries. The councils are entitled to meet central management once a year to receive a report outlining business prospects. The idea is to involve staff in consultation and decision-making about corporate matters such as changes in technology or production. They are made up of managers and employees. How could a business benefit from consulting with staff?

Quality circles
A quality circle is a small group of people from the same organisation (intra-organisational) who meet regularly to examine workplace issues such as quality, productivity, wastage, etc. The most effective quality circles have these features: the group consists of between five and ten people all involved in the same kind of work, membership is voluntary and people can choose their own issues/problems to examine, the group has access to management and can make suggestions and recommendations.

Quality circles and organisation culture
Quality circles are most effective when introduced in organisations where there is a participative, consultative management style, i.e. where workers' views are recognised as a valuable asset. However, this requires trust from both management and workers. Staff need to be empowered (given responsibility) to make decisions and create solutions – this only comes with adequate training. Overall they require complete commitment from management and from trade unions and staff committees. Otherwise they become 'talking shops' where nothing is achieved.

When they work, they give power and responsibility to workers who are able to share experiences and make concrete proposals. Using the ideas of Maslow and McGregor (see pages 295–97) they help put motivation theory into practice through team-building and co-operation. The employer may get cost reductions and improvements in productivity and greater employee involvement.

Intra-organisational groups
Do you speak to science, media or childcare students at your centre? If you do, well done, you are sharing experiences, breaking down barriers and building trust. If you don't, you will need to answer the question: Why not?

Intra-organisational groups are made up of employees working in the same organisation, e.g. full-time and part-time staff; production workers and marketing staff, management and workers. (One of the authors of this book once worked in a company where these groups never spoke to each other, which resulted in the organisation attempting to sell goods it was not capable of manufacturing!)

The important feature of these groups is that the membership cuts across traditional boundaries (i.e. departments or functions) within the organisation structure. Their purpose is to enable staff to share knowledge and build up trust through open, face-to-face and virtual communication. They can be transnational (across countries). Barclays Bank, for example, brings together staff from its centres in Tokyo, New York and London to develop new financial products. National work groups are used by the National Health Service, e.g. managers of the Wheelchair Assessment Service in local primary care trusts meet together in the National Wheelchair Managers' Forum to discuss mutual concerns. Site-specific groups (working party), e.g. all users of the new accommodation at your centre, could be involved in deciding how the space is allocated. What communication and interpersonal skills would be needed to reach a fair decision?

In tall organisations, where there is a formal hierarchy, there may need to be a major change in culture for intra-organisational groups to work effectively.

assignment focus

1   What are the possible benefits and drawbacks of employee membership of work groups from the point of view of both workers and managers (staff and students)?

2   Are students involved in the running of your centre? Is your group represented on a committee? Does anything positive happen?

Suggestion schemes

These are systems for encouraging employees to make positive suggestions for improving the product or work practices. Quality circles (see page 309) formally involve workers in upward communication and can result in substantial improvements. Schemes range from simple informal suggestion boxes to formal company-wide systems for continuous improvement (often with substantial prizes). Does your organisation have a suggestion scheme? Does it work?

Devolved authority and responsibility

Also called delegation, this is the process of giving authority to lower level managers/staff to make specific decisions. It may be necessary because each manager cannot do all the tasks that need to be done. The senior manager needs to ensure that the subordinate can do the work and that the work gets done. Senior managers remain responsible for all delegated work – they 'carry the can'. It may be desirable as a way of training and developing less experienced staff or 'fast tracking' capable staff for early promotion.

Empowerment

This is a situation where organisations give power and authority to all their staff to enable them to focus completely on the customer. This is achieved through training and good communication. Staff are actively encouraged to achieve their full potential. Management has to be prepared to delegate and trust staff, whilst staff have to be willing to accept responsibility. What does this say about Theory X and Theory Y?

Open communications

With open communication, there is no restriction on who sees or receives information. A restricted channel of communication refers to situations where particular information goes only to specified named people, 'for your eyes only'. This ensures that information is kept secure and confidential. Open communications between managers and operatives are generally more free, more relaxed and informal. Information and experiences can be shared which should result in better decisions.

Formal communication

Formal channels of communication are shown by the lines on an organisation chart. Information will flow from senior managers to middle managers to operatives, down the

Figure 16.14

hierarchy. Operatives will only be able to communicate upwards with managers through their supervisors. Formal channels are official and follow the chain of command in the organisation.

Informal communication

Whenever a group of workers get together, informal or unofficial channels of communication are likely to exist alongside the official ones. This is sometimes called the 'grapevine'. It can be a significant feature of the communications system because information is spread very quickly, although it may also be very destructive, e.g. when rumours are spread which are untrue.

Bottom-up and top-down communication

'Communication is a two-way process which requires information to flow up from employees as well as down from managers' (ACAS)

Most managers still consider that their main function is to give orders and direct the workforce, i.e. the emphasis is on top-down communication. However, much can be gained from involving employees in a positive and constructive way.

Bottom-up communication

The process whereby management formally obtain the views and ideas of the workforce is called bottom-up communication.

There are several methods available for improving bottom-up communication:

- *Employee surveys* In large complex organisations, this may be the only way to get employee views. The key to running a successful survey is to:
  - ask questions which are directly relevant to the workforce
  - be prepared to act on suggestions, otherwise the whole exercise will just be viewed as 'time wasting, what's the point, no one will do anything about our problems'
  - be prepared for a wide range of replies – workers may not think as highly of the organisation as senior management!

- *Appraisal interviews* Organisations which take training and development seriously, e.g. through the award of an Investors in People certificate (see page 314) will hold regular performance appraisal interviews with all their employees. These are an ideal occasion for obtaining employee views and attitudes. However they will only work if the culture of the organisation is open and honest and there is no fear of reprisals.

- *Managing by 'walking about'* With this approach, managers literally walk around the organisation. They can be seen and approached. Staff feel they are known, recognised and appreciated. Managers get a reputation for knowing what is going on and staff begin to volunteer information. Communication becomes less formal and more open and honest.

Top-down communication

This refers to communication that starts at the top of the organisation and passes down to the bottom. This has been the traditional approach in many UK companies. Senior management give orders to middle management, supervisors give orders to operatives. Workers in these organisations have always had a passive role.

> **remember**
> Top-down and bottom-up communication is sometimes called vertical communication.

However, there will always be a need for instructions and orders to be passed down the hierarchy. In tall complex organisations, there is still an emphasis on formal top-down communication. Compare this approach with flat organisations where workers are empowered, communications are more informal and more bottom-up communication occurs.

Lateral communication

When communication takes place across an organisation, e.g. across departments or functions, it is called lateral or horizontal communication. For example, the production manager would communicate with the marketing manager in the design and development of a new product. Lateral communication puts an organisation in a much better position to become customer focused as 'the right hand will know what the left hand is doing'. Everyone should know what is happening because everyone is involved in the decision-making.

assignment focus

1 How does open communication help the organisation gain committed employee co-operation?

2 How could communication be improved to achieve better motivation of employees?

Types of communication

Employee handbook

Here are some examples of information needed by employees, according to ACAS:

- health and safety requirements of their job and workplace
- terms and conditions of employment, e.g. hours of work, rates of pay, holiday pay, period of notice needed in order to leave the employer
- job description which sets out the requirements of the job
- disciplinary procedures.

This information is best given to employees in a company handbook when they join the organisation.

An employee handbook will tell you:

- how the business is run
- what the rules and regulations are
- what the arrangements are for holidays, pay, pensions, etc.
- how to complain if you have a problem with racial or sexual harassment
- what the disciplinary and grievance procedures are.

Newsletters and house journals

Newsletters, such as those produced by BP or Sainsbury's, usually appear regularly with information and news about the organisation and more chatty personal, social and sporty items. There could be a 'Who's Who' section, or even an interview with one of the managers and maybe a crossword. The purpose of the newsletter is to tell employees what is going on in their organisation before they find out from somewhere else. Today most newsletters are published on an internal intranet. Nationwide communicated its corporate plan to its employees on a DVD called 'Rising to the challenge'. This also included extracts on how its adverts were made.

Organisation bulletins

These are used for giving news or information within the business. They need to be restricted to really important events because if they appear too often they will not be read. They must be kept short.

assignment focus

1   On your own, prepare one item for your BTEC National group newsletter.

2   With your group, produce a newsletter which describes how organisations obtain the co-operation of employees through the contract of employment and employee involvement techniques. This must be word-processed, include graphics and should be distributed via e-mail.

Organisational culture

The culture of an organisation can be summarised by the phrase 'it's the way we do things here'. Do your classes always start and finish on time? Do you always turn up on time? What happens if you don't? Do you care? Do the staff care? The culture of an organisation is the set of customs, values, attitudes and behaviour adopted and shared by its members. Values can be seen in the mission statement.

Attitudes (the ethos) and behaviour may be seen in the way management treat workers, how colleagues treat each other, how staff treat customers, workers' attitudes towards the product they sell or the service they provide, even the clothes people wear at work and the language they use. The culture sets the standards for the organisation; it gives support and provides guidance. Winning companies have a strong set of values which are reflected in everything they do, they strive for excellence and continuous improvement. Does your organisation do this? Do you?

The culture of an organisation directly affects its structure – both have to work together for it to achieve its aims. Various classifications of types of culture have been suggested, e.g. those by Charles Handy on the following page.

Power or club culture

This type of culture has the following characteristics:

- It relies on the power or personality of the owner or directors who make all the key decisions. There can be problems if these people change.
- The organisation recruits like-minded people to join the 'club'.
- People who are not part of the 'club', i.e. do not share its views, do not succeed.
- The structure is loose and informal and tends to be organised by functions.

Role culture or bureaucracy

The characteristics of a role culture or bureaucracy are as follows:

- There is a formal structure which is hierarchical.
- The organisation chart defines the role of every individual.
- The job or role tends to be more important than the person.
- The limits of every job are strictly controlled.
- There is an emphasis on rules, routine and procedures.

Although the style can work well in large, stable organisations where there is little change, decision-making can be hampered by unnecessary and over-enthusiastic official procedures – 'Sorry it's more than my job's worth.'

Task culture

With this type of culture:

- The organisation is structured so as to complete tasks or projects.
- Teams and team players are important within a matrix structure.
- Individual specialists are needed to form the teams.
- There can be a high level of job satisfaction.

People-centred culture

The aim of the organisation is to satisfy the interests and motives of the owners. People are more important than the organisation. This style works best in relatively small, informal, flat organisations. It is found mostly in professional organisations, such as a management consultancy where each consultant works on individual projects.

Sir Terry Leahy, Chief Executive of Tesco, says: 'We changed our culture by understanding customers better than anyone else and by taking care of our staff'. Tesco is now number one.

 Charles Handy (1995) *Gods of Management: The changing work of organisations*, 4th edition, Oxford University Press

---

case study 16.9 — **Culture Club**

Carphone Warehouse

The Carphone Warehouse mission statement has 'Five Fundamental Rules':

'1 If we don't look after the customer, someone else will.

2 Nothing is gained by winning an argument but losing a customer.

3 Always deliver what we promise. If in doubt, under-promise and over-deliver.

4 Always treat customers as we ourselves would like to be treated.

5 The reputation of the whole company is in the hands of each individual.'

Source: Carphone Warehouse: www.cpwplc.com

'Our survey shows strong support for the firm's values — employees earn it an 81 per cent positive score for belief in these principles, the third highest score among the big firms.'

Source: http://business.timesonline.co.uk: 100 best companies to work for, 2006

In January 2007, Carphone Warehouse withdrew its sponsorship of Celebrity Big Brother after alleged racist remarks. The chief executive said, 'We are totally against all forms of racism and bullying and indeed this behaviour is entirely at odds with our brand values.'

KPMG voted No. 1 company to work for

'Company values have been formalised into the 'KPMG way' and the company records an 85 per cent positive score for belief in those values, the highest in our survey. A 'management for excellence' scheme has entrenched personal development and employees here think their job is good for their own personal growth (scoring 82 per cent). Progress is supported with mentoring and training, which staff say helps them (80 per cent).'

Source: http://business.timesonline.co.uk: 100 best companies to work for, 2006

activity

1   Use the classification of culture to analyse your group, centre, family and organisation.

2   Explain which culture is most likely to get the co-operation of employees through involvement.

3   How would you describe the culture of Carphone Warehouse?

National accreditation

Investors in People

Figure 16.15 Investors in People

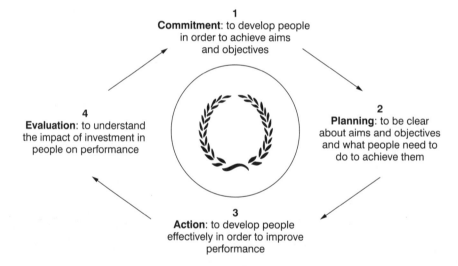

1 **Commitment**: to develop people in order to achieve aims and objectives

2 **Planning**: to be clear about aims and objectives and what people need to do to achieve them

3 **Action**: to develop people effectively in order to improve performance

4 **Evaluation**: to understand the impact of investment in people on performance

Charter Mark

To achieve the Charter Mark, organisations have to consult staff in the application process. So staff become involved and committed, making the organisation more efficient and improving customer service.

 Go to www.chartermark.gov.uk to find out more about Charter Mark.

International Organisation for Standardisation

The abbreviation for the International Organisation for Standardisation is ISO which is based on the Greek word isos meaning equal (as in isobar, a line which links places with the same atmospheric pressure, or isotherm, which links places with the same temperature). Here it applies to organisations with the same minimum quality standards.

To achieve ISO certification an organisation must have a written quality policy, quality manual, work procedures and instructions, plus systems for dealing with quality failures and customer complaints. It shows that the organisation consistently operates to recognised quality standards and that employees are committed to quality work and are fully involved in the quality process.

To find out more, visit www.iso.ch.

assignment focus

1   Does your organisation have a national accreditation? What benefits does it bring to various stakeholders, e.g. workers, management, employer, customer?

2   On a scale of 1–10, compare employee involvement techniques as a method of improving motivation.

3   For D1, if your organisation does not have a national accreditation, should it? Give reasons.

The importance of managing employee performance at work

Labour represents a significant investment for an organisation. Employment costs often account for a high proportion of total business costs, particularly in the service industries.

■ In 2005 Domino's Pizza employed 674 staff in the UK and Ireland at a total cost of £13.4 million (£12 million in wages and salaries plus £1.4 million in National Insurance and pensions costs). Domino's labour costs accounted for around 50% of total overheads.

■ Scottish & Newcastle plc employed 47,000 people across Europe and Central Asia at a total cost of £550 million – around 20 per cent of total running costs.

It is the job of human resources managers to ensure that the workforce operates as efficiently as possible (compare the average salary at Scottish & Newcastle and Domino's).

Measuring performance

Performance indicators

Which aspects of an individual's performance does an organisation need to measure? The precise answer will vary with the industry and the job in question. However, in each case the individual or team target should help the organisation as a whole to meet its goals. See Table 16.7.

Table 16.7 Performance indicators

Industry	Example of individual performance indicator	Example of organisational performance indicator
Manufacturing	A machinist's output, e.g. the number of t-shirts produced per day	Increased profits and market share
Retail	Sales achieved each week, e.g. the value of double-glazed windows sold	Increased profits and market share
Customer service	The number of customers dealt with per hour by a call centre operator	Customer satisfaction ratings
Education, e.g. college or school	Student retention and achievement, i.e. the number of students staying on and passing their exams	Schools are ranked by examination league tables
Health service, e.g. a hospital	The number of successful operations, the number of patients seen in a day	Health authorities are judged by the length of waiting lists
Transport, e.g. a coach or railway company, an airline	The percentage of services running to timetable, the number of passengers carried	Customer satisfaction. Poor performing companies may lose their franchise
The police	The number of arrests	Forces are judged on the crime clear-up rate (successful prosecutions)

In manufacturing and retail industries, clear and meaningful targets can be the basis for rewarding performance. In the public service sector, targets may be more problematic. Poorly thought out targets may encourage individuals to act only in their narrow self-interest rather than for the general good of the organisation.

assignment focus

1 Find out the precise targets that your school or college has to meet for:

a) GCSE passes

b) student retention

c) student achievement

d) success rate.

2 What can happen if these are not met?

Goal theory

Goal theory looks why people perform tasks (their goals). The theory can be applied to the workplace to show how leaders and situations can motivate employees by giving them a reason to work in a particular way.

The 'carrot' approach

Path-goal theory assumes (like Vroom's expectancy theory) that employees are motivated if they feel that they can do their work and that by doing so they will achieve a desirable outcome – perhaps a reward such as a bonus for meeting targets.

The 'stick' approach

Getting people to work to avoid an undesirable outcome seems to be less motivating. For example, hauling people before the boss if they fall short of targets may work but is not the best way to encourage performance.

It is important to set targets that are attainable and to support staff with effective leadership and appropriate training, facilities and systems.

case study 16.10

Don't call us ...

Converso runs a call centre in Southend. The telemarketers do 'outbound' work or cold-calling – ringing up the unsuspecting public and trying to sell to them. They take a lot of abuse in the process.

Of the 200 employees, most are teenagers who have not settled on a career; they will not stay long and absenteeism is high.

Prime selling time is 5 p.m. to 9 p.m. on weekdays – sunny summer evenings are bad for sales, so are televised sporting events. Bad weather is good for sales and teams will phone areas where they know it is raining.

Workers socialise before and after work. Team leaders are charismatic and experienced in the business. They give pep talks, explain tactics and encourage their teams against each other. Callers who exceed sales targets are applauded, whilst those who fail are publically 'roasted' with no excuses accepted. Pay is £7 per hour plus commission.

The owners of Converso see a limited future for 'outbound'. Competition from Indian centres has hit profit margins and the US may soon make it illegal. If so the UK will probably do the same.

activity

1 How are teleworkers motivated to perform? Does goal-theory apply?

2 What are the PESTLE factors that Converso must be aware of?

 Link

PESTLE factors are discussed in Unit 1, pages 43–51.

Remember the SMART objectives in Unit 1 (on page 24)? Business objectives need to be:
Specific,
Measurable,
Achievable,
Realistic and
Time-constrained.
The M is important here because measurable targets enable achievement to be monitored.

remember

SMART targets

The efforts of human resources managers are directed towards getting value for money from employees. We have seen that there is a growing trend for businesses to quantify performance by setting measurable targets – even in those industries where this was not traditionally done.

Remember that:

- the directors set strategic targets for the organisation as a whole. These show where the organisation is trying to go. For public sector organisations, these may be imposed from outside by regulators or government

- managers will work out how targets will be achieved by breaking them down into tactical targets for sections or departments within the business, e.g. to keep expenses within budget, to increase sales by 5 per cent

- at the operational level, individual workers and teams are set specific performance targets, e.g. completing a post round on time, answering a phone query every two minutes, etc.

Directors, managers and operatives are all employees and will stand or fall by their ability to achieve the targets set for them.

In January 2007, the following were in the news:

- Lord Browne stood down as chair of BP after a highly critical report on the company's safety record in the USA.

- Below target profits by EMI in the music industry led to a 'delayering' with directors and managers losing their jobs.

- Andriy Shevchenko missed his target literally by not scoring enough goals for Chelsea. He was left out of the team.

assignment focus

Find out the targets set for your school or college as a whole, for the business studies section, for your tutor.

Which targets are set?

Figure 16.16 Types of target

Financial performance

Targets commonly involve improving upon last year's performance and working towards financial ratios equal to industry benchmark standard.

Organisational targets might include increasing profits and providing sufficient cashflow. Managers will be set targets for cost and profit centres within the organisation (departments perhaps) and within these individuals and teams will have their own targets.

Profits may be the basis for pay awards – directors, whose job it is to generate value for shareholders, frequently justify their pay rises in this way. Where a business has a profit-sharing scheme (e.g. John Lewis, page 301) then employees too will be rewarded.

Sales targets

Sales may be expressed as either value or quantity. A college student enrolment target is quantitative; the Tesco data in Table 16.8 is financial.

Tesco has managed to increase the efficiency of its staff year on year, and they can measure this by:

Total sales ÷ Number of full-time equivalent employees
(i.e. two employees working half a week = one full-time employee)

Table 16.8 Tesco's turnover per full-time employee

Tesco plc	2001	2002	2003	2004	2005
Turnover per full-time employee	£159,678	£163,443	£160,157	£162,459	£166,534

assignment focus

Suggest why the average employee at Tesco is able to sell more in 2005 than in previous years? Sales are made on the shop floor and via the internet. Who has achieved this success: the operatives, the managers, the directors or all of them?

Sales staff may receive commission on sales as an incentive. This was the basis of the huge pay-outs to City bankers in December 2006 (page 299) and at Converso (page 316). High street retail staff key in a personal code before entering sales into the till; this enables their performance to be monitored.

Growth targets

- *Financial growth* Directors talk about 'adding shareholder value'. This results from increasing and 'ploughing back' profits so that a more valuable business results.
- *Geographical growth* A national business might grow by going international.
- *Sales growth* should be reflected in growing market share.

As with other targets, growth potential is identified by directors but is achieved by managers and operative workers. For instance, a college may grow because the business studies department offers a wider range of courses and recruits more students. If classes are larger as a result, the lecturers' performance will also appear more efficient (assuming that students pass).

In 2006 Domino's Pizza UK and IRL plc reported: sales up 15 per cent, profit up 27 per cent, earnings per share up 22 per cent, dividend up 38 per cent, 50 new stores opened and e-commerce sales up 69 per cent. The business is UK market leader in pizza delivery. They attributed this success to 'great people': their directors, management team and carefully chosen and trained franchises.

Source: Annual Report, January 2006

Targets for schools and colleges.

School success is judged by examination results with league tables based on GCSE passes from A* to C.

Colleges are required to perform up to national standards in attendance, retention, achievement and success rates. Failing courses will no longer be funded. These measures force management to impose targets upon course teams within their institutions.

Punctuality and attendance targets

Organisations will have internal standards. Unacceptable levels of absence and lateness will result in an interview with a manager and may lead to disciplinary procedures, loss of bonus payments and in extreme cases eventual dismissal. For example Camelot, who run the National Lottery, published the targets and performance indicators shown in Table 16.9.

Turnaround teams to help NHS hit financial targets

The NHS budget will have almost trebled between 1997 and 2008. Nevertheless around one third of health authorities is overspending.

'Turnaround teams' are being sent in to help meet the financial targets for 2006/7. These are experts who will look at more efficient working by staff, more efficient procurement of supplies and reorganisation of administrative jobs.

Other NHS targets:

- total waiting times for hospital treatment to be cut to18 weeks by 2008
- access to a GP within 48 hours
- a maximum four-hour wait for treatment in A&E (accident and emergency) departments.

Achievement will rely upon adequate numbers of trained staff working efficiently.

Source: Department of Health; http://www.dh.gov.uk

activity

1   Compare these targets with those for a profit-making company.

2   The NHS is a not-for-profit public service. Why is financial control so important?

Table 16.9 Camelot: performance indicators and targets

Performance indicator	2004/5	2005/6	Target
Attrition rate (staff turnover) p.a.	16.8%	22.9%	less than 15%
Training days per employee p.a.	5 days	11 days	3 days
Average sickness days per employee p.a.	8.26 days	8.86 days	6.8 days (CBI benchmark)
Employees participating in community activities	7.1%	10.9%	20%

Source: Camelot, *Corporate Responsibility Report 2006*

Technology has enabled management to monitor staff activity in ways not previously possible. Computer packages track the speed of data inputting, electronic tills count the number of items processed per minute by supermarket checkout staff, software is used in call centres to record the time it takes a receptionist to answer the telephone and log the number of calls taken per hour.

Retraining needs can be identified, ergonomically designed workstations installed to improve performance and incentives introduced.

Benchmarking

A benchmark is a standard or point of reference (look up the original meaning of the term).

Benchmarking within a business context involves identifying those organisations that are leaders in their field and then aiming to match their standards (the benchmarks). The process is shown in Figure 16.17.

Benchmarks can be identified in many areas, e.g.

- personnel – staff qualifications, skills and productivity (sales per employee at Tesco may be benchmarked by Sainsbury's). Camelot used a CBI benchmark for absenteeism
- use of IT – the effectiveness and use of the customer database, the type of equipment, the use of loyalty cards to capture data by leading companies
- product quality – the added value offered, the features included as standard (e.g. airbag and CD player) by successful competitors

Figure 16.17 The process of benchmarking

| **Stage 1**
Identify the benchmark

The organisation chosen will be in the same sector and usually of the same size.

The target must be relevant and achievable. | **Stage 2**
Find the secret of success

This may be difficult as secrets may be closely guarded.

The UK National Benchmarking Index and the local Business Link can help here.

Schools and colleges may co-operate with each other to learn best practice. | **Stage 3**
Do better

In the 1970s Japanese companies benchmarked the best Western manufacturers, reverse engineered their best products (took them apart) and then improved upon them by building in improved quality. |

- financial performance – ROCE (return on capital employed) and the other ratios are frequently compared with industry benchmarks
- management – management techniques used, such as TQM (total quality management) and motivational techniques.

 Link   Ratios are discussed in Unit 5, pages 220–28.

Managing performance

The term 'performance management' came into use in the 1980s. It refers to the practice of setting targets, measuring performance against these and taking action to rectify problems. This might include disciplinary measures, changes to the work environment, the introduction of a rewards system or staff development.

Probation (a trial period)

New staff may be asked to prove themselves over an initial probationary period of perhaps three or six months. There will be monitoring and support during this time. Satisfactory performance will mean the contract is confirmed, otherwise a further period of probation will be given. A second failure may lead to the contract being terminated.

Employee appraisal (or performance reviews)

Appraisal is an on-going process that looks at how well an employee is doing their job. It involves monitoring employee performance against agreed targets and then setting further targets that might include training and career opportunities as well as performance.

The process will look at the employee as an individual, but will also ask how the employee helps the organisation to achieve its objectives.

Setting up the appraisal system

- *Stage 1* The organisation will need to decide on the purpose of the appraisal. The usual aim is to review performance against targets, identify areas where the employees can become more effective and to set new targets both for performance and for personal development. The job itself may be reviewed, e.g. Has the job changed? What are the difficulties? Is training required?

Figure 16.18 Setting targets, monitoring and planning

Set targets   Monitor performance   Plan improvements

- *Stage 2* Decide what constitutes satisfactory performance and how this will be assessed. Interview, observation, discussion and checking performance figures are all possibilities. For example:
  - Performance may be compared with numerical targets (units produced, rate of answering telephone calls, number of sales made, etc.).
  - A checklist for observation may be used so that everyone is treated equally and also to provide a basis for feedback, e.g. teachers are observed taking a lesson.
  - Personality factors are contentious, e.g. 'lazy' is too vague, but 'late 20 per cent of the time' or '15 days absence' can be discussed.
- *Stage 3* Decide who the appraisers will be. Possibilities include:
  - *appraisal by managers* This is the most usual model. However, with the trend towards flattening of organisations, managers have a wider span of control and therefore less time. As a result other methods are growing in popularity
  - *peer appraisal* by employees at the same level, e.g. teachers observe each other's lessons and cross-mark work
  - *upward appraisal* by subordinates. This is a growing trend now used by companies such as British Airways and the Halifax Bank. Sometimes the management team as a whole, rather than an individual manager is appraised in this way
  - *360 degree appraisal* (or 'multi-source' assessment) by people at all levels (both above and below) in the organisation. Managers at Tesco, for example, are given 360 degree feedback to identify ways of improving their leadership skills
  - *self-appraisal* There is usually an element of self-appraisal with employees judging themselves against a list of criteria, e.g. How does the appraisee feel that they are progressing within the organisation? Where do they see themselves at this time next year? Are they ready for promotion? What staff development would they find useful?

Figure 16.19 shows the results of a survey carried out in 1995 into the use of different types of appraisal.

Figure 16.19 Appraisal techniques

Source: Saville and Holdsworth

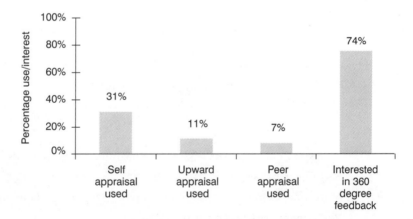

Appraisal is usually 'open'. The process is 'transparent' enabling the appraisee to take an active part and discuss the results.

Outcomes of appraisal

- There should also be a review of the trainee's potential and follow-up action should be agreed. This decides priorities for improvement, identifies any support that is needed, sets out development or training needs and agrees future targets and review dates.
- Appraisal may provide a basis for rewarding productivity in those occupations where the traditional bonus and commission schemes are difficult to apply.
- For employees who are taken on for a trial period the appraisal may determine whether or not their contract is renewed.

Making appraisal successful

Positive appraisal can motivate staff and improve performance. It can set out goals for improvement, identify opportunities for development of skills or for promotion. The employee feels valued and therefore committed to the organisation.

However, there are potential dangers:

■ It can be difficult to give useful feedback on poor performance. Telling the truth may cause an argument or destroy the employee's confidence so 'soft' appraisals may be given as a way out. Neither situation helps performance.

■ Praise is easier to give and can motivate. However, praising unsatisfactory performance can make people complacent.

■ Appraisals can be time-consuming. Busy managers may view them as a nuisance and a distraction and simply carry out a meaningless 'paper exercise'.

■ Appraisal that is regarded as unfair can lead to staff taking action under grievance procedures, or becoming unco-operative or disenchanted – especially if it is linked to performance-related pay, to promotion or to making people redundant.

case study 16.12

Performance management at Tesco

At Tesco, performance management applies to everyone. The aim is to make sure that all employees:

■ are aware of what the company is trying to achieve in its strategic plan

■ make plans to focus on their own part in making the company successful

■ have an on-going review of their progress.

There is an emphasis on continual improvement and staff are encouraged to develop themselves to do their jobs better.

The steering wheel

The 'steering wheel' is a central ideal in Tesco's planning. It is simply the company's way of illustrating the four main areas of concern that the business has: customers, operations, finance and people (its employees).

Communicating company objectives

Company objectives are communicated through the organisation from the top downwards:

1 Directors set out the strategic plan for the company – called the Corporate Wheel. This shows what the company aims to achieve for the next year in each of the four main areas. The plan is then cascaded down to:

2 heads of departments who plan to meet their departmental targets

3 to section managers who set out plans for their teams

4 and finally to the teams on the shop floor, in the warehouses and in the offices.

Performance management in action

The performance management process requires each employee to:

■ set out their individual objectives for the coming period – 'short simple descriptions of what needs to be achieved and how you will know when you have achieved it'

■ to write a personal development plan or PDP – 'a plan which describes how you will develop your skills to improve business performance and achieve your objectives'.

These plans will vary depending upon the employee's position in the organisation.

activity

Find out about the performance management system at the organisation you are studying. Try to speak to staff at different levels about their experiences. Do they have appraisals? If so, what type of feedback is there? Who is in charge? Who carries out the appraisal? Is it seen as useful, time-consuming, threatening?

Supporting employees

Mentoring

This can take a number of forms. Typically it involves an experienced member of staff supporting a new recruit through the initial stages after joining the organisation. The aim is to give the new recruit a point of contact where problems can be taken and advice given. The meetings are usually informal and supportive and the mentor is often someone at the same level in the organisation.

Mentoring takes place as part of management development and succession (promotion) planning. It can be a way of helping to fast-track recruits with potential into senior management roles.

It may also involve contact with members of other organisations who feel that they have experience and support to give. This may be a form of personal development for the mentor and good public relations for their employee.

The UK government's ICT Excellence awards have been designed to reward excellent schools and colleges. In the best institutions, the judges found self-assessment and peer assessment across all subjects; pupils taking responsibility for their own progress; teachers and pupils discussing and agreeing targets, regular peer mentoring among teaching staff.

Community Service Volunteers (CSV) helps business volunteers to mentor students in schools and colleges. In one scheme volunteers from the Financial Times acted as mentors for students at a south London college with the following aims:

■ The college aimed to improve key skills for students, improve student motivation, develop links with local employers, and improve student attendance, retention and achievement.

■ The *Financial Times* saw opportunities for staff to develop communication and interpersonal skills, links with members of the local community and an insight into vocational qualifications.

The mentors committed themselves to one student for either one or two years acting as role models in helping to develop students' study skills, aspirations and self-confidence.

assignment focus

1 Summarise the advantages of mentoring between colleagues.
2 What advantages can the *Financial Times* and their staff gain from mentoring college students?
3 Find out if your chosen organisation is involved in mentoring.

Monitoring

An organisation will constantly review the work of employees. Monitoring is an on-going process that may take a number of forms. There may be a check on the quality of work produced (e.g. a visit by a mystery shopper), regular meetings with reports on progress, a review of performance figures (e.g. sales made, costs incurred, customer feedback, queries answered), and so on.

This information can be used to inform the appraisal. According to Mayo, employees should respond well to the attention that is being paid to them.

Goal displacement

Systems for monitoring employee performance can become burdensome and time-consuming so that managers and employees become diverted away from their real jobs. There is also the problem that staff may concentrate only on what is being monitored – the bus driver who completes the journey on time by not stopping for passengers

Buddying

This involves pairing up inexperienced employees so that they can support and learn from one another. This is similar to peer mentoring except that the 'buddies' will be of similar experience. It can be useful where employees are new to an organisation or job.

Managing workloads

Today's dynamic and competitive business environment can be highly pressured. The potential for 'information overload', the need to hit targets and to respond to change all add to workload; ask your teachers about new initiatives in education!

Some people get a 'buzz' from pressure (a broker on the stock exchange for instance) and a certain level of stress can bring out the best in people. However, too much stress can become harmful, causing tension, sleeplessness, irritability and low confidence. The result can be absenteeism and an inability to face work. The courts are now taking this seriously.

> 'Stress is not always the demon king it is made out to be. A certain amount of stress is a necessary, even a beneficial, element in our lives. When the brain registers that a potentially stressful situation exists, we experience a surge of adrenaline, and this in turn can lead to an increase in performance.'

Source: Ursula Markham, *Managing Stress*, Element Books, 1989

case study 16.13 — Stressed out – but quids in?

Beverley Lancaster worked as a draughtswoman for Birmingham City Council. Without training, she was moved from her quiet office to a front-line job in housing where she had to deal with irate tenants. Ms Lancaster struggled to cope, became ill and eventually took early retirement. The Council admitted causing personal injury due to stress and was ordered to pay £67,000 damages.

Research funded by the HSE at Bristol University has found that one in five people feels 'very' or 'extremely' stressed at work. The reasons are:

- fewer people are in the workplace, as a result of 'downsizing', and they now have to work harder
- working hours can be very long – UK employees work some of the longest hours in Europe
- workers' performance is being monitored more thoroughly
- workers feel job insecurity through outsourcing of work
- changing job roles causes uncertainties.

The HSE believes that employers need clear guidelines and that some workplace cultures need to be changed.

activity

1 How do you think that the problems suffered by Beverley Lancaster could have been prevented by her employer?

2 What is the HSE and what is its role?

3 What do you understand by the term 'workplace culture'? Give other examples of culture – perhaps you can use your own experience.

Occupational health

Large organisations such as the rail companies and the Royal Mail have dedicated occupational health sections. Here medical staff with industry knowledge can advise on safe working practices, examine patients and make judgements about fitness for work, medical retirement, compensation claims, and so forth. Doctors at the Royal Mail, for example, gain experience of delivering letters to help understand the demands of the job.

The fact that the courts are now taking stress seriously and the recognition that stress can affect productivity through disputes, absenteeism, illness, etc. has also led to action. Initiatives include:

- greater physical security for staff, including security screens for staff handling customers' money, high-profile action taken against offenders (London Underground displays notices warning that physical abuse of staff will lead to prosecution), security guards in the workplace (does your local college have security passes?), closed-circuit TV, panic buttons, two-way radios to enable help to be summoned (e.g. in buses and trains)

- staff training in the prevention and resolution of customer conflict – particularly important in the public services such as health, social security and transport

- employee counselling services, either in-house or with external providers

- recognition of workload issues, training and development programmes to enable employees to prepare for and adapt to change in the workplace

- workplace ergonomics – to ensure that employees are comfortable with technological change, e.g. data inputters should have suitable breaks, and perhaps a change of activity, also chairs, keyboards and monitors that can be adapted by each user to avoid neck and arm strain.

Responsibility and autonomy

According to Herzberg, responsibility is a motivator. A job that affords an employee a degree of control and allows autonomy (independence or freedom) to make decisions should provide job satisfaction and result in better performance.

The Toyota case study on page 298 shows how this can work.

Sometimes staff may be given autonomy over a project alongside their daily work – setting up a database or updating the website content for example.

Promotion to higher level posts in the hierarchy will naturally increase responsibility and should also bring higher rewards. However, where an employee either lacks personal confidence or the necessary training or experience, responsibility can become a burden.

The Peter Principle

L.J. Peter pointed out that an excellent employee may not always be a suitable candidate for promotion. People may be promoted to 'the level of their own incompetence', i.e. from a job they can do into a job they cannot do.

The appraisal system must look realistically at an employee's potential as well as at their present performance.

Figure 16.20 Health and safety in an IT operation

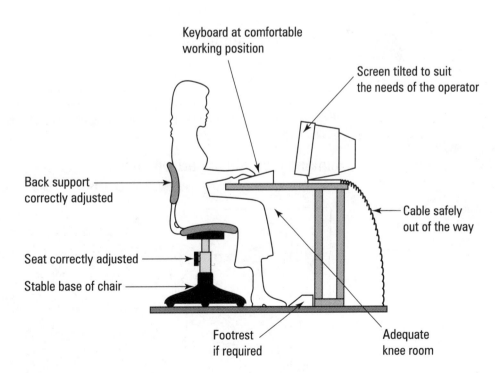

Keyboard at comfortable working position

Screen tilted to suit the needs of the operator

Back support correctly adjusted

Cable safely out of the way

Seat correctly adjusted

Stable base of chair

Footrest if required

Adequate knee room

Competence and capacity

Incompetence at work may not only lead to poor performance, but to serious consequences – loss of customers, damage to corporate image and even to legal action. Prevention is better than cure; HR managers must recruit suitable employees and train those already employed. Employee competence can be established in recruitment by:

- closely matching the job description and person specification to the requirements of the post
- ensuring that the selection process is valid and so that the right candidate is selected.

Figure 16.21 'But I've only applied for the part-time clerical assistant's post.'

Once in post, employees will be monitored and supported.

Change is now a major 'challenge' for all organisations (remember the PESTLE factors on pages 43–51?) and no job will remain the same. Employees need transferable skills (such as communication, number, ICT) so that they can adapt. Staff development becomes an essential means of giving staff the capacity to succeed.

Where a job is simply no longer needed (e.g. typesetters in the print trade), either an employee must be redeployed where possible or else made redundant.

Delegation of authority

The practice of delayering – cutting out layers of management to flatten the organisational structure – can lead to overworked managers delegating work (conferring responsibility) to those at a lower level. If this is seen as empowerment – putting the employee in control – then the job is enriched and the employee may be motivated by greater job satisfaction. On the other hand, delegation may be seen as giving an additional and unwelcome workload that has no reward.

Linking rewards to performance

Vroom's expectancy theory suggests that rewards can enhance employee performance.

Figure 16.22 A system of rewards can be used as an incentive

Performance-related pay

Pay rises earned by staff through increased productivity are acceptable to employers as they neither add to unit costs nor to inflation – staff earn more because they produce more.

Workers engaged in manufacturing and selling have traditionally received incentives for reaching targets. However, as we have seen, in parts of the service sector performance can be difficult to measure.

Recently there has been much debate about the government's attempts to introduce performance-related pay into teaching, the police, the health service and the civil service. The argument is that extra government spending on services can only be justified if these are seen to give value for money. How can performance in these occupations be measured accurately?

---

case study 16.14

A stick in carrot's clothing

In an attempt to get the taxpayer 'value for money' and raise standards, recent governments have sought to link the pay of public sector workers to output, results and performance. There are:

- rewards for the best performing and improving schools in the examination league tables, closure for the worst
- detailed performance indicators for hospitals. Doctors associated with high death rates will be stopped from performing operations.

Performance indicators to be used in the various services

Police:

- answering times for 999 calls
- incident response times
- percentage of all reported crimes where there is a result
- crimes detected per officer

Fire service:

- percentage of alarm calls where turn-out meets standards
- time taken to carry out inspections

Health authorities:

- length of hospital waiting lists

Schools:

- GCSE and GCE A-level results

On the other hand, much that is important cannot be measured. How do you measure the work of a nurse offering reassurance to a relative, or a police officer preventing a crime simply by being there?

---

activity

1 Identify the 'carrots' (incentives) and 'sticks' (punishments) in the case study.
2 Find out how the organisation that you are studying assesses performance. There may be a number of ways, depending upon the nature of a particular job.

Discipline

Employers will set out minimum standards of employee conduct in the contract of employment. There will be an agreed disciplinary code with standard procedures to ensure that all employees are treated equally and fairly.

 Link

See pages 306–307 for an explanation of disciplinary procedures.

Employee development

It is the role of HR managers to ensure that employees fulfil their potential. Staff development can take a number of forms.

Training

On-the-job training is appropriate where an employee has the necessary skills, but not the exact knowledge required for a job. In this case, the work can be explained and demonstrated in the workplace. For example, a new cashier will need to know how to work the till and procedures for accepting cheques, store cards and credit cards. A new clerical assistant will need to understand the filing system and how to use the computer software.

Off-the-job training takes place away from the job either in-house or out-of-house.

- *In-house training* An organisation may run internal staff development programmes using its own trainers or trainers 'bought in' from an external provider. For instance, BTEC trainers will visit schools and colleges to update teaching staff. In-house training will normally occur where the training involves a significant number of employees and will be tailored to the exact needs of the organisation.

- *External training* This is useful where few employees need training or where the training is highly specialised. Here staff are sent on day or residential courses outside the organisation. These may be held at the training agency's own premises or premises booked for the occasion – a hotel conference room perhaps. External training is normally of a general nature. For instance, employees may be sent on courses to learn IT packages, Microsoft Access, perhaps, or to learn new management techniques.

Training methods include:

- lectures, videos and demonstrations
- case studies involving role play or discussion
- simulations using software – engine drivers with Eurotunnel are given a simulation of the Channel Tunnel crossing
- interactive video where the trainee is required to respond – depending upon the response, the video will follow different sequences
- games and outdoor pursuits may be used to develop qualities such as problem-solving, team work, trust and initiative – although increasingly volunteering is being preferred as it is cheaper and often a more worthwhile option. Accidents and injuries sustained on the more extreme outdoor events have led to legal claims and the rising insurance costs have meant that these have been scaled down.

Figure 16.23 Rising insurance costs have hit the more extreme team-building events

Sometimes the purpose of training is to update knowledge. In this case an organisation may use 'cascading'. This involves training a small number of employees who will then teach other employees. The idea is to keep costs down and to avoid the practical problem of releasing a large number of staff at the same time.

Skills training

Skills may either be transferable or job-specific (non-transferable).

- Transferable skills, once learnt, may be applied in many different situations. The key skills of Application of Number, Communication and Information Technology are examples. Business letter-writing skills, business calculations, the use of standard business software (such as Microsoft Office) can be used in a variety of situations and industries – to request information, to apologise for a faulty product, to calculate percentage change, and so on.

- Non-transferable skills are narrow skills that are job-specific and apply only to a particular situation. They often require specific knowledge of a firm's procedures and processes, e.g. you may learn how your particular business completes its invoices and files them. Another business may do this differently and if you changed jobs you would need to learn the new system.

Investors in People (see page 314) is awarded for effective investment in the training and development of people (employees) in order to achieve business goals. It provides a framework for 'improving business performance and competitiveness'.

Figure 16.24 A page from Tesco's Excel Training Pack

Everyone who works for Tesco has the benefit of focused training and development.

We recognise that people are individuals and learn in different ways, so for training to be meaningful and measurable you need clear personal objectives.

Graduates start on our Excel programme as an excellent foundation, providing a combination of core business skills and knowledge. This is a unique opportunity to gain a broad understanding of the business before you choose to specialise in one particular area of our operation.

A framework approach ensures the programme is flexible and performance-based - so we both see results. The objective is to equip you to be a highly successful senior business manager.

Tesco Excel programme
Everyone's programme will be tailor-made to suit their needs encompassing the following broad areas:

- During your first year you will work through a series of placements, balancing on-the-job learning with a series of off-the-job training modules including: supply chain,

distribution, commercial, customers, finance and Tesco in Europe. Everyone starts in our stores - the front end of the business. No matter what area you end up working in, if you are going to contribute to our success you must understand the retail operation, particularly from the customer's perspective.

- You will also attend our Business Skills programme at Aston Business School, Birmingham. This intensive week course, leading to a Management Diploma, is designed to equip you with business skills including: business planning, financial management, marketing, human resources, IT and legal awareness.

- to 12 months in and you'll be looking for more responsibility. Typically graduates then go into a corporate placement; for example, as a member of a store senior team, or into marketing, distribution, commercial or our retail support office. Again you will work with your manager to set objectives and together will continually review your progress against these. You will then be ready take up a pre-appointment placement in your target job area. We expect that most graduates will have a permanent senior management position after about 18 months.

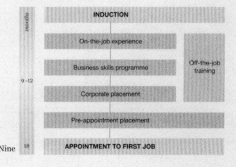

assignment focus

1 Research the types of training offered at your organisation.

2 Read the page from the Tesco training pack in Figure 16.24. List the different training activities under the headings:

   ■ on-the-job training

   ■ off-the-job training

   ■ transferable skills.

3 Now ask these questions of your chosen business.

The learning organisation

It is not just employees who need to learn. Successful organisations must also be prepared to adapt to new circumstances and develop the way they operate and treat their employees.

Job rotation

This is a Europe-wide scheme for small and medium-sized enterprises. Tailored training is provided for their staff whilst replacement workers are provided to cover for these employees until training is complete. Improved employee knowledge, skills and qualifications should increase worker effectiveness and improve job security.

Accelerated promotion

Where the needs of the workplace demand it, selected employees may be 'fast-tracked' into higher level work. The usual method is to compress the training period so that qualifications are achieved more quickly.

There are no minimum academic entry requirements to become a police constable but a good standard of education is expected and all applicants take the standard Police Initial Recruitment Test. However, there is a national accelerated promotion scheme for graduates wishing to move up the ranks. Some regional forces use accelerated promotion to fast-track ethnic minority candidates into positions of authority.

Personal development and professional development

Professional skills are developed through the organisational training programme often after development needs have been identified at appraisal. Increasingly, however, employers recognise the value of wider personal skills. Rounded individuals with developed life skills are likely to adapt to change more readily than those with vocational skills only. This is one reason why employers will encourage staff involvement in volunteering, mentoring and charity fund-raising.

The increased use of the term 'development' (as opposed to 'training') suggests that value is being placed upon a broader approach to the needs of employees.

assignment focus

To achieve P5, you will need to describe how employee performance is measured and managed. You will need to include the sorts of performance criteria that may be set and ways in which performance against these can be measured. Provide some examples and mention the difficulties in measuring performance in some occupations.

In describing how performance can be managed, you should include staff appraisals together with ways in which employees may be supported or sanctioned.

To achieve M3, you will need to explain how organisations are able to use performance measures to identify employee training and development needs. You should give examples of what these needs might be and the types of staff development that might be appropriate to them.

To achieve D2, you will need to assess why it is important for organisations to measure and manage employee performance at work Here you should look at the reasons staff are employed, the costs involved and how employee performance contributes to the achievement of business objectives. Again you should provide examples.

Introduction to the internet and e-business

This unit covers:

- How the internet has evolved
- Using the internet and related technology for a range of business activities
- Trends in the use of e-business
- The key features of planning for the use of e-business

You are living in a world where e-business is growing rapidly. This unit looks at the development and operation of the internet, and how businesses make use of it in their day-to-day activities. It considers the reasons for the growth in e-business and the factors to be considered by governments, organisations and individuals in planning to use e-business.

The unit has links with all the core units.

grading criteria	To achieve a **Pass** grade the evidence must show that the learner is able to:	To achieve a **Merit** grade the evidence must also show that the learner is able to:	To achieve a **Distinction** grade the evidence must also show that the learner is able to:
	P1 describe how the internet has developed and give examples of how it is used by eight selected contrasting business organisations	**M1** demonstrate how to solve problems in internet use for a range of different types of business activity	**D1** make justified recommendations as to how a selected business organisation and an individual could improve their preparation for the growing use of internet by business organisations
	P2 use the internet for a range of different types of business activity, taking actions to reduce the inherent risks to security and reliability	**M2** explain how two selected contrasting business organisations have responded to the competitive forces to develop or update their use of e-business and give reasons for their responses	
	P3 describe the competitive forces on two selected contrasting business organisations to develop or update their use of e-business		
	P4 describe (using examples) how the government, business organisations and individuals plan for the growing use of e-business		

How the internet has evolved

What is the internet?

Computer networks exist where computers are connected by cables or wireless links so that data can be exchanged between them.

- An internet (short for internetwork) is a group of computer networks linked together.

- The internet (sometimes denoted by a capital 'I') is a vast global network of computer networks. It links computers in organisations such as businesses, government departments, charities, universities, libraries, schools and private homes. The users are able to share information and communicate directly.

There is no single inventor of the internet and many of the most important features have been designed by volunteers working for no payment.

A brief history of the internet

1966   The US military began to use the system to connect defence laboratories. It was designed as a communications network that could not be brought down by an attack on a single centre. The system was next extended to the major US universities.

1982   William Gibson coined the term 'cyberspace' (the mythical place through which internet data travels).

1991   Sir Tim Berners Lee developed the World Wide Web (www) to enable researchers to send and receive scientific papers via the internet.

1991   The first free web-browser (MOSAIC) finally opened the World Wide Web to businesses and the general public.

Since 1995, the traffic on the internet has grown rapidly. Private users are attracted because it is free and uncensored, business users because it provides a global opportunity for marketing and e-commerce.

The popularity of the internet has been helped by, among other things, the increasing availability of low-cost, high-specification computers, government initiatives aimed at computer literacy, and the development of faster means of access such as broadband. More recently mobile phones and portable notebook computers have given travellers remote 'wireless' **online** access via the use of **hot-spot** locations.

We consider hot spot locations on page 335.

The rapid growth of online trading (or e-commerce) is one of the most notable of recent internet trends.

How the internet works

The internet is built around three levels of carriers rather like a tree with a trunk, branches and twigs.

- the trunk (called the 'backbone') consists of high-speed, high-capacity networks that carry internet traffic around the world. These are mainly the original military networks along with high-speed lines belonging to the major telephone companies

- mid-level networks form the branches

- smaller 'stub' networks are the twigs.

Many types of hardware and **protocols** (rules governing the exchange of data between computers) are involved. It is internet protocol (IP) that brings these together to form the internet. Particularly important are the systems for internet addresses and **domain names**.

Connecting to the internet

There are two principal methods of connection:

- Direct connection is used by large organisations and government agencies. These set up their own connection and pay to have a full-time link. Computers connected in this way are part of the net (Figure 29.1).

Figure 29.1 A direct internet connection

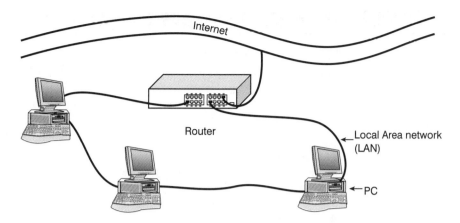

- **ISPs (internet service providers)** such as BT, AOL and Virgin, allow internet access for smaller organisations and individuals who register with them. The connection is dialled up as needed or, increasingly, connected permanently via broadband. Larger ISPs connect directly to the internet backbone, smaller ISPs gain access by connecting to larger ISPs (Figure 29.2).

Figure 29.2 Using an internet service provider

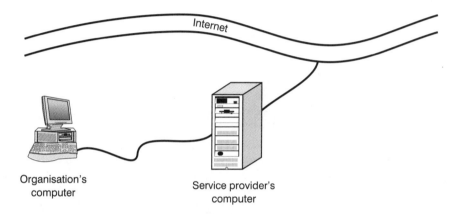

Unravelling the net – some internet terms

Figure 29.3 Internet terms

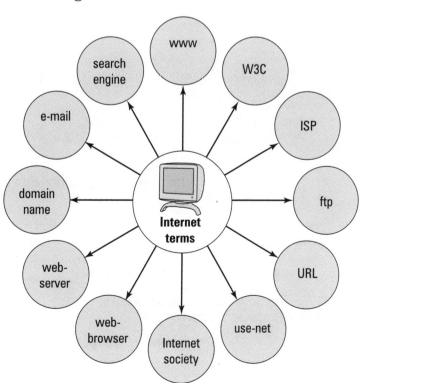

- A **URL (uniform resource locator)** is a string of characters used to identify a resource of the internet. A web address is an example of a URL.
- Internet service providers (ISP); see above.
- A **search engine** is used to locate relevant information on the World Wide Web, e.g. MSN, Ask (formerly Ask Jeeves), Yahoo and Google (the most popular).
- A web-server is a hard disc space where websites are stored once they are uploaded to the internet. ISPs will 'host' websites by making disc space available.
- Electronic mail (e-mail) is a service provided by an ISP or by Usenet.
- Usenet is a collection of newsgroups (online discussion forums) that began in 1979 before the internet. Discussions take place in text-only format and cover a wide range of subjects. Access is gained via ISPs such as BT and Virgin. It is also possible via search engines, such as the 'Groups' option on Google.
- File transfer protocol (ftp) is the principal protocol (set of rules) used to download files from the internet, especially from websites.
- A **web browser** is an application used to request and read pages from the World Wide Web. The best known browsers are Netscape Navigator and Microsoft's Internet Explorer.
- The World Wide Web (www) is a set of technology standards that enables multimedia documents (text, images, sound, video) to be read by anyone with access to the internet. The web organises its contents by subject matter to enable advanced information retrieval.
- The World Wide Web Consortium (W3C) is based at Cambridge, Massachusetts, USA. It develops and maintains common technology standards for use on the World Wide Web. These include the use of hypertext markup language (HTML) for web pages, acceptable graphics formats and new standards for use with interactive television and mobile phones. The Royal National Institute for the Blind (RNIB) is a member of W3C and has helped draw up the conventions for site design that will enable screen-reading software to perform effectively.
- The Internet Society (ISOC) is a non-profit, non-governmental, international organisation. Its mission is to 'promote the open development, evolution and use of the Internet for the benefit of all people throughout the world'. ISOC works towards making the internet a force for good and focuses upon the four 'pillars' of: standards, public policy, education and training, and membership.
- The domain name is the website name, e.g. www.levistrauss.com.
  The internet domain name system (DNS) lists all of the domain names on the internet together with their owners. Top level domain names include:
  - .co.uk or .com (for the USA) – for sites belonging to commercial, profit-making organisations. Some UK organisations now also use .com
  - .org – for a not-for-profit organisation
  - .ac.uk or .edu (USA) – for an academic institution
  - .gov.uk – a government site
  - .mil – a military site
  - .net – an organisation, such as an ISP, whose activities are related to the internet.

Figure 29.4 What the parts of the web address mean

http://www.eclipsepots.plus.com

| Protocol request/ response | World wide web | If the name of your website is already taken, you will need to choose another | ISP (internet service provider) hosting the site | The extension given. Other ISPs might offer: .co.uk |

A specific page within a site can be located by adding the appropriate page address to the end of the web address. For example:

http://www.eclipsepots.plus.com/contact —— The page showing contact details

With the exception of the USA, countries are usually identified within the domain name, e.g. .uk for the United Kingdom, .au for Australia, etc.

The Internet Society – www.isoc.org
The World Wide Web Consortium (W3C) – www.w3.org

Networking of computers

Networks

Computer networks can be either LANs or WANs:

- *LANs (local area networks)* link computers that are geographically close, perhaps in the same building or in buildings nearby. These computers normally belong to one organisation so that the LAN provides a form of internal communication.
- *WANs (wide area networks)* link computers that are geographically far apart, perhaps in different cities or across the world. Here communication is usually between different organisations. The internet is a WAN.

Wireless networks

Wireless application protocol (WAP) enables users of mobile phones and portable computers to receive e-mail and web-based information whilst on the move. Hot spots are being set up as areas where wireless (not plugged in) applications, such as notebook computers can access the internet. In 2002 there were 115 hot spots in the UK, by 2009 there will be over 10,000.

Current related technology

Wi-fi

Wi-fi (wireless fidelity or wide fidelity) uses short-range radio connections to create wireless LANs. It has a range of about 100 metres and is suitable for use by an organisation located on a single site. It can be used to send voice signals or data files over the internet via hot spot locations.

Bluetooth

Bluetooth is a short-range radio technology used to connect portable devices such as mobile phones, PDAs and notebook computers to a computer network (including the internet); there is no need for cables. Connecting and receiving devices must be within line of sight (must be able to see each other) and no more than 30 metres apart. (Harold Bluetooth was a tenth century Danish king.)

Figure 29.5 A hot spot at London's Heathrow Airport

Figure 29.6 Wi-fi

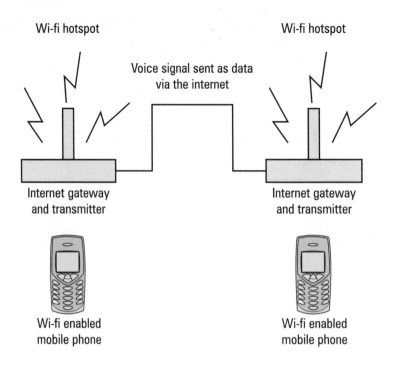

Wi-fi hotspot   Wi-fi hotspot

Voice signal sent as data
via the internet

Internet gateway   Internet gateway
and transmitter   and transmitter

Wi-fi enabled   Wi-fi enabled
mobile phone   mobile phone

3G (3rd generation) phones

3G technology aims to provide a worldwide standard for mobile computing devices so that they will work anywhere – so-called 'global roaming'. At the time of writing there is a battle for recognition between UMTS (the 3G standard for Europe and Japan) and CDMA2000 (the 3G standard for the USA).

3G devices are high-performance and require 500 times the bandwidth of 2G. Bandwidth relates to the frequencies needed for carrying data; these frequencies are in short supply and expensive.

PDAs (personal digital assistants)

John Scully of Apple computers first used this term to describe the Newton pocket computer. PDA now describes any pocket personal organiser that combines a calendar, diary and address book. The BlackBerry series combine PDA functions, wireless internet and e-mail connection with a mobile phone.

Smartphones

These are mobile phones incorporating the functions of a hand-held computer. They may offer address database, diary, fax, web browser and note-taking facilities.

VoIP (voice over internet protocol)

'Internet telephony' describes the use of the internet to make long distance phone calls. It requires software and a microphone or handset attached to the computer's soundcard. The advantages are low call charges. However, during busy periods, sound quality can be poor and callers may lose connection.

Figure 29.7 Watch this space! Look out for new developments in technology

Watch this space!
Look out for new
developments in
technology

Use of the internet and the world wide web by business organisations

In 2005, 88 per cent of UK business organisations had online access, reflecting a growing awareness that the internet is the way to do business. The main uses are banking and financial services, procurement of supplies and after-sales service, business-related market research and communication via e-mail.

Figure 29.8 How businesses use the internet

Source: Office for National Statistics, 2005

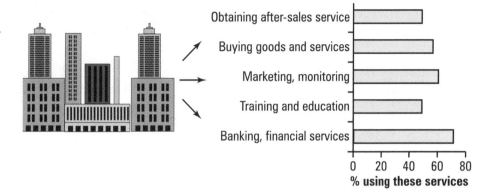

Procurement of supplies

Between 2004 and 2005, B2B online sales grew from £50 billion to £82 billion. Large organisations are most likely to be involved, although small business use is growing. Popular online purchases include office consumables (stationery and computer supplies) with firms such as Viking offering same or next day delivery to both businesses and households.

Businesses see electronic buying as advantageous because:

■ electronic ordering, processing, retrieval and storage of information eliminates errors – data passes directly from one computer to another with no possibility of inputting errors (as, for example, when details from a paper-based order are typed into the computer). This saves time and cost and avoids misunderstandings

■ it is open for business day and night (an advantage when dealing with overseas suppliers)

■ it enables comparison of terms and conditions and shopping around for better deals.

Manufacturers report that large retailers, including the supermarket chains, increasingly demand that they supply online.

Research

In October 2006, Prime Minister Tony Blair referred to 'the Google generation'. The phenomenal success of this search engine is down to its ability to find relevant sites from keywords. (Next time, notice how many sites are searched.)

Businesses use the research potential of the internet in numerous ways, e.g. finding suppliers or property, booking rail tickets, locating addresses, buying marketing data and checking on the competition. For example, the Upmystreet site enables businesses to identify local competitors, suppliers may buy competitors' products to check quality, customer service and value. Hospital doctors have even been encouraged to type patients' symptoms into Google when unsure of a diagnosis.

Development of an online presence

Increasingly businesses are establishing their own **online presence**. The Office for National Statistics reported that, by the end of 2005, 88 per cent of businesses surveyed had internet access and 70 percent had developed their own websites.

Having a business website is not an end in itself but should help the business to achieve its aims and objectives by communicating effectively with the business stakeholders. The main uses are shown in Figure 29.9.

Figure 29.9 Uses of a business website

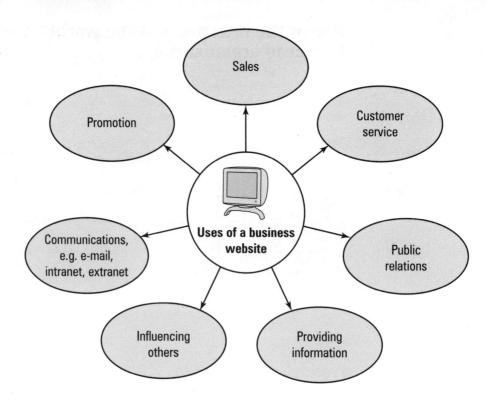

Sales and promotion

Most websites are designed primarily for marketing and sales purposes. The site acts as a virtual shop window for the organisation's goods and services. Increasingly customers are able to order online and pay via plastic card. The emergence of secure intermediary sites such as Pay-Pal makes this possible for smaller businesses.

 See the Tunde Jegede case study on page 360.

2B or not 2B?
We can distinguish between B2B and B2C websites.

B2B (business to business) sites provide industrial goods and commercial services for use by other businesses. For example, JCB makes earth-moving equipment for the construction industry, the haulage company Eddie Stobart delivers stock to manufacturers, wholesalers and retailers. Rolls-Royce enables industrial customers to order parts via its 'Sourcerer' site.

Figure 29.10 B2B and B2C

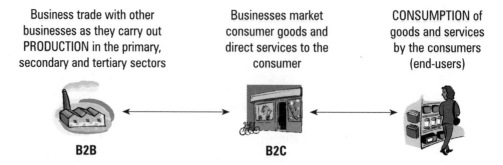

Business trade with other businesses as they carry out PRODUCTION in the primary, secondary and tertiary sectors

Businesses market consumer goods and direct services to the consumer

CONSUMPTION of goods and services by the consumers (end-users)

B2B   **B2C**

B2C (business to consumer) include the sites of retailers of consumer goods such as John Lewis, and providers of direct services such as Royal Mail, HSBC, Stagecoach and Thames Water. These also include the sites of charities and public services.

Many sites (such as Viking) operate as both B2B and B2C suppliers. The value of B2B sales within the UK is around four times that of B2C sales (Figure 29.11).

Sourcery at Rolls-Royce

Rolls Royce manufacturers aircraft engines as well as luxury cars. The company's Sourcerer site enables business customers (with a large shopping basket!) to order aerospace consumables online.

activity

Log on to Rolls-Royce's Sourcerer website: www.sourcerer-online.com.

1 What advantages can you see for Rolls-Royce and for their customers in buying supplies via the website?

2 View the different functions. (Be careful not to place an order.)

Figure 29.11 UK business – online sales

Source: Office for National Statistics

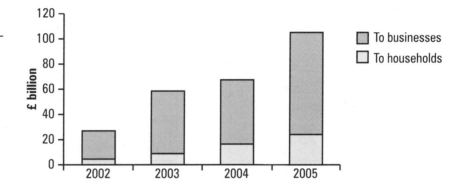

Customer service

The site of a computer retailer may provide technical advice, tips for trouble-shooting, free downloads of software drivers, frequently asked questions (FAQs), and so on. An online bank will enable customers to view their account balances, transfer money and pay bills. Online retailers will allow customers to track the delivery of goods purchased.

Public relations

A site may contain press releases and details of the organisation's social responsibility policy showing charitable donations, environmental policies, ethical practices, and so on. Some organisations encourage feedback, e.g. Shell's 'Tell Shell' forum and Sainsbury's 'Ask Justin' feature.

Information

It is usual for a site to provide links to specific stakeholder information, e.g. company shareholders will usually have access to the share price and to the annual report and accounts. Local authorities will list local services and contacts, central government provides details of legislation, government policies and statistical information on the state of the nation via the ONS site, the Edexcel site will provide details about this course.

Influencing others

Some sites exist to change the way that people behave. The sites of charities such as Greenpeace and the League Against Cruel Sports are interested in putting across a point of view. They will also hope to gain donations, try to recruit supporters and act as a pressure group on business and government.

Communication via e-mail, intranet and extranet

In addition to enabling communication with external stakeholders, an online presence may improve internal communication between employees in different functional areas. The use of mobile technology facilitates this.

case study
29.2

Sainsbury's website

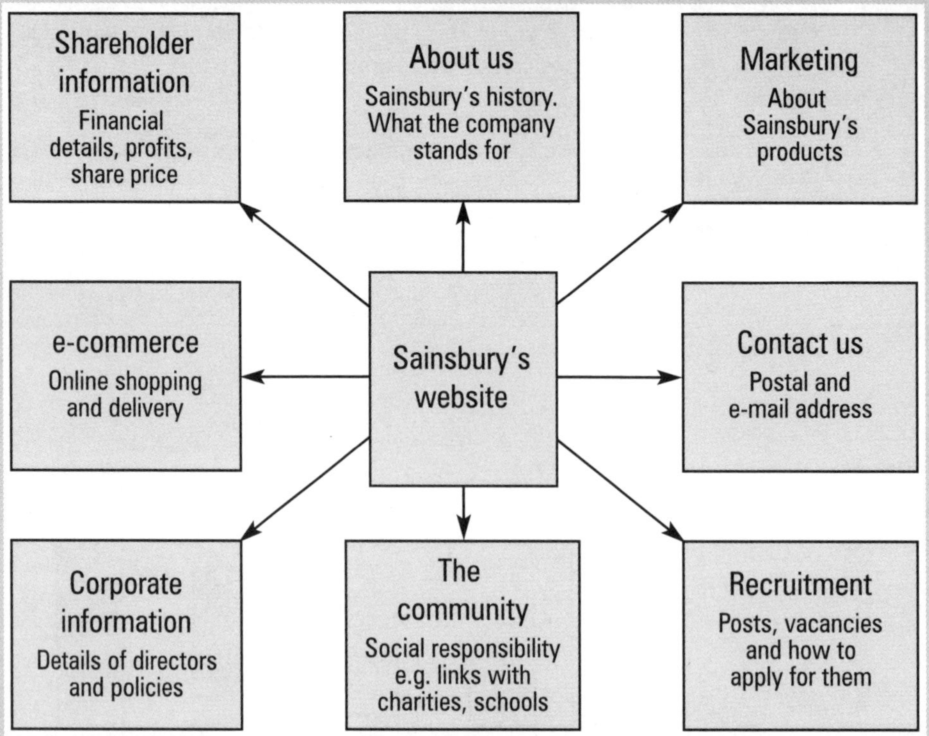

Figure 29.12 The content of
Sainsbury's website

Shareholder information
Financial details, profits, share price

About us
Sainsbury's history. What the company stands for

Marketing
About Sainsbury's products

e-commerce
Online shopping and delivery

Sainsbury's website

Contact us
Postal and e-mail address

Corporate information
Details of directors and policies

The community
Social responsibility e.g. links with charities, schools

Recruitment
Posts, vacancies and how to apply for them

activity

1   Re-read the section on key stakeholders on pages 17–21.

2   Identify the stakeholders targeted by Sainsbury's in each section of its site shown above. If you log on to the Sainsbury's site (www.sainsburys.co.uk) you will be able to give specific examples of content to help with this task.

3   What do you think is the main purpose of Sainsbury's site?

4   Whilst you are on the site, think about the usability. For example, is the site easy to navigate (can you find your way around)? Does it load quickly? Is it interesting? Is the information helpful to its audience in each case?

E-mail

E-mail is replacing the paper-based memorandum as the standard form of internal business communication. Increasingly it is also used as a convenient form of external communication, e.g. the website 'contact us' section will usually provide an e-mail link.

Advantages include:

- the speed of transmission (virtually instantaneous)
- the ability to check that it is received, to store and print copies
- the ability to attach files. With increasing bandwidth (the capacity of the electronic link), larger multimedia files can be attached including images and sound as well as text and number.

Intranet

This is the equivalent of a secure website that is available only to employees of the organisation. It provides all relevant details about the organisation in one place to be accessed as needed. Contents might include: organisational policies, forms, job vacancies and specifications, latest announcements, etc.

There is a considerable saving of time, duplication and storage space, with the added advantage that details are constantly updated.

Extranet

This an extension of the intranet. It permits access via the internet to authorised outside users such as salesforce, home workers, suppliers or customers.

Figure 29.13 Businesses using website, intranet and extranet

Source: Office for National Statistics, 2005 e-Commerce Survey of Business

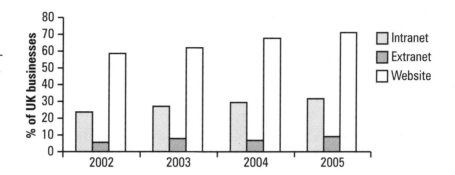

Uses of related mobile technology by business organisations

Increasingly, mobile technology allows employees to stay in touch whilst working away from the office. They may, for example, be at a meeting, working from home, on the road as part of the salesforce or travelling to a conference. In all of these situations, the business website provides a two-way information link between the employee and the business. It may allow e-mails or remote access to the company database. The technology enables users to print documents, check details, leave messages, send files, enter sales data, and so on.

The increasing need for 'real-time' (up to the minute) information requires mobile connection. The use of portable 'notebook' computers and PDAs, together with wireless technology, has facilitated access from a wide range locations.

---

case study 29.3 — Trains on line

GNER runs trains from London to Edinburgh under franchise from the Strategic Rail Authority. As part of the deal, it offers wi-fi to its passengers via the Orange 3G network.

The service allows travellers with a suitably-equipped laptop to access continuous high-speed internet and e-mail services. This is free to first-class passengers.

The company sees this 'mobile office experience' as a USP (unique selling point) that planes and cars cannot match; passenger wi-fi use increased from 45 minutes per person in June 2005 to around 70 minutes at the end of September.

GNER staff also make use of the internet link to communicate with staff in stations via wireless dual-mode PDAs.

Source: Martin Shaw, project manager at GNER

A number of modern football coaches begin a game by watching from a vantage point high in the stands where the pattern of play is clearer than at pitchside. Mobile technology, complete with microphone and earpiece, is used to communicate with the 'dug out' at pitch level. Sam Allardyce, manager of Newcastle United, uses Bluetooth technology to convey his instructions.

activity

1 Find out whether your school or college makes use of these techniques, and if so, for what purpose.

2 Do you or your friends have Bluetooth on your mobile phone? If so, what do you use it for?

Trends in internet development

case study 29.4   Internet use by households

Figures 29.14–29.17 show how the internet is used by households in the UK.

The main UK internet trends are:

- increasing penetration – 13.9 million (or 57 per cent) of households online

- increasing speed – a growing number of households (70 per cent of users) are connected to broadband

- falling costs – the trends are partly explained by falling costs of high specification hardware and cut-price, or even free, broadband advertised by some providers. The greater usability has in turn encouraged wider and more frequent use.

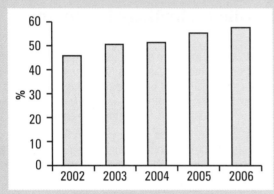

Figure 29.14 GB households with internet access

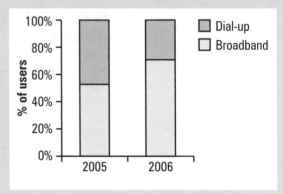

Figure 29.15 The use of broadband by internet households

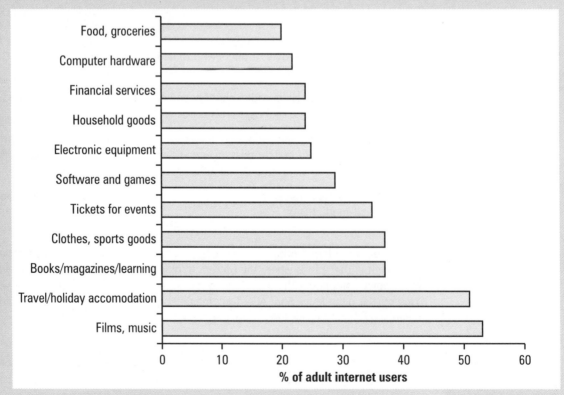

Figure 29.16 What why we buy online

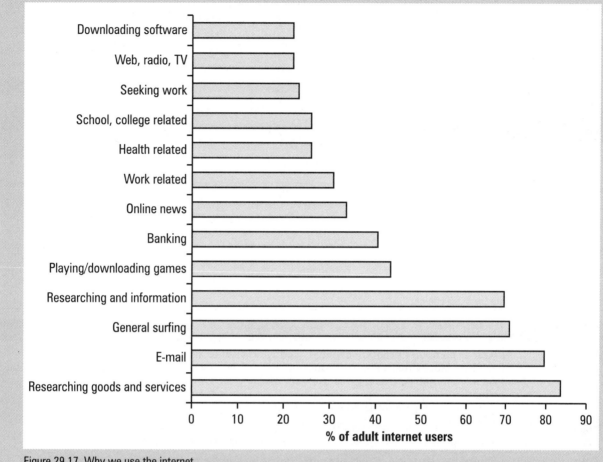

Figure 29.17 Why we use the internet

Source: all charts based on the National Statistics Omnibus Survey, 2006

activity

Use the details from the National Statistics Omnibus Survey 2006 (Figures 29.14–29.17) to write a brief newspaper article titled 'Households go online'. In your article indicate the main trends and the reasons for these.

assignment focus

You will need to select three contrasting businesses to illustrate the points that you will make about e-business.

To achieve P1, you must describe how the internet operates and give eight examples of how it is used by contrasting business operations.

How the internet and related technology can be used for a range of business activities

Setting up an internet linked computer

Equipment requirements

- Hardware: monitor, keyboard, mouse, computer, modem (inbuilt), internet link
- Connection: either dial-up telephone connection or broadband access

- Portable back-up facilities: USB stick, disk or CD
- Specification: it might be reasonable to assume that users will have at least Windows XP, 1024 x 768 screen resolution and a 56K modem. Websites should be designed to perform effectively on such equipment although optimum performance and use of all features will require higher specifications.

assignment focus

Computer specifications continue to develop. Find up-to-date information by researching:

- costs of a basic system and specifications offered
- costs and speed of broadband connection and operation
- any new developments in storage of data.

Risks

The internet brings undoubted benefits but its link with the outside world leaves machines vulnerable to unwanted software (Table 29.1). These risks are greater for users of broadband where the machine is permanently connected.

Table 29.1 Risks associated with the internet

Risks	Description
Virus	A small computer program capable of copying itself to 'infect' first one computer then another. Most viruses are malicious and can damage files. Today the majority are transmitted via the internet. A virus may lie dormant awaiting an event such as Friday 13th before it takes effect. In 2005, 1 in 43 e-mails contained viruses.
Trojan horse (or 'trojan')	Causes similar damage to a virus but is visible perhaps as an e-mail. It masquerades as a normal program until it is executed. Most e-mail viruses are Trojans.
Worm	Similar to a virus but affects networks rather than individual computers. Often spreads via e-mail.
Hacker	Originally computer programmers were called 'hackers'. More recently the term describes someone who gains unauthorised access to systems and networks. The motivation might be criminal, i.e. to steal data or money. Alternatively hackers may break into systems as a challenge; nevertheless this is likely to be illegal.
Spam	Unwanted e-mails – a sort of online junk mail. The name comes from a Monty Python sketch where the word 'spam' is repeated – just as e-mail spam keeps arriving. The motivation is often marketing. 65% of the 136 billion e-mails sent in 2005 were spam. Ed Gibson of Microsoft (talking at Westminster e-Forum) stated that the 'net would be unusable by 2008 unless things changed'.
Spyware	Any software that employs a user's internet connection without their knowledge or explicit permission. Poorly written spyware may also contain bugs or errors that can cause the web-browser to hang or freeze.

Adware	A software application in which advertising banners are displayed while the program is running. The ads appear as pop-up windows or through a bar on the screen.
	    It is claimed that revenue from the advertisements helps keep down the cost for internet users.
	    If adware tracks a user's personal information and passes it on to third parties, without the user's authorisation or knowledge, it is spyware.

Scams	The term 'scam' covers a variety of unethical and usually illegal practices in which users are mislead, usually with the intention of cheating them out of money. Phishing, for example, involves e-mails purporting to come from a bank. These seek confirmation of a customer's online password and other details. If provided, this is used to raid their account.
Loss of data	All computers, whether connected to the internet or not, may lose data through negligence (not saving or backing up), theft of equipment or files, physical damage (fire or flood for instance) or technical failure. Online computers run the additional risks of data loss through virus infection and hacking.
Computer freezes or 'hangs up'	This can be caused by problems in the software, incorrect installation or running files that are too large for the system.

In 2005, a survey of businesses with more that ten employees found that 1 in 7 experienced security problems (slightly down from the previous year). In October 2006 researchers monitoring a personal computer found that 'cyber criminals' made around 50 attempts to gain access in a single night.

Measures to reduce risks

Businesses use a variety of methods of reducing these risks (Figure 29.18).

Figure 29.18 Types of internet security used by businesses

Source: Office for National Statistics, e-Commerce Survey of Business, 2005

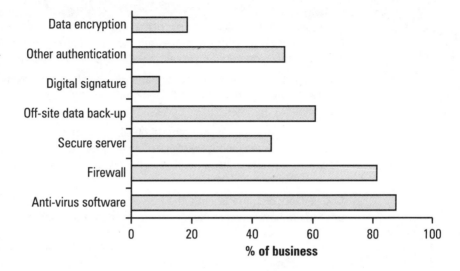

- Anti-virus software is essential. It is usually installed as standard with new systems but must be regularly updated. www.apple.com has started providing free anti-virus software to combat a virus that has 'infected' the Apple iPod.
- Firewall software filters out unwanted intrusion from the outside world. It can be used to block sites with undesirable content or to prevent breaches in security from hackers.
- Adware and spyware can be removed by specialist software.
- ISPs such as Yahoo provide spamguard software in an attempt to reduce the flow of unwanted e-mails.
- Data encryption involves the conversion of data into 'ciphertext' that cannot be understood by unauthorised users. Decryption uses a key to convert encrypted data back into its original form to be read. Encryption/decryption is especially important when using wireless communications where messages are easier to intercept, and when carrying out sensitive online transactions such as credit card purchases, or sending sensitive company information between departments.
- A digital (or electronic) signature is used to authenticate the identity of the sender of a message or the signer of a document. Digital signatures cannot be imitated, can be automatically time-stamped and may be used with any kind of message to verify the sender's identity and that the message arrived intact.
- Offsite data back-up. In an information-led economy data loss can be highly damaging to a business. Research following recent terrorist attacks showed that 90 per cent of businesses losing data as a result of incidents closed within two years. Where a building is destroyed (fire, flood, terrorism) on-site back-ups can be lost along with the original. For this reason it is becoming routine for businesses to store copies of data at a separate location. Increasingly organisations have reciprocal arrangements to store each other's data. Online storage (see case study 29.5) is another option.

Business internet technology policies

Organisations using ICT will have an information technology policy covering internet use. This will set out the rules for computer users within the business and will usually include:

- a description of the system
- what the system may be used for – this will be work-related
- what it may not be used for, e.g. playing games, accessing certain websites, downloading unauthorised files, sending material subject to copyright, etc.

- information about the Data Protection Act as it applies to the workplace
- an undertaking to use software in accordance with the licence and not to take or install pirate copies.

The user may need to sign that they will comply with the policy.

case study 29.5 — Lock it in the vault

In October 2006 BT launched its 'digital vault' – btdigitalvault.bt.com. This allows users to rent online space to store their files as an alternative to saving them on the home or office computer. It can act as main storage or back-up space.

The facility is particularly useful for large memory files such as music, videos and photos. It has the advantages of additional security (the data is encrypted during transmission) and files can be accessed from any location.

The 'vault' is part of a growing trend of 'digitisation' made possible by the use of broadband where computers are permanently online. For example, videos can be stored on Youtube whilst most ISPs supply webspace which is meant for websites but can be used for file storage.

Google Docs & Spreadsheets, the free equivalent of Microsoft Word and Excel, is an example of how software can be stored online rather than in the computer hard drive.

activity

BTs advertising plays heavily upon the dangers of losing files and how the 'vault' can help avoid this by providing a secure form of back-up.

Compare the 'vault' as a means of storage with more conventional saving on the computer hard drive or on portable devices, such as a USB stick or CD.

assignment focus

Check the policy for your organisation. You may well have been asked to sign a copy.

Use of the internet for business research
Types of data

The resources available to business are vast and growing. Important categories include the following.

Demographics

Population data is an essential element in market research. Sources include local authority sites, the government's ONS statistical website and private market research organisations, such as CACI who produce ACORN (a classification of residential neighbourhoods).

- Office for National Statistics – www.statistics.gov.uk
- CACI/ACORN – www.caci.co.uk/acorn

Competitor analysis

This can be done through logging onto their websites, much as a mystery shopper would do. Nick Jenkins of Moonpig.com buys greetings cards from his competitors to compare the price, quality and delivery times. By comparing invoice numbers, he can also estimate their monthly sales.

More conveniently, we could use a specialist site that has already done this research. Moneyfacts, for example, will give best buys in personal finance, whilst service providers such as AOL list sites that regularly scan the web and compare prices. Upmystreet provides a classified directory of businesses local to a given post code. This will enable small 'bricks and mortar' businesses to find out who their competitors are.

- Moneyfacts – www.moneyfacts.co.uk
- Upmystreet – www.upmystreet.com

Environmental analysis

The weather is an important factor for retailers. Rain in summer creates demand for umbrellas but wrecks the sales of barbecues and bottled water; sun will have the opposite effect. Retailers need to be ready with the right goods in stock. Similarly organisers of outdoor festivals need to be suitably insured. The internet can help businesses prepare for environmental factors in a number of ways:

- Weather forecasts for the short and long-term are available online from the BBC and the Met(eorological) Office.

- Transport information including real-time road travel conditions are available from the AA and RAC, whilst rail services are available from the sites of regional operators such as Midland Mainline and First Western. Online travel booking is a growth area through sites such as the Trainline and Travelocity.

- BBC – www.bbc.co.uk
- Met Office – www.metoffice.gov.uk
- AA and RAC – www.theaauk.co.uk; www.rac.co.uk
- Trainline – www.trainline.com (see the case study on page 351)
- Travelocity – www.travelocity.co.uk

Legislation

Details and advice about UK and EU legislation affecting business can be found from official sites, e.g. the Department of Trade and Industry (DTI), the Health and Safety Executive (HSE). The Business Link site will find legislation specific to a named business, e.g. the partners in Eclipse Pottery (Unit 37) could look up legislation relating to a pottery.

DTI – www.dti.gov.uk
- HSE – www.hse.gov.uk
- Business Link – www.businesslink.gov.uk

There are a host of specialist private consultants prepared to advise on new laws and how to comply. Type 'Employment Law + UK' into a search engine to see a sample of available sources.

Industry-specific legislation details will be provided for businesses by their trade associations – these range from the Association of British Travel Agents (ABTA) to the Aromatherapy Trade Council, the National Association of Fish Fryers and the British Christmas Tree Growers Association.

Specialist technical information

This will be available from product suppliers, e.g. when you buy a new PC, printer or USB flash drive you will find technical support information on the maker's website. This may involve instructions for setting up the equipment, trouble-shooting or registering for warranty purposes. Online facilities are replacing the telephone help-line as they are cheaper to provide (no staff needed), always available 24/7 and they should be free from human error.

Support may also be offered in the form of interactive online tutorials, downloads of firmware, software and product updates.

FAQs (frequently asked questions)

These are a feature of many business websites. These may deal with set-up, maintenance, trouble-shooting, upgrades, specifications and compatibility. The idea is to provide basic information so that this will not have to be repeated and explained constantly. Good **netiquette** (internet manners) demands that FAQs are read carefully before demanding e-mails are sent.

Effective searching of the internet

If you know the precise site that you are looking for, type in the URL (web address) into the address bar at the top of the browser screen. Failing this, you can type key words into a search engine in order to find a relevant site.

Bookmarking

Where a site is frequently used, it makes sense to bookmark it – to save it so that it can be activated by a mouse click. The browser does this through the 'Favorites' (sic) facility.

Figure 29.19 Favorites

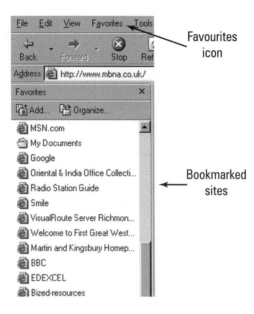

Using a search engine

Search engines, such as Google, MSN, Yahoo, Alta Vista and Excite, play a vital role in locating web pages for users. If the precise URL (web address) is not known, or you are simply 'surfing the net', relevant websites can be found by typing key words into a search engine. Once a site has been located, further searches may be possible via an in-site search facility.

case study 29.6   Search engines

Search engines look for key words. A search may be refined by linking key words together or narrowing the geographical area, e.g. searching the UK only.

Search engines do not search the whole web, rather each has an index of sites that it will search. This is why, for example, a particular search in Yahoo will turn up different sites from an identical search in Google, Excite or Alta Vista.

At the time of writing, Google has the largest index (check its home page to see how many sites it will use).

For a website to be successful, it must be included in the index of the major search engines otherwise surfers will not discover it. In order to improve their chances, many businesses will pay to submit their sites to search engines. Web designers can also help by using **metatags** to include those key words that search engines are likely to recognise.

activity

1   How many sites does Google currently search? (Look at the home page.)
2   Conduct an identical search in three different search engines.

Searching using key words

Google's success has been based on the way that it searches – it is the search engine most likely to find what we are looking for.

Our chances of success can also be improved by using compound searches. Suppose that we want to find the cult TV show *Monty Python's Flying Circus*, often referred to as 'Python' for short – see Table 29.2.

Table 29.2 Searching using keywords

Key word(s) entered into search engine	What it does	Search result
Python	Looks for sites containing the word 'python'.	Is likely to find references to snakes first.
Monty AND Python Alternatively: Monty + Python	This will pick up references to 'Monty' and to 'Python' that occur within 12 words of each other in the same site.	This could find Monty Python but will also find Monty the zoo-keeper who looks after Pythons.
Monty OR Python	Will find sites with either of these words as well as sites with both – literally the Full Monty!	It might find Monty Panasar, Field Marshall Montgomery, Pythons, etc.
"Monty Python"	Will only find sites where the two words appear together. This is the most precise search.	This will find Monty Python (TV comedy programme).

remember

Key Skill ICT from level 2 requires you to make compound searches using the Boolean operators of AND, OR, NOT.

Filtering sites

Search engines have filters that can prevent unwanted results and keep searches more relevant. www.google.co.uk for example has two radio buttons for 'Search the Web' and 'UK only'. The searches made in your course will be mainly UK only and using the filter will keep results more relevant.

Advanced searching

The more precise a search is, the more relevant will be the results. Search engines now include dialogue boxes that help us to pinpoint exactly what we are looking for.

Figure 29.20 Google advanced search

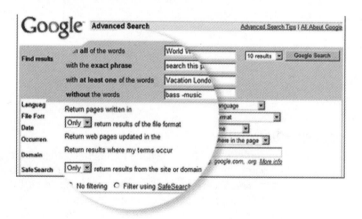

Validity of sources of data

Anyone can create a website containing anything and internet content is largely unregulated (although two of the most popular uses, gambling and pornography, are now subject to some attempts at control.) However, when searching the internet we need to find quality information, i.e. information that is up to date, accurate and unbiased. It is therefore essential to check the validity of any data researched.

We need to have some way of validating what we find – where has the information come from? Is it accurate? Does the author have a particular point of view? One internet bookseller has reportedly asked authors to write their own book reviews. Will these be useful for customers?

Customers purchasing on the web need to be assured that they are buying from a legitimate trader. Dell is an e-tailing success story. Their computers are not available in the shops, but they do have an established reputation as a quality brand, as do John Lewis and Tesco. But how do we judge the quality of brands we have never heard of?

Is the information provided correct? Some sites police their contributors, e.g. there are strict guidelines for those contributing learning materials to educational sites. However, for other sites there may be no such assurances.

Can you believe it?

Every time you make a search using Google, thousands of websites are searched and one thousand sites are suggested. Research shows that 42 per cent of the time users select the first result on the list and 12 per cent of the time the second. Sites in the first ten (i.e. the first page of results) are chosen 89 per cent of the time, with the remaining 990 sites chosen just 11 per cent of the time. No one in the research sample looked beyond site 449.

Just because something comes high on the list, is it automatically useful? One of the sites located most often by search engines is Wikipedia, the online encyclopaedia created by users. It is widely relied upon, often useful, but can be wrong.

Use of the internet for procurement

Selection of a suitable site

The rapid growth in e-commerce does not mean that every internet business is doing well. There is a lot of choice and customers (either businesses or households) will search for the most suitable site. Users need to have confidence in the information they are receiving and in the goods and services they buy. With digital services such as music, this may be gained via sampling – as with Tunde on Myspace (see page 360). When buying physical goods customers may want the reassurance of a known brand. This helps explain why household names such as Tesco and John Lewis have developed successful online operations.

Figure 29.21 Market share of internet searches

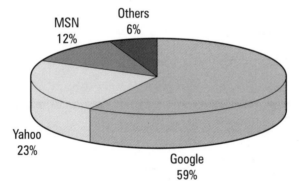

Intermediary sites

Although the internet can reduce the need for intermediaries in the supply chain a growing number of specialist sites are providing customer information, product comparisons and booking services. For example, www.moneyfacts.co.uk gives best buys for bank accounts, loans and mortgages and www.moneysavingexpert.com, run by Martin Lewis, the TV and radio broadcaster, tells consumers what to buy, what not to buy and how to take revenge on companies. Paypal is a web service that transfers funds free between any two parties with e-mail. It does a quarter of all eBay transactions. Again, see the Tunde case study on page 360.

Online services

Physical goods (printers, CDs, cars) need to be transported to the buyer in exactly the same way as goods bought from shops, by mail order or by telephone shopping. Research shows that each item is delivered 1.8 times (can you say why?). Online shopping over Christmas 2006 resulted in 200 million parcels being delivered.

Digital products and services on the other hand can be both purchased and delivered online.

case study 29.7

Get the train online

Rail information and tickets are available directly from the regional rail companies. Alternatively, www.trainline.com is an intermediary site providing these services across the whole rail network.

- Input: We enter our journey details – date, time of departure, destination, single or return.
- Process: The system will search the relevant rail company database and locate relevant services.
- Output: A tailored response appears on-screen, showing a choice of suitable trains with times of departure, details of any connections and times of arrival.

The site should operate in real-time, so that any last-minute changes (cancellations, etc.) are shown – something our printed timetable will not have.

Online ticket booking is paid for by credit or debit card.

As with any site, the usefulness will be dependent upon the amount of traffic on the line (which may affect speed), site design (which affects facility) and the effectiveness of delivery – will your ticket arrive on time, for example?

One regional rail operator sends out tickets three days before travel (leaving time for panic if there is a postal problem) and will not make changes to reservations booked online.

A more satisfactory solution is to e-mail a booking confirmation with a number that can be used to obtain an electronic ticket. Travelocity, the online travel agent, uses this system.

activity

1. Find a site providing booking arrangements such as those above. You may use a rail site, a cinema or theatre, a sports club, etc. Take the booking arrangement up until the point that you pay.
2. Briefly describe the site.
3. Evaluate the service in terms of speed and usability (facility).

Banking
The lower costs associated with e-banking have brought a number of new players into the financial services industry (Virgin, Tesco, Sainsbury's) and increased competition significantly. Online we can instantly view and print details of our account, make payments and transfer money (although we cannot get cash).

 Link

The case study on page 357 shows the advantages.

'Credit tarts' want jam on it
It used to be said that people were more likely to divorce than change their bank – not any more. In the new competitive environment, banks and credit card companies are making highly attractive offers to tempt new customers.

First Direct offered £50 to those opening a current account, whilst card companies might offer 0 per cent interest for the first six months to encourage new customers. In a society with so much personal debt, this can represent a considerable saving.

The internet makes it fast and painless to switch accounts so that a significant number of customers – so-called 'credit tarts' – make the change, and then move on again to the next good deal.

In an attempt to tie customers to their products, First Direct began charging current account customers in November 2006. The way to avoid the charges is to put in a certain amount of cash each month or take out another First Direct product – such as a credit card.

Music

Digital music (as opposed to music on CD, cassette or vinyl) can be downloaded and saved via formats such as MP3. Unauthorised file-sharing over the internet has been the subject of legal battles with Napster, a music site set up by a college student, the first to be sued by the major record companies. Recently, however, the music industry has realised that downloading is here to stay and that it is better to regulate the trade and treat it as an opportunity rather than a threat:

■ Record companies have now set up their own music download sites with payment per track or by subscription, whilst Napster now operates as one of the growing legal download sites with music available only to paying members.

■ The Apple i-Pod has become a huge success on the back of the popularity of both legal and illegal downloading.

■ High street music retailers, such as Virgin and HMV have launched their own download sites (although their files cannot be played on the i-Pod).

case study 29.8

Downloads hit the charts

In January 2007, the UK Official Charts Company included downloaded music in the pop music charts for the first time with the first revamped Top 40 aired on JK and Joel's Radio 1 Chart Show.

Now any music, whether oldies, album tracks or digital-release only, can be included. Downloaders tend to be 'older and richer' and, according to the BPI (British Phonographic Industry), 96 per cent male, so chart music is changing.

Despite the considerable level of illegal downloading that persists, the sale of singles has been transformed by the introduction of downloaded music.

By 2008 it is predicted that 25 per cent of all music sales will be downloads, but oddly there is still a strong niche market for vinyl discs.

Figure 29.22 UK single sales 2004–06

Source: BPI/OCC

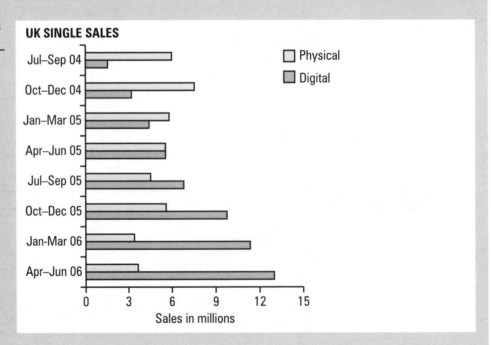

UK SINGLE SALES

activity

1 Are there any unlikely tracks currently in the charts?

2 What exactly is an MP3 file?

3 Name some sites that offer legal downloads of music files. How much do they charge?

Software downloads

New editions of software may be downloaded from the supplier's website as they become available – the latest version of Internet Explorer or drivers for a USB stick might be examples. These are usually free of charge for existing users. Firmware (something between hardware and software originally held in a ROM chip) is now stored in such a way that it too can be updated in this way.

Travel

We have seen that travel information and bookings are increasingly provided online by sites such as Travelocity, e-bookers and Trainline. Online booking enables electronic ticketing, whilst BA enables users to print their own boarding passes. These help offset some of the delays caused by airport security.

Information services

The internet is excellent for transmitting information, although it is important to ensure that it is good quality, by checking the date and source. Documents that are relevant to businesses include:

- electronic journals, newspapers and annual reports. These can be saved to file or printed
- subscription information services from companies such as Mintel, Reuters and Dunn & Bradstreet, available as immediate downloads in various formats.

> **remember**
>
> Look for the security symbol when doing business online.

Methods of reducing risks

Along with the benefits of e-business come a number of significant risks.

---

case study 29.9

Security on the line

HSBC is to review its online security after finding that hackers could access customers' online accounts.

'Keylogger' software is able to capture the keystrokes made on a particular computer. Using these, a hacker can find the password needed to successfully log onto an account. However, HSBC has said that online fraud accounted for only a minor part of total fraud. A bigger problem is that people do not dispose of financial documents properly. Fraudsters can use bank statements and utility bills to 'steal' users' identity and access their bank accounts and credit cards.

Security experts warn that few online bank accounts are safe from determined hackers.

Problems include failings in bank security systems, multiple identity and password checks are needed, and customers not keeping their anti-virus software up to date. Most home computers are vulnerable to software such as spyware and keyloggers.

Gone phishing – with the net

Phishing is a multimillion pound problem. It involves criminals gaining passwords in order to steal funds from internet bank accounts.

The usual method is to send an e-mail that appears to come from your bank asking you to confirm your password on a fake website set up by the thieves. The internet security firm Messagelabs says it is intercepting 50,000 such emails and more than 80 new phishing websites every day. Around £4.5m has already been refunded to about 2,000 customers.

The problem for banks is that the crooks are getting smarter. Cyber crime experts have warned internet banks to take more care with security or run the risk that people will stop using their services.

---

activity

1 Banks tend to keep quiet about cyber crime. Why do you think this is?

2 Identify the possible risks to security in the businesses you have chosen to study. Carry out some research on viruses, worms, etc. Using this research and the information above, produce a leaflet advising customers of potential dangers and measures they should take to counter these. See page 344.

Legal protection and limitations when using the internet for procurement

All businesses operating online or using email are bound by the provisions of the E-Commerce Regulations 2002. These protect customers' interests by placing limitations upon the activities of online traders. The idea is to promote online business by promoting customer confidence in the net.

We provide details of the regulations on page 366.

Use of the internet for promotion

The internet provides an ideal medium for promoting organisations together with their goods and services. Many advertisers are turning to the web in preference to traditional media such as Commercial TV.

The revenue from advertisers means that many facilities on the web are made available to the user free of charge; this is one of the cases made in favour of using adware. Google, Yahoo and other search engines fund themselves via advertising revenue.

Most business websites are designed to promote the organisation and its products. Along the way it may also promote the goods and services of other businesses via banner advertisements along the top or down the side of the site, or pop-ups (advertisements that suddenly appear and obscure part of the screen).

Viral advertising (word of mouth)

News travels fast on the web – like a virus. The Arctic Monkeys became known because their fans spread the word via e-mail, blogs (weblogs) and chatrooms. Will Chase of Tyrrell's Potato Chips believes that this is one of the most effective forms of advertising.

Link registrations

Websites can earn money via 'revenue sharing affiliate schemes'. This is how it works. A website makes an agreement to carry advertising (perhaps banners or pop-ups) carrying a link to the advertiser's site. The host site receives money for each customer who clicks through and makes a purchase via the link.

Direct e-mails

The internet provides a rapid and inexpensive way of contacting customers with newsletters, promotional offers, details of bookings, receipts, password confirmations, etc. A particular advantage is the ability to respond to customers as individuals so that information is targeted.

In the next section (on page 359), we see how cookies and customer databases make this possible.

Use of internet for business communication

E-mail

The same rules that apply to business letters also apply to business e-mails. Some general points:

- The footer should give the business name and address.
- Content must not be discriminatory, illegal or offensive – emails can be sent round the world in seconds. The employer is responsible for staff e-mails and can be sued.
- It is illegal to attach other people's intellectual property without permission, e.g. photographs or articles.
- E-mails can be contractually binding.
- It is illegal to use personal data for direct marketing if you are asked not to do so.

The Regulation of Investigatory Powers Act permits employers to monitor e-mails sent by staff for specific business purposes. This might be done to check for abuse.

Figure 29.23

Digital cameras

Photographs taken with digital cameras have a number of advantages. Most notably, they can be sent via e-mail attachment, posted on websites and the intranet, and manipulated for use in brochures and in-house publications.

Estate agent rightmove.co.uk is able to photograph properties and upload the images to the website or e-mail them to potential clients.

Increasingly mobile phones are being used to capture digital photographs and video images.

Voice-over internet protocol (VoIP)

Telephone calls can be transmitted via the internet. To enable this, specialist software together with a microphone or a handset is connected to the web browser (perhaps MS Explorer or Netscape Navigator). There is potential for considerable savings on long distance calls.

We also look at VoIP on page 336.

Video-conferencing

Video-conferencing involves holding meetings via a video link capable of relaying a picture of the caller as well as the voice. Considerable savings are possible in accommodation, travelling and time, as well as in the associated carbon footprint.

Broadband systems (such as ISDN) give satisfactory results, but participants claim that it is difficult to pick up cues such as body language and asides (notice the delay when a news presenter speaks to the Washington correspondent). Big deals are not usually closed in this way.

Webcams

Webcams (or netcams) are low cost video cameras that can be connected to a computer and relayed via the internet to a website. Those logging onto the site can see images from the camera in real-time (as they happen).

Some small retailers are using webcams to show customers their products. Simon Bennett has installed a webcam in his fish shop in Lyme Regis in Dorset. He uses this to show customers his 'catch of the day' and as a result has been swamped with orders from all over the country. (Source: *The Metro*, 9 January 2007)

A cheap video-conference can be conducted by using a webcam along with Microsoft's NetMeeting software. You may have tried this in an ICT class.

---

assignment focus

To achieve P2, you will need to describe and illustrate through examples how the internet can be used for different types of business activity. In doing this, you should provide at least one example of each of the following:

■ processes involved in setting up an internet-related computer (Suggested activity: produce a booklet explaining the hardware and software needed, the risks of internet use and sensible precautions that might be taken.)

■ conducting a compound search to find business information (Suggested activity: conduct relevant searches to find legislation relevant to an organisation involved in e-business. Bookmark the relevant sites. Summarise the findings.)

■ use of the internet for procurement (Suggested activity: locate online suppliers for one of the businesses you have chosen to study for this unit.)

■ use of the internet for promotion (Suggested activity: design a web promotion for a chosen business. Explain how the promotion will work and where it will be seen.)

■ use of the internet for business communication (Suggested activity: write an e-mail to your teacher/lecturer on the business use and abuse of e-mails. You might write a brief e-mail and attach a file containing the main details.)

To achieve M1, you will need to demonstrate that you can solve internet problems that might occur in six of the activities carried out above. Examples might be system crashing, the firewall denying access to selected web-pages, etc. You will need to provide evidence in the form of screen dumps and witness statements.

Trends in the use of e-business

What are the trends?

In May 2006 the BBC closed down the e-commerce section in its business index because people no longer want to read about e-commerce – they prefer to do it.

The Office for National Statistics reported that online sales by UK businesses (both B2B and B2C) rose from £18.6 billion in 2002 to £103.3 billion in 2005. Figure 29.24 shows the trends in retail (B2C) online sales.

Figure 29.24 Online retail sales in the UK

Source: Verdict Research

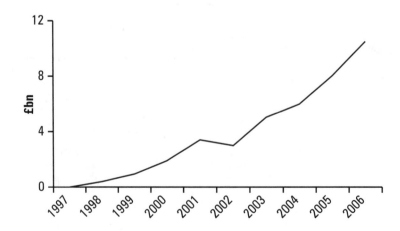

For some items, online sales form a significant proportion of the total (Figure 29.25).

Figure 29.25 Percentage of UK retail sales made online

Source: Mintel

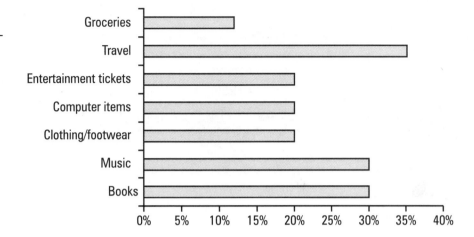

Mathew Hardcastle of eBay gives four reasons for the acceleration of online retailing:

- the growing use of broadband
- people are, as a result, spending more time online than watching TV
- the growth in online advertising
- consumers are more confident about buying over the internet, e.g. methods of payment are now seen as more secure.

People do not just buy small items – eBay sells a car in Britain every two minutes. At the time of writing, traditional shopping chains such as Tesco, John Lewis and Next are getting involved.

Why do businesses develop an online presence? Many of the advantages to a business of using a website are shown in case study 29.10.

case study 29.10 — Internet banking aims for net profits

The financial services industry provides a good example of e-tailing (online retailing). Traditionally any business wishing to enter the banking industry would need to acquire and maintain a network of branches in expensive high street locations.

From the 1980s the growth in popularity of postal and telephone accounts showed that there was a market for home banking. Internet banking is a logical extension of this trend.

In recent years new players such as Virgin, Tesco, Sainsbury's and the Prudential (through Egg) have entered the market as 'clicks'-only banking businesses. The existing banks have responded by moving into 'clicks and mortar' through their own e-banking brands, such as Cahoots (Abbey National) and Smile (Co-operative Bank).

Figure 29.26 Why e-banking is attractive to customers

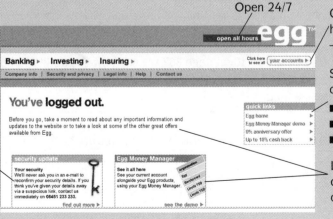

Open 24/7

Convenience of home banking – no queues

Shop around for better deals resulting from:
- lower costs
- more competition
- increased choice

Less pressure to make a decision. Work at your own pace

Security through:
- passwords at log-in
- encryption of details

Advantages of e-banking to the banks:

There is an initial cost of setting up the site but thereafter:

- e-banking avoids the expense of running branches in expensive high street locations
- staff costs are reduced – the customers browse the site and serve themselves. The site processes transactions automatically
- the sites have a global presence and are always open to take business
- more competitive offers result from lower costs
- the site is maintained centrally and so should be up to date.

activity

1   Not all consumers will have access to e-commerce.
- a)   Which groups in society are less likely to have internet access? (See the chart in Fig. 29.31 on page 365.)
- b)   Which groups may have internet access but not the ability to buy online? (Think what you need to make an online purchase.)

2   Explain any other disadvantages of buying online from the customer's viewpoint.

Marketing benefits

Round the clock promotion to a global audience

A website is open for business 24/7 (24 hours a day/7 days a week).

case study 29.11   **Net Cord**

Tennis becomes a national obsession for two weeks each year during the Wimbledon lawn tennis championships. However, the Wimbledon All England Club website provides the 'brand' with constant, year round, global availability.

activity

Visit the site of the Wimbledon All England Lawn Tennis Club, or if you prefer, the site of another sports club.

1   To what extent is the club engaged in e-commerce?

2   What other financial benefits will the site bring to the club?

Increased flexibility of location

A dot.com business is free from the need to maintain a 'bricks and mortar' presence in expensive high street premises. Such businesses can locate so as to gain cost savings.

 Link

In case study 29.10 on page 357 we see how the ability to build a business without a physical high street presence has reduced barriers to entry into the financial services industry.

Data collection and use in the marketing mix

Successful marketing involves targeting customers effectively and a website provides an effective means of capturing and storing the necessary data. As customers use a site, their details are recorded, e.g. when they register, make enquiries or make purchases.

This information is stored in a database and used to build up a picture of an individual's buying habits.

Figure 29.27 A website provides an effective means of capturing and storing customer data

Name	Age
Lee J	32
Mo R	23
Phu S	29
Rowe T	45
Simon P	60
Timms B	39

The 'Front-End' – the web page on screen is the interface between the user and the web-site software

Customer details →

The 'Back-End' – the part the user cannot see. This may include a database of user details on the web-server

The customer profile built up from the database can also be used to attract revenue from companies wishing to advertise on the site.

Capturing data is possible whenever a site allows for user interaction. For example:

- The 'contact us' facility allows users to make queries or pass on opinions about the business.

- On sites where goods and services can be ordered and paid for by plastic card, the customer will have to create an account by inputting a password and a user ID, input details of the order, the delivery address and debit or credit card details for payment.

- Sites providing free information, such as newspapers, educational sites, football clubs, etc., may still require users to register in order to monitor site usage. Users may need to log in at subsequent visits using their ID and password.

Suits you, sir!

Terrestrial TV stations such as ITV1 are rapidly losing advertisers to the internet. One reason is that advertisers are unhappy with viewing figures, but another is that promotions on the web can be targeted more precisely.

In August 2006, for example, e-Bay signed up with Google to create a range of online adverts tailored individually to each of its customers. Whenever a customer searches for a product on eBay, the Google search engine will come up with relevant promotional links. A 'click-to-call' feature will enable the shopper to talk to the advertiser via online phone links at the click of a button.

At the time of writing, Google is the most successful advertising-funded internet company.

Source: Adapted from the *Guardian*, 29 August 2006

Opportunities for competitor analysis

Businesses will routinely act as mystery shoppers by visiting the sites of their competitors. They will even buy their products to compare quality, prices and customer service. Comparing invoice numbers between purchases provides a means of estimating a competitor's monthly sales.

Feedback from customers

A business will succeed by keeping its customers satisfied. In a constantly changing market environment, it is vital for suppliers to understand what they are doing well and how they might improve. A feature of most sites will be the 'contact us' section allowing for customer comments.

Almost every page on BBC Online, for example, has a link to a feedback form, the 'Tell Shell' forum is another example, whilst Sainsbury's invites its customers to 'Tell Justin'.

Opportunities to communicate with customers

Online communication provides an opportunity to recognise individual customers and to speak to them directly. A cookie is a file that is saved onto a user's hard disk when they first access a website. It enables the site to recognise the user whenever they log in and then to welcome them by name on later visits ('Hello, Roger ...'). The cookie can track the searches that a customer makes, record what they buy and add these details to those already on the customer database.

According to *My Big Idea* by Rachel Bridge, it is between eight and 20 times cheaper to sell to existing customers than to find new ones. Communicating with customers, understanding their needs and meeting expectations for price, quality and service will help build brand loyalty and repeat business.

Some customers object to cookies as an 'intrusion' and most web browsers allow them to be disabled.

case study 29.12 — Tunde Jegede

Tunde Jegede, performer and composer, produced his first album 'Lamentation' in 1995 and his second 'Malian Court Music' the following year.

Figure 29.28 Tunde Jegede

Both recordings were made by his own company with pressing and distribution outsourced. The marketing was impressive, with a BBC2 documentary and radio exposure. Meanwhile 'Lamentation' was nominated Wire magazine album of the year and gained plaudits from acts such as the Pet Shop Boys. The problem, said Tunde, was one of 'synchronicity' – of tying in the marketing with physical distribution. CDs were not in the shops when people wanted them and the shops did not know where the music should be displayed: 'When music falls between categories it gets lost.'

Tunde is one of the growing number of musicians who has decided that the internet is the place to market his music. He uses his own site www.tundejegede.com and has a presence on myspace.com. Both sites have links with iTunes and Paypal.

Tunde sees a number of advantages in selling online:

Figure 29.29 How Tunde uses the internet to market his music

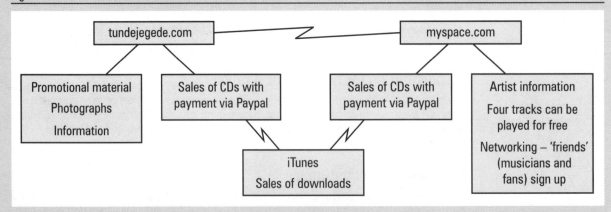

■ Marketing:

- It provides a global shop window from three sites with 24/7 availability for information and products.
- Different musical classifications are possible for people with different tastes. On iTunes 'Lamentation' is classical, 'Still Moment' is New Age.
- 'Still Moment' appears on the first page of the European iTunes cross-over site. This attracts interest and boosts sales on a scale not previously possible.
- Customers can try out tracks before buying.

- Distribution:
  - iTunes has world-wide distribution for downloads.
  - For CDs the market now comes to Tunde. Paypal (a secure third party site) enables customers to pay.
- Cashflow:
  - CDs are no longer pressed ahead of demand. Customers now pay before delivery.
  - Downloads have no cost to Tunde (although he still prefers the quality of CDs).

With thanks to Tunde Jegede.

activity

1 Why is online selling appropriate for niche products such as Tunde's?
2 Online music sales are hugely popular. As a customer, explain the advantages and disadvantages of buying music online.
3 It has been claimed that things last for ever on the internet ('The Long Tail'). Explain what this means with reference to music.

Cost benefits of going online

There are a number of clear savings to be made from online operations.

Reduced staffing costs

Staff costs are reduced as people are replaced by technology (notice in the John Lewis example (page 368) how 150 employees outperformed 700 over a Christmas period. The customers browse the site and serve themselves. The site processes these transactions automatically.

Flexibility of location

The opportunities for flexibility in location bring reduced storage and premises costs. Flexible location may also bring tax advantages. Tesco, for example, is able to avoid charging VAT on CDs by basing its online sales operation overseas. Their original operation was in Jersey but was moved to Switzerland in March 2007 following a change in local laws.

Reduced requirement for premises

Traditionally businesses have traded from 'bricks and mortar', i.e. a physical base, such as a factory, warehouse or shop. Internet trading has enabled a shift 'from bricks to clicks' – to electronic trading by clicking on a mouse. Here location becomes less important.

This has given rise to two new possibilities:

- 'clicks'-only businesses – the dot.com organisations – selling only online. Successful examples include book and music retailer Amazon, computer retailer ebuyer and auction site eBay
- 'clicks and mortar' businesses operating part physical and part electronic trading. Increasingly established B2C businesses including the major supermarkets, the retail banks and a growing number of high street stores are developing internet sales alongside their traditional high street operations.

Economies of scale are made possible by global sales. Where fixed costs (such as rents, electricity and salaries) are spread over a large volume of products, each item attracts a smaller proportion of the cost. Further economies can be achieved by the bulk-buying which becomes possible where orders are large.

Cashflow advantages

Cashflow advantages arise from a number of factors. Online novelty card company Moonpig.com is a good example:

- Internet customers place orders and pay immediately by plastic. The product is price insensitive – people will pay a lot for a unique card.
- Very small stocks are carried (paper, card, envelopes, etc.) and more is ordered as needed. Suppliers allow 60 days credit.
- The technology helps keep down costs of staffing and operations are conducted from small premises.

Chief executive, Nick Jenkins, believes that printing cards is almost like printing money.

The disintermediation of the supply chain (cutting out the middleman)

Efficiencies in the supply chain are encouraged by online trading. Dell is a good example of how direct selling from manufacturer to the consumer may be encouraged. No Dell products are available in the shops, yet the company succeeds by combining a strong brand with keen pricing.

For digital services, with no need for physical delivery, there is a distinct price advantage: Digital music sites need only one copy of a track to deliver an indefinite number of downloads, the low cost airlines easyJet and Ryanair sell their flights directly online to avoid travel agents' commission; users print out their own details.

The 2004 Office for National Statistics survey into e-business noted that many businesses now routinely refer customers to websites rather than to their address or telephone number. We can see the advantages for business in educating us to do this and in discouraging us from contacting them directly. (If you telephone or write to a business as part of your research, you may well be told, 'It's all on our website'. How helpful this is depends upon the site itself and how good you are at searching it.)

Benefits to customers

A significant number of people still do not use the internet and many continue to prefer the reassurance of personal service. However, assuming that they have internet access, are confident with it and the technology is working, the customer should also gain. There are a number of potential advantages.

24/7 availability

This means that we can shop when it pleases us: day, night, weekend or bank holiday.

Flexibility of location

The internet is a 'one-stop shop' that can be used at any time, from home, office and, increasingly, on the move. There is no need to travel and should be no need to queue. Information can be retrieved from sources across the globe, downloaded, printed or saved.

Working hours in the UK are amongst the longest in the EU so that home shopping provides significant attractions.

Easier cost comparisons

Internet users can rapidly compare product prices, either by moving from the site of one provider to another, or by using one of the sites dedicated to making price comparisons.

- www.uswitch.com will compare the cost of gas and electricity.
- www.moneysavingexpert.com provides a comparison of bank accounts, investments, loans and mortgages.
- www.doorone.co.uk provides a comparison of various household goods.

Lower prices

Insurance from Churchill ('give the dog a phone') is 10 per cent cheaper if bought online, the interest rate earned from Abbey's online bank, Cahoot, is higher than on their other accounts. In general the lower operating costs of internet trading are likely to translate into lower prices for customers.

Figure 29.30

Add to this the ease with which internet traders can enter the market. This leads to more customer choice as we saw in our study of the banking industry on page 353. Increased competition helps keep prices down.

An ITV investigation by Trevor McDonald, not surprisingly, found the internet to be both cheaper and significantly faster – hours compared to days – when shopping for the same range of goods.

Personalised offers

The customer database and the use of cookies can be used to encourage further purchases. Ebuyer, for example, sends personalised e-mails with details of new offers, Tesco.com identifies 'favourites'. Amazon identifies books or CDs likely to be of interest when the user logs on; 'if you have already bought an iPod we will display the latest headsets'.

Operational implications of trends on organisations

Customers on the internet are looking for convenient and rapid access to information and products that are available 24/7. They have come to expect increased choice and lower prices. The global reach and searching capabilities of the internet also gives customers the chance to locate specialist items; those things that are impossible to find in the high street either because they are too rare or because they are a minority taste.

Gone fishing – but without the net

Before the internet became widely accessible, *Yellow Pages* ran an award-winning advert showing a fictional character called J.R. Hartley trawling second-hand bookshops in search of a copy of *Fly Fishing*; an out-of-print book that he had written many years before.

His problem was solved by the 'Good Old *Yellow Pages*' which supplied a list of second-hand bookshops in the area. He still had to telephone each shop on the list, and even then his search was restricted to the local area. He was lucky to find a copy.

Had the internet existed, JR could have searched for the book itself across the world. The traditional *Yellow Pages* has now been supplemented by an online version that enables users to search locally or nationwide for businesses, contact details, maps, car parks and consumer advice.

Operational implications of trends on organisations

Online selling is not without its problems and businesses may have to do some things differently.

Mouse-trap?

The two most common complaints from online customers are:

- not being in when the delivery arrives (remember the average parcel is delivered 1.8 times)
- ordering goods that turn out to be unsuitable.

Online retailers find that a higher percentage of goods are returned than for high street shops where the customer can examine products before buying.

John Lewis believes that all online businesses will have this problem. However, they identify three things that they can do to avoid this unwelcome cost:

- Make sure that customers have enough information when they buy.
- Understand how to help customers choose correctly.
- Have enough staff to deal with phone calls and customer requests.

The Citizens Advice Bureau says there is a problem of trust. Customers need to be able to speak to the trader if there is a problem.

Ikea, the Swedish furniture company, is being cautious about going online for these reasons. It wants to get it right.

Digivate, a company that builds e-commerce websites, sees the need to make online retailing a more exciting experience. Some sites already try this – the Dulux 'paint a virtual room' feature is an example.

Source: Adapted from *The Sunday Times*, 22 October 2006

E-business has brought pressure upon traditional retailers as they have encountered competition from new providers.

Strategic implications of trends on organisations

The internet is the T in PESTLE and businesses that are affected have to respond to the challenge by refocusing their businesses. In 2005, for example, illegal downloads cost the UK music industry £414m. We have seen that the major record stores have decided to set up their own music download sites in response, that traditional banks now offer internet accounts and that high street retailers are also beginning to sell online.

Sony has adapted its portable music players to allow it to use MP3 files and compete with the Apple iPod (it previously used its own Atrac format).

Although e-commerce is accelerating rapidly, it accounted for just 3.1 per cent of UK retail sales in 2006. Analysts suggest that it could reach 7 per cent by 2010 and then slow down. 'Online is just another channel to market albeit a pretty big one and one that is having a lot of impact in some product areas.' However, businesses are unlikely to be able to ignore the web.

Table 29.3 Some winners and losers

Winners	Losers
Tesco: the first supermarket to make a profit from its internet service, www.tesco.com. In 2006 online grocery profits were £56.2 million. Tesco Direct has launched a second online service to sell non-food goods.	HMV: Profits down 20% in 2006 because it did not anticipate the online threat from iTunes and Amazon.com. It now has its own download site.
John Lewis: made big online profits in 2006 and they look set to grow. Furniture and electrical goods did well with a rush on flat screen TVs for the football World Cup in Germany.	Dixons: falling profits caused Dixons to close down all high street branches in April 2006. It now operates online only.
	Woolworths ignored the internet at first and paid the price. Its internet operation will now enable customers to shop online and collect goods at the stores.

For PESTLE, see Unit 1, pages 43–51.

Implications of trends on customers

Not everyone has access to the internet (Figure 29.31). A number of people do not see it as relevant to their lives, whilst others give cost or lack of skills as the reason.

Figure 29.31 People in the
UK who have never used the
internet

*Source: Internet Access – House-
holds and Individuals,* 2006 (Office
for National Statistics)

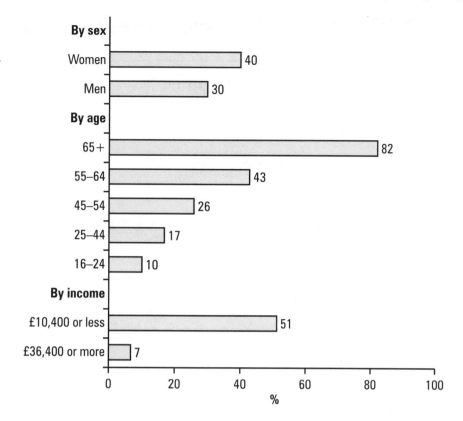

The lower a person's income the less likely they are to have used the internet. Not surprisingly older people are also less likely to be users.

The increasing trend for organisations to place essential information on websites and to offer better deals for online users is clearly putting certain sections of the population – notably the older and the poorer – at a disadvantage.

As demand for traditional services is hit, some may find it more difficult to access a full range of services.

'2,500 more Post Offices to close'
The government has announced that another 2,500 post offices will close by 2009 because fewer people are using them.

Trade Secretary Alistair Darling told MPs that losses were running at £4 million a week with 4 million fewer customers than 2 year ago. He said 'Internet, e-mail and text messaging have meant that young and old alike increasingly use the phone or internet banking, cashpoints or direct debits to pay bills.'

Source: Adapted from *The Metro*, December 2006

There is a need for increased education in technical literacy if people are to get the services they need. The launch by the government of UK Online in 2001 aimed to tackle this problem by providing local internet access for those who wanted it.

assignment focus

You will need to study two contrasting businesses which are being affected by competition from e-business.

To achieve P3, you should describe the competitive forces that are driving them to develop or update their use of e-business.

To achieve M2, you should explain how these two businesses have responded (or are responding) by developing their e-business operations. Give reasons why the two organisations have responded in the way they have.

The key features of planning for the use of e-business

Government support

At national level, the government recognises the growing importance of e-business and provides support to help businesses plan for its use. Legislation, help and advice, education and training are all a part of this.

Legislative framework

Changes in technology bring the need for new laws to regulate online traders and protect their customers.

The Electronic Commerce (EU Directive) Regulations 2002

This directive aims to boost e-commerce by promoting consumer confidence. It applies to any business operating online via the web or using e-mail, including both B2B and B2C traders.

Under the directive, an online business must:

- display the business name on its materials
- display the business registration number or proprietor's name (as in a letter)
- show the geographic address (number, street, town and not just a PO box)
- show contact information, such as the business phone number and e-mail address
- show the VAT number (if VAT registered)
- refer to trade or professional recognition schemes, with registration number, if applicable (e.g. 'Member of The Association of British Travel Agents')
- provide clear information on price, tax and delivery
- show clear terms and conditions and acknowledge orders.

The Consumer Protection (Distance Selling) Regulations 2000 as amended by the Consumer Protection (Distance Selling) (Amendment) Regulations 2005

These regulations relate to businesses selling online, by mail order or by telephone to consumers. They do not apply to business to business transactions.

The key points are:

- Clear information about terms and conditions must be provided to the consumer before a purchase is made. Extras such as VAT and carriage must not be added after the consumer has decided to purchase.
- The consumer must be provided with a written confirmation of order following a purchase.
- There is a 'cooling off' period of seven working days for most goods, although perishable or digital goods may be exceptions. Customers must be informed of their right to cancel with no charge, although it may be permissible to charge for carriage on cancelled goods.

The Office of Fair Trading conducts 'sweeps' of the internet in order to identify and crackdown upon rogue traders who are ignoring the law.

Data Protection Act 1998

This applies to any business that collects information about people (employees, customers, visitors, etc.) such as names, addresses and phone numbers. This information may be paper-based or stored on computer.

Under the Act, a business must:

- state honestly how the data collected will be used. A Privacy Statement may be displayed to make this clear
- register with the Information Commissioner, a government official that oversees data protection. The cost of registration is £35 per year (2007)
- not export the data outside the EU without permission from the data subject (i.e. the person on whom the data is held)
- keep the data secure, reveal it and delete it if requested by the data subjects.

Government help and advice for e-business

Government sources of help and advice to e-business include:

- the Department of Trade and Industry (DTI) – a range of business information and advice about e-communications is provided via its website

- Business Link – the government enterprise agency provides information and advice to small businesses via a network of local Business Link offices. There is an e-commerce section on its website

- information on the Data Protection Act is available from the website of the Information Commissioner

- grants – some local authority small business promotion schemes make e-commerce funding available up to a maximum of £1,000. Business Link has a page dedicated to finance and grants.

- DTI – www.dti.gov.uk
- Business Link – www.businesslink.gov.uk
- Information Commissioner – www.ico.gov.uk

Education and training

Government ICT education and training initiatives are delivered through schools and colleges, where there is a growing emphasis on the application of ICT in teaching and learning.

In addition to online help and information, local Business Links also provide a variety of e-business courses tailored to the needs of local organisations. For example:

---

e-marketing and e-commerce £30

What you will learn in 3 hours

- Search engine marketing, online advertising and how to write interesting advertising copy
- How to analyse past results to guarantee a return on future investment
- How to drive traffic to your website
- Benefits of e-commerce to your business

Specialist e-business training is a growth area (a PESTLE opportunity) for private sector providers. Type 'education+e-business' into Google and you will find pages of sites offering internet-related training courses.

Planning for e-business at organisational level

Careful planning for online operating will be critical to its success.

Strategic decisions

Top management will decide at board level on the aims and objectives of a move to online trading. For example, the directors of a traditional retailer looking at a move into 'clicks and mortar' might consider:

- Do we actually need an online business? Woolworths took the view that it was not necessary until falling sales caused it to change its mind in late 2006.

- Which items will be sold online? The supermarkets began with groceries, but having seen the potential have now moved into non-food items.

- How will the online business fit with the traditional business? PC World, for example, sells online but customers come to the stores to view and collect. John Lewis delivers through its partner Ocado and Amazon uses Royal Mail, whilst other suppliers use a variety of private courier services.

- Should we be 'clicks and mortar' or a 'clicks-only' business? Dixons, for example, has responded to the e-business revolution by becoming internet only; no high street Dixons stores remain.

John Lewis – mission possible

The John Lewis Partnership is divided into the John Lewis department store business and Waitrose supermarkets. Its mission is to run the business 'for the happiness of its members', i.e. the 65,000 partners, or workers, who own the business and share the profits. The business boasts that it is 'never knowingly undersold' – you can't find the same item cheaper elsewhere.

The organisation retains its values but has changed with the times. In 2001, John Lewis still refused to accept credit cards, closed on Mondays as well as Sundays and took no interest in the internet. After four years of declining profits, senior management drew up a plan. There would be more focus on customers, improved marketing (with own-brand products renamed John Lewis instead of Jonelle), revamped stores and … online sales.

Whilst many retailers made a slow start to Christmas 2006, John Lewis took record profits. The online business was a major success with John Lewis Direct run by 150 employees taking more cash per week than the Oxford Street store (650,000 sq. ft. of the best retail space in Britain) employing 700 staff. The online operation sells 20,000 product lines as against 300,000 in a John Lewis 'physical' store.

The success of the online operation has to be seen as part of the whole – people buying by internet need to be sure what they are buying and that it is secure. The evidence is that customers trust the John Lewis brand, its values, quality and pricing. In September 2006 Waitrose, also with online sales delivered by Ocado, was named the 'greenest supermarket chain' by the National Consumer Council.

activity

What were the competitive pressures that forced John Lewis to think about developing e-business operations?

Location of manufacture and service provision

Businesses have much more flexibility in their choice of location when business is online. There is, for example, the option to locate in low cost areas where this is appropriate.

- *Location of manufacture* Improved communication links with suppliers makes it possible to outsource manufacture to low-cost producers across the world. James Dyson's relocation of manufacture from Malmesbury to Malaysia is an example.

- *Location of service provision* The outsourcing of call centre provision (see case study 16.3, page 292) to India is a cost-saving measure. On the other hand, John Lewis operates its online business from Chelsea in West London – by no means the cheapest location – but this is because it already owns the premises (a former Peter Jones store).

Business process re-engineering (BPR)

BPR is the introduction of improved business processes, organisation and culture. It is claimed that a change to a customer-centred approach can bring significantly improved performance.

Internet technology can support BPR in many ways: software can be used to gather information on customers (so-called data mining), to analyse flow of work within the organisation and to set up business simulations used to predict results.

BPR is part of the service@swansea e-service project introduced in 2004 and the council expects to be making £3.8m a year in savings by 2008. However, a trades union official said:

'We would suggest that BPR is a euphemism for job losses because it identifies savings as a result of the introduction of the new technology – in terms of customer contact services and in terms of back office support, in payroll, personnel and finance.'

Redefining of the supply chain

Business to business online communication enables the sourcing of goods and services through more responsive links with the supply chain (the chain of businesses involved in bringing a product from the producer to the customer). This allows delivery from the supplier just-in-time (JIT) to meet customer demand.

As a result, e-tailing businesses do not need to carry large stocks— sites such as Amazon and ebuyer show their stock levels online. Lower stock also reduces the associated storage costs of rent, insurance, warehouse wages, damage to goods and obsolescence.

The net also makes possible rapid online connections with the various links in the supply chain. For example, a business selling on the internet can take an online order from a customer, use the internet to source the product from the supplier (either a manufacturer or wholesaler), arrange with a courier (such as UPS or Royal Mail) for delivery, provide delivery dates and enable the customer to track the progress of the order.

Investment in information technology

Clearly an organisation must invest in effective equipment and update this as required.

Laura Tenison owns JoJo Mamam Bebe, the baby clothes company. She says that technology is vital and must work. On one occasion her company lost £20,000 worth of online orders because the computers were unable to cope with demand. It would have cost less than this to upgrade the system.

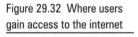

assignment focus

Look in the annual report of the businesses you are studying. How many years is the computer equipment deemed to be useful before it is written off?

(Hint: Look in the 'accounting policies section' under 'depreciation' and the assignment focus on page 203)

Acquisition and development of appropriate skills

The human resources plan must take into account the need to recruit, train and retain staff with appropriate skills. At high levels within the organisation exceptional staff may be 'head-hunted' (or enticed away from their present employer).

ICT is continually developing so that regular skills audits and updating will be necessary to keep staff abreast of changes in technology and familiar with new software.

Planning for use of e-business at individual level
Growth of home computing

Computer ownership has steadily grown since the 1980s when affordable home computers first came onto the market. Alongside this, the government has promoted computer literacy in schools so that students have adapted readily to the internet revolution.

By 2006, almost 60 per cent of households had home internet access (page 342) and for those without the internet there exists a variety of other ways of getting online (Figure 29.32).

Figure 29.32 Where users gain access to the internet

Source: Office for National Statistics, 2006

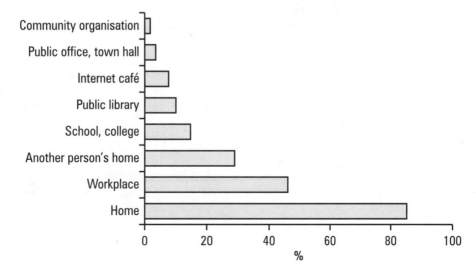

The pattern is not consistent and varies with region, income and age. We have seen that the benefits of choice and cost brought by the internet are less likely to be available to older people and those on lower incomes. To counter this, a number of schemes have been introduced to help people at a local level.

UK online

UK Online centres started out in 2001 when the Department for Education and Skills (DfES) identified the growing gap between those with a PC and those without. People who could afford it were using computers and the internet to do lots of useful and interesting things, while others without the same opportunities were being left behind.

The DfES started UK Online centres to provide computer access to people in the community and help them learn new skills. Centres were located in libraries, community centres and schools. Initially there were about a thousand centres around the country – now we have over 6,000.

These days, UK Online centres are part of a wider network of learning venues run by the University for Industry (Ufi), which includes learndirect centres and other further education sites such as colleges. This has created a single network which gives large numbers of people access to the internet and e-government services.

Every UK Online centre is unique. From state-of-the-art centres with 200 PCs, to the small room at the back of a church hall which has just one or two computers, each one plays its part in making a positive contribution to the community, by helping all sorts of people learn new skills.

Source: UK Online; www.ufi.com/ukol

Employability and ICT skill requirements

Employers will assume that students leaving school and college will be ICT literate. In an information-based economy with a growing service sector such skills are likely to be essential. We have seen that increasingly internal communication is via e-mail and that intranet use is growing.

Higher level technical work, such as setting up and maintaining computer networks and website design and site maintenance, requires specialist skills.

Increase in flexible working models

Internet communication enables changes from the traditional patterns of working. Increasing use of websites, extranets and e-mail enables:

- teleworking – this has been used for some years by companies such as BT. Employers benefit from lower office costs whilst employees avoid the cost and time spent travelling

- job sharing – where there are clear systems it is possible for two or more people to share one job, perhaps working on alternate days.

We discuss flexible working in detail, including teleworking and job sharing, in Unit 16, page 284.

Secondments

Internet-based services are frequently outsourced to specialist providers. Employees from the hiring firm may second employees to work with the new provider for a period of time

E-services are being developed by local councils across the UK. The need to bring in private sector firms to run the services has resulted in hundreds of council IT staff being outsourced to the private sector.

In one arrangement, Bradford City Council agreed for staff to be seconded to the private firm running the IT service – the staff would remain council workers but would work within the private organisation for an agreed period of time.

Contracting

Transaction costs (the costs of doing business) are often cheaper outside the organisation. It becomes worth outsourcing (or contracting) work to outside organisations.

De-skilling and re-skilling

No job is for life. Rapid changes in technology mean that existing skills are no longer required. Employees are de-skilled as computers take over from people; this is one area in which e-businesses can make cost savings.

In response, employees must constantly retrain and develop new skills in order to keep up with developments.

---

assignment focus

To achieve P4, you will need to describe with examples:

- how the government supports e-business developments. You should mention legislation, support, advice and grants, and education and training

- how and why businesses make strategic plans for e-business

- how and why individuals could plan to take advantage of e-business, e.g. what opportunities exist for using and for learning to use e-business.

To achieve D1, you should:

- look at an organisation that has become engaged in e-business. Assess its progress so far and make justified recommendations for further development. You should use factual data about business performance and current trends it might take advantage of

- recommend with reasons how you could improve your use of the internet and why you might wish to do this.

Starting a small business

This unit covers:

- Presenting the initial business idea using relevant criteria
- The skills and development needed to run the business successfully
- The legal and financial aspects that will affect the start-up of the business
- Producing an outline business start-up proposal

According to businessdynamics (the business education and enterprise charity), 'One in three young people want to work for themselves.' Is this true of the students in your group? Are you one of these?

This unit helps you to identify the skills needed to run a successful small business and the skills you may need to develop. You will need to identify a business idea and consider how it will be financed, what the market and competition are, and the legal factors that may be involved. Finally, you will look at how to write a proposal for the business.

<table>
<tr><th>To achieve a **Pass** grade the evidence must show that the learner is able to:</th><th>To achieve a **Merit** grade the evidence must also show that the learner is able to:</th><th>To achieve a **Distinction** grade the evidence must also show that the learner is able to:</th></tr>
<tr><td>**P1** present the initial business idea using relevant criteria</td><td>**M1** explain and justify methods used to identify the target market for the proposed business</td><td>**D1** present a comprehensive business proposal that addresses all relevant aspects of business start up</td></tr>
<tr><td>**P2** describe how to identify the target market</td><td>**M2** analyse the development needed to run the business successfully</td><td></td></tr>
<tr><td>**P3** describe the skills needed to run the business successfully and what areas require further development</td><td>**M3** assess the implications of legal and financial aspects that will affect the start up of the business</td><td></td></tr>
<tr><td>**P4** describe the legal and financial aspects that will affect the start up of the business</td><td></td><td></td></tr>
<tr><td>**P5** produce a written outline proposal for starting up a new small business following an acceptable business model</td><td></td><td></td></tr>
</table>

grading criteria

Presenting the initial business idea using relevant criteria

Why work for yourself?

Your answer to this is likely to include:

- 'To be my own boss'
- 'To get job satisfaction'
- 'I can make more money that way'

There could be negative reasons such as:

- 'Can't get a job that I like'
- 'There isn't much work round here'.

Can you suggest any others?

businessdynamics concludes that, 'Enterprise certainly isn't for everyone. It is insecure, frustrating and exhausting, but it's also exciting, challenging and rewarding.'

Certainly the popularity of TV programmes such as Dragon's Den have shown that there is no shortage of people with initiative who are willing to put their ideas on the line. These programmes also show that it is important to think these ideas through.

It is unlikely that a new business will just appear. The owner(s) will have spent many hours thinking through all that will be needed to make it a reality. Financial backing is often needed to cover start-up costs and get the idea off the ground. It will be necessary to make a convincing presentation of the business idea in order to interest a financial backer.

Criteria

In this section we will look at the main criteria that need to be considered in presenting our business idea effectively.

What type of start-up?

A new entrepreneur (one who undertakes the risks of establishing and running a business enterprise) has the option of:

- setting up a new business
- buying an existing business that is up for sale
- buying into a franchise to take advantage of a tried and tested product.

Starting a brand new business

Many entrepreneurs will start-up an entirely new business. This means having the right business idea and bringing it to the marketplace. Involved in this are a variety of practical and legal considerations including finding the funds, getting the right premises and equipment, buying suitable stock, marketing the right product at the right price and delivering it to satisfied customers.

We will look at these in the course of this chapter. We provide a sample business plan on pages 404–411.

Buying an existing business – under new management

Sometimes an entrepreneur may prefer to buy an existing business that comes up for sale. An advantage is that there are likely to be a ready-made client base and fixed assets already in place. There may also be experienced employees and, hopefully, a sound reputation. There are risks too. It is wise to ask, is the previous owner key to the business success? Does the business have a future (why is the owner selling?) and is it worth the asking price?

In Unit 5, we saw that the balance sheet should give a true and fair view of the value of business assets including any goodwill (the value placed on the good name and reputation of the business). Ideally you should study the audited final accounts for the last four years. Remember though that accounts are purely about finance, they will not tell you about conflicts amongst the staff or that a large plc is about to locate nearby and take most of your customers.

See the section on the balance sheet in Unit 5, pages 216–17.

Figure 37.1 MFI, the furniture retailer was sold in September 2006 for £1. Why?

Buying into a franchise

A franchise enables a new entrepreneur to run their own business using an established brand name trusted by customers. This minimises the start-up risk and in addition the franchisor may provide support in fitting out the premises and with regional or national advertising. On the down side, the franchisee will be monitored for quality and, if standards fall, approval to operate may be withdrawn.

'We are highly selective about the franchisees we allow ...'

Source: Domino's Pizza Annual Report, 2006

Burger King franchises are on sale for £70,000. Public concern about healthy eating led to poor UK profits in late 2006 with some of the franchises reported to be in financial difficulty.

Business aims

Success is relative; it must be measured against what a business sets out to achieve.

Link In Unit 1, pages 28–33 we examined the most common strategic aims set by organisations.

Survival is likely to come high on the list in the first three years. A new business with limited resources must be realistic and ask hard questions such as: How much do we need to make each month to break-even? Can we survive the first six months? Can we live off the business in the first year?

Gap in the market

In 1993 Claire Owen lost her job. Despite having a young child, her response was to set up her own award-winning marketing recruitment agency, Stopgap.

Claire believes that any new entrepreneur must have personal self-confidence and enough cash to survive for the first 18 months without drawing money from the business. In her experience, banks are unlikely to lend cash to a brand new business unless it can provide security to guarantee repayment.

Risk

Setting up an enterprise inevitably involves risk. As Figure 37.2 shows, many businesses fail often leaving their owners in financial difficulty. This will be particularly true if the business is a sole trader or partnership with unlimited liability.

Figure 37.2 Business failures in England and Wales, 1999–2004

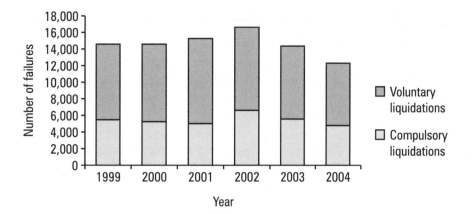

On pages 401–403, we look at how drawing up a business plan will help avoid some of the more predictable problems.

What's the big idea?

The business idea is all-important – this may be an entirely new concept, or a variation on a product that already exists. YouTube.com (sold to Google for £876m in October 2006) was born when two friends found it difficult to send each other digital film clips via the internet.

Paul Cleghorn started TIOTI.com (Tape It Off The Internet) after trying to download the latest series of the US drama The West Wing: 'I thought it would be easy ... it's not, it's a nightmare.' TIOTI tells users where and when shows are available on line. Mr Cleghorn says he was astonished no one had done it already.

case study 37.1 — Innocent drinks – a case of organic growth

Key people

Innocent Drinks was set up in August 1999 by three friends, Adam Balon (sales director), Richard Reed (marketing director) and Jon Wright (operations director). At the time, they all had jobs but were looking for a business idea. They had previously looked at (and rejected): a plastic alternative to house keys (they kept losing theirs) and a way to stop baths overflowing.

The product

They finally came up with an idea for 'smoothie' drinks made only from crushed fruit.

The USP (unique selling point) was that they would use pure ingredients, with no artificial sweeteners or concentrates. They are 'not made from fruit – they are fruit'.

A gap in the market

This is a lifestyle product based on people's increasing interest in healthy eating, and their willingness to pay for it. The three friends found from experience that many of the smoothies they bought in the shops used fruit concentrates rather than whole fruit. They knew that they could make better drinks at home using a blender, but this was very time-consuming and left a lot of washing up. Perhaps cash rich/time poor people would pay for 'natural, fresh, goodness' made easy.

Market research

The friends bought £500-worth of fruit, made up a batch of smoothies and took them to the Jazz on the Green festival in West London.

Instead of a questionnaire, they asked punters to put the empty bottles either into a YES bin (yes they should make the drinks full-time) or a NO bin. The response was overwhelmingly 'yes', so they gave up their jobs next day and formed the company Innocent Drinks.

▶

Funding

The owners' savings did not provide enough capital and they spent nine months looking for backing. No banks were interested. They e-mailed all of their friends and work acquaintances. Eventually they found an American business angel (financial backer), Maurice Pinto; he believed in their idea and supplied the funds.

Development and growth

Innocent sold its first smoothie on 28 April 1999. They had planned to raise more finance but sales grew so quickly that the company immediately became self-financing.

Performance

The figures show that this has been a smooth operation. The company has achieved dramatic growth over eight years of trading with 2006 figures showing:

- 183 employees at offices in: London, Manchester, Dublin, Paris, Amsterdam, Copenhagen
- sales revenue of £80m, with £120m projected for 2007. Sales growth has ranged from 50 to 100 per cent a year
- UK market share of 65 per cent with 1 million smoothies sold a week
- a growing product range, including yogurt, vanilla bean and honey 'thickie'.

Opportunities and threats

The UK market for natural lifestyle foods and drinks is growing and Innocent has plans to freeze the smoothies to produce deserts – a healthy alternative to ice cream. There are also ideas for cosmetics.

Supermarkets have seen the potential and are producing own-label copies.

Corporate image

The company has a strong set of principles. It will not compromise on quality and all ingredients are natural, bottles are 50 per cent recycled plastic (100 per cent is the target), the labels are made of mango-leaf paper.

Ten per cent of profits go to their charity, The Innocent Foundation, set up to fund projects in those areas of the world where the company sources its products.

Innocent uses electric cars and 'green' electricity for production.

The future

Global firms are keen to add ethical brands to their portfolio and are bound to be interested in buying a strong growing brand such as Innocent.

There are a number of precedents. Ben & Jerry's, the American ice cream manufacturer, developed with similar principles to Innocent. Although their advertising retains the small, friendly, home-made feel (the number of nuts you get depends on who threw them in ...), they are now owned by the Anglo-Dutch giant, Unilever. Similarly L'Oriel has bought the Body Shop and Green & Black's chocolate is now owned by Cadbury.

The team at Innocent say they are not ready to sell yet.

activity

1   What suggests that the three friends were the right types of people to form a business?

2   Do you think that they planned the business start-up well, or were they lucky?

3   What is a 'business angel' and why was this one so important?

4   Was primary or secondary market research carried out at the Jazz on the Green festival?

5   Was this a suitable venue for the market research? Why do you think it was chosen?

6   Conduct a SWOT analysis for the company.

7   Explain the term 'lifestyle product'. Give examples of such products that you use (not necessarily food).

For SWOT analysis, see Unit 3, pages 131–32.

Innocent Drinks – www.innocentdrinks.co.uk

USP – competitive edge

Few businesses produce a unique product. Most operate in a competitive market and will need to develop a USP (unique selling point) – the reason why people will buy their products rather than those of their rivals.

Examples of a USP might be:

- competitive pricing – 'never knowingly undersold', 'find it cheaper and we'll refund the difference'
- outstanding customer service – 'no quibble returns policy for unwanted purchases', 'same day delivery', '2 year warranty on parts and labour'
- the product – 'hand-crafted', 'pure wool', 'smooth and creamy'
- the location – 'at a high street near you', 'beat the queues buy online now'.

Often it may be a combination of these and other factors.

case study 37.2

Woodworm – a competitive edge and perfect timing

In 2001, Joe Sillett repaired an old cricket bat that had woodworm. Shortly afterwards he scored a century with it. This became the inspiration for a cricket equipment company he set up the following year.

Joe needed someone special to use his equipment and approached Andrew Flintoff, whose England batting average was only 19 at the time.

The sponsorship of Flintoff followed by that of fellow international Kevin Peterson were timed perfectly as England's ashes win over the Australians in the summer of 2005 turned both players into national heroes.

'The company has grown dramatically because of the endorsement of two role-model figures,' according to Brand Rapport, the sports marketing and sponsorship agency.

The year to September 2006

- Turnover: £2m+ (forecast to double in 12 months)
- Cricket bat sales: 45,000 (up from 15,000 in 2005)
- New offices in Billingshurst, West Sussex will house a cricket and golf showroom
- Six people on the payroll: 'We have pretty much outsourced everything.'
- 15 per cent of the UK and Australian cricket bat market
- A growing product range including accessories (pads, stumps) and clothing

What's next?

A move into the lucrative golfing market with the sponsorship of Ernie Els. Products will include shirts, sweaters, rainwear and summer shorts.

The aim?

Woodworm to be one of the biggest four or five sporting brands in the world: 'We have a proven formula' that can be used for other sports.

activity

1   What is the USP here?

2   Can you think of other products or businesses that benefit from the endorsement of celebrities? What can go wrong with the use of celebrity endorsements?

3   What are the advantages to the company of outsourcing the manufacture of their equipment?

4   Joe Sillet says there is a strong link between the markets for cricketing and golfing equipment. Can you suggest what this is?

Woodworm website – www.woodworm.tv

Business trends – will there be a demand for our products?

The business environment is dynamic (ever changing). Whilst this can threaten existing products, it provides a constant opportunity for new ones. Successful businesses are those most able to identify and support the emerging trends

assignment focus

Which external factors might present an opportunity for the following?

a)   Nicotine patches

b)   Blacks – retailers of outdoor clothes and equipment

c)   Nelson Thornes – educational publishers

d)   A web designer

e)   A training agency helping firms keep up with employment regulations

f)   An estate agent

For small businesses, the local economy is important.

---

remember

PESTLE analysis (see Unit 1, pages 43–51) is a useful way of looking at the factors causing changes in the external business environment. Trends that have given opportunities for new business ideas can be found under all six headings.

Figure 37.3 Balancing personal and business needs

Balancing personal and business needs

Being your own boss will be hard work. You need to be sure what you want from self-employment, whether you have what it takes to succeed and that your personal circumstances will allow you to see it through. What working for yourself does not do (at least at first) is give you lots of time off.

Business and personal needs may well come into conflict, particularly in the early stages. The entrepreneur will often need to put the business first to gain success. There may be sacrifices, but in the long-term there may be significant rewards.

When Justin Cooke set up his media company he was 25. In the early stages, he frequently worked so late at the office that he took his sleeping bag and slept under the desk. Would you do this if your boss at work asked you to? So why did Justin do this?

Business needs	Personal needs
• survival – enough cash to pay the bills. Borrowing may be needed • growth – create profit (sales – cost) and reinvest into the business	• independence – takes own decisions • power – the boss, in charge • achievement – your business is successful. People want your products • high rewards – all of the profit belongs to the owner

---

The section on motivation in Unit 16, pages 293–303 explains those factors most likely make us to work harder.

assignment focus

To achieve P1, you must decide on a business idea, set out an outline business start-up proposal and present this to your group.

In your presentation include those items on the checklist in table 37.1 below. You may wish to use visual display material (e.g. PowerPoint slides or handouts) to emphasise the main points and enhance your presentation.

In preparing to present your business idea, it is a good idea to check yourself against the checklist in Table 37.1. If satisfactory, this will provide the basis for the later, more detailed stages of:

- drawing up the business plan
- checking for feasibility.

Table 37.1 Checklist

Personal aims Why do I want to run a business?	Work for self Self-esteem Independence Power Achievement Other
Personal circumstances	Am I in a position to run a business? Funding Skills and personality Family support Other
Type of business start-up	New Existing Franchise
Business aims convert to SMART targets	Profitability Survival Ethical Other
Business idea	Competitive edge USP
External trends giving rise to demand	PESTLE factors
Balance of business and personal needs	Areas of conflict and proposed solutions

Identifying target market – Is there anyone out there?

The actions and choices of customers are vital for business survival. It is essential to understand who your customers are so that you can target your message effectively and meet their precise product needs.

Market segmentation

The market segment that a business targets may be based upon one or a combination of consumer characteristics, including age, sex, lifestyle, income, culture and ethnicity.

Sometimes a product has an unexpected appeal beyond its intended audience. This can be a bonus:

- The Range Rover, initially designed as a 4 x 4 off-road vehicle for farmers unexpectedly sold to aspirational city dwellers. It became the original 'Chelsea Tractor'.

Wider appeal may, however, present an image problem:

- The stylish checks of Burberry clothes became such a favourite with trouble-making 'chavs' that Leicester nightclubs at one time refused entry to anyone wearing them.

case study 37.3   Woman's Own

From 2004, Marks & Spencer achieved a 41 per cent sales increase in women's lingerie (worth £6.6m a year) by advertising in Celebrity Women's magazines. These adverts targeted women aged 25–45 in the higher income ABC1 socio-economic groups.

It is vital for advertisers to understand which newspapers, magazines, TV programmes their target market will use. The website www.ipcadvertising.com shows the market segments for a variety of magazines. For example:

Woman's Own key facts:

- Launched: 1932
- Circulation: 356,811 weekly (ABC, Jul–Dec 06)
- Female readership: 1,112,000 (NRS, Jul–Dec 06)
- Target market: busy mums and housewives aged 25–54
- Median age of reader: 46
- Full-page advert: £23,650.

activity

1   Who are the market segments for: 18–30 holidays, Saga Insurance, *Loaded* magazine, the Apple i-Pod, the *Sun* newspaper, *The Financial Times*, Innocent Drinks, Waitrose supermarkets?

2   Use www.ipcadvertising.com to view the readership and advertising charges for a variety of different magazines.

Market research

Business plans are driven by the sales we expect to make. It is necessary to research the market in order to forecast what these sales levels will be.

Market research investigates the potential customers of a business and the competition it may expect. This should show us whether there is a market for our product (think of the Yes/No bins for Innocent Drinks). We may find that our product needs to be adapted, or perhaps we need to develop a different product altogether (remember the earlier ideas discarded by the Innocent Drinks team before they developed 'smoothies').

Market research should also confirm the nature of our target market. For example, will our potential customers be male or female? How old are they? What is their occupational group? Ethnic group? Geographical area? Post code? Such knowledge will enable us to market our products more effectively. Why did Innocent Drinks trial their drinks at a music festival?

Primary (or field) research collects data for the first time. Here researchers try to discover the likely demand for a new product through a number of methods, including:

- interviews
- direct observation
- questionnaires and surveys
- trialling products
- sampling the population.

Primary research is covered in detail in Unit 3, pages 117–123.

Page 271 shows the primary research methods used by Eclipse Pottery.

Secondary research uses existing published information to identify business trends.

Sources of information for secondary research are covered in full in Unit 3, pages 123–26.

The BTEC National 'Guidance and units' specification also provides sources of secondary research.

Strengths and weaknesses

SWOT analysis

SWOT analysis (also known as situational analysis) is a technique used in business planning for comparing or matching an organisation's internal strengths and weaknesses with the opportunities and threats found in the external environment. It can help to identify both threats to survival and potential for growth

SWOT analysis is discussed in detail in Unit 3, pages 131–32.

PESTLE factors (the Opportunities and Threats part of SWOT) are discussed in detail in Unit 1, pages 43–51 and in Unit 3 pages 131–33.

---

case study 37.4

Alliance Boots: SWOT analysis

Alliance Boots is a retail company engaged in operating drug stores. The company's business is concentrated in the UK, although it sells its products in more than 130 countries.

Table 37.2 Alliance Boots: SWOT analysis

Strengths	*Weaknesses*
• Strong brand ownership in growth markets • Network of stores in the UK • Restructuring efforts to concentrate on 'core business'	• Uncompetitive on pricing • High dependence on the UK market • Declining profitability
Opportunities	*Threats*
• Grow local customer base through promotions • Trend towards self-medication • Growth in online retailing	• Maturity in certain UK markets • Price competition has pressurised margins (medicines and pharmacies available in supermarkets) • Slowdown in the UK economy

Source: Data Monitor, 7 May 2005

activity

Complete a SWOT analysis for your school or college.

'Green' is the colour of money.

In October 2006 scientists announced that we had four years left to prevent 'irreversible and catastrophic' climate change. The race is on to find solutions – and the rewards could be high.

Some examples of environmental opportunities and threats:

■ Manufacturers will have to produce totally recyclable products.

■ Electrical goods such as TVs and DVD players will no longer be allowed to have standby modes.

■ With the switch from fossil fuels to renewable energy, manufacturers of 'green' fuels will make huge profits. BP (Beyond Petroleum) and Shell are looking at renewables.

■ B&Q are selling solar panels and wind turbines for generating domestic electricity. They also provide an installation service.

Can you suggest others?

Market trends

Some examples of market trends include:

- **P** – the involvement of voluntary organisations in the public services
- **E** – the rise in house prices that is leading to the buy-to-let boom and the import of prefabricated timber dwellings
- **S** – the growth in camping and outdoor activities that has led to the growth of retailers such as Black's (see the case study on page 31) and an increase in members of the Caravan Club
- **T** – the growth in broadband and mobile internet technology that has led to an increase in business online trading (see page 339)
- **L** – the ban on smoking that is causing pub chains to sell off businesses that do not sell food and is threatening bingo halls
- **E** – the demand for renewable forms of energy has led B&Q to stock wind electricity generators (as used by David Cameron) and power companies to sell 'green' electricity (see Innocent Drinks, page 375).

- For PESTLE, see Unit 1, pages 43–51 and Unit 3 pages 132–33.
- In the business plan at the end of the unit we show how the partners at Eclipse identify their target market.

---

assignment focus

To achieve P2, you must describe the methods by which a business might identify its target market. Here you should look at a range of information sources involving both primary and secondary market research.

To achieve M1, you will need to identify the target market for your proposed business and then explain and justify the methods that you have used to do this.

The skills and development needed to run the business successfully

You need not only to be sure what you want from self-employment but also whether you have what it takes to succeed. Could you run a business? According to businessdynamics, 53 per cent of young people will try at some point.

---

assignment focus

1 What sort of qualities do you feel you will need to be an entrepreneur?
2 What sort of assets might you use as 'security' for a loan?
3 Is there anyone in your group whose family owns a business? If so, ask them to give a brief talk on the: type of business activity, form of organisation (sole trader, partnership, etc.), the pros and cons. Why did they set up on their own? Are they pleased that they did?

What does a successful entrepreneur look like? What line of business are these entrepreneurs engaged in?

Skills

Is self-employment right for me?

Setting up in business requires a considerable investment of time, funds and energy. It also requires an ability to take risks. Before going ahead, it is sensible to be sure that you really have what it takes.

Figure 37.4 Richard Branson

Figure 37.5 Meena Pathak

Your own contribution

Everyone has their strengths and weaknesses and it is important to recognise these. Richard Branson's huge empire is built upon his ability to come up with the right ideas, but few of these would have turned into workable business ideas without the support of others. Similarly you must decide on your own role. Can you run the business unaided, do you need a partner with special expertise or will you engage skilled employees?

Depending on your product you may need to consider the following.

Technical/operational skills
These will be necessary for example if you manufacture or are engaged with information technology. James Dyson had such skills but still worked for 14 years to get his bagless vacuum cleaner onto the market. These days, however, production is outsourced to the Far East.

Selling
A business stands or falls on its ability to sell its goods or services. A good idea still needs to be brought to the market as the right product, at the right price, in the right place, and promoted in such a way that the customer is persuaded to buy. How were Innocent Drinks and Woodworm cricket bats able to place their products? Do you have the ability to sell your idea or do you have a partner who does? The creators of Innocent Drinks work as a team with Adam Balon in charge of sales.

Management
Management skills become particularly important once a business takes on employees and an organisation structure develops. There will be a need to communicate ideas, co-ordinate the different functions, listen to feedback, set appropriate targets and monitor progress. When Richard Branson began *Student* magazine – his first venture – he saw himself as a journalist. Increasingly he needed management skills as his business grew. Could you do this?

Recording and checking performance
A business must keep accurate records of its transactions both for management purposes and for legal reasons.

We discuss financial reporting in more detail in Unit 5, pages 197–201.

Computerised accounting systems such as Sage Line 50 are a convenient way of maintaining financial records and producing instant reports. Training in the use of such systems may be an important development need.

Figure 37.6 Purpose of
business records

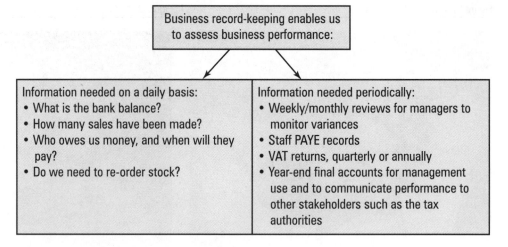

Figure 37.7 A computerised
accounting system

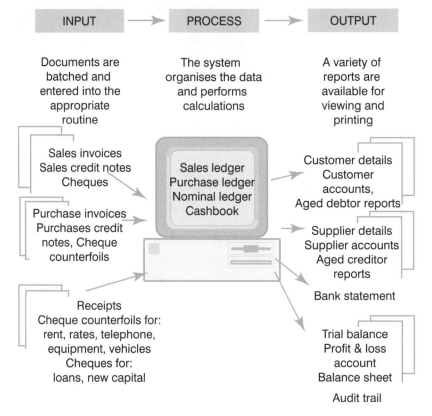

Administration

A business will need to establish systems, i.e. correct ways in which things are to be done. As well as enabling the business to work efficiently and meet customer needs, this will also be necessary ensure that the business fulfils its many legal requirements such as following health and safety procedures, paying staff salaries or maintaining accurate accounts for HM Revenue & Customs.

Previous experience

If you have prior experience of work in business, perhaps as an employee, from a family contact or from a previous venture, this will be an advantage.

If this is your first involvement in business, there will be a 'steep learning curve' and expert support and training may be needed.

Assessing your strengths and weaknesses

What skills do you currently possess?

Business Link, the business support organisation, suggests that would-be entrepreneurs rate themselves against the list of key qualities shown in Table 37.3 (the rating scale is ours).

Table 37.3 Is self-employment right for me?

Desirable personal qualities	Strong	Satisfactory	Weak
Are you prepared for the personal demands of setting up a new business?			
How well do you handle uncertainty?			
Do you have a positive attitude?			
Are you prepared to take chances and gamble on your own ideas?			
Do you have any of the key qualities of a typical entrepreneur? (e.g. initiative, dedication, energy, the right attitude)			
Do you have an absolute determination to succeed?			
Can you bounce back from setbacks and take criticism?			
Are you able to delegate?			
Do you have core business skills? (e.g. communication, number and ICT skills, financial ability, judgement, etc.)			
Are you prepared to spend time carrying out in-depth market research?			
Do you have sufficient funds to set up a new business? (Funds needed can vary considerably.)			
Are you willing to draw on expert help when you need it?			

Source: Adapted from Business Link

---

assignment focus

1 Make a copy of Table 37.3 and complete it to identify your strengths and weaknesses.

2 Now identify your development needs. What additional skills do you need in order to run your proposed business effectively?

Development needs

Once skills gaps have been identified, it is important to plan ways in which these personal development needs are to be met.

Training opportunities – planning and accessibility

Training may involve self-study, research, attending courses or mentoring or **coaching** by professionals. Opportunities may be accessed in a number of ways:

The local college of further education will run a variety of evening courses to meet local skills needs. Relevant subjects may include accounting, web-design, management skills, office and administration skills and business planning.

Small business support agencies such as the local Business Link, the Chamber of Commerce or trade associations will provide information on the various aspects of starting up and running a small business. This may involve personal visits and interviews, alternatively the websites may be accessed via the internet.

The Department for Communities and Local Government sells online courses offered via learndirect.

case study 37.5

Business Link

Business Link is the official government new and small business support agency.

Businesses can register to obtain information tailored to their particular form of business activity and locality. Links are provided to other relevant information sources such as the Department of Trade and Industry (DTI), HM Revenue & Customs (HMRC), Health and Safety Executive (HSE), as well as relevant local authorities and trade associations.

The site acts as a free and accessible one-stop shop for business information providing:

- spreadsheet models for financial forecasting, such as cashflow and break-even
- advice booklets on aspects of business start-up and running
- searches for laws and licences that apply to your own particular business.

activity

1 Log onto the Business Link site: www.businesslink.gov.uk.
2 Identify the sections that will be of particular help to you in your proposed business start-up.

 Link

We also look at sources of business advice on pages 391–93.

Cost implications of development

Whilst much information can be accessed free of charge via the web, college evening courses, perhaps web design, accounting, marketing or management skills, may cost several hundred pounds depending upon teaching hours and available support funding (look at the prospectus of your local FE college). Intensive one-day courses at private training agencies are likely to be more expensive.

Small Firms Training Loans (SFTL) are available from some banks to help pay certain training costs.

Time scales

The T in SMART stands for 'time-related'. Training and development plans must be scheduled so that the appropriate skills are acquired by the time they are needed. Remember that it is vital to be aware of the legal implications of running your business and to obtain any necessary licences before trading can begin.

Link

For SMART, see page 24.

Maximise your strengths

Very few entrepreneurs are strong in all of the areas required. Family support is often essential, yet Karan Bilimoria made a success of Cobra beer despite his father's opposition.

Lena Bjorck arrived in the UK from Sweden with no qualifications or business experience, yet was able to recognise a viable business opportunity. Whilst working as a kitchen porter, she realised that service to customers was poor and that she could do it better. She now runs one of the country's most successful catering companies.

The key is to make the most of your assets and take action to address any gaps. Remember that the skills gap may be bridged by personal development, or by bringing in partners with appropriate skills, by appointing skilled employees or by outsourcing.

To summarise, succeeding in business is about ideas, motivation and ambition. However, you also need the confidence to sell yourself and your ideas; this is clearly easier when you believe that your idea is a good one. Finally, you must know your own strengths and weaknesses and when to take advice.

Figure 37.8 Make the most of your assets and take action to address any gaps

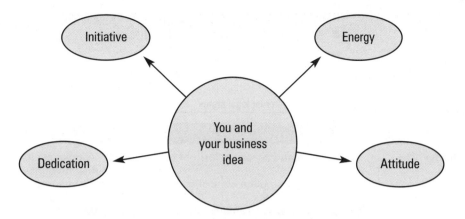

assignment focus

To achieve P3, you must describe the skills needed to run your business successfully. You should also identify those areas where you need further development.

To achieve M2, you must also analyse realistically those development needs that you have identified. For example, how and where you will gain the necessary development, what it will cost and when it will be completed. You should identify any on-going needs, such as the need to keep up with changes in the law.

You may use a time line or Gantt chart to show that your development will be completed in readiness for the business launch or by the appropriate point in the first financial year.

See page 277 for an example of a Gantt chart.

The legal and financial aspects that will affect the start-up of the business

Legal aspects

The legal status of the business

The choice of legal status for your business will depend upon:

- the funds required to set up and run the business
- the type of business activity (e.g. some professional associations do not allow their members to form limited companies)
- the level of risk involved (limited liability may be needed)
- whether you wish to remain in personal control.

We also look at legal status in Unit 1 on pages 14–15.

Whether you decide to start up a new business or buy an existing business, your enterprise will be small-scale so that your choice of legal status is likely to be one of those listed in Table 37.4. Notice the different levels of liability for business debts; this may be important.

Contracts – trading terms and conditions

In buying and selling goods and services your business will enter into legal contracts with customers and suppliers and there is an obligation on both parties:

Figure 37.9 A legal contract

The supplier undertakes to provide appropriate goods and services at a given time for an agreed price.

The buyer undertakes to pay a given price at an agreed date.

It is essential to be clear about of terms and conditions so as to avoid:

■ legal action and the loss of valuable suppliers

■ late arrival of supplies

■ cashflow problems and bad debts from poor paying customers.

Table 37.4 Advantages and disadvantages of different legal status

Legal status	Advantages	Disadvantages

Sole trader
 	
One owner
	• The simplest and cheapest form of business to set up
	• You will have complete control and can keep all of the profits.
	• Your business affairs remain confidential
		• The initial capital comes from your savings
		• It may be difficult to raise extra finance without some form of security
		• You will have:
		  – personal unlimited liability for all business debts
		  – a heavy work load
		  – all of the responsibility and you cannot afford to be ill

Partnership 2–20 owners	• Simple and cheap to set up • Partners bring extra capital, and perhaps valuable experience and expertise • The work-load and business liabilities are shared. • Business affairs remain confidential	• You are no longer in overall control; decisions and profits are shared • All partners have unlimited liability for business debts and a contract made by one partner is legally binding on all others • Problems may result if: partners cannot work well together or if one wishes to leave

Private limited company
 	
No maximum number of shareholders
	• Business affairs are separate from the affairs of the shareholders (the owners)
	• Extra capital may be raised by selling shares
	• Shareholders have limited liability for business debts so that their personal property is not at risk
	• Shares can only be sold by permission of existing shareholders; this avoids unwelcome take-over attempts
		• Usually more expensive and complex to set up than a sole trader or partnership
		• Under the Companies Acts, a company must:
		  – register their details with the Registrar of Companies at Companies House
		  – submit an annual financial summary to the Registrar for inspection by the general public

Public limited company (plc)	Not appropriate for a small business start-up	
Franchise May be sole trader, partnership or limited company	• Sells an established branded product trusted by the consumer; this minimises the start-up risk • Support from the franchisor may include help with setting up premises and regional or national advertising	• Disadvantages depend upon the legal status chosen by the franchisee • The franchisor will monitor the franchisee for quality and may withdraw approval to operate
Charitable status	• Organisations providing certain services to the community may gain charitable status to reduce the tax liability of the business	• Charitable status is not available to all businesses

National laws, local bylaws, regulations and regulatory bodies

Legal requirements are many and complex, and they vary from business to business. The Business Link website provides an electronic questionnaire to show individual entrepreneurs the laws applying to their own particular businesses. Here we provide general details.

Consumer law

■ The Supply of Goods and Services Act (1982) states that goods must be of 'satisfactory quality' and 'fit for the purpose for which they are sold'. A buyer who has a genuine complaint about faulty goods can ask for money to be refunded by the supplier or for compensation if the goods are retained. It may be costly to take a supplier to court, although the small claims court will make this less expensive.

■ The Consumer Safety Act (1987) protects the consumer from harmful goods.

Figure 37.10 Laws
affecting small businesses

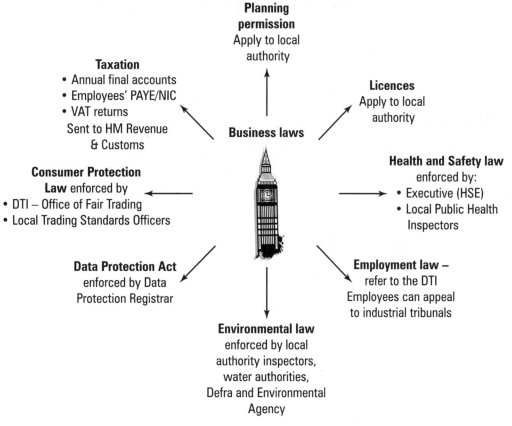

Planning permission
Apply to local authority

Taxation
- Annual final accounts
- Employees' PAYE/NIC
- VAT returns
  Sent to HM Revenue & Customs

Licences
Apply to local authority

Business laws

Consumer Protection Law enforced by
- DTI – Office of Fair Trading
- Local Trading Standards Officers

Health and Safety law
enforced by:
- Executive (HSE)
- Local Public Health Inspectors

Data Protection Act
enforced by Data Protection Registrar

Employment law –
refer to the DTI Employees can appeal to industrial tribunals

Environmental law
enforced by local authority inspectors, water authorities, Defra and Environmental Agency

- The Trades Descriptions Act states that goods must be 'as described', including quantity and size (weights and measures), quality, specification, ingredients, features, date and place of manufacture. For example, 'ice cream' must contain a given amount of cream and a 1 kg bag of sugar must contain 1 kg. Trading standards inspectors from the local town hall enforce this Act.

Employment law

Relevant laws include the Employment Act (2002), Sex Discrimination Act (1975), Equal Pay Act (1970), Race Relations Act (1976), Disability Discrimination Act (1975), European Working Time Directive (2002), Employment Equality (Age) Regulations 2006.

The most important legal provisions are as follows.

- Discrimination on grounds of race, sex, disability, sexual orientation, religion or philosophical belief or age is illegal.

- You must be prepared to make 'reasonable adjustments' to enable disabled people to work or continue working.

- You must provide a secure, safe and healthy working environment.

- Within the first two months of employment, an employee must receive a written contract of employment showing terms and conditions.

- Most employees are entitled to work a 48-hour maximum average working week and minimum rest periods.

- Employees are entitled to a minimum of four weeks' paid leave a year and may also be entitled to maternity leave, paternity leave, adoption leave and leave for family reasons.

- Part-time workers must be treated no less favourably than full-time staff.

- Your employees have the right to the current national minimum wage. What is the present rate? At times they may be entitled to statutory sick pay (SSP) or statutory maternity pay (SMP).

- You must deduct income tax and National Insurance (NI) contributions from your employees' wages under PAYE (Pay As You Earn), and send these to HM Revenue & Customs. Employees must be given a payslip itemising pay and deductions.

Data Protection Act 1998

If your business holds personal information about clients or employees (whether on computer or on paper), you may need to notify the Data Protection Commissioner and abide by their conditions.

Health and safety

The Health and Safety at Work Act (HASAWA) makes you, as a business owner, responsible for the health and safety of everyone affected by your business and its activities. This includes:

- employees working at your premises, from home or at another site
- visitors, such as customers or subcontractors
- members of the public (even if outside your premises).

You are also responsible for anyone affected by products and services you design, produce or supply.

HASAWA is enforced by the Health & Safety Executive (HSE): www.hse.gov.uk.

Fire regulations

Under the Regulatory Reform (Fire Safety) Order 2005, the business owner or an appointed employee is responsible for:

- removing the risk of fire as far as possible
- drawing up emergency plans for dealing with a fire should it occur.

All who use the premises must be able to escape, all fire equipment should be in working order and regular fire drills and training must take place. The law is enforced by the local fire authority

Financial record-keeping

Every business, whatever its legal structure, must keep accurate financial records to enable tax to be calculated on business profits. Each business must:

- send final accounts comprising an income statement (or profit and loss account) and a balance sheet (showing the value of the business) to HM Revenue & Customs at the end of each financial year. Sole traders and partners are taxed as private individuals whereas companies pay corporation tax
- register for VAT where annual turnover (sales value) exceeds the threshold set in the Chancellor's budget. Any surplus of output tax (VAT collected on sales) over input tax (VAT paid on purchases) must be sent to HM Revenue & Customs every three months (or annually for small businesses)
- deduct PAYE (income tax) and NIC (National Insurance Contributions) from employees' pay and send them to HM Revenue & Customs.

In addition, under the Companies Acts (see page 200), limited companies must publish an annual report and accounts, present this to the shareholders for approval at the AGM (annual general meeting). A copy of the report and accounts must be sent to Companies House where it will be made available to the general public for a small fee.

Local authorities

Local authorities have the power to introduce laws that apply to their own geographical area, e.g. the traffic congestion charge in central London and the car parking restrictions introduced by different boroughs. They can also give planning permission and specify building regulations.

Local authorities are also responsible for enforcing much national legislation at a local level.

Planning permission

Alterations to the structure or to the use of a building must be approved by the local authority planning committee and local residents' views may be taken into consideration. The Emirates Stadium project (see page 21) was approved only after lengthy consultations between the Arsenal Football Club, Islington Borough Council and local community groups.

Licences

Certain trades require a licence from the local authority. These include businesses dealing with food, alcoholic drinks, gaming, animals, caring, operating a freight delivery service and the entertainment business.

Licences may also be required for practices which discharge waste into water or the air. These are regulated by the Environment Agency, the local water authority or the local authority.

Compulsory insurance

Some business risks can be reduced, at a price, by means of insurance. Self-insurance (where the business does not insure but bears the risk itself) may be preferred where either risks are remote or insurance is too costly.

However, insurance for some risks is compulsory. Motor insurance (third party at least) is one example, whilst buildings insurance and life assurance may be necessary as a condition of a mortgage.

Intellectual property – protecting the business idea

It is illegal to use ideas from other businesses where they have taken out protection under the Copyright, Designs and Patents Act 1988.

Intellectual property, including patents, trade marks, copyright and registered designs, is covered in detail in Unit 2, pages 65–69.

Sources of help and advice for small businesses

Various forms of support are available to new businesses depending upon their size, activity, geographical location and the age of the entrepreneurs.

Government and EU support

The Department of Trade and Industry (DTI) co-ordinates government support for UK business. Information, funding and advice are available. There are grants for up to 50 per cent of the cost of some projects and a variety of development programmes some of which contain financial help.

Go to www.open.gov.uk.

Small Business Service

Local Learning and Skills Councils (LLSCs) in England, the regional offices of Education and Learning in Wales (ELWa) and Local Enterprise Companies (LECs) in Scotland help businesses to set up, grow and evolve. They also fund vocational qualifications. (No similar body exists for Northern Ireland.)

Small Firms Loan Guarantee Scheme (SFLGS)

The government Small Business Service guarantees a percentage of a bank loan. The aim is to encourage banks to make loans available to small businesses which would otherwise have difficulty in borrowing.

Small Firms Training Loans (SFTL)

Some banks make loans available for training costs that could otherwise not be afforded.

Export Credit Guarantee Department (ECGD)

This is a UK government department that insures UK exports sold on credit against non-payment. It also provides long-term cover for certain foreign investment projects. The aim is to encourage firms to export by removing some of the risks.

Business Link

This is a government source of help and advice to new and small businesses. The website has a comprehensive section on starting a business with spreadsheet templates useful for financial planning. Advice is provided on all aspects of starting up and running a new business.

Regional development grants

The government provides financial assistance for firms setting up in certain regions of the country. The aim is to encourage businesses to relocate into areas where employment is needed.

Objective One funding

Objective One was devised to help reduce differences in social and economic conditions within countries of the EU. It targeted regions with prosperity at 75 per cent or less of the

European average, with £350m of European investment made available to the UK. As an example, Cornwall and the Isles of Scilly (a region suffering from the decline of traditional industries such as mining, farming and fishing) used Objective One funds to assist local businesses and improve the prosperity of the region.

From 2007 to 2013, Objective One is replaced by a Convergence Programme. This will continue economic development in the regions by investing in skills to help people into work; helping develop a knowledge-based economy and aiding business productivity and innovation.

Non-governmental support to small businesses

Prince's Trust
The Prince's Trust was set up in 1983 by Prince Charles to provide support and advice for young entrepreneurs aged 18–30. It offers low interest loans of up to £5,000 and pre-start marketing grants of up to £250.

Shell Livewire
Shell Livewire runs a Young Entrepreneur of the Year Award Scheme. It also gives free business advice covering business planning, sales, marketing, finance and funding.

businessdynamics
businessdynamics was founded in 1977 (as Understanding Industry) by 3i to provide information and events for 14–19-year-old students interested in business enterprise.

High street banks
The small business adviser will consider business proposals to decide whether the bank will be prepared to provide financial support. Template business plans and information packs are made available and loans, overdrafts or factoring arrangements may be made available on condition that the adviser continues to visit the business to provide ongoing monitoring and support

Trade associations
These provide information, help and advice to businesses engaged in particular types of activity. Associations cover a diverse range of industries.

The British Phonographic Institute (BPI) is a trade association that represents British music recording companies. It has five main aims:

- To put the views of the recording industry to Government, the European Commission and other relevant organisations

- To research and publish statistics that help recording companies with market information

- To give advice on legal and regulatory developments of relevance to the industry

- To provide a forum for the exchange of non-competitive information. (Remember that BPI members are competing in the same industry)

- To promote the British recording industry.

The website shows some issues that concern its members.

Source: BPI website: www.bpi.co.uk

---

assignment focus   Identify the appropriate trade association for your proposed business by referring to the Trade Association Forum website.

Trade Association Forum – www.taforum.org.uk

Solicitors
Solicitors provide help with legal matters such as conveyancing (purchase of property), drawing up contracts and setting up companies.

Accountants

These assist with financial matters including planning, setting up recording systems, tax advice and auditing accounts at the end of each financial year

Local Chambers of Commerce

Chambers of Commerce represent local businesses of all sizes and from all sectors. Their aim is to promote, help and support the businesses within their area by providing information, arranging events and pressing for changes that they feel will stimulate economic activity.

Federation of Small Businesses

This exists to support small businesses within the UK as a whole.

- Prince's Trust – www.princes-trust.org.uk
- Shell Livewire – www.shell-livewire.org
- businessdynamics – www.businessynamics.org.uk
- Federation of Small Businesses – www.fsb.org.uk

Financial aspects

Personal survival budget – what will you live on?

The business plan must recognise that the owner must survive as well as the business.

On page 374 we quoted Claire Owen as saying that a new entrepreneur should have sufficient savings to live for 18 months without withdrawing cash from their business. Where this is not possible a realistic allowance for owners' drawings should be built into the business cashflow and break-even forecasts.

Figure 37.11 Types of financial need

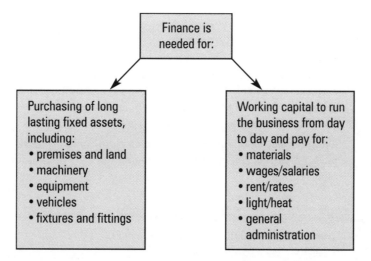

Start-up costs and running costs

In Unit 5 we identified these two types of business expense as:

- capital expenditure
- revenue expenditure.

 See Unit 5, pages 202–204 for explanations of these.

Sources of finance

Capital and revenue expenditure require different types of finance.

Capital provided by the owners (or equity funding)

Owners' capital can be used for either the purchase of fixed assets in the start-up phase, or as a source of working capital used for daily running costs.

Figure 37.12 Sources
of finance

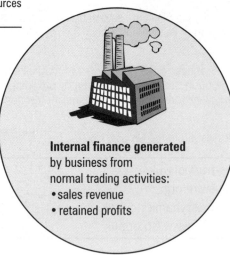

External finance
raised from:

Owner(s) capital
including:
• venture capital
• business angels
} Risked by the owners in the hope of profits

Grants } From government and non-government bodies

Long term liabilities:
• loans
• mortgaes

Current liabilities:
• trade credit
• overdrafts
} External borrowing that must be repaid

Internal finance generated
by business from
normal trading activities:
• sales revenue
• retained profits

The amount of capital required is a major factor in determining the appropriate form of business organisation. Whilst sole trader status can support a small organisation, a project such as the Channel Tunnel will need access to the millions of pounds that only a plc can raise.

Capital is regarded as permanent in that it does not have to be repaid. Instead, the owners risk their savings in the hope that they will be rewarded from future profits. Sole traders and partners will take their share of the profit as drawings whilst company shareholders will receive dividends.

case study 37.6

Sweet success

For many years the shareholders of Ben & Jerry's, the niche market ice cream, received no dividends at all. The firm ploughed back all profits, with the shareholders' approval. It grew as a result into a valuable premium brand. The shareholders were rewarded when the company was bought by Unilever.

On the other hand, Thornton's, the chocolate company, after a disappointing 2003, paid out virtually all of its £4.4 million profits as dividends. This left only £1,000 to plough back.

activity

1   How would ploughing back profits help Ben & Jerry's to grow? Why would the shareholders agree to this?
2   Why do you think that Thornton's chose to reward its shareholders rather than plough back profit?

As a business grows, extra capital may be raised by changing the form of business organisation. A sole trader may bring in partners or form a limited company. In turn, a limited company may 'float' on the stock market as a plc. Tesco has been through all of these stages as it has grown.

Grants

Grants may be available from UK government for specific types of business activities or those located in regeneration areas. Funding from the EU Convergence Programme and Regional Development grants are examples.

Short-term borrowing is suitable for providing working capital.

■   Trade credit is offered when suppliers agree to accept payment for goods or services at a future date. The typical credit period is 30 days.

■   Bank overdrafts enable a business to overspend (overdraw) on its current bank account. Overdrafts are repayable on demand (at any time the bank wishes).

case study
37.7

Nothing ventured ...

New and developing companies may raise further capital with the help of **venture capital** trusts (VCTs)or business angels.

Venture capital trusts are companies that will purchase shares in new or expanding businesses. Potentially large amounts of new capital can be raised in this way. 3is (formerly Investors in Industry) is one of the major providers of venture capital to UK businesses.

Business angels are individuals with funds to invest. (see the Innocent Drinks case study). To protect their investment, they may wish to take some part in the management of the business and they normally have considerable skills and experience to offer. As a reward for their risk, business angels will be interested in gaining a return of perhaps 25–30 per cent on their investment. They may also put a time limit on their involvement.

Figure 37.13 3is

activity

1   What percentage interest would you get from investing in a bank savings account? Use the weekend newspapers or a bank website to find out.

2   Why does a business angel require a much higher return?

3   Refer to the website for further details of its activities.

Borrowing (or debt funding)

Borrowing, unlike owners' capital, must be repaid at some point.

Long-term borrowing is suitable for the purchase of fixed assets.

■   Bank loans are offered for a period of between one to ten years and repaid in regular instalments at an agreed rate of interest. A new business may need security for any borrowing, i.e. a guarantee that the loan will be repaid.

■   Loans from friends and relatives may be offered for lower rates of interest or even interest-free. The time period for repayment may also be more flexible.

■   Commercial mortgages are long-term loans used to buy land or buildings. The property acts as security and will be repossessed and sold if the borrower cannot repay. Repayment may be over 25 years.

Debt funding versus equity funding

This allows the owners to remain in control of the business, assuming that they can repay with equity funding (selling a share in the business, perhaps to venture capitalists or to business angels) the original owners risk losing control of the business.

Other methods of financing

■   *Leasing* A business can hire rather than buy a fixed asset such as vehicles or machinery. The main benefit is that the asset is made available for immediate use without the need to buy it outright.

■   *Factoring* A business that allows its customers credit may run short of cash whilst awaiting payment. Here a bank will pay 80 per cent of all invoices immediately. It will then collect the debts as they become due. At this point, it will pay the remaining 20 per cent, less a commission for providing the service.

■   *Advertising and sponsorship* Certain businesses are attractive to advertisers and sponsors and some organisations depend almost entirely upon it. Obvious examples are independent TV companies (why not the BBC?), the press (see the case study on page 380), sporting teams and events (e.g. shirt sponsorship), and transport companies (bus advertising).

See also Unit 2, page 69, The need for finance.

Pricing policy

As we saw in Unit 1 (pages 9–10), there may be times when a business may be prepared to sell for cost or even below cost – special promotional offers, for example. Ultimately, however, a business must charge sufficient for its products to cover costs and provide a suitable reward for its owners. There are a number of approaches to pricing and a business may use more than one depending upon circumstances.

Pricing policies include:

- pile 'em high and sell 'em cheap
- penetration pricing
- premium pricing (perceived value pricing)
- skimming pricing
- cost-plus pricing
- marginal cost pricing
- positioning pricing
- demand-based pricing
- competitive pricing
- discount pricing
- differential pricing.

These pricing policies are explained in detail in Unit 9, pages 242–44.

Cashflow forecasting

Whilst a director of Tottenham Hotspur FC, Sir Alan Sugar spoke of 'the prune-juice effect' – the way in which huge quantities of cash continually flowed out of the business.

Businesses must be able to pay their bills on time. The cashflow forecast enables them to estimate their ability to do this over the forthcoming period – normally six or 12 months. A new business will include a cashflow forecast in its business plan – the bottom line estimates the monthly cash surplus or deficit.

Read pages 207-212 in Unit 5 where we look in detail at cashflow forecasting. The business plan at the end of this unit shows the cashflow forecast for Eclipse pottery (page 409).

---

remember

There are three sections to the cashflow forecast:
- receipts
- payments
- a summary of the cash position, comprising:
  - net cashflow
  - opening balance
  - closing bank balance.

See Unit 5, page 207.

Greenco Ltd's cashflow problem

Greenco will have a cashflow problem during each of the first two months with the shortage of £2,900 in December being the worst. Unless action is taken, some bills will not be paid. Consequences of cash shortages might include: unpaid staff refusing to work, unpaid suppliers refusing to deliver, electricity being cut off, and so on.

The cause of the problem is the £12,000 paid out for equipment in October. Possible solutions might be to:

- raise a loan to help pay for these fixed assets
- lease the equipment or buy it on credit so that payments are spread over the coming months
- arrange for a bank overdraft. This is not a usual way to fund fixed assets but in this case the problem is short-term and will be solved by December
- issue more shares so that the company has sufficient working capital available.

case study 37.8 — Greenco Ltd

Greenco Ltd will begin trading in October with a share capital of £15,000. The marketing department has set a sales target for the first six months (Table 37.5). The sales price will be £10 a unit.

Table 37.5 Greenco's sales targets

	Oct	Nov	Dec	Jan	Feb	Mar	Total
Sales volume (no. of units)	1,000	1,500	2,000	2,500	2,000	3,000	12,000

The production department agrees that it can produce these goods and estimates the variable costs of production as £5 per unit, made up of:

materials: £4 a unit

production wages: £1 a unit.

Estimated fixed costs of the various functional areas are £44,500, thus:

- salaries: £6,000 per month
- rent and rates: £1,500 in October and £1,500 in January
- insurance: £2,400 in October
- light and heat: £800 in December and £800 in March
- general administration: £1,000 in October, thereafter £100 per month.

Additionally, equipment costing £12,000 will be paid for in October.

The finance department at Greenco feeds all of these estimates into the cashflow forecast (Table 37.6).

Table 37.6 Cashflow forecast of Greenco Ltd, six months to March 2000

	Oct £	Nov £	Dec £	Jan £	Feb £	Mar £	Total £
Receipts:							
Sales (of stock) @ £10	10,000	15,000	20,000	25,000	20,000	30,000	120,000
New capital	15,000						15,000
Loans, grants, etc.							0
Total receipts (A)	**25,000**	**15,000**	**20,000**	**25,000**	**20,000**	**30,000**	**135,000**
Payments:							
Purchase (of materials)	4,000	6,000	8,000	10,000	8,000	12,000	48,000
Production wages	1,000	1,500	2,000	2,500	2,000	3,000	12,000
Salaries	6,000	6,000	6,000	6,000	6,000	6,000	36,000
Rent/rates	1,500			1,500			3,000
Insurance	2,400						2,400
Light/heat			800			800	1,600
General administration	1,000	100	100	100	100	100	1,500
Equipment	12,000						12,000
Total payment (B)	**27,900**	**13,600**	**16,900**	**20,100**	**16,100**	**21,900**	**116,500**
Net cashflow (A–B)	(2,900)	1,400	3,100	4,900	3,900	8,100	18,500
add opening bank balance	0	(2,900)	(1,500)	1,600	6,500	10,400	0
Closing bank balance	**(2,900)**	**(1,500)**	**1,600**	**6,500**	**10,400**	**18,500**	**18,500**

▶

Before reading on, look at the bottom line in Greenco's cashflow forecast.

1   a) In which months will Greenco have a cash shortage?

    b) In which month will the problem be greatest?

2   Which item is the cause of the problem?

3   What might be the consequences if no action is taken to avoid this problem?

Figure 37.14 Causes of and solutions to cashflow problems

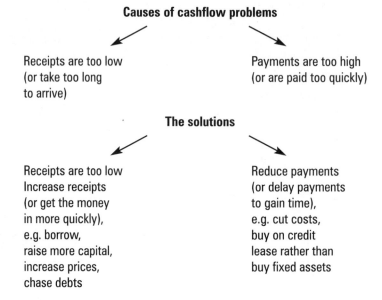

Causes of cashflow problems

Receipts are too low
(or take too long
to arrive)

Payments are too high
(or are paid too quickly)

The solutions

Receipts are too low
Increase receipts
(or get the money
in more quickly),
e.g. borrow,
raise more capital,
increase prices,
chase debts

Reduce payments
(or delay payments
to gain time),
e.g. cut costs,
buy on credit
lease rather than
buy fixed assets

Break-even forecasting

A business breaks even when the sales revenue generated in a trading period is sufficient to cover running costs so that there is neither a profit nor a loss. Sales beyond break-even will bring a profit, whereas failure to break even results in a loss.

In order to forecast the break-even point, we need to understand the nature of business costs and how they behave as output rises and falls.

Remember that business costs are not the same as payments. Costs used in the profit calculation are those items whose value is consumed (used up) in the course of production.

The following are therefore not classed as costs:

■ the capital expenses – buying fixed assets such as premises, plant, machinery, equipment and vehicles. These remain available for future periods and are not wholly consumed in production

■ money paid to the owners for personal, rather than business, use (i.e. drawings of sole traders and partners and dividends paid to company shareholders).

We can identify fixed costs and variable costs:

■ Variable costs are directly related to the units that we produce and sell. They change in proportion to the level of output and sales so that if output doubles then variable costs will double. Variable costs include: raw materials, stocks purchased for resale, wages of employees directly engaged in production, direct expenses such as royalties paid to patent-holders and variable selling costs such as sales-force commission.

■ *Fixed costs* (or overheads) are not affected by the level of output but remain unchanged as production levels rise and fall. They are generally related to time periods rather than to production. Fixed costs include rent, rates, light, heat, salaries, depreciation on fixed assets, finance costs, and, for our purposes, any other costs not regarded as variable. Note that fixed costs are fixed only in the short term and within present production capacity. For example, if we move to a larger factory then rent will rise, if we employ more supervisors then salaries will rise.

Link Case study 2.4 on pages 76–77 shows how to draw a break-even chart.

case study 37.9 — Forecasting Greenco's profit

Greenco uses the same financial estimates as above to calculate the break-even point and draw a break-even chart. The calculation is:

$$\text{Break-even point} = \frac{\text{Fixed costs}}{\text{Contribution per unit}} = \frac{£44,500}{(£10 - £5)}$$
$$\text{(sales per unit} - \text{variable cost per unit)}$$

Break-even point = 8,900 units *or* £89,000 (8,900 units @ £10)

Table 37.7 Financial estimates

Units	Fixed costs for period	Variable cost per unit £5		Sales revenue per unit £10	
	Fixed costs	Variable costs	Total costs	Sales	Profit/(loss)
0	44,500	0	44,500	0	(44,500)
2,000	44,500	10,000	54,500	20,000	(34,500)
4,000	44,500	20,000	64,500	40,000	(24,500)
6,000	44,500	30,000	74,500	60,000	(14,500)
8,000	44,500	40,000	84,500	80,000	(4,500)
10,000	44,500	50,000	94,500	100,000	5,500
12,000	44,500	60,000	104,500	120,000	15,500

Figure 37.15 Greenco's break-even chart

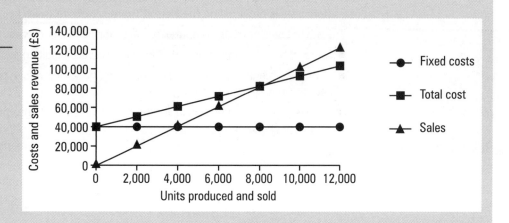

Table 37.8 shows that the business will make a profit of £15,500 in the first six months:

Table 37.8 Forecast trading and profit and loss account

	£	£
Sales Revenue		120,000
less Purchases	48,000	
Direct Wages	12,000	
Variable cost of sales		60,000
Gross profit		60,000
less Overheads (fixed costs)		
Salaries	36,000	
Rent/rates	3,000	
Insurance	2,400	
Light/heat	1,600	
General admin.	1,500	
Net Profit		44,500
		15,500

Note: capital items (buying machinery, etc.) are not costs.

At the end of the year, the business will be taxed on its profits. Remaining profits can then be paid as dividends to shareholders or ploughed back into the business to find future growth.

Cash versus profit

Notice that the forecast cash (£18,500) is not the same as the forecast profit (£15,500). The two are calculated differently and so it is possible for a business to have profit and no cash, or cash and no profit. You will consider this in detail if you study the specialist financial units.

Using computer software to draw up financial forecasts

Financial forecasts may be drawn up by using either:

■ commercially designed software – suitable templates are available from the Business Link website and from the high street banks

■ a spreadsheet – a spreadsheet model that may be used for cashflow and break-even forecasts is provided on the Nelson Thornes website (www.nelsonthornes.com).

The advantages of using computer software for financial forecasting include:

■ automatic calculations provide fast and accurate results once data are entered

■ 'what if?' scenarios can be used – data can be varied to see the effects of different possibilities such as changing sales prices or costs

■ charts can be linked to illustrate the figures. These will automatically update when data are changed.

activity

1   Set up an electronic cashflow forecast using the template on the Nelson Thornes website (www.nelsonthornes.com/btec). Enter Greenco's figures to check that it works.

2   Try out each of the alternative 'what if?' scenarios by changing the relevant figures:

   a)   What if the cost of the equipment is spread evenly over the first six months?

   b)   What if Greenco buys takes out a loan of £3,000?

   c)   What if Greenco pays £12,000 in October for equipment but buys materials on 30-day credit? In this case, the purchases figures will be moved back a month – October to November, etc. October will read zero, and the purchases for March will appear as creditors (they will be paid in April).

   d)   Suggest and try out one other solution.

3   In your opinion, which of the above is the best solution? Provide your reasons. (Note that none of them will affect the break-even point or the final profit.)

Cash budgets and profit and loss budgets

The cashflow and profit forecasts may need to be reworked a number of times before they are acceptable to the owners of the business.

It may be useful to review the diagram of the budgeting process in Unit 1, page 25 – Fig 1.14.

Once these forecasts are acceptable they become the cash budget and the profit and loss budgets, i.e. the targets for the period. The owner or managers will be given responsibility for meeting them. Progress will be monitored at regular intervals and action taken to correct any variances.

assignment focus

To achieve P4, you will need to describe the legal and financial aspects that will affect the start up of your proposed business.

To achieve M3, you should assess how each aspect will impact upon the business start-up. For example, you will need to look at how you will raise sufficient start-up funds, how you will maintain a suitable level of working capital throughout the year and whether you will break even.

You will need to look at whether you can meet the relevant legal requirements and the costs and other resources involved in doing so.

Producing an outline business start-up proposal

The business proposal and its purpose

The business plan will set out the business idea and how it will achieve its goals over the coming year. The plan is a professionally presented document that may be used as evidence in raising finance from banks or other backers, such as business angels.

Reviewing information and ideas

It is likely that the original plan will be amended several times before it becomes a workable idea. The use of spreadsheet models for cashflow and break-even forecasts will be invaluable here.

Setting targets and goals – where are we going?

The plan will set out the business aims and tactics for achieving these. It will identify the resources needed and realistically examine the possibilities of success by comparing the costs and revenues that are likely to be involved. Details will be shown for marketing, operations (including legal aspects) and finances.

The financial plan will test the feasibility of the proposal by bringing together the estimated costs and revenues to see if there will be sufficient cash to run the business on a monthly basis and sufficient profit to reward the owners for their enterprise.

Contingency planning

A business is wise to prepare for the unexpected.

Insurance

One way to minimise risk is to insure. It is not possible to insure against being a bad entrepreneur. However, it is wise to insure against a variety of other business risks.

Liability insurance will help pay any compensation and legal costs that occur if an employer is found to be at fault. Examples are:

- employers' liability insurance, covering damage to employees
- public liability insurance, covering damage to the public
- product liability, covering damage resulting from a faulty product.

Other insurances are available for:

- premises and contents – covering buildings, stock and equipment
- consequential loss (business interruption) – to help with on-going fixed costs if a disaster, such as a fire or flood, closes the businesses for some time
- theft from buildings and vehicles breakages including goods in transit
- fidelity – what if an employee runs off with the money?
- personal insurance, e.g. income protection and critical illness insurance
- motor insurance – the law requires at least third party insurance to protect innocent bystanders and their property
- life assurance – in a partnership each partner will have an insurable interest in other partners.

---

case study 31.10   **Boscastle**

On 16 August 2004, the Cornish coastal village of Boscastle was devastated by a flash flood when heavy rain caused local rivers to overflow.

The main livelihood of the village is tourism and many businesses including gift shops and restaurants had their stock ruined. Vehicles were washed into the sea and premises badly damaged or even destroyed.

Figure 37.16

activity

The events at Boscastle in 2004 show the importance of planning for the unexpected and in particular the need to insure.

1   Which insurance policies would protect businesses affected by such a disaster?

2   'Self-assurance' exists where a business chooses not to insure, but instead to bear the risk itself. Can you explain why a business may choose to do this for certain risks?

3   Name some risks that must be insured by law. Why is this?

Loss of data

In an information-led economy, businesses are wise to keep back-up copies of data on a separate site and to protect computers from hackers.

Link

We look at this in more detail in Unit 29, pages 344–46.

Investigations following post-2000 terrorist attacks showed that:

- 80 per cent of businesses directly involved in incidents closed within 18 months
- 90 per cent of businesses losing data as a result of incidents closed within two years.

Worst case scenarios – what if?

Spreadsheet models enable us to examine worst-case scenarios (the worst that can happen) to see how the business finances will be affected under a variety of circumstances.

For example, what if a major customer goes elsewhere? What if interest rates go up by 0.25 per cent?

Models

Model business plans and spreadsheet templates are available from a variety of sources including: the high street banks, TEC/LEC, Business Link and local Chambers of Commerce.

Components of the plan

The business plan will comprise the components shown in Figure 37.17.

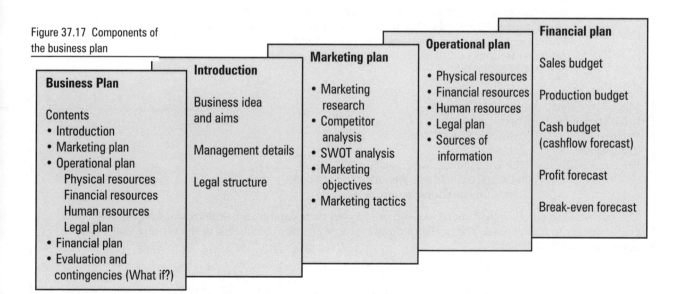

Figure 37.17 Components of the business plan

Business Plan

Contents
- Introduction
- Marketing plan
- Operational plan
  Physical resources
  Financial resources
  Human resources
  Legal plan
- Financial plan
- Evaluation and contingencies (What if?)

Introduction

Business idea and aims

Management details

Legal structure

Marketing plan
- Marketing research
- Competitor analysis
- SWOT analysis
- Marketing objectives
- Marketing tactics

Operational plan
- Physical resources
- Financial resources
- Human resources
- Legal plan
- Sources of information

Financial plan

Sales budget

Production budget

Cash budget (cashflow forecast)

Profit forecast

Break-even forecast

Sample business plan

The following is an example of a business plan for the fictional Eclipse Pottery.

Della Moon and Wayne Moon, trading as Eclipse
The Wheelhouse, Wateringham PL14 3CN
Tel (010101) 820541 Fax: (010101) 820557
E-mail: moon&son@netprobe.net

BUSINESS PLAN

Contents
Introduction
Marketing plan
Operational plan
Financial plan
Evaluation and contingencies

Introduction

Business idea and aims
The business will produce and sell earthenware/ceramic 6-piece dinner sets to a standard design registered as 'Eclipse'. The finish will be to the specification of individual clients with whom we will work closely.

Our mission is to:
- provide a quality product supported by a quality service for customers
- establish a reputation for excellence initially at an area level
- establish the presence of the 'Eclipse' trade mark in the marketplace
- maximise profits through operations in a niche market
- concentrate on quality rather than quantity.

Management details
Key people: Della Moon (Design and production)
             Date of birth: 18/08/51
             Experience: Local government finance officer 22 years
             Qualifications: 4 O-levels, OND Business and Finance
             Expertise: Pottery exhibitions locally, won local design award 2004, sales to local business
             Address: 23 Factory Row, Wateringham PL6 2QF
             Tel: 01010 454545

             Wayne Moon (Marketing)
             Date of birth: 07/10/76
             Occupation: Commercial artist (freelance)
             Experience: 6 years of working on major contracts
             Qualifications: 2 A-levels, Higher Diploma in Art & Design, Crossley College of Art
             Expertise: Has working relationships with numerous potential business clients
             Address: Roundwood, Warren Place, Penleigh
             Tel: 01101 663410

Legal structure
The business will operate as follows:
Legal structure: Partnership
Partners: Della and Wayne Moon
Trading as: Eclipse
Business address: The Wheelhouse, Wateringham PL14 3CN
                     Tel (010101) 820541 Fax: (010101) 820557
                     E-mail: moon&son@netprobe.net

The partnership structure will enable the owners to pool their capital and skills whilst keeping regulatory requirements to a minimum. The partners do not foresee any significant risk in the venture that would necessitate limited liability.

Start-up finance will be raised as follows:

	£
Partners' capital:	
D. Moon	5,000
W. Moon	10,000
Bank loan	5,000
Total	20,000

It is intended that the Moon family retain control of the business. A bank loan secured against the property of W. Moon is therefore preferred to raising further capital by bringing in new partners.

Marketing plan

Marketing research

Primary research has been concentrated on local businesses which we see as our initial market. Our investigations have taken the form of:

■ a survey by questionnaire of a representative sample of potential consumers
■ a survey of local businesses – we used a combination of visits, telephone calls and mailshots to ask a series of key questions.

Secondary research into the existing competition and the economic prospects for the area has used a variety of sources including the *Yellow Pages*, the local *Thomson Directory* and local statistics supplied by the local Business Link and Chamber of Commerce. In addition we have consulted the *Population Census*, *Labour Force Survey*, *ONS Unemployment Rates*, *Social Trends* and *Business Monitors*.

The trends that we have identified in tourism, local employment and population all support our belief that there is a gap in the market for our product.

We expect our customers to be:

■ local restaurants
■ local craft and gift shops
■ one-off contracts for special commissions.

The market is expected to grow by roughly 5 per cent a year and we believe that there will be a continuing demand for quality pottery items that are distinctive and hand-crafted.

Competitor analysis

The tableware that is generally available from retailers is not a substitute for our goods, which are differentiated by the quality of the designs and the image. We would therefore expect to have a local monopoly with all the benefits this would give us.

SWOT analysis

Table 37.9 SWOT analysis

Strengths:	Weaknesses:
• We are a local business. We understand our customers and will sell personalised products. • Our emphasis on quality and concentration on a niche market allows a potentially high mark-up. • A relatively small capital investment is required and we will incur little financial risk. • We have excellent premises, new equipment, and low running costs. • The flexibility allowed by sub-contracting production to a local potter will allow us to respond to market demand in the short term and to keep down fixed costs.	• 30-day credit terms are necessary to gain sales but cash purchase of stock means that the business will need external finance in the early stages. • The business is initially dependent upon one large contract. • Maximum production is limited to 60 units per month at present. Increasing turnover will require expansion and may bring the danger of overtrading.
Opportunities:	Threats:
• The trend towards eating out will continue (source: *Household Expenditure Survey*) providing the potential for increased sales to restaurants. • The South-West tourist season may lengthen as cheap flights from Stansted to Newquay encourage short-break visitors. • There is potential for reaching a niche market via the internet. • Eclipse pottery with its natural wholesome image is well placed to benefit from consumers' growing preference for organic foods and a green lifestyle. • Our premises allow for future expansion and eventual workshop sales. • Students from the art college could be employed on a casual basis during peak times to provide additional flexible labour.	• Increased legislation from the European Union in: health and safety, employment, the environment and consumer protection may place a burden on small businesses. • New competitors may enter the market via the internet.

Marketing objectives

Our objectives are to:

- establish a reputation in our niche market as a provider of distinctive, quality products
- achieve a turnover of £36,000 in the first six months by selling 300 units at a guide price of £120 for each dinner set:

Table 37.10 Sales forecasts

	Apr	May	Jun	Jul	Aug	Sept	Total
Sales volume (units)	30	40	50	60	70	50	300
Sales revenue (@ £120 per unit)	3,600	4,800	6,000	7,200	8,400	6,000	36,000

Marketing tactics

We will achieve our objectives through the following marketing mix.

Product

We will specialise in dinner sets bearing the distinctive 'Eclipse' motif. Our USP (unique selling point) will be our emphasis on personal designs using local knowledge, quality materials and craft.

We will concentrate on quality rather than volume in order to secure a niche in the market.

Price

In discussion with potential clients, we have identified an optimum unit price of £120. Potential sales are likely to fall sharply above this and there will be no significant rise with lower prices. Trade sales will be on 30-day credit.

Although we believe that people are willing to pay premium prices for goods, our low operating costs enable us to set prices that will deter new entrants to the market.

Promotion

All promotion will be geared towards portraying an image of quality.

The business name 'Eclipse' and logo have been carefully chosen to appeal to the ABC1 groups who will be our target market.

We have produced a brochure of sample designs for mailing to interested parties together with business stationery. A 'brochureware' website is currently in preparation.

The business launch will consist of an open evening at 'The Wheelhouse' by invitation only with a guest list of local dignitaries and business people who may be potential clients. The local press have agreed to write a feature.

Della Moon's work is well known locally and examples, together with business contact details, are displayed in galleries in the area.

Eclipse will exhibit at craft fairs and exhibitions to gain exposure and we anticipate that much custom will come from reputation by 'word of mouth'.

The business name and telephone number have been entered in the *Yellow Pages* and *Thomson's Directory*, a website is under development and we will build a database of all enquiries to add to Mr W. Moon's existing contacts.

Promotional costs will be relatively modest with initial outlay likely to be:

- launch evening: £500
- brochures, business cards, stationery and mail-shot to selected customers: £700.

Place

Initially we intend to sell within a radius of approximately 50 miles. Sales will be on the following basis:

- direct to some customers such as the chain of vegetarian restaurants with whom we have already had discussions
- batches commissioned by selected local retailers
- individual commissions from customers at craft fairs, shows and exhibitions within the area. Where customers cannot collect the goods themselves, we will arrange delivery by independent carrier

- our website will act as a promotional brochure initially, although there will be a facility for contacting us about commissions.

We will not be dependent upon passing trade, although potential customers can come and visit our workshop by arrangement. In future we may develop a showroom on the premises perhaps with a cafe.

Operational plan

A unit of production is one place-setting (six pieces of pottery).

Maximum production capacity is 60 units per month. This means that some orders must be produced in advance so as to meet sales deadlines.

Unit production costs will be:

- raw materials: £20 per unit
- labour: £15 per unit.

Table 37.11 Production schedule

	Apr	May	Jun	Jul	Aug	Sept	Total
Production volume (units)	40	45	50	60	60	45	300
Production cost (£)							
raw materials (@ £20)	800	900	1,000	1,200	1,200	900	6,000
labour (@ £15)	600	675	750	900	900	675	4,500

Quality assurance

Each batch will be inspected carefully before distribution to customers. Items will be carefully sealed in boxes and stamped and dated as 'passed'.

Since our aim is to establish a reputation for quality in a niche market, all 'seconds' will be destroyed – none is to be sold off cheaply.

Physical resources

Capital expenditure:

The following fixed assets will be purchased at start:

Table 37.12 Fixed assets

	Cost (£)
'Jet Heat' electric kiln	9,000
'Multi-rev' potters' wheels	4,000
Specialist tools	2,000
Desk-top computer, laser printer	2,400
Office furniture	1,600
Total capital expenditure:	**19,000**

Premises:

'The Wheelhouse' premises with appropriate workshop and storage facilities will be rented.

Raw materials:

Raw materials (clay, glaze and paints) will be purchased on a JIT, cash-on-delivery basis from a local supplier who provides same-day delivery. Stocks will not be held as supplies are guaranteed.

Financial resources

£20,000 of start-up finance will be raised as shown in the introductory section.

Ultimately the partnership hopes to secure credit from suppliers, although this may not be possible in the early stages of the business.

Properties owned by both partners may be used as security against further loans or overdrafts.

Overhead costs:
Estimates for the first six months are:

Table 37.13 Estimated overhead costs for first six months

Overheads	£	Details
Transport/distribution	240	£40 monthly
Rent/rates	3,300	£2,200 in April, £1,100 in July
Insurance	2,000	£2,000 paid at start in April
Light/heat	1,400	£700 per quarter (June and Sept)
Advertising	1,200	£1,200 initial launch in April
Interest charges	60	£10 monthly
General administration	300	£50 monthly
Total	8,500	

Human resources

D. Moon will concentrate on design, W. Moon will run the marketing and finance aspects of the business. Initially each partner will take drawings of £1,000 a month.

Pottery production will be carried out by a contract potter working to D. Moon's design instructions. Production will be carried out on the firm's premises to ensure quality control. Payment will be £15 per saleable unit.

Legal plan

The premises are already designated for commercial use and comply with health and safety regulations. The remote location means that there will be no disruption to neighbouring properties and there is ample space for parking and loading.

Advice has been taken from the local authority concerning health and safety issues and the workshop is passed as safe.

Employment laws are not applicable as the potter is self-employed and works on a sub-contract basis.

Initially the business will not register for VAT as annual turnover will be below the Chancellor's most recent threshold.

All financial transactions will be recorded by D. Moon on an integrated computerised accounting package. An accountant will be engaged each year to draw up the business final accounts for the Department of Revenue & Customs.

No licence is required to operate a pottery although this will change if it is decided to open a cafe. The partnership will not need to register under the Data Protection Act.

After balancing the cost of insurance premiums against the expected, risk cover has been arranged for: premises, contents, breakages, product liability, public liability and personal accident. Both partners already have life assurance policies.

Sources of information

In drawing up this plan the following sources of information have been invaluable:

- Business Link for Devon and Cornwall: http://www.blinkdandc.com/
- JMB Solicitors, Bodmin
- Accounting Associates, St Austell
- Federation of Small businesses
- St Austell Chamber of Commerce: http://www.staustellchamber.org.uk/.

Financial plan

Table 37.14

SALES BUDGET (units)							
	Apr	May	Jun	Jul	Aug	Sept	Total
Sales volume (units)	30	40	50	60	70	50	300
SALES REVENUE BUDGET (£)							
Sales @ £120 per unit	3,600	4,800	6,000	7,200	8,400	6,000	36,000

Note: please see the marketing plan for details.
Receipts will be 1 month later than above owing to 30-day credit.

Table 37.15

PRODUCTION BUDGET (units)							
	Apr	May	Jun	Jul	Aug	Sept	Total
Production volume (units)	40	45	50	60	60	45	300
PRODUCTION REVENUE BUDGET (£)							
Raw materials @ £20 per unit	800	900	1,000	1,200	1,200	900	6,000
Direct labour @ £15 per unit	600	675	750	900	900	675	4,500

Note: please see the operational plan for details.
Payment will be in the months shown above.

Table 37.16 Cash budget

Notes	Figures to nearest £	At start £	Apr £	May £	Jun £	July £	Aug £	Sept £	Total £	Notes
	Receipts									
	Cash sales									
30 day credit	Cash from debtors		0	3,600	4,800	6,000	7,200	8,400	30,000	Debtors £6,000
	New capital	15,000							15,000	
	Bank loan	5,000							5,000	
	Total receipts (A)	20,000	0	3,600	4,800	6,000	7,200	8,400	50,000	
	Payments									
Materials	Cash purchases		800	900	1,000	1,200	1,200	900	6,000	Creditors 0
	Cash to creditors									
	Drawings		2,000	2,000	2,000	2,000	2,000	2,000	12,000	
	Production wages		600	675	750	900	900	675	4,500	
	Transport/ distribution		40	40	40	40	40	40	240	
Fixed assets	Capital items	19,000							19,000	
	Rent/rates		2,200			1,100			3,300	
	Insurance		2,000						2,000	
	Light/heat				700			700	1,400	
	Advertising		1,200						1,200	
	Loan repayments		80	80	80	80	80	80	480	
	Interst charges		10	10	10	10	10	10	60	
	General admin		50	50	50	50	50	50	300	
	Total payments (B)	19,000	8,980	3,755	4,630	5,380	4,280	4,455	50,480	
	Net cashflow (A–B)	1,000	(8,980)	(155)	170	620	2,920	3,945	(480)	
	add Opening balance b/d	0	1,000	(7,980)	(8,135)	(7,965)	(7,345)	(4,425)	0	
	Closing balance c/d	1,000	(7,980)	(8,135)	(7,965)	(7,345)	(4,425)	(480)	(480)	

Note: Please see the marketing plan and operational plan for details.
Column 1 shows the start-up funding required.

Table 37.17 Forecast income statement (profit and loss) for period ending 30 September 200–

	£	£
Sales		36,000
Variable production cost		10,500
GROSS PROFIT		25,500
Fixed cost		8,500
NET PROFIT		17,000
less Partner's drawings		12,000
Retained profits		5,000

Table 37.18 Break-even point

	Period fixed costs £8,500	Unit variable costs £35		Unit sales revenue £120	
Units	**Fixed costs £**	**Variable costs £**	**Total costs £**	**Sales revenue £**	**Profit/(loss)**
0	8,500	0	8,500	0	(8,500)
60	8,500	2,100	10,600	7,200	(3,400)
120	8,500	4,200	12,700	14,400	1,700
180	8,500	6,300	14,800	21,600	6,800
240	8,500	8,400	16,900	28,800	11,900
300	8,500	10,500	19,000	36,000	17,000
360,	8,500	12,600	21,100	43,200	22,100

Break-even point = 100 dinner sets
or £12,000 (100 units sold @ £120 each)

Figure 37.18 Break-even chart

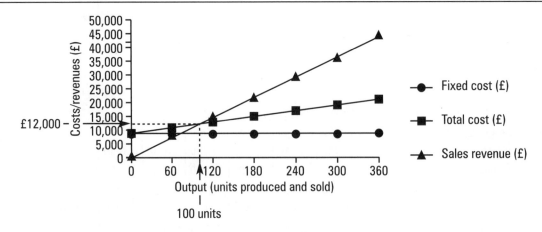

Evaluation and contingencies
Marketing
The sales estimates are based partly upon firm orders and partly upon enquiries from prospective customers who have shown genuine interest in the products.

Operations

The production budget shows that orders can be produced to time under present constraints. Should there be further demand, the business has capacity to produce an extra 60 units worth £7,200 revenue

Finance
Cashflow:

There will be a cash shortfall over the period partly due to start-up costs and partly to the need to pay production costs immediately whilst giving customers 30-days' credit. Additional funding of just over £8,000 is needed in the initial stages and it is hoped to raise an overdraft using one partner's property as security. When the September customers pay the £6,000 due in October, the bank can be repaid.

Profitability:

The business will break-even at 100 units and generate a net profit of £17,000 for the six-month period. This will enable the partners to take their drawings of £12,000 and to plough back £5,000 for future growth.

   Assuming that the bank overdraft is forthcoming, the business plan is viable. It is acceptable to the partners who are prepared to operate with minimal drawings during the first year

Monitoring and review

The financial forecasts will be monitored on a monthly basis and any significant variances investigated.

Contingencies

The partners feel that there is little risk in this business proposal: the sales forecast is based upon firm orders, there will be no unmanageable debt (see cashflow above) and sales are within production capacity. The plan is to grow the business gradually as W. Moon has other business interests; hence there will be no danger of overtrading.

   Nevertheless the following **contingency plans** are in place:

- In the event of a cash shortage beyond that forecast, both partners are prepared to forego drawings during year one. This would save £2,000 per month.
- Any increase in the cost of supplies can be absorbed by the business in the short-term. The break-even point is low (at 27 per cent of capacity) so the business will remain in profit.
- The potter works on a sub-contract basis. In the case of illness there is no liability to pay wages and D. Moon can take over manufacture until a replacement is found.
- Suitable insurance has been arranged.

This business plan was submitted for and on behalf of Eclispe by the partners:

Della Moon .... Date: 20 Jan 200–

Wayne Moon .... Date: 20 Jan 200–

To achieve P5, you will need to write up your business proposal in outline using a suitable model. This should include information from P1, P2, P3 and P4.

You will achieve D1 if your business proposal is comprehensive, accurate, professionally produced and addresses all relevant aspects of business start-up.

Ensure that there are clear links between the sections, e.g. the financial forecasts should be accurately based upon the estimated sales revenue from the marketing plan and the estimated costs of the business operations.

You should be prepared to present the plan to a bank manager in an attempt to secure financial backing for your proposal. You must therefore be able to comment accurately on the figures presented and respond to questioning.

Glossary

Accessibility
Meeting audience needs effectively using readable, legible text; sounds; images, etc.

Advertising
Paid for impersonal communication or message intended to inform or persuade an audience

Advertising agency
Marketing business that will design, plan and implement an advertising campaign

AIDA
Attention, Interest, Desire, Action

AIO inventory
Questions to find consumers' activities, interests and opinions

Appraisal
A system for gaining feedback on employees' performance, by looking at what a job is, how well it is performed, and what action should be taken in future

B2B
Business to business, e.g. wholesaler, retailer

B2C
Business to consumer

Balance sheet
A statement of the worth of a business at a given date. It lists assets, liabilities and capital, usually in the form: Assets – Liabilities = Capital

Benchmarking
Process of identifying then improving on best practice in another organisation, best practice is the standard or benchmark

Body language
Non-verbal communication comprising gestures and facial expressions (e.g. smiles) which can help or hinder communication

Brand
Used by a supplier to identify their products from those of competitors. It may be a name, a symbol or a term. Brands are often given a particular image or value

Branding
Giving a product a distinctive identity through trademarks, design, packaging, etc.

Break-even point
The level of production and sales at which a business covers its costs so that there is neither a profit nor a loss. It can be measured either in units or in revenue

Broadband
A system that can carry many signals of varying frequencies. For the user the advantage is more information (text, audio, video, etc.) at greater speed

Budget
An agreed plan that serves as a target for a future period, e.g. sales, production or revenue. It may be quantitative (units) or financial

Business
An organisation that produces or distributes goods or services

Business angel
An individual willing to risk funds by investing in a new or risky business venture

Business objectives
Goals or aims of an organisation which are **SMART**

Cashflow
Cash inflows and outflows as a business produces and sells

Cashflow problem
A shortage of working capital (available cash) to pay bills.

Central government
The government at Westminster, as opposed to local government

Centralised control
Where all important decisions are taken by managers at the top of the organisation

Coaching
An expert helps others to develop specific skills

Contingency plans
Plans drawn up in case the unexpected happens

Glossary

Contract of employment
Legal agreement between an employee and employer which sets out terms and conditions of a job

Copyright
Exclusive legal ownership to e.g. music, text, software (Copyright Act 1988)

Copywriter
Person who writes the words (known as 'copy') for an advertisement

Corporate image
View that an organisation projects of itself to its stakeholders (consumers, employees, etc.)

Critical path analysis
Sequence of activities which show the shortest time in which a project can be completed. Critical tasks must be completed before subsequent tasks can be started

Culture
The set of beliefs, values and attitudes that shape and drive an organisation

Current assets
Assets which can quickly be turned into money; sometimes known as liquid assets; they include stock in trade, trade debtors, cash in bank and cash in hand

Current liabilities
Creditors who must be paid in the short-term (certainly within a year)

Decentralised control
Where important decisions are taken by divisional managers further down the organisation, e.g. a business may have different divisions for geographical areas or for different products

Demographic segmentation
Splitting consumers into similar groups based on demographic features

Demographics
Features of the potential buyers such as age, gender or income

Deregulation
Removal of restrictions to allow private businesses to run services that were previously operated by the state.

Direct marketing
Communication from the seller direct to the buyer such as mail, text or e-mail

Direct selling
Selling directly to the buyer, e.g. door to door and home parties

Disability Discrimination Act
States that it is illegal to discriminate against someone because they have a disability

Disciplinary procedure
Formal systems which must be followed when staff are disciplined. Beginning with an informal verbal warning, the process could end in dismissal of an employee

Distribution channel
Means by which goods reach the final user can include retailers and wholesalers

Domain name
The address used by an organisation. It is used as a way of locating information and reaching other users. In an e-mail address, for example, everything following the @ is the domain name

E-commerce
Electronic commerce, i.e. all commercial transactions conducted via the internet. This includes selling, banking, investing and bill paying

Efficiency ratio
A ratio used to measure the efficiency of a business; includes debtors' payment period, creditors' payment period, rate of stock turnover

Elasticity
Responsiveness of demand to a change in price

Encryption
Use of mathematical algorithms to make data unintelligible to all but the intended recipient. Sensitive data, such as credit card numbers, is protected in this way

E-tailers
Electronic retailers, i.e. online retailers

Financial accounting
The process of collecting financial data and using this to report on the historical (or past) performance of the business

Fixed assets
Assets which will be of use to the business for a substantial length of time (certainly more than a year)

Fixed costs (or overheads)
Costs that do not rise or fall with changes in output and sales. Fixed costs are usually related to time periods, e.g. rent

Focus group
Market research interview method, a small group is assembled to discuss a particular topic

Formal communication
Communication which follows the formal lines of authority in an organisation

Franchise
An arrangement under which one business (the franchisor) allows another business (the franchisee) to supply its products

Freedom of Information Act
States that anybody can request information from a public authority in England, Wales or Northern Ireland and has the right to receive that information

FTSE-100 (the 'footsie')
An index showing changes in the share prices of the 100 most valuable companies listed on the London Stock Exchange

Functional activities
The different departments within a business such as: R&D, production or operations, distribution, marketing, human resources, finance, administration, MIS

Functions
Activities within an organisation such as administration, personnel, finance, etc.; separate departments may be set up to carry these out

Gantt chart
Chart or matrix which shows how project activities have to be achieved by a set time

Geographic segmentation
Dividing consumers into similar groups based on where they live

Global
World-wide

Goods
Tangible items – we can touch, feel and see them

Grievance procedure
Formal systems which must be followed when staff have a grievance/complaint for unfair treatment against an organisation or another worker

Hierarchy
Layers or grades of formal management with clear lines of authority and control

Horizontal integration
When a business expands its present operations

Hot spot
An area where wireless (not plugged in) applications, such as notebook computers, can access the internet

Incentives
Methods of motivating employees into working more effectively, may be monetary (bonus) or non monetary (perks such as a company car)

Industrial sectors
Primary sector, secondary sector and tertiary sector

Informal communication
Ways of communicating which do not follow the formal lines of authority in the organisation, commonly called the grapevine

Infrastructure
The services that support a business

Intellectual property (IP)
An organisation's intangible assets such as trade marks, patents, copyrights logo, brand name, etc.

International
Over more than one country

Investors in People (IIP)
A national government-backed quality standard, awarded to organisations for effective investment in the training and development of their staff

Internet Service Provider (ISP)
A company that provides software to allow your computer to connect to the internet, e.g. BT, AOL, Virgin

JIT (just in time)
Stock is bought in just as it is needed

Job description
Written document setting out the duties, responsibilities and reporting procedures of a job

Lateral integration
When a business diversifies its product range to gain access to different markets

Limited liability
The amount an owner must pay creditors if a business fails is limited to the amount they have invested in the business

Liquidity
The ability of a business to turn its assets (items owned by a business) into cash

Liquidity (or solvency) ratio
A ratio used to measure business solvency, i.e. its ability to pay its creditors; includes current ratio (or working capital ratio), acid test ratio (or quick ratio or liquid capital ratio)

Local business
A business serving the immediate area

Local government
The local council with headquarters at the town hall. It is responsible for local services such as education and road maintenance

Management accounting
Uses the same business accounts as financial accounting to provide information purely for internal use by managers to help them draw up forecasts, set up plans and make decisions about the future

Market segments
Specific part of the market defined by particular characteristics such as age or income (consumers) type of retail outlet (business)

Market share
Proportion of a total market (often measured by sales value) held by a business or product. A market leader has a larger market share than competitors

Marketing mix
The combination of the 4Ps (Price, Product, Promotion, Place) or the 7Ps (the 4Ps plus: People, Processes, Physical evidence) which are within the control of the business

Media mix
Combination of media (press, TV, etc.) used to reach a particular segment

Glossary

Mentoring
Someone with experience supporting someone with less experience

Merger
A merger (or amalgamation) involves combining two organisations to form a single business. This is agreed by management and shareholders of the businesses concerned

Metatags
Can be used to describe the contents of a website. They enable search engines to index the site and locate it when users make searches

Mixed economy
Where a country has businesses operating in all three sectors: public, private and voluntary

Multilingual support
Providing translation or interpreting facilities for an audience

Multimedia
Use of images, sounds, video to create a presentation

National
Across the nation. This may be a country such as France or a group of countries such as the UK

Netiquette
Internet ethics, e.g. use the spell-checker, don't ask before reading the FAQs (frequently asked questions)

niche market
A small or specialised market segment, e.g. expensive sports cars

online
Activities on the internet

online presence
A website

outsourcing
Buying from an outside provider, e.g. a business may use a security firm rather than employing their own security staff

partnership
Business with between two and 20 owners

patents
An exclusive legal right to sell, use or make an invention

PAYE (pay as you earn)
Income tax deducted from an employee's pay. These are a main source of government income

PEST
Political, economic, social and technological factors that affect businesses

PESTLE
Political, economic, social, technological, legal and environmental factors that affect businesses

Private limited company
A business owned by shareholders and run by a board of directors

Private sector
Those businesses not run by the state but by private individuals. Profit is a usual motive of the private sector

Privatisation
Changing state owned businesses into privately owned business. This involves selling the shares to private buyers

Product
Features and benefits associated with goods and services-one of the 4Ps

Product mix
The range of products provided or produced by an organisation

Product range
The total number of product/service lines and items sold or produced by a business

Production
The process for transforming inputs such as materials, labour and capital into goods and services

Profit
The surplus or additional money created when goods or services are sold at a price higher than the cost of producing them: Sales revenue − Total production cost (Variable + Fixed costs)

Profit and loss account
Shows the profit generated by a business over a trading period: Sales − Direct costs of sales = Gross profit − Overheads = Net profit. The sections calculating gross profit is sometimes referred to as the trading account

Profitability ratio
A ratio used to measure business profits against sales or investment; includes ROCE (return on capital employed), gross margin (or gross profit %), net margin (or net profit %)

Promotion
Process of informing, persuading or influencing businesses or consumers into making a purchase

Promotional mix
Combination of methods such as advertising and public relations used to promote a product

Protocols
Rules governing the exchange of data between computers

Public relations
An organisation's relationships with its stakeholders intended to create a favourable impression

Public sector
The part of the economy owned by local or national government

Publicity
Unpaid form of attracting attention to a product/person, by using the media; may be favourable or unfavourable

Public–private partnerships (PPPs)
Where private sector businesses help fund public projects

Qualitative analysis
Uses 'soft' data based on attitudes, interests and opinions

Quantitative analysis
Uses 'hard' measurable, numerical data

Search engines
Search the World Wide Web to locate pages with a given content, e.g. Google, MSN, Yahoo, Ask Jeeves

Segmentation
Splitting whole markets into smaller units (segments) in order to target promotion and other marketing activities at specific groups of people

Service
An action providing a benefit such as banking or education

Shareholder value
The value of each share. This should increase if the company makes profits

SMART targets/objectives
Precise quantifiable targets that are: specific, measurable, achievable, realistic and timed

Sole trader
Business with one owner

Span of control
The number of employees over whom a manager or supervisor has authority

Stakeholders
The people and communities who have an interest in a business because they are affected by its activities

Strapline
Slogan or phrase associated with a product or organisation

Strategic plan
Corporate/organisation-wide plan to achieve goals and objectives at some specific time in the future

Strategy
Plans by which a business will achieve its objectives, e.g. increasing sales by 10 per cent

SWOT
An assessment of a business under the headings: strengths, weaknesses, opportunities and threats

Take-over
One business taking control of another by buying sufficient shares

Teleworking
Working at home for an organisation using the telephone and/or computer

Trade association
An organisation representing firms operating in the same industry

Trading account
The first section of the profit and loss account showing: Sales – Direct costs = Gross profit. Some service-sector businesses do not calculate gross profit and therefore do not produce a trading account

Trial balance
A list of ledger balances in which the total debit balances should equal the total credit balances. If it does not balance, there is an error in the ledger entries

Unlimited liability
Where the owners of a business must pay in full all money owed to creditors

URL (uniform resource locator)
Used to identify a website address, web page, a file or a server on the internet

USP (unique selling point)
The reason why customers go to one business rather than another, e.g. quality or low prices

Variable costs
Costs that change proportionately as output rises and falls i.e. twice the output means twice the cost

VAT (value added tax)
A tax on the value added during production. A business pays input tax to suppliers of goods and services. It reclaims this by charging output tax on the sales of goods and services to customers. Any excess is sent to HM Revenue & Customs

Venture capital
Loan or share capital made available to new businesses or those that have a significant amount of risk

Verbal communication
Face-to-face or telephone communication where specific skills such as listening are needed

Vertical integration
When a business grows into other activities along the supply chain

Voluntary sector
The part of the economy in which businesses have at least some volunteer workers. These are not-for-profit businesses providing a service to a group in society

Web-based presentation
The layout, structure and design of an organisations website and other online activity

Web browsers
Request and read pages from the World Wide Web, e.g. for example: Netscape Navigator, Internet Explorer

Working capital
Money needed to run the business from day to day

World Wide Web Consortium (W3C)
Organisation which provides standards on web accessibility

Index